ESSENTIAL PAPERS IN PSYCHOANALYSIS

Essential Papers on Borderline Disorders
Michael D. Stone, M.D., Editor

Essential Papers on Object Relations
Peter Buckley, M.D., Editor

Essential Papers on Narcissism
Andrew P. Morrison, M.D., Editor

Essential Papers on Depression
James C. Coyne, Editor

Essential Papers on Psychosis
Peter Buckley, M.D., Editor

Essential Papers on Countertransference
Benjamin Wolstein, Editor

Essential Papers on Character Neurosis and Treatment
Ruth F. Lax, Editor

Essential Papers on the Psychology of Women
Claudia Zanardi, Editor

Essential Papers on Transference
Aaron H. Esman, M.D., Editor

Essential Papers on Dreams
Melvin R. Lansky, M.D., Editor

D1512322

ESSENTIAL PAPERS ON DREAMS

Melvin R. Lansky, M.D.
Editor

NEW YORK UNIVERSITY PRESS
NEW YORK AND LONDON
1992

NEW YORK UNIVERSITY PRESS
New York and London

Library of Congress Cataloging-in-Publication Data
Essential papers on dreams / Melvin R. Lansky, editor.
p.   cm. — (Essential papers in psychoanalysis)
Articles previously published in various journals or books.
Bibliographical references and index.
ISBN 0-8147-5061-3 (cloth)—ISBN 0-8147-5062-1 (pbk.)
1. Dreams.   2. Psychoanalysis.   3. Dreams—Therapeutic use.
4. Psychotherapy.   I. Lansky, Melvin R.   II. Series.
[DNLM: 1. Dreams—collected works.   WM 460.5.D8 E78]
BF175.5.D74   1992
154.6'3—dc20
DNLM/DLC
for Library of Congress   92-1410
                                                            CIP

New York University Press books are printed on acid-free paper,
and their binding materials are chosen for strength and durability.

Manufactured in the United States of America

10 9 8 7 6 5 4 3 2

For Karen, Madeleine, and Joshua

A dream which is not interpreted is like
a letter which is not read.

TALMUD BERAKOTH, 55a

Contents

Preface

This book is an attempt to assemble in one volume essential and enduring contributions that will take the psychoanalytically sophisticated reader from the origins of psychoanalytic thinking about dreams set forward in 1900 in *The Interpretation of Dreams* to the present-day complexity and controversy of psychoanalytically informed thinking about dreams. It is, therefore, unlike many of the recent single-author books or anthologies on dreams that are listed in appendix 2.

The book follows, as do all psychoanalytic books on dreams, in the wake of *The Interpretation of Dreams*. My attempt has been not only to give the reader a reasonable sampling of significant works that portray the unfolding and direction of psychoanalytic thinking about dreams, but also to place them in the perspective of the great issues, controversies, and shortcomings that constitute the legacy of *The Interpretation of Dreams*. The papers, however enduring and worthwhile in their own right, can profitably be seen as attempts to deal with the ''unfinished business'' of Freud's monumental dream book. Toward that end, I have attempted to outline those issues in an introductory chapter that emphasizes some of the consequences of the fact that *The Interpretation of Dreams* is basically a prepsychoanalytic work that arose largely—though, of course, not completely—as a result of Freud's self-analysis and the analysis of his own dreams, using the associative method but without the vantage point of the psychoanalytic process.

The importance of the psychoanalytic process, undisputed in psychoanalytic theory and practice since the publication in 1905 of the Dora case, are highlighted in papers by Lewin and by Greenson. Freud's almost radical mistrust of the manifest content is modified by papers by Federn and by Erikson. Ego-psychological emphasis on synthesis and adaptation, an expanding aspect of psychoanalytic thought since 1923, foreshadowed perhaps but not explicit in *The Interpretation of Dreams,* is developed in the contributions of Fromm and French, Brenner, and Weiss. *The Interpretation of Dreams* is concerned with what the mind is like—with its ability to deceive itself with wishes represented in dreams as though fulfilled. Although such wishes invariably involve others—both as objects of desire and as those in whose eyes the dreamer has, loses, or regains esteem—the notions of self and object are at the very earliest stage of psychoanalytic understanding. I have chosen a short work by Hanna Segal, a Kleinian, and self-psychological works by Fosshage and by Stolorow and Atwood—the latter written especially for this volume—as up-to-date exemplars of highly sophisticated thinking about self and object in dreams.

In the section on special topics I have, for reasons of limited space, confined contributions on trauma and psychosis to papers by Blitzsten and the Eisslers and by Levitan. I have provided the reader with a relatively long section on the nightmare, consisting of contributions by Lidz, Mack, Hartmann, and Lansky, because the current explosion of knowledge from nonpsychoanalytic sources about trauma and about sleep tends to minimize, obscure, or outright dispute that nightmares, even post-traumatic nightmares, are true dreams. The issue of whether or not dreams, nightmares, and even post-traumatic nightmares *have a function,* and whether an understanding of that function is of potential use in the overall treatment of the nightmare sufferer, is a crucial one, among the most crucial in psychoanalytic dream theory today. The readings in the nightmare section complement not only those in the preceding section on trauma and psychosis but also those by Fisher and Hobson in the final section that deal with dreams in the light of findings in laboratory sleep research.

A concluding chapter attempts to conceptualize the dream as an investigative tool, originally in understanding the workings of the mind, later in the study of the psychoanalytic process and of predicaments—developmental, traumatic, and pathological—and finally as a tool to be combined with and compared to other methods of investigation.

I have included two appendices that will guide the reader to other psychoanalytic or psychoanalytically informed texts on dreams. Appendix 1 is a list of Freud's works on dreams reprinted from the *standard edition.* Appendix 2 is a list of psychoanalytically informed books by authors since Freud, both single-author books and anthologies.

My own thinking about dreams has evolved over many years in the consulting room and in the classroom with students, patients, and colleagues. I am grateful to Richard Baker, Carol Bley, Richard Fox, Judith Karger, and Benjamin Kilborne, my valued collaborators, colleagues, and friends throughout many years of investigating and theorizing about dreams in clinical and theoretical settings. My thanks also to Allan Compton and to Jack Katz for helpful and creative commentaries on my writings on dreams.

PART I

PSYCHOANALYTIC CLASSICS

1. The Legacy of *The Interpretation of Dreams*

Melvin R. Lansky

I.

Freud saw *The Interpretation of Dreams* as his major and most significant contribution to psychoanalysis and the study of the mind. The book, conceptualized except for its introductory chapter by 1896, remained in his own mind his magnum opus and, despite its many revisions, his basically unaltered view of the significance and meaning of dreams until his death in 1939. *The Interpretation of Dreams* provided the foundations for the psychoanalytic theory not only of dreaming but also, more generally, of consciousness and the unconscious, of the imagination, and of the processes underlying self-deception.

Of the great books to have influenced the history of scientific ideas, none in modern times has so dominated the field it founded as *The Interpretation of Dreams*. The written works of Newton, Copernicus, and Darwin—considered apart from the ideas put forward in these works—are mostly of historical interest. The written works of these authors are not today texts of comparable pedagogical and research interest. Despite its shortcomings, *The Interpretation of Dreams* still holds sway not only as the most essential basic text in psychoanalytic training but also as an introduction to the psychoanalytic conception of the mind.

Indeed, the work has been so influential that it has erroneously been taken to be a textbook on psychoanalytic dream interpretation. It has also been taken to be the embodiment of the psychoanalytic theory of mental functioning to such a great extent that for decades its last chapter needed no more citation than "chapter 7" in the psychoanalytic literature. It is only slowly and with great difficulty that the clinical, philosophical, and theoretical underpinnings of the book could be separated from each other and put to the same examination for basic soundness of theoretical and clinical viability as could other works.

Despite its overwhelming and enduring influence as a basic psychoanalytic manifesto, *The Interpretation of Dreams* is in large part a prepsychoanalytic book. The major ideas were developed by 1896 during Freud's self-analysis near the time that his father died and with the intense and ambivalent relationship to Wilhelm Fleiss dominating Freud's emotional life. *The Interpretation of Dreams* represents a decisive step from the—at that time unpublished—*Project for a Scientific Psychology* (1895) toward a purely psychological theory of the mind.

Much of the data in the dream book—that is, the dreams subjected to the most detailed and most meticulous scrutiny—are Freud's own dreams, analyses of which were the results of dream analysis, not psychoanalysis proper. Dream analysis—which consists of systematic tracings of the dreamer's associations to the elements in the written text of the dream—resulted in a body of data that provides in unusual detail the connection between conscious or preconscious worries and sensory impressions of the preceding day and the manifest dream text. But, when judged by subsequent psychoanalytic standards, the method is extremely limited in its perspective on objects, on self, and on emotion or affect.

II

The work itself is far from being a straightforward exposition. Freud tells us many times in the text that he has tried to present his views on dreams without getting too involved in the psychology of the neuroses. The latter effort resulted both from Freud's hope that his views would be considered without being discredited as products of deranged minds, and also, as he quite candidly states, because there were limitations to the extent to which he was willing to reveal intimate details concerning his inner life. Because of the book's format, thorough analyses of dreams—that is, analyses in which the associative method reveals a truly convincing connection between the instigation in the events of the dream day and the infantile conflict discovered in the latent dream thoughts—are surprisingly scant even in the rich abundance of clinical material.

The book evolved chronologically in three parts: chapters 2 through 6 deal with clinical considerations; chapter 7, with the psychology of the dream processes; and chapter 1, written several years later, with a consideration of the contributions of previous authors.

Chapters 2 to 6 form the clinical material addressing the associative method (chapter 2); a preliminary (i.e., psychological rather than metapsychological) statement of the wish fulfillment hypothesis (chapter 3); distortion in dreams (chapter 4); material and sources of dreams with special emphasis on infantile conflict (chapter 5); and the dream work (chapter 6).

Despite Freud's Herculean attempt at evenhandedness, the exposition and the data supporting it do not go hand in hand. Throughout his exposition, Freud gives examples of points to be made, but very few dreams are analyzed with significant completeness. The celebrated "specimen dream" put forward in chapter 2, for example, is analyzed only to the point of demonstrating that the associative method leads to Freud's preconscious preoccupation concerning the circumstances of Irma's mishandled treatment and especially with exculpating himself in the eyes of his colleagues in the face of charges of incompetence. Schur (1966) has pointed out that even the aspects of the day residue concerning Freud's protection of and his competitiveness with Wilhelm Fleiss—convincingly evident from his correspondence to Fleiss at the time—have not been revealed in the text of *The Interpretation of Dreams* at all.

Many of the major dreams presented in chapters 2 through 6 are Freud's own (Grinstein 1980). For example, the dream of Irma's injection (chapter 2), the dream of the botanical monograph (chapter 5A) and the Count Thun (chapter 5B) dream reveal aspects of dream formation in the context of Freud's own psychology—his aspirations, his desires, his fears, and his neurosis. Of the many dreams catalogued in *The Interpretation of Dreams,* only the Count Thun dream seems to have been completely enough analyzed in print so that the relationship of the infantile neurosis to the conflict in the dream day stands out, even in the midst of Freud's indirect prose, and becomes available for the reader's consideration. Scrutiny of those dreams reveals Freud as a fierce sexual competitor whose competitive nature emerges at times of felt rejection, exclusion, or narcissistic injury. Actual sexual desire does not seem to be a major factor in the evidence directly presented to the reader in *The Interpretation of Dreams*. The latent dream thoughts, in the early part of the text especially, seem to hover more in the here and now and to deal especially with Freud's status among others.

Chapter 7, "The Psychology of the Dream Processes," draws not only from the material presented in chapters 2 through 6 but also from the deeper parts of Freud's self-analysis and his strictly psychoanalytic work with neurotics to consider the nature of the mind, the unconscious, and the imagination in such a way as to account for the phenomena presented in the earlier chapters. There is both a philosophical and a theoretical basis for chapter 7 that can be usefully distinguished.

Viewing the clinical material from which the expositions in chapters 2 thrugh 6 derive, Freud asks, What is the mind like such that all of this is so? Chapter 7 is an attempt to answer that question. It is important to keep in mind that difficulties—of which there are many—in Freud's answer to the question do not remove the basic problems posed by the question and by the compelling clinical material that generates the question.

Freud's exposition in chapters 2 to 6 expounds a wish fulfillment theory, a theory of distortion, disguise, and deception, and a method—that of the association of ideas—for getting from the one to the other. The wish fulfillment hypothesis is an elaboration of the fundamental presumption that dream formation must, for reasons that transcend the specific psychological issues in the dream—that is, *metapsychologically*—proceed in such a way as to move the psyche to a state of lesser rather than greater disturbance. Dreams, then, have a *function,* as do any other forms of ideation. They serve to restore homeostasis to a disrupted psyche or prevent disruption or further disruption that would result from disturbing awarenesses—for example, of one's wishes or of conflicts that involve wishes that have been repressed. The essence of the task of diminishing or avoiding disruption is that of self-deception. Every dream, even simple dreams of convenience in which wishes appear undisguised, is an act of self-deception. The dream work comprises specific operations by which one deceives oneself, usually about what one's wishes are and always in the experiencing of them as fulfilled. *The Interpretation of Dreams,* and chapter 7 in particular, is a treatise on the ubiquity of self-deception. Every act of repression, any defense against awareness, is an act of self-deception. The essential question posed in chapter 7 is, What is the mind like such that it can deceive itself?

The problem of self-deception has remained a difficult and unresolved one, not only for psychoanalysis but also for psychology and philosophy generally. How is the mind ordered so that it deceives not only about wishes, but also about deception itself? It is an acknowledgment of this question that the enduring philosophic value of *The Interpretation of Dreams* and its place in the history of ideas transcends that of the specific theories of the psyche that Freud put forward to explain the particulars of the activity of repression, that is, of self-deception.

Freud's *theoretical* approach to the problem of self-deception contains assumptions about discharge phenomena that are controversial and seen by many contemporary critics as outmoded. His treatment of theory in chapter 7 involves a notion of what may be called "the picture with the charge on it," or the cathected neuron. For reasons that go beyond the scope of this discussion, that theory is seen by many as being in considerable need of revision (Basch 1976). Freud's entire notion of psychoneurosis and of dreams in the 1890s had as its central feature a retained, that is to say repressed, picture—a memory or a latent dream thought—with a charge, that is, a quota of affect, on it. The idea of a feared object was displaced in phobias; the idea of a bodily dysfunction appeared in consciousness in the conversions; the idea of forbidden act, in the obsessions and compulsions; the idea of a persecutor, in the delusions. Each was presumably derived from a pathogenic "picture," a memory; or, in the case of dreams, the idea of the fulfilled wish derived from the latent dream thoughts. I shall return to these points.

Chapter 1 of *The Interpretation of Dreams,* written just before its publication in 1900, is a lengthy consideration of writings of other authors that is usually, but erroneously, in this writer's view, seen as a simple literature review and is either given short shrift or dismissed altogether in crowded psychoanalytic curricula. This tendency to underrate or omit chapter 1 is a serious error that works against appreciating the text as a whole. A cursory reading of the table of contents of *The Interpretation of Dreams* will show the interested reader that chapter 1 closely parallels chapters 5 and 7 in topics discussed. Chapter 1 presents theses and antitheses in the works of others in respect to which chapter 5, and especially chapter 7, are the syntheses. Freud's questions of the existing literature are essential complements to his own clinical material put forward in chapters 2 through 6, and in light of this, chapter 1 should be seen along with the clinical chapters as an overture to chapter 7. If the preliminary framing of basic issues that is accomplished in chapter 1 is not borne in mind, the formulations in chapter 7 are likely to impress the reader as inextricably linked to Freud's emplanatory notion of the cathected neuron. As a result, the metapsychology of chapter 7 is likely to be confused with Freud's neurophysiologic theorizing.

III

A detailed history of Freud's writings after 1900 that deal with dreams is beyond the scope of this introduction.[1]

Freud's subsequent theoretical considerations centered mostly around the issue of trauma, both adult and infantile. Reports from younger colleagues in World War I of the repetition in dreams of battlefield traumas caused Freud to postulate in 1920 the wish to master a wish from (what was soon to be called) the "ego." Freud thought that mastery involved a repetition and reexperience of a past traumatic situation with the opportunity to form anticipatory anxiety. Such repetition was in the service of this ego wish, that is, the attaining of that mastery or mental preparedness to face the trauma.

In one of his last statements on dreams in 1933, Freud noted, "Only two serious difficulties have arisen against the wish fulfillment theory of dreams. . . . The first of these difficulties is presented by the fact that people who have experienced the shock, a severe psychic trauma—such as happened so often during war and such as affords the basis for traumatic hysteria—are regularly taken back in their dreams to the traumatic situation. According to our hypothesis about the function of dreams, this should not occur. What wishful impulse could be satisfied by harking back in this way to this exceedingly distressing traumatic experience?" (Freud 1933, 28)

The second problem concerned the repetition of dreams in painful traumatic experience from early infantile life: "If for the sake of studying it, we isolate one particular psychical function, such as dreaming, and the psychical machinery as a whole, we make it possible to discover the laws that are peculiar to it; but when we insert it once more into the general context, we must be prepared to discover that these findings are obscured or impaired by collision with other forces. We say that a dream is a fulfillment of a wish; but if you want to take these latter objections into account, you can say nevertheless that the dream is an *attempt* at the fulfillment of a wish" (Freud 1933, 28–29). In these passages, Freud somewhat uncharacteristically theorizes about the nature of dreams without adducing specific clinical material in the context of which the problems arise. He assumes, as he does in *Beyond the Pleasure Principle* (1920), that the dream is a simple replay of the event without intervening dream work and hence without the distinction of manifest from latent content. Since these dreams seem to generate rather than diminish

1. The interested reader will find a list of these writings in appendix B to *The Interpretation of Dreams* in the Standard Edition.

anxiety, they appear to be counterinstances to the wish fulfillment theory—
or disruption lowering function attributed to dreams generally.

IV

I shall discuss the legacy of *The Interpretation of Dreams* briefly insofar as
that legacy pertains to the following topics: the psychoanalytic situation and
the idea of psychoanalytic process; manifest and latent content and problems
in the clinical application of radical associationalism; adaptation and synthesis and the topic of problem solving; object, self, and affect and the limitations of self-analysis; wish-fulfillment and the problem of post-traumatic
dreams; and the relationship of clinical data to philosophy, to theory, and to
laboratory data. My intent falls short of being systematic, historically complete, or comprehensive. Rather, it is to illuminate some of the sources of
current controversy about dreams as those sources continue to deal with
unresolved issues in the text.

A. The Psychoanalytic Situation

It is important to realize that the bulk of the clinical material presented in *The
Interpretation of Dreams* does not arise from the analytic situation as we
know it. The observations put forward in *The Interpretation of Dreams* are
not formulated in terms of the analytic situation or the analytic process at all.
Most of the book derives from Freud's exhaustive associations among the
elements of written texts of his own dreams and his tracing idea and affect in
the dream collage—the manifest dream—both to recent and to indifferent
material from the preceding twenty-four hours—the day residue or the dream
day and memories of early events. Other material comes from psychoanalytic
treatment at the very earliest stage of the development of psychoanalysis at a
time when the true process was only beginning to emerge. It was only on the
last day of the nineteenth century—when Dora left her analysis—that Freud
(1905a) began to appreciate the significance of the transference, that is to
say, of the existence of the analytic process.

It should also be kept in mind that Freud was preoccupied with his
psychoanalytic conceptualization of the psychoneuroses. Psychoneuroses, as
opposed to *aktualneuroses,* were characterized by the presence of a patholog-
.ical idea, *a picture derived from another idea, a repressed memory, that had
an affective charge on it.* Such pathological ideas included phobias, compul-

sions, obsessions, delusions, and conversions. The model of a symptomatic idea defending against awareness of a pathologically trapped idea with a quota of affect on it was one that held Freud captive in this period of his investigations. As is the case with dreams, such pathological ideas are compromise formations serving both expressive and defensive functions.

Freud's preoccupation with "the picture with the charge on it" was not limited to dream analysis. It was a theoretical preoccupation that influenced his view of the psychoneuroses and one that he wished to transplant to the study of other products of the imagination—dreams, jokes, and slips.

Subsequent psychoanalytic understanding has made it clear that it is not just dreams and symptoms that are compromise formations of expressions of wishes and of defenses against those wishes. Early conceptualizations regarding symptoms and dreams came to be generalized to memory and to mental activity generally. Insights originally gleaned from the study of dreams came to be seen as so much a part of all of mental life that it seemed questionable whether the dream was unique in actual clinical practice or merely unique historically in having provided a venue for discoveries later found to apply to the whole spectrum of mental life. Mindful of the extent to which all thoughts and actions are compromises between expressive and defensive functions, some have challenged the specialness of the dream in analytic practice (Brenner 1976): Is the dream still the royal road to the unconscious or just a historically early and somewhat fascinating item of psychoanalytic research?

From the point of view of dream analysis, the specialness of dreams seems harder to delineate than it was early in the investigative days of what should not be called psychoanalysis proper but, rather, dream analysis. Only in the context of the analytic process does the specialness emerge. And the psycho-analytic process itself is not discussed in *The Interpretation of Dreams*.

We still lack a truly unambiguous notion of psychoanalytic process that could be utilized in an expanded theory of dreams. Bertram Lewin (1955) formulated a view of the analytic situation and the analytic process entirely in terms of the vicissitudes of self-absorption and involvement with the other; that is, he developed a conception of the psychoanalytic process solely in the language of sleeping, waking, and dreaming. Lewin's brilliant and original work has tended to be neglected by psychoanalysts who are not comfortable working with dreams. Greenson (1970), challenging the notion put forward in a monograph of the Kris Study Groups that dreams were less special than traditionally regarded, defended his views with a dramatic portrayal of the interplay between analyst and patient in the analytic situation. It is only in the context of a deepening analytic process that the psychoanalytic study of the dream can be appreciated. And it is only in this context that the nature of interpretation—at first thought by Freud to be a simple reversal of the dream work—can be understood.

B. Manifest Content and Latent Content

On the very first page of *The Interpretation of Dreams*, Freud emphasized that dreams could be interpreted so that a dream could be placed in the meaningful continuity of mental life. To reconcile the notion of an attitude toward dreams as scientifically understandable with the alien and often absurd quality of the dream experience, Freud developed the notion of latent content, that is to say, of latent dream thoughts that were indeed continuous with the whole of mental life. These latent dream thoughts were, so to speak, "behind" the manifest dream, fully formed but woven into the manifest dream by the operations of the dream work. This distinction and the subsequent emphasis on distortion and dream work in chapters 4 and 6 of *The Interpretation of Dreams* enabled Freud to presume the basic wish fulfillment hypothesis put forward partially in chapter 3, that is, that it was not necessarily the manifest content of the dream that represented a wish as fulfilled but, rather, the latent dream thoughts represented wishes as fulfilled. The manifest dream was the result of transformation of the latent content through the operation of the dream work. It was the latent content, like the repressed memory in the psychoneuroses, that was in continuity with the mainstream of mental life and it is this continuity that is the object, not only of dream analysis, but of psychoanalysis.

This basic distinction in chapter 4 enabled Freud to reconcile many clinical phenomena with the wish fulfillment hypothesis, which is nothing more than a hypothesis to reaffirm the basic notion that *dreams have a function,* the function of keeping tension in the psychic apparatus at relatively manageable levels.

Dreams, then, are not simply the guardians of sleep but bits of ideation, woven, so to speak, to keep the apparatus in equilibrium, as are other types of mental activities. Freud had to account for the presence in his clinical material of anxiety dreams, punishment dreams, unpleasant dreams, absurd and nonsensical dreams, and others that seemed to defy the idea that dreams were simple wish fulfillments and, hence, appeared to challenge the notion that dreams have a function. The process of analytic interpretation as Freud then saw it, that is to say, the reversal of the dream work through interpretation, leading from manifest content to latent dream thoughts, was an attempt to reconcile apparent counterinstances with the wish fulfillment hypothesis. This view of the nature of conflict and defense led Freud to a radical distrust of the manifest content, which, in a famous metaphor, he likened to the facade of an Italian church, the appearance of which gave no real sense of what was behind it. This model was basically the same model that he had developed for the psychoneuroses of a manifest idea with an affectively laden latent idea behind it. The model held Freud captive, so much so that he put forward the notion of manifest and latent content somewhat inconsistently.

The model of latent content with a quota of affect on it allowed him to view the dream like a psychoneurotic symptom: a phobia, a conversion, an obsession, a delusion, so to speak, with a memory behind it. That is, just as the psychoneuroses "contained" a latent (i.e., unconscious) memory with a quota of affect, so the dream "contained" latent dream thoughts with a quota of affect attached to them. So Freud's views derived not simply from his views of dreams according to the procedure of his self-analysis—done in isolation and with a good deal of oblivion to some powerful interpersonal processes. They were also colored by his method of working self-analytically with a dream text—not the experience of the dream but a written text describing it—and also from the model of neuroses he had before him and from his earliest efforts at psychoanalysis.

Freud contrasted the "lexicon" method of dream interpretation—one in which dreams or elements of dreams could be decoded, no matter what their context—with a radical associationalism he put forward in chapter 2. Each dream interpretation was an independent research product, so to speak. Hence, there is an absolute severance between the manifest and the latent content. Freud was not only suspicious of the manifest content per se, but was also suspicious of methods of dream interpretation that essentially allegorized the dream and sought to get its message as would a literary critic (see Reed 1987; Greenson 1970).

In clinical practice, however, Freud did not stick to this extreme of radical associationalism. There is widespread agreement that his manifesto put forward in chapter 2 and alluded to elsewhere is overstated. Pulver (1987) has noted that the concept of a manifest dream is somewhat ambiguous. The actual text of the dream is not the dream experience—mostly visual—but a translation of the dream back into verbal language. Charles Brenner (1976) has observed that this really constitutes a set of associations to the dream, not the dream itself.

Freud actually used manifest content of dreams in a number of different ways, especially symbols, typical dreams, and traumatic dreams. The notion of typical dreams is a somewhat misleading one. By typical dreams, Freud actually means typical wishes or typical unconscious predicaments such as ambivalence toward loved ones, the wish to exhibit oneself, and so forth. So Freud uses the vehicle of typical dreams to discuss his collection of findings about the unconscious. Freud's use of the word "symbol" as applied to dreams also requires explication. He does not use the word in the same sense as would a literary critic. His usage derives from his exhaustive study of dream text in his own self-analysis. By "symbol," he means material in the dream that, after exhaustive associations, did not prove to be derived from recent and indifferent material found in the day residue, that is, was not reducible to recent or indifferent impressions of the previous day. This specific context in which Freud uses the word "symbol" has not been sufficiently appreciated in the psychoanalytic literature nor has the problem of *how one knows that a symbol is indeed a symbol,* an element with a transcendent meaning, rather than something to be analyzed afresh using only the associative method. Freud wavers on this issue but in the end tends to see translation of symbols as only an adjunctive rather than a mainstay of psychoanalytic interpretation. Indeed, the very presumption that one can know without fail that a symbol is a symbol and that one can know what that symbol means is a return to the lexicon method of dream interpretation and a violation of the principle of radical associationalism.

In discussing traumatic dreams—which he does only in 1920 and after, Freud has a tendency to presume both that the traumatic dream is an exact replay of the traumatic situation and that what overwhelmed the patient in the dream is the same thing that overwhelmed the patient in real life. Uncharacteristically, Freud theorizes about these dreams without providing clinical examples. It is striking, particularly in view of Freud's radically skeptical view of inferences based solely on manifest content, that he tends to regard traumatic dreams more like memories than true dreams and to presume, without clinical investigation or other convincing evidence, that they have no latent content whatsoever.

In actual psychoanalytic practice, most clinicians use an interplay of manifest and latent content. The first significant person after Freud to use manifest content was Paul Federn (1932), who pointed to ego feeling, the actual bodily feeling in the manifest content of the dream and its relationship to the dreamer's attitude toward his own will. Federn's unique and strikingly original researches tend to be neglected because his use of the word "ego" differed somewhat from the accepted usage as the organ of adaptation by the later ego psychologists.

A paper on the "Specimen Dream" by Erik Erikson (1954) was a landmark contribution that pointed to rich connections between manifest and latent content and served to stimulate much of the literature that has come after it. Erikson's work was influential: Fine, Moore, and Waldhorn (1969), summarizing the investigations of the Kris Study Groups of the New York Psychoanalytic Institute, produced detailed material on the manifest content of the dream. Spanjaard (1969) carefully reviewed the literature and recommended supplementing the associative method with manifest dynamic aspects of the dream so that the dream could be interpreted in the light of the current transference conflict. Rosenbaum (1965), in an unusual statistical study, concluded that the clinical significance of the analyst appearing undisguised in dreams was not shown even in a quite large sample to be as ominous prognostically as it had been felt to be in common clinical lore. Other useful contributions are those by Stewart (1967) and Pulver (1987), both of whom point to a usable interrelationship between manifest and latent content of dreams.

In actual practice, there is a tendency to use an interplay of manifest and latent content, and it is only seldom that psychoanalytic literature contains case reports that really partake of the radical associationalism that Freud advocated in chapter 2 of *The Interpretation of Dreams*.

Nonetheless, distortion and self-deception remain basic features that differentiate psychoanalysis from less depth-psychologically oriented psychology. Self-deception is a major part of the analytic experience for both analyst and patient and is an inescapable part of the analytic process. It is the products of mental activity resulting from self-deception (i.e., repression or defense) in the service of modulating disturbance that is material to be analyzed, be that material a dream, a symptom, an imago, or the entire meaning of any given analytic hour or situation that comes to the patient's mind for discussion. It is a general feature of mentation and it is what psychoanalysis deals with, whether it be neurotic symptoms, dreams, memories, self- or object-representations, or more complex bits of mentation that are woven into everyday thinking.

Chapter 7 deals with this problem on a more general level that is apart from the specific clinical situation. In this chapter, Freud asks, What must the structure of the mind be like such that it can deceive itself? The reader thinking that chapter 7 is only an elaborate theory of discharge dynamics fails to understand the significance of chapter 7. The basic distinction into manifest and latent concerns the problem of self-deception. The issue of self-deception, be it clinical, philosophical, or theoretical, is an extremely difficult and poorly understood one.

The legacy of contempt for and suspicion of the manifest content of dreams systematically undercuts psychoanalytic research into dreams: How does one classify dreams and study them if one is to hold everything about the manifest content untrustworthy? Even if one modifies this view somewhat, the problem still remains that we cannot proceed to classify dreams in a surefooted manner so that we can then meaningfully study them. The alternative to a classificatory approach is, of course, the view that each dream is indeed an independent psychoanalytic research project to be solved using the associative method. Yet few psychoanalysts in actual psychoanalytic practice today would go that far. We inevitably ask, What about the story in the dream, the self state in the dream, self and object images in the dream, affect in the dream? What about symbols, typical dreams, traumatic dreams, first dreams, dreams representing the analyst, dreams of turning points in the analytic process, or dreams of termination? Do psychotics have psychotic dreams and borderline patients have borderline dreams? Even though such implied classification seems to violate the radical associationalism that Freud espoused in chapter 2, the time may be nearing for a theoretical psychoanalytic understanding of the place extra-associative methods in studying specific types of dreams.

C. Adaptation and Synthesis

Freud's conclusion in chapters 6 and 7 of *The Interpretation of Dreams* is that dreaming per se is not a type of thinking but only a processing of already existing thoughts, the latent dream thoughts being processed by the dream work so that they are disguised and transformed into the manifest dream experience, which is less distressing. Freud continues the expansion of his earlier notion of the psychoneuroses applied in the case of dreams not to symptom and repressed memory, but to the manifest and latent content of the dream. In that theory of the psychoneuroses, the actual latent content, that is to say, the repressed affectively charged memory, is what has become sequestered and separated from the patient's sense of psychic continuity. The actual process of symptom formation is less a focus of psychoanalytic attention than is the conflict revealed in the (repressed) memory. So with the latent dream thoughts as compared to the dream work.

All this, of course, is based on the metapsychological—not just psychological—presumption that the motive of the dream is invariably to decrease disruption. Put metapsychologically, of course, that means that a dream deals with a wish as fulfilled, that is, a source of disturbance as removed. This is metapsychological rather than psychological and is based on a notion of tension reduction rather than on psychological factors such as desire or conscious wish.

This basically metapsychological view toward wish fulfillment—the view that the dream (as does every act of mentation) has the purpose of modulating tension in the psychic apparatus—is still accepted today by most psychoanalysts. There is very little opposition, however, to the acknowledgment of a problem-solving synthetic adaptive aspect to dream life, acceptance of which is virtually ubiquitous in psychoanalytic thinking. Thus, the element of reduction of disturbance (wish fulfillment), that of self-deception (distortion), must be complemented by a notion of adaptation, synthesis, problem solving, planning, or decision making. Most psychoanalytic thinkers have arrived at a balance of all these factors, although a few (e.g., Fosshage 1983) have tended to adopt the synthetic adaptive point of view and to deemphasize or dispute altogether the disturbance-lowering and self-deceptive function of dreams.

Freud in chapter 5 of *The Interpretation of Dreams* saw a major and hitherto unacknowledged source of the instigation of the dream: disruption caused by an unconscious wish. The dream as the distorted representation of a wish as fulfilled dealt with the disruption in the same way that a dream of convenience dealt with a somatic disturbance such as thirst, hunger, or a need to urinate.

Chapter 5 of *The Interpretation of Dreams* emphasized the unconscious as a dream instigator that is only stimulated by the day residue. In Freud's famous metaphor, the unconscious wish was the capitalist, the day residue merely the entrepreneur. Just as Freud devalued the manifest content in chapter 4 of *The Interpretation of Dreams,* so he tends to devalue the day residue in chapters 5, 6, and 7; that is, he sometimes underestimates the extent to which a specific current conflict stirred up an unconscious response to which the dream was an attempted solution (see Palombo 1988).

Freud repeatedly emphasizes that the dream work only processes. It does not think. The manifest dream is literally a collage of sensory impressions, both recent and indifferent, made from the day residues and serving to express what fundamentally was an unconscious, infantile wish that had been stirred up by a current conflict or a preconscious worry.

But Freud at the end of chapter 6 of *The Interpretation of Dreams* discussed one aspect of the dream work that did not come from processing in the unconscious, that is to say, from displacement, condensation, or symbol formation. This was a bit of preconscious mental activity that made the dream appear more coherent and consistent to the dreamer than the actual dream experience was. Freud's term ''secondary elaboration'' or ''secondary revision'' was applied to this aspect of the dream work, which was contributed by the preconscious (or, later, the ego).

Since the developments in ego psychology that followed publication of *The Ego and the Id* in 1923, there has been more and more attention to synthesis and thinking, not just thoughts being processed but actual thinking. Prominent thinkers in emphasizing ego psychology and the structural theory were Arlow and Brenner (1964), Brenner (1969; 1976), Erikson (1954), and Thomas French (Fromm and French 1962). More recently, the work of Joseph Weiss and his collaborators (1986) has emphasized the problem-solving function of dreams from the point of view of unconscious decision making.

It is important to realize that not only the so-called ego psychologists but virtually every school of psychoanalysis has seen dream activity as a process of active thinking and problem solving. The object relations theorists and Kleinians (Meltzer 1984; Segal 1981) and the self psychologist (Kohut 1971; 1977; Ornstein 1987; Stolorow and Atwood 1992) have all described problem-solving synthetic aspects to dream formations. Some (Fosshage 1983) have gone as far as to devalue the tension-lowering, wish-fulfiling, and self-deceptive aspects of dreams entirely in favor of the problem-solving adaptive or planning functions.

D. Object, Self, and Affect

The limitations in Freud's conceptualization of object, self, and affect in *The Interpretation of Dreams* is very much colored by the fact, noted previously, that the book, developed essentially by 1896 during Freud's self-analysis, is a prepsychoanalytic work. Freud pays meticulous attention to the dream collage constructed from impressions of the dream day, but the context of the dream is drawn from Freud's conscious mind facing the written text of the dream and using his association to verbal elements of the dream. This is dream analysis and self-analysis, but not psychoanalysis as we understand it today, that is, an unfolding of consciousness that is very much in steady state with the experience of self and emotions seen increasingly in relationship to the analysand's bond with the other, the analyst, a relationship of which the analysand becomes more and more aware. Freud's self-analysis was powerfully affected by his strong attachment to and ambivalence toward Wilhelm Fleiss, which was by and large not acknowledged. This has been pointed out by many authors (Schur 1966; Grinstein 1980).

It is easy to get from the interpretation of the dreams a distorted view of the psychoanalytic attitude toward dreams insofar as they reflect object relations, the self, and affect. I shall treat these points (somewhat arbitrarily) as though they were separate.

Object. Freud's preoccupation with his self-analysis allowed him only minimal awareness of the transference to Fleiss and of his own dependency, his competitiveness, his devaluation, and his anger at Fleiss, which was so typical of his relationships with previous and subsequent male figures (e.g., Breuer, Jung, Adler, Ferenczi) with whom he became involved. Brilliant and lasting though his researches were, they were basically not integrated into the context of the relationship of the other, that is to say, the day-to-day or minute-to-minute fluctuation of the transference.

It would probably be reasonable to say that the entire range of current psychoanalytic thinking is oriented to "object[2] relations" as compared with the original self-analytic researches on which *The Interpretation of Dreams* is based. There is not now and never has been a school of psychoanalytic

2. The word "object" as it is used in the *Three Essays on Sexuality* (1905b), that is, in relation to an instinct that has source, aim, and object, does not give full play to the sense of the significance of "the other" that is inherent in psychoanalysis from the very earliest times onward.

thought that did not stress the relationship with the other and, of course, the significance of the transference.

The notion of an internal world with internal objects in the presence of whom one exists in the context of a relationship and by virtue of which one is defined as a self was put forward perhaps most brilliantly and decisively by Melanie Klein. Klein developed the notion of the object world in her rich, phenomenologically descriptive notion of an internal world containing part objects (functions) and whole objects (actual people, who are more ambivalently regarded). Klein's writings, although they may seem difficult at first, trace phenomenology of unconscious fantasy regarding others. Her writing and her clinical material have served, more perhaps than any others, to make it clear that much if not all of internal mental life is object related, that is, endowed with an unconscious animism and experienced as thinking or theorizing *about or in relation to internal objects.* The (at times ubiquitous) illusion that one acts independently of objects and even that the psychoanalytic discourse takes place out of the context of the analytic relationship is what Jacques Lacan (1977) has called the "mirage of monologue." Klein's conceptualization of the internal world—colored by early conflicts but not entirely equatable with them—has been an influential point of view, and most analysts today would probably agree with Donald Meltzer (1984), who wrote, "Neurotics would not be seen as 'suffering from reminiscences' but could be thought of as *living in the past* represented in the immediate present qualities of the internal world."

Melanie Klein's work, stressing as it does the phenomenology of unconscious fantasy, has required theoretical elaboration. This has come especially from the work of Wilfred Bion (1977), but also from that of Herbert Rosenfeld (1952) and of Hanna Segal (1981). Bion conceptualized primitive mental states (beta elements) that could not be processed, for example, as dream thoughts of neurotics could be processed by the "primary processes." This defect in capacity doomed the sufferer of these states to constant pathological repetition until (perhaps as a result of psychoanalytic treatment) they could be processed using the alpha function, as Bion called it, that is, an interpersonal process often coming from early nurturance that enabled "thoughts" to be processed, dreamed, thought about, and symbolized. In Bion's view, once thoughts could actually be thought or dreamed, "metabolized," as it were, they could be transformed, used, symbolized, and somehow assimilated so that the thinker could learn from experience. In the absence of such a capacity, primitive mentation generates inchoate tensions that simply stimulate repetitive and often self-defeating action, cycling over and over again in self-destructive, chaotic patterns of relating or thinking. Hanna Segal (1981) has elaborated these points in her discussions of evacuative dreams and predictive dreams. In both of these kinds of dreams, primitive tension that cannot be processed in the same way as can neurotic ideational material is dealt with in the dream as though it could be evacuated or gotten rid of. In evacuative dreams, the fantasy is that one has rid oneself of the part that cannot really be comprehended, understood, or empathized with. In predictive dreams, the process of dreaming is insufficiently effective for evacuation so that an acting out, a mise-en-scène thematically similar to the dream, often follows the dream in an attempt to further rid oneself of the tension that the dream tried unsuccessfully to split off and evacuate.

None of the current major psychoanalytic schools—developmental, Kleinian, British middle, self psychological, ego psychological—fail to place strong emphasis on the patient's internal world in relation to internal objects.

Self. Detailed examination of the dreams and analysis of dreams in *The Interpretation of Dreams* reveals that narcissistic aspects of the day residue are rampant in *The Interpretation of Dreams*. Despite Freud's emphasis on sexuality, very little of the dreams concern lust or drives as such, wishing to culminate in orgasm. Rather, they reveal the self, or in particular Freud's (often neurotic) self, as a narcissistically involved sexual competitor. The Irma dream (the "specimen dream" in chapter 2), the dream of the Botanical Monograph, and the Count Thun dream all show these competitive narcissistic aspects of Freud's personality. It is noteworthy that, except for the Count Thun dream, Freud's analyses of the more detailed dreams earlier in the book do not go very deeply into the unconscious. In part the superficiality serves purposes of exposition since Freud is building up to more complex points and going deeper and deeper into the unconscious as the text proceeds; but the superficiality of the material is due also to the limitations Freud placed on how much of his analysis he wanted to reveal and on the limitations of the (self-) analysis itself. The dreams are addressed in large part—the ones in the early chapters especially—to Freud's standing before others and particularly his professional status as a manifestation of his competitiveness, and sexual competitiveness especially. Although he writes about the object as an object of desire, in fact a close reading of *The Interpretation of Dreams* shows that the clinical material reveals Freud to be a sexual competitor with a good deal of vulnerability to loss of standing or lack of recognition in the professional community. These narcissistic conflicts cannot be dismissed as simple replays of a more basic infantile conflict.

Since Freud did not do his (self-) analysis in the immediate context of an ongoing relationship to an analyst, he was not able to note the vicissitudes of his narcissistic vulnerability as it affected his self-analysis. Modern-day psychoanalysis would always be mindful of the relationship of dream interpretation to the state of the transference and the particular sense of self that the patient felt before the analyst at the particular time when a dream is interpreted.

Heinz Kohut (1977) carried the issue of the patient's sense of self somewhat to extremes by postulating a "self-state dream," a representation by the healthier parts of the personality of an incohesive ego desperately searching for concrete circumstances under which it could be experienced as cohesive. Grinstein (1983) has pointed out that self-state dreams have much in common with traumatic dreams. Kohut's formulation (Kohut 1977; Ornstein 1987) raises methodological problems since he maintains that the understanding of this type of dream does not deepen with the associative process and so seems to be something that is taken entirely on the level of manifest content. The problem with Kohut's formulation is that it gives us no reliable method with which to distinguish a self-state dream from one that is not a self-state dream (Reed 1987). Some self psychologists put so much emphasis on the synthetic, expressive, creative aspect of the dream and not the disguise, self-deception, or distortion (Fosshage 1983) that the difference between self-state dreams and others appears not to matter.

In work that expands on Kohut's notion of self objects, that is, objects that are not so much objects of desire as objects necessary for the maintenance of a cohesive sense of self, Robert Stolorow and George Atwood (1992) have conceptualized dreams such that the need for self-object relationships is seen as a part of all dreams. All dreams can be seen as creating concrete circumstances for a self that is in search of cohesion-producing relationships. Stolorow and Atwood's formulation has as one of its many advantages the fact that it does not seek to replace one of the bulwarks of psychoanalytic theory, the need for an appreciation of self-deception, distortion, and disguise, with an overly simplistic view of the dream that sees it simply as an allegory and basically without a function. Stolorow and Atwood, by stressing the function of concretization, see the dream as a creative act constructing concrete circumstances to perform its functions, which are in part the maintenance of cohesion, in part wish fulfillment. The dream is seen as rich in a truly psychoanalytic complexity that does not beg the question of distortion, disguise, or self-deception. These authors abandon discharge dynamics as an ultimate explanation of the dreaming process.

Affect. The expanded view of object, self, and affect has inevitably resulted in more attention to the affect of shame as the central emotion signaling danger to interpersonal bonds. Freud's self-analysis was not public, was not before the other (i.e., another analyst) and as a result, shame, the emotion that is felt *before the other,* the *public* emotion, the emotion signaling *threat to the sense of self* and to the *bond to the other* tends to be minimized or ignored and replaced by anxiety, guilt, and anger. Freud's descriptions are rich in realization of his competitiveness, his anger, his hostility, his death wishes, and his guilt. Yet examination of the dreams reveals shame, embarrassment, exposure as inadequate, and narcissistic rage at being excluded in many of the most significant dreams in the book. In the Specimen Dream, the Count Thun Dream, and the Dream of the Botanical Monograph, these are especially prominent.

Freud's very earliest conceptualizations—based on his work with patients in *Studies in Hysteria* (Breuer and Freud 1895)—conceptualized shame quite adequately. Nonetheless, he had a great deal of difficulty theorizing about shame or recognizing it in himself. As his emphasis shifted to unconscious fantasy and transgression, he paid more and more attention to the internalized fear of punishment or fear of the superego that he called guilt. While almost all the material in the early chapters in *The Interpretation of Dreams* concerns reversals of shaming situations, Freud seldom if ever mentions shame, but develops a notion of affect that results from an emphasis on unconscious desire: anger, lust, sexual competitiveness. All of these seem to be very peripheral parts of the actual clinical material, at least insofar as he presents that material to the reader.

These more modern notions of object, self, and affect somewhat unite in a more up-to-date view of relationships, one that sees every self being much more dependent as a self on the relationship with the other to give one a sense of self. Shame arises when either that need is exposed or the bond is risked. Shame is the master emotion signaling danger to meaningful bonding (Scheff 1990). Although often veiled or invisible, shame is an accompaniment of every encounter in which exposure as unlovable or unworthy can threaten meaningful bonding. This is the kind of conflict that every analyst sees in every hour in the context of the transference, implicitly or explicitly, but one that only in the last twenty years with the pioneering work of Heinz Kohut (1971) and of Helen Block Lewis (1971) has begun to be acknowleged in psychoanalytic circles.

E. Pathology and Trauma

Psychopathology in Freud's early writings was entirely a pathology of ideas, a model that derived from his notion of retention hysteria and that basically had to do with a "picture with a charge on it," a traumatic memory with a quota of affect, in the phobias, compulsions, conversions, and delusions. In *The Interpretation of Dreams,* the latent dream thoughts with the quota of affect attached to them adhere to the same model of disturbance handled by repression. The method of *association of ideas* in each case was used to uncover the traumatic memory or the latent dream thought with subsequent affective release. Pathology, then, was portrayed simplistically as that of traumatic tension of an unconscious idea—in the case of the dream, of the latent dream thoughts. There was, in this earliest model, no conception of pathological structure—modification of the ego or pathological self struc-ture, lack of cohesion of the self.

The idea of pathological structures of ego and eventually of self and self structure evolved only later in the history of psychoanalysis. Its influence on the theory of dreams was not apparent for many years.

The idea that the structure of the ego could be altered or modified to deal with pathological, even psychotic, parts of the personality became clearly conceptualized only after the ascendancy of psychoanalytic ego psychology. The work of Blitzsten, Eissler, and Eissler (1950) was a landmark contribu-tion in conceptualizing the relation of ego modification to clinical dream analysis. These authors noted that hidden tendencies, often psychotic ones, in the ego and the central issues of the analysis could often be foreshadowed by the overall attitude of the dreamer's ego toward his dreams, which in retrospect revealed these difficulties taking place.

Dissociation, depersonalization, and splitting of the ego were also slow to be assimilated into the theory of dreams. Kleinian authors, including Melanie Klein (1946) herself, Bion (1977), Segal (1981), and Rosenfeld (1952), conceptualized splitting as a defensive operation more primitive than repres-sion and one in which parts of the self that were unacceptable were evacuated or gotten rid of. These have been mentioned in the preceding section. Levitan (1967), following the work of Bertram Lewin (1955), emphasized the process of dissociation and depersonalization in the dream with his nuanced study of the vicissitudes of dream life in a patient with severe depersonalization. Levitan's work, as in the case with that of Lewin, has had less influence than its originality and usefulness merit, probably because of the lack of comfort that most analysts have had working with dreams.

F. Wish Fulfillment and the Problem of Post-Traumatic Dreams

Freud, establishing the primacy of the wish fulfillment theory in his assertion that dreams have function, dealt with apparent counterexamples to the wish fulfillment theory. Punishment dreams could be seen as wishes for punishment and later as superego wishes. Anxiety dreams, an apparent counterexample to the wish fulfillment hypothesis, were so only superficially. It was not the case that the dream generated anxiety but rather that the wish generated anxiety in the face of censorship. It was the latent content, not the manifest content, that was the source of the anxiety.

It cannot be emphasized too strongly that it is the metapsychological, not the psychological significance of the wish fulfillment hypothesis that is of central theoretical importance. That is, it is not so much that dreams always reflect the psychology of wish and desire as that dreams have a disturbance-lowering and tension-reducing function that serves to keep the organism in some sort of homeostasis or equilibrium.

The problem of post-traumatic anxiety dreams was not taken up in *The Interpretation of Dreams,* nor was the problem of traumatic dreams, whether or not they awakened the dreamer. Freud, in *Beyond the Pleasure Principle* (1920) and in the *New Introductory Lectures* (1933), talks about both of those types of traumatic dream as though they were simple replays of the traumatic event. Although he does not say so, his line of thinking—one, uncharacteristically, never drawn from clinical material that he presents to the reader—tends to assume that the dream is a simple replay of the traumatic event. Hence, there seems to be no difference between the manifest and latent content, no dream work, no distortion, and the entire model of "the picture with the charge on it" seems to be at the manifest level of the symptomatology rather than at a latent level. From this point of view, the whole idea of psychoneurosis and the dream as basically a psychoneurotic structure seems to collapse.

Freud attempted to resolve this serious problem in 1920 by positing a wish for mastery, a wish *from the ego* rather than the id, a wish that precedes and goes beyond the pleasure principle. He argued that the purpose of the replay, so to speak, was to allow the ego to prepare itself with anticipatory anxiety so that then the situation could be mastered. Freud does not adduce clinical material, and he also makes the blatantly incorrect presumption that traumatic situations are never preceded by anticipatory anxiety. Certainly, combat veterans, Holocaust sufferers, and a host of other traumatic victims of childhood or adult trauma do have the opportunity to form anticipatory anxiety in the face of the trauma. Accordingly, Freud's line of thinking seems to be only dubiously derived from clinical evidence.

A significant contributor to the study of nightmares, but not of the theory of nightmares, was Ernest Jones, whose monograph *On the Nightmare* (1931) hypothesized that the feeling of weight, the breathlessness, and the paralysis so frequently reported by nightmare sufferers had to do with fantasies of being the passive partner in intercourse. Theodore Lidz (1946), studying acute combat nightmares, noted suicidal wishes and severe family dysfunction in his nightmare sufferers. The nightmare, then, served in part to screen disruptions that were due to familial trauma and the anger resulting from it.

J. O. Wisdom (1949) put forward an interesting hypothesis with the presumption that a traumatic dream was an exact replay of the traumatic situation. Wisdom conjectured that, even if traumatic dreams were seen as exact replays of the traumatic event, there might be significant dream work and latent content. Wisdom assumed that the victim in the nightmare was an internal object that the dreamer wished to attack—that is, only a part of the dreamer that the dreamer wished to be rid of, and not the entire person.

John Mack (1970), studying dreams and nightmares of children in his careful developmental studies, enlarged the theory of nightmares to include both anger and helplessness. Ernest Hartmann's (1984) book represents a fine synthesis of descriptive and laboratory psychiatry with psychoanalytic principles. Hartmann seems to ignore the familial pathology in nightmare sufferers.

Lansky and his coworkers (Lansky 1990; Lansky and Karger 1989; Lansky 1991) have pointed to the screening function and affect-transforming quality of post-traumatic nightmares in a sample comprised mostly of combat veterans. In this study, there was unmistakable latent content and dream work that seemed to use the return to the combat situation as a screen for sustained familial trauma throughout the life cycle. This hypothesis is strengthened by the fact that, in this sample, the choice to encounter the trauma, that is, to enlist not only for military service but also for combat, was a voluntary one in almost every case. The intensity of affect in the nightmares of these patients does not gainsay the idea that dreams have a function and that that function consists of an attempt to lower tension by representing the wishes fulfilled. Considering the intense and overwhelming shame and narcissistic disorganization in the dream day of these patients and shame-engendering conflicts in the day residue, it became apparent that the dream text seemed to transform shame into fear.

It does not seem necessary to evoke the idea of a "picture with a charge on it" for post-traumatic dreams or nightmares. If, rather than assuming that *memory contains affect,* one allows that *awareness itself evokes affect,* then one might imagine a screening function for traumatic dreams if the scene being reexperienced (even if it reflects a seemingly minor change in emphasis from the original traumatic scene) is somehow less disturbing than either the original traumatic scene or the emotional turbulence in the patient's immediate dream day. It is probable that the effects of the post-traumatic state in generating disturbing affect, especially shame, in the day residue have been overlooked in our conceptualization of traumatic dreams.

G. Beyond Clinical Data

Freud, in chapter 7 of *The Interpretation of Dreams,* turned to theory and philosophical considerations to attempt to make sense of the clinical material and the psychology of the dream processes. There tends to be a mistrust of philosophical thinking among analysts, although the reader contemplating the clinical data in chapters 2 through 6 of *The Interpretation of Dreams* is led strongly to the book's major philosophical question: What must the mind be like so that it can deceive itself? This level of questioning is on a different level from neurophysiological speculation.

Actual theorizing in chapter 7 occurs both on the metapsychological and the theoretical levels. On the metapsychological level, Freud presumes that *dreams have a function,* basically that of restoring homeostasis in the psyche, and that dreams—and indeed all mental activities—have a disturbance-lowering function that involves distortion and self-deception in the service of keeping disturbance within reasonable bounds. This metapsychology, fundamentally a type of philosophical hedonism, arguing that the mind operates to go from relative unpleasure to relative pleasure, is different from the drive theory, the theory of discharge dynamics, or the idea of the cathected neuron that Freud posits in this chapter to explain the clinical phenomenon. Metapsychology transcends the particulars of discharge dynamics that Freud used to theorize about metapsychology. The latter are more immediately dependent on the model of neurophysiology to which Freud adhered, that is to say, of the cathected neuron—"the picture with a charge on it"—or the idea or memory or latent dream thought with its quota of affect. The relationship of ideation to affect is presumed to be such that the *idea* (conscious or unconscious) *carries* a quota of affect (as opposed to a view of *awareness or consciousness itself such that it generates affect*). That is to say, awareness of one's wishes, especially conflictual ones, can be expected to generate affect and this awareness in turn may prove overwhelming if it is not in some way regulated. The fact that aspects of awareness are upsetting is a matter quite apart from any discharge phenomena involving desire (i.e., of the psychology or physiology of desire). One might imagine—viewing the process of distortion and self-deception—that the varying capacities to alter ideation would also alter affect that is a response to it, and hence in effect transform affect by distorting ideas. Consciousness or the capacity to be conscious would remain, therefore, a resultant of what affects are tolerable once consciousness is attained. Consciousness still remains secondary, so to speak, not primary, and the problem of self-deception—that is, the fact that the mind alters ideation to keep itself from being too disturbed—is still in focus.

There have been recent attempts to look at the theory of dreams and the function of dreams utilizing the results of laboratory investigation of sleep and dreams. Charles Fisher (1978), one of the very few psychoanalysts who was a qualified laboratory researcher, reached perhaps the highest level of synthesis between psychoanalytic data, psychoanalytic theory, and sleep data. The newer generation of sleep researchers tends to be so dominated by the particular technology available and particular research methods at hand that the result has been either a dismissal of the meaning of dreams altogether or an overemphasis on phenomena correlated with the presence or absence of REM (rapid eye movement) sleep to the point where scientific observation seems to be overshadowed by the narrow range of particular technology at hand. In some of these studies (Hobson 1988) there seems to be an assumption that newer methods overshadow both clinical evidence and theoretical implications so completely as to render them utterly invalid. There seems to be in the writings of many sleep researchers either an ignoring of the function of dreams altogether (ironically, the state of affairs to which chapter 1 of *The Interpretation of Dreams* is addressed) or a tendency to assume that the parameters of REM or NREM sleep govern our ability to think about dreams altogether.

V

Theoretical controversy and accumulation of empirical knowledge about dreams have had much less effect on the overall understanding of dreams in psychoanalysis than has the increased understanding of psychoanalytic phenomena seen in terms of the analytic process.

Freud's earliest self-analytic researches took place in the form of self-analysis and dream analysis. As has been pointed out by Erikson (1954) and Schur (1966), these investigations took place in the presence of an unacknowledged, intense transference to Wilhelm Fleiss. It is a major feature of the legacy of *The Interpretation of Dreams* that some of our most detailed knowledge of dream formation took place in the context of an intense transferential process that was not acknowledged.

Freud's discovery of the transference (1905a) and of the analytic process, in fact, took place in his attempt to encourage Dora to engage in a type of dream analysis in the famous case that originally bore the title "Dreams and Hysteria." Very little of Freud's subsequent contributions on dreams or of his revisions of *The Interpretation of Dreams* concern the psychoanalytic process itself.

Every major school of psychoanalytic thought after Freud—I shall touch here on ego psychological, Kleinian, and self psychological points of view —has evolved new and more precise conceptualizations of the analytic process. The result has been in each school to involve an approach to dreams that is difficult to disentangle from the view of the analytic process as a whole. Ego psychology emphasizes synthetic and decision-making facets of the ego in relation to the transference and the analytic process (Fromm and French 1962; Arlow and Brenner 1964; Brenner 1969; Weiss 1986). Kleinians (Bion 1977; Segal 1981; Meltzer 1984) use process-oriented concepts such as projective identification and a newer view of countertransference that sees the countertransference as a response to the patient's projective identification, that is, in terms of the psychoanalytic process. Self psychologists (Kohut 1977; Stolorow and Atwood 1992), with heightened understanding of fragmentation phenomena and a more refined concept of empathy as an intersubjective phenomenon, also attain a more process-oriented view of the psychoanalytic enterprise.

Each of these schools has evolved conceptualizations·of analytic data that move away from Freud's (1900) original preoccupation with the nature of the mind considered more or less in isolation and toward a consideration of the mind in the context of self in relation to the other—to psychoanalytic data in terms of the transfernce, that is, the analytic process.

The status of psychoanalytic dream theory at any given time is a function of the status of conceptualization of the analytic process. Developments in the theory of dream proceed pari passu with enhancement of conceptualization of the psychoanalytic process. The theory of dreams has, since Dora left her analysis on the last day of the nineteenth century, been in steady state with psychoanalytic appreciation of the process. This dependence on context makes it difficult and always somewhat arbitrary to separate the current theory of dreams from the current status of psychoanalytic knowledge generally. This burden to return to the context of the psychoanalytic situation is the legacy of *The Interpretation of Dreams*. The student of dreams is left with the formidable task of conceptualizing particular clinical contribtuions about dreams in terms of the prevailing view of the analytic process in which those dreams are examined or of integrating nonclinical viewpoints into the analytic situation as it is currently understood.

REFERENCES

Arlow, J., Brenner, C. (1964) *Psychoanalytic Concepts and the Structural Theory.* New York, International Universities Press.

Basch, M. (1976) Theory formation in chapter 7: A critique. *J. Am. Psychoanalyt Assoc* **24:** 61–100.

Bion, W. R. (1977) *Seven Servants.* New York, Aronson.

Blitzsten, N. L., Eissler, R. S., Eissler, K. R. (1950) Emergence of hidden ego tendencies during dream analysis. *Int. J. PsAn.* **31:**12–17.

Brenner, C. (1969) The dream in clinical psychoanalytic practice. *J. Nerv. Ment. Dis.* **149:** 122–32.

——— (1976) *Psychoanalytic Technique and Psychic Conflict.* New York, International Universities Press.

Breuer, J., Freud, S. (1895) *Studies in Hysteria. Standard Edition.* London, Hogarth, 1956.

Erikson, E. H. (1954) The dream specimen of psychoanalysis. *J. Am. Psychoanalyt. Assoc.*2: 5–56.

Federn, P. (1932) Ego feeling in dreams. *PsAn Quart* **1:**511–42.

Fine, B., Moore, B., Waldhorn, H. (1969) *The Manifest Content of the Dream.* Kris Study Group Monograph III. New York, International Universities Press.

Fisher, C. (1978) Experimental and clinical approaches to the mind body problem through recent research in sleep and dreams. In Rosenzweig, N., Griscom, H. (Eds.), *Psychopharmacology and Psychotherapy: Synthesis or Antithesis.* New York, Human Sciences Press.

Fosshage, J. (1983) The psychological function of dreams: A revised psychoanalytic perspective. *Psychoanal. & Contemp. Thought* 6:641–69.

Freud, S. (1895) *Project for a Scientific Psychology. Standard Edition*, vol. I. London, Hogarth, 1966.

—— (1900) *The Interpretation of Dreams. Standard Edition*, vols. IV, V. London, Hogarth, 1953.

—— (1905a) *Fragment of an Analysis of a Case of Hysteria. Standard Edition*, vol. VIII:7–122. London, Hogarth, 1953.

—— (1905b)*Three Essays on Sexuality. Standard Edition*, vol. VII. London, Hogarth, 1953.

—— (1920) *Beyond the Pleasure Principle. Standard Edition*, vol. XVIII. London, Hogarth, 1955.

—— (1923) *The Ego and the Id. Standard Edition*, vol. XIX. London, Hogarth, 1961.

—— (1933) Revision of the theory of dreams. In *New Introductory Lectures on Psychoanalysis. Standard Edition*, vol. XXII. London, Hogarth, 1964.

Fromm, E., French, T. (1962) Formation and evaluation of hypotheses in dream interpretation. *J. Psychol.* 54:271–83.

Glover, E. (1929) The screening function of traumatic memories. *Int. J. Psychoanal.* 10:90–93.

Greenson, R. (1970) The exceptional position of the dream in psychoanalytic practice. *PsAn Quart,* 39:519–49.

Grinstein, A. (1980) *Sigmund Freud's Dreams*. New York, International Universities Press.

—— (1983) *Freud's Rules of Dream Interpretation*. Madison, CT, International Universities Press.

Hartmann, E. (1984) *The Nightmare: The Psychology and Biology of Terrifying Dreams*. New York, Basic.

Hobson, J. A. (1988) *The Dreaming Brain*. New York, Basic.

Jones, E. (1931) *On the Nightmare*. London, Hogarth.

Klein, M. (1946) Notes on some schizoid mechanisms. In *Int. J. Psychoanal.* 27:99–110.

Kohut, H. (1971) *The Analysis of the Self*. New York, International Universities Press.

—— (1977) *The Restoration of the Self*. Madison, CT, International Universities Press.

Lacan, J. (1977) *Ecrits*. A. Sheridan, tr. New York, Norton.

Lansky, M. (1990) The screening function of post-traumatic nightmares. *Brit. J. Psychother.* 6:384–400.

—— (1991) Transformation of affects in post-traumatic nightmares. *Bull. Menninger Cl.* 55:470–90.

Lansky, M., Karger, J. (1989) Post-traumatic nightmares and the family. *Hillside J. Clin. Psychiat* 11:169–83.

Levitan, H. (1967) Depersonalization and the dream. *PsAn Quart.* 36:157–71.

Lewin, B. (1955) Dream psychology and the analytic situation. *Psychoanal. Quart.* 24:168–99.

Lewis, H. B. (1971) *Shame and Guilt in Neurosis*. New York, International Universities Press.

Lidz, T. (1946) Nightmares and the combat neurosis. *Psychiatry* 9:37–49.

Mack, J. (1970) *Nightmares and Human Conflict*. Boston, Little Brown.

Meltzer, D. (1984) *Dream-Life: A Reexamination of Psychoanalytic Theory and Technique*. London, Clunie.

Ornstein, P. (1987) Self state dreams. In Rothstein, A. (Ed.), *The Interpretations of Dreams in Clinical Pracitce*. Madison, CT, International Universities Press.

Palombo, S. (1988) Day residue and screen memory in Freud's dream of the botanical monograph. *J. Am. Psychoanalyt Assoc* 36:881–904.

Pulver, S. (1987) The manifest dream in psychoanalysis: A clarification. *J. Am. Psychoanalyt. Assoc.* **35**:99–118.

Reed, G. (1987) Rules of clinical understanding in classical psychoanalysis and in self psychology: A comparison. *J. Am. Psychoanalyt. Assoc.* **35**:421–46.

Rosenbaum, M. (1965) Dreams in which the analyst appears undisguised: A clinical and statistical study. *Int. J. Psychoanal.* **46**:429–37.

Rosenfeld, H. (1952) *Psychotic States.* London, Hogarth.

Scheff, T. (1990) *Microsociology.* Chicago, University of Chicago Press.

Schur, M. (1966) Some further "day residues" of "the specimen dream of psychoanalysis." In Lowenstein, R. M., Schur, M., Solnit, A. (Eds.), *Psychoanalysis: A General Psychology.* New York, International Universities Press.

Segal, H. (1981) The function of dreams. In Grotstein, J. (Ed.), *Do I Dare Disturb the Universe: A Memorial to Wilfred Bion.* Beverly Hills, Caesura Press.

Spanjaard, J. (1969) The manifest dream content and its significance to the interpretation of dreams. *Int. J. Psychoanal.* **50**:221–35.

Stewart, W. (1967) Comments on the manifest content of certain types of unusual dreams. *Psychoanalyt. Quart.* **36**:329–41.

Stolorow, R., Atwood, G. (1992) Dreams and the subjective world. Chapter 12 in this volume.

Weiss, J. (1986) Dreams and their various purposes. In Weiss, J., Simpson, H., *The Psychoanalytic Process.* New York, Guilford.

Wisdom, J. (1949) A hypothesis to explain trauma reenactment dreams. *Int. J. Psychoanal.* **31**:13–20.

2. Revision of the Theory of Dreams

Sigmund Freud

Ladies and Gentlemen,—If, after an interval of more than fifteen years, I have brought you together again to discuss with you what novelties, and what improvements it may be, the intervening time has introduced into psycho-analysis, it is right and fitting from more than one point of view that we should turn our attention first to the position of the theory of dreams. It occupies a special place in the history of psycho-analysis and marks a turning-point; it was with it that analysis took the step from being a psycho-therapeutic procedure to being a depth-psychology. Since then, too, the theory of dreams has remained what is most characteristic and peculiar about the young science, something to which there is no counterpart in the rest of our knowledge, a stretch of new country, which has been reclaimed from popular beliefs and mysticism. The strangeness of the assertions it was obliged to put forward has made it play the part of a shibboleth, the use of which decided who could become a follower of psycho-analysis and to whom it remained for ever incomprehensible. I myself found it a sheet-anchor during those difficult times when the unrecognized facts of the neuroses used to confuse my inexperienced judgement. Whenever I began to have doubts of the correctness of my wavering conclusions, the successful transformation of a senseless and muddled dream into a logical and intelligible mental process in the dreamer would renew my confidence of being on the right track.

It is therefore of special interest to us, in the particular instance of the theory of dreams, on the one hand to follow the vicissitudes through which psycho-analysis has passed during this interval, and on the other hand to learn what advances it has made in being understood and appreciated by the contemporary world. I may tell you at once that you will be disappointed in both these directions.

Let us look through the volumes of the *Internationale Zeitshrift für (ärztliche) Psychoanalyse [International Journal of (Medical) Psycho-Analysis]*, in which, since 1913, the authoritative writings in our field of work have been brought together. In the earlier volumes you will find a recurrent sectional heading 'On Dream-Interpretation', containing numerous contributions on various points in the theory of dreams. But the further you go the rarer do these contributions become, and finally the sectional heading disappears completely. The analysts behave as though they had no more to say about dreams, as though there was nothing more to be added to the theory of dreams. But if you ask how much of dream-interpretation has been accepted by outsiders—by the many psychiatrists and psychotherapists who warm their pot of soup at our fire (incidentally without being very grateful for our hospitality), by what are described as educated people, who are in the habit of assimilating the more striking findings of science, by the literary men and by the public at large—the reply gives little cause for satisfaction. A few formulas have become generally familiar, among them some that we have never put forward—such as the thesis that all dreams are of a sexual nature —but really important things like the fundamental distinction between the manifest content of dreams and the latent dream-thoughts, the realization that the wish-fulfilling function of dreams is not contradicted by anxiety-dreams, the impossibility of interpreting a dream unless one has the dreamer's associations to it at one's disposal, and, above all, the discovery that what is essential in dreams is the process of the dream-work—all this still seems about as foreign to general awareness as it was thirty years ago. I am in a position to say this, since in the course of that period I have received innumerable letters whose writers present their dreams for interpretation or ask for information about the nature of dreams and who declare that they have read my *Interpretation of Dreams*, though in every sentence they betray their lack of understanding of our theory of dreams. But all this shall not deter us from once more giving a connected account of what we know about dreams. You will recall that last time we devoted a whole number of lectures to showing how we came to understand this hitherto unexplained mental phenomenon.[1]

Let us suppose, then, that someone—a patient in analysis, for instance— tells us one of his dreams. We shall assume that in this way he is making us one of the communications to which he had pledged himself by the fact of having started an analytic treatment. It is, to be sure, a communication made by inappropriate means, for dreams are not in themselves social utterances, not a means of giving information. Nor, indeed, do we understand what the dreamer was trying to say to us, and he himself is equally in the dark. And now we have to make a quick decision. On the one hand, the dream may be, as non-analytic doctors assure us, a sign that the dreamer has slept badly, that not every part of his brain has come to rest equally, that some areas of it, under the influence of unknown stimuli, endeavoured to go on working but were only able to do so in a very incomplete fashion. If that is the case, we shall be right to concern ourselves no further with the product of a nocturnal disturbance which has no psychical value: for what could we expect to derive from investigating it that would be of use for our purposes? Or on the other hand—but it is plain that we have from the first decided otherwise. We have—quite arbitrarily, it must be admitted—made the assumption, adopted as a postulate, that even this unintelligible dream must be a fully valid psychical act, with sense and worth, which we can use in analysis like any other communication. Only the outcome of our experiment can show whether we are right. If we succeed in turning the dream into an utterance of value of that kind, we shall evidently have a prospect of learning something new and of recieving communications of a sort which would otherwise be inaccessible to us.

Now, however, the difficulties of our task and the enigmas of our subject rise before our eyes. How do we propose to transform the dream into a normal communication and how do we explain the fact that some of the patient's utterances have assumed a form that is unintelligible both to him and to us?

As you see, Ladies and Gentlemen, this time I am taking the path not of a genetic but of a dogmatic exposition. Our first step is to establish our new attitude to the problem of dreams by introducing two new concepts and names. What has been called the dream we shall describe as the text of the dream or the *manifest* dream, and what we are looking for, what we suspect, so to say, of lying behind the dream, we shall describe as the *latent* dream-thoughts. Having done this, we can express our two tasks as follows. We have to transform the manifest dream into the latent one, and to explain how, in the dreamer's mind, the latter has become the former. The first portion is a *practical* task, for which dream-interpretation is responsible; it calls for a technique. The second portion is a *theoretical* task, whose business it is to explain the hypothetical dream-work; and it can only be a theory. Both of them, the technique of dream-interpretation and the theory of the dream-work, have to be newly created.

With which of the two, then, shall we start? With the technique of dream-interpretation, I think; it will present a more concrete appearance and make a more vivid impression on you.

Well then, the patient has told us a dream, which we are to interpret. We have listened passively, without putting our powers of reflection into action.[2] What do we do next? We decide to concern ourselves as little as possible with what we have heard, with the *manifest* dream. Of course this manifest dream exhibits all sorts of characteristics which are not entirely a matter of indifference to us. It may be coherent, smoothly constructed like a literary composition, or it may be confused to the point of unintelligibility, almost like a delirium; it may contain absurd elements or jokes and apparently witty conclusions; it may seem to the dreamer clear and sharp or obscure and hazy; its pictures may exhibit the complete sensory strength of perceptions or may be shadowy like an indistinct mist; the most diverse characteristics may be present in the same dream, distributed over various portions of it; the dream, finally, may show an indifferent emotional tone or be accompanied by feelings of the strongest joy or distress. You must not suppose that we think nothing of this endless diversity in manifest dreams. We shall come back to it later and we shall find a great deal in it that we can make use of in our interpretations. But for the moment we will disregard it and follow the main road that leads to the interpretation of dreams. That is to say, we ask the dreamer, too, to free himself from the impression of the manifest dream, to divert his attention from the dream as a whole on to the separate portions of its content and to report to us in succession everything that occurs to him in relation to each of these portions—what associations present themselves to him if he focuses on each of them separately.

That is a curious technique, is it not?—not the usual way of dealing with a communication or utterance. And no doubt you guess that behind this procedure there are assumptions which have not yet been expressly stated. But let us proceed. In what order are we to get the patient to take up the portions of his dream? There are various possibilities open to us. We can simply follow the chronological order in which they appeared in the account of the dream. That is what may be called the strictest, classical method. Or we can direct the dreamer to begin by looking out for the 'day's residues' in the dream; for experience has taught us that almost every dream includes the remains of a memory or an allusion to some event (or often to several events) of the day before the dream, and, if we follow these connections, we often arrive with one blow at the transition from the apparently far remote dream-world to the real life of the patient. Or, again, we may tell him to start with those elements of the dream's content which strike him by their special clarity and sensory strength; for we know that he will find it particularly easy to get associations to these. It makes no difference by which of these methods we approach the assocations we are in seach of.[3]

And next, we obtain these associations. What they bring us is of the most various kinds: memories from the day before, the 'dream-day', and from times long past, reflections, discussions, with arguments for and against, confessions and enquiries. Some of them the patient pours out; when he comes to others he is held up for a time. Most of them show a clear connection to some element of the dream; no wonder, since those elements were their starting-point. But it also sometimes happens that the patient introduces them with these words: 'This seems to me to have nothing at all to do with the dream, but I tell it you because it occurs to me.'

If one listens to these copious associations, one soon notices that they have more in common with the content of the dream than their starting-points alone. They throw a surprising light on all the different parts of the dream, fill in gaps between them, and make their strange juxtapositions intelligible. In the end one is bound to become clear about the relation between them and the dream's content. The dream is seen to be an abbreviated selection from the associations, as selection made, it is true, according to rules that we have not yet understood: the elements of the dream are like representatives chosen by election from a mass of people. There can be no doubt that by our technique we have got hold of something for which the dream is a substitute and in which lies the dream's psychical value, but which no longer exhibits its puzzling peculiarities, its strangeness and its confusion.

Let there by no misunderstanding, however. The associations to the dream are not yet the latent dream-thoughts. The latter are contained in the associations like an alkali in the mother-liquor, but yet not quite completely contained in them. On the one hand, the associations give us far more than we need for formulating the latent dream-thoughts—names all the explanations, transitions, and conections which the patient's intellect is bound to produce in the course of his approach to the dream-thoughts. On the other hand, an association often comes to a stop precisely before the genuine dream-thought:

it has only come near to it and has only had contact with it through allusions. At that point we intervene on our own; we fill in the hints, draw undeniable conclusions, and give explicit utterance to what the patient has only touched on in his associations. This sounds as though we allowed our ingenuity and caprice to play with the material put at our disposal by the dreamer and as though we misused it in order to interpret *into* his utterances what cannot be interpreted *from* them. Nor is it easy to show the legitimacy of our procedure in an abstract description of it. But you have only to carry out a dream-analysis yourselves or study a good account of one in our literature and you will be convinced of the cogent manner in which interpretative work like this proceeds.

If in general and primarily we are dependent, in interpreting dreams, on the dreamer's associations, yet in relation to certain elements of the dream's content we adopt a quite independent attitude, chiefly because we have to, because as a rule associations fail to materialize in their case. We noticed at an early stage that it is always in connection with the same elements that this happens; they are not very numerous, and repeated experience has taught us that they are to be regarded and interpreted as *symbols* of something else. As contrasted with the other dream-elements, a fixed meaning may be attributed to them, which, however, need not be unambiguous and whose range is determined by special rules with which we are unfamiliar. Since *we* know how to translate these symbols and the dreamer does not, in spite of having used them himself, it may happen that the sense of a dream may at once become clear to us as we have heard the text of the dream, even before we have made any efforts at interpreting it, while it still remains an enigma to the dreamer himself. But I have said so much to you in my earlier lectures about symbolism, our knowledge of it and the problems it poses us, that I need not repeat it to-day.[4]

That, then, is our method of interpreting dreams. The first and justifiable question is: 'Can we interpret *all* dreams by its help?'[5] And the answer is: 'No, not all; but so many that we feel confident in the serviceability and correctness of the procedure.' 'But why not all?' The answer to this has something important to teach us, which at once introduces us into the psychical determinants of the formation of dreams: 'Because the work of interpreting dreams is carried out against a resistance, which varies between trivial dimensions and invincibility (at least so far as the strength of our present methods reaches).' It is impossible during our work to overlook the manifestations of this resistance. At some points the associations are given without hesitation and the first or second idea that occurs to the patient brings an explanation. At other points there is a stoppage and the patient hesitates before bringing out an association, and, if so, we often have to listen to a long chain of ideas before receiving anything that helps us to understand the dream. We are certainly right in thinking that the longer and more roundabout the chain of associations the stronger the resistance. We can detect the same influence at work in the forgetting of dreams. It happens often enough that a patient, despite all his efforts, cannot remember one of his dreams. But after we have been able in the course of a piece of analytic work to get rid of a difficulty which had been disturbing his relation to the analysis, the forgotten dream suddenly re-emerges. Two other observations are also in place here. It very frequently comes about that, to begin with, a portion of a dream is omitted and added afterwards as an addendum. This is to be regarded as an attempt to forget that portion. Experience shows that it is that particular piece which is the most important; there was a greater resistance, we suppose, in the path of communicating it than the other parts of the dream.[6] Furthermore, we often find that a dreamer endeavours to prevent himself from forgetting his dreams by fixing them in writing immediately after waking up. We can tell him that that is no use. For the resistance from which he has extorted the preservation of the text of the dream will then be displaced on to its associations and will make the manifest dream inaccessible to interpretation.[7] In view of these facts we need not feel surprised if a further increase in the resistance suppresses the associations altogether and thus brings the interpretation of the dream to nothing.

From all this we infer that the resistance which we come across in the work of interpreting dreams must also have had a share in their origin. We can actually distinguish between dreams that arose under a slight and under a high pressure of resistance.[8] But this pressure varies as well from place to place within one and the same dream; it is responsible for the gaps, obscurities and confusions which may interrupt the continuity of even the finest of dreams.

But what is creating the resistance and against what is it aimed? Well, the resistance is the surest sign to us of a conflict. There must be a force here which is seeking to express something and another which is striving to prevent its expression. What comes about in consequence as a manifest dream may combine all the decisions into which this struggle between two trends has been condensed. At one point one of these forces may have succeeded in putting through what it wanted to say, while at another point it

is the opposing agency which has managed to blot out the intended communication completely or to replace it by something that reveals not a trace of
it. The commonest and most characteristic cases of dream-construction are
those in which the conflict has ended in compromise, so that the communicating agency has, it is true, been able to say what it wanted but not in the
way it wanted—only in a softened down, distorted and unrecognized form.
If, then, dreams do not give a faithful picture of the dream-thoughts and if
the work of interpretation is required in order to bridge the gap between
them, that is the outcome of the opposing, inhibiting and restricting agency
which we have inferred from our perception of the resistance while we
interpret dreams. So long as we studied dreams as isolated phenomena
independent of the psychical structures akin to the, we named this agency the
censor [9] *of dreams.*

You have long been aware that this censorship is not an institution peculiar
to dream-life. You know that the conflict between the two psychical agencies, which we—inaccurately—describe as the 'unconscious repressed' and
the 'conscious', dominates our whole mental life and that the resistance
against the interpretation of dreams, the sign of the dream-censorship, is
nothing other than the resistance due to repression by which the two agencies
are separated. You know too that the conflict between these two agencies
may under certain conditions produce other psychical structures which, like
dreams, are the outcome of compromises; and you will not expect me to
repeat to you here everything that was contained in my introduction to the
theory of the neuroses in order to demonstrate to you what we know of the
determinants of the formation of such compromises. You have realized that
the dream is a pathological product, the first member of the class which
includes hysterical symptoms, obsessions and delusions, [10] but that it is
distinguished from the others by its transitoriness and by its occurrence under
conditions which are part of normal life. For let us bear firmly in mind that,
as was already pointed out by Aristotle, dream-life is the way in which our
mind works during the state of sleep. [11] The state of sleep involves a turning-
away from the real external world, and there we have the necessary condition
for the development of a psychosis. The most careful study of the severe
psychoses will not reveal to us a single feature that is more characteristic of
those pathological conditions. In psychoses, however, the turning-away from
reality is brought about in two kinds of way: either by the unconscious
repressed becoming excessively strong so that it overwhelms the conscious,
which is attached to reality, [12] or because reality has become so intolerably

distressing that the threatened ego throws itself into the arms of the unconscious instinctual forces in a desperate revolt. The harmless dream-psychosis is the result of a withdrawal from the external world which is consciously willed and only temporary, and it disappears when relations to the external world are resumed. During the isolation of the sleeping individual an alteration in the distribution of his psychical energy also sets in; a part of the expenditure on repression, which is normally required in order to hold the unconscious down, can be saved, for if the unconscious makes use of its relative liberation for active purposes, it finds its path to motility closed and the only path open to it is the harmless one leading to hallucinatory satisfaction. Now, therefore, a dream can be formed; but the fact of the dream-censorship shows that even during sleep enough of the resistance due to repression is retained.

Here we are presented with a means of answering the question of whether dreams have a function too, whether they are entrusted with any useful achievement. The condition of rest free from stimulus, which the state of sleep wishes to establish, is threatened from three directions: in a relatively accidental manner by external stimuli during sleep, and by interests of the previous day which cannot be broken off, and in an unavoidable manner by unsated repressed instinctual impulses which are on the watch for an opportunity of finding expression. In consequence of the diminishing of repressions at night there would be a risk that the rest afforded by sleep would be interrupted whenever an instigation from outside or from inside succeeded in linking up with an unconscious instinctual source. The process of dreaming allows the product of a collaboration of this kind to find an outlet in a harmless hallucinatory experience and in that way assures a continuation of sleep. The fact that a dream occasionally awakens the sleeper, to the accompaniment of a generation of anxiety, is no contradiction of this function but rather, perhaps, a signal that the watchman regards the situation as too dangerous and no longer feels able to control it. And very often then, while we are still asleep, a consolation occurs to us which seeks to prevent our waking up: 'But after all it's only a dream!'

This was what I wanted to say to you, Ladies and Gentlemen, about dream-interpretation, whose task it is to lead the way from the manifest dream to the latent dream-thoughts. When this has been achieved, interest in a dream, so far as practical analysis is concerned, is for the most part at an end. We add the communication we have received in the form of a dream to the rest of the patient's communications and proceed with the analysis. We, however, have an interest in dwelling a little longer on the dream. We are tempted to study the process by which the latent dream-thoughts were transformed into the manifest dream. We call this the 'dream-work'. As you will recall, I described it in such detail in my earlier lectures [13] that I can restrict my present survey to the most concise summary.

The process of the dream-work, then, is something entirely new and strange, nothing resembling which was known before. It has given us our first glimpse of the processes which take place in the unconscious system and has shown us that they are quite other than what we know from our conscious thinking and are bound to appear to the latter preposterous and incorrect. The importance of this finding was then increased by the discovery that in the construction of neurotic symptoms the same mechanisms (we do not venture to say 'processes of thought') are operative as those which have transformed the latent dream-thoughts into the manifest dream.

In what follows I shall not be able to avoid a schematic method of exposition. Let us assume that in a particular case we have before us all the latent thoughts, charged with a greater or less amount of affect, by which the manifest dream has been replaced after its interpretation has been completed. We shall then be struck by one difference among these latent thoughts, and that difference will take us a long way. Almost all these dream-thoughts are recognized by the dreamer or acknowledged by him; he admits that he has thought this, now or at some other time, or that he might have thought it. There is only one single thought that he refuses to accept; it is strange to him or even perhaps repellent; he may possibly reject it with passionate feeling. It now becomes evident to us that the other thoughts are portions of a conscious, or, more accurately, a preconscious train of thinking. They might have been thought in waking life too, and indeed they were probably formed during the previous day. This one repudiated thought, however, or, properly speaking, this one impulse, is a child of night; it belongs to the dreamer's unconscious and on that account it is repudiated and rejected by him. It had to wait for the nightly relaxation of repression in order to arrive at any kind of expression. And in any case this expression is a weakened, distorted and disguised one; without our work of dream-interpretation we should not have found it. This unconscious impulse has to thank its link with the other, unobjectionable, dream-thoughts for the opportunity of slipping past the barrier of the censorship in an inconspicuous disguise. On the other hand, the preconscious dream-thoughts have to thank this same link for the power to occupy mental life during sleep as well. For there is no doubt about it: this unconscious impulse is the true creator of the dream; it is what produces the psychical energy for the dream's construction. Like any other instinctual impulse, it cannot strive for anything other than its own satisfaction; and our experience in interpreting dreams shows us too that that is the sense of all dreaming. In every dream an instinctual wish has to be represented as fulfilled. The shutting-off of mental life from reality at night and the regression to primitive mechanisms which this makes possible enable this wished-for instinctual satisfaction to be experienced in a hallucinatory manner as occurring in the present. As a result of this same regression, ideas are transformed in the dream into visual pictures: the latent dream-thoughts, that is to say, are dramatized and illustrated.

This piece of the dream-work gives us information about some of the most striking and peculiar features of dreams. I will repeat the course of events in dream-formation. As an introduction: the wish to sleep and intentional turning away from the external world. Next, two consequences of this for the mental apparatus: first, the possibility for older and more primitive methods of working to emerge in it—regression; secondly, the lowering of the resistance due to repression which weighs down upon the unconscious. As a result of this last factor the possibility arises for the formation of a dream and this is taken advantage of by the precipitating causes, the internal and external stimuli which have become active. The dream which originates in this way is already a compromise-structure. It has a double function; on the one hand it is ego-syntonic,[14] since, by getting rid of the stimuli which are interfering with sleep, it serves the wish to sleep; on the other hand it allows a repressed instinctual impulse to obtain the satisfaction that is possible in these circumstances, in the form of the hallucinated fulfilment of a wish. The whole process of forming a dream which is permitted by the sleeping ego is, however, subject to the condition of the censorship, which is exercised by the residue of the repression still in operation. I cannot present the process more simply: it is not more simple. But I can proceed now with my description of the dream-work.

Let us go back once more to the latent dream-thoughts. Their most powerful element is the repressed instinctual impulse which has created in them an expression for itself on the basis of the presence of chance stimuli and by transference on to the day's residues—though an expression that is toned down and disguised. Like every instinctual impulse, it too presses for satisfaction by action; but its path to motility is blocked by the physiological regulations implied in the state of sleep; it is compelled to take the backwards course in the direction of perception and to be content with a hallucinated satisfaction. The latent dream-thoughts are thus transformed into a collection of sensory images and visual scenes. It is as they travel on this course that what seems to us so novel and so strange occurs to them. All the linguistic instruments by which we express the subtler relations of thought—the conjunctions and prepositions, the changes in declension and conjugation—are dropped, because there are no means of representing them; just as in a primitive language without any grammar, only the raw material of thought is expressed and abstract terms are taken back to the concrete ones that are at their basis. What is left over after this may well appear disconnected. The copious employment of symbols, which have become alien to conscious thinking, for representing certain objects and processes is in harmony alike with the archaic regression in the mental apparatus and with the demands of the censorship.

But other changes made in the elements of the dream-thoughts go far beyond this. Such of those elements as allow any point of contact to be found between them are *condensed* into new unities. In the process of transforming the thoughts into pictures, preference is unmistakably given to such as permit of this putting-together, this condensation; it is as though a force were at work which was subjecting the material to compression and concentration. As a result of condensation, one element in the manifest dream may correspond to numerous elements in the latent dream-thoughts; but, conversely too, one element in the dream-thoughts may be represented by several images in the dream.

Still more remarkable is the other process—*displacement* or shifting of accent—which in conscious thinking we come across only as faulty reasoning or as means for a joke. The different ideas in the dream-thoughts are, indeed, not all of equal value; they are cathected with quotas of affect of varying magnitude and are correspondingly judged to be important and deserving of interest to a greater or less degree. In the dream-work these ideas are separated from the affects attaching to them. The affects are dealt with independently; they may be displaced on to something else, they may be retained, they may undergo alterations, or they may not appear in the dream at all. The importance of the ideas that have been stripped of their affect returns in the dream as sensory strength in the dream-pictures; but we observe that this accent has passed over from important elements to indifferent ones. Thus something that played only a minor part in the dream-thoughts seems to be pushed into the foreground in the dream as the main thing, while, on the contrary, what was the essence of the dream-thoughts finds only passing and indistinct representation in the dream. No other part of the dream-work is so much responsible for making the dream strange and incomprehensible to the dreamer. Displacement is the principal means used in the *dream-distortion* to which the dream-thoughts must submit under the influence of the censorship.

After these influences have been brought to bear upon the dream-thoughts the dream is almost complete. A further, somewhat variable, factor also comes into play—known as 'secondary revision'—after the dream has been presented before consciousness as an object of perception. At that point we treat it as we are in general accustomed to treat the contents of our perception: we fill in gaps and introduce connections, and in doing so are often guilty of gross misunderstandings. But this activity, which might be described as a rationalizing one and which at best provides the dream with a smooth façade that cannot fit its true content, may also be omitted or only be expressed to a very modest degree—in which case the dream will display all its rents and cracks openly. It must not be forgotten, on the other hand, that the dream-work does not always operate with equal energy either; it often restricts itself to certain portions of the dream-thoughts only and others of them are allowed to appear in the dream unaltered. In such cases an impression is given of the dream having carried out the most delicate and complex intellectual operations, of its having speculated, made jokes, arrived at decisions and solved problems, whereas all this is a product of our normal mental activity, may have been performed equally well during the day before the dream as during the night, has nothing to do with the dream-work and brings nothing to light that is characteristic of dreams. Nor is it superfluous to insist once more on the contrast within the dream-thoughts themselves between the unconscious instinctual impulse and the day's residues. While the latter exhibit all the multiplicity of our mental acts, the former, which becomes the motive force proper of the forming of the dream, finds its outlet invariably in the fulfilment of a wish.

I could have told you all this fifteen years ago, and indeed I believe I did in fact tell it you then. And now let me bring together such changes and new discoveries as may have been made during the interval. I have said already that I am afraid you will find that it amounts to very little, and you will fail to understand why I obliged you to listen to the same thing twice over, and obliged myself to say it. But fifteen years have passed meanwhile and I hope that this will be my easiest way of reestablishing contact with you. Moreover, these are such fundamental things, of such decisive importance for understanding psycho-analysis, that one may be glad to hear them a second time, and it is in itself worth knowing that they have remained so much the same for fifteen years.

In the literature of this period you will of course find a large quantity of confirmatory material and of presentation of details, of which I intend only to give you samples. I shall also, incidentally, be able to tell you a few things that were in fact already known earlier. What is in question is principally the symbolism in dreams and the other methods of representation in them. Now listen to this. Only quite a short while ago the medical faculty in an American University refused to allow psycho-analysis the status of a science, on the ground that it did not admit of any experimental proof. They might have raised the same objection to astronomy; indeed, experimentation with the heavenly bodies is particularly difficult. There one has to fall back on observation. Nevertheless, some Viennese investigators have actually made a beginning with experimental confirmation of our dream symbolism. As long ago as in 1912 a Dr. Schrötter found that if instructions to dream of sexual matters are given to deeply hypnotized subjects, then in the dream that is thus provoked the sexual material emerges with its place taken by the symbols that are familiar to us. For instance, a woman was told to dream of sexual intercourse with a female friend. In her dream this friend appeared with a traveling-bag on which was pasted the label 'Ladies Only'. Still more impressive experiments were carried out by Betlheim and Hartmann in 1924. They worked with patients suffering from what is known as the Korsakoff confusional psychosis. They told these patients stories of a grossly sexual kind and observed the distortions which appeared when the patients were instructed to reproduce what they had been told. Once more there emerged the symbols for sexual organs and sexual intercourse that are familiar to us —among them the symbol of the staircase which, as the writers justly remark, could never have been reached by a conscious wish to distort.[15]

In a very interesting series of experiments, Herbert Silberer [1909 and 1912] has shown that one can catch the dream-work red-handed, as it were, in the act of turning abstract thoughts into visual pictures. If he tried to force himself to do intellectual work while he was in a state of fatigue and drowsiness, the thought would often vanish and be replaced by a vision, which was obviously a substitute for it.

Here is a simple example. 'I thought', says Silberer, 'of having to revise an uneven passage in an essay.' The vision: 'I saw myself planing a piece of wood.' It often happened during these experiments that the content of the vision was not the thought that was being dealt with but his own subjective state while he was making the effort—the state instead of the object. This is described by Silberer as a 'functional phenomenon'. An example will show you at once what is meant. The author was endeavouring to compare the opinions of two philosophers on a particular question. But in his sleepy condition one of these opinions kept on escaping him and finally he had a vision that he was asking for information from a disobliging secretary who was bent over his writing-table and who began by disregarding him and then gave him a disagreeable and uncomplying look. The conditions under which the experiments were made probably themselves explain why the vision that was induced represented so often an event of self-observation.[16]

We have not yet finished with symbols. There are some which we believed we recognized but which nevertheless worried us because we could not explain how *this* particular symbol had come to have *that* particular meaning. In such cases confirmations from elsewhere—from philology, folklore, mythology or ritual—were bound to be especially welcome. An instance of this sort is the symbol of an overcoat or cloak [German *'Mantel'*]. We have said that in a woman's dreams this stands for a man.[17] I hope it will impress you when you hear that Theodor Reik (1920) gives us this information: 'During the extremely ancient bridal ceremonial of the Bedouins, the bridegroom covers the bride with a special cloak known as "Aba" and speaks the following ritual words: "Henceforth none save I shall cover thee!" ' (Quoted from Robert Eisler [1910, 2, 599 f.]). We have also found several fresh symbols, at least two of which I will tell you of. According to Abraham (1922) a spider in dreams is a symbol of the mother, but of the *phallic* mother, of whom we are afraid; so that the fear of spiders expresses dread of mother-incest and horror of the female genitals. You know, perhaps, that the mythological creation, Medusa's head, can be traced back to the same *motif* of fright at castration.[18] The other symbol I want to talk to you about is that of the *bridge*, which has been explained by Ferenczi (1921 and 1922). First it means the male organ, which unites the two parents in sexual intercourse; but afterwards it develops further meanings which are derived from this first one. Is so far as it is thanks to the male organ that we are able to come into the world at all, out of the amniotic fluid, a bridge becomes the crossing from the other world (the unborn state, the womb) to this world (life); and, since men also picture death as a return to the womb (to the water), a bridge also acquires the meaning of something that leads to death, and finally, at a further remove from its original sense, it stands for transitions or changes in condition generally. It tallies with this, accordingly, if a woman who has not overcome her wish to be a man has frequent dreams of bridges that are too short to reach the further shore.

In the manifest content of dreams we very often find pictures and situations recalling familiar themes in fairy tales, legends and myths. The interpretation of such dreams thus throws a light on the original interests which created these themes, though we must at the same time not forget, of course, the change in meaning by which this material has been affected in the course of time. Our work of interpretation uncovers, so to say, the raw material, which must often enough be described as sexual in the widest sense, but has found the most varied application in later adaptations. Derivations of this kind are apt to bring down on us the wrath of all non-analytically schooled workers, as though we were seeking to deny or undervalue everything that was later erected on the original basis. Nevertheless, such discoveries are instructive and interesting. The same is true of tracing back the origin of particular themes in plastic art, as, for instance, when M. J. Eisler (1919), following indications in his patients' dreams, gave an analytic interpretation of the youth playing with a little boy represented in the Hermes of Praxiteles. And lastly I cannot resist pointing out how often light is thrown by the interpretation of dreams on mythological themes in particular. Thus, for instance, the legend of the Labyrinth can be recognized as a representation of anal birth: the twisting paths are the bowels and Ariadne's thread is the umbilical cord.

The methods of representation employed by the dream-work—fascinating material, scarcely capable of exhaustion—have been made more and more familiar to us by closer study. I will give you a few examples of them. Thus, for instance, dreams represent the relation of frequency by a multiplication of similar things. Here is a young girl's remarkable dream. She dreamt she came into a great hall and found some one in it sitting on a chair; this was repeated six or eight times or more, but each time it was her father. This is easy to understand when we discover, from accessory details in the interpretation, that this room stood for the womb. The dream then becomes equivalent to the phantasy, familiarly found in girls, of having met their father already during their intra-uterine life when he visited the womb while their mother was pregnant. You should not be confused by the fact that something is reversed in the dream—that her father's 'coming-in' displaced on to herself; incidentally, this has a special meaning of its own as well. The multiplication of the figure of the father can only express the fact that the event in question occurred repeatedly. After all, it must be allowed that the dream is not taking very much on itself in expressing frequency by multiplicity.[19] It has only needed to go back to the original significance of the former word; to-day it means to us a repetition in time, but it is derived from an accumulation in space. In general, indeed, where it is possible, the dream-work changes temporal relations into spatial ones and represents them as such. In a dream, for instance, one may see a scene between two people who look very small and a long way off, as though one were seeing them through the wrong end of a pair of opera-glasses. Here, both the smallness and the remoteness in space have the same significance: what is meant is remoteness in *time* and we are to understand that the scene is from the remote past.

Again, you may remember that in my earlier lectures I already told you (and illustrated the fact by examples) that we had learnt to make use for our interpretations even of the purely *formal* features of the manifest dream— that is, to transform them into material coming form the latent dream-thoughts.[20] As you already know, all dreams that are dreamt in a single night belong in a single context. But it is not a matter of indifference whether these dreams appear to the dreamer as a continuum or whether he divides them into several parts and into how many. The number of such parts often corresponds to an equal number of separate focal points in the structural formation of the latent dream-thoughts or to contending trends in the dreamer's mental life, each of which finds a dominant, even though never an exclusive, expression in one particular part of the dream. A short introductory dream and a longer main dream following it often stand in the relation of protasis and apodosis [conditional and consequential clauses], of which a very clear instance will be found in the old lectures.[21] A dream which is described by the dreamer as 'somehow interpolated' will actually correspond to a dependent clause in the dream-thoughts. Franz Alexander (1925) has shown in a study on pairs of dreams that it not infrequently happens that two dreams in one night share the carrying-out of the dream's task by producing a wish-fulfilment in two stages if they are taken together, though each dream separately would not effect that result. Suppose, for instance, that the dream-wish had as its content some illicit action in regard to a particular person. Then in the first dream the person will appear undisguised, but the action will be only timidly hinted at. The second dream will behave differently. The action will be named without disguise, but the person will either be made unrecognizable or replaced by someone indifferent. This, you will admit, gives one an impression of actual cunning. Another and similar relation between the two members of a pair of dreams is found where one represents a punishment and the other the sinful wish-fulfilment. It amounts to this: 'if one accepts the punishment for it, one can go on to allow oneself the forbidden thing.'

I cannot detain you any longer over such minor discoveries or over the discussions relating to the employment of dream-interpretation in the work of analysis. I feel sure you are impatient to hear what changes have been made in our fundamental views on the nature and significance of dreams. I have already warned you that precisely on this there is little to report to you. The most disputed point in the whole theory was no doubt the assertion that all dreams are the fulfilments of wishes. The inevitable and every recurring objection raised by the layman that there are nevertheless so many anxiety-dreams was, I think I may say, completely disposed of in my earlier lectures.[22] With the division into wishful dreams, anxiety-dreams and punishment dreams, we have kept our theory intact.

Punishment-dreams, too, are fulfilments of wishes, though not of wishes of the instinctual impulses but of those of the critical, censoring and punishing agency in the mind. If we have a pure punishment-dream before us, an easy mental operation will enable us to restore the wishful dream to which the punishment-dream was the correct rejoinder and which, owing to this repudiation, was replaced as the manifest dream. As you know, Ladies and Gentlemen, the study of dreams was what first helped us to understand the neuroses, and you will find it natural that our knowledge of the neuroses was later able to influence our view of dreams. As you will hear,[23] we have been obliged to postulate the existence in the mind of a special critical and prohibiting agency which we have named the 'super-ego'. Since recognizing that the censorship of dreams is also a function of this agency, we have been led to examine the part played by the super-ego in the construction of dreams more carefully.

Only two serious difficulties have arisen against the wish-fulfilment theory of dreams. A discussion of them leads far afield and has not yet, indeed, brought us to any wholly satisfying conclusion.

The first of these difficulties is presented in the fact that people who have experienced a shock, a severe psychical trauma—such as happened so often during the war and such as affords the basis for traumatic hysteria—are regularly taken back in their dreams into the traumatic situation. According to our hypotheses about the function of dreams this should not occur. What wishful impulse could be satisfied by harking back in this way to this exceedingly distressing traumatic experience? It is hard to guess.

We meet with the second of these facts almost every day in the course of our analytic work; and it does not imply such an important objection as the other does. One of the tasks of psycho-analysis, as you know, is to lift the veil of amnesia which hides the earliest years of childhood and to bring to conscious memory the manifestations of early infantile sexual life which are contained in them. Now these first sexual experiences of a child are linked to painful impressions of anxiety, prohibition, disappointment and punishment. We can understand their having been repressed; but, that being so, we cannot understand how it is that they have such free access to dream-life, that they provide the pattern for so many dream-phantasies and that dreams are filled with reproductions of these scenes from childhood and with allusions to them. It must be admitted that their unpleasurable character and the dream-work's wish-fulfilling purpose seem far from mutually compatible. But it may be that in this case we are magnifying the difficulty. After all, these same infantile experiences have attached to them all the imperishable, unfulfilled instinctual wishes which throughout life provide the energy for the construction of dreams, and to which we may no doubt credit the possibility, in their mighty uprush, of forcing to the surface, along with the rest, the material of distressing events. And on the other hand the manner and form in which this material is reproduced shows unmistakably the efforts of the dream-work directed to denying the unpleasure by means of distortion and to transforming disappointment into attainment.

With the traumatic neuroses things are different. In their case the dreams regularly end in the generation of anxiety. We should not, I think, be afraid to admit that here the function of the dream has failed. I will not invoke the saying that the exception proves the rule: its wisdom seems to me most questionable. But no doubt the exception does not overturn the rule. If, for the sake of studying it, we isolate one particular psychical function, such as dreaming, from the psychical machinery as a whole, we make it possible to discover the laws that are peculiar to it; but when we insert it once more into the general context we must be prepared to discover that these findings are obscured or impaired by collision with other forces. We say that a dream is the fulfilment of a wish; but if you want to take these latter objections into account, you can say nevertheless that a dream is an *attempt* at the fulfilment of a wish. No one who can properly appreciate the dynamics of the mind will suppose that you have said anything different by this. In certain circumstances a dream is only able to put its intention into effect very incompletely, or must abandon it entirely. Unconscious fixation to a trauma seems to be foremost among these obstacles to the function of dreaming. While the sleeper is obliged to dream, because the relaxation of repression at night allows the upward pressure of the traumatic fixation to become active, there is a failure in the functioning of his dream-work, which would like to transform the memory-traces of the traumatic event into the fulfilment of a wish. In these circumstances it will happen that one cannot sleep, that one gives up sleep from dread of the failure of the function of dreaming. Traumatic neuroses are here offering us an extreme case; but we must admit that childhood experiences, too, are of a traumatic nature, and we need not be surprised if comparatively trivial interferences with the function of dreams may arise under other conditions as well.[24]

NOTES

For full citation of abbreviated reference, the reader is urged to consult the original source.

1. [Cf. the whole of Part II of *Introductory Lectures on Psycho-Analysis* (1916–17).]
2. [Some illuminating remarks on reflection will be found, in a similar connection, in Chapter II of *The Interpretation of Dreams* (1900a), *Standard Ed.*, 4, 101–2.]
3. [A slightly different list of these alternative methods is given in 'Remarks on the Theory and Practice of Dream-Interpretation' (1923c), *Standard Ed.*, **19,** 109.]
4. [See *Introductory Lectures* (1916–17), Lecture X.]
5. [Freud had recently written a special note on 'The Limits to the Possibility of Interpretation' (1925i), *Standard Ed.*, **19,** 127.]
6. [Cf. *The Interpretation of Dreams* (1900a), *Standard Ed.*, **5,** 518–19.]
7. [Cf. 'The Handling of Dream-Interpretation in Psycho-Analysis' (1911e), *Standard Ed.*, *12,* 95–6.]
8. [Cf. Section II of 'Remarks on the Theory and Practice of Dream-Interpretation' (1923c), *Standard Ed.*, **19,** 110.]
9. [This is one of the very rare occasions on which Freud uses the personified form *'Zensor'* instead of the impersonal *'Zensur'* (censorship). See an Editor's footnote in *Introductory Lectures*, XXVI, *Standard Ed.*, **16,** 429.]
10. [This part of the sentence is repeated almost word for word from the second sentence in Freud's preface to the first edition of *The Interpretation of Dreams* (1900a), *Standard Ed.*, 4, xxiii.]
11. [*The Interpretation of Dreams*, ibid., **4,** 2.]
12. [The notion occurs already in one of Freud's very earliest psychological papers, his first one on 'The Neuro-Psychoses of Defence' (1894a), *Standard Ed.*, **3,** 55.]
13. [*Introductory Lectures*, XI.]

14. [In conformity with the ego.]

15. [Longer descriptions of these experiments will be found in Chapter VI (E) of *The Interpretation of Dreams* (1900a), *Standard Ed.*, **5**, 384.]

16. [Freud gave a very much fuller account of Silberer's experiments, with a great many quotations, in some passages added in 1914 to *The Interpretation of Dreams* (1900a), *Standard Ed.*, **5**, 344–5 and 503–6.]

17. [The symbol is referred to in the *Introductory lectures*, *Standard Ed.*, **15**, 155 and 157, but the fact that this applies to *women's* dreams is only mentioned among some 'Observations and Examples' published earlier (Freud, 1913h), *Standard Ed.*, **13**, 196.]

18. [Cf. a posthumously published note by Freud on the subject (1940c [1922]).]

19. ['*Häufigkeit*' and '*Häufung*' in German. Both words are derived from '*Haufen*' — a 'heap'.]

20. [Cf. *Introductory Lectures*, XI, *Standard Ed.*, **15**. 177. See also *The Interpretation of Dreams*, ibid., **4**, 329 ff.]

21. [*Introductory Lectures*, XII, *Standard Ed.*, **15**, 186. For all of this see also *The Interpretation of Dreams*, ibid., **4**, 314 ff. and 332 ff.]

22. [See *Introductory Lectures*, XIV.]

23. [In Lecture XXXI.]

24. [The topic of the last three paragraphs was first raised by Freud in Chapters II and III of *Beyond the Pleasure Principle* (1920g). Further allusions to it will be found in Lecture XXXII, p. 106 below.]

3. Dream Psychology and the Analytic Situation

Bertram D. Lewin

This paper will try to apply some of our knowledge and theory about sleep and the dream to an understanding of the analytic situation, which is here defined, empirically, as the familiar standard hour, or loosely, as 'what happens on the couch'; and sometimes the word 'couch' will be used metaphorically as synonymous with 'analytic situation'. Included in the idea of analytic situation are the phenomena of free association, resistance, transference, repetition, and others well known and generally admitted as working concepts.

Genetically, the analytic situation is an altered hypnotic situation, as the analytic hour is an altered hypnotic session. The analytic patient takes his origin from the hypnotic patient, for originally Freud's patients were attracted to therapy by their knowledge of cures due to hypnosis. The development of analysis from hypnosis has been studied and told with much detail and perspicacity by Ernest Jones (1953). It seems that some patients could not be hypnotized, or they 'countersuggested' too vigorously; that is, they had a resistance to being hypnotized or, more likely, a fear of being put to sleep. The refractory patient made the following *as if* proposal that the treatment be modified: 'Although I cannot, for reasons of my own, let myself be put to sleep,[1] or into a state resembling sleep, nevertheless, I promise to relax as if I were in bed and to tell everything that comes to me in this quasi-hypnotic or quasi-hypnagogic state. In return for this concession, I accept more responsibility for what I say.'

We may put it that a resistance appeared in therapy even before psychoanalysis was properly born and was of major importance in its subsequent development. It changed the hypnotic situation into an analytic situation. It should be noted that the time of this change coincides with the time in the embryology of psychoanalysis, when hypnosis was being used not to produce

Reprinted by permission of David Lewin and *The Psychoanalytic Quarterly*, Vol. 24, 1955.

suggestive, irrational cures, but to uncover traumatic, repressed memories; so that this purpose is tacitly assumed in the above-stated bargain.

With this modification of the hypnotic session into the analytic hour, the therapist's theoretical interest was diverted from the problems centering about sleeplike states and became more and more focused on the contents of the patient's remarks and behavior. The study of the patient as a quasi-sleeper or quasi-dreamer was completely subordinated to the therapeutic and theoretical study of his symptoms. The theory of the neuroses was developed, and it seems in retrospect inevitable that the writings on technique should have been couched largely in terms of this theory. The patient on the couch was prima facie a neurotic person and only incidentally a dreamer. It is well, however, to question the complete inevitability of this particular choice of formulation and terminology. We may plausibly speculate whether an alternative path could not have been chosen; namely, to regard the analytic material and 'what happens on the couch' not as something like a neurosis, but instead, something like a dream, and to introduce dream concepts and dream psychological terminology. If this path had been taken, quite possibly we would have developed a poorer and less useful terminology than we have now, but that is not the issue. We are not raising the question of better or worse, merely of difference.

The relationship between neurosis theory and dream theory seems to have been a slippery one for analysts to hang on to. Thus, Freud (1950) confessed that he discovered the essential unity of the two, then forgot, and had to rediscover it. Perhaps it is necessary for all of us to repeat this rediscovery. So much of our analytic phylogeny recapitulates Freud's scientific ontogeny that we may not have, even now, thoroughly 'worked through' this insight and taken in all its implications. We have no doubt that the dream is the royal road to the unconscious and that dream analysis is an indispensable instrument in therapeutic practice. We know that the dream is a wish fulfilment and a communication, and we bank heavily on this knowledge. But we have paid little attention to the chief function of dreaming, its guardianship of sleep. Attention to the interpretation of contents and to the dream work has distracted us, here too, from the problem of sleep and from a consideration of the analytic subject as a fractional dreamer or sleeper. Again in retrospect, Freud's rejection of Breuer's ideas of hypnoidal states appears consistent with the general turning from an interest in the sleeper as such.

We all know the psychoanalytic dictum that whatever is rejected in the course of conflict-solving may return and find a disguised place in that which is accepted. So, sleep, excluded by agreement from the analytic situation, gained access to it in another form—the method of free association. I developed this idea in a recent paper (1954), where I pointed out that the wish to be put to sleep, which the patient brought to the hypnotic situation, has been supplanted by the wish to associate freely in the analytic situation. The patient lies down, not to sleep, but to associate. The interpretation of free association as the substitute for sleep in the therapeutic situation was based not only on the tacit bargain cited above, but also on one of Freud's definitions of free association, given in *The Interpretation of Dreams* (Standard Edition, IV, p. 102), where it is likened to the state of mind that precedes sleep (also to the hypnotic state).

For our present purposes, then, we shall project the metapsychology of sleep and the dream on to the analytic situation. We readily note certain coincidences. Thus the narcissism of sleep, an element assumed in dream psychology, coincides with narcissism on the couch, and the rare blank 'sleep dreams' are analogous to the rare transient falling asleep on the couch, both phenomena being the unusual near zeros of their respective domains. The manifest dream text coincides with the manifest analytic material, expressing, in processed form, latent thoughts become preconscious. Dream formation is to be compared with 'analytic-situation formation'; it is the 'exception', to use Freud's word, to the basic narcissism. Other analogies suggest themselves, but because there are so many differences of detail and elaboration, due to the opposite paths taken in the psychic apparatus by the dream process and the analytic-situation process (one terminating mainly in visual hallucinations, the other mainly in words), it is well to consider at first only the broader coincidences.

NARCISSISM

Since we mentioned the concept of *narcissism* as an element of the psychoanalytic theory of sleep and the dream, and suggested its application in the analytic situation, it would be well to come to terms with this word and its meaning. To ignore its origin in sexology, *narcissism* was introduced into psychoanalysis as a definition of an erotic relationship in which the self was the object, that is to say, self-love; but the youth gazing at his image in the fountain always had a more abstract and symbolical quality, as a representation of a form of love, than did, for example, the picture conjured up by the word, *libido,* with its etymology of sexual desire and its implication of the excited genital and sexual congress as the representation of object relationship. Narcissism has always seemed to be more conceptual, to be something behind the phenomena, and as far as factual existence is concerned, it has some of the shadowy and absent quality of its mythological eponym's forlorn sweetheart, the nymph Echo.

I mean that narcissism is an abstraction, with visible correlates in childhood psychology, in neurosis, in sleep, and in the love life. Narcissism, as a concept, is behind the dream, behind the depression and elation, behind somatic symptoms, etc. We must carefully distinguish between narcissism the concept and narcissistic phenomena as we distinguish the conceptual points and lines of pure mathematics from the ink dots and strokes that we see and measure (cf. Hartmann, Kris and Loewenstein's discussion of theory [1953]). But as the dot is the *approximate* concrete representative of the abstract point, so, I believe, we may take a certain type of blank dream as a sort of concrete, approximate, 'inkspot' picture of the abstract 'point' narcissism. This blank dream (1953), though concrete, approximates the narcissism of sleep, and as a manifestation , epitomizes what *narcissism* can mean not only in dream and sleep psychology but also in the phrase *narcissistic neurosis,* its content signifying an intense, primitive, direct experience of the baby in the nursing situation, inclusive of sleep at the breast.

The revelance of this discussion of narcissism to the theme, the application of dream psychology to the analytic situation, depends on a rather subtle point. Despite our theory, in ordinary dream interpretation, narcissism is left to one side, and to a certain extent this is also true in our ordinary interpretation of the standard analytic situation. However, certain narcissistic phenomena that appear on the couch (some of them related to sleep) will help us to understand the nature and psychology of the standard situation, as the 'narcissistic dream' throws light on the psychology of sleep and ordinary dreaming.

TOXIC TECHNIQUE

Before entering into an investigation of the standard analytic hour, it will be profitable to take up another, simpler modification of the older hypnotist's seance. I refer to what might be called the *toxic therapeutic situation,* where one or another drug is used as an adjuvant or an initiator of something like a cathartic situation. Here it is easy to apply dream psychology to interpret the situation, for the drug produces something like a sleep or a half-sleep state, and the fantasies that appear are readily compared to dream formations. For theoretical purposes, however, let us approach the matter indirectly, and treat the situation as a toxic neurosis.

In *Mourning and Melancholia,* Freud states that a 'toxic' condition might of itself lead to narcissistic regression and depression (and presumably also elation) without the intervention of any object loss. But toxins may initiate many other types of mental states. In psychiatry, it has long been known that the psychological contents of a drug psychosis may include not only manifestations of direct impairment of the cerebral cortex (disorientation, torpor, intellectual inhibition, etc.), but also others called 'psychogenic' and due to individual mental factors, such as significant life experiences. In other words, a drug delirium has somewhat the structure of a dream, the drug being the incentive to a kind of sleep or 'state of narcissism', the psychogenic symptoms being cast in a form resembling a dream.

When 'narco' drugs are used in combined sleep- and psychotherapy, they produce a comparable state, where the narcissistic regression of anesthesia, like the narcissism of natural sleep, is made imperfect by an 'exception', which is like a dream. Excluding such heavy methods as the *Dauerschlaf,* which would be dreamless, the desideratum in the therapies I have in mind is not deep sleep nor hallucinosis, but a state nearer 'muttering delirium with sense in it'; that is, something not too far from intelligible or interpretable hypnagogic free association and catharsis.

From our present standpoint of historical reconstruction, we may say that the therapist acts here to supply a different answer to the problem raised by the Anna O type of patient, the type which resists and 'cannot be hypnotized'. The primitive resistance to being put to sleep is overcome by pharmacological aid. The drug promotes the relaxation and submission which is undertaken voluntarily in the hypnotic or standard analytic situation.

FEAR OF SLEEP AND DEATH

The wish for a soothing drug, or the fear of it, often comes up in associations during an analytic hour, among other reasons because of conflicts centering about sleep. The interpretation of this wish or fear throws light on the resistance of patients to hypnotism, which was not interpreted when historically the bargain of free association was struck. Some of the ambivalence about sleep and anesthesia was discussed in a previous paper (1954), where I recounted some of the fantasies of seduction, or of being disgracefully uninhibited in language and action, and the moral objections that were raised to the introduction of the use of chloroform. In his 1888 paper, Freud tried to allay some of the public's and the medical profession's fear of harm coming from hypnotism by reminding his readers that anesthesia had been feared in the same way, but that this fear had gradually been dispelled through familiarity and reason.

It is true, as Freud says, that common sense and familiarity have overcome some of the irrational alarm over being put to sleep by chloroform, and its social sanctioning *(accouchement à la reine)* has caused some of the anxiety to be ignored. Nevertheless, there still remain certain fears of being anesthetized, and the commonest one is not the fear of being uninhibited and losing self-control but the fear of dying. There is no need here to repeat arguments or furnish evidence for the idea that this fear is symptomatic and covers other latent ones. I shall merely name some of the pregenital varieties of the fear of death, or the fear of being put to sleep, which is the same. These are: the fear of being devoured, of being poisoned, of being suffocated; and finally, a variety which is not so much a fear of dying in the sense of losing consciousness (sleeping) as a fear of the afterlife (and bad dreams), a fear rather ignored in our materialistic era. The equivalence of sleep and death and its clinical applicability is demonstrated in the following account, kindly placed at my disposal some years ago by Dr. Maxwell Gitelson.

'The patient was a fifty-six-year-old man, seen in consultation, who had had a coronary attack, and who after recovery from this was suffering from an aversion to food, from a feeling that food did not go down, and from breathing difficulties, subjectively experienced as "inability to get enough of what I need". After much emotional distress and subjective torture, at one point he burst out to his wife and daughter, who were standing by, "I am going to stop fighting this thing. I am going to let myself die." Thereupon he collapsed on the pillow, fully believing that he was going to die, and instead dropped into the first peaceful sleep that he had had in many months.' Dr. Gitelson comments: 'This resignation to death really represented in his critical emotional state the development of a capacity to accept a profound oral regression with which death and sleep were equated'. A not irrelevant illness in this patient was peptic ulcer of many years' standing. (Cf. Stone [1947], who describes sleep on the analytic couch in a duodenal ulcer patient.)

It would not be difficult to imagine that Dr. Gitelson's patient might have shown the same behavior if he had tried to accommodate himself to the analytic couch. The resistance to analysis, like the resistance to sleep or to anesthesia, may, particularly at the beginning, be due to a fear of death or its corollaries. Being hypnotized, anesthetized, killed, put to sleep, are equivalents, and all may be represented by lying down on the analytic couch. Many patients have dreamed of their analysis as a surgical operation, the table (the surgical one this time, not the dining table) representing the bed or couch. By extension, and for other reasons that come from medical education, physicians often think of themselves being dissected when they dream of their analysis, and sometimes they even turn the autopsy into a cannibal procedure. In the literature we have a record of a famous dream in which a young physician with strong scientific curiosity sees himself as a cadaver undergoing dissection. The analysand was of course Freud (Standard Edition, V, p. 452), and since it was a self-analysis, appropriately he is also the anatomist. The dream begins: 'Old Brücke must have set me some task; strangely enough it related to a dissection of the lower part of my own body, my pelvis and legs, which I saw before me as though in the dissecting room, but without noticing their absence in myself and also without a trace of any gruesome feeling. . . . The pelvis had been eviscerated . . .', etc. It is significant historically that the founder of psychoanalysis could see himself as a prosector and at the same time as the anatomical preparation, and later we shall have more to say about the identification of an analysand with a physically ill patient or a cadaver.

At this point, however, I should merely like to emphasize once more the natural unconscious equivalence of sleep and death, both of them states of narcissism, psychologically. Also that the exception to the narcissism of sleep, to wit, the dream, is the same as the exception to the narcissism of death, to wit, the afterlife. But more to the present purpose, I wish to indicate by these examples the sort of resistances there might be to lying down on the analytic couch, and how the couch and the analytic situation itself need interpretation. In all its variety, the most obvious interpretation, not necessarily the deepest, is that the couch is a place for sleeping.

RANK'S FALLACY

In the above exposition I have tried to tie up some loose ends, many of them historical, which are related to the main theme of this paper, and to offer some justification for applying sleep metapsychology to the analytic situation. I should like now briefly to discuss an important error, which has a position in the history of psychoanalysis, and which involved both the theory

of the analytic situation and the matter of sleep. I refer to the theory pro-
pounded by Otto Rank, and by him embodied in a technique, that in analysis
patients relive their stay in the uterus and with its termination, their birth.

Rank, I believe, always had an unconscious feeling that the analytic
situation was somehow a sleep and that the associative material was the
equivalent of manifest dreaming. This I infer from an article of his called
Eine Neurosenanalyse in Träumen (1924), a tour de force, based on the tacit
assumption that an entire analysis and the whole process of the analytic
situation could be understood as if it were a dream. A reading of this paper
clarifies some of Rank's later erroneous views.

Rank's argument (1924-a) that the analytic situation represents an intra-
uterine state and its termination a rebirth begins with the observation, correct
enough, that rebirth fantasies accompany the resolution of the analytic situation, that patients dream of leaving the analyst as a being born. In this Rank
saw not a metaphorical expression of separation, but a 'so to speak biological' repetition of the act of birth, *'meist in allen seinen Einzelheiten getreu'*
(for the most part accurate in all details), so that the time spent on the couch
is a true and immediate replica and reliving of that spent in the uterus. This
idea Rank got directly from his patients, and he says, *'psychologisch hat also
der Pazient recht'*, a quotation which conceals evident special pleading. It
seems that Rank fell into the same sort of error which so distressed Freud
when, at a critical moment in psychoanalytic history, he found that he had
been misled by hysterical women's fantasies during analysis into believing
that they had really been seduced in early childhood by their father or a near
male relative. Freud took the hard step, then, of recognizing his error and
realizing that he was dealing with the memory of an infantile fantasy. Rank
was not aware that he had been deceived in the same way. He did not take
into account the comparable alternative to his interpretation of the rebirth
fantasy, namely, that it was a fantasy of waking up. For, among the fantastic
elaborations of the fact of pleasurable sleep is the idea that one is *in utero*, or
rather, within the mother's body, and this intramaternal fantasy is a later,
more complicated and more highly processed fantasy of the œdipal period,
which contains later knowledge and impressions about gestation.

In other words, Rank could equally well have thought that the fœtal
postures adopted by patients on the couch and other signs and symptoms of
the 'intramaternal situation' were fantasy attempts to fulfil the wish to sleep;
similarly he could have interpreted the 'birth trauma' manifestations as the
correlated resistance to waking up from the analytic bed. The insight that

really resides in Rank's theory, if one analyzes his elaborations and misunderstandings, is expressed in his statement that '. . . *die eigentliche Übertragungsliebe, die wir bei beiden Geschlechtern analytisch aufzulösen haben, die mütterliche ist . . .*', which is blurry and an overstatement, but nevertheless contains an intuition of the whole precedipal development and approximates in a way an interpretation of the position on the couch as a relationship to the mother. That it is, though hardly so directly and 'biologically' (whatever that implies) as Rank states. The couch is reminiscent of *sleep* and therefore an important element of the nursing situation. Rank felt the importance of the fact that the patient was lying down, and that somehow this was connected with the precedipal relationship to the mother, but in his qualification of the statement quoted above, he himself fell into a fantasy in the clause, '. . . *wie sie in der pränatalen physiologischen Bindung zwischen Mutter und Kind gegeben war'*. Here he was believing a fantasy to be a literal statement of genetic facts.

To Rank, in fact, as to Jung, the story of Œdipus seemed only a myth, not a genetic fact. However, the point here is that Rank's analysis of the analytic situation and his failure to see that he was observing symptoms of sleeping and waking, led him to theorize falsely, and along with Ferenczi for a while, to regress in his technique to a quasi catharsis, where the patient relived fantasies on the couch and acted out the script suggested, and this acting out Rank identified with the therapeutic process. His active injunction, the setting of a definite terminal date, provoked the patient into a regressive protest to having his stay on the couch cut short, and the patient then portrayed being 'untimely ripp'd' from the analytic couch as an anxious, painful awakening, the traumatic 'birth'. In the œdipal setting, the regressively expressed formula for this would read: the father is waking and weaning me betimes from my sleep with the mother.

Rank was not saved from his fallacy by his knowledge of the theory of the neuroses, which indeed was shattered when he applied it to the analytic situation; but he might have been saved from his mistake if he had followed and analyzed thoroughly his perception about the 'prenatal state', which meant that the analytic situation was some kind of sleep and the associative material some kind of dreamlike production; that is, if he had consistently applied the metapsychology of the dream. Instead, he built his theory of the analytic situation on unanalyzed infantile fantasies about the unborn child and childbirth.

The reason I have dealt here so extensively with Rank's theory may not be immediately evident. But I regard it as an attempt, thwarted by a mistake, to do what I am attempting now, that is, to project upon the couch and the analytic situation the idea that the patient is as if somewhat asleep.

FREE ASSOCIATION

From such general expositions of the analytic situation in terms of sleep and dream psychology, we may turn to individual elements in it, and to begin with, the very important one of free association. It is often profitable and instructive to see a familiar fact in a different context—to see the dream, for instance, as something that occurs in nature as well as in an analytic procedure, which as a matter of fact Freud's own dreams gave us a chance to do. We must, in other words, remind ourselves occasionally that God could not care less whether a dream is reported to an analyst or not; and we may well look for the phenomenal elements of the analytic situation in their natural habitats.

Let us, therefore, consider a solitary individual who is contemplating his own thoughts, feelings, memories and impulses. Let him approximate Freud's idea of free association by having him limit action to a minimum and by letting him put his mental processes into words with no care for style or form. That he should report these words to anyone is, for the time being, irrelevant. In any event, we have as yet no 'analysis', not even a self-analysis, for many persons have used very much this method of introspection for many purposes.

Freud tells us that he came upon this method of giving free rein to the contents of consciousness in the writings of the German author, Boerne. In an essay, "The Art of Becoming an Original Writer in Three Days" (1827), Boerne concludes his exposition with the following words: 'Take a sheet of paper and for three days in succession write down, without any falsification or hypocrisy, everything that comes into your head. Write what you think of yourself, of your women, of the Turkish War, of Goethe, of the Funk criminal case, of the Last Judgment, of those senior to you in authority— and when the three days are over, you will be amazed at what novel and startling thoughts have welled up in you. This is the art of becoming a writer in three days.[2] Boerne evidently intended to use the scribbling as the raw material for his literary work. He had as his purpose the liberation of the imagination, or as we might prefer to say, the exploration of the preconscious system, for the advancement of literary composition. In *The Interpretation of*

Dreams (Standard Edition, IV, p. 102), Freud calls attention to Schiller's use of a method very like free association for the same purpose. We see, therefore, that from the start analysts have known that there was involved not merely a way of thinking, but also purposes and intentions that determined its use.

These intentions may be various. If we consider the works of Herbert Silberer (1909, 1912), another solitary associator, we see two evident motives for his recording freely arising ideas and feelings. One of these motives was psychological investigation in the narrower sense; he was interested in examining the why and how of this variety of thinking. His second purpose might be called, loosely, philosophical or mystical. Pursuing his first intention, Silberer noted his associations and the contents of his dreams and hypnagogic reveries, making scientific inferences and assumptions concerning the representation of waking up, the nature of symbols, and the way certain states of the dreamer enter the manifest dream text. His scientific psychological interest lay not in dream interpretation in Freud's sense of unearthing unconscious contents and wishes, but in establishing the nature of certain formal properties in the manifest contents. In addition to this interest, Silberer had another which he called 'anagogic'. He used the dream thoughts and associations as incentives and directives for philosophic and theologic speculation, and possibly for the evocation of moods and feelings that went with them. In both endeavors, there was of course nothing like the 'analytic situation' or a 'therapeutic intention'. Silberer was led from verbal associations—a cardinal requirement in Freud's definition of free association—into visual and symbolic representation, and in reveries, during states of fatigue, he came very near to dreaming.

Jung was much influenced by Silberer, and it is fair to assume that he was describing his own variant of free association when (1911) he spoke of 'undirected thinking', which, he says, starts in words but is later replaced by visual images and after that by dreamlike fantasies. The latter he came to regard as the basic or elemental contents of the unconscious, and he held them in a certain awe, much as the ancients had for dreams that emerged through the gates of horn and ivory to bring to mortals the messages of the gods. They suggested to him ethical and religious beliefs and goals, and reminded him of parallels in myth and fable. As Boerne took notes for literary composition, so Jung (and in part, Silberer) used associations and reveries for metaphysical and mythological constructions. In fact, as Glover (1950) noted, Jung's psychological constructions resemble an Olympus, and his allegedly basic concepts are themselves the complex condensations, distortions, and symbols of a sort of manifest dream text.

Given any fantasy which arises during free and solitary ruminations, such as Silberer's while he gazed into his crystal globe, it is clear that one or another feature will be more likely to impress the observer when he retrospectively assesses them, and that he will be guided by his purposes, special interests and education. One observer will be struck by the similarity of the given fantasy to ideas he held as a child or which possibly he has heard expressed by children. Another person, with little empathy for children but well-versed in cultural history or anthropology, will be more aware that the fantasy resembles a certain series of myths. Consequently, the first observer would ultimately try to construct a psychology of the child, while the second might contribute to anthropology or the history of culture. A third-observer, departing form the principle of putting the fantasy into words and running into complex reveries and unusual absorbed states, might come to accept these manifest, processed, ideas and qualities as the final disiderata of the method. Still another observer could ignore all the frames of reference mentioned; in fact from Zilboorg's account (1952) of Francis Galton's use of the method, an academic psychologist of the old school, interested in the study of the mind according to the old canons of the science, might view the associations simply as novel, static 'enlargements of consciousness'. Clearly, all such observers have brought to the field their own measures and coördinates.

Freud's self-analytic intentions and purposes can be indicated in a few words. He approached his own associations as he did those of his patients, and he was guided by the same medical and analytic intentions, little concerned, to begin with, as to their nonmedical application. However, when one uses the word *medical* in connection with Freud, it must be in a very broad and enlightened sense, not synonymous with *therapy,* and including all the connotations and implications of science and research. Free association for him was calm self-observation and the verbal reporting or recording of the associations, which rules out of the method some of the 'inexpressibles' to which Jung refers, or at least insists on attempting to verbalize. This verbalization is by no means impossible; witness the brilliant descriptions of mystical experiences by many saints and poets.

We might use as an instance of Freud's attitude toward nonverbalization his pursuit through indirect associations of the forgotten name, *Signorelli,* when he could bring to mind only the visual images of the artist's frescoes.

Under the same circumstances, it is conceivable that some other person, say an artist, not particularly interested in the problem of forgetting, might have been sidetracked into aesthetic moods, and he might have lost his interest in the painter's name. Freud's special interest in remembering and forgetting outweighed any tendency toward pleasurable aesthetic memories. From the purely psychoanalytic point of view or according to Freud's rules, many of the reveries and states of mind in question represent resistances to putting thoughts into words and to the hidden implications and associative links to these same thoughts. In his reference to calm self-observation, as well as in the account of resistance and transference which immediately follows this in *The Introductory Lectures,* Freud leaves aside the problem of the relative awakeness of the person who is freely associating.

There are doubtless many other purposes that free association might be made to serve. Those mentioned are: 1, literary creation; 2, psychological science; 3, mystical experience; 4, ethical and philosophical guidance or inspiration; 5, therapy. As a drug is only *materia medica* in itself and variously utilizable for experiment or therapy or pleasure, so are free associations capable of varied employment. They can be elaborated, superseded, used 'anagogically' for moral illumination, or permitted to lead to buried memories, according to the interests and intentions, conscious or unconscious, of the self-observer. The thoughts and reveries of the relaxed, solitary person may lead off in many directions, guided by the pleasure principle, by impulses to action (Hartmann [1947]), or by intellectual and secondary intentions. Actions may include gestures or fugues or 'rational behavior'. The spontaneous ideas of the solitary self-observer can belong to various parts of his personality: different ego interests and pleasure strivings can seize upon the newly arisen ideas and feelings, progressively or regressively (E. Kris [1950]). They may be turned into practical channels, such as literary production or problem solving, go over into aesthetic or athletic action, or be passively enjoyed or tolerated.

For the purposes of this discussion, it will be noted that the conception of free association is given a very loose construction. But at its core, again for our purposes, stands Freud's special, tight definition of a 'condition of calm self-observation . . . something which is quite different from reflection without precluding it', an attention to what is on the conscious surface of the mind, with a relinquishing of all objections to what might appear there, no matter from what source, or what the form or content. Around this nuclear, strictly defined norm, radiate these states of consciousness of all degrees of awakeness and sleepiness, including the artificial 'toxic' states; and there are insensible transitions toward reveries and dreams in one direction, and, in the other, toward directed, secondarily processed, structured mental work.

Indeed, what William James (1890, II, pp. 325–326) has to say about primitive reasoning may be interesting in this context. 'It is', he says, 'by no means easy to decide just what is meant by reason, or how the peculiar thinking process called reasoning differs from other thought sequences which lead to similar results. Much of our thinking consist of trains of images suggested one by another, a sort of spontaneous reverie, of which it seems likely enough that the higher brutes should be capable. This sort of thinking leads nevertheless to rational conclusions, both practical and theoretical. . . . As a rule in this sort of irresponsible thinking, the terms which fall to be coupled together are empirical concretes, not abstractions. A sunset may call up the vessel's deck from which I saw one last summer, the companions of my voyage, my arrival into port, etc.; or it may make me think of solar myths, of Hercules' and Hector's funeral pyres, of Homer and whether he could write, of the Greek alphabet, etc. If habitual contiguities predominate, we have a prosaic mind; if rare contiguities, or similarities, have free play, we call the person fanciful, poetic, or witty. The upshot of it may be that we are reminded of some practical duty: we may write a letter to a friend abroad, or we may take down the lexicon and study our Greek lessons.'[3]

Evidently, James was associating pretty freely himself, and he goes on to say that such actions as he mentioned, although 'rational', are not performed as the result of reasoning. (Cf. Hartmann, loc. cit.) Later under the rubric of *resistance,* we shall refer to a special sort of action that may issue under such circumstances. Here it will suffice to call attention to James's quietly inspired differentiation of the prosaic and the poetic mind in free association, which contains *in nuce* premonitions of psychoanalytic formulations. Writing in 1889, James often astonishes us by what he might have called 'poetic' prophecy; for after trying to sum up thinking, he says, 'if we could say in English "it thinks" as we say "it rains" or "it blows", we should be stating the fact most simply and with the minimum of assumption. As we cannot, we must simply say that thought goes on' (ibid., p. 224).

I might of course have omitted James's remarks and simply referred to E. Kris's exposition (1950) of preconscious thinking, which covers this field; yet, James's words seemed worth quoting for themselves.

We must now ask how this big, loose process of solitary thinking or associating differs from the association desirable on the analytic couch. We may say, first of all, that there is probably no transference situation; we say *probably,* for there may be an occult one, such as we believe existed in Freud's thinking in relation to Wilhelm Fliess, and we cannot be too sure whether some of the accounts of self-analysis are entirely accurate when their reporter assumes that there was no analyst. I have in mind Pickworth Farrow's account (1945) and Freud's comments thereon. Certainly, if one has been in an analytic situation, subsequent self-analytic procedures will contain elements of the original transference. However, in nature, there would probably be no analyst in a self-analysis in the narrower sense.

On the other hand, there would certainly be resistances, in the freudian sense. These Freud observed in his own self-analysis, and he constantly alludes to them in his work with his own dreams. Nor is it hard to make them out in Silberer's or in Jung's writings. Indeed, the recognition that there are resistances to free thought ranks as one of Freud's great technical discoveries. Although some of the persons mentioned near the beginning of this discussion, like Boerne and Schiller, had an inkling that they were overcoming some sort of impediment to thinking, and although some mystics write of the 'darkness' when no ineffable experiences can be reached, yet it remained for Freud to note that certain paths of thought 'led nowhere', or to a halt, or *ins Unendliche* (into the endless, as he says in one place), and in general certainly away from the place that Freud was interested in—from repressed material which is not egosyntonic. In short, in free solitary association, there may be no transference but there is surely resistance. If, for terminological reasons, one wishes to reserve the word *resistance* for the situation on the couch,[4] then one would still have to say *repression* or *defense.*

RESISTANCE, SLEEP, AND THE DREAM

The analytic resistance is a pragmatic concept. After hypnotism was abandoned, Freud found that the patient would or could not live up completely to his promise to associate freely in a useful way; and it is well to emphasize the word *useful* and to specify the use. Freud had a therapeutic and scientific intention, and the resistance was directed against the instrument of this intention. I follow Freud in calling free association an instrument, for he compares analytic resistance to the resistance a person might offer to the use of dental forceps. The resistance was discovered in the analytic situation; but in his self-analysis also, Freud felt his resistances as he felt those of his neurotic patients. They felt like a counterforce that reminded him of the

countersuggestion he knew from his prepsychoanalytic work, which recalci-
trants used against being hypnotized. Resistance, therefore, is something that
exists in self-analysis too, but, be it noted, in self-analysis which coincides
with freudian intentions. It also exists in free association and rumination that
resembles free association, but if this occurs without freudian intentions, it
may not be noted or, if it is, not considered to be of practical importance.

There is no need here to repeat the insight into resistances which came
from further experience with the neuroses. I shall merely mention the ad-
denda to *The Problem of Anxiety*, Anna Freud's classic account in *The Ego
and the Mechanisms of Defense*, and call attention to Loewenstein's recent
paper, "Defenses, Autonomous Ego, and Technique" (1954), and to its
bibliography.

I wish to go back to nature and the more general field of solitary association outside the analytic situation. Solitary meditators, or whatever we may
choose to call them, who do not have the specific freudian intent have no
objection to the appearance of resistances. When they encounter what we call
resistances, they do not face them as Freud had to, for they are swayed by
other motives. They are not co-signers of the contract with Anna O. They
elaborate the resistances, act them out, enjoy them, or use them in some
other way, but they do not recognize them. The intentions and the point of
view are crucial. Freudians must call such manifestations *resistance*, but
others may be content with manifest, processed material not to be further
analyzed. Boerne and Silberer and William James arrive at ends different
from Freud.

On the couch, however, the resistance to being hypnotized or put to sleep
shown by Anna O has been replaced by the resistance to free association, its
substitute. In the resistance to free association, the old agreement about being
put to sleep may be placed on the agenda for reconsideration. The patient, in
conflict about free association, may suggest that he be hypnotized or be given
a drug. Or he may depart form the basic contract by getting into a mystic
state of mind, or into some of the sleepy states described by Silberer. I have
indicated in a previous paper that the resistive patient may become either too
sleepy or too alert for useful free association. His behavior may come to
resemble that of the solitary associator with no freudian intentions.

If you recall William James's hypothetical case of associations to a sunset,
one outcome of the undirected thinking was action: the person was led by his
associations to take down a Greek lexicon and study his Greek lesson. Such
an action, from our standpoint, would not be an end, though it might have

been for James's nonfreudian; we should consider it, even in self-analysis, an evasion of the fundamental rule. We should say, This man has quit associating. In a discussion, Rado once compared a certain resistive acting out to sleepwalking, thus correlating phenomena of resistance with those of the dream, and R. Sterba (1946) reported instances where persons have acted out the dream contents of the previous night. More often action in place of association should be considered a waking-up analogue. But Rado's reference to sleepwalking, perhaps the least 'rational' of actions, brings out hyperbolically the fact that, to a freudian, motion is not in itself an end. It may be as disturbing to free association as to sleep. Aphoristically, one might say that the dream is the guardian of sleep, but the analyst is the guardian of free association.

In the cathartic cure and in early psychoanalysis, did the listening doctor relinquish the use of sleep? Perhaps not entirely, on close inspection, for when the patient found communication impeded, he was encouraged to associate freely (even by the laying on of hands), and in effect he was set to work to produce more or less dreamlike fantasies, to approach therefore in quality the mentation of sleep. At the point of resistance, to put it strongly, the patient was soothed a little, encouraged to be 'more asleep'. In this context, resistance meant too much alertness, which thwarted the doctors' intentions. Other resistances were soon encountered, in which, contrariwise, the patient let himself be in too much of a dream and eliminated too much responsibility and reality testing. With the years, after much study of the neuroses and psychoses, a good deal of this behavior was clarified, and the knowledge that accumulated was formulated in terms of a theory, and finally organized in *The Problem of Anxiety* and the literature that stems from this work.

AFFECTS

Affects on the couch or arising during solitary association are like those that appear in dreams. They are part of the manifest content. The freudian intention is to analyze them, and as in dream analysis determine whether a 'happy mood' may not conceal a fear of death, or whether an anxiety is a signal and a repetition. The solitary meditator may take the affect at its face manifest value and go on from there, taking the elated and depressed feelings especially as warranted.

THE ANALYST

We may approach the matter of the analyst and where he fits into the metapsychology of the dream by a preliminary consideration of the solitary associator. If he is following Freud's rules, i.e., if he is a self-analyst, there may be a kind of occult analyst, or at least an occult transference figure, as we learn from the role which Wilhelm Fliess played in Freud's self-analysis. Let us assume, however, for the general situation of self-analysis, that it is possible to do what Freud did in his self-study without someone else (real or ideal), therefore, without a transference.

As to the unanalytic free associator, for his unanalytic purposes he may wish to confide, so that we may speak of a possible confidant for such solitary meditations who would be the recipient of ideas that go through his mind. It is needless to list here the possibilities of such a relationship, which might include any kind of human communication from the most primitive to the most sophisticated, nor do I wish to document them. We again encounter the matter of purpose. Hanns Sachs has described one variety of such communication in his article, Daydreams in Common (1920), where the common ground was originally the sharing of masturbation fantasies, later of more elaborate stories. Supposing Boerne or Schiller had sought a confidant; then the other person could have been called an editor or a collaborator. Silberer might simply have considered such a person an intruder.

It was during the transition from hypnotic treatment to catharsis and analysis that the neurotic patient changed from being a hypnotic subject to being a confider, and the therapist *pari passu* became a psychoanalyst. Freud's and Breuer's first subjects came to them with the stated purpose of relief from symptoms, and to the end persons continued to go to Freud either to be cured or to learn, by sampling the cure, a therapeutic method. But before there was an official psychoanalysis, patients had come to be put under hypnosis, which they knew of as a sort of magical sleep. The idea that sleep is a magical healing method must be very ancient, more ancient than the sleep of the Æsculapian temple; and the general prevalence of this idea in the unconscious may well have attracted patients to hypnotists. 'And God put Adam into a deep sleep', the early anesthetists reminded their theologically oriented opponents and their reluctant patients, and certainly sleep has its rational place in therapy even today. In its origins, however, the therapeutic use of sleep quite possibly depended on fantasy, and the original hypnotic patients may have asked for it with the idea that after sleep should come a better waking, one into a new world, a dreamworld or heaven, in short, into a wish-fulfilling world where the blind see, the mute speak, the lame walk and are whole. Baudelaire called the drug addict's goal an artificial paradise, and this it was that the seeker after hypnotic sleep desired. The hysterical person, having been hypnotized, acted out many fantasies and miracles of therapy, and we still see often enough flights into health of the same shaky order.

The magical sleep-maker became a confidant, and the analytic situation arrived in history. But the confidant listening to associations as they appear is a very special kind of listener. Sometimes the person on the couch is hardly aware of his presence and is even surprised by it at the end of an analytic session; at other times, the patient can think of nothing but the analyst's person. We speak of the transference, thinking of the building up of fantasies about the analyst which are new editions of older ones in the patient's history. Evidently the analyst is not a unitary element that can be directly mapped to a unitary spot in the diagram of the psychic apparatus and into the psychology of sleep and the dream. In fact, in what follows it will become clear that the analyst belongs in several places in the diagram, also 'around' the diagram, and that he can be mapped in terms of dream psychology as a day residue, as an external excitant, and as an external or 'border' soother.

As the focus for infantile transference fantasies, the analyst was compared by Otto Rank, with Freud's approval (1916, footnote), to a day residue, a recent stimulus of the immediate environment which is processed into manifest material by the addition of unconscious ideas. In this sense, the analyst is a perception, he is recent material. Rank's point was made in refuting some of Silberer's views of 'anagogy' and in reference to dreams about the analyst, but the waking fantasies on the couch use him in the same way in this context. That the analyst is a sleep-maker or waker needs more elaboration, and will receive it in the discussion that follows. Also, it will be necessary to analyze in dream metapsychology the superego role often attributed to him.

Let us leave the patient side for a moment and consider the analyst as an interpreter, where his wishes and actions are central. Is the patient still clothed for him in traces of the sleep or part-sleep from his phylogenetic history as a hypnotic and cathartic subject? Or has the concept of the recumbent sleeper and dreamer been repressed? In the latter case we might look for some return of the repressed, and possibly see it when analysts turn to drugs as an adjuvant to cathartic or analytic therapy. However, let us consider two psychoanalytic aphorisms which epitomize the aim of analysis. The first is: 'Where id was, there let ego be!' Let us combine this with another familiar remark, that the ego rejoins the id in deep sleep. The inference is that the analyst is a waker. To confirm this inference, we have another aphoristic statement, much quoted, *'Ich verstand, dass ich von jetzt ab zu denen gehörte, die "am Schlaf der Welt gerührt" haben, nach Hebbels Ausdruck'*, (Freud [1914]). ['I understood that from now on, I belonged among those who "disturbed the sleep of the world", as Hebbel says.'] Inescapably the analyst is an arouser, as well as a day residue. As an external neutral fact, regardless of his intentions, he may become part of the subject's analytic-situation manifest content, and he is in the structure of the analytic situation as if a dream-day residue. But when the analyst's intentions come into play, and he interprets and analyzes, he is often not in the structure but an external waker or disturber of the situation. We shall see later that he may also at times play the role of a soother.

I suggested in a previous paper (1954) that coincidental with all other effects of the analyst's remarks or perhaps even of his presence, there is a deep effect, which I likened to the musical: the analyst continuously operates either to wake the patient somewhat or to put him to sleep a little, to soothe or to arouse; and this effect may be quite unconscious both for subject and analyst.

There are apparently some simple therapeutic situations, comparable to the standard analytic but different nevertheless, in which the aim is more nearly the simple one of arousing or wakening the patient. The idea that a psychosis is a kind of dream is ancient, and many maneuvers used in the treatment of schizophrenia have a rousing intention, as those most experi-enced in the field have stated or indicated. Zilboorg (1930), for example, as a preliminary to using the classical technique, put his schizophrenic patient through a course of training in reality discrimination, as if to insert into a dream some of the functions of the waking state. K. R. Eissler (1951) insists on dealing directly with 'the primary process', which is a concept of dream psychology, so that the maneuver is a concession to the patient's dreaming. In a somewhat different context, Eissler (1951, 1943) states that at one stage of the treatment, the intellectual content of what is told the patient is not as important as the therapist's voice or manner—that one could influence the patient perhaps even by mumbling, surely a 'musical' remark. John Rosen says explicitly and generally, 'What is the psychosis but an interminable nightmare in which the wishes are so well disguised that the psychotic does not awaken? Why not then awaken him by unmasking the real content of his psychosis? Once the psychosis is stripped of its disguises, will not this dreamer awaken too?' (1953).

Other, less clearly understood, methods of dealing with schizophrenia put the patient to 'sleep' by more or less drastic means. Empirically they often wake up different, and often they speak of the experience as a 'rebirth'. The 'rebirth' fantasy is the counterpart of the 'intrauterine fantasy'; the latter is an infantile fantasy which takes the child asleep as its model for life before birth; the 'birth' fantasy uses the child's waking up, or perhaps its 'waking up' into a dream. In any case, the therapist appears to have the intention of fulfilling the sleeper's wish for a healthy paradise, as I suggested in discussing the use of hypnotic sleep as an implementation of this idea in neurotics. We can gain some insight into the sleep-making intention of the physician by considering the ambivalence of physicians toward patients, their vacillation between a preference for a live or a dead patient, which I partly analyzed as due to their double experience in medical school, where they dealt with cadavers as their first patients and later had to transfer some of their conception of the patient as cadaver to live persons (Lewin [1946]). But as the sleep therapies of schizophrenia are organized, the doctor's wish to put the patient to sleep is subordinated to his wish to waken him and to cure him. As in surgery, the physician's sleep-making enters the larger therapeutic activity with its arousing intention, as a 'feed-back' and regulator or subordinate action.

To return to the topic of arousing, and the analyst's excitant role in this direction, we may again consider a schizophrenic case. I refer to Nunberg's classic analysis (1920, 1921) of the patient who had had a catatonic attack. He constantly referred to the attack as 'my dream', and he called his desire for recovery a wish to forget this dream completely. Elsewhere (1953) I have shown how the wish to forget a dream is equivalent to a wish to be completely awake, and in Nunberg's patient the way this was expressed is worth noting. For he set the physician up as a father and ego ideal, endowed him with tremendous power, expressed deep submission, and stated that he wished to be cured by the 'power' of this father's words. That is, as I interpret it, he wished the father to awaken him through powerful loud noises. In infancy, words and noises are powerful excitants and arousers, and apparently the same holds in the case of the dream.

Here I rely on Isakower's studies (1939, 1954), according to which manifest words that appear just at the end of dreams during wakening moments represent wakener-superego, and because they ave not been caught by the full dream work, they retain their verbal and environmental sense. Reasoning further, to be wakened is to be weaned, and as a variant, to be brought back to this world, which returns us to Rank and his fallacy. It also reminds us of Rank's insight into the preoedipal transference situation, and of his attempted analysis of the 'couch' and of the analytic situation *per se*. The 'couch' means sleep, with its maternal implications; and the spoor of the preœdipal father, who is not a dream element but a wakener, is sublimated in the therapy into the analyst who is not an element of the 'couch situation', but one who disturbs the sleep of the world and its inhabitants. The 'auditory sphere', which borders on the atmosphere where the sound waves travel, catches most of the stimuli (though surely not all) that awaken the child, the dreamer, and the analysand.

That the analyst is on the border of the dream becomes evident, by contrast, in those dreams where he is represented as a soother, and where there is no border. I am referring to those unprojected, blank, 'sleep', or 'narcissistic' dreams in which the analyst is represented. For example, in the dream reported by Rycroft (1951), where the border of the dreamer is vague, and the dream is not visually projected but is 'pure feeling', the analyst is a soothing atmosphere and the homologue of the breast or dream screen. In Rycroft's report, the patient said he felt as if he were being taken under the analyst's wing, but that there was no visual content, and that it was an allegorical way of expressing a feeling which was more like an emotion. I have encountered comparable 'transference remarks' in patients who expressed their preœdipal wish to sleep at the breast by fantasies of occupying the same space as the analyst, as if they could walk right into or through him. This is an unusual mapping of the analyst; it puts him in the place of sleep itself.

Nunberg's patient wished to be thoroughly awake and to forget his catatonic 'dream'. Rycroft's patient, not psychotic, in dreaming portrayed his analyst as the bland 'spirit of sleep' and enjoyed the best night's sleep he had ever had. Both patients centered their relationship about the fact of *sleep*, reminding us again of Freud's bargain with Anna O, and suggesting that both of these patients sensed the relationship *as if* in terms of the old prepsychoanalytic days, when the hypnotist put his patient to sleep and awakened him. Their manifest thoughts referred to this latent doctor-patient relationship.

Other clinical examples might be given, but they are readily available in analytic practice. Therefore, I shall be content to summarize some of the results of our mapping of the elements of dream psychology to the couch situation. With ingenuity, it is possible to find the couch situation's counterparts in *The Interpretation of Dreams*. In the sense of 'transference figure', the analyst is to be paired with what seemed in dream interpretation a very minor piece of material: he is the opposite number of indifferent precipitates or day residues to which unconscious ideas lend their cathexis. As interpreter, he stands for another minor element—a current external stimulus, which may threaten to arouse the dreamer, like the real fire in Freud's paradigm of the dream in Chapter VII, that of the burning child. He is also the opposite number of certain external stimuli which did not interest Freud in connection with the dream—the stimuli which promote sleep. These were taken for granted and did not need to be counteracted by the guardianship function of the dream, for they too assisted the maintenance of sleep and ordinarily were not registered in the dream. We know a great many of these differing at different ages: lulling and crooning, the full meal, and other satisfactions, all in a way wish fulfilments too. There are also soporific drugs, and as an interesting psychological example, the memory of the nursing situation, which, when it appears, often coincides with sound and happy sleep. In this context, the analyst's position is that of peripheral stimulus.

It will be noted that the analyst is at both ends and around the diagram of the psychic apparatus; that he is 'around' the couch as the external world is around the dream.

The rest of the mapping on to the couch of dream psychology is not difficult, for 'analysis-formation' is like dream-formation and involves the same memory traces and psychic systems, though usually in different proportions. Blank dreams are approximated by the 'blank couch', that is, sleep on the couch where the narcissism of sleep which is 'under' the dream comes out into the open as 'couch narcissism'. I omit what the analyst does besides lulling and rousing from the present statement; that is, I omit most of analytic technique, the contents of the specific interpretations and other operations, which of course matter very much. To fall back on Freud's old comparison of hypnosis and chloroform anesthesia, it is what one does after the patient is chloroformed that matters most, and this is what we call technique and not situation. As the surgeon cannot always ignore or completely forget the basic situation of anesthesia, so we cannot always ignore the ratio between sleep and waking in the analytic patient.

NOTES

1. The wording of the 'patient's proposal' does not mean that hypnosis is necessarily sleep, any more than 'to be put to sleep by ether' means that drug anesthesia is absolutely the same thing as natural sleep. No assumption of the sort is necessary. The assumption merely is that the patient regards being hypnotized, as he might regard being anesthetized, as such an action, and that he has the same attitude toward being hypnotized as he might have toward going to sleep. See Freud (1888); also Lewis (1954).
2. Ernest Jones (1953). Zilboorg (1952).
3. William James said that if you have a noble emotion such as you might get from going to The Symphony, you should do something about it, act on it, even go and pay a call on your great-aunt.
   I wish to thank Dr. Carl Binger for this reference, which he rightly calls 'the apotheosis of the pragmatic'.
4. One should not take the phrase *on the couch* too physically and literally. Free association, and an analytic situation too, occur with a person sitting up or in other positions. But this alters only a few obvious details; the person can also daydream, doze, and even sleep in the sitting position, and he can 'associate'.

REFERENCES

Eissler, Kurt R.: *Some Psychiatric Aspects of Anorexia Nervosa.* Psa. Rev., XXX, 1943.
————: *Remarks on the Psychoanalysis of Schizophrenia.* Int. J. Psa., XXXII, 1951.
Farrow, E. Pickworth: *Psychoanalyze Yourself.* New York: International Universities Press, Inc., 1945.
Freud, Anna: *The Ego and the Mechanisms of Defense* (1936). London: Hogarth Press, 1937.
Freud, S.: *Hypnotism and Suggestion* (1888). Coll. Papers, IV.
————: *The Interpretation of Dreams* (1900). Standard Edition, IV and V. London: Hogarth Press, 1953.
————: *Introductory Lectures on Psychoanalysis* (1916). London: G. Allen and Unwin, 1922.
————: *Mourning and Melancholia* (1915). Coll. Papers, IV.
————: *Metapsychological Supplement to the Theory of Dreams* (1916-a). Coll. Papers, IV.
————: *On the History of the Psychoanalytic Movement* (1914). Coll. Papers, I.
————: *The Problem of Anxiety* (1926). New York: The Psychoanalytic Quarterly, Inc. and W. W. Norton and Co., Inc., 1936.
————: *Aus den Anfängen der Psychoanalyse.* London: Imago Publishing Co., 1950.
Glover, Edward: *Freud or Jung.* New York: W. W. Norton and Co., Inc., 1950.
Hartmann, Heinz: On Rational and Irrational Action. In: *Psychoanalysis and the Social Sciences, I.* New York: International Universities Press, Inc., 1947.
————; Kris, Ernst; and Loewenstein, Rudolph M.: The Function of Theory in Psychoanalysis. In: *Drives, Affects, Behavior.* (Edited by Rudolph M. Loewenstein.) New York: International Universities Press, Inc., 1953.
Isakower, Otto: *On the Exceptional Position of the Auditory Sphere.* Int. J. Psa., XX, 1939.
————: *Spoken Words in Dreams.* Psychoanalytic Quarterly, XXIII, 1954.
James, William: *The Principles of Psychology.* New York: Henry Holt and Co., 1890.

Jones, Ernest: *The Life and Work of Sigmund Freud. Vol. I.* New York: Basic Books, Inc., 1953.

Jung, Carl G.: *The Psychology of the Unconscious* (1911). New York: Moffat, Yard and Co., 1916.

Kris, Ernst: *The Significance of Freud's Earliest Discoveries.* Int. J. Psa., XXXI, 1950.

————: Introduction to: *Aus den Anfängen der Psychoanalyse.* (See reference under Freud.)

————: *On Preconscious Mental Processes.* Psychoanalytic Quarterly, XIX, 1950.

————: See also Hartmann.

Lewin, Bertram D.: *Countertransference in Medical Practice.* Psychosomatic Med., VIII, 1946.

————: *Reconsideration of the Dream Screen.* Psychoanalytic Quarterly, XXII, 1953.

————: The Forgetting of Dreams. In: *Drives, Affects, Behavior.* (Edited by Rudolph M. Loewenstein.) New York: International Universities Press, Inc., 1953.

————: *Sleep, Narcissistic Neurosis and the Analytic Situation.* Psychoanalytic Quarterly, XXIII, 1954.

Loewenstein, Rudolph M.: "Defenses, Autonomous Ego, and Technique." Int. J. Psa., XXXV, 1954.

————: See also Hartmann.

Nunberg, Herman: *Practice and Theory of Psychoanalysis* (1920, 1921). New York: Nervous and Mental Disease Monographs, 1948.

Rank, Otto: *Eine Neurosenanalyse in Träumen.* Vienna: Internationaler Psychoanalytischer Verlag, 1924.

————: *Das Trauma der Geburt.* Vienna: Internationaler Psychoanalytischer Verlag, 1924 (a).

Rosen, John N.: *Direct Analysis.* New York: Grune and Stratton, 1953.

Rycroft, Charles: *A Contribution to the Study of the Dream Screen.* Int. J. Psa., XXXII, 1951.

Sachs, Hanns: The Community of Daydreams (1924). In: *The Creative Unconscious.* Cambridge, Mass.: Sci-Art Publishers, 1942.

Silberer, Herbert: *Bericht über eine Methode gewisse symbolische Halluzinations-Erscheinungen hervorzurufen und zu beobachten.* Jahrb. f. psa. Forschungen, I, 1909.

————: *Symbolik des Erwachens und Schwellensymbolik überhaupt.* Jahrb. f. psa. Forschungen, III, 1912.

Sterba, Richard F.: *Dreams and Acting out.* Psychoanalytic Quarterly, XV, 1946.

Stone, Leo: *Transference Sleep in a Neurosis with Duodenal Ulcer.* Int. J. Psa., XXVIII, 1947.

Zilboorg, Gregory: *Affective Reintegration of Schizophrenias.* Archives of Neurology & Psychiatry, XXIV, 1930.

————: *Some Sidelights on Free Associations.* Int. J. Psa., XXXIII, 1952.

PART II

CURRENT PSYCHOANALYTIC VIEWS

A. General

4. The Exceptional Position of the Dream in Psychoanalytic Practice

Ralph R. Greenson

INTRODUCTION

Freud considered *The Interpretation of Dreams* his major work. He wrote in the third (revised) English edition, published in 1932, 'It contains, even according to my present-day judgement, the most valuable of all the discoveries it has been my good fortune to make. Insight such as this falls to one's lot but once in a lifetime' (*17*, p. xxxii). At the end of Part E in the seventh chapter Freud said: '*The interpretation of dreams is the royal road to a knowledge of the unconscious activities of the mind*' (p. 608). A further indication of how important Freud considered this work to be is that he revised and amplified the book on dreams on eight different occasions, the last time in 1930 (*55*, p. xii).[1]

You may wonder why I chose to present a paper on the exceptional position of the dream since all this would seem to be common knowledge. A careful reading of the psychoanalytic literature in recent years, however, reveals that a number of psychoanalysts believe either that the dream has declined in clinical importance over the last forty years and is of no special value for psychoanalytic therapy or they use techniques which indicate that they have disregarded Freud's theory and methods of understanding and using the dream in clinical practice. I am also impressed that some influential

Reprinted by permission of Daniel P. Greenson and *The Psychoanalytic Quarterly*, Vol. 39, 1970.

The A. A. Brill Memorial Lecture, November 11, 1969.

I am indebted to Max Schur, Milton Wexler, Alfred Goldberg, and Nathan Leites for many of the ideas in this paper, a collaboration made possible by the foundation for Research in Psychoanalysis, Beverly Hills, California.

1. It is fitting on the occasion of the Brill Memorial Lecture to note that the first English edition of the book was translated by A. A. Brill in 1913.

psychoanalysts contend that this downgrading of the significance of the dream in clinical practice has come about because, (a) the structural theory was introduced, (b) Freud's great work on dreams has discouraged attempts at emulation or elaboration, and (c) Freud's concept of the topographic theory has become useless (*58,* pp. 52, 53). These conclusions and more can be found in a monograph titled The Place of the Dream in Clinical Psychoanalysis *(58)* which is the result of a two-year study of dreams by the Kris Study Group under the Chairmanship of Charles Brenner with Herbert Waldhorn serving as Reporter. Most of the members of this group appear to have concluded that (1) the dream is, clinically speaking, a communication in the course of analysis similar to all others; (2) it does not provide access to material otherwise unavailable; (3) it is simply one of many types of material useful for analytic inquiry; (4) it is not particularly useful for the recovery of repressed childhood memories; (5) Freud's theory that the dream-work is governed by the interplay between the primary process and the secondary process is not compatible with the structural theory and ought to be discarded.

I disagree with every one of the conclusions stated above. I am happy to point out that I am not alone in my beliefs, for I have discovered that some members of that section of the Kris Study Group, with Leon Altman as their spokesman, opposed many of those opinions. Altman has recently published a book, *The Dream in Psychoanalysis,* in which he suggests other reasons for the decline in clinical use of the dream. He expressed the opinion that since the coming of the trend toward ego psychology, many analysts have not had the experience of having their own dreams properly analyzed and the lack of this type of personal experience has deprived the psychoanalyst of the conviction that the interpretation of dreams is of outstanding importance for psychoanalysis (*1,* p. 1).

Besides that section of the Kris Study Group reported in *The Place of the Dream in Clinical Psychoanalysis,* there are prominent analysts of Kleinian persuasion who also work with patients' dreams in ways which are far removed from what Freud, Isakower *(34, 35),* Sharpe *(52),* Lewin *(41, 42),* Erikson *(10),* and a host of others have described in their writings on this subject. In this paper I shall attempt to contribute some clinical material and formulations which I hope will demonstrate how those analysts who seem to operate from divergent theoretical and technical convictions differ from analysts who believe in the exceptional position of the dream.

It is my belief, after many years of psychoanalytic therapy with private patients and candidates in psychoanalytic training, that one cannot carry out genuine analysis in sufficient depth if one does not understand the structure of dream formation *as well as the patient's and the analyst's contributions to the technique of dream interpretation.*

SOME GENERAL FORMULATIONS

The dream I believe is a unique form of mental functioning which is produced during a special phase of sleep. This phase is unlike any other phase of the sleep cycle and differs also from the waking state. The psychophysiological research of Dement and Kleitman *(6)*, Charles Fisher *(13, 14)*, and Ernest Hartmann *(32)*, among others, has made this emphatically clear. Recent research suggest the likelihood that dream deprivation may be the cause of severe emotional and mental disorders. We may well have to add to Freud's dictum that the dream is the guardian of sleep, that sleep is necessary in order to safeguard our need to dream.

The altered balance of mental forces in the dream is produced by bursts of psychic activity that seek sensory release because sleep diminishes contact with the external world and also cuts off the possibility of voluntary motor action. The dream state allows for a reduction and regression of conscious ego activities and of the censorship function of the superego. It is important to realize, however, that in a sense, one is never fully awake nor fully asleep. These are relative and not absolute terms. Kubie *(38)*, Lewin *(40)*, and Stein *(54)* have stressed the merits of keeping in mind the sleep-waking ratio in studying any kind of human behavior. This helps explain the fact that in the dream the perceiving function of the ego, being deprived of the external world during sleep, turns its energy toward internal psychic activity. Freud wrote that when people go to sleep they undress their minds and lay aside most of their psychical acquisitions *(21, p. 222)*. Lewin added that the dreamer generally sheds his body. The dream usually appears to us as a picture and is recorded only by an indefinite 'psychic' eye *(42, p. 86)*.

If we follow the notion of a variable sleep-waking ratio, we are immediately reminded of phenomena similar to dreams: free association, parapraxes, jokes, symptom formations, and acting out. But there are crucial differences. No production of the patient occurs so regularly and reveals so much so graphically of the unconscious forces of the mind as the dream. Dream interpretation can uncover in more immediate and convincing ways not only what is hidden, but how it is hidden and why it is hidden. We gain special access to the interplay and the transitions between the unconscious psychic activities governed by the primary process and conscious phenomena which follow the laws of the secondary process. The proportion between input and output, in terms of reported phenomena and obtained knowledge of unconscious material, is in no other type of psychic phenomena as favorable as it is in dreams *(9)*.

So long as psychoanalytic therapy focuses on the resolution of neurotic conflicts in which the crucial components are unconscious, it makes no sense to consider every production of the patient of equal potential value. Affects, body language, and dreams are all, in most ways, nearer to those almost unreachable depths we search out so persistently in our analytic work. We attempt to present our findings to the patient's conscious and reasonable ego with the hope of providing him with a better understanding of his way of life and an opportunity for change.

These same points can be expressed structurally by stating that the dream reveals with unusual clarity various aspects of the id, the repressed, the unconscious ego and superego, and to a lesser degree certain conscious ego functions, particularly its observing activities. However, limiting the approach to the dream to the structural point of view is an injustice because it neglects the fact that we also have in the dream more open access to dynamic, genetic, and economic data of basic importance. Small wonder then that the dream experience itself, often without interpretation, leads more directly and intensely to the patient's affects and drives than any other clinical material. This makes for a sense of conviction about the reality of unconscious mental activity unequalled by any other clinical experience. This is particularly true of transference dreams.

The dream is in closer proximity to childhood memories by dint of the fact that both make use essentially of pictorial representations. Freud *(17, 22)* and Lewin *(42)* have emphasized that primitive mentation takes place in pictures and is closer to unconscious processes than verbal representation. Even after the child learns to speak, his thinking is essentially dominated by pictorial representations. Things heard get turned into pictures, as we know from certain screen memories *(42, 49)*. If an event is to become a memory in early childhood, it has eventually to become concretized, a mental representation, a memory trace. Lewin states that then we search for lost memories as if they can be found somewhere. This type of memory, the recall of an objectified experience, is a step which seems to occur at the end of the first or beginning of the second year of life *(53, 57)*. There are more primitive 'imprintings' which are derived from infantile body and feelings states that are not capable of being remembered but which may give rise to mental images and sensations in dreams. Lewin's ideas on blank dreams and the dream screen and his discussion of related problems are especially worthy of note *(39, 42,* pp. 51–55).

To return briefly to the special importance of the psychic eye for the dreamer and the interpreter of dreams. The dream is essentially a visual experience and most adult recollections of early childhood come to us as pictures or scenes. The analyst interpreting to his patient is often working upon a fragment of historical experience which he hopes will lead to a memory. Such fragments or details may appear in dreams. When the analyst tries to fill in the gaps between single interpretations, he is making a construction, he is trying to re-create a series of interrelated forgotten experiences. Such conjectures may lead to recollections but, even if they do not, they may lead to a sense of probability or conviction that the reconstruction is correct. This may then appear in a dream as an event *(25)*. Lewin describes this as trying to re-create a story in pictures of the patient's forgotten past. By doing so we attempt to get the patient to scan his past along with us; we are engaged in conjoint looking *(42,* p. 17). The ultraclarity of some dream details also indicates that there is a special relationship between the cathexis of looking and the search for memories. This wish to see what actually took place, to be 'in' on it, adds to the special sense of conviction that the correct interpretation of a dream can convey.

Ernst Kris decried the one-sided emphasis on analyzing defenses and stressed the importance of reconstructing past historical events so that the patient could 'recognize' the pictures drawn as familiar *(36,* p. 59). He believed that memory plays a central role in a circular process which, if integrated, makes it possible for the patient to reconstruct his total biographical picture, change his self-representation and his perspective of the important persons in his world. In Kris's paper on the 'good analytic hour', it is remarkable how often he chose examples of hours which contained dreams and recovered memories *(37)*.

The predominant elements in the psychic activities that occur in dreams are heavily weighted on the side of the id, the repressed memories, the primitive defensive mechanisms of the ego, and the infantile forms and functions of the superego. Occasionally one can observe more mature ego functions but they are rarely dominant. All this testifies to the high degree of regression that occurs in dreaming, but as in all regressive phenomena, the quality and quantity of regression is uneven and selective in the different psychic structures and functions, as Freud pointed out as early as 1917 *(21)*, Fenichel in 1945 *(11)*, and Arlow and Brenner in 1964 *(2)*. The clearest and most comprehensive description of the unevenness and selectivity of regression can be found, in my opinion, in Anna Freud's book, *On Normality and Pathology in Childhood* (*16*, pp. 93–107).

Free association is a similar regressive phenomenon; it is an attempt to approximate something between wakefulness and sleep. The use of the reclining position, the absence of external distractions, the patient's attempt to consciously suspend his ordinary censorship, to abandon strict logic and coherence in his communications, all attest to that. However, real spontaneous free associations are rarely achieved by most patients and are then defended against with far greater sophistication. The point I wish to make is that the dream is the freest of free associations. Slips of the tongue may quickly reveal some deep unconscious insights but they occur rarely; insight is localized and the old defenses are very readily reinstituted. Acting out is by definition ego-syntonic to the patient and its infantile origins are strongly rationalized away and defended. By contrast, as bizarre and incomprehensible as the dream may appear, the patient recognizes the dream as his, he knows it is his own creation. Although the strange content of the dream may make it seem alien, nevertheless it is irrevocably his, like his symptoms, and he is quite willing to work on his dreams, provided his analyst has demonstrated how working together on dreams is helpful in achieving greater awareness of the patient's unknown self.

A few words before turning to some clinical examples. In 1923 Freud himself recognized that *some* of his ideas subsumed under the topographic point of view conflicted with the descriptive and dynamic attributes of unconscious mental activities and he introduced the structural point of view *(22)*. This new division of the psychic apparatus into id, ego, and superego clarified the role of the conscious and unconscious ego and the conscious and unconscious superego in its conflicts with the totally unconscious id. I agree with Fenichel *(11)*, with Rapaport and Gill *(48)*, as well as with Arlow and Brenner *(2)*, who stress the superiority of the structural theory in affording a clearer and more logical explanation for the origin and fate of neurotic conflicts. I do not agree with Arlow and Brenner, however, that Freud's hypotheses concerning the primary process, the secondary process, and the preconscious should be discarded or that they are incompatible with the structural point of view. Even Merton Gill *(27)*, who believes that the topographic point of view is conceptually not on a par with the other metapsychological points of view, agrees that some topographic conceptions have an important place both clinically and theoretically. I find this to be particularly true in working with dreams. It is equally important in dealing with patients who suffer from defects and deficiencies in ego formation and the parallel difficulty in building constant internal object-representations, problems which go below and beyond the conflict theory of the psychoneuroses. I do not wish to dwell on theory—it is not my strong point, but those interested may turn to the writings of Hartmann *(33)*, Loewenstein *(45)*, Benjamin *(3)*, Eissler *(8)*, Schur *(50)*, Loewald *(43)*, Mahler *(46)*, and Fisher's remarks in the panel on The Psychoanalytic Theory of Thinking *(12)*, for a more thorough discussion of the subject.

CLINICAL EXAMPLES

Some clinical examples of how different analysts work with dreams illustrate the divergencies in technique and theoretical orientation. I shall begin with clinical material from the publications of psychoanalysts who work with dreams in ways that seem to me to be unproductive, wasteful, and at times even harmful.

A clinical illustration presented in *The Place of the Dream in Clinical Psychoanalysis* (*58*, pp. 59–67) was that of a thirty-year-old writer in the second year of her analysis. Essentially, she seemed to be an as-if character, exceedingly immature and dependent. There was a childhood history of social failure in competition with her younger sister because of the patient's ineptitude and gaucheness. The patient had severe acne of the face, neck, and back in adolescence and had occasional recurrent active lesions. She was also thin and flat-chested. She entered treatment because of mild depressions, poor concentration, and inability to sustain an intimate relationship with a man. The patient had several brief affairs accompanied by a dread of losing the man and was always flooded by remorse and loss of self-esteem when the affair ended. In the weeks prior to the dream reported, the patient had had sexual relations with a man named John, whom she had known only a short time. He had left town for several weeks and, in spite of knowing better from past disappointments, she found herself imagining that John loved her and they would be married. During this interval she brought in a dream. Now I quote verbatim from the monograph.

'She began the hour as follows: "I had a very bad dream. I had cancer of the breast. A doctor, a woman, said it would have to be removed. She said that there would be after-effects which I would feel in my neck. My friend R. had this operation. I was scared and I panicked, and wondered how I could get away, run away, and not have to have this done.'' She continued with the following associations: ''I tried to think why I should have such a dream. I thought it must be related to my idea that I am not complete by myself and that I need some sort of union with a remarkable man to make myself complete. This might be related to my worry that John was gone and maybe this was symbolized by my breast being removed. Actually, I am very frightened by things like that. Many people do have an obsession about such fears. For example, Paul does. Some people can face these things with great courage and strength, but not me. I am very frightened when I think about the danger of the scorpions in Mexico [she was planning a trip in a few months] . . .'' ' (pp. 61, ff.)

The patient awoke, fell asleep, and had another dream but I shall omit it because the presenter and the group did not touch upon it. After a few innocuous associations, the analyst finally spoke and I shall quote his first remarks verbatim.

'At this point the analyst intervened, asking, ''about your dream. What do you associate to the business about the doctor?'' The patient responded: ''She was a matronly type of woman, stern. She didn't seem to feel sorry for me or anything like that, but just said what would have to be done. I was thinking, how could a man make love to me without one breast? I would be terribly self-conscious. . . .'' After a pause the analyst asked: ''What about the part in the dream about the neck?'' She responded: ''Sometimes I make a wrong movement and my neck muscles can hurt. That area is vulnerable for me because of my complexion problems involving my chin and neck, about which I have always felt so self-conscious. . . .'' The analyst then added: ''When you speak of self-consciousness about your skin and neck, does it remind you of the self-consciousness you have recently been describing when you told me about how terrible you felt before you had any breast development?'' The patient said: ''So, do you think that the fact that John did not call me made me re-experience those feelings of inadequacy? They may still be present'' ' (pp. 62, ff.).

The analyst then offered a long intellectual interpretation and the patient responded in kind.

The Study Group's discussion of this presentation included the following excerpt. 'The discussion of this report was initiated by the remarks of the analyst presenting the data. He maintained that the clinical material supported the belief that dreams can best be treated in the same way as other associations in the hours, and not necessarily accorded extraordinary or exhaustively detailed procedural attention as some would insist. Here, in the hours described, the analytic work is focussed on the problems highlighted by the repetitive life experience of the patient. . . . Accordingly, some portions of the dream can be neglected in favor of others, and a dream need have no specific attention directed to it if spontaneous associations are meager and the work with the dream (as opposed to other material) seems less likely to be rewarding. The rich amount of symbolically understandable elements in the second half of the first dream was not explored at all, but it was the analyst's clinical judgment that nothing was lost in the process . . .' (pp. 64, ff.).

I shall limit myself to a few remarks about the patient's manifest dream, her associations, the analyst's interventions, and the group discussion. In the first dream the patient is terrified upon discovering she has a cancer of the breast. She is told this by a female doctor who warns her there will be after-effects. The patient's associations sound to me intellectualized and a rote repetition of old interpretations given her by her male analyst. There does not seem to be any attempt on the part of the analyst to point out her intellectualization or to get to her terror of this malignant thing growing inside her. The analyst did not pursue the only spontaneous free association the patient produced, namely her fear of scorpions in Mexico. After the patient reported the second dream and a few innocuous associations, the analyst asked: 'About your dream. What do you associate to the business about the doctor?' To me, the way the question was put gives the impression the analyst is either defensive and hostile or even contemptuous, otherwise he would not use a phrase like 'what about the business about the doctor'. Furthermore, it is all too intellectual. Words like 'what do you associate' push the patient in the direction of intellectual compliance; not the best way to get to feelings or really free, free associations. In general, there was no sign that the therapist was trying to reach or establish contact with the patient's affects; he shows no signs of being 'tuned in' on her feelings; on the contrary, he seems to play right along with her intellectualized defensiveness.

If you read the second dream, it seems to express in obvious symbolic terms the patient's envy of her sister and her aunt, but it was completely ignored. Apparently the analyst and the group did not discern any possible connections between cancer, breast, mother, and envy. There also was no apparent awareness of how frequently heterosexual promiscuity is used as a defense against helpless childhood dependency needs with the resultant urges and fears of fusing or becoming reunited with the pregenital mother. There was also no mention of a hostile transference to her male analyst or a wish to have a female analyst. The analyst and the group seemed content to maintain a highly intellectual contact with the patient, and were reluctant to open up the patient's fantasy life and follow wherever it might lead. Toward the end of this discussion in the monograph, there are a few sentences that deserve special comment. 'Such axiomatic procedures as the desirability of working with transference elements before nontransference material, or affect-laden before nonaffect-laden material, or the necessity of drawing the patient's attention to evident omissions or to an addendum, were all mentioned. The consensus was that these were best considered as tactical maneuvers, subordinated to an overall strategy of the conduct of the analysis, which would, of course, change with the progress of the treatment' (p. 66).

In my opinion there is no place for 'axiomatic procedures' in trying to do psychoanalytic therapy. It is true that some of us follow certain time-tested technical guidelines in beginning the exploration of such oft-recurring clinical constellations as may occur in associating to dreams or in free association in general. These approaches are tools for investigation. I find the concept of an 'overall strategy of the conduct of the analysis' an impressive, high-sounding phrase but, in reality, with our present state of knowledge, this 'overall strategy' is at best loose, subject to frequent changes and revisions, and full of unknowns. Only psychoanalysts with preconceived and rigid theoretical notions are sure of an 'overall strategy'. And they also have prefabricated interpretations for all types of patients and disregard the fact that each individual human being is unique, as well as the fact that there is still much even the best of us do not know and cannot predict about our patients. Freud had the humility to say that we should let the patient determine the subject matter of the hour *(18)*; he attached great importance to following the patient's free associations. In 1950b Eissler severely criticized Alexander and his followers for making decisions about the definitive strategy for treatment of a case. Eissler felt that Alexander was more interested in validating his own hypotheses than in really analyzing his patients *(7)*.

This leads to another type of distortion in working with dreams which can be found in the writings of some of the Kleinian analysts. Hans Thorner in studying the problem of examination anxiety illustrated his ideas by describing a patient, a dream, and his interpretations. Again, limitations of space permit me to present only the highlights.

A man of early middle age complained of impotence and that all his love relationships came to a premature end. At times he could begin a relationship but as soon as he felt the woman was interested in him, he had to break off. He was impotent in other spheres of his life as well. Although he had reached a high standard of proficiency in music he was unable to play in public or before his friends. It became clear that all these situations approximated an examination situation. When he applied for a new job he was terrified of being interviewed because of what he considered to be his 'black record', although realistically there was little black in his record. During one of these intervals he reported a dream which shed new light upon the nature of his black record. In the dream red spiders were crawling in and out of the patient's anus. A doctor examined him and told the patient that he was unable to see anything wrong with him. The patient replied, 'Doctor, you may not see anything, but they are there just the same'.

Thorner reports his interpretations to the patient as follows: 'Here the patient expresses his conviction that he harbours bad objects (red spiders) and even the doctor's opinion cannot shake this conviction. The associative link between "black record" and "red spiders" shows the anal significance of his "black record". He himself is afraid of these object against which he, like the man in the dream, asks for help. This help must be based on a recognition of these objects and not on their denial;—in other words he should be helped to control them. It is clear that we are here dealing with a feeling of persecution by bad internal objects' (56, pp. 284, ff.).

I believe this a prime example of interpreting the manifest content of a dream according to the analysts's theoretical convictions. The patient's associations are interpreted in a narrow, preconceived way. The patient's reproach to the examining physician, 'Doctor, you may not see anything, but they are there all the same' is not recognized as a hostile transference nor is it acknowledged as a possible justifiable reproach to the analyst that he really may be missing something. I wonder if the red spiders crawling in and out of the patient's anus are not the patient's reaction to his analyst's intrusive and painful interpretations. But now I, too, am guilty of interpreting without associations.

Another example of a similar type can be found in Hanna Segal's book (51). She describes a patient, his dream, and her interventions as follows.

'Powerful unconscious envy often lies at the root of negative therapeutic reactions and interminable treatments; one can observe this in patients who have a long history of failed previous treatments. It appeared clearly in a patient who came to analysis after many years of varied psychiatric and psychotherapeutic treatments. Each course of treatment would bring about an improvement, but deterioration would set in after its termination. When he began his analysis, it soon appeared that the main problem was the strength of his negative therapeutic reaction. I represented mainly a successful and potent father, and his hatred of and rivalry with this figure was so intense that the analysis, representing my potency as an analyst, was unconsciously attacked and destroyed over and over again. . . . In the first year of his analysis, he dreamt that he put into the boot of his little car tools belonging to my car (bigger than his), but when he arrived at his destination and opened the boot, all the tools were shattered.'

Dr. Segal interprets: 'This dream symbolized his type of homosexuality; he wanted to take the paternal penis into his anus and steal it, but in the process of doing so, his hatred of the penis, even when introjected, was such that he would shatter it and be unable to make use of it. In the same way, interpretations which he felt as complete and helpful were immediately torn to pieces and disintegrated, so that it was particularly following good sessions which brought relief that he would start to feel confused and persecuted as the fragmented, distorted, half-remembered interpretations confused and attacked him internally' (pp. 29–30).

Here too, I believe one can see how the analyst's conviction about the correctness of her insights and interpretations tempts her to make detailed interpretations without any of the patient's associations for confirmatory clinical evidence. Once again I do not see in this case presentation any evidence of an analyst and patient working together on a dream. I see instead, an analyst forcing a patient to submit to her interpretation. By doing so this analyst is acting in a way which proves she is really like the patient's hated and envied potent father. No wonder he dreams that all his tools are shattered. To quote Freud: 'But dream interpretation of such a kind, without reference to the dreamer's associations, would in the most unfavorable case remain a piece of unscientific virtuosity of very doubtful value' (23, p. 128). I must add that many analysts of non-Kleinian affiliation also disregard the patient's associations.

At this point, I will present some work with dreams that I believe exemplifies how an analyst who appreciates the exceptional position of the dream utilizes it in his practice. For the sake of clarity and demonstrability, the dreams I have chosen for illustrations are those from my recent clinical experience with which I was able to work fruitfully. They are not everyday examples of my work with dreams. There are many dreams I can understand only vaguely and partially and some I can hardly understand at all. There are also occasions when the dream is not the most productive material of the hour, but this has been rare in my experience. Freud wrote as far back as 1911 that dream interpretation should not be pursued for its own sake, it must be fitted into the treatment, and all of us agree on this obvious point *(19)*.

I realize that no clinical demonstration of the value of dream interpretation will change the opinions of those who are predominantly devoted to theory conservation or theoretical innovations. Their theories seem to be more real to them than the memories and reconstructions of their patient's life history. Working with dreams is not only an enlightening experience for the patient, but it may be a source of new clinical and theoretical insights of the analyst, if he has an open mind. Furthermore, there are some analysts who have no ear or eye for dreams, like people who find it hard to hear and visualize the beauty of poetry, or like the tone-deaf who cannot appreciate the special imagery and language of music, or those who have no facility for wit and humor. Such analysts will lower the importance of dream interpretation, no matter what evidence you present. Finally, there are analysts who, for some other reasons, have never had the opportunity to learn how to listen to, understand, and work with dreams.

The two dreams I shall present are from the analysis of the same patient, a thirty-year-old writer, Mr. M., who came for analytic treatment because of a constant sense of underlying depressiveness, frequent anxiety in social and sexual relations, and a feeling of being a failure despite considerable success in his profession and what appeared to be a good relationship to his wife and children. He had a great fear that he would not be able to do free association at all, and that if he did I would find him empty or loathsome and send him away. We worked on these resistances for several weeks and he was then able on occasion to do some relatively spontaneous free association on the couch. One of the major sources of his resistances in the beginning was his experience with several friends who were also currently in psychoanalytic treatment. They talked freely and often in social situations about their œdipus complexes, their positive and negative transference reactions, their castration anxiety, their superegos, their incestuous desires, etc., all of which my patient felt was 'textbooky', 'artificial', and 'a load of crap'. Mr. M. was afraid that he would not be able to genuinely accept such interpretations, and yet also dreaded that unknowingly he too might turn out to be a 'junior psychoanalyst' socially. I want to present the highlights from an hour in the sixth week of his analysis in which he reported his first dream. He had often had the feeling of having dreamed, but until this point could never remember any of his dreams.

One day he began the hour by stating: 'I had a dream but it seems unrelated to anything we have been talking about'.

I was making a phone call to some guy in a men's clothing store. I had ordered some clothes made to order and they didn't fit. I asked the guy to take them back but he said I had to come in myself. I told him I was not going to pay for the clothes until they fit. I said it seems like you just took them off the rack. I repeated, I won't pay for the clothes until they fit. As I said that I began to vomit, so I dropped the phone and ran into the bathroom to wash out my mouth. I left the received dangling and I could hear the guy saying, 'What did you say, what? What?'

I remained silent and the patient spontaneously began to speak: 'The most striking thing to me is the vomiting. I just can't vomit, I never, never vomit. I can't even remember the last time I did, probably as a child sometime. It is like a biological thing, it's so strong. Like in yesterday's hour, I couldn't get myself to talk. [Pause] Free association is like vomiting.' I intervened at this point and said, 'Yes, free association becomes like vomiting when things are trying to come up in your mind that you would rather keep inside yourself and away from me. The dream says it has to do with something not fitting you properly.' The patient quickly replied, 'Yes, it's about clothes, but that is too silly. Why clothes? Clothes not fitting? [Pause] Oh my God, this can't have anything to do with the analysis. The man saying, what is it, what, what, that could be you. [Pause] I leave you talking and go to vomit in the bathroom—buy why, why do I do that?' I answered, 'When I give you an interpretation that doesn't seem to fit you, you must resent it and feel that I just took it off my "psychoanalytic rack", like the other "textbooky" analysts you have heard about'. The patient: 'Oh Jesus, I can't believe it, I thought things like this only happened in books. How funny!'

At this point, the patient began to roar with laughter and tears streamed down his face. He gathered himself together and said: 'I never thought things like this would happen to me. You are right. When you say things that don't seem to fit me, sometimes I do get annoyed, but I keep it in. [Pause] I get scared here when I feel angry. It's like being afraid of my father when I was a kid. [Pause] I now suddenly see a vague picture of me vomiting when I was about three or four years old. [Pause] It was with my mother, right on her, she must have been holding me. She was so nice about it, too, she took me to the bathroom and cleaned me up and herself too. Amazing, this whole thing.' I answered: 'Yes, apparently you were not afraid to vomit up things in front of your mother, but you must have been very scared of doing that with your father and now you feel the same way here with me. But you see these kinds of things do tend to come out in dreams or in such things like your forgetting to pay me this month.' The patient was startled and blurted out: 'This is too much. I had your check in my wallet, but in the last minute I decided to change my jacket and left my wallet at home. And I never even thought of it when I was telling you the dream, all about not wanting to pay that man. Something must really be cooking inside of me.' The patient paused, sighed, and after a while I asked him just to try to say what was going on. His associations then drifted to his shame about revealing his toilet activities, masturbation, his hemorrhoids, a history of an anal fistula, and other matters.

I believe this clinical example demonstrates how it is possible to work productively with a first dream, which is contrary to the opinions expressed in the monograph *The Place of the Dream in Clinical Psychoanalysis.* Avoidance of dream interpretation by the analyst can frighten the patient, because the patient may sense the analyst's fear of the dream contents. An analyst's timid approach to a dream may add to a patient's suspicion that he, the patient, is especially full of internal evils or may convince him that he has a frightened analyst. On the other hand, deep interpretations given too early will either frighten the patient into leaving the analysis or it will persuade him that the analyst is omniscient and convert the patient into a devout follower and not a working ally. One has to assess carefully with each patient how much and how little one can do with early dreams and early material in general.[2]

Let us scrutinize more carefully what I tried to do with that first dream. Once the patient was spontaneously able to connect his fear of vomiting with his fear of free association, I first confirmed this representation of his resistance by saying out loud what he had already become conscious of—his dread of losing control over the horrible things inside of himself: vomiting is equated to free association and he vomits into the sink and not into the phone, the analysis. I then felt I could lead him in the direction of trying to discover

2. See Berta Bornstein *(4)*, Loewenstein *(44)*, and Greenson *(30)* for examples of their method of dealing with this delicate problem.

what was making him vomit. The obvious symbolism of the ill-fitting clothes delivered to him ready-made and not made to order, symbols which he himself could grasp, encouraged me to point out his suppressed anger at me for my ill-fitting, ready-made interpretations, taken off my psychoanalytic rack. His laughter was a relief from the fear that he lacked an unconscious mind and was a freak, and also that I might be harsh with him for such thoughts. It was confirmation of the correctness of my interpretation and also an early sign of conviction that there is an active but unconscious part of his mind which does contain specific and personal meanings and they are not as terrible as he had imagined.

My referring to myself as the 'textbooky guy' who is unable to tailor his interpretations to suit the patient must have given Mr. M. enough trust in my motherliness so that he could recall an early childhood memory of vomiting on his mother. Here vomiting is loving and not hating. He was then able to contrast this with his dread of vomiting up things in the presence of his father. His later association to the toilet, masturbation, and so forth, indicated an increase in his ability to let things come up in free association in my presence, a lessening of his resistances. Apparently my way of communicating to him helped me establish a working alliance with his reasonable, observing ego.

There are many elements in this dream which I did not point out to Mr. M. but which are of interest to us as examples of the function of the dream work and of the interaction of the primary process and the secondary process as well as of the interaction of the id, ego, and superego. The patient's very first sentence before telling the dream: 'I had a dream but it seems unrelated to anything we have been talking about', is an attempt to contradict and deny the very essence of the dream, namely, that it concerns his feelings about me and the analysis. The psychoanalytic situation is depicted as a telephone conversation, only a verbal exchange, and even that is held at a distance. The man he speaks to is referred to as a 'guy working in a store', not the most awesome or flattering representation of a psychoanalyst. The insights and interpretations I gave him were represented by clothes, and clothes conceal rather than reveal, an example of reversal and the use of opposites. Psychoanalysis does not strip you, it is supposed to clothe you, a reassurance, a wish-fulfilment. His fear of close emotional contact with the analyst is demonstrated by his refusal to come in person to the store. His leaving the phone dangling and hearing the 'guy's voice' saying 'what is it, what, what', is a beautiful and hostile caricature of my analytic technique. It is as well his revenge against me for leaving him dangling hour after hour; it is not he who keeps asking desperately, but I. The vomiting is not only an expression of his forbidden instinctual impulses but it is also a self-punishment for his hostility. It is as well a rejection of the interpretations I have been forcing him to swallow and also his spiteful obedience: 'You want me to bring things up. O.K., here it is'. This is an example of the coexistence of opposites in the primary process.

One can see that the vomiting is derived from both the id and the super-ego. It also serves the resistances, a defensive function of the ego, by breaking off our line of communication. All this and more is in the dream *and* in the patient's associations, facilitated by the interpretations. Only a fraction of this material can be meaningfully conveyed to the patient in a single hour, but it serves a valuable service for the analyst as source material for clues that will be of use in the future.

Mr. M. continued with the theme of clothes and concealment in the next several hours. As a child of impoverished parents he was embarrassed by his shabby, dirty clothing. He was also ashamed of being skinny and had tried to hide this by wearing several sweatshirts and sweaters on top of each other when he was young. When he later became affluent he bought bulky tweed sport coats and often wore turtle-neck sweaters with a leather jacket and boots. During the post-dream interval he recalled stealing money from his father to buy a zoot suit, which was fashionable in his youth, because he wanted to make a good impression at a school dance. He also recalled having severe acne which he attributed to masturbation and which he attempted to cover with various facial creams and lotions. He tried to rationalize his stealing from his father by recalling that his father cheated his customers at times. All this material had the meaning: 'I have to hide my true self. If anyone sees beneath my surface he will find me ugly and unlovable. I am a fraud, but so is most of the world. How do I know you are genuine and sincere in your treatment of me and will it change once I am stripped of all my superficial disguises?' (I was not merely working with the manifest dream in the following days, but with the latent dream thoughts which the patient's associations and my intervention had uncovered.)

The second dream of Mr. M. occurred about two and one half years later. The patient had to interrupt his analysis for six months because of a professional assignment abroad and returned some three months before the dream. During this three-month interval of analytic work Mr. Mr. was in a chronic state of quiet, passive depression. I had interpreted this as a reaction to his wife's fourth pregnancy, which must have stirred up memories and feelings in regard to his mother's three pregnancies after his birth. It seemed clear to me that he was re-experiencing the loss of the feeling and fantasies of being his mother's favorite, the only child and the favorite child. The patient accepted my interpretations submissively and conceded they had merit, but he could recall nothing about the birth of his three siblings nor his reactions, although he was over six when the youngest was born. My interpretations had no appreciable influence on his mood.

Mr. M. came to the hour I shall now present, sadly and quietly, and in a somewhat mournful tone recounted the following dream:

I am in a huge store, a department store. There are lots of shiny orange and green plastic raincoats on display. A middle-aged Jewish woman is arranging other articles of clothing. Nearby is a female manikin dressed in a gray flannel dress. I go outside and see a woman who looks very familiar but I can't say specifically who she is. She is waiting expectantly and eagerly for me near a small surrey, putting clothes in it. I feel sorry for the poor horse and then realize the surrey is detached form the horse. I lift up the surrey to connect it and I am surprised how light the surrey is, but I don't know how to hitch it up to the horse. I also realize then that I was silly to feel sorry for the horse.

Mr. M.'s associations were as follows: 'The three women in the dream were so different from one another. The older Jewish woman was a motherly type, working, doing, arranging, like my own mother used to before she became bedridden. The manikin reminds me of how I used to think of gentile girls when I was a kid; beautiful, pure, and cold, like my wife. But they taught me different. The best sex I have ever experienced was only with gentile girls. Jewish women just don't turn me on. They never did. Since my wife's pregnancy our sex life is practically nil. She isn't feeling well and I must say I'm in no mood for sex. I would like to be close to her in bed, but I don't want her to think it is a sexual demand so there is no talking even. I'd like to just be close and cuddle. My wife is so quiet of late. I feel she is getting revenge on me for all my past wrongs. I never realized before I had had such a bad temper and that she had been and still is so afraid of me. [Pause] I feel so alone in that big house of ours. I work like a horse to pay for it. Maybe I am the horse in the dream that I felt sorry for.'

I intervened. 'It might be so. You think he had such a big load to carry, but then you lift up the buggy and you are surprised to discover how light it is.' The patient interrupted me. 'That buggy is so light, it's a baby buggy, it's a baby carriage. No wonder it was so light, it was so tiny, and the woman was putting clothes on it, like diapers.' [Pause] I interrupted. 'A baby buggy is very heavy for a little boy, he has to work like a horse to push it.' Mr. M. burst in with, 'I can remember trying to push my baby sister in her buggy but it was too heavy for me. Now I see my father carrying the baby carriage downstairs as if it were a toy. I can even remember my brother and me together trying to push it.' I interpreted and reconstructed: 'I believe you have been depressed ever since your wife got pregnant because it stirred up memories of how you reacted when you were a small boy and your mother got pregnant and delivered your brother and sisters. You didn't want to face the fact that your father was hitched up to the coming of the babies. You wished you could have been the father of the babies. But you weren't—you didn't know how to do it as a little boy and you felt left out in the cold, detached. You have been depressed about this ever since.' After a pause, Mr. M. said, 'I've always felt I'm not a real man. I act like one, but inside I still feel a real man should be like my father; strong physically, tough, and unafraid. I can fly airplanes but my hands sweat whenever I want to screw my own wife.'

In the next hour the meaning of the green and orange raincoats became clear. the patient spontaneously recalled some dirty jokes from early puberty in which the terms 'raincoat' and 'rubbers' were used to refer to condoms. He then remembered finding condoms in his father's chest of drawers and later stealing some for his own use, just in case an opportunity presented itself, which, he wistfully said, 'didn't occur for several years'. By that time the 'rubbers', the raincoats, had disintegrated in his wallet. It is worth noting how the hidden old shreds of 'rubbers' in the patient's associations were changed into the shiny new raincoats on display in the dream. Here you can see the attempt at wish-fulfilment in the the manifest content of the dream: 'I can buy conspicuous sexual potency in a store or in analysis'. Later it also became clear that I too was the poor horse who had him as a big load to carry and also I was the 'horse's ass' who could not help him make proper sexual connections with his wife or any other woman.

To me the outstanding element in the manifest dream was the surrey which turned out to be so tiny and light. My translation of the word 'surrey' into 'buggy' was the crucial technical point. I got from surrey to buggy by visualizing a surrey, which I have never seen in actual life but which brought to mind a popular song, A Surrey with a Fringe on Top. This led me to baby buggies with fringes on top. Not wanting to push the patient into *my* association of baby buggy, I dropped the baby part and said just buggy, to see where it would lead him. (All this flashed through my mind quickly and was not as carefully thought out as it sounds here.) But I believe I was on the right track as it helped the patient pictorialize a baby buggy. And this enabled him to recall early childhood memories that had been repressed. Once his associations became freer, I could see how the dream work had condensed, reversed, and disguised the agony of feeling abandoned, unloved, inept, and depressed, by pictorializing an attractive woman waiting eagerly for him to join her. The tininess and lightness transforms the surrey into a baby buggy and changes the adult Mr. M. into a jealous, rivalrous small boy who cannot make babies as his big father can. The dream work tries to negate the fact that the father is connected with the mother's pregnancies; the surrey and horse are not hitched together—the patient is unable to hitch a male and female together. The familiar but unrecognizable woman is the mother of his childhood years, whom he has tried to ward off in his memories, in his sexual life, and in the analysis. The hugeness of the department stores is a plastic representation of him as a little boy in a situation too big for him, as his present big house makes him feel like a tired old horse. He is full of jealousy, envy, and depression, and sorry for himself.

It was not possible to work on all these points in one hour, but the surrey-baby-buggy dream led in the next hours to the conviction that his present depression and the old underlying depression from childhood, which had brought him into the analysis, were directly connected, hitched up, to his mother's pregnancies and deliveries. The repression, isolation, and denial were temporarily broken through by our work with this dream and there were several tearful and angry hours in contrast to the quiet sadness of the previous months. Making available to the patient's conscious ego the memories and affects related to trying to push the baby carriage made it possible to reconstruct a crucial phase of this man's conflicts in early childhood, which were emotionally inaccessible to him until our work on the dream.

I believe this clinical vignette demonstrates the exceptional position of the dream. Months of what I believe to have been good psychoanalytic work on the patient's acting out or reenactment of the childhood depression provided insight and some understanding, but no emotional or behavioral change although I am fairly sure that it prepared the way for the surrey-buggy dream. It was the dream, however, plus the patient's and analyst's work on it, that made possible the breakthrough to the hidden memories and affects. Only then did the patient develop a conviction and certainty about the reconstruction—and when he clearly understood and felt the connection between the seemingly strange, remote, and symbolic elements of the dream and the events in his present and past life. For me this is convincing evidence of the special proximity between the dream, childhood memories, and affects. To a great extent this depends on whether the patient and the analyst can use their capacity to oscillate between the primary and secondary processes in helping one another reach the latent dream thoughts hidden beneath the manifest dream. The patient contributes by his free associations; the analyst contributes by associating as if he were the patient and then translating his findings in ways that provide links or bridges to the vital and alive psychic activities in the patient which are capable of becoming conscious at the moment. This is dependent on the analyst's capacity for empathy, his ability to visualize the verbal productions of his patient, and then to translate his findings at a time and in a style and form which are real and plausible to the patient *(28, 29,30)*.

CONCLUSION

The dream is an exceptional and unique production of the patient. It is his special creation but can only be fully understood if the analyst and the patient work together by means of the patient's free associations and the analyst's interpretations. To work effectively with a patient's dream the analyst must subordinate his own theoretical interests, his own personal curiosity, and attempt to make contact with what is living, accessible, and dominant in the patient's psychic life at the time. He must associate emphatically with the patient's material, as if he had lived the patient's life. Then he must translate the pictures he gets from the patient's verbal rendering of the dream back into thoughts, ideas, and words. Finally, he must ask himself what of all of this will be valuable to the patient's conscious and reasonable ego and how he can say it effectively to the patient.

This can be learned in one's personal analysis and in supervision in clinical work, if the training and supervising analysts are competent in working with their patients' dreams. It can be learned to a lesser degree in dream seminars and even from books and papers if the writer is a skilful teacher and uses clinical examples from his own experience. Dream interpretation cannot be taught to people who are not at home or are ill at ease with the form and content of unconscious mental activities. Obviously you cannot teach dream interpretation to those who are blind and deaf to the beauty and wit in the blending of dream formation, free association, and interpretation. Working with dreams makes extraordinary demands on the patient and the analyst. In a sense the dream is the most intimate and elusive creation of the patient; it is so easy to forget! The patient is then asked to associate as freely as possible to the different elements of this strange material, in the presence of his psychoanalyst. He will be torn between the desires to reveal and to conceal the hidden contents which have unexpectedly risen to the surface. The analyst must listen with free-floating attention, oscillating between the patient's and his own primary and secondary processes. Eventually, he will have to formulate his ideas in words which are comprehensible, meaningful, and alive to the patient. Sometimes he may only be able to say, 'I do not understand the dream—perhaps we shall sometime later'.

Some psychoanalysts deny the exceptional position of the dream because they have a special difficulty in learning the technique of dream interpretation. Others decrease the importance of dream interpretation to enhance certain theoretical convictions or to attack or defend the beliefs of some honored teacher. I believe that the dream is the royal road to a knowledge of unconscious activities for both the patient and the analyst, provided the psychoanalyst is not seduced into narrow bypaths and dead-end streets by technical or theoretical prejudices. My conviction of the exceptional position of the dream has been confirmed by daily work with patients, in particular their clinical responses, both immediate and long-range. This conviction has been substantiated by the results of literally hundreds of analysts whose work on dreams are listed in the texts of Fliess, Altman, the *Annual Survey of Psychoanalysis,* the *Index of Psychoanalytic Writings,* the *Psychoanalytic Quarterly Cumulative Index,* and the *Chicago Psychoanalytic Literature Index (15, 1, 26, 31, 47, 5).*

I shall close with two quotations Kurt Eissler has graciously permitted me to paraphrase from a personal communication: 'With hard work and fortunate circumstances an analysis may stop all neurotic symptomology, all acting out, all neurotic slips and errors, and it may make the former patient the epitome of normalcy. Nevertheless, the person will never stop dreaming irrational, instinct-ridden, bizarre dreams, a perpetual proof of the ceaseless activity of the unconscious mind' *(9).* And from Freud, who wrote in 1933, 'Whenever I began to have doubts of the correctness of my wavering conclusions, the successful transformations of a senseless and muddled dream into a logical and intelligible mental process in the dreamer would renew my confidence of being on the right track' (*24*, p. 7).

REFERENCES

1. Altman, Leon L.: *The Dream in Psychoanalysis*. New York: International Universities Press, Inc., 1969.
2. Arlow, Jacob A. and Brenner, Charles: *Psycholoanalytic Concepts and the Structural Theory*. New York: International Universities Press, Inc., 1964.
3. Benjamin, John D.: Prediction and Psychopathological Theory. In: *Dynamic Psychopathology in Childhood*. Edited by Lucie Jessner and Eleanor Pavenstedt. New York: Grune & Stratton, Inc., 1959, pp. 6–77.
4. Bornstein, Berta: The Analysis of a Phobic Child: Some Problems of Theory and Technique in Child Analysis. In: *The Psychoanalytic Study of the Child, Vol. III–IV*. New York: International Universities Press, Inc., 1949, pp. 181–226.
5. *Chicago Psychoanalytic Literature Index*. Chicago Institute of Psychoanalysis, 1953–1969.
6. Dement, William C. and Kleitman, Nathan: *The Relation of Eye Movements during Sleep to Dream Activity: An Objective Method for the Study of Dreaming*. J. Exper. Psychol., LIII, 1957, pp. 339–346.
7. Eissler, Kurt R.: *The Chicago Institute of Psychoanalysis and the Sixth Period of the Development of Psychoanalytic Technique*. J. Genet. Psychol., XLII, 1950, pp. 103–157.
8. ———: On the Metapsychology of the Preconscious: A Tentative Contribution to Psychoanalytic Morphology. In: *The Psychoanalytic Study of the Child, Vol. XVII*. New York: International Universities Press, Inc., 1962, pp. 9–41.
9. ———: Personal Communiation.
10. Erikson, Erik H.: *The Dream Specimen of Psychoanalysis*. J. Amer. Psa. Assn., II, 1954, pp. 5–56.
11. Fenichel, Otto: *The Psychoanalytic Theory of Neurosis*. New York: W. W. Norton & Co., Inc., 1945.
12. Fisher, Charles: Discussion in Panel Report on *The Psychoanalytic Theory of Thinking*. Reported by Jacob A. Arlow. J. Amer. Psa. Assn., VI, 1958, pp. 143–153.
13. ———: *Psychoanalytic Implications of Recent Research on Sleep and Dreaming*. J. Amer. Psa. Assn., XIII, 1965, pp. 197–303.
14. ———: Dreaming and Sexuality. In: *Psychoanalysis—A General Psychology. Essays in Honor of Heinz Hartmann*. Eedited by Rudolph M. Loewenstein, Lottie M. Newman, Max Schur, and Albert J. Solnit. New York: International Universities Press, Inc., 1966, pp. 537–569.
15. Fliess, Robert: *The Revival of Interest in the Dream*. New York: International Universities Press, Inc., 1953.
16. Freud, Anna: *Normality and Pathology in Childhood. Assessments of Development*. New York: International Universities Press, Inc., 1965.
17. Freud, S.: *The Interpretation of Dreams* (1900–1901). Standard Edition, IV–V.
18. ———: *Fragment of an Analysis of a Case of Hysteria* (1905 [1901]). Standard Edition, VII.
19. ———: *The Handling of Dream-Interpretation in Psycho-Analysis* (1911). Standard Edition, XII.

20. ———: *Introductory Lectures on Psychoanalysis. Part II. Dreams.* (1916 [1915–16]). Standard Edition, XV.

21. ———: *A Metapsychological Supplement to the Theory of Dreams* (1917 [1915]). Standard Edition, XIV.

22. ———: *Remarks on the Theory and Practice of Dream Interpretation* (1923 [1922]). Standard Edition, XIX.

23. ———: *Some Additional Notes on Dream-Interpretation as a Whole* (1925). Standard Edition, XIX.

24. ———: *New Introductory Lectures in Psycho-Analysis* (1933 [1932]). Standard Edition, XXII.

25. ———: *Constructions in Analysis* (1937). Standard Edition, XXIII.

26. Frosch, John and Ross, Nathaniel, Editors: *Annual Survey of Psychoanalysis, Vol. IX.* New York: International Universities Press, Inc., 1968.

27. Gill, Merton M.: *Topography and Systems in Psychoanalytic Theory. Psychological Issues, Vol. III, No. 2, Monograph 10.* New York: International Universities Press, Inc., 1963.

28. Greenson, Ralph R.: *Empathy and Its Vicissitudes.* Int. J. Psa., XLI, 1960, pp. 418–424.

29. ———: *That 'Impossible' Profession.* J. Amer. Psa. Assn., XIV, 1966, pp. 9–27.

30. ———: *The Technique and Practice of Psychoanalysis, Vol. I.* New York: International Universities Press, Inc., 1967.

31. Grinstein, Alexander: *The Index of Psychoanalytic Writings.* New York: International Universities Press, Inc., 1959.

32. Hartmann, Ernest: *The D-State.* New England J. Med., CCLXXIII, 1965, pp. 30–35, 87–92.

33. Hartmann, Heinz: *Technical Implications of Ego Psychology.* Psychoanalytic Quarterly, XX, 1951, pp. 31–43.

34. Isakower, Otto: *A Contribution to the Pathopsychology of Phenomena Associated with Falling Asleep.* Int. J. Psa., XIX, 1938, pp. 331–345.

35. ———: *Spoken Words in Dreaming. A Preliminary Communication.* Psychoanalytic Quarterly, XXIII, 1954, pp. 1–6.

36. Kris, Ernst: *On Some Vicissitudes of Insight in Psycho-Analysis.* Int. J. Psa., XXXVII, 1956, pp. 445–455.

37. ———: *The Recovery of Childhood Memories in Psychoanalysis.* In: *The Psychoanalytic Study of the Child, Vol. XI.* New York: International Universities Press, Inc., 1956, pp. 54–88.

38. Kubie, Lawrence S.: *A Reconsideration of Thinking, the Dream Process, and 'The Dream'.* Psychoanalytic Quarterly, XXXV, 1966, pp. 191–198.

39. Lewin, Bertram D.: *Reconsideration of the Dream Screen.* Psychoanalytic Quarterly, XXII, 1953, pp. 174–199.

40. ———: *Dream Psychology and the Analytic Situation.* Psychoanalytic Quarterly, XXIV, 1955, pp. 169–199.

41. ———: *Dreams and the Uses of Regression.* Freud Anniversary Lecture Series, New York Psychoanalytic Institute. New York: International Universities Press, Inc., 1958.

42. ———: *The Image and the Past.* New York: International Universities Press,Inc., 1968.

43. Loewald, Hans W.: Review of: *Psychoanalytic Concepts and the Structural Theory,* by Jacob Arlow and Charles Brenner. Psychoanalystic Quarterly, XXXV, 1966, pp. 430–436.

44. Loewenstein, Rudolph M.: *The Problem of Interpretation.* Psychoanalytic Quarterly, XX, 1951, pp. 1–14.

45. ———: *Some Remarks on Defences, Autonomous Ego and Psycho-Analytic Technique.* Int. J. Psa., XXXV, 1954, pp. 188–193.

46. Mahler, Margaret S.: *On Human Symbiosis and the Vicissitudes of Individuation: Volume I, Infantile Psychosis.* New York: International Universities Press, Inc., 1968.

47. *Psychoanalytic Quarterly Cumulative Index, Vols. I–XXXV, 1932–1966.* New York: The Psychoanalytic Quarterly, Inc., 1969.

48. Rapaport, David and Gill, Merton M.: *The Points of View and Assumptions of Metapsychology.* Int. J. Psa., XL, 1959, pp. 153–162.

49. Schur, Helen: An Observation and Comments on the Development of Memory. In: *The Psychoanalytic Study of the Child, Vol. XXI.* New York: International Universities Press, Inc., 1966, pp. 468–479.

50. Schur, Max: *The Id and the Regulatory Principles of Mental Functioning.* New York: International Universities Press, Inc., 1966.

51. Segal, Hanna: *Introduction to the Work of Melanie Klein.* New York: Basic Books, Inc., 1964.

52. Sharpe, Ella Freeman: *Dream Analysis, A Practical Handbook in Psycholoanalysis.* London: Hogarth Press, 1949.

53. Spitz, René A.: *The First Year of Life.* New York: International Universities Press, Inc., 1965.

54. Stein, Martin H.: States of Consciousness in the Analytic Situation. In: *Drives, Affects, Behavior, Vol. II.* Edited by Max Schur. New York: International Universities Press, Inc., 1965, pp. 60–86.

55. Strachey, James: Editor's Introduction: *The Interpretation of Dreams* (1900). Standard Edition, IV, pp. xi–xii.

56. Thorner, Hans A.: Three Defences against Inner Persecution. In: *New Directions in Psychoanalysis.* Edited by Melanie Klein, Paula Heimann, and Roger E. Money-Kyrle. New York: Basic Books, Inc., 1957, pp. 282–306.

57. Waelder, Robert: *The Problem of the Genesis of Psychical Conflict in Earliest Infancy.* Int. J. Psa., XVIII, 1937, pp. 406–473.

58. Waldhorn, Herbert F., Reporter: *Indications for Psychoanalysis: The Place of the Dream in Clinical Psychoanalysis.* (Monograph II of the Kris Study Group of the New York Psychoanalytic Institute.) Edited by Edward D. Joseph, New York: International Universities Press, Inc., 1967.

B. Manifest Content

5. Ego Feeling in Dreams

Paul Federn

Federn was the first to study extensively and intensively the actual states and changes of ego feeling in falling asleep, in dreaming, and in awakening. He discusses such neglected yet evident phenomena as the absence of bodily ego feeling in most dreams. The mental ego, in its passive rather than its active state, carries on in the dream; only exceptionally does the bodily ego participate, and when such participation becomes too intense, the sleeper awakes, the dream is ended. Active bodily ego feeling in dreams represents volition.

—E. W., ed.

EGO FEELING

I cannot assume that every reader interested in this study of the dream will care to read or reread my previous communications; therefore, by way of introduction, I should like to review the more important results of my previous studies of ego feeling and outline the conception of the ego which grew out of them.

Ego feeling is the sensation, constantly present, of one's own person— the ego's own perception of itself. This statement reaffirms the idea, emphasized especially by Oesterreicher, that "the ego" is not a mere abstraction devised to convey in a single word the idea of the "ego participation" *(Ichbezogenheit)* of actions and events. Neither is the ego solely the sum of these ego participants, nor do I regard it merely as the sum of the ego functions (Nunberg), nor yet simply as the "psychic representation" of that which refers to one's own person (Sterba): these are all aspects of the ego— they represent functions performed by the ego or which belong within the ego. The ego, however, is more inclusive; more especially, it includes the

Reprinted by permission of Basic Books, Inc., Publishers, New York, from *Ego Psychology and the Psychoses,* by Paul Federn. Edited by Edoardo Weiss, M.D. © 1952 by Basic Books, Inc.

subjective psychic experience of these functions with a characteristic sensation. This self-experience is a permanent, though never equal, entity, which is not an abstraction but a reality. It is an entity which stands in relation to the continuity of the person in respect to time, space, and causality. It can be recognized objectively and is constantly felt and perceived subjectively. We possess, in other words, an enduring feeling and knowledge that our ego is continuous and persistent, despite interruptions by sleep or unconsciousness, because we feel that processes within us, even though they may be interrupted by forgetting or unconsciousness, have a persistent origin within us, and that our body and psyche belong permanently to our ego. Many authors have therefore used the term "ego consciousness" *(Ichbewusstsein)* to designate this phenomenon. The expression "ego feeling" has occasionally been used by Freud and by other psychologists and also, as a self-explanatory term, by laymen. If I prefer this latter expression to the term "ego consciousness" and single out "ego feeling" to mark the integrating part of the ego, I do so not because of an arbitrary preference for this designation but for the following reasons. The ego's experience of itself does not consist simply in the knowledge and consciousness of the qualities of the ego mentioned above; the experience also includes a sensory element for which the words "feeling" or "sensation" are appropriate, and the term "ego consciousness" ignores this feeling quality. Not only in clinical pathology but also in the psychopathology of everyday life—in sleep, fatigue, distraction, and daydreams—we can distinguish, often accurately, between ego *feeling* and ego *consciousness*. Ego consciousness, in the pure state, remains only when there is a deficiency in ego feeling. And the mere empty knowledge of one's self is already a pathological state, known as estrangement[1] or depersonalization. The term "ego consciousness," then, would cover our ego experience only if "estrangement" were the normal state of all human beings.

It is also incorrect to identify ego feeling with consciousness, though numerous authors, of whom I believe Janet was the first, have described and defined "becoming conscious" as becoming attached to the ego. At the present time, we know that the property of belonging to the ego may become, be, or remain conscious or unconscious; and from the study of pathological states, we know that ego feeling may disappear from previously conscious portions of the ego and later reappear. In every psychological process, ego feeling may or may not accompany consciousness. When ego feeling does not accompany consciousness, the individual is only aware that an experience —which may be the perception of a somatic or external reality, a memory, or merely an affect—is or has been taking place within, but this knowledge is accompanied, under these circumstances, by a sense of strangeness; or, in other words, a feeling of estrangement appears instead of ego feeling. That the cardinal feature of "ego experience" *(Icherlebnis)* is not thought or knowledge but sensation was first noted in cases of pathological disturbances in ego feeling. The symptom of estrangement, since it was first discovered, has always been referred to as a *feeling* of estrangement, never as a *knowledge* or *consciousness* of estrangement.

Ego feeling, then, is the totality of feeling which one has of one's own living person. It is the residual experience which persists after the subtraction of all ideational contents—a state which, in practice, occurs only for a very brief time. This total ego feeling is always a combination of changing and unvarying elements, and the total subjective experience of one's ego orientation toward an act is qualified by the ego feeling that is present at the time. I consider it more correct to speak of the "ego orientation *toward* an act" than of the "ego orientation of an act," at least in a discussion of ego feeling.[2] Consideration of the fact that ego feeling constantly fluctuates in extent, so that its content is constantly shifting, and of the fact that it nevertheless is constantly uniting all relations and parts of the ego into a single whole, leads us to the conclusion that the "ego" always includes both total and partial experience and must always be investigated both analytically and synthetically. These conceptions of ego feeling cause us to reject as misleading the temptation to distinguish between viewing a thing exclusively as a whole or exclusively as a part. Psychoanalysis has always sought to comprehend the parts as well as the whole, laying more stress, however, on analysis than on synthesis. My study of ego feeling further emphasizes this double orientation of psychoanalysis.

A theorist might still query whether what we have here designated as ego feeling is not merely the intellectual experience of that which remains constant while ever-changing experiences, relations and reactions pass through consciousness; that is, whether it is not merely a *knowledge* on the part of the ego, the content of which escapes attention because it does not change. This question is answered conclusively by the observation that even the clearest *knowledge* of one's own ego is experienced as something insufficient, uncomfortable, incomplete, and unsatisfying, even akin to fear; and that even for the purest "self experience" something affective in quality is requisite for normality.[3]

Ego feeling, therefore, is the simplest and yet the most comprehensive psychic state which is produced in the personality by the fact of its own existence, even in the absence of external or internal stimuli. As has been said, it is true that unmixed ego feeling can form the whole content of consciousness for a very short time only, as there are always too many stimuli ready to enter consciousness. To repeat our formulation: combined with the consciousness of the self, there is also an affective sense of the self, which we designate briefly as "ego feeling." In other articles,[4] I have studied "ego feeling" more intimately and have shown in pathological and normal cases that *somatic* and *psychic* ego feeling may be separate from each other, and that we must distinguish within the varying extensions of ego feeling a nucleus of ego feeling which remains constant; and, in particular, that we have a precise sense of the degree to which our psychic processes and our body are invested with ego feeling. Whenever there is a change in ego feeling cathexis, we sense the "boundaries" of our ego. Whenever an impression impinges, be it somatic or psychic, it strikes a boundary of the ego normally invested with ego feeling. *If no ego feeling sets in at this boundary, we sense the impression in question as alien.* So long as no impression impinges upon the boundaries of ego feeling, we remain unaware of the confines of the ego. Psychic and bodily ego feeling can both be active or passive. In different persons the quality of the ego feeling depends also upon what special instinctual forces (eg., tender, sadistic, masochistic, exhibitionistic) exercise a continuous dominance over the personality or else are ready at all times to find expression. Further, we have confirmed Nunberg's finding that all neuroses and psychoses begin with a condition of estrangement of shorter or longer duration. We also found that the withdrawal of ego feeling from an ego boundary can be a defensive measure of the ego, which can occur with or without repression, or which can initiate repression and itself disappear. The development of the individual is accompanied by a development, qualitative and quantitative, of ego feeling, the stages of libido development also being characterized by various types of ego feeling. Therefore, ego feeling is capable of fixation at, or regression to, an earlier stage, in respect to both quality and extent.

The hypothesis based on these points, which is useful as a psychoanalytic conception of ego feeling, states that ego feeling is the original narcissistic investment of the ego. As such it has at first no object; I designated it intermediate *(medialer)* narcissism. Not until much later, after the object libidinal cathexes have reached the ego boundary, or have invested it and again been withdrawn, does reflexive narcissism arise.

This hypothesis is supported by numerous clinical observations. If it is correct, the study of "ego feeling" has furnished us with a working method of adding to our knowledge of cathexes with narcissistic libido and also, indirectly, of the functioning of object cathexes.

Dreams, considered as topics for study, are met with so regularly in healthy individuals that it is difficult to say whether they should be included in normal or in abnormal psychology. In any case, as regards the ego in dreams we are dealing with a disturbed condition; hence, the study of "ego feeling" in dreams must logically follow a clinical investigation of estrangement. Therefore, using mainly data derived from patients suffering from estrangement, I shall first discuss the relations between estrangement, dreams, and sleep, and only then present our subject proper, the quality and the quantity of ego feeling during dreams.

ESTRANGEMENT AND DREAMING

Very many persons who are suffering from estrangement state that they see reality as in a dream, or, that they feel as if they were in a dream. This is a surprising statement which requires explanation. This statement would not have been surprising if our feeling in regard to a dream, while we are dreaming, were similar to the one which the estranged individual has in regard to reality. This is not the case, however. The dreamer subjectively feels that his dream is real. The surprising, incomprehensible, even absurd, character of much that is dreamed does not prevent the dreamer from believing in the reality of his dream as long as he is dreaming, even though what he dreams may be inconsistent with whatever knowledge of reality remains over from the waking state in the mind of the dreamer.

In contrast, the estranged individual must actually coerce himself to believe that his impressions are real. Intelligence, common sense, memories, and inferences from memories compel him to admit intellectually something which he does not feel to be evident. To the dreamer, on the contrary, the reality of what he dreams is self-evident—aside from well-known exceptions —even though the dream may contradict all his rational experience.

However, except in cases of extreme depersonalization, we can readily understand what estranged individuals mean when they say that they see the world as if they were dreaming, if we remember that they make this statement only in retrospect. For, everyone who remembers a dream after he awakens feels in it a certain alien quality. This quality is due to the incoherence and impermanence of the dream, the illogical nature of its content, and the manner in which it vanishes. In retrospect, dream figures are usually shadowy, unsubstantial, or unreal. The process of secondary elaboration not only improves the internal logic of the dream; usually, the same process alters the dream, also, so that it comes to resemble more closely a sequence of waking events. Dreams without secondary elaboration have, when recalled, more of the quality of strangeness. It may well be that this very quality leads to secondary elaboration. We arrive, then, at the curious conclusion that while they are in operation, the processes of dreaming and estrangement are basically different, and that they appear to resemble each other only in the impression which they leave behind. If we disregard the dream's importance as a portal to the unconscious and as an object of study, and if we except dreams of unusual personal significance, a dream is a "nothing"—a series of unreal images, which have disappeared from consciousness and which, even as memories, have automatically lost their content and vividness. But the estranged individual, also, feels an indifference in regard to his experiences during his estranged state. He can only recall that he was in an abnormal state. Persons severely affected by estrangement even say that their reality is less vivid than their dreams, and this is true—for estranged and normal persons do not dream differently.

Another analogy obtains between dreams and estrangement. A dreamer, one might say, is passively overcome by the dream, and the dream develops or unfolds itself *upon* or *with* the dreamer passive. A dreamer also feels that he is passively seized by the dream, for, as a rule, he cannot fix the elements of the dream in order to form deliberate judgments in regard to them. Only rarely can he voluntarily react to any of the dream elements or bring them back to mind, for the dream enters consciousness more or less as a finished picture, and it arouses only such small parts of consciousness as are necessary to receive the dream picture. These awakened parts, as soon as they are not needed, instantly fall back into sleep. The will is conspicuously absent from dreams. Scherner, in many passages of his book, depicts this lack of centrality of the ego and the weakness of the will in very plastic language. The estranged individual also feels more passive than a normal individual toward what he experiences. However, his reasons for this feeling are different from those of the dreamer: his attention is always diverted to his own condition; he becomes inattentive and his interest in other things is disturbed; so that, as a result of his disorder, he becomes apathetic and passive toward the whole of reality.

Up to the present point, we have been discussing well-known characteristics of the states under comparison. On turning our attention to "ego feeling" (which, it is true, patients do not mention of their own accord) we at once discover a feature common to both states, the dream and estrangement. In both, "ego feeling" is deficient. This is particularly true of those patients with severe depersonalization, whose ego is not invested with full ego feeling either at its boundaries or in its nucleus. These individuals feel their ego only partially and with decreased intensity and suffer a subjective loss in their sense of importance, their feeling of well-being, and the unity of their personality. However, as we shall see, disturbances of the ego in the dream and in estrangement are, for the most part, not alike. We have already drawn attention to the fact that dreams are experienced as real, and the objects of the individual's estrangement as unreal. We conclude that in the case of dreams, the ego boundary at which dream experiences impinge is invested with ego feeling, and that this is not the case for experiences during estrangement. However, neither the waking judgment of the depersonalized individual, nor the partially awakened judgment of the dreamer, is able to recognize as *false* the "unreality" of experience (in estrangement), or the "reality" of experience (in dreams). Neither individual can prevail against the abnormal cathexis of the ego boundary, which in the case of estrangement is too small and in dreams is relatively too great. This impotence in the face of a disturbance of ego cathexis is characteristic of both states.

We have, consequently, discovered two reasons why estranged individuals use the words "as in a dream" to describe their state. The more important reason is the one mentioned last—the recollection that there was a deficiency of ego feeling. This disorder of the ego is not a disturbance of consciousness, nor a feeling of giddiness, unclarity, obscurity or haziness, but an impairment of ego feeling. Before we look for its significance let us discuss a few relations between estrangement and sleep.

ESTRANGEMENT, FALLING ASLEEP, AND AWAKENING

We know from clinical observation that states of estrangement vary in their intensity and extent at different times in the same patient. Only rarely do patients complain constantly of the same degree of estrangement. Usually, the fact that they are speaking with the physician is enough to bring about an improvement in their condition. Their own interest, and their satisfaction in arousing the attention of the physician and feeling his interest, bring about an increase in the cathexis of the ego boundaries, which in milder cases appears to abolish the sense of estrangement. Usually such patients, after learning to accept their feeling of estrangement as a symptom, can describe the curve of intensity of their feelings of estrangement since the last visit. Less severely affected new patients, in the excitement of the first visit, do not feel any sense of estrangement, nor do they mention it spontaneously or at all unless direct questioning draws their attention to the fact that these states, also, are the concern of the physician. Then, as experience constantly bears out, the patients reward the physician who wishes to know about these subtle variations in their permanent condition, and who spontaneously suspects the presence of such states of estrangement, by immediately giving him their complete confidence. Even if for no other reason, an acquaintance with these states is of practical importance for physicians in general as well as for psychoanalysts.

However, although such mildly affected patients report about their states of estrangement only in the past tense, estrangement does occur even under the protected conditions of a consultation hour. Curiously enough, many such patients have merely forgotten that previously, in health, they had a stronger contact with the world and with themselves, a contact which gave a full sense of well-being but which no longer spontaneously comes to mind even as a basis of comparison.

The intensity of the estrangement depends on many factors which do not always have the same effect, but differ in their effect according to the degree of severity, or stage of development of the case. There are patients who develop feelings of estrangement as soon as they are left alone or feel themselves abandoned, whereas the presence of a person invested with libido abolishes the disturbance, or at least diminishes it to such a point that they feel practically no estrangement. Observations of this order long gave rise to the belief that estrangement consisted in a withdrawal of object libido. In some cases the estrangement sets in just when the patient meets persons who are invested with object libido, and, conversely, in other cases just when there is *no one* in his company in whom he can take an actual interest. Often merely to direct his object libido toward another person temporarily suffices to protect him from estrangement; but soon his capacity to invest his ego boundary with ego feeling is exhausted, and he is suddenly seized with a sense of the strangeness and unreality of external and internal perceptions. In most cases the severity of the estrangement also depends, fundamentally, on somatic factors. Fatigue and exhaustion or intense exertion predispose to estrangement—then, his ego frontiers crumbling under such bodily or psychic strain, the patient, gradually or suddenly, intermittently or abruptly, finds himself in a condition of estrangement. Hartmann and Nunberg were the first to show that sudden emotionally charged experiences which were followed, for only partly conscious reasons or more usually for unconscious reasons, by a so-called object loss, may produce traumatic estrangement. Theoretically, the effect of all these factors can be explained, economically, by making a distinction between two questions relating to libidinal cathexis; namely, first, whether ego feeling can be sufficiently established at all for the ego boundary in question, and secondly, whether the libido reserve is great enough to maintain the cathexis of the ego boundary. The severity of estrangement is therefore dependent not only, dynamically, on the inhibition of cathexis at the time, but also, economically, on the magnitude of the libido supply. We can formulate this distinction, which applies in general in pathological states, by contrasting a withdrawal of libido due to an external or internal frustration with what we might call an exhaustion *(Versiegen)* of libido.

Observation teaches us that in chronic cases of estrangement, improvement, other things being equal, consists in a re-establishment of ego feeling, but that in each situation a sufficient cathexis of the ego boundary can be set up only slowly and after repeated efforts. For this reason, often, very subtle differences in ego disturbance are described in terms of whether or not the environment is sharply observing the patient or is friendly toward him. It is especially during improvement that patients describe such differences.

Analogously, we know from clinical experience that estranged persons whose condition has already improved do not always, like normal persons, regain their normal orientation toward the inner and the outer world; indeed, they feel more estranged after sleeping than at other times. Even in patients not improving, this symptom is more severe in the morning than later in the day, resembling in this respect the symptoms of depressive patients insofar as there are no exacerbations caused by the above mentioned factors of fatigue and strain. Thus, we see that melancholia and estrangement are characterized by similar daily curves of severity and similar reaction curves to strain and exhaustion. This morning increase of symptoms is directly connected with the state of ego feeling during sleep. This morning exacerbation would not have been expected on the basis of previous experience with normal individuals. On the contrary, according to our experience with healthy persons, we might have anticipated that after the libido reserve was completely replenished by sleep, the ego, in its nucleus and at its boundaries, would, at least for a time, be fully invested with ego feeling. Then, according to the severity of the case and the demands made upon the individual, the ego disturbance would reappear in the course of the day. According to this, the disturbance of libido economy would appear at awakening only potentially, and would only become actual sooner or later in the course of the day in response to the demands of the individual. In fact, such a curve is really present in all estranged persons in whom the disturbance shows any fluctuation. However, it does not become effective immediately in the morning, because the abnormally long transition from sleeping to waking postpones the mechanism of simple dependence on the magnitude of the libido reserve. In the estranged individual, as we have said above, there is a disturbance in the displaceability or, better, in the displacement of the libido, insofar as it has to invest the ego boundaries.

The investment of object representations with object libido may at the same time hardly be disturbed. The fact explains why, in spite of their estrangement, patients can work with interest and accuracy, and why they do not cease to show selection in their object relations, at least within certain limits, insofar as there is no concomitant difficulty in maintaining object cathexis. The latter difficulty may be secondary or, as Nunberg has shown, may have been the precipitating cause of the estrangement. But even in the latter case the object cathexis may persist. The very fact that it persists in the presence of a defective ego boundary causes this particular object to arouse a special feeling of strangeness. What was called ''object loss'' consists in this loss of capacity to perceive an object with one's full ego feeling: with the loss of the ego feeling, the narcissistic satisfaction in having the object is lost, too. Of this I have been fully convinced by a case of pathological mourning. After the death of the patient's mother all relationships, things, and recollections in any way connected with her mother were particularly strongly invested with object libido. Repeatedly, new and often very minor events from the past were coming into the patient's mind; everything connected with her mother took on great significance. The patient did not sleep day or night because of the press of ideas and associations belonging to her mother complex. These object representations were disturbingly vivid in content and deeply depressive in affect. At the same time, there was present a complete estrangement from this intensive repetition of all her past object relationships with her mother, which extended both to their ideational content and to the affect of grief itself. She said, ''I have the grief but I do not feel it.'' Although her grief was manifest in her facial expression and in its somatic effects, the patient continually complained that she did not "really" feel her grief, an assertion which, for an inexpert observer such as I was at the time, was absolutely inconsistent with her whole condition and appearance. Years later a similar case permitted me to understand the situation: the object cathexes evoked the pain of bereavement, but the ego boundary in question[5] was without feeling, as though dead. We must therefore designate "pathological mourning" (Freud) as a narcissistic psychosis, not only because of its genesis and in its character as an unconscious identification, but also for its libidinal mechanism, a statement that holds equally true for melancholia. In recalling all the cases of pathological mourning and melancholia in my analytic experience, I do not remember one patient who failed to express the paradoxically complaint that he felt nothing but suffering and yet did not really feel the suffering.

Though this field is somewhat remote from the present topic, I have treated it in detail here, because, for the reader to be convinced of what follows, it is important for him to recognize that there is a real distinction between *object* cathexis and the *narcissistic* cathexis of the corresponding ego boundary. The difference between the normal and the abnormal mechanism of narcissistic cathexis of the ego boundary is seen most clearly in the morning in the speed of recovery of the ego after sleep. It is because of this delayed mechanism that both estranged and depressed individuals feel an exacerbation of their symptoms every morning. And the increased difficulty of cathexis of the ego boundary is surely one reason why the restoration and strengthening of the ego during sleep fails to cause an improvement in ego feeling immediately on awakening. In melancholia there must be additional unfavorable influences, for relative improvement does not set in until evening. The investigation of these factors in melancholia is not in the scope of the present discussion. Provisionally, the morning exacerbation in estrangement seems to me adequately explained by the physiological processes in sleep. However, I have not as yet paid special attention to the problem whether, in the narcissistic psychoses, sleep itself is not subject to special disturbance.

One statement can be made which is unquestionably true: In dreamless sleep ego feeling is extinguished. I have dealt with this point in detail in "Some Variations in Ego Feeling" (Chapter 1). I first recognized the existence of ego feeling during the act of going to sleep—that is, not in *statu nascendi* but in *statu exeundi*. When an individual falls asleep rapidly, ego feeling is suddenly extinguished. A sudden disappearance of ego feeling of this nature is also found in narcolepsy. When the process of falling asleep is disturbed, the loss of ego feeling is only partial and gradual. Falling asleep is promoted if one learns to withdraw ego feeling as much as possible from the body, leaving only the ego feeling connected with breathing. Such an intentional withdrawal of ego feeling is well-known to the Yogis. But it should be used only in harmony with the regular periodicity of sleeping and waking, which in itself predisposes to the disappearance of ego cathexis. If one coerces oneself to sleep in opposition to this periodicity, sleep itself becomes an effort, and one is more likely to awake fatigued and unrefreshed.

As long as a sleeper does not dream, he does not feel his ego. Whether an unconscious ego persists, or whether Friedrich Kraus's "basic personality" *(Tiefenperson)* corresponds to an ego or to the id, are still insoluble questions. It must be assumed that even in dreamless sleep, much psychic and even intellectual work, shrewd and intelligent arrangement and construction, takes place in the unconscious. Freud has compared the unconscious with the "good folk" in fairy tales who help us with our work during our sleep. But as far as we know, all the unconscious accomplishments during sleep are biologically centered through the unity of the body, not psychologically through the unity of the ego. Hence Freud's statement that sleep is a narcissistic state refers to unconscious narcissistic cathexes which, if they are attached to any entity at all, at least are not attached to the ego of waking life. It is probable that Freud wished this statement merely to express in an extreme fashion the fact that with the exclusion of sensory stimuli, object cathexes are withdrawn to an incomparably greater degree than during waking life. The withdrawal of object cathexes permits narcissistic cathexes to become object cathexes, as when the person of the dreamer is wholly projected and appears in the dream as another person. Here, in our discussion of the manifest expression of narcissism in ego feeling, we must establish that in dreamless sleep this narcissistic cathexis of the ego is absent.

When, on falling asleep, consciousness is lost, ego libido ceases to be in the ego and all ego feeling disappears. It is mostly a matter of taste whether one says that the ego libido vanishes *(versiegt)*, that it is asleep, that it is withdrawn into the id, or that it is distributed among the partial functions. However, this narcissistic cathexis always stands ready to return to the ego, as we see from the fact that, except in pathological conditions, every stimulus which wakes the individual immediately re-establishes ego feeling. This is readily understood if it is recalled that ego feeling perpetuates the most primordial sensation of living substance, phylogenetically and ontogenetically, and that its disappearance is probably a direct expression of the sleep of the cells. These are facts gleaned from biology. Mysticism, on the other hand, would say that the mind leaves the body during sleep and returns to it on waking. The mind carries away all its knowledge with it, and during dreams is supposed to reside, not in the body, but in the place where the dream takes it. This theory is an expression of the fact that the ego feeling in dreams is, for the most part, a purely psychic one.

On awakening from sleep, ego feeling is established immediately. On waking from a dream, it is exceptional for the ego feeling to be continuous with that in the dream. In health, the ego feeling on waking is vivid and undiminished and fills body and mind with satisfaction and vigor. The ego also immediately regains its security as to its temporal continuity with its own past and its own future. This is not the case in many neurotics. They feel their inadequacy in the morning. This is true in most cases of phobia and of "premelancholia" (with this term I refer to the daily depressive moods which may exist for years before the onset of melancholia) and, as mentioned above, in cases of estrangement. Were one to inquire for symptoms of estrangement among all those who complain of beginning the day badly, it is possible that one might even find that they were constantly present. It is true that the patient does not mention them himself, because his bed and his bedroom are his fortress, remote from the demands of the day and of object relations. The estrangement first becomes fully perceptible when the individual turns toward an object. The disorder causes the full ego feeling to become established only gradually. It would be interesting to investigate to what extent disturbances and delays in the everyday habits of dressing, etc., are connected with a morning ego deficiency.

As an example of how severely a marked case of estrangement can be disturbed in the morning, I will cite a case which was materially improved by prolonged analysis. The patient's sister was in an advanced state of severe catatonia. The patient, also, had symptoms which went beyond mere estrangement, and every six months there were transitory exacerbations lasting only a few days, with uncertainty of orientation, hypochondriacal sensations, and severe anxiety, which corresponded to an abrupt but mild catatonic disturbance. This very intelligent patient understands the nuances of ego cathexis and the problem of estrangement so well, from his own experience, that he can give the most precise information concerning his condition. He can accurately distinguish estrangement for sense perceptions, for affect, and for thinking; he states that today he no longer has these disturbances, well-known to himself and to me, but that the total intensity of his ego continues to be diminished, particularly after awakening. It takes a long time before his full ego feeling is established. He feels that this is related to his sexual potency. Sometimes he is better, and then he has the same sexual excitement and general vigor in the morning which he had in his years of health. Usually, however, this normal libidinous feeling is replaced by a mixture of mild anxiety and trembling lust which he senses throughout his body and which does not permit a normal bodily ego feeling to appear. This represents a regression of ego feeling to an earlier, masochistic stage. This peculiar feeling quiets down only gradually, to be superseded by a state of moderately diminished ego feeling which, for him is usual. All patients with severe estrangement give remarkable accounts of how they regain their ego in the morning. They are and feel strange, until they "become themselves," as far as the disturbance in the economy and mobility of their ego libido permits. I should like to add that a morning disturbance of ego feeling of this type usually causes the function of the will to be re-established more slowly in the morning.

Up to the present we have in part discussed, and in part only indicated, the relations which exist—subjectively and objectively—between estrangement, dream, and sleep. But I had other reasons for turning to this problem, and introduced the discussion of these relations chiefly for didactic purposes. I wished to use them to renew the reader's interest in the difference between narcissistic and object cathexis, in the phenomenon of ego feeling, and in the inconstancy of the ego boundary, so that he might be more interested in the subject of this paper proper, ego feeling in dreams. This subject became important to me because from the ego feeling in dreams it is possible to demonstrate the distinction between psychic and bodily ego feeling, utilizing a special method of self-observation.

EGO FEELING IN DREAMS

Dreams which one hears, reads, or recalls have undergone secondary elaboration, not only as regards their content, but also as regards the manner in which things happen in them. It is almost impossible to remember them exactly. Involuntarily one tends to recall the events of the dream as if one had followed them as an awake, unified, and complete personality and had experienced them with one's whole being. The more we have ourselves done and seen in the dream, the more strongly do we hold this belief.

Once we have begun to pay attention to ego feeling and ask ourselves or another dreamer on awaking what the ego feeling in the dream was, we will discover, first of all, that a consciousness of the self was always present and that it was the right one. The dreamer is always identical with the waking person, and knows this with certainty. This feature enables the dreamer to free himself of some troublesome portions of the ego by projecting them into other persons. The dream ego itself, however, always remains one's own ego, with a consciousness of the continuity of one's own psychic processes.

However, in the majority of dreams, and in the greater part of each dream, this dream ego differs from that of waking life in that there is a sense of one's identity *(Eigengefühl)* only as regards one's psychic processes, while the body is, so to say, ignored. In waking life, psychic and bodily ego feeling are not easy to distinguish, because both are so obviously permanently inherent in the ego. As regards dreams, however, it is quite clear to retrospective memory that these two forms of ego feeling are entirely distinguishable.

In spite of the fact that everything dreamed is experienced as wholly real, we do not—in the great majority of all dreams—feel that we are corporally present. We do not feel our body with its weight and its form. We have no bodily ego feeling with its ego boundaries, as in normal waking life. However, we are not at all aware of this deficiency of the body ego, while we would feel it dreadfully during waking life. I have already mentioned that even an estranged person need know nothing of his estrangement if he has no immediate task to perform or, for instance, if he is in the protection of his bed. But dreaming is only a very partial awakening from the state of "egolessness." The unconscious and preconscious processes, which become the manifest dream content, awaken the ego where they strike its boundaries, so that there is an ensuing new investment with ego feeling; and as long as a dream picture may have need for it, an ego boundary is never without cathexis. The evanescence of the dream and the impossibility of bringing it back to mind and considering it, are due to the fact that the narcissistic investment of the psychic ego boundaries is constantly being withdrawn as soon as one dream picture is finished and another appears.

There are exceptions to this. A scene may persist for a time; the dreamer may even recall a previous scene. Under what circumstances these two exceptions occur is a special problem. If the whole dream takes its course very slowly and in apparently re-enforced pictures, the sleep is a pathological state, a state of severe overfatigue analogous to that of a fatigued retina in which the ability to receive new images is established more slowly, and the previous image remains longer than normally. The consciousness of the normal dreamer regains its receptivity to new images as quickly as does the healthy retina.

The dream state ordinarily contents itself with the psychic ego and its variable boundaries: a bodily ego feeling appears only under certain conditions. When the dream picture impinges on the psychic ego boundary it awakens consciousness. Because it strikes the *psychic* ego boundary from without, as an object cathexis, it is felt as real, even though it may contradict reality. In the dream we are certain of the reality of what happens; we sense it psychically. Exceptionally, we see it with lifelike or even greater vividness. We see it as real; therefore, the visual ego boundary must be to some extent awakened; but we do not have a sense of our presence as a body among bodies. It is this bodiless condition of the dreamer to which I wish to draw special attention in this article.

After awakening, one cannot usually remember where and how one felt one's body to be; even in the most interesting dream scene one cannot remember whether one was sitting or standing, the direction of one's gaze, or even the posture one assumed—this even though the dream scene may be so well ordered that one can draw it. In some dreams, the remembered events, such, for example, as seeking an object in a store, meeting a number of people, or the pursuit of an individual, directly require that the dreamer himself must have been in a certain place at a certain time, but nevertheless was there only as an observing psychic ego, or even a moving observing psychic ego, without any bodily ego feeling and without consciousness of one's body. The latter has not been awakened from the sleeping state of being without cathexis. The dream has shown no interest in the body of the dreamer. The dream awakens the sleeper no more than is necessary, and in this shows a precise selection, which may be attributed to the dream function or perhaps to the dream work. In any case, there must have been a disaggregation of ego functions in sleep which permits such a partial awakening of the ego. Thus, the dream work has a selective and condensing action both on the dream material and on the ego boundaries.

In sleep we not only recuperate from the stimuli of daily life and reactions of the ego to these daily irritants, but we also permit the ego as a whole to rest. And if sleep is disturbed by undischarged reactions, wishes or stimuli, the dream affords it additional protection by permitting only a partial awakening of the functions of consciousness and of the ego cathexis. The nucleus of ego feeling, which is connected with the function of the labyrinths and with orientation in space, need be awakened only enough to permit of the dream scenes appearing correctly oriented in space (as regards up and down). It is probable that without this nucleus there can be *no ego feeling at all,* for the intact ego apparently never feels disoriented in space. However, in order to use as little as possible of the ego feeling of the ego nucleus, bodily ego feeling awakes as little and as seldom as possible. Even as regards the ego nucleus, noteworthy exceptions do occur in dreams, e.g., a sudden turning upside down of the whole dream environment, exceptions which, as we know, are used to represent certain typical experiences.

This economizing of ego cathexis in dreams is so strict that there are even dreams of movement in which bodily ego feeling is lacking. We would all assume that a dream experience of such definite bodily character as that of flying and floating could not occur without a strong and complete bodily ego feeling. But even this is not true. I wish to demonstrate the differences, by means of this well-known and well-understood typical dream, between cathexis with bodily and with psychic ego feeling.[6]

It often happens that in flying the dreamer has a sense of his whole body, particularly when an exhibitionistic wish, a desire to show himself, is present. But even in exhibitionistic flying dreams, as in other exhibitionistic dreams, the body ego is seldom complete. Ego feeling may be distinct only for the upper part of the body, the remainder of the body being entirely without cathexis or only vague in consciousness and feeling. But particularly in these dreams, it happens at times that there is a painful sense that ego feeling is deficient, as for example in dreams of floating on staircases, in which the lack of feeling in the chest and in the arms can be quite unpleasant. However if, as often happens, the flying is done in a flying machine, bodily ego feeling is as a rule wholly lacking. The dreamer remembers the direction and course of the flight and, also, the machine, but he obtained no exact impression of the machine during the flight; he was not conscious of his body or of its position in the machine. It is still more surprising that bodily ego feeling may be quite deficient not only in these strongly displaced and symbolic representations of the sexual act, but even in direct sexual dreams. Often the feeling is limited to the sexual organs; often there is present only the specific pleasure sensation, entirely without bodily ego feeling.

Psychic ego feeling in dreams, which, as we said, is the form of cathexis regularly present, is incomparably more often passive rather than active in character. When psychic ego feeling is active, however, bodily ego feeling is usually present also. A particular type of dream associated with active psychic ego feeling is the peeping dream, which includes the bodily ego feeling of the eyes but no feeling of the remainder of the body.

In a few dreams, bodily ego feeling is present either during the whole dream or only in single parts of it. The difference between those parts in which bodily ego feeling is present and those in which it is absent is quite definite. Whoever has once become aware of it can usually tell quite definitely in which scenes of the dream he experienced bodily ego feeling. Bodily ego feeling may be very vivid and accentuated, it may be of ordinary quality, or, on the other hand, it may be expressly felt as vague and indistinct. The most extreme case of a particularly vivid bodily ego feeling with a specific quality was reported by a patient who, in childhood, had had typical somnambulistic dreams of a constant nature.

He related that he would arise from his sleep with great effort in order to save someone or something. He would have to forestall a danger. The danger would consist in something falling down and striking the endangered person or object. The sleeper would get up with the sense that it was his duty to help and to forestall the danger. This was a dream action commanded by his superego. The act of getting up was difficult; the dreamer had a sense of anxiety or oppression connected with the fact that he must get up. He would feel this oppression as in a nightmare; but, while in a typical nightmare the feeling of weight would be projected from the chest on to the incubus which weighed upon it, in our somnambulist it could be felt in the body itself as a difficulty in lifting the body. He sensed the weight of his body which had to be lifted; that is, it would remain within the dreamer's ego as a burden and an impediment to getting up and subsequently walking. During the act of walking, the bodily ego feeling was exceptionally intense.

Contrasting in one aspect to this type of somnambulistic dream—I do not know to what extent it is typical—are the inhibition dreams. In an inhibition dream a movement is intended but is held up at the last moment. Then, in the last moment before waking, a strong bodily ego feeling appears in the inhibited limb or limbs. But this somatic ego feeling in the inhibited limb differs from normal bodily ego feeling, not only in intensity, but also in the fact that the organ thus invested with ego feeling is felt as *outside* the ego.[7] Just as during waking an intense bodily pain is *felt*, by the normal individual (not by the hypochondriac), as if it hit the ego from without, although one knows that the painful organ belongs to the body—so the painful immovability and rigidity of the inhibited limb during the dream is felt as striking the ego from without. Only after awaking does the ego regain the feeling of command over and possession of the organ.

In somnambulistic dreams, on the contrary, the feeling of bodily weight remains within the ego. Common to both types of dream is the fact that a contrast between superego and ego comes to expression in them. In the inhibition dream the ego wishes to do something; the wish, arising from the id, is concurred in by the will of the ego, and the bodily movement would begin if the ego were not forced, by command of the awakening superego, to inhibit the execution of the wish and its own desire. In the end, the opposing wish prevents the execution of the previous act of will. In contrast, in the somnambulistic dream the will of the ego is incited by the superego to a positive action which is burdensome to the ego. To summarize, in the inhibition dream the ego says "I am not allowed to do it"; while in the somnambulistic dream the ego says "I am required to do it."

My somnambulist patient, throughout the whole process of sleepwalking, was able to clearly observe and, later, recall another curious double orientation of the ego. During the whole process there was present an opposing command, which resisted getting up and which retarded and impeded movement. However, this opposing will does not, as in the inhibition dream, arise from the superego, but from a part of the ego. The sense of being oppressed by the task, mentioned above, was rationalized throughout the dream by the "sensible" thought, "You are asleep and dreaming; wait until tomorrow morning and see if the danger cannot be removed then, or if, perhaps, it does not exist at all." It is as if the ego were divided. One part is very close to the thinking of waking life, while the other part sleeps so profoundly that it can carry out movements without waking. That this sleep must be very deep to permit such division of the ego follows from the feeling which occurs when the sleepwalking is interrupted by waking up, either as a result of an external stimulus or occasionally as a result of a decision of the somnambulist himself. This feeling is always one of being torn from the deepest sleep. That such an exceptional depth of sleep—that is, "being a good sleeper"—is sufficient in itself to explain the possibility of such complex muscular activity during sleep is inadequate. We know, besides, that deep sleep can be established just to allow the sleeper to express contradictory wishes and tendencies of will. All sleepwalking consists in going from the bed and returning to the bed. That this dream is a compromise is shown even in these two phases of walking. I shall discuss the somnambulistic dream elsewhere; it was introduced into the present paper only because it is the dream in which I have, so far, found the most marked bodily ego feeling—namely, the feeling of a hindering body ego, of a resistance arising from the body ego. The somnambulistic dream also forms an exception to the rule that when the psychic ego feeling is active, the bodily ego feeling is active too; for in this case psychic ego feeling was active while the body ego was passive, that is, was felt as a hindrance. During the sleepwalking, however, the body ego became active.

As a rule bodily ego feeling, when it occurs in dreams, is much less marked than in the abnormal dreams of which I have just spoken. When bodily ego feeling does not involve the whole body, but only parts of it, the parts are usually those which stand in relation with the external world of the dream, either through movements or through sensations, as I noted previously in the case of floating dreams. But it must not be thought that in dreamed movements the moving limbs are always invested with bodily ego feeling. I remarked, above, the absence of bodily ego feeling in dreams of flying in machines; the same statement applies to many other movement dreams which are devoid of any bodily ego feeling, even of the partial type. In the following study of the interpretive value to be ascribed to the different types of investment with bodily ego feeling, we shall find that the apparently unimportant, never heeded feature, whether the dreamer does or does not feel the limb while it is being moved, is of crucial importance in the interpretation of the dream; not, indeed, for the uncovering of the latent content, but as regards the attitude which the ego takes toward the latent dream thoughts.

THE SIGNIFICANCE OF DIFFERENCES IN EGO FEELING IN DREAMS

If the reader is convinced of the wide range of variations in ego feeling, and of the preciseness of our information concerning the appearance of bodily ego feeling in dreams, he will, I hope, share my expectation that so precise a symptom cannot be without significance. The meaning of this phenomenon can be understood only in the light of psychoanalytic methods; and psychoanalysis may be able to utilize this understanding in practical work also. Finally, our new knowledge leads us to a general problem of psychology which is so difficult that every new approach must be welcome—namely, the problem of the will.

When, purely from observation, I learned what great differences there may be in the ego feeling of dreams, I tried to list different explanations which occurred to me and apply them first of all to my own dreams, in which

I could state with certainty whether bodily ego feeling was present or not. At first, I thought that I could find a reciprocal relation between the degree to which the ego is emphasized and the intensity of the dream pictures, because this relation held true in a few dreams. However, this assumption proved to be erroneous, as did a second assumption that bodily ego feeling occurs when the dream deals with the total problem of the dreamer's personality, his own fate. These two misleading relations were derived merely from peculiarities of individual dreams.

It then occurred to me that in many dreams a partial ego feeling could be explained simply, and at first without theoretical interest, by the fact that very often, in dreams, an especially strong affect is accompanied by strong bodily ego feeling. This holds true particularly for anxiety dreams, but it also is true of dreams in which the dreamer feels pity or pride. By analogy, a stronger ego feeling makes its appearance when an instinctual impulse becomes conscious in the dream, as in masochistic or exhibitionistic dreams. A careful study of bodily ego feeling as conditioned by affect and instinct would be very profitable. From knowledge gained in other fields, it is certain that we must distinguish between active and passive ego feeling, and this point proves to be useful in this instance. We have one sort of ego feeling corresponding to the active functions and another sort corresponding to the passive functions of the body. In dreams in which there is a strong affect of shame or fear, in masochistic dreams, and in exhibitionistic dreams, the bodily ego feeling is a passive one.

I suspect that definite affects have a corresponding cathexis of definite parts of the body with passive ego feeling. If such a relation can be demonstrated as a constant finding, we may suppose that, also, in dreams in which there is no affect but in which a part of the body is invested with a particular passive ego feeling, one might be able to deduce the presence of an affect which belongs to the dream, but which was not "awakened." For dreams are poor in affect; it is a necessary condition for sleep that affects be not fully produced.

As regards *active* bodily ego feeling, observation of my own dreams and the dreams of others proved that it appears when the dreamer not only *wishes* what the dream signifies, but also sanctions the dream wish or part of it with his *will*. For this reason, dreams are seldom accompanied, in their entirety, by active bodily ego feeling, for generally we are dealing with forbidden wishes which, disturbing sleep, are fulfilled in the dream. Only rarely does the ego venture to desire the forbidden. But the ego may do so partially, and individual parts of the dream action may correspond to the will of the dreamer, even though during waking life these actions might be opposed by the remaining portions of the ego. A consistent "state of mind" exists only as a phrase in books on jurisprudence, where it is supposed even to solve the problem of guilt. We psychoanalysts, and today we may well say "we psychologists," know how little undivided conviction and will man possesses, and how often, in the course of the day, the waking man wills to do something and does not do it. What he willed was his real desire. But in spite of his willing and desiring, the ego obeyed the superego, and not only did not fulfill the wish, but also repressed it. In the dream the wish awakens the psychic ego by means of the manifest dream pictures, and then the whole ego can sanction the wish in the dream, because while awake the ego wanted this wish too. Then, not only does the corresponding psychic ego boundary receive cathexis, but the bodily ego is aroused as well. However, such an arousal does not allow sleep to persist for long. For this reason it is possible, in waking from a dream with exceptionally strong and complete active bodily ego feeling, to observe oneself and to become completely convinced of the fact that on waking one had a strong sense of still wanting what he wanted at the end of the dream. In this manner, in the past few years, I have been able to establish by self-observation the typical significance of dreams with full bodily ego feeling, just as in previous years I was able to determine the significance of this feeling in the inhibition dream. My interpretation was confirmed when it was tested by the analysis of dreams. A concurrence of the will with the dream wish is an enhanced fulfilment of the pleasure principle, and, as a matter of fact, these intensive "will dreams" are particularly pleasurable. We know, however, that the opposing will of the superego easily changes them into inhibition dreams. Actually, *the explanation of dreams with bodily ego feeling as "will dreams"* was already tacitly included in the explanation of inhibition dreams. The explanation, that toward the end of the sleep the body ego might be expected to be awakening, is invalidated by the fact that more frequently it does not do so.

The observation that a partial bodily ego feeling so often accompanies dreamed movements very well fits our explanation that active bodily ego feeling discloses the will of the dreamer. For these correspond to a volitional impulse magnified into an action. It is more curious that such movements should ever occur without bodily ego feeling. Dream analysis shows that such a lack of bodily ego feeling is not accidental. If a movement is made and no bodily ego feeling accompanies it to reveal that the patient willed it, this movement is intended to emphasize his ability, not his desire, to make the motion. The dream wish, then, refers to the ability. For this reason, the typical flight dream of an impotent man is that of flying in a machine. In this type of flying, as we recall, bodily ego feeling is usually absent. In fact, many impotent men do not wish the sexual act or an erection for sexual reasons; instead they wish that they were able to carry out the act, that is to say, that they were potent in general. This is true particularly in the case of neurotics for whom impotence fulfills an unconscious wish which runs counter to masculine sexuality, or of those neurotics in who impotence is due to the desire not to have intercourse with particular sexual objects. Similarly, on the other hand, we can understand why some flying dreams occur *with* full bodily ego feeling; that is, because they represent fulfilment of actual willing, not merely wishing to be able to do it.

By observing bodily ego feeling, we have been able to determine the way in which "I want to" *(ich will)* and "I can" are expressed in dreams. From this we can see that this method of expression quite corresponds to the meaning of these verbs as auxiliaries of mode in the grammatical sense. For the mode of a verb expresses the attitude which a person's ego takes toward the activity or experience conveyed in the verb. In the case of "I will," the ego affirms the action and causes it to be carried out. "I can" states that, as far as the ego is concerned, the action is possible. It is therefore meaningful and logical that in dreams "I will" is expressed by the presence of active bodily ego feeling, and "I can" by the presence of psychic ego feeling only, and an absence of ego feeling. These findings should encourage us to look for other expressions of modality in dreams.

The somnambulist, referred to above, presented a special increase in bodily ego feeling, which he perceived not as active ego feeling but, at first, as a burden; and yet at the same time he willed to do the difficult thing. Accordingly, as far as I gather from his description, there was a *passive bodily* ego feeling and an *active psychic* ego feeling. His superego had commanded him to carry out the action. This curious combination expresses in a characteristic way "I should" *(ich soll)*—a volition in the service of the superego and an unwillingness of the ego. It must be added that in the course of his sleepwalking, his body ceased to be a burden and his bodily ego feeling became active. Therefore, after the resistances were overcome, and in the presence of the feeling that it was only a dream, an active will accompanied the dream activity. Similarly, in waking life, in the case of "I should," there are present, simultaneously, an activity of the willing ego and a resistance from a part of the ego. Both are expressed in the dream by the constituents of ego feeling. If we now turn to the inhibition dream—already explained by Freud in *The Interpretation of Dreams*—my own investigations have shown that it expresses "I want to but am not allowed" *(ich darf nicht).*[8] In this the influence of the superego is unconscious; there is only an awareness of the fact that the body or a part of it, strongly invested with bodily ego feeling, cannot be moved. A muscular apparatus invested with bodily ego feeling is withdrawn from the psychic ego.

The recognition of the meaning of ego feeling in dreams gives rise to a need for a new detailed investigation of these typical dream forms. My present communication is, therefore, a preliminary one. However, it can be safely asserted that the different types of investment with ego feeling—either purely psychic ego feeling or psychic plus bodily ego feeling, active or passive, total or partial—expresses the various modalities of dream occurrences. Conversely, we shall be able to deduce the modality of the dream occurrences from the condition of ego feeling in cases where the analysis of the dream does not give it, and thereby advance psychoanalytic interpretation. The observation of ego feeling in dreams opens a new path for dream interpretation, so that we shall be able to apply the appropriate auxiliary verbs to the dream action. For, as we have shown above, these verbs express the attitude of the ego and of the superego toward the action, whereas the main verb conveys the alteration of the object brought about by means of an effector organ or instrument. That "I want to," "I can," "I am not allowed," and "I should" are expressed in the dream by the ego cathexis, fully corresponds to the processes in waking life. ("I have took," "I cannot," and "I am allowed" still await interpretation.) In waking life the whole ego and superego take definite stands in relation to an action corresponding to these auxiliary verbs; for example, in the case of "I want to," there is active psychic and bodily ego feeling, thought, impulse, and motor activity. In dreams, however, because of the withdrawal of cathexis, both motor and thought activity are usually lacking. For this reason, the differences of ego feeling are the only means which remain at the disposal of the dream to express modality. The difference between "I want to" *(ich will),* "I should," "I must," "I am allowed to," and "I can," which are so great in waking life, are expressed in dreams only by means of subtle, long-overlooked differences of ego feeling; that is to say, they are barely more than indicated. However, the poverty of this means of expression need not surprise us, for we have long since been taught by Freud that even the most powerful instinctual desires are often represented in dreams by a remote symbolism, in itself almost indiscernible and long overlooked.

In waking life, all power is returned to the ego, in particular the will. *The will is the turning of the whole active ego cathexis to particular activities,*[9] *whether they be mere thinking or action.* To believe that the will is only a foreknowledge of an event which would occur in any case is a completely erroneous intellectualistic conception, as Klages long since proved. The ego *as a whole* has at its disposal a certain active libido cathexis which it can send out or withdraw, and *this* is the will. Active bodily ego feeling in waking life represents the materially smaller permanent cathexis of the ego. In dreams it represents the will.

The will is not mentioned in Freud's book on dreams, for the reason that the will belongs to consciousness and to the ego.[10] My contribution aims to amplify our knowledge of dreams, particularly by showing that willing, also, can be recognized in dreams. It is consistent with the theory of dream interpretation to believe that even small differences in cathexis with ego feeling are not insignificant and accidental, but that they too are determined —determined in the same way as the modality or the latent affect which they indicate. When future studies have added to our knowledge, these determinations will also be found of use in the interpretation of dreams.

NOTES

1. There is no exact English equivalent for *Entfremdung.* This phenomenon is usually described as "sense of unreality," which does not convey the meaning of *Entfremdung.* The word is therefore translated literally.
2. This statement does not imply a dispute with Schilder, who referred to the "ego orientation of an act" for other purposes.
3. To designate the feelings themselves as perceptions of autonomic processes, and to consider such perceptions as equivalent to those with intellectual content (Behaviorism), does not touch the problem. For we are basing our investigation on the empirical fact that there is a difference between intellectual and affective experiences.
4. See Chapters 1, 2, and 15.
5. Concerning the reasons for the exhaustion *(Versiegen)* of libido in melancholia, see Federn, "The Reality of the Death Instinct, Especially in Melancholia." *Psa. Rev.,* XIX (1932).
6. Federn, "Über zwei typische Traumsensationen" ("On Two Typical Dream Sensations"), *Jahrb. d. Psa.,* VI (1914).
7. I know that this description sounds paradoxical, but the paradox is connected with the sensation, not with the description. The organ lies partially within the sensory ego boundary, but outside that for motor activity.
8. *Ibid.*

9. My previous theory (see "Narcissim in the Structure of the Ego," Chapter 2) that the death instinct is intimately associated with the act of willing, as I hope to show in a future paper, is probably true and does not conflict with the above statement.

10. When willed actions appear themselves in the manifest dream content, they are derived, like thinking processes, from the dream material.

6. The Dream Specimen of Psychoanalysis

Erik Homburger Erikson

I. ORIENTATION

Before embarking on advanced exercises in the clinical use of dream interpretation, it seems an attractive task to return, once more, to the "first dream ever subjected to an exhaustive interpretation." This, of course, is Freud's dream of his patient Irma (6). While Freud has by no means published a full account of his exhaustive analysis, he, nevertheless, has offered this dream to his students as the original dream "specimen." For this reason [and for others, only dimly felt up to the time when Freud's letters to Fliess (9) were published] the "Irma Dream" has imprinted itself on the minds of many as a truly historical document; and it seems instructive to discuss this dream once more with the specific purpose of enlarging upon some aspects of dream interpretation which we today, half a century later, would consider essential to an exhaustive analysis.

As we review in our minds the incidents of dream analysis in our daily practice and in our seminars and courses, it must be strikingly clear that the art and ritual of "exhaustive" dream analysis has all but vanished. Our advanced technique of psychoanalysis, with its therapeutic zeal and goal-directed awareness of ever-changing transference and resistances, rarely, maybe too rarely, permits that intellectual partnership, that common curiosity between analyst and patient which would take a good-sized dream seriously enough to make it the object of a few hours' concerted analysis. We know too well that patients learn to exploit our interest in dreams by telling us in profuse nocturnal productions what they should struggle and learn to tell us in straight words. And we have learned (or so we think) to find in other sources what in Freud's early days could be garnered only from dreams. Therefore, we feel that even a periodic emphasis on dreams today is wasteful

Reprinted by permission of International Universities Press, Inc., from the *Journal of the American Psychoanalytic Association*, Vol. 2, 1954.

and may even be deleterious to therapy. But let us admit that such restraint, more often than not, is a policy of scarcity rather than abundance; and that the daily choice of dream data, made necessary by such restraint, is more arbitrary and often whimsical than systematic. The truth is that the privilege of using choice and restraint in the interpretation of dreams must be earned; only sufficient regard, at least during the years of training, for the art of total dream analysis, brought up to date at each state of the development of psychoanalysis, can help a candidate in psychoanalytic training to graduate to that much more advanced practice (now freely granted to beginners) of picking from a patient's daily dream productions whatever dream fragments, symbols, manifest images, and latent dream thoughts support the prevalent trend of interpretations. It stands to reason that a psychoanalyst can know which dream details he may single out for the purposes of the day only if, at least preconsciously, he has somehow grasped the meaning of the whole dream in relation to the course of the analysis and in relation to the course of the patient's life.

Such grasp can become a firm possession of the analyst's preconscious mental activity only if he has acquired by repeated exercise the potential mastery of the whole inventory of manifest leads, associational trends, and relevant life data which make up a whole dream. If he can learn this in his own analysis, so much the better. Some must learn it later, when dream analysis becomes the main vehicle of self-analysis. In the course of formal training, however, "exhaustive" dream analysis can best be studied in connection with those seminars, usually called "continuous," in which the study of the history of a whole treatment permits a thorough assessment of the inventory of forces, trends, and images in a patient's life—including his dream life. I propose that we prepare ourselves for the task of this total analysis by taking up once more Freud's dream of his patient Irma.

To reinterpret a dream means to reinterpret the dreamer. Let me, therefore, discuss first the spirit in which we undertake such a reinterpretation.

No man has ever consciously and knowingly revealed more of himself, for the sake of human advance, than did Freud. At the same time, he drew firm lines where he felt that self-revelation should come to an end, because the possible scientific gain was not in proportion to the pain of self-exhibition and to the inconvenience of calumny. If we, in passing, must spell out more fully than Freud did certain latent dream thoughts suggested by him, we are guided by the consideration that the most legitimate didactic use of the personal data of Freud's life concerns a circumscribed area of investigation, namely, the dynamics of creative thought in general and, specifically, in psychoanalytic work. It seems to us that the publication of Freud's letters to Fliess points in this direction (2).

In reviewing the dream of Irma, we shall focus our attention, beyond the fragmentary indices of familiar infantile and neurotic conflicts, primarily on the relation of this very dream to the moment in Freud's life when it was dreamed—to the moment when creative thought gave birth to the interpretation of dreams. For the dream of Irma owes its significance not only to the fact that it was the first dream reported in *The Interpretation of Dreams*. In a letter sent to his friend Fliess, Freud indulges in a fancy of a possible tablet which (he wonders) may sometimes adorn his summer home. Its inscription would tell the world that "In this house, on July 24, 1895, the Mystery of the Dream unveiled [*enthüllte*] itself to Dr. Sigm. Freud" (9). The date is that of the Irma Dream. Such autobiographic emphasis, then, supports our contention that this dream may reveal more than the basic fact of a disguised wish fulfillment derived from infantile sources; that this dream may, in fact, carry the historical burden of being dreamed in order to be analyzed, and analyzed in order to fulfill a very special fate.

This, then, is our specific curiosity regarding the dream of Irma. We can advance this approach only in the general course of demonstrating the dimensions of our kind of "exhaustiveness" in the interpretation of dreams.

But first, the background of the dream, the dream itself, and Freud's interpretation.

II. THE IRMA DREAM, MANIFEST AND LATENT

The dreamer of the Irma Dream was a thirty-nine-year-old-doctor, a specialist in neurology in the city of Vienna. He was a Jewish citizen of a Catholic monarchy, once the Holy Roman Empire of German Nationality, and now swayed both by liberalism and increasing anti-Semitism. His family had grown rapidly; in fact, his wife at the time was again pregnant. The dreamer just then wished to fortify his position and, in act, his income by gaining academic status. This wish had become problematic, not only because he was a Jew but also because in a recent joint publication with an older colleague, Dr. Breuer, he had committed himself to theories so unpopular and, in fact, so universally disturbing that the senior co-author himself had disengaged himself from the junior one. The book in question *(Studies in Hysteria)* had emphasized the role of sexuality in the etiology of the "defense neuropsychoses,'' i.e., nervous disorders caused by the necessity of defending consciousness against repugnant and repressed ideas, primarily of a sexual nature. The junior worker felt increasingly committed to these ideas; he had begun to feel, with a pride often overshadowed by despair, that he was destined to make a revolutionary discovery by (I shall let this stand) undreamed-of means.

It had occurred to Freud by then that the dream was, in fact, a normal equivalent of a hysterical attack, "A little defense neuropsychosis." In the history of psychiatry, the comparison of normal phenomena with abnormal ones was not new: the Greeks had called orgasm "a little epilepsy." But if hysterical symptoms, if even dreams, were based on inner conflict, on an involuntary defense against unconscious thoughts, what justification was there for blaming patients for the fact that they could not easily accept, nor long remember, and not consistently utilize the interpretations which the psychiatrist offered them? What use was there in scolding the patient, as Bernheim has done: *"vous vous contre-suggestions, madame?"* "Defense," "transference," and "resistance" were the mechanisms, the concepts, and the tools to be elucidated in the years to come. It was soon to dawn on Freud that in order to give shape to these tools, a basic shift from physiologic concepts (to which he was as yet committed) to purely psychological ones, and from exact and sober medical and psychotherapeutic techniques to intuitive observation, even to self-observation, was necessary.

This, then, is the situation: within an academic milieu which seemed to restrict his opportunities because he was a Jew; at an age when he seemed to notice with alarm the first signs of aging, and, in fact, of disease; burdened with the responsibility for a fast-growing family—a medical scientist is faced with the decision of whether to employ his brilliance, as he had shown he could, in the service of conventional practice and research, or to accept the task of substantiating in himself and of communicating to the world a new insight, namely, that man is unconscious of the best and of the worst in himself. Soon after the Irma Dream, Freud was to write to his friend Fliess with undisguised horror that in trying to explain defense he had found himself explaining something "out of the core of nature." At the time of this dream, then, he knew that he would have to bear a great discovery.

The evening before the dream was dreamed, Freud had an experience which had painfully spotlighted his predicament. He had met a colleague, "Otto," who had just returned from a summer resort. There he had seen a mutual friend, a young woman, who was Freud's patient: "Irma." This patient, by Freud's effort, had been cured of hysterical anxiety, but not of certain somatic symptoms, such as intense retching. Before going on vacation, Freud had offered her an interpretation as the solution of her problems; but she had been unable to accept it. Freud had shown impatience. Patient and doctor had thus found themselves in a deadlock which made a righteous disciplinarian out of the doctor and a stubborn child out of the patient: not a healthy condition for the communication of insight. It was, of course, this very kind of deadlock which Freud learned later on to formulate and utilize for a working through of resistance. At the time, Freud apparently had heard some reproach in Otto's voice regarding the condition of the patient who appeared "better, but not well"; and behind the reproach he thought to detect the stern authority of "Dr. M.," a man who was "the leading personality in our circle." On his return home, and under the impression of the encounter, Freud had written a lengthy case report for "Dr. M.," explaining his views on Irma's illness.

He had apparently gone to bed with a feeling that this report would settle matters so far as his own peace of mind was concerned. Yet that very night the personages concerned in this incident, namely, Irma, Dr. M., Dr. Otto, and another doctor, Dr. Leopold, constituted themselves the population of the following dream (6, pp. 196–197).

A great hall—a number of guests, whom we are receiving—among them Irma, whom I immediately take aside, as though to answer her letter, and to reproach her for not yet accepting the "solution." I say to her: "If you *[du]*[1] still have pains, it is really only your own fault."—She answers: "If you *[du]* only knew what pains I have now in the throat, stomach, and abdomen—I am choked by them." I am startled, and look at her. She looks pale and puffy. I think that after all I must be overlooking some organic affection. I take her to the window and look into her throat. She offers some resistance to this, and like a woman who has a set of false teeth. I think, surely she doesn't need them *[sie hat es doch nicht nötig]*.—The mouth then opens wide, and I find a large white spot on the right, and elsewhere I see extensive grayish-white scabs adhering to curiously curled formations which are evidently shaped like the turbinal bones of the nose.—I quickly call Dr. M., who repeats the examination and confirms it. Dr. M. looks quite unlike his usual self; he is very pale, he limps, and his chin is clean-shaven *[bartlos]*. . . . Now my friend, Otto, too, is standing beside her, and my friend Leopold percusses her covered chests and says: "She has a dullness below, on the left," and also calls attention to an infiltrated portion of skin on the left shoulder (which I can feel in spite of the dress). M. says, "There's no doubt that it's an infection, but it doesn't matter; dysentery will follow

and the poison will be eliminated." . . . We know, too, precisely *[unmittelbar]* how
the infection originated. My friend, Otto, not long ago, gave her, when she was
feeling unwell, an injection of a preparation of propyl. . . . propyls. . . . propionic
acid. . . . trimethylamin (the formula of which I see before me, printed in heavy
type). . . . One doesn't give such injections rashly. . . . Probably, too, the syringe
[Spritze] was not clean.

I must assume here that Freud's associations to this dream are known to
all readers, in all the literary freshness which they have in *The Interpretation
of Dreams*, and in all the convincing planlessness of true associations, which,
unforeseen and often unwelcome, make their determined entrance
like a host of unsorted strangers, until they gradually become a chorus
echoing a few central themes. Here I must select and classify.

Irma proves, first of all, to be the representative of a series of *women
patients*. Freud remembers a number of *young women* in connection with the
question whether or not they were willing to accept their therapist's "solution." Besides Irma, who we now hear is a rosy young *widow, a governess*
comes to memory, also of youthful beauty, who had resisted an examination
because she wanted to hide her false teeth. The dreamer remembers that it
had been this governess about whom he had had the angry thought (which in
the dream he expresses in regard to Irma), namely, *"Sie hat es doch nicht
nötig"* (incorrectly translated as, "She does not need them"). This trend of
association establishes an analogy between women patients who will not
accept solutions, who will not yield to examination, and who will not submit
to advances, although their status promises an easy yielding: young widows,
young governesses. Fifty years ago as well as today, suspicions concerning
young women patients and especially "merry widows" found their way into
medical wit, rumor, and scandal. They were accentuated at the time by the
common but not officially admitted knowledge that the large contingent of
hysterical women was starved for sexual adventure. On the sly it was suggested that the doctor might as well remove their inhibitions by deeds as well
as words. It was Freud who established the fact that the hysterical patient
transfers to the doctor by no means a simply sexual wish, but rather an
unconscious conflict between an infantile wish and an infantile inhibition.
Medical ethics aside, neither satisfaction nor cure could ensue from a sexual
consummation of the transference.

But then other kinds of patients—men, women, and children—impose
themselves on the dreamer's memory: *"good ones"* who fared *badly,* and
"bad ones" who maybe, were *better off.* Two hysterical ladies had accepted

his "solutions" and had become worse; one had died. As to *obstreperous* patients, the dreamer must admit that he thinks of a very occasional patient, his own wife, and he must confess that even she is not at ease with him as the ideal patient would be. But are there any easy, any ideal patients? Yes, *children*. They do not "put on airs." In those Victorian days, little girls were the only female patients who undressed for examination matter-of-factly. And, we may add, children oblige the dream interpreter by dreaming simple wish fulfillments where adults build up such complicated defenses against their own wishes—and against the interpretation of dreams.

In speaking of his *men patients,* the dreamer is ruthless with himself and his memories. Years ago he had played a leading role in research which demonstrated the usefulness of cocaine for local anesthesia, especially in the eye. But it took some time to learn the proper dosage and the probable dangers: a dear friend died of misuse of cocaine. Other men patients come to mind, also *badly off.* And then there are memories concerning the *dreamer himself* in his double role as patient and as doctor. He had given himself injections for swellings in the nose. Had he *harmed himself?*

Finally the dreamer, apparently looking for a friend in his dilemma, thinks of his oldest and staunchest admirer, a doctor in another city, who knows all his *"germinating ideas,"* and who has fascinating ideas regarding the relationship of *nose and sexuality* and regarding the phasic aspect of conception; but, alas, he too has a *nasal affliction.* This far-away doctor is no other than Dr. Fliess, whom Freud at the time was consulting, confiding his emotions and his ideas, and in whom he was soon to confide his very self-analysis.

To state the case which Freud at the time wished to make we shall quote from his lengthy summary (6, pp. 204–207).

The dream fulfills several wishes which were awakened within me by the events of the previous evening (Otto's news, and the writing of the clinical history). For the result of the dream is that it is not I who am to blame for the pain which Irma is still suffering, but that Otto is to blame for it. Now Otto has annoyed me by his remark about Irma's imperfect cure; the dream avenges me upon him, in that it turns the reproach upon himself. The dream acquits me of responsibility for Irma's condition, as it refers this condition to other causes (which do, indeed, furnish quite a number of explanations). The dream represents a certain state of affairs, such as I might wish to exist; *the content of the dream is thus the fulfillment of a wish; its motive is a wish.*

This much is apparent at first sight. But many other details of the dream become intelligible when regarded from the standpoint of wish fulfillment. I take my revenge on Otto. . . . Nor do I pass over Dr. M.'s contradiction; for I express in an obvious allusion my opinion of him: namely, that his attitude in this case is that of an ignoramus ("Dysentery will develop, etc.") Indeed, it seems as though I were appealing from him to someone better informed (my friend, who told me about trimethylamin), just as I have turned from Irma to her friend, and from Otto to Leopold. It is as though I were to say: Rid me of these three persons, replace them by three others of my own choice, and I shall be rid of the reproaches which I am not willing to admit that I deserve! In my dream the unreasonableness of these reproaches is demonstrated for me in the most elaborate manner. Irma's pains are not attributable to me, since she herself is to blame for them in that she refuses to accept my solution. They do not concern me, for being as they are of an organic nature, they cannot possibly be cured by psychic treatment. —Irma's sufferings are satisfactorily explained by her widowhood (trimethylamin!); a state which I cannot alter. —Irma's illness has been caused by an incautious injection administered by Otto, an injection of an unsuitable drug, such as I should never have administered. —Irma's complaint is the result of an injection made with an unclean syringe, like the phlebitis of my old lady patient, whereas my injections have never caused any ill effects. I am aware that these explanations of Irma's illness, which unite in acquitting me, do not agree with one another; that they even exclude one another. The whole plea—for this dream is nothing else—recalls vividly the defense offered by a man who was accused by his neighbor of having returned a kettle in a damaged condition. In the first place, he said, he had returned the kettle undamaged; in the second place, it already had holes in it when he borrowed it; and in the third place, he had never borrowed it at all. A complicated defense, but so much the better; if only one of these three lines of defense is recognized as valid, the man must be acquitted.

Still other themes play a part in the dream, and their relation to my non-responsibility for Irma's illness is not so apparent. . . . But if I keep all these things in view they combine into a single train of thought which might be labeled: concern for the health of myself and others; professional conscientiousness. I recall a vaguely disagreeable feeling when Otto gave me the news of Irma's condition. Lastly, I am inclined, after the event, to find an expression of this fleeting sensation in the train of thoughts which forms part of the dream. It is as though Otto had said to me: "You do not take your medical duties seriously enough; you are not conscientious; you do not perform what you promise." Thereupon this train of thought placed itself at my service, in order that I might give proof of my extreme conscientiousness, of my intimate concern about the health of my relatives, friends and patients. Curiously enough, there are also some painful memories in this material, which confirm the blame attached to Otto rather than my own exculpation. The material is apparently impartial, but the connection between this broader material, on which the dream is based, and the more limited theme from which emerges the wish to be innocent of Irma's illness, is, nevertheless, unmistakable.

I do not wish to assert that I have entirely revealed the meaning of the dream, or that my interpretation is flawless. . . .

For the present I am content with the one fresh discovery which has just been made: If the method of dream-interpretation here indicated is followed, it will be found that dreams do really possess a meaning, and are by no means the expression of disintegrated cerebral activity, as the writers on the subject would have us believe. *When the work of interpretation has been completed the dream can be recognized as a wish-fulfillment.*

We note that the wish demonstrated here is not more than preconscious. Furthermore, this demonstration is not carried through as yet to the infantile sources postulated later in *The Interpretation of Dreams*. Nor is the theme of sexuality carried through beyond a point which is clearly intended to be understood by the trained reader and to remain vague to the untrained one. The Irma Dream, then, serves Freud as a very first step toward the task of the interpretation of dreams, namely, the establishment of the fact that dreams have their own "rationale," which can be detected by the study of the "work" which dreams accomplish, in transforming the latent dream thoughts into manifest dream images. Dream work uses certain methods (condensation, displacement, symbolization) in order to derive a set of manifest dream images which, on analysis, prove to be significantly connected with a practically limitless number of latent thoughts and memories, reaching from the trigger event of the preceding day, through a chain of relevant memories, back into the remotests past and down into the reservoir of unconscious, forgotten, or unclearly evaluated, but lastingly significant, impressions.

Our further efforts, then, must go in two directions. First, we must spell out, for the Irma Dream, certain latent connections, which in "The Interpretation of Dreams," for didactic reasons, are dealt with only in later chapters: here we think primarily of the dream's sexual themata, and their apparent relation to certain childhood memories, which in Freud's book follow the Irma Dream by only a number of pages. And we must focus on areas of significance which are only implicit in "The Interpretation of Dreams" but have become more explicit in our lifetime. Here I have in mind, first of all, the relationship of the latent dream thought to the dream's manifest surface as it may appear to us today after extensive studies of other forms of imaginative representation, such as children's play; and then, the relationship of the dream's "inner population" to the dreamer's social and cultural surroundings.

I propose to approach this multidimensional task, not by an immediate attempt at "going deeper" than Freud did, but, on the contrary, by taking a fresh look at the whole of the manifest dream. This approach, however, will necessitate a brief discussion of a general nature.

III. DIMENSIONS OF THE MANIFEST DREAM

The psychoanalyst, in looking at the surface of a mental phenomenon, often has to overcome a certain shyness. So many in his field mistake attention to surface for superficiality, and a concern with form for lack of depth. But the fact that we have followed Freud into depths which our eyes had to become accustomed to does not permit us, today, to blink when we look at things in broad daylight. Like good surveyors, we must be at home on the geological surface as well as in the descending shafts. In recent years, so-called projective techniques, such as the Rorschach Test, the Thematic Apperception Test, and the observation of children's play, have clearly shown that any segment of overt behavior reflects, as it were, the whole store: one might say that psychoanalysis has given new depth to the surface, thus building the basis for a more inclusive general psychology of man. It takes the clinical psychoanalytic method proper to determine which items of a man's total behavior and experience are amenable to consciousness, are preconscious, or unconscious, and why and how they became and remained unconscious; and it takes this method to establish a scale of pathogenic significance in his conscious and unconscious motivations. But in our daily work, in our clinical discussions and nonclinical applications, and even in our handling of dreams, it has become a matter of course that any item of human behavior shows a continuum of dynamic meaning, reaching from the surface through many layers of crust to the "core." Unofficially, we often interpret dreams entirely or in parts on the basis of their manifest appearance. Officially, we hurry at every confrontation with a dream to crack its manifest appearance at if it were a useless shell and to hasten to discard this shell in favor of what seems to be the more worthwhile core. When such a method corresponded to a new orientation, it was essential for research as well as for therapy; but as a compulsive habituation, it has since hindered a full meeting of ego psychology and the problems of dream life.[2]

Let us, then, systematically begin with the most "superficial": our first impression of the manifest dream. After years of practice one seems to remember, to compare, and to discuss the dreams of others (and even the reports given to us of dreams reported to others) in such a matter-of-fact manner that one reminds himself only with some effort of the fact that one has never seen anybody else's dream nor has the slightest proof that it ever "happened" the way one visualizes it. A dream is a verbal report of a series of remembered images, mostly visual, which are usually endowed with affect. The dreamer may be limited or especially gifted, inhibited or over-eager in the range of his vocabulary and in its availability for dream reports; in his ability to revisualize and in his motivation to verbalize all the shades of what is visualized; in his ability to report stray fragments or in the compulsion to spin a meaningful yarn; or in his capacity or willingness to describe the range of his affects. The report of a dream, in turn, arouses in each listener and interpreter a different set of images, which are as incommunicable as is the dream itself. Every dream seminar gives proof that different people are struck by different variables of the manifest dream (or, as I would like to call them, by dream configurations) in different ways, and this by means only because of a different theoretical approach, as is often hastily concluded, but because of variations in sensory and emotional responsiveness. Here early overtraining can do much harm, in that, for example, the immediate recognition of standardized symbols, or the immediate recognition of verbal double meanings may induce the analyst to reach a premature closure in his conviction of having listened to and "understood" a dream and of understanding dreams in general. It takes practice to realize that the manifest dream contains a wealth of indicators not restricted to what the listener happens to be receptive for. The most important of these indicators are, it is true, verbal ones; but the mere experiment of having a patient retell toward the end of an analytic hour a dream reported at the beginning will make it quite clear to what extent a verbal report is, after all, a process of trying to communicate something which is never completely and successfully rendered in any one verbal formulation. Each completed formulation is, of course, a complete item for analysis; and once told, the memory of the first verbal rendering of a dream more or less replaces the visual memory of it, just as a childhood experience often retold by oneself or described by others becomes inextricably interwoven with the memory itself.

I pause here for an illustration, the shortest illustration, from my practice. A young woman patient of German descent once reported a dream which consisted of nothing but the image of the word S[E]INE (with the "E" in brackets), seen light against a dark background. The patient was well-traveled and educated and it therefore seemed plausible to follow the first impression, namely, that this image of a word contained, in fact, a play of words in a variety of languages. The whole word is the French river SEINE, and indeed it was in Paris (France) that the patient had been overcome with agoraphobia. The same French word, if heard and spelled as a German word, is SEHN, i.e., "to see," and indeed it was after a visit to the Louvre that the patient had been immobilized: there now existed a complete amnesia for what she had seen there. The whole word, again, can also be perceived as the German word SEINE, meaning "his." The letter "E" is the first letter of my name and probably served as an anchorage for the transference in the dream. If the letter "E" is put aside, the word becomes the Latin SINE, which means "without." All of this combined makes for the riddle "To see (E) without his . . . . in Paris." This riddle was solved through a series of free associations in which, by way of appropriate childhood memories of a voyeuristic character and through the analysis of a first transference formation, led to the visual recovery of one of the forgotten pictures: It was a "Circumcision of Christ." There she had seen the boy Savior without that mysterious loincloth which adorns Christ on the Crucifix—the loincloth which her sacrilegious eyes had often tucked at during prayers. (The dream word SEINE also contains the word SIN.) This sacrilegious and aggressive curiosity had been shocked into sudden prominence by the picture in the Louvre, only to be abruptly repressed again because of the special inner conditions brought about by the state of adolescence and by the visit to the capital of sensuality. It had now been transferred to the analyst, by way of the hysterical overevaluation of his person as a therapeutic savior.

The presence of meaningful verbal configuration in this dream is very clear. Less clear is the fact that the very absence of other configurations is equally meaningful. That something was only *seen,* and in fact focused upon with the exclusion of all other sensory experiences (such as spatial extension, motion, shading, color, sound, and, last but not least, the awareness of a dream population) is, of course, related to the various aspects of the visual trauma: to the symptom of visual amnesia, to an attempt to restore the repressed image in order to gain cure by mastery, and to a transference of the original voyeuristic drive onto the person of the analyst. We take it for granted that the wish to revive and to relive the repressed impulse immediately "muscles" its way into the wish to be cured. That the dream space was dark and completely motionless around a clear image was an inverted representation of the patient's memory of the trauma: an area with a dark spot in the center (the repressed picture) and surrounded by lively and colorful halls, milling crowds, and noisy and dangerous traffic, in bright sunlight. The lack of motion in the dream corresponds to the patient's symptoms: agoraphobia and immobilization (based on early determined defense mechanisms) were to end the turmoil of those adolescent days and bring to a standstill the struggle between sexual curiosity and a sense of sin. There was no time dimension in the dream, and there was none in the patient's by now morbid psychic life. As is often the case with hysterics, a relative inability to perceive the passage of time had joined the symptom of spatial avoidance, just as blind anxiety had absorbed all conflicting affects. Thus, all the omitted dimensions of the manifest dream, with the help of associations, could be made to converge on the same issues on which the one overclear dimension (the visual one) was focused. But the choice of the manifest dream representation, i.e., the intelligent use of multilingual word play in a visual riddle, itself, proved highly overdetermined and related to the patient's gifts and opportunities: for it was in superior esthetic aspirations that the patient had found a possible sphere of conflict-free activity and companionship. In the cultivation of her sensitive senses, she could see and hear sensually, without being consciously engaged in sexual fantasies; and in being clever and witty she had, on occasion, come closest to replacing a son to her father. The whole area of functioning, then, had remained more or less free of conflict, until, at the time of accelerated sexual maturation and under the special conditions of a trip, sacrilegious thoughts in connection with an esthetic-intellectual endeavor had brought about a short-circuit in her whole system of defenses and reasonably conflict-free intellectual functions: the wish to see and feel esthetically, again, converged on sexual and sinful objects. While it is obvious, then, that the desublimated drive fragment of sacrilegious voyeurism is the force behind this dream (and, in this kind of case, necessarily became the focus of therapeutic interpretation) the total dream, in all of its variables, has much more to say about the relationship of this drive fragment to the patient's ego development.

I have temporarily abandoned the Irma Dream for the briefest dream of my clinical experience in order to emphasize the fact that a dream has certain formal aspects which combine into an inventory of configurations, even though some of these configurations may shine only by their absence. In addition to a dream's striving for *representability,* then, we would postulate a *style of representation* which is by no means a mere shell to the kernel, the latent dream; in fact, it is a reflection of the individual ego's peculiar time-space (2), the frame of reference for all its defenses, compromises, and achievements (3). Our "Outline of Dream Analysis" (Chart 6.1), consequently, begins with an inventory of Manifest Configurations, which is meant to help us, in any given dream or series of dreams, to recognize the interplay of commissions and omissions, of overemphases and underemphases. As mentioned before, such an inventory, once having been thoroughly practiced, must again become a preconscious set of general expectations, against which the individual style of each dream stands out in sharp contour. It will then become clear that the dream life of some (always, or during certain periods, or in individual dream events) is characterized by a greater clarity of the experience of *spatial* extension and of motion (or the arrest of motion) in space; that of others by the flow or the stoppage of *time;* other dreams are dominated by clear *somatic* sensations or their marked absence; by a rich *interpersonal* dream life with an (often stereotyped) dream population or by a pronounced aloneness; by an overpowering experience of marked *affects* or their relative absence or lack of specificity. Only an equal attention to all of these variables and their configurations can help the analyst to train himself for an awareness of the varieties of manifest dream life, which in turn permits the exact characterization of a given patient's manifest dream life at different times of his treatment.

Chart 6.1:
Outline of Dream Analysis

I. *Manifest Configurations*

Verbal
    general linguistic quality
    spoken words and word play
Sensory
    general sensory quality, range and intensity
    specific sensory focus
Spatial
    general quality of extension
    dominant vectors
Temporal
    general quality of succession
    time-perspective
Somatic
    general quality of body feeling
    body zones
    organ modes
Interpersonal
    general social grouping
    changing social vectors
    "object relations"
    points of identification
Affective

quality of affective atmosphere
inventory and range of affects
points of change of affect
Summary
    correlation of configurational trends

II. *Links between Manifest and Latent Dream Material*

Associations
Symbols

III. *Analysis of Latent Dream* Material

Acute sleep-disturbing stimulus
Delayed stimulus (day residue)
Acute life conflicts
Dominant transference conflict
Repetitive conflicts
Associated basic childhood conflict
Common denominators
    "Wishes," drives, needs
    methods of defense, denial, and distortion

IV. *Reconstruction*

Life cycle
    present phase
    corresponding infantile phase
    defect, accident, or affliction
    psychosexual fixation
    psychosexual arrest
Social process: collective identity
    ideal prototypes
    evil prototypes
    opportunities and barriers
Ego identity and lifeplan
    mechanisms of defense
    mechanisms of integration

As for Part II of our "Outline" (Links between Manifest and Latent Material), the peculiar task of this paper has brought it about that the dreamer's associations have already been discussed, while some of the principal symbols still await recognition and employment.

IV. VERBAL CONFIGURATIONS

In the attempt now to demonstrate in what way a systematic use of the configurational analysis of the manifest dream (in constant interplay with the analysis of the latent content) may serve to enrich our understanding of the dream work, I find myself immediately limited by the fact that the very first item on our list, namely, "verbal configurations," cannot be profitably pursued here, because the Irma Dream was dreamed and reported in a German of both intellectual and colloquial sophistication which, I am afraid, transcends the German of the reader's high school and college days. But it so happens that the English translation of the Irma Dream which lies before us (6) contains a number of conspicuous simplifications in translation, or, rather, translations so literal that an important double meaning gets lost. This, in a mental product to be analyzed, can be seriously misleading, while it is questionable that any translation could avoid such mistakes; in the meantime we may profit from insight into the importance of colloquial and linguistic configurations. Actually, what is happening in this translation from one language into another offers analogies with "translations" from any dreamer's childhood idiom to that of his adult years, or from the idiom of the dreamer's milieu to that of the analyst's. It seems especially significant that any such transfer to another verbal system of representation is not only accidentally to mistranslate single items, but to become the vehicle for a systematic misrepresentation of the whole mental product.

There is, to begin with, the little word *du,* with which the dreamer and Irma address one another and which is lost in the English "you." It seems innocent enough on the surface, yet may contain quite a therapeutic burden, a burden of countertransference in reality and of special meaning in the dream. For with *du* one addressed, in those days and in those circles, only near relatives or very intimate friends. Did Freud in real life address the patient in this way—and (a much more weighty question) did she address the Herr Professor with this intimate little word? Or does the dreamer use this way of addressing the patient only in the dream? In either case, this little word carries the burden of the dreamer's sense of personal and social obligation to the patient, and thus of a new significance in his guilt over some negligence and in his wish that she should get well—an urgency of a kind which (as Freud has taught us since then) is disadvantageous to the therapeutic relation.

To enumerate other verbal ambiguities: there is a very arresting mistranslation in the phrase, "I think, surely she doesn't need *them,*" which makes it appear that the dreamer questions the necessity for Irma's false teeth.. The German original, *"sie hat es doch nicht nötig,"* means literally, "she does not need *it,*" meaning her resistive behavior. In the colloquial Viennese of those days a richer version of the same phrase was *"das hat sie doch gar nicht nötig, sich so zu zieren,"* the closest English counterpart to which would be: "Who is she to put on such airs?" This expression includes a value judgment to the effect that a certain lady pretends that she is of a higher social, esthetic, or moral status than she really is. A related expression would be the protestation brought forth by a lady on the defense: *"Ich hab das doch gar nicht nötig, mir das gefallen zu lassen";* in English, "I don't need to take this from you," again referring to a misjudgment, this time on the part of a forward gentleman, as to what expectations he may cultivate in regard to a lady's willingness to accept propositions. These phrases, then, are a link between the associations concerning patients who resist "solutions," and women (patients or not) who resist sexual advances.

Further mistranslations continue this trend. For example, the fact that Dr. M.'s chin, in the dream, is *bartlos,* is translated with "clean-shaven." Now a clean-shaven appearance, in the America of today, would be a "must" for a professional man. It is, therefore, well to remember that the German word in the dream means "beardless." But this indicates that Dr. M. is minus something which in the Europe of those days was one of the very insignia of an important man, to wit, a distinctive beard or mustache. This one little word then denudes the leading critic's face, where the English translation would give it the luster of professional propriety: it is obvious that the original has closer relations to a vengeful castrative impulse on the part of the dreamer than the translation conveys.

Then, there is that little word "precisely" which will become rather relevant later inn another context. In German one would expect the word *genau,* while one finds the nearly untranslatable *umittelbar* ("with a sense of immediacy"). In relation to something that is suddenly felt to be known (like the cause of Irma's trouble in the dream) this word refers rather to the degree of immediate and absolute conviction than to the precise quality of the knowledge; in fact, as Freud points out in his associations, the immediacy of this conviction really stood in remarkable contrast to the nonsensical quality of the diagnosis and the prognosis so proudly announced by Dr. M.

There remains the brief discussion of a play of words and of a most relevant simplification. It will have occurred to you that all the mistranslations mentioned so far (except "precisely") allude to sexual meanings, as if the Irma Dream permitted a complete sexual interpretation alongside the professional one—an inescapable expectation in any case.

The word play "propyl . . . . propyls . . . . propionic acid," which leads to the formula of trimethylamin, is so suggestive that I· shall permit myself to go beyond the data at our disposal in order to provide our discussion of word play in dreams and in wit with an enlightening example. Freud associated "propyl" to the Greek word *propylon* (in Latin *vestibulum*, in German *Vorhof*), a term architectonic as well as anatomic, and symbolic of the entrance to the vagina; while "propionic" suggests *priapic*—phallic. This word play, then, would bring male and female symbols into linguistic vicinity to allude to a genital theme. The dream here seems to indulge in a mechanism common in punning. A witty word play has it, for example, that a mistress is "something between a mister and a mattress"—thus using a linguistic analogy to the principal spatial arrangement to which a mistress owes her status.

Finally, a word on the instrument which dispenses the "solution." The translation equips Dr. Otto with a "syringe" which gives the dream more professional dignity than the German original aspires to. The German word is *Spritze*, which is, indeed, used for syringes, but has also the colloquial meaning of "squirter." It will be immediately obvious that a squirter is an instrument of many connotations; of these, the phallic-urinary one is most relevant, for the use of a dirty syringe makes Otto a "dirty squirter," or "a little squirt," not just a careless physician. As we shall see later, the recognition of this double meaning is absolutely necessary for a pursuit of the infantile meaning of the Irma Dream.

The only verbal trend, then, which can be accounted for in this English discussion of a dream reported and dreamed in German induces us to put beside the interpretation of the Irma Dream as a defense against the accusation of medical carelessness (the dispensation of a "solution") and of a possible intellectual error (the solution offered to Irma) the suggestion of a related sexual theme, namely, a protest against the implication of some kind of sexual (self) reproach.

In due time, we shall find the roots for this sexual theme in the dream's allusion to a childhood problem and then return to the dreamer's professional predicament.

We will then appreciate another double meaning in the dream, which seems to speak for the assumption that one link between the medical, the intellectual, and the sexual themes of the dream is that of "conception." The dream, so we hear, pictures a *birthday reception* in a great hall. "We receive" stands for the German *emplangen,* a word which can refer to conception *(Empfängnis)* as well as to reception *(Empfang).* The dreamer's worries concerning the growth of his family at this critical time of his professional life are clearly expressed in the letters to Fliess. At the same time, the typical association between biological *conception* and intellectual *concept formation* can be seen in the repeated reference to "germinating ideas."

V. INTERPERSONAL CONFIGURATIONS IN THE DREAM POPULATION

For a variety of reasons, it will be impossible to offer in this paper a separate discussion of each of the configurational variables listed in our "Outline." The medical implications of the sequence of *somatic* configurations must be ignored altogether, for I am not sufficiently familiar with the history of medicine to comprehend the anatomical, chemical, and procedural connotations which the body parts and the disease entities mentioned in the dream had in Freud's early days. The *sensory* configurations happen in this dream to fuse completely with the dreamer's *interpersonal* activities. Only once— at a decisive point in the middle of the dream—there occurs a kinesthetic sensation. Otherwise, at the beginning as well as at the end of his dream the dreamer is "all eyes."

Most outstanding in his visual field, so it seems, is, at one time, Irma's oral cavity, and, at another, the formula Trimethylamin, printed in heavy type. The infinite connotations of these two items of fascination become clearer as we see them in a variety of dimensions.

The Irma Dream, to me, suggests concentration on the dreamer's interaction with the people who populate his dream, and relate this interaction to changes in his mood and to changes in his experience of space and time. Chart 6.2 lists contemporaneous changes in the dream's *interpersonal, affective, spatial,* and *temporal* configurations.

Given a diagrammatic outline, we have the choice between a horizontal and a vertical analysis. If we try the vertical approach to the first column, we find the dreamer, immediately after having abandoned the receiving line, preoccupied with an intrusive and coercive kind of examination and investigation. He *takes* the patient aside, reproaches her, and then *looks* and *thinks;* finally he finds what his is looking for. Then his activities of examining fuse with those of the other doctors, until at the end he again *sees,* and this time in heavy type, a formula. It is obvious, then, that investigation, in isolation or co-operation, is the main theme of his manifest activities. The particular

Chart 6.2
Selected Manifest Configurations

	I Interpersonal		II Affective	III Spatial	IV Temporal
	The Dreamer	*The Population*			
1.	WE are receiving	WIFE receives with him	Festive mood?	Spacious hall	Present
2.	I take Irma aside / I reproach her	IRMA has not accepted the solution	Sense of urgency / Sense of reproach	Constricted to a "space for two"	Present / Past reaches into
3.	I look at her	Complains, feels choked	Startle		Present, painful
4.		Looks pale and puffy	Worry		Present, painful
5.	I think				Present, painful
6.	I take her to window / I look I think	Offers resistance	Impatience	Close to window	Present, painful
7.		THE MOUTH opens		Constricted to parts of persons	
8.	I find, I see organic symptoms		Horror		
9.	I quickly call Dr. M.	Dr. M. confirms symptoms	Dependence on authority		Present co-operative effort
10.		Looks pale, limps, is beardless			Present co-operative effort
11.		OTTO, LEOPOLD, join examination			Present co-operative effort
12.		LEOPOLD points to infiltration			Present co-operative effort

13. I "feel" infiltration	Fusion with patient. Pain?	
14. Dr. M. gives nonsensical reassurance	Sense of reassurance	Future brighter
15. WE know cause of infection	Conviction, faith	Future brighter
16. OTTO gave IRMA injection		Past guilt displaced
17.		
18. I see formula		
19. (judges)	Sense of righteousness	Present, satisfactory
20. THE SYRINGE was not clean		Past, guilt localized

mode of his approach impresses one as being *intrusive,* and thus somehow related to phallic.[3] If I call it a singularly male approach, I must refer to research in another field and to unfinished research in the field of dreams. Observations on sex differences in the play construction of adolescents (4) indicate that male and female play scenes are most significantly different in the treatment of the space provided, i.e., in the structuring of the play space by means of building blocks and in the spatial vectors of the play activities. I shall not review the criteria here, because without detailed discussion a comparison between the task, suggested by an experimenter, of constructing a scene with a selection of building material and toys, is too different from the inner task, commanded by one's wish to sleep, to represent a set of images on the dream screen. Nevertheless, it may be mentioned that Dr. Kenneth Colby, in following up the possibility of preparing an analogous kind of psychosexual index for the formal characteristics of dreams, has found temporal suddenness, spatial entering, the sensory activity of looking, concern with authority, and a sense of ineffectualilty, to be among the numerous items which are significantly more frequent in male dreams.[4] Dr. Colby has been able to isolate some such regularities in spite of the fact that the dream literature at the moment indulges in every possible license in the selection, description, and connotation of dream items. It seems to me that such studies might prove fruitful for research and technique, especially if undertaken in the frame of standardized inquiry into the variables of dream experience, as suggested in our inventory of configurations. It is possible that the dream has hardly begun to yield its potentialities for research in personality diagnosis.

But now back to the "interpersonal" configurations, from which we have isolated, so far, only the dreamer's activities. If we now turn to the behavior of the dream population, it is, of course, a strangely intrapersonal social life which we are referring to: one never knows whether to view the cast of puppets on the dreamer's stage as a microcosmic reflection of his present or past social reality or as a "projection" of different identity fragments of the dreamer himself, of different roles played by him at different times or in different situations. The dreamer, in experimenting with traumatic reality, takes the outer world into the inner one, as the child takes it into his toy world. More deeply regressed and, of course, immobilized, the dreamer makes an autoplastic experiment of an alloplastic problem: his inner world and all the past contained in it becomes a laboratory for "wishful" rearrangements. Freud has shown us how the Irma Dream repeats a failure and turns to an illusory solution: the dreamer takes childish revenge on Otto (*"he* did it") and on Dr. M. ("he is a castrate and a fool"), thus appeases his anxiety, and goes on sleeping for a better day. However, I would suggest that we take another look at the matter, this time using the horizontal approach to the diagrammatic outline, and correlating the dream's changing interpersonal patterns with the dreamer's changing mood and perspective.

The dreamer at first is a *part of a twosome,* his wife and himself, or maybe a family group, *vis-à-vis* a number of guests. "We receive," under festive circumstances in an opulent spatial setting. Immediately upon Irma's appearance, however, this twosomeness, this acting in concert, abruptly vanishes. The wife, or the family, is not mentioned again. The dreamer is suddenly *alone* with his worries, *vis-à-vis* a complaining patient. The visual field shrinks rapidly from the large hall to the vicinity of a window and finally to Irma's oral aperture; the festive present is replaced by a concern over past mistakes. The dreamer becomes active in a breathless way: he looks at the patient and thinks, he looks into her throat and thinks, and he finds what he sees ominous. He is startled, worried, and impatient, but behaves in a punitive fashion. *Irma,* in all this, remains a complaining and resistive vis-à-vis, and finally seems to become a mere part of herself: *"The mouth* opens." From then on, even when discussed and percussed, she neither acts nor speaks—a good patient (for, unlike the proverbial Indian, a good patient is a half-dead patient, just alive enough to make his organs and complexes accessible to isolation and probing inspection). Seeing that something is wrong, the dreamer calls *Dr. M.* urgently. He thus establishes a *new twosome:* he and the "authority" who graciously (if foolishly) confirms him. This twosome is immediately expanded to include a professional group of younger colleagues, Dr. Otto and Dr. Leopold. Altogether they now form a small community: *"We know . . . ."*

At this point something happens which is lost in the double meaning of the manifest words, in the German original as well as in translation. When the dreamer says that he can *"feel"* the infiltrated portion of skin on the (patient's) left shoulder, he means to convey (as Freud states in his associations) that he can *feel this on his own body:* one of those fusions of a dreamer with a member of his dream population which is always of central importance, if not the very center and nodal point of a dream. The dreamer, while becoming again a doctor in the consenting community of doctors, thus at the same time turns into his and their *patient.* Dr. M. then says some foolish, nonsensical phrases, in the course of which it becomes clear that it had not been the dreamer who had harmed Irma, not at all. It is clear with the immediacy of a conviction that Dr. Otto who had infiltrated her. The dreams ends, then, with Otto's professional and moral isolation. The dreamer (first a lonely investigator, then a patient, now a *joiner*) seems quite righteous in his indignation. The syringe was not clean: who would do such a thing? "Immediate" conviction, in harmony with authority, has clarified the past and unburdened the present.

The study of dreams and of culture patterns and ritualizations reveals parallels between interpersonal dream configurations and religious rites of conversion or confirmation. Let me repeat and underscore the points which suggests such an analogy. As the isolated and "guilty" dreamer quickly calls Dr. M., he obviously *appeals for help from higher authority*. This call for help is answered not only by Dr. M., but also by Dr. Leopold and Dr. Otto, who now, together with the dreamer, form a group with a *common conviction* ("we know"). As this happens, and the examination proceeds, the dreamer suddenly feels as if he were the sufferer and the examined, i.e., he, the doctor and man, fuses with the image of the *patient* and *woman*. This, of course, amounts to a surrender analogous to a spiritual conversion and a concomitant sacrifice of the male role. By implication, it is now *his* mouth that is open for inspection (passivity, inspiration, communion). But there is a *reward* for this. Dr. M. (symbolically castrated like a priest) recites with great assurance something that makes *no logical sense* (Latin, Hebrew?) but seems to be *magically effective* in that it awakes in the dreamer the *immediate conviction* (faith) that the causality in the case is now understood (magic, divine will). This common conviction restores in the dream a "We-ness" (congregation) which had been lost (in its worldly, heterosexual form) at the very beginning when the dreamer's wife and the festive guests had disappeared. At the same time it restores to the dreamer a *belongingness* (brotherhood) to a hierarchic group *dominated by an authority* in whom *he believes implicitly*. He immediately benefits from his newly won *state of grace:* he now has sanction for *driving the devil* into Dr. O. With the *righteous indignation* which is the believer's reward and weapon, he can now make *"an unclean one"* (a disbeliever) out of his erstwhile accuser.

Does this interpretation of the Irma Dream as a dream of conversion or confirmation contradict that given by Freud, who believed he had revenged himself on the professional world which did not trust him? Freud, we remember, felt that the dream disparaged Dr. M., robbing him of authority, vigor, and wholeness, by making him say silly things, look pale, limp, and be beardless. All of this, then, would belie as utterly hypocritical the dreamer's urgent call for help, his worry over the older man's health,[5] and his "immediate" knowledge in concert with his colleagues. This wish (to take revenge on his accusers and to vindicate his own strivings) stands, of course, as the dream's stimulus. Without such an id wish and all of its infantile energy, a dream would not exist; without a corresponding appeasement of the superego, it would have no form; but, we must add, without appropriate ego measures, the dream would not work. On closer inspection, then, the radical differentiation between a manifest and a latent dream, while necessary as a means of localizing what is "most latent," diffuses in a complicated continuum of more manifest and more latent items which are sometimes to be found by a radical disposal of the manifest configuration, sometimes by a careful scrutiny of it.

Such double approach seems to make it appear that the ego's over-all attitude in dream life is that of a withdrawal of its outposts in physical and social reality. The sleeping ego not only sacrifices sense perception and motility, i.e., its reactivity to physical reality; it also renounces those claims on individuation, independent action, and responsibility which may keep the tired sleeper senselessly awake. The healthy ego, in dreams, quietly retraces its steps; it does not really sacrifice its assets, it merely pretends that, for the moment, they are not needed.[6]

I shall attempt to indicate this systematic retracing of ego steps in a dream by pointing to the *psychosocial criteria* which I have postulated elsewhere (2) (3) for the ego's successive graduations from the main crises of the human life cycle. To proceed, I must list these criteria without being able to enlarge upon them here. I may remind the reader, however, that psychoanalytic theory is heavily weighed in favor of insights which make dysfunction plausible and explain why human beings, at certain critical stages, should fail, and fail in specific ways. It is expected that this theory will eventually make adequate or superior human functioning dynamically plausible as well (12,13). In the meantime, I have found it necessary to postulate tentative criteria for the ego's relative success in synthesizing, at critical stages, the timetable of the organism, and the representative demands and opportunities which societies universally, if in different ways, provide for these stages. At the completion of infancy, then, the criterium for the budding ego's initial and fundamental success can be said to be a Sense of *Basic Trust* which, from then on, promises to outbalance the lastingly latent Sense of *Basic Mistrust*. Such trust permits, during early childhood, the critical development of a Sense of *Autonomy* which henceforth must hold its own against the Senses of *Shame* and *Doubt*, while at the end of the oedipal phase, an unbroken Sense of *Initiative* (invigorated by play) must begin to outdo a more specific Sense of *Guilt*. During the "school age," a rudimentary Sense of *Workmanship* and Work-and-Play companionship develops which, from then on, must help to outbalance the Sense of *Inferiority*. Puberty and Adolescence help the young person sooner or later to consummate the selective gains of childhood in an accruing sense of *Ego Identity* which prevents the lasting dominance of a then threatening Sense of *Role Diffusion*. Young adulthood is specific for a structuring of the Sense of *Intimacy* or else exposes the individual to a dominant Sense of *Isolation*. Real intimacy, in turn, leads to wishes and concerns to be taken care of by an adult Sense of *Generativity* (genes, generate, generation) without which there remains the threat of a lasting Sense of *Stagnation*. Finally, a Sense of *Integrity* gathers and defends whatever gains, accomplishments, and vistas were accessible in the individual's life time; it alone resists the alternate outcome of a Sense of vague but over-all *Disgust*.

This, of course, is a mere list of terms which point to an area still in want of theoretical formulation. This area encompasses the kind and sequence of certain universal psychosocial crises which are defined, on the one hand, by the potentialities and limitations of developmental stages (physical, psycho-sexual, ego) and, on the other, by the universal punctuation of human life by successive and systematic "life tasks" within social and cultural institutions.

The Irma Dream places its dreamer squarely into the crisis of middle age. It deals most of all with matters of *Generativity*, although it extends into the neighboring problems of Intimacy and of Integrity. To the adult implications of this crisis we shall return later. Here we are concerned with the dream's peculiar "regression." The doctor's growing sense of harboring a discovery apt to *generate new thought* (at a time when his wife harbored an addition to the *younger generation*) had been challenged the night before by the impact of a doubting word on his tired mind: a doubting word which was immediately echoed by self-doubts and self-reproaches from many close and distant corners of his life. At a *birthday* party, then, the dreamer suddenly finds himself *isolated*. At first, he vigorously and angrily asserts his most experienced use of one of the ego's basic functions: he examines, localizes, diagnoses. Such *investigation in isolation* is, as we shall see later on, one of the cornerstones of this dreamer's sense of *Inner Identity*. What he succeeds in focusing on, however, is a terrifying discovery which stares at him like the head of the Medusa. At this point, one feels, a dreamer with less flexible defenses might have awakened in terror over what he saw in the gaping cavity. Our dreamer's ego, however, makes the compromise of abandoning its positions and yet maintaining them. Abandoning independent observation the dreamer gives in to a *diffusion of roles:* is he doctor or patient, leader or follower, benefactor or culprit, seer or fumbler? He admits to the possibility of his *inferiority in workmanship* and urgently appeals to "teacher" and to "teacher's pets." He thus forfeits his right to vigorous *male initiative* and guiltily surrenders to the inverted solution of the oedipal conflict, for a fleeting moment even becoming the feminine object for the superior males' inspection and percussion; and he denies his sense of stubborn *autonomy,* letting *doubt* lead him back to the earliest infantile security: childlike *trust.*

In his interpretation of the Irma Dream, Freud found this trust most suspect. He reveals it as a hypocritical attempt to hide the dream's true meaning, namely, revenge on those who doubted the dreamer as a worker. Our review suggests that this trust may be overdetermined. The ego, by letting itself return to sources of security once available to the dreamer as a child, may help him to dream well and to sustain sleep, while promising revengeful comeback in a new day, when "divine mistrust" will lead to further discoveries.

VI. ACUTE, REPETITIVE, AND INFANTILE CONFLICTS

I have now used the bulk of this paper for the demonstration of a few items of analysis which usually do not get a fair share in our routine interpretations: the systematic configurational analysis of the manifest dream and the manifest social patterns of the dream population. The designation of other, more familiar, matters will occupy less space.

Our "Outline of Dream Analysis" suggests next a survey of the various segments of the life cycle which appear in the dream material in latent form, either as acutely relevant or as reactivated by associative stimulation. This survey leads us, then, back along the path of time.

OUTLINE OF DREAM ANALYSIS

III. *Analysis of Latent Dream Material:*

Acute sleep-disturbing stimulus
Delayed stimulus (day residue)

Acute life conflicts
Dominant transference conflict
Repetitive life conflicts
Associated basic childhood conflicts
Common denominators
   "Wishes," drives, needs
   methods of defense, denial, and distortion

The most immediately present, the *acute dream stimulus* of the Irma Dream, may well have been triggered by discomfort caused by swellings in nose and throat which, at the time, seem to have bothered the usually sound sleeper: the prominence in the dream of Irma's oral cavity could be conceived as being codetermined by such a stimulus, which may also have provided one of the determinants for the latent but all-pervading presence in the dream of Dr. Fliess, the otolaryngologist. Acute stimulus and *day residue* (obviously the meeting with Dr. Otto) are associated in the idea as to whether the dreamer's dispensation of solutions may have harmed him or others. The *acute life conflicts* of a professional and personal nature have been indicated in some measure; as we have seen, they meet with the acute stimulus and the day residue in the further idea that the dreamer may be reproachable as a sexual being as well.

Let us now turn to matters of childhood. Before quoting, from *The Interpretation of Dreams*, a few childhood memories, the relevance of which for the Irma Dream are beyond reasonable doubt, I should like to establish a more speculative link between the dream's interpersonal pattern and a particular aspect of Freud's childhood, which has been revealed only recently.

I must admit that on first acquaintance with regressive "joining" in the Irma Dream, the suggestion of a religious interpretation persisted. Freud, of course, had grown up as a member of a Jewish community in a predominantly Catholic culture: could the overall milieu of the Catholic environment have impressed itself on this child of a minority? Or was the described configuration representative of a basic human proclivity which had found collective expression in religious rituals, Jewish, Catholic, or otherwise?

It may be well to point out here that the therapeutic interpretation of such patterns is, incidentally, as violently resisted as in any id content (5). Unless we are deliberate and conscious believers in a dogma or declared adherents to other collective patterns, we dislike being shown to be at the mercy of unconscious religious, political, ethnic patterns as much as we abhor sudden insight into our dependence on unconscious impulses. One might even say that today when, thanks to Freud, the origins in instinctual life of our impulses have been documented and classified so much more inescapably and coherently than impulses rooted in group allegiances, a certain clannish and individualist pride has attached itself to the free admission of instinctual patterns, while the simple fact of the dependence on social structures of our physical and emotional existence and well-being seems to be experienced as a reflection on some kind of intellectual autonomy. Toward the end of the analysis of a young professional man who stood before an important change in status, a kind of graduation, a dream occurred in which he experienced himself lying on the analytic couch, while I was sawing a round hole in the top of his head. The patient, at first, was willing to accept almost any other interpretation, such as castration, homosexual attack (from behind), continued analysis (opening a skull flap), and insanity (lobotomy), all of which were indeed relevant, rather than to recognize this dream as an over-all graduation dream with a reference to the tonsure administered by bishops to young Catholic priests at the time of their admission to clerical standing. A probable contact with Catholicism in impressionable childhood was typically denied with a vehemence which is matched only by the bitter determination with which patients sometimes disclaim that they, say, could possibly have observed the anatomic difference between the sexes at any time in their childhood, or could possibly have been told even by a single person on a single occasion that castration would be the result of masturbation. Thus, infantile wishes to belong to and to believe in organizations providing for collective reassurance against individual anxiety, in our intellectuals, easily join other repressed childhood temptations—and force their way into dreams. But, of course, we must be prepared to look for them in order to see them; in which case the analysis of defenses gains a new dimension, and the study of social institutions a new approach.

The publication of Freud's letters to Fliess makes it unnecessary to doubt any further the possible origin of such a religious pattern in Freud's early life. Freud (9) informs Fliess that during a most critical period in his childhood, namely, when he, the "first-born son of a young mother," had to accept the arrival of a little brother who died in infancy and then the advent of a sister, an old and superstitiously religious Czech woman used to take him around to various churches in his home town. He obviously was so impressed with such events that when he came home, he (in the words of his mother) preached to his family and showed them how God carries on *("wie Gott macht")*: this apparently referred to the priest, whom he took to be God. That his mother, after the death of the little brother, gave birth to six girls in succession, and that the Irma Dream was dreamed during his wife's sixth pregnancy, may well be a significant analogy. At any rate, what the old woman and her churches meant to him is clearly revealed in his letters to Fliess, to whom he confessed that, if he could only find a solution of his "hysteria," he would be eternally grateful to the memory of the old woman who early in his life "gave me the means to live and to go on living." This old woman, then, restored to the little Freud, in a difficult period, a measure of a sense of trust, a fact which makes it reasonably probable that some of the impressive rituals which she took him to see, and that some of their implications as explained by her, appear in the Irma Dream, at a time when his wife was again expecting and when he himself stood before a major emancipation as well as the "germination" of a major idea. If this is so, then we may conclude that rituals impress children in intangible ways and must be sought among the covert childhood material, along with the data which have become more familiar to us because we have learned to look for them.

For a basic childhood conflict more certainly reflected in the Irma Dream, we turn to one of the first childhood memories reported by Freud in *The Interpretation of Dreams* (6, p.274):

Then, when I was seven or eight years of age another domestic incident occurred which I remember very well. One evening before going to bed I had disregarded the dictates of discretion, and had satisfied my needs in my parents' bedroom, and in their presence. Reprimanding me for this delinquency, my father remarked: "That boy will never amount to anything." This must have been a terrible affront to my ambition, but allusions to this scene recur again and again in my dreams, and are constantly coupled with enumerations of my accomplishments and successes, as though I wanted to say: "You see, I have amounted to something after all."

This memory calls first of all for an ethnographic clarification, which I hope will not make me appear to be an excessive culturalist. That a seven-year old boy "satisfies his needs in his parents' bedroom" has sinister implications, unless one hastens to remember the technological item of the chamber pot. The boy's delinquence, then, probably consisted of the use of one of his parents' chamber pots instead of his own. Maybe he wanted to show that he was a "big squirt," and instead was called a small one. This crime, as well as the punishment by derisive shaming, and, most of all, the imperishable memory of the event, all point to a milieu in which such character weakness as the act of untimely and immodest urination becomes most forcefully associated with the question of the boy's chances not only of ever becoming a man, but also of amounting to something, of becoming a "somebody," of *keeping what he promises*. In thus hitting the little exhibitionist in his weakest spot, the father not only followed the dictates of a certain culture area which tended to make youngsters defiantly ambitious by challenging them at significant times with the statement that they do not amount to much and with the prediction that they never will. We know the importance of urinary experience for the development of rivalry and ambition, and therefore recognize the memory as doubly significant. It thus becomes clearer than ever why Dr. Otto had to take over the severe designation of a dirty little squirt. After all, he was the one who had implied that Freud had promised too much when he said he would cure Irma and unveil the riddle of hysteria. A youngster who shows that he will amount to something is "promising"; the Germans say he is *vielversprechend,* i.e., he promises much. If his father told little Freud, under the embarrassing circumstance of the mother's presence in the parental bedroom, that he would never amount to anything, i.e., that the intelligent boy did not hold what he promised—is it not suggestive to assume that the tired doctor of the night before the dream had gone to bed with a bitter joke in his preconscious mind: yes, maybe I did promise too much when I said I could cure hysteria; maybe my father was right after all, I do not hold what I promised; look at all the other situations when I put dangerous or dirty "solutions" in the wrong places. The infantile material thus adds to the inventory of the doctor's and the man's carelessness in the use of "solutions" its infantile model, namely, exhibitionistic urination in the parents' bedroom: an incestuous model of all these associated dispensations of fluid.

But it seems to me that this memory could be the starting point for another consideration. It suggests not only an individual trauma, but also a pattern of child training according to which fathers, at significant moments, play on the sexual inferiority feelings and the smoldering oedipal hate of their little boys by challenging them in a severe if not viciously earnest manner, humiliating them before others, and especially before the mother. It would, of course, be difficult to ascertain that such an event is of a typical character in a given area or typical for a given father; but I do believe that such a "method" of arousing and testing a son's ambition (in some cases regularly, in some on special occasions) was well developed in the German cultural orbit which included German Austria and its German-speaking Jews. This matter, how-

168 ERIK HOMBURGER ERIKSON

ever, could be properly accounted for only in a context in which the relation of such child-training patterns could be demonstrated in their relation to the whole conscious and unconscious system of child training and in their full reciprocity with historical and economic forces. And, incidentally, only in such a context and in connection with a discussion of Freud's place in the evolution of civilized conscience could Freud's inclination to discard teachers as well as students (as he discards Dr. O. in his dream after having felt discarded himself) be evaluated. Here we are primarily concerned with certain consequences which such a cultural milieu may have had for the sons' basic attitudes: the inner humiliation, forever associated with the internalized father image, offered a choice between complete submission, a readiness to do one's duty unquestioningly in the face of changing leaders and principles (without ever overcoming a deep self-contempt and a lasting doubt in the leader); and, on the other hand, sustained rebellion and an attempt to replace the personal father with an ideological principle, a cause, or, as Freud puts it, an "inner tyrant." [7]

Another childhood memory, however, may illuminate the personal side of this problem which we know already from Freud's interpretation of the Irma Dream as one of a vengeful comeback.

I have already said that my warm friendships as well as my enmities with persons of my own age go back to my childish relations to my nephew, who was a year older than I. In these he had the upper hand, and I early learned how to defend myself; we lived together, were inseparable, and loved one another, but at times, as the statements of older persons testify, we used to squabble and accuse one another. In a certain sense, all my friends are incarnations of this first figure; they are all *revenants*. My nephew himself returned when a young man, and then we were like Caesar and Brutus. An intimate friend and a hated enemy have always been indispensable to my emotional life; I have always been able to create them anew, and not infrequently my childish idea has been so closely approached that friend and enemy have coincided in the same person; but not simultaneously, of course, nor in constant alternation, as was the case in my early childhood [6, p. 451].

This memory serves especially well as an illustration of what, in our "Outline," we call *repetitive conflicts*, i.e., typical conflicts which punctuate the dreamer's life all the way from the infantile to the acute and to the outstanding transference conflicts. The fact that we were once small we never overcome. In going to sleep we learn deliberately to return to the most trustful beginning, not without being startled, on the way, by those memories which seem to substantiate most tellingly whatever negative basic attitude (a sense of mistrust, shame, doubt, guilt, etc.) was aroused by the tiring and discouraging events of the previous day. Yet this does not prevent some, in the restored day, from pursuing, on the basis of their very infantile challenges, their own unique kind of accomplishment.

VII. TRANSFERENCE IN THE IRMA DREAM

Among the life situations in our inventory, there remains one which, at first, would seem singularly irrelevant for the Irma Dream: I refer to the "current transference conflict." If anything, this dream, dreamed by a doctor about a patient, would promise to contain references to countertransference, i.e., the therapist's unconscious difficulties arising out of the fact that the patient may occupy a strategic position on the chessboard of his fate. Freud tells us something of how Irma came to usurp such a role, and the intimate *du* in the dream betrays the fact that the patient was close to (or associated with somebody close to) the doctor's family either by blood relationship or intimate friendship. Whatever her personal identity, Irma obviously had become some kind of key figure in the dreamer's professional life. The doctor was in the process of learning the fact that this made her, by definition, a poor therapeutic risk for him.

But one may well think of another kind of "countertransference" in the Irma Dream. The dreamer's activities (and those of his colleagues) are all professional and directed toward a woman. But they are a researcher's approaches: the dreamer takes aside, throws light on the matter, looks, localizes, thinks, finds. May it not be that it was the Mystery of the Dream which itself was the anxious prize of his persistence?

Freud reports later on in *The Interpretation of Dreams* (6) that one night, having exhausted himself in the effort of finding an explanation for dreams of "nakedness" and of "being glued to the spot," he dreamed that he was jumping light-footedly up a stairway in a disarray of clothes. No doubt, then, Freud's dreams during those years of intensive dream study carry the special weight of having to reveal something while being dreamed. That this involvement does not necessarily interfere with the genuineness of his dreams can be seen from the very fact, demonstrated here, that Freud's dreams and associations (even if fragmentary and, at times, altered) do not cease to be fresh and almost infinitely enlightening in regard to points which he, at the time, did not deliberately focus upon.

In our unconscious and mythological imagery, tasks and ideals are women, often big and forbidding ones, to judge by the statues we erect for Wisdom,

Industry, Truth, Justice, and other great ladies. A hint that the Dream as a mystery had become to our dreamer one of those forbidding maternal figures which smile only on the most favored among young heroes (and yield, of course, only to sublimated, to "clean" approach) can, maybe, be spotted in a footnote where Freud writes, "If I were to continue the comparison of the three women I should go far afield. Every dream has at least one point at which it is unfathomable; *a central point,* as it were, connecting it with the unknown." The English translation's "central point," however, is in the original German text a *Nabel—*" a navel." This statement, in such intimate proximity to allusions concerning the resistance of Victorian ladies (including the dreamer's wife, now pregnant) to being undressed and examined, suggests an element of transference to the Dream Problem as such: the Dream, then, is just another haughty woman, wrapped in too many mystifying covers and "putting on airs" like a Victorian lady. Freud's letter to Fliess spoke of an "unveiling" of the mystery of the dream, which was accomplished when he subjected the Irma Dream to an "exhaustive analysis." In the last analysis, then, the dream itself may be a mother image; she is the one, as the Bible would say, to be "known."

Special transferences to one's dream life are, incidentally, not exclusively reserved for the author of *The Interpretation of Dreams.* In this context I can give only a few hints on this subject. Once a dreamer knows that dreams "mean" something (and that, incidentally, they mean a lot to his analyst), an ulterior *wish to dream* forces its way into the *wish to sleep by way of dreaming.* That this is a strong motivation in dream life can be seen from the fact that different schools of dynamic psychology and, in fact, different analysts manage to provoke systematically different manifest dreams, obviously dreamed to please and to impress the respective analysts; and that members of primitive societies apparently manage to produce "culture pattern dreams," which genuinely impress the dreamer and convince the official dream interpreters. Our discussion of the style of the Irma Dream has, I think, indicated how we would deal with this phenomenon of a variety of dream styles: we would relate them to the respective cultural, interpersonal, and personality patterns, and correlate all of these with the latent dream. But as to the dreamer's transference to his dream life, one may go further: in spurts of especially generous dream production, a patient often appeals to an inner transference figure, a permissive and generous mother, who understands the patient better than the analyst does and fulfills wishes instead of interpreting them. Dreams, then, can become a patient's secret love life and may elude the grasp of the analyst by becoming too rich, too deep, to unfathomable. Where this is not understood, the analyst is left with the choice of ignoring this rival, the patient's dream life, or of endorsing its wish fulfillment by giving exclusive attention to it, or of trying to overtake it with clever interpretations. The technical discussion of this dilemma we must postpone. In the meantime, it is clear that the first dream analyst stands in a unique relationship to the Dream as a "Promised Land."

This, however, is not the end of the transference possibilities in the Irma Dream. In the letters to Fliess, the impression is amply substantiated that Freud, pregnant with inner experiences which would soon force upon him the unspeakable isolation of the first self-analysis in history—and this at a time when his father's death seemed not far off—had undertaken to find in Fliess, at all cost, a superior friend, an object for idealization, and later an (if ever so unaware and reluctant) sounding board for his self-analysis. What this deliberate "transference" consisted of will undoubtedly, in due time, be fully recorded and analyzed. Because of the interrelation of creative and neurotic patterns and of personal and historical trends in this relationship, it can be said that few jobs in the history of human thought call for more information, competence, and wisdom. But it furthers an understanding of the Irma Dream to note that only once in all the published correspondence does Freud address Fliess with the lone word *Liebster* ("Dearest"): in the first letter following the Irma Dream (August 8, 1895). This singular appeal to an intellectual friend (and a German one at that) correlates well with the prominence which the formula for Trimethylamin (a formula related to Fliess' researches in bisexuality) has in the dream, both by dint of its heavy type and by its prominent place in the play of configurations: for it signifies the dreamer's return to the act of independent observation—"I see" again.

The Irma Dream, then, in addition to being a dream of a medical examination and treatment and of a sexual investigation, anticipates Freud's self-inspection and with it inspection by a vastly aggrandized Fliess. We must try to visualize the historical fact that here a man divines an entirely new instrument with unknown qualities for an entirely new focus of investigation, a focus of which only one thing was clear: all men before him, great and small, had tried with every means of cunning and cruelty to avoid it. To overcome mankind's resistance, the dreamer had to learn to become his own patient and subject of investigation; to deliver free associations to himself; to unveil horrible insights to himself; to identify himself with himself in the double roles of observer and observed. That this, in view of the strong maleness of scientific approach cultivated by the bearded savants of his day and age (and represented in the dreamer's vigorous attempts at isolating and localizing Irma's embarrassing affliction), constituted an unfathomable division within the observer's self, a division of vague "feminine yielding" and persistent masculine precision: this, I feel, is one of the central meanings of the Irma Dream. Nietzsche's statement that a friend is a lifesaver who keeps us afloat when the struggling parts of our divided self threaten to pull one another to the bottom was never more applicable; and where, in such a situation, no friend of sufficient superiority is available, he must be invented. Fliess, to a degree, was such an invention. He was the recipient of a creative as well as a therapeutic transference.

The "mouth which opens wide," then, is not the oral cavity of a patient and not only a symbol of a woman's procreative inside, which arouses horror and envy because it can produce new "formations." It is also the investigator's oral cavity, opened to medical inspection; and it may well represent, at the same time, the dreamer's unconscious, soon to offer insights never faced before to an idealized friend with the hope that (here we must read the whole dream backwards) *wir empfangen:* we receive, we conceive, we celebrate a birthday. That a man many incorporate another man's spirit, that a man may conceive from another man, and that a man may be reborn from another, these ideas are the content of many fantasies and rituals which mark significant moments of male initiation, conversion, and inspiration (11); and every act of creation, at one stage, implies the unconscious fantasy of inspiration by a fertilizing agent of a more or less defied, more or less personified mind or spirit. This "feminine" aspect of creation causes tumultuous confusion not only because of man's intrinsic abhorrence of femininity but also because of the conflict (in really gifted individuals) of this feminine fantasy with an equally strong "masculine" endowment which is to give a new and original form to that which has been conceived and carried to fruition. All in all, the creative individual's's typical cycle of moods and attitudes, which overlaps with neurotic mood swings (without ever coinciding with them completely), probably permits him, at the height of consummation, to identify with father, mother, and newborn child all in one; to represent, in equal measure, his father's potency, his mother's fertility, and his own reborn ideal identity. It is obvious, then, why mankind participates, with pity and terror, with ambivalent admiration and ill-concealed abhorrence, in the hybris of creative men, and why such hybris, in these men themselves, can call forth all the sinister forces of infantile conflict.

VIII. CONCLUSION

If the dreamer of the Irma Dream were the patient of continuous seminar, several evenings of research work would now be cut out for us. We would analyze the continuation of the patient's dream life to see how his inventory of dream variations and how his developing transference would gradually permit a dynamic reconstruction of the kind which, in its most ambitious version, forms point VI of our "Outline."

IV. *Reconstruction*

Life cycle
  present phase
  corresponding infantile phase
  defect, accident, or affliction
  psychosexual fixation
  psychosexual arrest
Social process: collective identity
  ideal prototypes
  evil prototypes
  opportunities and barriers
Ego identity and lifeplan
  mechanisms of defense
  mechanisms of integration

In the case of the Irma Dream, both the material and the motivation which would permit us to aspire to relative completeness of analysis are missing. I shall, therefore, in conclusion, select a few items which will at least indicate our intentions of viewing a dream as an event reflecting a critical stage of the dreamer's life cycle.

As pointed out, the Irma Dream and its associations clearly reflect a crisis in the life of a creative man of middle age. As the psychosocial criterion of a successful ego synthesis at that age I have named a Sense of Generativity. This unpretty term, incidentally, is intended to convey a more basic and more biological meaning than such terms as creativity and productivity do. For the inventory of significant object relations must, at this stage, give account of the presence or absence of a drive to create and secure personal children—a matter much too frequently considered merely an extension, if not an impediment, of genitality. Yet any term as specific as "parental sense" would not sufficiently indicate the plasticity of this drive, which may genuinely include works, plans, and ideas generated either in direct connection with the task of securing the life of the next generation or in wider anticipation of generations to come. The Irma Dream, then, reflects the intrinsic conflict between the partners and objects of the dreamer's intimate and generative drives, namely, wife, children, friends, patients, ideas: they all vie for the maturing man's energy and commitment, and yet none of them could be spared without some sense of stagnation. It may be significant that Freud's correspondence with Fliess, which initiates an *intellectual intimacy* of surprising passion, had begun a few months after Freud's marriage: there are rich references to the advent and the development of the younger generation in both families, and, with it, much complaint over the conflicting demands of family, work, and friendship. Finally, there is, in the material of the Irma Dream, an indication of the problem which follows that of the generative conflict, namely, that of a gradually forming *Sense of Integrity* which represents man's obligation to the most mature meaning available to him, even if this should presage discomfort to himself, deprivation to his mate and offspring, and the loss of friends, all of which must be envisaged and endured in order not to be exposed to a final Sense of Disgust and of Despair. The fact that we are dealing here with a man of genius during the loneliest crisis of his work productivity should not blind us to the fact that analogous crises face all men, if only in their attachments and allegiances to trends and ideas represented to them by strong leaders and by coercive institutions. Yet again, such a crisis is raised to special significance in the lives of those who are especially well endowed or especially favored with opportunities: for the "most mature meaning available to them" allows for deeper conflict, greater accomplishment, and more desperate failure.

A discernible relationship between the dreamer's acute life problem and the problems left over from corresponding infantile phases has been indicated in the previous section. Here I shall select two further items as topics for a final brief discussion: psychosexual fixation and arrest; collective identity and ego identity.

In our general clinical usage we employ the term fixation alternately for that infantile stage in which an individual received the relatively greatest amount of gratification and to which, therefore, his secret wishes persistently return and for that infantile stage of development beyond which he is unable to proceed because it marked an end or determined slow-up of his psychosexual maturation. I would prefer to call the latter the point of *arrest*, for it seems to me that an individual's psychosexual character and proneness for disturbances depends not so much on the point of fixation as on the *range* between the point of fixation and the point of arrest, and on the *quality* of their interplay. It stands to reason that a fixation on the oral stage, for example, endangers an individual most if he is also arrested close to this stage, while a relative oral fixation can become an asset if the individual advances a considerable length along the path of psychosexual maturation, making the most of each step and cultivating (on the very basis of a favorable balance of basic trust over basic mistrust as derived from an intensive oral stage) a certain capacity to experience and to exploit subsequent crises to the full. Another individual with a similar range but a different quality of progression may, for the longest time, show no specific fixation on orality; he may indicate a reasonable balance of a moderate amount of all the varieties of psychosexual energy—and yet, the quality of the whole ensemble may be so brittle that a major shock can make it tumble to the ground, whereupon an "oral" fixation may be blamed for it. Thus, one could review our nosology from the point of view of the particular field circumscribed by the points of fixation and arrest and of the properties of that field. At any rate, in a dream, and especially in a series of dreams, the patient's "going back and forth" between the two points can be determined rather clearly. Our outline, therefore, differentiates between a point of psychosexual fixation and one of psychosexual arrest.

The Irma Dream demonstrates a great range and power of pregenital themes. From an initial position of phallic-urethral and voyeuristic hybris, the dreamer regresses to an oral-tacutal position (Irma's exposed mouth and the kinesthetic sensation of suffering through her) and to an anal-sadistic one (the elimination of the poison from the body, the repudiation of Dr. Otto). As for the dreamer of the Irma Dream (or any individual not clearly circumscribed by neurotic stereotypy), we should probably postpone any over-all classification until we have thought through the suggestions contained in Freud's first formulation of "libidinal types." In postulating that the ideal type of man is, each in fair measure, narcisstic *and* compulsive *and* erotic, he opened the way to a new consideration of normality, and thus of abnormality. His formulation does not (as some of our day do) focus on single fixations which may upset a unilinear psychosexual progression of a low over-all tonus, but allows for strong conflicts on each level, solved by the maturing ego adequate to each stage, and finally integrated in a vigorous kind of equilibrium.

I shall conclude with the discussion of ego identity (2, 3, 5). This discussion must, again, be restricted to the Irma Dream and to the typical problems which it may illustrate. The concept of identity refers to an over-all attitude (a *Grundhaltung*) which the young person at the end of adolescence must derive from his ego's successful synthesis of postadolescent drive organization and social realities. A sense of identity implies that one experiences an over-all sameness and continuity extending from the personal past (now internalized in introjects and identifications) into a tangible future; and from the community's past (now existing in traditions and institutions sustaining a communal sense of identity) into foreseeable or imaginable realities of work accomplishment and role satisfaction. I had started to use the terms ego identity and group identity for this vital aspect of personality development before I (as far as I know) became aware of Freud's having used the term *innere Identität* in a peripheral pronouncement and yet in regard to a central matter in his life.

In 1926, Freud sent to the members of a Jewish lodge a speech (8) in which he discussed his relationship to Jewry and discarded religious faith and national pride as "the prime bonds." He then pointed, in poetic rather than scientific terms, to an unconscious as well as a conscious attraction in Jewry: powerful, unverbalized emotions *(viele dunkle Gefühlsmächte)*, and the clear consciousness of an inner identity *(die klare Bewusstheit der inneren Identität)*. Finally, he mentioned two traits which he felt he owed his Jewish ancestry: freedom from prejudices which narrow the use of the intellect, and the readiness to live in opposition. This formulation sheds an interesting light on the fact that in the Irma Dream the dreamer can be shown both to belittle and yet also temporarily to adopt membership in the "compact" majority of his dream population. Freud's remarks also give added background to what we recognized as the dreamer's vigorous and anxious preoccupation, namely, the use of *incisive intelligence* in *courageous isolation,* the strong urge to investigate, a unveil, and to recognize: the Irma Dream strongly represents this ego-syntonic part of what I would consider a cornerstone of the dreamer's identity, even as it defends the dreamer against the infantile guilt associated with such ambition.

The dream and its associations also point to at least one "evil prototype" —the prototype of all that which must be excluded from one's identity: here it is, in the words of its American counterpart, the "dirty little squirt," or, more severely, the "unclean one" who has forfeited his claim to "promising" intelligence.

Much has been said about Freud's ambitiousness; friends have been astonished and adversaries amused to find that he disavowed it. To be the primus, the best student of his class through his school years, seemed as natural to him ("the first-born son of a young mother") as to write the *Gesammelten Schriften*. The explanation is, of course, that he was not "ambitious" in the sense of *ehr-geizig:* he did not hunger for medals and titles for their own sakes. The ambition of uniqueness in intellectual accomplishment, on the other hand, was not only ego-syntonic, it was ethno-syntonic, almost an obligation to his people. The tradition of his people, then, and a firm inner identity provided the continuity which helped Freud to overcome the neurotic dangers to his accomplishment which are suggested in the Irma Dream, namely, the guilt over the wish to be the one-and-only who would overcome the derisive fathers and unveil the mystery. It helped him in the necessity to abandon well-established methods of sober investigation (invented to find out a few things exactly and safely to overlook the rest) for a method of self-revelation apt to open the floodgates of the unconscious. If we seem to recognize in this dream something of a puberty rite, we probably touch on a matter mentioned more than once in Freud's letters, namely, the "repeated adolescence" of creative minds, which he ascribed to himself as well as to Fliess.

In our terms, the creative mind seems to face repeatedly what most men, once and for all, settle in late adolescence. The "normal" individual combines the various prohibitions and challenges of the ego ideal in a sober, modest, and workable unit, well anchored in a set of techniques and in the roles which go with them. The restless individual must, for better or for worse, alleviate a presistently revived infantile superego pressure by the reassertion of his ego identity. At the time of the Irma Dream, Freud was acutely aware that his restless search and his superior equipment were to expose him to the hybris which few men must face, namely, the entry into the unknown where it meant the liberation of revolutionary forces and the necessity of new laws of conduct. Like Moses, Freud despaired of the task, and by sending some of the first discoveries of his inner search to Fliess with a request to destroy them (to "eliminate the poison"), he came close to smashing his tablets. The letters reflect his ambivalent dismay. In the Irma Dream, we see him struggle between a surrender to the traditional authority of Dr. M. (superego), a projection of his own self-esteem on his imaginative and far-away friend, Fliess (ego ideal), and the recognition that he himself must be the lone (self-)investigator (ego identity). In life he was about to commit himself to his "inner tyrant," psychology, and with it, to a new principle of human integrity.

The Irma Dream documents a crisis, during which a medical investigator's identity loses and regains its "conflict-free status" (10, 13). It illustrates how the latent infantile wish that provides the energy for the renewed conflict, and thus for the dream, is imbedded in a manifest dream structure which on every level reflects significant trends of the dreamer's total situation. Dreams, then, not only fulfill naked wishes of sexual license, of unlimited dominance and of unrestricted destructiveness; where they work, they also lift the dreamer's isolation, appease his conscience, and preserve his identity, each in specific and instructive ways.

NOTES

1. German words in brackets indicate that the writer will question and discuss A. A. Brill's translation of these words.
2. "Formerly I found it extraordinarily difficult to accustom my readers to the distinction between the manifest dream-content and the latent dream-thoughts. Over and over again arguments and objections were adduced from the uninterpreted dream as it was retained in the memory, and the necessity of interpreting the dream was ignored. But now, when the analysts have at least become reconciled to substituting for the manifest dream its meaning as found by interpretation, many of them are guilty of another mistake, to which they adhere just as stubbornly. They look for the essence of the dream in this latent content, and thereby overlook the distinction between latent dream-thoughts and the dream-work. The dream is fundamentally nothing more than a special *form* of our thinking, which is made possible by the conditions of the sleeping state. It is the dream-work which produces this form, and it alone is the essence of dreaming—the only explanation of its singularity" (6, pp. 466–467).
3. See the chapter "Zones, Modes, and Modalities" in (2).
4. According to a report presented to the Seminar on Dream Interpretation in the San Francisco Psychoanalytic Institute.
5. In another dream mentioned in "The Interpretation of Dreams" (6), Freud accuses himself of such hypocrisy, when in a dream he treats with great affection another doctor whose face ("beardless" in actuality) he also alters, this time by making it seem elongated and by adding a yellow beard. Freud thinks that he is really trying to make the doctor out to be a seducer of women patients and a "simpleton." The German *Schwachkopf*, and *Schlemihl*, must be considered the evil prototype which serves as a counterpart to the ideal prototype, to be further elucidated here, the smart young Jew who "promises much," as a professional man.
6. See Ernst Kris' concept of a "regression in the service of the ego" (11).
7. As pointed out elsewhere (2), Hitler, also the son of an old father and a young mother, in a corresponding marginal area, shrewdly exploited such infantile humiliation: he pointed the way to the defiant destruction of all paternal images. Freud, the Jew, chose the way of scholarly persistence until the very relationship to the father (the oedipus complex) itself became a matter of universal enlightenment.

BIBLIOGRAPHY

1. Erikson, E. H. Studies in the interpretation of play. *Gen. Psychol. Mon.*, *22*:557–671, 1940.
2. Erikson, E. H. *Childhood and Society.* New York: W. W. Norton & Co., 1950.
3. Erikson, E. H. Growth and crises of the "healthy personality" (for Fact-Finding Committee, Midcentury White House Conference). New York: Josiah Macy Jr. Foundation, 1950. Somewhat revised in *Personality in Nature, Culture and Society,* ed. C. Kluckhohn and H. R. Murray, New York: Knopf, 1953.
4. Erikson, E. H. Sex differences in the play constructions of pre-adolescents. *Am. J. Orthopsychiat.*, *21*:667–692, 1951.
5. Erikson, E. H. Identity and young adulthood. Presented at the 35th Anniversary of the Institute of the Judge Baker Guidance Center in Boston, May, 1953 (to be published).
6. Freud, S. The interpretation of dreams. In *The Basic Writings of Sigmund Freud.* New York: Modern Library, 1938.
7. Freud, S. The history of the psychoanalytic movement. In *The Basic Writings of Sigmund Freud.* New York: Modern Library, 1938.
8. Freud, S. Ansprache an die Mitglieder des Vereins B'nai B'rith (1926). *Gesammelte Werke,* Vol. XVI. London: Imago Publishing Co., 1941.
9. Freud, S. *Aus den Anfängen der Psychoanalyse.* London: Imago Publishing Co., 1950.
10. Hartmann, H. Ichpsychologie und Anpassungsproblem. *Internat. Ztschr. f. Psychoanal. u. Imago, 24*:62–135, 1939. Translated in part in Rapaport (13).
11. Kris, E. On preconscious mental processes. *Psychoanal. Quart.*, *19*:540–560, 1950. Also in *Psychoanalytic Explorations in Art.* New York: International Universities Press, 1952.
12. Kris, E. On inspiration. *Internat. J. Psycho-Anal.*, *20*:377–389, 1939. Also in *Psychoanalytic Explorations in Art.* New York: International Universities Press, 1952.
13. Rapaport, D. *Organization and Pathology of Thought.* New York: Columbia University Press, 1951.

C. Synthesis and Adaptation

7. Formation and Evaluation of Hypotheses in Dream Interpretation

Erika Fromm and Thomas M. French

In an earlier paper Fromm (1) discussed French's (2) approach to the interpretation of dreams. French attempts to reconstruct and visualize the functioning of the Ego at the moment of dreaming through study of the dream work. This complements the classical approach of Freud. Freud's interest was focused on the dream as a distorted and disguised fulfillment of an infantile wish. French, starting with the classical approach, supplements it by studying the dream as a cognitive, integrative attempt of the Ego to solve a *current, Here-and-Now* conflict. French has called this the "Focal Conflict." This focal conflict is always based ultimately on one or more infantile conflicts, although in a particular case it may not be easy to trace it back to its roots in the dreamer's past.

I

The authors consider dreams to be artistic products of the thinking, groping mind. The dreamer uses simultaneously ideation and more formally organized logical thought in producing the dream, just like the poet, the composer, and the painter do in their creative activities. And dreams, when once fully understood, are fascinating works of beauty.

In order to understand a dream, the interpreter must involve himself open-mindedly in a parallel re-creative, non-schematic process. It is an intuitive activity. But if it is to be more than a hit-or-miss spouting off of the analyst's own brainstorms it requires also scientific self-discipline and the willingness to evaluate critically and conscientiously the ideas and hypotheses one has

Reprinted with permission of the Helen Dwight Reid Education Foundation. Published by Heldref Publications, 4000 Albemarle St., N.W., Washington, D.C. 20016. Copyright © 1962, from the *Journal of Psychology,* Vol. 54, pp. 271–83.

arrived at intuitively. Only then can the interpreter find out whether his intuitive hypotheses are correct, need modification and/or refinement, or whether they should be discarded because they are wrong.

At the start of a dream interpretation the interpreter is in a situation similar to that of M. Broussard when he came upon the Rosetta Stone. The message of the dream—or parts of it—are written in hieroglyphs (the language of the patient's Unconscious) on a slab of black basalt. It must be translated faithfully into consciously understandable language (the language of the Conscious). How does the interpreter go about this task?

The interpreter should not just decode the "symbols." Like the *good* translator of poetry from a foreign language and culture, who tries faithfully and artistically to recreate in the language of the translation the specific poetic atmosphere and quality of the original poem, so the dream interpreter must also recreate the dream's specific, elusive atmosphere in order to understand it fully and make it meaningful to the patient's conscious mind.

Sometimes the interpreter intuitively grasps the central meaning of a dream. He then must proceed to see whether all the details fit in as parts of the whole—which his hypothesis. (If they do not, he must discard his hypothesis as being wrong, or modify it.) The following dream and its interpretation may serve as an example of an intuitive (re-) creative, correct hypothesis:

A. The Cement Dream

1. Dream. In the fifteenth analytic hour a 35-year-old male married patient,[1] father of three children, who came to analysis in order to be cured of his neurodermatitis, reported that a few nights ago he dreamt he "was mixing cement." That was all.

2. Associations. Immediately upon awakening he felt as if he really knew exactly how to mix cement. But actually, he says, he does not.

He associates in the analytic hour that his house recently needed tuckpointing; that he was going to do it himself, but did not know how to mix concrete. So, he hired somebody. The patient further associated: "My dear wife went to a bingo game last night." He had to take care of the children, put them to bed, and wait till she got home. Because she went out to play bingo, he came too late to his night job.

Then he talked about a hit-and-run driver who killed a child. The patient "cannot see how people can leave the scene—I couldn't do such a thing."

Later he tells of his wife's accusing him of wanting to get rid of everything, not enjoying his family, just tolerating them.

3. Interpretative Process. That the hiring somebody might refer to the analyst whom he had just hired recently to help him with his problems, was easy to figure out (on the basis of parallels). And the dream in connection with the first association upon awakening stated clearly that "mixing cement" was a "problem" that the patient felt he could not solve alone (again a parallel).

But *what* is the specific problem that the patient wants the analyst to help him with at this time? That is the basic question we had to answer in interpreting this dream.

In order to do so we let our imaginative processes play over the material. We visualized a house, tuckpointing, cement.

Suddenly it occurred to us that in "tuckpointing" cement is used to *hold the bricks of a house together.* The *function* of tuckpointing is to prevent the house from crumbling apart. . . . Our next thoughts were: A house is a home, a home for a *family.*

In a flash, we felt that now intuitively we may have grasped the central meaning of the dream; and we hypothesized that the patient's problem may be one of holding his family together.

This hypothesis immediately proved to be the key for understanding all the associations as well as the dream:

In all of the associations the patient refers to a wish to be a good family man . . . and a fear that he is not. He asks himself: Am I or am I not a good family man? He wants to be. He says his wife is the one who neglects her duties to the family and acts like a "hit-and-run" driver, he "couldn't do such a thing." But his wife accuses him of "wanting to get rid of" the family, just tolerating them. The dream expresses the patient's hope that in therapy the analyst will help him to hold his family together. The patient dreamt the dream in an *effort to solve* the problem of how to be a good family man. But this problem is expressed in the dream in a deanimated, de-vitalized symbolic form: instead of interacting with his wife and children directly, he "mixes (lifeless) cement."

II

Rarely are a dream and its associations so concise, short, clear and simple that the dream's total latent meaning can be grasped by the interpreter at once, as a whole with all its constituent subparts.

Usually dreams are too complicated to be encompassed by the interpreter's integrative Ego span right at the beginning of the interpretive process.

This process starts in the majority of the cases with *scanning* of the material (usually followed by letting it "simmer" in the analyst's mind). Like a radar instrument, the interpreter lets his thoughts and feeling processes sweep, in a random fashion, over the patient's dream material, the associations and the preceding hour, until he gets one or more clues.

Listening for clues . . . what are these clues?

There may be parallels in the material of the dream and the associations. Or incongruencies. Or a feeling of empathic resonance within the analyst. Or the interpreter may look first for the general affect of the dream, which so often indicates the reactive motive. Or perhaps the totality of the situation in which the patient puts himself in the dream—or with which dream and associations seem to be pervaded—become a first clue to the interpreter.

Perhaps, on the other hand, the interpreter may be struck by strange, curious parts of the dream and get the feeling: this detail must mean something . . . but what?

III

The *nature* of the clues often determines which particular method of further approach to the understanding of the dream the interpreter then follows. If he thinks he has caught on to the focal conflict as a whole, he must proceed to find the evidence in the constituent parts of the dream . . . evidence *for* as well as *against* his hypothesis. In Rorschach terminology, we shall call this approach from the whole to the parts the W→D→d approach.

Let us show on an example of modern art what we mean. Look at this picture by Joan Miro (see Figure 7.1).

The first impression is one of lightness, grace, freedom, wit—on account of the mostly upward slithering, quicksilvery, mischievous movement in the picture. The brilliant reds, blues, greens, yellows and whites in the actual painting contribute to the feeling of playfulness and gaiety. These are W impressions.

Figure 7.1
Joan Miro, *Harlequins' Carnival* (1924–25). Room of Contemporary Art Fund, 1940, Albright-Knox Art Gallery. Buffalo, New York. Photo, courtesy, Museum of Modern Art, New York.

Then the viewer may become aware of details:

Clown-like cats which play with a ball of wool and pay no attention to a fish behind them. Tentatively the viewer makes an hypothesis that this could be a circus picture. He looks further and sees a ladder near which two people are swinging from a high trapeze. This confirms the circus idea.

Then he sees a jack-in-the-box who throws a ball into the left hand of a long-necked, round-headed man with a fancy mustache. The man holds a pipe in his mouth. His stomach seems to be a bouncing ball in a body contorted out of shape. What could that mean?

There are musical notes, and eyes in the painting. Why? the viewer asks himself. Could they symbolize that the act of looking and music are important features of what the artist wants to express? It fits with the circus. The viewer then recognizes other animated, circus-like creatures that move and twirl about in amiable confusion. But he is still vaguely disturbed by the representation of the man whose throat seems to be so painfully elongated and whose stomach looks like a bouncing ball. He cannot make this jibe with the gay circus idea until he learns about one historical fact: Miro painted this picture when he was poverty-stricken and starving (4). Miro called the painting "Harlequins' Carnival."

The danger in the W→D→d type approaches lies in the temptation to use a Procrustean Bed technique to make the details fit the hypothesis; or to discard as "unimportant" those details that do not fit in with one's hypothesis.

The greater the emotional commitment the interpreter has to his hypothesis the easier can he succumb to the Procrustean temptation. The scientist does get committed to his hypothesis. It's his baby. He has great Ego involvement in it (5). Anyone who has ever gone through the emotional process of hypothesis making—with its hours of "labor," toil, happy excitement, despair, and utter joy—can have no doubt about this.

If the initial clue has been but a detail—a minor (d, Dd) or major (D) piece of the mosaic of the dream pattern—the interpreter will look for other (meaningful) pieces until he recognizes the total Gestalt of the dream; usually with a joyful "Aha Erlebnis." In these cases he proceeds from d or D to W.

Let us—as a simile—show you another picture by Miro (Figure 7.2). You cannot begin to understand the idea that Miro wants to express in this picture until you recognize that the lower left hand detail is a female breast in profile—with a small human figure close to it. Then, perhaps, you go to the upper right hand design and figure out that it could be a breast seen full face—and a child attached to it. It is an infant. The painter has given it typically infantile random movements. The lower right and upper left designs you now comprehend as being symbolic representations of breast and child, too, and the fine-spun lines connecting the elements in the opposite corners as indicating a *relationship*. After understanding all of these details, you now can "interpret" the whole, you say to yourself: oh, Miro wants to depict the idea of Maternity (and this, indeed, is the name of the picture). You still have a little trouble with that golden horn. It's a horn of plenty, symbolizing the rich experience that maternity is for mother and child. It fits in with and enriches the interpretation given.

The interpretative process here described in making a surrealist painting intelligible is the same as the one the dream interpreter goes through when he deciphers a dream by means of the D→W approach. We shall use this approach in:

Figure 7.2
Joan Miro, *Maternity* (1925). Collection Mrs. Roland Penrose. Photo, courtesy, Museum of Modern Art, New York.

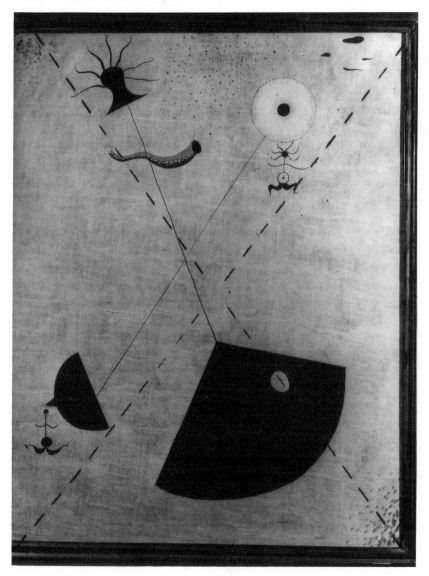

B. The Army Mess Hall Dream

In the ninety-eighth hour, the analyst praised the patient whose Cement Dream we discussed above, for having been able to allow himself to become aware of tender feelings towards his wife. The patient expressed pleasure and embarrassment in relation to this compliment at the end of the ninety-ninth hour. The next night the patient had a dream.

1. Dream.

I was in the Army again. Went into the mess hall with another guy. Had a little trouble getting food. Then saw a couple of guys I recognized. A Southerner, called "the Colonel"—he was really a private—said: "Sit down, I'll take care of you. I'll serve you like a king, on gold plates." I replied: "Never mind the plates, just get me good food." Then this guy's appearance changed . . . he looked like Jack Benny. He said he was Jack Benny's brother. I said: "Are you related?" Everybody laughed. Then the scene changed. We were both being chased. We were going through a tunnel. I said: "This is ridiculous! If you are Jack Benny's brother and he owns millions, why doesn't he help out?"

2. Associations.
The patient associated that he had been close to "the Colonel" in the Army. The "Colonel" had been willing to do quite a bit for him.

The gold plate business seemed odd to the patient. He said he "Didn't care for a lot of bullshit, just facts—don't flower it up. Sometimes people will give you a medal and then lay an egg."

He returned to thinking about the "Colonel," and about a lieutenant in the Army (a medical officer) for whom the "Colonel" worked. This doctor was rough. He said the patient was goldbricking, using his dermatitis as an excuse for discharge. The patient denied it. The lieutenant's superior officer overruled the lieutenant and got the patient discharged.

3. Interpretative Process.
The manifest content of this dream as a whole at first seems ununderstandable. Perhaps the interpreter is struck by a curious detail of the dream, the "Colonel's" words: "I'll take care of you . . . will serve you on gold plates."

It is incongruous to be served on gold plates in an Army mess hall. The juxtaposition of these two details seemed odd to the patient, too. Obviously they must be an important clue to the latent content of the dream.

The interpreter may make a mental note that an Army mess hall is a stark, uncozy, purely masculine place; a place where men use rough language (see the word bullshit in the associations) in order to hide or disparage sentiments.

Then the interpreter's attention may turn to the patient's next association: "Sometimes people will give you a medal and then lay an egg." A curious association. It sticks out like a sore thumb. To what perceptions, thoughts or feelings could the patient refer by quoting this saying?

As a working hypothesis, the interpreter may begin now to ask himself: does the patient symbolize in the dream the thought that someone who serves him is trying to flatter him? (Serve him—a mere army sergeant—"on gold plates like a king"; "flower it up"; "give a medal.") Who could the flatterer who takes care of him be? The analyst? Very possibly so. The analyst, after all, has praised the patient recently about being able to express tender feelings towards his wife.

Now the association "Sometimes people will give you a medal and then lay an egg" falls into place and a part of the dream's puzzle becomes intelligible. The patient is pleased by the analyst's praise, but also intensely embarrassed about his tender feelings; and he fears the analyst's praise will lead to something unpleasant. What this unpleasant consequence is, we don't know yet. Nor can we be *fully* sure at this point that the " 'Colonel' who really was a private" stands for the analyst.

Why does the "Colonel" change into the brother of Jack Benny, i.e., the brother of a famous and rich man? And why is he chased out through a tunnel together with the patient? We could find no answer to these two questions and thus could not understand the last half of the dream until it occurred to us that the young analyst was the Chief Psychiatric Resident at the clinic at which the patient was seen, that he occupied an office next to the office of the Chief Psychiatrist who was a famous man, and that a tunnel connected the Psychiatric Clinic with other parts of the hospital—and led out to the street.

We can now be certain that the " 'Colonel' who really was a private," and whose physiognomy changes so he looks like Jack Benny's brother represents the analyst. What is more, now the total latent dream content forms an organic, intelligible, cognitive whole.

The patient felt pleasure at being warmly praised by the analyst for expressing gentle tenderness towards his wife. But he blusteringly must deny this in the dream because he also feels shame. According to his Teutonic ego ideal, a real he-man should not be tender. Therefore, in the second half of the dream his thoughts turn to depreciating his analyst's importance. ("He said he was Jack Benny's brother. I said: Are you related? Everybody laughed.") Furthermore, the patient fears that the hospital authorities will chase him out of treatment—and the "sissy" analyst with him—if they hear that this resident who takes care of him has "flattered" him for being able to express tenderness. As the patient's masculine pride disapproves of gentle tenderness within himself, so he thinks the men in charge of the hospital must do; and the director of the psychiatric clinic, his resident psychiatrist's big brother, "doesn't help out."[2]

IV

Which method of approach the interpreter will use in solving the riddle of a dream is an intuitive decision.

In some cases the nature of the dream material itself "demands" a particular interpretative approach. In trying to open a heavy, tightly nailed-down wooden case you don't use your finger nails, you use a crow bar—that's what "the thing asks for."

In other cases the manner of approach may be determined by subtle factors residing within the interpreter's own personality structure—and we don't mean counter-transference. Neo-Gestalt theoretical research on perception (Klein (6), Witkin, et al. (7)) and on cognition (Klein (8), Scheerer and Huling (9)) has shown that, within certain subtle limits, personality charac-teristics and/or the particular psychic and somatic state a person is in (e.g., hunger) determine whether and how he perceives an objective stimulus or a problem. It is for these reasons that certain clues may immediately be perceived (in a certain context) by one interpreter, and not by another.

Also: on the basis of their own personality structure and their characteristic mode of working, some interpreters may naturally tend to use one interpre-tive approach rather than another.

Frequently, without necessarily being consciously aware of it, one uses several methods in succession . . . or in combination . . . in the interpreta-tion of one dream.

There is only *one*[3] fully correct Focal Conflict interpretation for every dream . . . but there is not just one road that leads to it. Important is only that one gets there, and is not satisfied with being merely somewhere in the vicinity of the correct understanding.

V

The question arises now: What makes for failure in dream interpretation? Failure can be due to the interpreter's unwillingness to evaluate critically his intuitive hunches. It occurs when instead of checking and rechecking for correctness, he deïfies his intuition and allows no doubt about it. If challenged, some analysts will burn at the stake those that advocate scientific controls.

In the more enlightened, less fanatic believer in "pure" intuition, failure to find the Focal Conflict frequently is due to his getting side-tracked on a Sub-Focal Conflict.

Another possible cause of failure may be the interpreter's commitment to an (incorrect) hypothesis he has made at an earlier stage of the interpretative process, and his resistance to letting go of it. This point was touched upon above but deserves further consideration here:

An intuitively made hypothesis is the interpreter's artistic creation. He has a great deal of Ego involvement in it. The *purely* intuitive analyst makes *one* hypothesis. He puts all of his eggs in *one* basket. Naturally, he is not willing to drop it.

The intuitive interpreter with the Scientific Critical Attitude—he who looks for evidence that could prove or disprove his hypothesis and who also looks for possible gaps—is committed to his hypothesis too. But he is *mainly* committed to his hypothesis, *not solely*. Some of his Ego involvement is taken up by the sporty pursuit of proving his own hypothesis wrong or insufficient.

Actually, after his hypothesis has occurred to him he makes two more: *(a)* my hypothesis is correct; and *(b)* it may be wrong; with the major Ego involvement, of course, on *(a)*.

Because he is not totally committed to his one artistic-intuitive creation, he has some free-floating "committability" left and is able to evaluate his own creation critically, to let intuitive emphases shift, and to find new solutions if necessary.

Still another cause for failure is the fact that so frequently an important clue to the dream lies right under the interpreter's nose but is not recognized as a clue. Or it is recognized only after a good deal of "simmering," incubating about the dream—and shifting of emphasis for and against certain hypotheses the interpreter has made. The clue has been "camouflaged" as a subpart in the context of another cognitive whole. Suddenly the overlooked clue jumps out of its camouflaged position and stands out by itself (or ties up with another part into a more meaningful whole). And the interpreter asks himself: Why, in Heaven's name, didn't I see that before?

Scheerer and Huling (9) published a beautiful paper on "Cognitive Embeddedness in Problem Solving" which deals with the same topic in near-to-ordinary-life problem solving situations.

VI

How, in the end, can the interpreter be sure that he has faithfully, i.e., correctly, caught the Focal Conflict and the exact total meaning of a dream? The answer to this question is: The interpretative hypothesis is correct if it illuminates or explains every bit of the dream text plus every single association given to it as parts of *a total response the dreamer has made to his actual current emotional situation*. Fidelity is measured by the degree to which the interpretation approximates the ideal of such total illumination and explanation.

Two types of checks are possible. One is of a scientific nature. The other is an artistic kind of validation which we shall call the Esthetic Experience.

In the process of seeking scientific evidence, the interpreter carefully, minutely, checks and rechecks the material for inconsistencies with his hypothesis. The interpretative hypothesis about the dream is correct, if in the end the interpreter does not need to resort to subsidiary or extraneous side hypotheses to tie up loose ends; and futhermore, if he has been totally honest in his critical evaluation as to whether or not all the material fits in with his hypothesis. He must not violate any of it by using a Procrustean Bed Technique.

The other evidence for the correctness of an interpretation is a more subjective artistic experience the interpreter has with some—not all—interpretations he makes. This is what we propose to call *the Esthetic Experience*.

The Esthetic Experience is a close relative to the Aha-Erlebnis, but not its identical twin.

What happens in the interpreter—who may be the therapist, or the patient, or preferably both searching together—while he is trying to solve the riddle of the dream?

He has found some clues. Perhaps has brought some or even most of them into a meaningful relationship with each other. But there has remained some part of the material that has defied explanation. Or the whole did not make "real sense" to him. The analyst sits back and "simmers," lets his radar-like, freely suspended attention wander over the dream again.

Suddenly he arrives at a new or modified artistic insight about the dream. And feels: Oh, . . . that's it! That's beautiful! That illuminates the whole meaning of the dream and I now can see it in all its plasticity as the beautiful work of art that it is. He feels exhilarated, excited, joyous, and experiences esthetic pleasure.

Is the Esthetic Experience the interpreter has, real proof that he has arrived at the correct interpretation? Subjectively it certainly feels like it. And frequently it really is. Particularly, if the patient comes to this sudden insight or if the therapist's interpretation "hits home" with the patient and, like a sunburst, illuminates to him too, the dark landscape of his unconscious struggle.

When the interpretation is made in the process of research—from a written record, post hoc, in the absence of the patient—some additional, consensual proof can be gained if the esthetic feeling is experienced by your colleagues when you present to them the patient's dream and your interpretation. We hope you felt it when we gave you the Cement Dream and our interpretation of it. And perhaps some of you felt only what we should like to call the *Hm-hm Erlebnis*. This can be described as the arriving at an insight which proves someone else's hypothesis rather than one's own. It contains insight . . . nodding-agreement insight. But it is not as creative an insight as that experienced in the Aha-Erlebnis and in the Esthetic Experience.

Nearly always the Esthetic Experience is subjectively felt by the one who experiences it as pretty strong proof. But it *can* have its pitfalls: The investigator may get so enchanted by it that he fails to finecomb the material for details that might not fit in with his hypothesis. The Esthetic Experience does not necessarily suffice. It always must be followed, at least for check-up purposes, by the process of finding the Scientific Evidence.

Much of what has been said in relation to dream interpretation here perhaps applies to all creative scientific hypothesis formation and evaluation.

NOTES

1. This patient was analyzed by Dr. David Hamburg. The authors express thanks to him for allowing them to use the notes he took during the analytic hours for the interpretations they are making in this paper.

2. The transference meaning of this dream will be discussed in our forthcoming book, *Method of Dream Interpretation*.
3. It is true that there are many overdetermined meanings of a dream. But these meanings vary greatly in the intensity of their cathexis at a particular time. The Focal Conflict is the one that it most intensely cathected at the time of dreaming.

REFERENCES

1. Fromm, E. The Psychoanalytic Interpretation of Dreams and Projective Techniques. *Am. J. Orthopsychiat.*, 1958, 28, 67–72.
2. French, T. M. The Integration of Behavior. Vol. I–III. Chicago: Univ. Chicago Press, 1952, 1953, 1958.
3. Freud, S. The Interpretation of Dreams (1900). The Basic Writings of Freud, New York: Modern Library, 1938.
4. Erben, W. Joan Miro. München: Prestel Verlag, 1959, p. 119.
5. Roe, A. Creativity and the Scientist. Lecture given at the Ill. Psychol. Assoc. Conv. Chicago, October 9, 1959.
6. Klein, G. S. The Personal World through Perception. *In* Blake, R. R., & Ramsey, G. V. *(Eds.), Perception: An Approach to Personality.* New York: Ronald Press, 1951, pp. 328–355.
7. Witkin, H. A., Lewis, H. B., Hertzman, M., Machover, K., Meissner, P. B., & Wapner, S. Personality through Perception. New York: Harper, 1954.
8. Klein, G. S. Cognitive Control and Motivation. *In* Lindzey, G. *(Ed.), Assessment of Human Motives.* New York: Rinehart, 1958, pp. 87–118.
9. Scheerer, M., & Huling, M. D. Cognitive embeddedness in problem solving. A theoretical and experimental analysis. *In* Kaplan, B., & Wapner, S. *(Eds.), Perspectives in Psychological Theory.* New York: Int. Univ. Press, 1960, pp. 256–302.

8. Dreams in Clinical Psychoanalytic Practice

Charles Brenner

Freud began his psychotherapeutic attempts to cure hysterical patients of their symptoms by attempting to undo the patients' amnesia concerning the origin of their symptoms with the help of hypnotic suggestion. He was not, at that time, particularly interested in his patients' dreams, and his earliest articles on hysteria, particularly the *Studies in Hysteria,* which he wrote together with J. Breuer (4), contain no special references to the subject of dreams or dream interpretation. It was not long after he gave up hypnosis and began to develop the psychoanalytic method, however, that Freud's attention was directed to his patients' dreams and to his own dreams. His quick and brilliant success in elucidating so much of dream psychology contributed substantially toward convincing him of the value of his newly discovered method of investigation and treatment—the psychoanalytic method. More than likely it helped give him the courage to persist in his devotion to psychoanalysis in the face of the disdain and disapproval it engendered, obstacles which would have discouraged a man who was less confident of himself and of the work he was doing. As Freud (6) himself wrote, in the preface to one of the later editions of *The Interpretation of Dreams,* such a discovery comes only once in a lifetime.

The publication of that monumental work in 1900 aroused little interest in either the medical or the scientific world at first. In 1905 Freud (5) published a case history, *Fragment of an Analysis of a Case of Hysteria,* the Dora case, which was intended primarily to illustrate the practical value of dream analysis in psychoanalytic work. As analysts other than Freud began to appear on the scene, they accepted, or were soon convinced of, the correctness of Freud's emphasis on the usefulness of analyzing patients' dreams. The clinical use of dream analysis very early became one of the hallmarks of genuine,

Reprinted by permission of the author and Williams and Wilkins, from *The Journal of Nervous and Mental Disease,* Vol. 19, 1969, pp. 122–32.

Freudian analysis. It is still so viewed by many, although it is now less often referred to explicitly in this regard, particularly in the psychoanalytic literature proper. As psychoanalysts, we take it for granted today as a part of psychoanalytic practice, but it is interesting to see evidences in the early psychoanalytic literature of very explicit emphasis on the clinical importance of dream interpretation. For example, if one refers to early volumes of the *Internationale Zeitschrift für Psychoanalyse,* one finds a special section in each issue devoted to short communications concerning dream interpretation: a new symbol, an unusual dream, an interesting latent content, *etc.*

Psychoanalytic journals do not currently have such a section, to the best of my knowledge, but it is still usual, if not universal, for the curricula of psychoanalytic institutes to devote a considerable amount of time to the study of dream interpretation. In the United States, at any rate, our curricula devote no such amount of time to the study of the interpretation of symptoms, or of character traits, or of parapraxes or jokes. Dreams and their interpretation still occupy a special place in our minds—our professional minds—whether we acknowledge it explicitly or not.

I recall a panel discussion at the Edinburgh Congress, in 1961, at which Dr. M. Balint and Miss A. Freud participated. In the course of the discussion, Dr. Balint said that it is his practice to insist that every psychoanalytic candidate whom he analyzes stick with at least one of his dreams until it has been thoroughly analyzed, no matter how many analytic sessions it may take. Dr. Balint explained that, in this way, he assured himself that every one of his candidates had at least one opportunity to understand a dream thoroughly and to learn what the unconscious mind is really like. Miss Freud, to my surprise, expressed enthusiasm for the idea, although she said that she had never done such a thing and, on being pressed, admitted that it might be undesirable to do so, even in a training analysis. I might add that, in one of the courses I took with him in the early 1940's, Dr. H. Sachs described it as his usual practice to continue the analysis of a patient's dream over two or more sessions, *i.e.,* to tell a patient at the end of a session, "Well, we still don't understand that dream. We'll have to spend more time on it tomorrow." At that time, I was too early in my analytic career for Dr. Sachs' comment to make any particular impression on me, but what I heard in Edinburgh did stimulate a lively response, since it differed so markedly from my own practice and was so at variance with what I had until then assumed to be generally accepted procedure among analysts today.

I shall begin my presentation by a brief discussion of dream psychology —of dream theory, if you will.

In the seventh chapter of his *Interpretation of Dreams*, Freud (6) proposed a theory of mental organization and functioning which seemed to him to explain satisfactorily the diverse phenomena of dream psychology, of neurotic symptom formation, of parapraxes, and of jokes. All of these psychic phenomena, both normal and pathological, Freud believed could be explained only if one assumed the operation of a mental apparatus, much of whose workings are unconscious, and, indeed, inaccessible to consciousness as such. This theory was reviewed and expanded somewhat in the paper which he published in 1915 (8) as *The Unconscious,* without, however, being substantially altered. As a matter of convenience, it is often referred to as the "topographic theory." Subsequently Freud revised his theories about the mental apparatus and its functioning in rather substantial ways. His revised theory, again for the sake of convenience, is referred to generally as the "structural theory."

I do not propose to enter into a discussion of the revisions of Freud's earlier theories which constitute the differences between the topographic and the structural theories; for such a discussion I shall merely refer to *Psychoanalytic Concepts and the Structural Theory,* by Arlow and myself (1). There has rarely been any discussion of the question whether these theoretical revisions imply, or entail, any new view of dream psychology.

We are familiar with the fact that the revisions have had such an effect with respect to certain pathological phenomena. We have a very different view today from that which analysts had some 50 years ago concerning the psychology (psychopathology) or neurotic symptom formation as well as of the unconscious determinants of many character traits. In particular, we have a different view of the relationship between symptom and anxiety, as well as a much different, and, we believe, more accurate view of the role of conflict, of defense, and of superego tendencies in the production of both neurotic symptoms and normal as well as abnormal character traits. In fact, it was the accumulation of new data from the application of the psychoanalytic method to clinical work with these very phenomena and the reassessment of those data, both new and old, that led to the theoretical revisions to which I refer. Moreover, as we know, it is the theoretical revisions in question which have made possible what we call defense analysis and character analysis in a systematic and effective way, thus enlarging the scope of psychoanalysis therapeutically as well as improving its therapeutic efficacy and diminishing the dangers previously attendant on its use.

It is all the more interesting, therefore, that there have been so few attempts to revise psychoanalytic theories of dream psychology in the light of the structural theory, that is, in the light of the theoretical revisions in the theory of the mental apparatus and its functioning which have proved so valuable clinically. As far as I am aware, the first such attempt was the one I made myself in the chapter on dreams in my *Elementary Textbook of Psychoanalysis* (2). In that chapter I presented an exposition of dream psychology which included reference to Freud's later theoretical revisions. In 1964 Arlow and I (1) reviewed in detail the psychoanalytic data acquired since 1900 which speak in favor of revising dream theory and presented the suggested, necessary revisions in concise form.

The present paper offers a revised theory of dream psychology which is based on the structural theory of the mind. Like the structural theory, this dream theory is more consonant with the facts of mental functioning available through application of the psychoanalytic method than is the dream theory outlined by Freud in 1900. Like the structural theory also, it widens the range of our clinical work with dreams and refines our ability to use dream analysis to our patients' best advantage.

The new theory, like the old, begins with the assumption that, despite the general quiescence of mental functioning during sleep, there are certain energies of the mind which remain active, at least during those times when dreaming, *i.e.,* the dream work, is going on. It is these energies which initiate dreaming. They, or, more exactly, the mental representations which are associated with them, constitute the latent content of the ensuing dream. This latent content stems from the instinctual derivatives of the id on the one hand and from the impressions and cares of the preceding day on the other. So far, we are on familiar ground. However, when we leave the question of the initiation of a dream and of its latent content and turn instead to the dream work, the new theory shows some significant differences from its predecessor.

To be specific, the new theory assumes that the mental energy which is associated with the latent dream content activates various unconscious ego and superego functions, just as might happen during waking life. Some of the ego functions assist or guide the instinctual energies toward satisfaction. Other ego functions, to which we refer as defenses (counterinstinctual ego functions), oppose the gratification just referred to, acting in accordance with superego demands. It may be added parenthetically that the instinctual gratification which is characteristic of dreaming is a gratification in fantasy— what Freud called an "hallucinated wish-fulfillment." At times, however, somatic gratification may occur as well, *e.g.*, a sexual orgasm.

To continue with our description of the dream work, the interplay among instinctual (id) derivatives, ego functions, and superego demands and prohibitions is not always as simple as we have just outlined. For example, defenses (ego functions) may be directed against superego demands as well as against instinctual derivatives. Moreover, on occasion, superego demands may join forces with an id impulse, *e.g.*, a masochistic or a sadistic one. Our theory assumes, therefore, that the dream work consists of an interplay among id, ego, and superego. This interplay may be quite simple or extremely complex. In any case, its final result is the manifest dream—what the dreamer experiences consciously during his sleep.

I should like to emphasize that the description I have just given of the dream work is not essentially different from what we understand to be the way in which the mental apparatus operates during waking life. In waking life, too, we have reason to assume that conscious thoughts, ideas, fantasies, *etc.* are the end result of a compromise, an interplay, among instinctual forces, ego functions, and superego demands and prohibitions. This is what is meant by the principle of "multiple functioning," a term first introduced by Waelder (9). To be sure, it was Freud who introduced the notion of compromise formation into psychoanalytic theories of mental functioning. He recognized very early that hysterical symptoms are, in fact, a compromise between the gratification of a sexual wish and the infliction by the patient of punishment on himself for permitting himself to gratify such a forbidden wish while, at the same time, the wish itself is barred from consciousness by repression. It was not until many years later, however, that it was clearly recognized that the tendency to compromise formation among id, ego, and superego is as characteristic for normal mental functioning as it is for neurotic symptom formation. It may be added, again parenthetically, that the full significance of the principle of mental functioning is still often overlooked. A conscious fantasy, a thought, an action, much less a symptom is never *purely* a defense, a self-punishment, or an instinctual gratification. It may be predominantly one or the other, to be sure. It may be proper, as a matter of analytic technique, to draw a given patient's attention to one or another of the several determinants just mentioned. However, it is essential to be clear in one's own mind that whatever one *observes* of the conscious mental life of any person, whether a patient or not, is the result of an interaction among the various forces and trends in the mind, forces which are most conveniently subsumed under the headings of id, ego, and superego.

So far, then, we have postulated that during dreaming, as during waking mental life, instinctual energies plus the influences of the outer world—day residues in dreaming, perceptions in waking life—impel or drive the mind in the direction of compromise formation. In other words, the principle of multiple functioning is operative during dreaming just as it is during waking life. Yet we know that the net result of an interplay among the conflicting and cooperating tendencies of id, ego, and superego during waking life is not a dream. A dream occurs only when one is asleep. How can one account for the difference?

Our answer is as follows. 1) There is a regressive alteration in many of the functions of the ego during dreaming. 2) There is a similar regressive alteration in superego functioning during dreaming. 3) Instinctual wishes and fantasies stemming from the id play a larger role in dreaming than they do in most adult, waking, mental phenomena. Each of these points will be discussed in turn.

First, with respect to regression of ego functions during dreaming, we must assume that it is a consequence of the sleeping state (7). More than this we cannot say at the present time. We can say much more, however, by way of description of the nature of these regressive alterations and of their consequences. Let us begin by specifying, as far as possible, just what regressive changes characterize ego functions during sleep.

In any list of the ego functions which are regressively altered during sleep, we must certainly include reality testing, thinking, language, defenses, integrative ability, sensory perception, and motor control. Some of these obviously overlap, others might be subdivided, but since any list would be subject to some qualification, let us take the one just given and consider each of its items.

We shall begin with reality testing. More specifically, we are concerned with that aspect of reality testing which has to do with the ability to distinguish between what is perceived of the outer world and what is the result of something going on in one's own mind: the ability to distinguish fact from fancy. Generally speaking, the dreamer is unable to do this. His ability to test reality, to distinguish between a stimulus from the outer world and a stimulus from the inner world, has regressed to a stage characteristic of infancy, to a time of life when he was unable to distinguish between events of the outer world and those of the inner one. Traces of this stage normally persist well into childhood, as witnessed by the child's tendency to treat his fantasies and games as real, at least during playtime. As an extreme example of this tendency, one may note that it is by no mean rare for a young child to have an imaginary companion for months or even years, a companion who is as real and present to the child as any of the objectively real persons of his environment. To an adult dreamer, the conscious result of the dream work, that is, the images of the manifest dream, are as real as are waking fantasies (of the sort just mentioned) to a small child. The dreamer's function of reality testing has regressed to a stage characteristic of early childhood.

Since thinking and the use of language are so intimately associated, we may conveniently consider them together. There are numerous manifestations of the regressive alteration of these functions during dreaming. For example, a dreamer tends to think as a child does, in concrete sensory images, usually visual, rather than in words, as is characteristic for adult, waking thought. This regression to an infantile mode of thought accounts for the fact that most manifest dreams consist of visual images. Characteristically, a dream is something that the dreamer sees in his sleep. It will be recalled that Freud (6) originally accounted for this characteristic of dreams by postulating a need for plastic representability as one of the attributes of the dream work. In addition to thinking in visual images to a large extent, the dreamer deals with words and language in a regressive way. There is a clearly evident tendency in the dream work to play with words and to equate words that sound alike, as there is in childhood. There is likewise clearly evident a regression in other, closely related aspects of thinking. The dream work is full of representation by allusion, representation by the opposite, representation of the whole by the part, or the part by the whole. In a word, the dream work is characterized by that type of mentation normally dominant in childhood which is generally referred to in the psychoanalytic literature as "primary-process thinking." In particular, the dream work is characterized by the use of symbols in the psychoanalytic sense of the word.

Finally, as Freud pointed out, a realistic attitude toward time, toward space, and toward death, as well as the usual adult requirements of logic and syntax, are either grossly defective or absent. All of these changes are attributable to a regressive alteration of various aspects of the ego functions of language and of thinking. In each case, we can observe that the dreamer's mind is functioning in a primitive or infantile manner.

The ego's integrative function is also regressively altered during sleep.

Freud noted the participation of this function in the dream work from the start of his researches, identifying it at that time as the tendency to secondary revision. However, despite many exceptions, dreams are not, as a rule, harmonized and integrated with respect to their various component parts to nearly the same degree as we expect ordinary waking thoughts, or even daydreams, to be. The dreamer, like the child, is less concerned with unity and consistency than is the waking adult, even though, as Freud noted, the integrative function of the ego does play a part in dream formation.

One of the most striking of the changes in ego functioning during dreaming, and one of the most significant in clinical work, is the diminution of the ego's defenses. Freud related this diminution to the paralysis of motility during sleep: since action is impossible, wishes are not so dangerous. It seems likely, however, that more is involved than a realistic appraisal by the dreamer of the defensive value of his own immobility during sleep. The dreamer's diminished defensive opposition to his own instinctual wishes does, in fact, resemble the limited defensive capacities of the ego of a small child. If this resemblance is significant, the diminution of ego defenses during dreaming should be considered to be at least in part a regressive alteration of the defensive functions of the ego.

Finally, as we know, ego functions of sensory perception and of motor control are also profoundly altered during sleep. In the case of these two functions, however, it is not so clear that the alterations to be observed are a result of regression. They seem to be caused rather by a diminution or suspension of the particular ego function in question rather than by regression to patterns of functioning which are characteristic of infancy or early childhood. In any case, the alterations in these particular ego functions are of less interest to us than are the others, since they do not seem to be directly involved in or to influence directly the dream work proper. For that reason, we need not discuss them in particular detail.

Another aspect of the diminution and regression of ego functions during sleep is that the degree to which it occurs with respect to any particular function may vary considerably from dream to dream and from one part of a dream to another. This fact should occasion no surprise from analysts, who are accustomed to observing evidences of such alterations from day to day and from minute to minute in their analytic patients. In dreams, the dream work may regressively utilize nonverbal, visual thinking in one part of a dream, while verbal thoughts, characteristic of mature mental functioning, appear in another part. Indeed, visual elements and verbal thoughts may appear in a manifest dream simultaneously. It is important to remember this fact in utilizing dream interpretations in one's clinical practice. It is as necessary to obtain a patient's associations to dream thoughts expressed verbally as it is to obtain his associations to visual or other sensory elements of the manifest dream if one is to arrive at a satisfactory understanding of the dream's latent content. One must not ignore a manifest dream element simply because it is verbal rather than visual.

One may also conclude from such observations of ego functioning as those noted here that the dream work, as waking mentation, is characterized by the simultaneous interplay of mature ego functioning and primitive or infantile ego functioning: to use more familiar, although less correct terms, the simultanous interplay of primary and secondary process thinking. It is only that, in waking life, the more mature forms of ego functioning tend to predominate while, in the dream work, less mature forms of ego functioning predominate; at least they are more conspicuous and relatively more impor- tant than they normally are in waking life. It is apparent from all of these considerations why the mental phenomena of waking life to which dreams bear the closest relationship are those in which ego functioning of a primitive or infantile sort plays a substantial part: neurotic or psychotic symptoms, parapraxes, and such phenomena as daydreams, jokes, reverie, etc.

Superego functions also show clear evidence of regressive alteration dur- ing dreaming, although superego regression has attracted less general atten- tion than has regression of such ego functions as defenses and reality testing. It appears, nevertheless, that superego regressions contribute substantially to the infantile character of the mental processes involved in the dream work and in the manifest dream as well. For example, when unpleasure accompan- ies the direct or distorted fantasy of instinctual gratification in a manifest dream, it is far more often anxiety than guilt. What would produce guilt or remorse in waking life is more apt to produce fear of punishment during a dream, just as it normally does during early childhood when the superego is still in process of formation. Similarly, the dreamer, like the child, seems to be more nearly exclusively guided by the principle of "an eye for an eye and a tooth for a tooth" than is the waking adult. He is also more prone to project his guilty impulses onto the person of others, while he identifies himself, in the dream, with the disapproving and punishing judge. Finally, he is more likely to instinctualize punitive suffering, i.e., to react masochistically. It is apparent that each of these characteristics of dream life represents a regression on the part of the dreamer to a more childish stage of superego development and functioning.

Finally, one may surmise that the fact that instinctual wishes often find a more direct and conscious expression in dreams than would be permitted in waking life bespeaks a diminution of the superego's functioning to a more childish level as well as a diminution of the ego's defenses. We must remember in this connection that the link between superego functioning and the institution and maintenance of anti-instinctual defenses by the ego is a particularly close one. The defenses against the drives are normally maintained by the ego at the behest of the superego, once the superego has been firmly established as a system of the mind.

Now for the third point that we proposed to discuss, namely, the fact that instinctual wishes and fantasies stemming from the id play a larger role in dreaming than they do in most adult, waking, mental phenomena. That this is true seems self-evident. The explanation for it seems equally evident: during sleep, the mental representations of external reality are largely decathected. Broadly speaking, the only things that matter to us in our sleep are our own wishes and needs. This is one aspect of what Freud emphasized as the increase in narcissism during sleep. Since the instinctual fantasies which comprise the id aspect of the latent content of a dream are so largely infantile in content, it is understandable that they too impart an infantile character to the dream which they stimulate.

I shall attempt now to summarize the theory of dream psychology which I have just described to you. I shall begin by repeating that, despite the general quiescence of mental functioning during sleep, certain energies of the mind remain active. They, and the mental processes associated with them, constitute the latent content of the dream. This latent content takes its origin, on the one hand, from the instinctual derivatives of the id and on the other from the impressions and cares of the preceding day. The dream work consists of a mutual interplay among the various tendencies of id, ego, and superego, tendencies which may reinforce one another, may cooperate with one another, or may oppose one another. Such an interplay occurs as a regular state of affairs during waking life as well. However, during sleep various ego and superego functions are regressively altered. Moreover, a relatively large part is played in the dream work by infantile, wish-fulfilling fantasies, since a relatively smaller part is played by the claims of external reality, which are largely decathected during sleep. As a result, mental activity during dreaming is much more infantile in many ways than is mental activity during waking life. Condensation, displacement, representation by allusion, by opposites, by symbols, representation in concrete, visual images, disregard for time, space, and death, in a word, all of the familiar characteristics of the dream work are caused by ego and superego regression, plus the infantile nature of much of the latent content from which the dream work takes its origin. Finally, it is as a result of regressive alteration of the ego function of reality testing that the dreamer believes that what he dreams is not fantasy but reality.

Having presented to you this revised theory of the psychology of dream formation, my next task is to explain what relevance it has for clinical psychoanalytic work. In my opinion, its relevance can best be summarized under two headings. First, it suggests that dream analysis has more to tell than merely the content of the dreamer's unconscious, repressed, sexual childhood wishes or fantasies. Second, it suggests likewise that dream analysis is not as uniquely important as a method of investigating unconscious memories and unconscious mental processes as some psychoanalysts believe it to be.

What do I mean by saying that dream analysis has more to offer than a view of the dreamer's unconscious, infantile wishes? We know that it was to these wishes that Freud pointed when he described every dream as a wish fulfillment. When dreams are described as the highway to the unconscious mind of man, what is usually meant by "the unconscious" are repressed, infantile wishes. What more is there?

Let me give an example to illustrate what I have in mind. A 35-year-old, unmarried man, who had been in analysis for several months, dreamed that he was on a toboggan, rushing swiftly downhill on an icy slide. At first, the ride was exciting and enjoyable. Soon, however, he grew frightened. He was going too fast. An accident seemed inevitable. He did not awaken, but the dream, or his memory of it, ended.

The following information is pertinent. The patient had come to analysis depressed and unhappy over certain events in his life. During the course of the first few months of analysis, he had become more cheerful, even optimistic. Shortly before the dream just reported, however, he had begun to bring to his analysis memories and fantasies that pointed to conflict over frightening, homosexual wishes which were closely related to his jealousy of a younger sister, the family's favorite, as well as to a prolonged separation from his mother in early childhood. The emergence of this material made him noticeably uneasy, although he was not himself aware that this was so.

In associating to his dream about tobogganing, the patient spoke about a number of experiences he had had in another winter sport, namely, skiing. He was a fairly proficient skier and had never been injured while skiing. Friends of his had been injured, however. He recalled a doctor who had once fallen and fractured his clavicle on a downhill run. The man behaved like a child—like a sissy. No real man would have carried on like that over a little pain. The patient himself would certainly have been ashamed to show such weakness. Other associations had to do with the seating arrangements on a toboggan. Each passenger holds up the legs of the one behind. It's lots of fun if one is between two girls but embrassing to have a man sitting in front of one, or behind one, either, for that matter, the patient felt.

I assume you will agree with me that part of the latent content of my patient's dream was an unconscious, homosexual wish, originating in child-hood and revived in the transference. He wished that I, the man seated behind him, would make love to him as though he were a girl. What I wish to emphasize, however, is how much more the dream has to tell us. We learn from it that the patient is far more than just uneasy about his feminine wishes. He is very frightened that their consequence will be a painful physical injury, presumably the loss of his penis. We learn, also, some of the defenses he used in the dream work and in his associations to the dream in his effort to avoid, or at least to minimize, his anxiety. For one thing, he projected his expectation of bodily injury, as well as his feeling of unmanliness, onto his skiing companion. For another, he emphasized both is own stoicism and his love of sports. We can infer that both of these character traits serve impor-tantly the function of defending him against frightening, homosexual wishes. Indeed, some months later, in order to reassure himself about his manliness, he undertook, successfully, a hazardous athletic feat, of a sort for which he was quite untrained—a typical, counterphobic bit of acting out.

It is clear, therefore, that superego of this patient's dream affords a view of unconscious *conflict,* rather than merely an opportunity to identify an unconscious, infantile wish. We learn from the analysis of the dream not only the wish itself but also the fears that it arouses and the defenses which are directed against it. It is necessary to have a clear recognition of this fact in order to make the maximum use of dream analysis in one's clinical work with patients. In the present instance, what seemed to me most useful to interpret to the patient was that he was much more frightened by the recent references to homosexuality that had come up in his analysis than he consciously realized. At the time he reported the dream that we have been discussing, the state of the analytic work was such that it would have been premature to interpret to him that he did, indeed, have frightening homosexual wishes, although unconscious ones, to be sure. It would have been equally inappropriate at that time to have interpreted the defensive function of his athletic prowess. However, the decision as to what was appropriate and useful to interpret at the time is determined by factors other than dream interpretation proper. One is influenced by the previous course of the patient's analysis, by one's knowledge of what has already been interpreted to him, how he has responded to previous interpretations, the state of the transference, the general level of resistance, one's knowledge of special events that may be upsetting in the patient's life outside the analysis; *i.e.,* under different analytic circumstances, it might have been quite proper to interpret to him not only his fear of homosexuality but also his sexual wishes of a feminine nature toward me, or the fact that his interest in dangerous sports served to reassure him against the castration fears aroused by his wish to be loved as a girl. The point that I wish to make is that dream analysis tells one more than his patient's infantile wishes. It also tells us the anxiety (or guilt) associated with those wishes and the defenses which are directed against them in an effort to avoid anxiety. Not infrequently, it tells one something about the dynamics of character traits, as in the case just cited, or about the psychopathology of a symptom.

My second point is that our present understanding of dream psychology suggests that dream analysis is not as *uniquely* important as a method of investigating unconscious mental processes as some psychoanalysts believe it to be. *All* conscious mental phenomena and all behavior are multiply determined. It is not only the case with dreams that they are a compromise formation among instinctual (id) wishes, defenses motivated by anxiety or guilt, and superego demands or prohibitions. The same is true of neurotic symptoms, parapraxes, slips, jokes, many character traits, one's choice of a profession, one's sexual practices and preferences, daydreams, conscious childhood memories, including screen memories, one's reactions to a play, film, or book, one's social habits and activities in general and, above all, every patient's so-called free associations. They are no more free than is a manifest dream. Like every dream, they are the outcome of an unconscious interplay among the various forces and tendencies within the mind, forces which are most conveniently grouped under the headings id, ego, and super-ego. It is not possible to predict in general, I believe, which conscious phenomena will lead most quickly and easily to the fullest knowledge of unconscious mental processes. Nor is it, in my opinion, the same phenomena which are most advantageous for analysis at every stage of any one patient's analysis. Sometimes a dream is best; at another time, something else. What I wish to emphasize is the incorrectness of the view that dream analysis is, generally speaking, outstandingly the *best* method for learning about unconscious mental processes. It is essential in analysis to pay attention to patients' dreams; it is important, sometimes very important, to analyze them. It is equally important to pay attention to and to analyze many other aspects of what our analytic patients tell us.

In my experience, it is not rare for students to conclude from their analytic education that dreams are treated differently from other analytic material, in the following sense. When a patient tells a dream, one expects him to associate to it; when a patient tells a daydream, fantasy, or symptom, *etc.*, one doesn't ask for such associations. Apparently, the idea is not rare that dreams or, rather, dream analysis is different from the rest of analytic practice. This, I believe, is the basis for what Balint said in Edinburgh, for example. I am firmly of the opinion that this view is wrong. In my experience it is as important for patients to associate to symptoms, to fantasies, to physical sensations and images experienced during an analytic hour, *etc.*, as it is for them to associate to a dream. The results are just as likely to be illuminating and rewarding. I might add that I believe it is as risky to interpret the unconscious meaning of a neurotic symptom without the patient's associations to it as it is to interpret the unconscious meaning of a dream without the dreamer's associations. One may do either correctly with the skill born of long experience if one has an intimate knowledge of the psychological context in which the dream was dreamed or the symptom appeared. However, one may also go far astray or miss much of importance.

For example, a few days ago I learned from a young, married woman who had been in treatment for two months that she had been quite uncomfortable a couple of weeks before on a recent trip to a bank. She had been invited to have lunch with a friend who worked in the bank in a windowless dining room below street level but couldn't stay in a room down there with only one door for an exit. It made her anxious; why she didn't know. At that moment she realized that she had thought of this example of her habitual claustrophobia just after telling me about her mixed feelings for a sibling who had died before the patient was born, whose picture had been kept in the patient's room all through her childhood, and with whom she felt she was often unfavorably compared. Her first thought was that her fear of closed spaces, her worry that she would be unable to get out, was a result of her rage at her dead baby sister, whom her parents refused to let be dead and gone. Her second thought was to object that such an explanation couldn't be correct, since her sister's body is not buried; it is in a vault above ground. This reminded her that the underground bank rooms in which she had felt so anxious were next to the bank's vaults. She went on then to tell me for the first time that it frightens her to be in tunnels or elevators, especially if she can't get out, *i.e.*, if traffic stops in a tunnel or if an elevator's doors fail to open promptly.

I hope I have given enough material in this very brief vignette to illustrate the point that I wish to make, namely, that associations to a symptom are just as valuable and just as necessary to the understanding of the symptom's unconscious determinants as are associations to a dream for its interpretation. It is just as important for a patient to associate to symptoms, daydreams, or fantasies, in a word, to any of the many consequences of unconscious conflict, as it is for him to associate to the conscious elements of a dream.

In summary, I have presented a revision of psychoanalytic dream theory. According to the theory that I have presented, dreams, like many other features of mental life, are best understood as the result of an interplay among id, ego, and superego. Put into other words, a dream is multiply determined. The consequences of this understanding of dream formation are two-fold. First, dream analysis leads to an understanding not only of the unconscious, infantile wishes which the dream endeavors to fulfill in fantasy but also of other aspects of unconscious mental functioning of which those wishes are a part: to the fears and guilt feelings associated with them, to defenses against them and, often, to related symptoms or character traits. Second, while dream analysis is even more useful clinically than we are accustomed to considering it to be, it is not unique in this respect. Other consequences of inner conflict are as important to analyze as are dreams and may, on occasion, be quite as useful a road to the understanding of a patient's inner conflicts, of his unconscious mind, as a dream would be.

REFERENCES

1. Arlow, J. A., and Brenner, C. *Psychoanalytic Concepts and the Structural Theory.* International Universities Press, New York, 1964.
2. Brenner, C. *An Elementary Textbook of Psychoanalysis.* International Universities Press, New York, 1955.
3. Brenner, C. Some comments on technical precepts in psychoanalysis. J. Amer. Psychoanal. Ass., **17**: 333–352, 1969.
4. Breuer, J., and Freud, S. *Studies in Hysteria,* Vol. 2. 1895.
5. Freud, S. *Fragment of an Analysis of a Case of Hysteria,* Vol. 7. 1905.
6. Freud, S. *The Interpretation of Dreams,* Vols. 4 and 5. 1900.
7. Freud, S. *Metapsychological Supplement to the Theory of Dreams,* Vol. 14. 1917.
8. Freud, S. *The Unconscious,* Vol. 14. 1915.
9. Waelder, R. The principle of multiple function. Psychoanal. Quart., *5:* 45–62. 1936.

9. Dreams and Their Various Purposes

Joseph Weiss

In this chapter I shall present observations about dreams that support the theory of the mind proposed in this book. This theory was developed mainly from observations of the behavior of the analytic patient. However, a theory of the mind would rest on a weak foundation unless it could account for important phenomena, such as dreams, which are different from the phenomena it was developed to explain. Moreover, a theory of the mind that did not account well for dreams would be of little or no interest to analysts. An investigator, in developing a theory, should cast a wide net; he should use whatever evidence is pertinent, including informal observations as well as observations obtained in rigorous research.

In the present chapter I shall attempt to show that dreams reflect the same processes as those underlying the behavior of the patient during analytic treatment. They are products of the dreamer's thoughts (his higher mental functions), and they reflect the dreamer's unconscious concerns, as well as his plans and policies for dealing with these concerns. Moreover, the dreamer exerts control over his unconscious mental life. He regulates the production of dreams in accordance with the criteria of safety and danger.

My thesis may be put in the language of Freud's tripartite model as follows: The ego produces dreams in an attempt to deal adaptively with its problems, including those that arise from the demands on it of the instincts, of conscience, and of current reality. It produces dreams as part of its task of self-preservation.

My conception of dream formation rests ultimately on observation. However, this conception is compatible with certain ideas that Freud stated, but did not develop fully, in certain of his late works and that have subsequently been discussed by other writers.

Reprinted by permission of the Guilford Press, from *The Psychoanalytic Process*, edited by J. Weiss and H. Sampson, New York, 1986.

A BRIEF HISTORY OF FREUD'S IDEAS ABOUT DREAM FORMATION

Freud based his original theory of dream formation on the automatic functioning hypothesis. In *The Interpretation of Dreams* (1900), in which Freud presented his original theory in considerable detail, he assigned the ego a relatively small part in the formation of dreams. He assumed here that dreams express a primitive mental process (the primary process) in which unconscious wishes seek gratification by cathecting memories of gratification (p. 566); for example, the hungry infant hallucinates the image of the mother's breast.

In the primary process as Freud defined it, infantile wishes seek gratification in hallucinatory images in which they are depicted as fulfilled. This process is regulated by the pleasure principle and is carried out automatically without regard for thought, belief, or assessment of current reality. Freud stated explicitly in *The Interpretation of Dreams* that although dreams may contain judgments, criticisms, appreciations, explanations, or arguments, the thought processes which produce them are not an essential part of the formation of dreams. Thus, Freud wrote: *"Everything that appears in dreams as the ostensible activity of the function of judgment is to be regarded not as an intellectual achievement of dream work, but as belonging to the material of the dream-thoughts and as having been lifted from them into the manifest content of the dreams as a ready-made structure"* (1900, p. 445, italics Freud's).

Freud, however, assumed here that the production of dreams is regulated to a certain extent by considerations of danger and safety. He argued that the censor (he later assigned the censor's task to the ego) may permit repressed impulses to find expression in dreams because it has turned off the power of motility so that impulses unable to find expression in action may be allowed to become conscious without danger to the dreamer.

In discussing particular dreams (1900), Freud was not confined by his theory of dream formation. He implied, but did not state explicitly, that certain dreams are formed not automatically but by unconscious thought and that their purpose is not wish fulfillment but preparation for action. For example, in his discussion of examination dreams, Freud assumed that the dreamer unconsciously anticipates a certain task (similar to the examination) that he fears he will not be able to carry out successfully. In the dream he remembers that sometime in the past he had worried about a similar task but had carried it out successfully. He thereby reassures himself about the impending task. In Freud's words: "It would seem then that anxious examination dreams (which, as has been confirmed over and over again, appear when the dreamer has some responsible activity ahead of him next day and is afraid there may be a fiasco) search for some occasion in the past in which great anxiety has turned out to be unjustified and has been contradicted by the event" (1900, p. 274).

Examination dreams are intended not to fulfill an infantile wish but to reduce anxiety about an impending task. They are therefore oriented to reality and are a preparation for real action. The dreamer, in creating an examination dream, makes prominent use of a kind of thought process that the id is unable to carry out. The dreamer anticipates the impending task and, in the light of certain past achievements, assesses his capacity to carry it out. The dreamer's purpose is to prepare himself for the upcoming task by offering himself encouragement. Thus the dreamer, in producing an examination dream, does something that in the *Outline* Freud assumed is done by the ego.

Freud's discussion of examination dreams anticipated developments in the theory of dreams that he did not make explicit and general until the *Outline*. Freud changed his theory of dream formation gradually. His first change, a relatively modest one, concerned the production of punishment dreams. Such dreams are challenges to Freud's earlier view, because in both their manifest and latent contents they are so unpleasant. If a dream is so unpleasant, how can it be regarded as the fulfillment of an infantile libidinal wish? Freud solved this problem by maintaining that punishment dreams are wish fulfillments, but that they fulfill wishes derived not from the system Unconscious, but from the unconscious ego (in particular from the part of the ego that Freud was later to refer to as the superego). Punishment dreams, according to Freud, suggest that the ego may contribute more to the formation of dreams than heretofore recognized.

It must be admitted that their recognition means in a certain sense a new addition to the theory of dreams. What is fulfilled in them is equally an unconscious wish, namely a wish that the dreamer may be punished for a repressed and forbidden wishful impulse. To that extent dreams of this kind fall in with the condition that has been laid down here that the motive force for constructing a dream must be provided by a wish belonging to the unconscious. A closer psychological analysis, however, shows how they differ from other wishful dreams. In the cases forming Group B [dreams in which distressing dream-thoughts make their way into the manifest content of the dreams] the dream-constructing wish is an unconscious one and belongs to the repressed, while in punishment-dreams, though it is equally an unconscious one, it must be reckoned as belonging not to the repressed but to the "ego." Thus, punishment-dreams indicate the possibility that the ego may have a greater share than was supposed in the construction of the dreams. . . . The essential characteristic of punishment-dreams would thus be that in their case the dream-constructing wish is not an unconscious wish derived from the repressed (from the system *Ucs.*), but a punitive one reacting against it and belonging to the ego, though at the same time an unconscious (that is to say, preconscious) one. (added to *The Interpretation of Dreams* [1900] in 1919, pp. 556–558)

The next change Freud made in his theory of dreams was more fundamental. It was inspired by certain dreams of patients suffering from traumatic neuroses, who in these dreams relived the painful and frightening traumatic experiences from which their neuroses arose. Such dreams, Freud wrote, inevitably lead the dreamer back to the situation in which the trauma occurred (1920). Such dreams are concerned with experiences which, as Freud pointed out, are not and could never have been pleasurable. They cannot be conceptualized as regulated by the pleasure principle, as expressing an infantile wish arising in the unconscious, or as the expression of an unconscious wish for punishment. They are, Freud concluded, motivated by a wish for mastery, a wish Freud was later to assign to the ego. Indeed, Freud was later to emphasize the importance of the task of mastering external and internal stimuli by considering it among those things the ego does in the interest of self-preservation (1940, pp. 145–146).

Freud, in 1920, stated directly that traumatic dreams are an exception to the proposition that dreams are wish fulfillments: "It is impossible to classify as wish-fulfillments the dreams we have been discussing which occur in traumatic neuroses or the dreams, during psychoanalysis, which bring back to memory the psychical traumas of childhood" (p. 32).

Freud stated directly, too, that traumatic dreams are not produced in accordance with the pleasure principle: "We may assume, rather, that dreams are here helping to carry out another task which must be accomplished before the dominance of the pleasure principle can even begin. These dreams are endeavoring to master the stimulus retrospectively, by developing the anxiety whose omission was the cause of the traumatic neuroses" (1920, p. 22).

In the *Outline* Freud presented his entire theory of dream formation in a mere seven pages and he discussed the ego's part in the formation of dreams in just two or three paragraphs. About the ego's role, he wrote that though the motive for the formation of dreams may originate in the id or in the ego, it is the ego that produces dreams. He maintained his earlier view that dreams are wish fulfillments, but offered a new explanation of how in a dream a wish becomes fulfilled. In *The Interpretation of Dreams* Freud had assumed that infantile wishes, as a consequence of automatic processes, may be depicted as fulfilled. In the *Outline*, however, Freud stated that certain wishes (which may or may not be infantile), as a consequence of a decision made by the ego, may be depicted as fulfilled.

As regards the ego's part in the formation of dreams, Freud wrote in the *Outline* (1940):

It remains for us to give a dynamic explanation of why the sleeping ego takes on the task of the dream-work at all. The explanation is fortunately easy to find. With the help of the unconscious, every dream that is in process of formation makes a demand upon the ego—for the satisfaction of an instinct, if the dream originates from the id; for the solution of a conflict, the removal of a doubt or the forming of an intention, if the dream originates from a residue of preconscious activity in waking life. The sleeping ego, however, is focused on the wish to maintain sleep; it feels this demand as a disturbance and seeks to get rid of the disturbance. The ego succeeds in doing this by what appears to be an act of compliance: it meets the demand with what is in the circumstances a harmless *fulfilment of a wish* and so gets rid of it. (pp. 169–170)

Freud illustrated this ego activity by three examples, one of which was: "A need for food makes itself felt in a dreamer during his sleep: he has a dream of a delicious meal and sleeps on. The choice, of course, is open to him either of waking up and eating something or continuing to sleep. He *decided* in favor of the latter and satisfied his hunger by means of the dream" (1940, p. 170, italics mine).

Since Freud, other analysts have written that the ego plays a central part in the formation of dreams. For example, according to Arlow and Brenner, "It [the structural theory] postulates that ego functions, in this case defenses and integrative functions, participate in the dream work throughout its course" (1964, p. 135). Moreover, "We expect to learn from the analysis of our patient's dreams about the nature of the fears associated with their instinctual wishes, about their unconscious need to punish themselves, and even about the defenses which at the moment they are unconsciously employing in their struggles against their wishes" (p. 141). I shall add that we also expect to learn about the patient's pathogenic beliefs, his unconscious plans, policies, purposes, and goals. Thomas French went even further than Arlow and Brenner. He emphasized the problem-solving function of dreams: "We have postulated that the dream work, like the thought processes directing our ordinary waking activity, is dominated by the need to find a solution for a problem" (1954, p. 15).

DREAMS OF PRISONERS OF WAR AND THEIR
ADAPTIVE FUNCTIONS

The pertinence of the concept that the ego produces dreams and that it does so for certain vitally important adaptive purposes (such as warning, consoling, or working for mastery) is evident from the study of persons who are under great stress or who have undergone great stress. It was from his observations of patients with traumatic neuroses that Freud discovered that dreams may be produced by the ego as part of its task of mastering excitation. Extreme situations are, in general, likely to reveal factors that may not be obvious under normal circumstances. In situations where survival is at stake, the great part played in the production of dreams by the ego (which Freud tells us in the *Outline* is responsible for self-preservation) is particularly clear.

The part played by the ego in the production of dreams may be illustrated by dreams of former prisoners of war. My account here of such dreams is based on a study carried out by Dr. Paul Balson while he was Director of Psychiatric Research at Letterman Army Hospital (1975). Balson studied the dreams of five former prisoners of war, each of whom was interviewed intensively and three of whom received psychotherapy. Balson's procedure of studying the veterans' dreams years after they were produced seems justified for the following reasons: The dreams had been especially vivid in their imagery, and had made such powerful impressions on the veterans that they were confident that they remembered their dreams fairly accurately. In addition, the dreams were typical; all five tended to produce the same kinds of dreams. It seems highly unlikely that the five veterans would distort their memories of their dreams in the same ways.

The veterans produced a variety of dreams. However, I shall confine my discussion to three kinds, each of which was both typical and adaptive. (Each veteran, of course, did not necessarily produce all three kinds of dreams.) The three kinds of dreams corresponded, respectively, to three quite different (and, in each case, stressful) situations in which the veterans found themselves. These were the situations of the soldiers (1) before their capture, (2) during prolonged imprisonment in which they were mistreated, and (3) after their release from prison camp. The fact that in each of these situations the soldiers produced typical dreams suggests that each situation was so compelling that the feelings it mobilized (and the tasks it required the soldiers to perform) more or less overrode individual differences.

In Balson's opinion, each of the three kinds of dreams that the veterans produced was adaptive: "In all of these subjects these distinctive dream styles and patterns clearly enabled each individual prisoner to adapt to each successive stage of this prolonged and multifaceted psychological and physical trauma. The value of these dreams and their sequential patterning before, during, and immediately following the captivity appeared beyond objective or subjective refutation" (1975, p. 21).

WARNING DREAMS OF PRISONERS OF WAR

Before he was captured, a soldier who was exposed to the danger of capture typically produced frightening dreams that he was being captured. This kind of dream may be described as a warning dream. It performs in sleep the same function as, according to Sharpe (1950), certain fantasies foretelling danger perform in waking life. In warning dreams, the dreamer, to use Sharpe's phrase, is producing a "cautionary tale." The dreamer tells himself, "If I am not careful, I will be captured." The dream, as Freud told us in *The Interpretation of Dreams* (1900), has no way of representing such conjunctions as "if" in pictorial form. The best the dream can do to represent the possibility of capture is to depict the situation of capture.

The soldier's warning dream is adaptive. It orients him throughout the night to the grave danger he is facing, and it thereby prepares him for it. In Balson's (1975) words:

It can reasonably be assumed that the dream patterns from the period of time prior to capture . . . provided evidence of ego adaptive maneuvers directed towards enabling the individual to prepare for anticipated major environmental alterations, e.g., "I kept dreaming of death . . . being trapped in a burning helicopter . . . when I actually was burned and captured it seemed almost familiar somehow . . . almost expected." (p. 18)

The warning dream performs its function whether or not it is interpreted or the dreamer is able to explain its meaning. (In Balson's examples, the soldiers understood the meaning of their warning dreams.) It keeps the dreamer aware of the possibility of capture and, by preventing him from sleeping too soundly, may make him more able to react adaptively to the danger of capture and therefore be less vulnerable to capture.

A soldier's dream of being captured cannot readily be explained as the direct expression of an infantile wish. This is because the possibility of capture is, to the soldier, terrifying. He could, if captured, be killed. A dream of being captured could, of course, be explained as the direct expression of an unconscious wish for punishment. However, such an explanation is implausible. It either fails to connect the soldier's dangerous situation with his dreams, or it assumes that soldiers in danger of capture typically develop a wish to be punished by being captured. Moreover, a much more compelling explanation is at hand, which assumes that the dream is produced by the ego as a warning to the dreamer. According to this assumption, the ego, in producing a warning dream, is carrying out the same vital function that it carries out in waking life when it produces an anxiety signal. It carries out this function, as Freud tells us in the *Outline* (1940), as part of its task of self-preservation.

BLISSFUL DREAMS OF PRISONERS OF WAR

Immediately after capture a soldier typically produced traumatic dreams in which he relived the circumstances of his capture. However, after prolonged internment (in which the soldiers were treated badly) he produced blissful dreams of gratification, of power, or of being serene.

The theory presented in *The Interpretation of Dreams* is able to some extent to explain the captured soldier's production of blissful dreams, but it cannot explain it completely. The theory of *The Interpretation of Dreams* assumes that dreams are produced when powerful unconscious wishes that cannot find gratification in action find gratification instead in hallucinatory wish fulfillment. That theory assumes, moreover, that the process by which dreams are formed (the flowback of excitation to perception) is regulated automatically by the pleasure principle without regard for the dreamer's unconscious beliefs or his unconscious assessments of his current reality. That theory accounts well for the content of the captured soldier's blissful dream. A soldier, after a prolonged and tortured stay in prison camp, no doubt felt intensely deprived and frustrated. He no doubt longed to be gratified, powerful, or serene. He could not satisfy this wish in reality. He could satisfy it in his dreams by depicting it as fulfilled.

The theory presented in *The Interpretation of Dreams*, however, cannot account for the observation that a soldier did not produce blissful dreams either before his capture or after he had escaped. The soldier in the field who was in danger of being captured should have had as strong a wish to be gratified, powerful, or serene as the soldier after his capture, yet he produced not blissful dreams but warning dreams.

Moreover, both the content and the timing of the captured soldier's blissful dreams are well explained by the concept that the dreamer (or his ego) regulates the production of dreams and does so for an adaptive purpose. The dreamer, according to my formulation, assesses his situation. He concludes that he cannot change it; his fate has been taken out of his hands, so that he has nothing to lose by temporarily relinquishing any efforts to further his cause. The dreamer then decides to permit a blissful dream. He carries out a policy of denial. By producing such a dream, the dreamer not only denies his present situation, he offers himself consolation and a measure of hope. The decision of the dreamer to produce such a dream is adaptive, and its value does not depend on the dreamer's conscious understanding of it. This is because a blissful dream, by relaxing the dreamer, helps him to indulge in a deep sleep and thus to restore himself. If permits him to relax without putting him in any more danger than he is already facing, and it offers the dreamer a measure of hope during a period of despair.

In Balson's view, too, the soldiers' blissful dreams were adaptive: "The dreams functioned as partial attempts at mastery. When the subject was being severely deprived, propagandized, or physically abused and tortured, the dreams would be seen as an escape and as a means of 'gaining back my strength to go on' " (1975, p. 12). In one dream reported by Balson, a soldier who had been made to feel extremely helpless pictured himself as powerful and able to eat, drink, and have sex according to his wishes. He enjoyed the dream immensely, stating, "I felt so serene and powerful" (p. 12).

TRAUMATIC DREAMS OF PRISONERS OF WAR

After he was released and was out of danger, a soldier typically produced the kind of traumatic dreams that Freud referred to in *Beyond the Pleasure Principle* (1920). In these dreams the soldier repeated the frightening experiences of his life in prison camp. As Freud (1920) has convincingly argued, traumatic dreams of this kind are not produced in accordance with the pleasure principle. They repeat experiences that are not and could never have been pleasurable. Their purpose may be self-punishment; escaped prisoners may suffer from survivor guilt. However, Freud emphasized another function of traumatic dreams, which he considered more fundamental than the attainment of pleasure: It is to master traumatic experiences. This purpose (mastery) is, in the *Outline* (1940), ascribed to the ego, which, according to

Freud, seeks mastery of its inner and outer world as part of its task of self-preservation.

Repetition for mastery, as Freud (1920) pointed out, is a part of children's play. A child who has suffered a trauma passively attempts by repeating it actively to master it. However, an adult's reaction to a trauma is not so different from a child's. An adult who, for example, has been traumatized by an automobile accident may, after the accident, become preoccupied with it. He may spend a great deal of time mentally reviewing the circumstances of the accident. He may even go to the scene of the accident to better understand just how it came about. Moreover, he may develop a neurosis. He may become quite anxious about driving, or he may be temporarily unwilling or unable to drive.

How does the driver develop this problem, and how, by going over it in his mind, does he work to solve it? According to my thesis, an adult driver may react to an accident in much the same way as a child may react to a traumatic experience. Both may develop a neurosis. Moreover, they may develop their neuroses in much the same way: by developing a pathogenic belief. The driver may develop a pathogenic belief about his responsibility for the accident and about the likelihood that he will suffer a similar accident in the future. He may also partially repress the pathogenic belief, as well as the circumstances of the accident and the feelings of horror he was in danger of experiencing at the time of the accident. Thus, after the accident the traumatized driver may not be able to understand just how it happened, not only because he did not have the attention at the time to encompass it, but also because he has repressed his memories of it. A driver who has repressed his traumatic memories of an accident may maintain his repressions for varying lengths of time. He may remain calm and avoid thinking about the accident for just a few hours, until he is in the security of his home, surrounded by his family. He may then begin to lift his repressions and bring forth the circumstances of the accident and the previously repressed feelings of terror and horror. Or he may repress the memories of the accident for a much longer time. Eventually, however, the driver, by repeatedly going over the details of the accident, may permit himself, in a gradual and controlled manner and at his own pace, to face the circumstances of the accident and to remember the terror and horror. He ordinarily permits himself to remember the accident and to face these feelings only as rapidly as he can safely do so. He may, by gradually facing his feelings, become able to lift the repressions warding off the traumatic experience, to become conscious of and master the emotions connected with the experience, and to bring forth and change the pathogenic beliefs derived from it.

The soldier, whose primary task during prolonged internment was to console himself and to keep himself hopeful, faced an entirely different kind of task once he had escaped. His greatly improved situation now gave him the security and strength to face the same kind of task as the driver had faced after the accident, which was to master his traumatic experiences. According to Balson(1975):

The traumatic dreams of reliving which occurred immediately following capture and immediately following release clearly appeared to serve the same adaptive and restorative psychological functions as any dream pattern characteristic of a period of intense stress or trauma. These traumatic dreams of reliving appeared to allow the individual an opportunity for partial psychological mastery and affect expression in relationship to the traumatic events. (p. 19)

The soldier's task was similar to that of the driver, but more difficult. The soldier was more severely traumatized than the driver. He experienced more horror and terror. His repressions were deeper, and his pathogenic beliefs (which, as Balson pointed out, may include the belief that he was captured as a punishment for some wrongdoing) were more dire.

The soldier, like the moviegoer, kept the traumatic experiences repressed until he was out of danger. Then he attempted, by repetitively going over the experiences of his capture and imprisonment, to master them. However, at first he kept the repressions intact during his waking life and began the task of lifting them only in his dreams. The soldier's beginning this crucial task in his dreams is an example of my thesis that in dreams a person expresses his major unconscious plans, purposes, and goals.

Both the soldier's repression of his traumatic experiences while in danger and his attempts to lift his repressions once safe were adaptive. During an emergency it is adaptive for a person to institute repressions to prevent himself from being paralyzed by overwhelming feelings. However, it is equally adaptive for him after an emergency has passed to lift the repressions. It is only by lifting his repressions that a person may gain a clear understanding of the horrifying traumatic events he has experienced. He may then, by understanding these traumas, overcome both the emotions connected with them and the pathogenic beliefs inferred from them.

DREAMS AS THE EXPRESSION OF POLICY

Each of the kinds of dreams discussed above is about the dreamer's major current concerns and each expresses the dreamer's (or his ego's) policy toward these concerns. The chief concern of the soldier before capture was the danger of being captured. His policy toward the danger as he expressed it in his warning dreams was "Be careful!" The chief concern of the soldier after prolonged capture was his despair and hopelessness. His policy toward this despair, as expressed in his blissful dreams, was to offer himself denial, consolation, and hope. (The soldier's blissful dreams should not be regarded simply as a maladaptive turning away from reality. Such dreams do turn the dreamer away from reality. However, in a hopeless situation, denying current concerns and offering oneself a degree of hope may be adaptive.) The chief concern of the escaped soldier was to overcome the effects of the experiences he had been through. In his traumatic dreams he expressed a policy toward these concerns and began to carry it out; he told himself, "Remember the experiences you have been through, understand them, and master the feelings and ideas which they aroused in you." Examination dreams, too, illustrate my thesis that in his dreams a dreamer expresses a policy. In an examination dream the dreamer encourages himself by telling himself, "Don't take your worries so seriously!"

For each of the kinds of dreams discussed above (but not in all kinds of dreams) the plot or story of the dream contributes to its meaning. The story carries the message the dreamer must convey to himself and creates the mood or affect the dreamer needs to experience. Such was the case, too, in the example reported by Freud in the *Outline* of the dreamer who appeased his appetite by dreaming that he was eating a meal. The fact that this dream of eating was in visual imagery and hence closer to experience than verbal thought helped the dream to perform its function of appeasing the dreamer's appetite and enabling him to sleep.

Such was the case, too, in the dreams produced by the former prisoners of war. These, Balson tells us, were depicted in especially vivid visual imagery. The vividness of these dreams may reflect the urgency of the task which the dreams were intended to perform. A vivid realistic dream about being captured may serve as a more effective warning than a pallid and vague dream, and more effective still than the verbal thought, "Be careful or you will be captured." Similarly, a vivid realistic dream of a situation in which he is satisfied, powerful, or serene may be a greater blame to a troubled soldier's spirits than a pallid, vague one and a greater balm still than a verbal thought such as, "Console yourself by forgetting your troubles." Indeed, the soldier, during such a dream and even after awakening, may experience some of the relaxation and happiness he would feel if he really were in the situation his dream depicts.

The vividness of the escaped soldier's dreams may also be adaptive. His vivid dreams about the circumstances of his capture and of his life in prison camp may help him to remember and ultimately to master these experiences better than his conscious attempts to remember them.

The dreams discussed above, as already noted, perform their functions whether or not the dreamer is able consciously to interpret them. The soldier who, before capture, dreamed that he was being captured, was reminded in his dreams of his chief danger and indeed his chief concern—capture. He was warned of this danger whether or not he consciously wished to be warned of it, and whether or not he consciously recognized that to be warned of danger was the purpose of the dream. He was, in addition, induced by the dream to sleep lightly and thus to be more alert to danger.

The soldier who, after capture, permitted himself blissful dreams, was offering himself consolation and enabling himself to enjoy a deep and restful sleep. He consoled himself whether or not he consciously wished for consolation, and whether or not he consciously realized that to console himself was the purpose of the dream.

The soldier who, after his escape, dreamed of the circumstances of his capture, was beginning to do the work he needed to do to overcome the effects of his traumatic experiences. He was beginning to do this work whether or not he consciously wanted to do it or consciously realized that he was doing it. Similarly, the person who, according to Freud, dreamed of eating to appease his appetite and so was enabled to remain asleep was helped by his dream to stay asleep whether or not he consciously understood the meaning of the dream.

THE SUBJECT MATTER OF DREAMS

A person's dreams, as I have said, reflect his chief concerns, in particular those concerns that he is unable by conscious thought alone to sort out or put in perspective, or toward which he is unable consciously to develop a policy or plan. A person, for various reasons, may be unable by conscious thought alone to deal successfully with certain problems. The veterans whose dreams

I have just described could not by conscious thought alone deal successfully with their problems because their problems were so overwhelming. Likewise, a person may be unable by conscious thought to deal successfully with a problem because, as a result of his repressions, he cannot permit himself consciously to face it. In either case, a person who cannot deal successfully with a crucial problem consciously may attempt to deal with it in his dreams.

The dreams of analytic patients generally reflect problems that the patient cannot face as a consequence of his repressions. Therefore, during a period of his analysis in which he is working unconsciously to solve a particular problem, a patient may produce a particular kind of dream. After he has succeeded in making that problem conscious and has acquired the capacity to deal with it successfully by conscious thought, he may stop producing that kind of dream.

Such was the case in the analysis of Mr. Q, who, for a time during his treatment, was not conscious of his profound distrust of the analyst. During that period, he produced dreams in which he warned himself that, were he to trust the analyst, he would put himself in a situation of danger. After he became conscious of his distrust of the analyst and was able consciously to tolerate not trusting him, he stopped producing such dreams.

Mr. Q was a successful businessman whose childhood problem was similar in certain ways to that of the typical case presented by Freud in the *Outline* (1940). Mr. Q was the son of young parents and their only son until he was 5 years old, when his younger sister was born. Like the patient described in the *Outline,* Mr. Q in early childhood was close to his mother and interested in her sexually. His mother would take him into her bed when his father, an insurance executive, was away on a business trip. Mr. Q dreaded his father's return, not only because it meant that he had to stop sleeping with his mother, but because he hated and feared his father.

Mr. Q described his father as cruel, punitive, and rejecting. Mr. Q was competitive with his father and assumed that his father was competitive with him. Moreover, he assumed that his father was envious of his close relationship with his mother, for, as he experienced it, his mother preferred him to his father.

In short, Mr. Q developed a typical Oedipal constellation as described by Freud. He also developed typical castration anxiety. He literally (as opposed to metaphorically) believed that he would be castrated for his sexual interest in his mother. He did not remember being threatened with castration by either of his parents, but he did remember that his uncle, a pediatrician, threatened to castrate him if he did not stop squirming during a physical exam.

Mr. Q, during the period of his analysis on which I shall report, repeated with the analyst the childhood conflicts about trust that he had experienced with his father. During this period the patient consciously admired the analyst and wanted to like and trust him. He believed that unless he liked and trusted the analyst he would not be successfully analyzed. He also wanted to experience with the analyst closeness such as he had been unable to experience with his father. Unconsciously, however, Mr. Q was deeply distrustful of the analyst. He felt intensely guilty about his distrust, and was afraid to experience it. He unconsciously feared that were he to experience or express it, he would hurt the analyst and thus provoke punishment and rejection from him.

Although Mr. Q was struggling consciously to like the analyst, he wished unconsciously to overcome his fear of him and his need to placate him by being compliant, noncompetitive, and admiring.

During the period of his analysis described above, Mr. Q would wake up early with frightening dreams on the days he was to see the analyst (two or three times a week). Often he would be unable to get back to sleep. Mr. Q's associations to the dreams made it clear that the dreams were intended to warn him that although the analyst might appear friendly and trustworthy, he was in fact malicious and not to be trusted.

In one such dream the patient depicted the analyst as a friendly, pleasant plantation owner who genially led the patient on a tour of his mansion but who was indifferent to the misery of the slaves, who were being tortured in their quarters. In another dream, the patient depicted himself as a young circus performer and the analyst as an older performer who told the patient about a fantastic stunt. If the patient and the older performer had attempted this stunt, the patient would have been injured or killed and the older performer would have been completely safe.

Mr. Q produced warning dreams of this kind for about two months. As he became able, with the analyst's help, to consciously tolerate both his distrust of the analyst and his contempt for him, he stopped having this kind of dream. He had no need for such dreams after he realized that he was required neither to like the analyst nor to comply with him, and that he could reject any of the analyst's comments with which he did not agree.

During this period of his analysis, Mr. Q prepared himself unconsciously for his analytic sessions by reminding himself in his dreams about his belief that the analyst was not to be trusted.

In the next example, the patient, an analytic candidate, prepared himself in a dream for an analytic session by offering himself reassurance that he could not permit himself consciously to feel. The patient, who had developed a father transference, had been wary about telling the analyst about his successes with women. He feared consciously that by bragging to the analyst he would make him jealous, as he believed he had made his father jealous. He had begun to realize that his conception of the analyst as vulnerable stemmed from a father transference, but he had been unable consciously to retain an image of the analyst as strong and generous.

In his dream the patient was watching in a matter of fact way as one of his own patients, a young PhD student, made love with a girlfriend in a park. As the dreamer's associations made clear, one purpose of the dream was to prepare the dreamer to tell the analyst about his sexual relationship with his own girlfriend. He was enjoying it and feared that in describing it to the analyst, he would make the analyst jealous. In the dream, he told himself, "Since I am not jealous when watching my patient making love, I should assume that my analyst will not be jealous when hearing about my lovemaking."

In the following example, a patient, Mr. K, produced a series of terrifying warning dreams. They all had the same message: that if he were to break away from his mother by dating a woman, he would kill his mother. The patient understood his dreams. He had been conscious of his separation guilt, but not of its intensity. He was made aware by his dreams of the intensity of his guilt. He experienced the dreams as telling him that he was not yet ready to form a heterosexual relationship.

The patient, a professional musician in his 30s, decided during his analysis to struggle against his homosexuality by forcing himself to have sexual relations with women. Early in life, the patient had developed a symbiotic relationship with his mother, whom he described as highly emotional, angry, seductive, and possessive. She would sleep with the patient when his father, a remote figure, was out of town. She would also, at times, punish the patient by beating him.

Mr. K was almost conscious of his belief that, were he to develop a sexual relationship with a woman, he would kill his mother, whom he believed lived primarily for him. He decided, largely out of unconscious compliance to the analyst and despite great anxiety, to date an attractive woman he met at work. Almost immediately after starting to date her, he began to have horrible nightmares of his mother dying. Mr. K visualized his mother, emaciated and pale, lying in her coffin, calling him in a weird voice to return to her. The nightmares were so vivid and frightening that the patient dreaded going to sleep, and they continued until the patient stopped dating the woman. Mr. K was able to interpret his dreams himself; he knew consciously that their message was untrue. Yet his dreams were so vivid, realistic, and terrifying that he could not ignore them.

Punishment dreams, along with warning dreams and encouragement dreams, are relatively common. They are much more common, for example, than blissful dreams, which are relatively rare. (A person, in my experience, may produce a blissful dream in two circumstances: if he is without hope and thus is in no danger of being lulled into a false sense of security, or if he assumes that a certain important person is watching over him and protecting him from danger.)

In the following dream, which is a punishment dream, the dreamer, who felt guilty about defeating his rivals, attempted to relieve himself of his guilt by a dream in which he turned the tables on himself, and so identified with the victim.

An analytic patient in his 20s attained a position that he expected would put him in the center of a number of interesting activities while relegating his rivals to the sidelines. He felt guilty about his rivals. He found relief in a dream in which he depicted himself in the sixth grade, sitting with the girls from his class while watching the popular athletic boys compete in a baseball tournament.

ARE DREAMS FORMED AUTOMATICALLY OR BY THE EGO? ABSURD DREAMS AS A CASE IN POINT

In *The Interpretation of Dreams* (1900), Freud stated that two separate functions may be distinguished in mental activity during the construction of a dream: the production of the dream thoughts (day residues), and their transformation by the dream work into the dream. The mind, according to Freud, employs all of its faculties in the production of dream thoughts. These are normal (secondary process) thoughts that are formed in waking life by the preconscious and retain their charge of interest during sleep. These thoughts are concerned with various things, including problem solving and the forming of intentions. However, these thoughts are not an *essential* part of the dream, and the solutions they propose or the intentions they form are not part of the dream's interpretation.

The *essential* part of the dream, according to the theory presented in *The Interpretation of Dreams,* is the dream work. The dream work is not like normal thinking. Rather, it functions automatically in accordance with the laws governing the primary process. "The dream work is not simply less cautious, more careless, more irrational, more frightful, more forgetful, or more incomplete than waking thought: It is different from it qualitatively and for that reason not completely comparable with it. It does not think, calculate, or judge in any way at all; it restricts itself to giving things a new form" (1900, p. 507). The dream work, Freud tells us, is the *essence* of dreaming. "At bottom dreams are nothing more than a particular form of thinking made possible by the conditions of the state of sleep. It is the *dream work* which creates that form and it alone is the essence of dreaming" (1900, footnote, pp. 506–507).

Freud gradually changed his conception for dream formation. In the *Outline* he no longer assumed that dreams are formed automatically by the primary process, but rather that they are formed by the ego, which "takes on the task of the dream work" (1940, p. 169).

The views proposed here, like Freud's views in the *Outline,* assume that the ego plays a central part in the construction of dreams, and that in forming them it makes use of thought similar to conscious thought. The ego may express its plans, purposes, and goals in dreams, and it may attempt to solve problems. Moreover, the plans, purposes, and goals that the ego expresses and the solutions to problems that it offers are an essential part of the meaning of dreams.

In order to compare Freud's early theory of dream formation with the theory he presented in the *Outline* and on which the views presented here are based, I shall discuss absurd dreams. In *The Interpretation of Dreams,* Freud conceived of the formation of absurd dreams as taking place in two steps: Before going to sleep, the person produces normal thoughts that contain an element of derision or criticism. Then the dream work, which does not function logically but by the primary process, transforms the thought into the dream, using absurdity to express the derision or criticism.

According to the views proposed here (which are compatible with those which Freud presented in the *Outline*), the use of absurdity in dreams is not the result of automatic processes, nor is it qualitatively different from its use in normal conscious thought (i.e., in the exercise of certain higher mental functions) and should be attributed not to the primary process but to the ego. The ego may use absurdity in dreams in a logical and normal way, just as it may in normal conscious argumentation in order to make a point. In some dreams the ego uses absurdity in a way which is akin to the method of logical proof employed by Greek geometers and called "reduction to absurdity." Such dreams have the structure of an argument: A particular premise that the dreamer would like to disprove is shown to lead to an absurd conclusion. This kind of dream may be illustrated by the following example:

Miss F, a woman in her early 20s, had, throughout childhood, been very close to her identical twin sister. She was, however, at the time of the dream, separating herself from her twin and experiencing considerable guilt. She had begun an affair but feared that this would hurt her sister. It was in these circumstances that Miss F produced a dream in which she pictured herself and her sister as married to one another and about to have a baby. She woke up thinking, "How absurd." As her associations made clear, the patient was by this dream telling herself that, however much she loved her sister, she would not be able to have a baby with her, and therefore that her happiness depended on leaving her sister and developing a relationship with a man.

In constructing this dream Miss F began with the premise that she should love her sister, and that she could in a love relationship with her achieve everything that she wanted in any relationship. In the dream, she proceeded to carry this premise to its logical conclusion, by depicting her sister and her having a baby, and she showed herself by the manifestly false conclusion that the premise she began with was false: She could not achieve with her sister everything that she wanted in a relationship. Miss F could not directly disavow her idea that she should seek happiness in her relationship with her sister to the exclusion of other relationships. However, she could reduce this idea to absurdity.

This dream no doubt expresses derision. However, it is best understood not primarily as the expression of an impulse toward derision but as a normal thought about a particular problem and directed to the solution of that problem. The derision is a part of the thought and an inherent part of its logic. Miss F used derision to mock a premise she had held out of guilt. Her purpose was to weaken the hold on her of this premise.

This dream illustrates a fundamental difference between Miss F's experience and the experience of the person who uses irony or reduction to absurdity in waking life: The difference is the dreamer's relative lack of self-observation. The dreamer generally does not know he is being ironic or using reduction to absurdity until after awakening.

A dream that, in my opinion (although not necessarily in the opinion of Dr. Renik) makes use of reduction to absurdity, has been reported by Owen Renik (1981, p. 159). He described a patient who out of guilt would falsely accuse herself of plagiarism. She dreamt that she stole a bicycle, but on waking up she remembered that it belonged to her. She thereby reduced to absurdity her idea that she was a plagiarist.

A young professional man was frequently worried that none of his hopes would be realized. Like his mother, who had often warned him to take advantage of his opportunities, he was afraid to stop worrying for fear that if he did so he would indeed miss some opportunity. In his dream, which he recognized as absurd, he sat down happily to a large, delicious meal, only to be disappointed when it walked away from him.

In this dream, the patient mocked his mother's teaching and, by doing so, reassured himself that he need not be constantly concerned with the possibility of losing his opportunities.

A young businessman, out of compliance to his father, believed that he should do everything scientifically, including choosing a wife. After he fell in love with an attractive woman he was inclined to forget his father's advice, but he could not quite bring himself to do so However, as he came to understand his spiteful obedience to his father, he eventually became able to forget his father's advice and marry the woman. While he was working on this problem, the patient dreamt that he found himself in a store measuring numerous socks with a ruler to find the pair that fit him perfectly.

In general, a person who uses absurdity in his dreams also uses it in his waking thoughts. A good example of this occurred in the analysis of a young college student who had suffered a severe loss around her 13th year. Afterward, she developed the magical idea that unless she were worried about losing something which she valued, she would, in fact, lose it.

In the first year of her analysis, she began one hour by telling me in a worried voice that she was concerned about the four-month vacation I was about to take. However, after I had questioned her about it she made clear that she knew my vacation was to be only 3 weeks. Later in the same hour, the patient reported a recent dream in which she experienced an intense longing to be accepted at a certain university. After waking up she realized the dream was absurd because she was already in her junior year at that university. In both her dream and her waking thought she showed herself that her fear of loss was absurd.

In the following example, the dreamer reassures himself in a patently false way that his wife is healthy. Since the reassurance is false and indeed absurd, the purpose of the dream is not to reassure the dreamer but to warn him.

The patient, who was not completely aware of his worry about his wife, produced a dream that was simply a vivid image of a woman's torso endowed with large breasts. The patient's first comment on the dream was that he experienced the breasts as overwhelming, as though the woman were an Amazon. Then he thought that the dream image indicated how a woman's torso might have appeared to him when he was a young child.

Next the dreamer commented that his wife has large breasts and is quite proud of them. His wife, he then remembered, has seemed worried about herself lately. She has had a persistent unexplained fever and certain confusing symptoms. The patient then began to realize that he too has been worried about his wife but has been denying his worry about her.

It occurred to him then that the dream might express an attempt to reassure himself about his wife. However, further investigation revealed that it meant just the opposite. That is, it told the dreamer, "Though your wife is proud and sexy, she nonetheless may be ill and should see a doctor. Stop attempting to offer yourself false reassurances about her health!"

As the dreamer became aware of the meaning of the dream, he remembered something that he had not understood earlier; namely, that he had awakened from the dream with a feeling of anxiety appropriate to the dream's message: that he stop denying his worry.

I shall end this chapter with a dream that is akin to the dreams of prisoners of war, in that it occurred under extremely dire circumstances; it was vivid and realistic; its purpose—to offer consolation—was evident; and it offered great consolation and relief both at the time it was dreamt and for quite a while afterward.

The dreamer, a 30-year-old carpenter who was the father of two children, came to therapy after he killed his wife in a shooting accident while unloading a defective gun. The shooting was truly an accident, and the patient's wife died instantly. The patient, at the beginning of his treatment (which was not an analysis), was distraught and indeed suicidal. He felt intense grief and guilt. His therapist focused on the accidental nature of the killing and in various ways supported the patient in his struggle not to think of himself as a murderer. After 8 months of therapy, the patient attained enough relief of guilt to permit himself to produce the following vivid, realistic dream: "I accidentally shot my wife. She staggered to where I was sitting, then lay dying in my arms. As she was dying, she told me that she knew that my shooting her was accidental, and she forgave me for it."

The patient was able in this dream to offer himself much-needed relief and consolation. He kept the dream in mind for a long period of time. He reacted to the dream as though to a real event—that is, as though his wife had in fact forgiven him. He was relieved by the dream despite the fact that he knew it was only a dream and that his wife was dead and could not forgive him.

This dream makes apparent the power of dreams, with their vividness and closeness to experience, to carry a message to the dreamer. The patient could not offer himself comparable relief by simply telling himself, "My wife would surely forgive me." This dream, like the blissful dreams of captured soldiers, offered a desperate dreamer an experience he could remember and use to console himself for a long time after he produced it.

REFERENCES

Arlow, V. and Brenner C. *Psychoanalytic Concepts and the Structural Theory.* New York: International Universities Press, 1964.
Balson, P. Dreams and fantasies as adaptive mechanisms in prisoners of war in Vietnam.

Unpublished paper written in consultation with M. Horowitz and E. Erikson, 1975. (On file at the San Francisco Psychoanalytic Institute.)

French, T. *The integration of behavior.* Vol. 2; *The integrative process in dreams.* Chicago: University of Chicago Press, 1954.

Freud, S. *The interpretation of dreams* (1900). *Standard Edition* 4:1–338, 5:339–627. London: Hogarth Press, 1953.

——— *Beyond the pleasure principle* (1920). *Standard Edition* 18:3–64. London: Hogarth Press, 1955.

——— *New introductory lectures on psychoanalysis* (1933). *Standard Edition* 22:3–182. London: Hogarth Press, 1964.

——— *An outline of psychoanalysis* (1940). *Standard Edition* 23:141–207. London: Hogarth Press, 1964.

Renik, O. Typical examination dreams, "superego dreams" and traumatic dreams. *Psychoanalytic Quarterly* 50 (1981): 159.

Sharpe, E. *Collected papers in psychoanalysis.* London: Hogarth Press, 1950.

D. Object, Self, Affect

10. The Function of Dreams

Hanna Segal

Doctor Segal is herein re-exploring some intriguing notions about dreams and dreaming. In employing Bion's conceptions about alpha and beta elements (and functioning) conjoined to her own discovery of the symbolic equation aspect of concrete thinking (in a state of projective identification) the patient confuses (a) himself with the object to be symbolized and (b) the object to be symbolized with the symbol for it. With these tenets Segal seeks to advance from Freud's simple notion of dreams as formations to a more sophisticated notion that dreams are veritable "bowel movements" in which painful states of mind can be dreamed away by evacuation, provided the elements of the experience have been "alphabetized" by alpha function. Elements which resist alpha function become beta elements (to use a Bionian term) and are suitable for prediction of future acting-out. Thus the predictive dream is part of a more elaborate procedure in which the undigested beta elements must be dreamed and acted-out in order to achieve ultimate evacuation.

Jones tells us that to the end of his life Freud considered *The Interpretation of Dreams* his most important work. This is not surprising. Whereas his studies on hysteria revealed the meaning of symptoms, it was his work on dreams that opened up for him and us the understanding of the universal dream world and dream language. The structure of the dream also reflects the structure of personality.

To recap briefly the classical theory of dreams, repressed wishes find their fulfillment in the dream by means of indirect representation, displacement, condensation, etc., and by use of symbols which Freud puts in a slightly

Reprinted by permission of Hanna Segal, James S. Grotstein, and H. Karnac (Books) Ltd., from *Do I Dare Disturb the Universe? A Memorial to Wilfred Bion,* edited by James S. Grotstein, London, 1983.

different category from other means of indirect presentation. Dream work is the psychic work put into this process. By means of dream work a compromise is achieved between the repressing forces and the repressed and the forbidden wish can find fulfillment without disturbing the repressing agencies. Freud did not revise much the theory of dreams in the light of his further work. For instance, he did not tell us how his views on dreams were affected by his formulation of the duality of instincts and the conflict between libidinal and destructive dreams. He also, at the time of his basic formulations about the dream, did not yet have available to him the concept of working through. I myself feel rather uneasy about the dream being conceived as nothing but a compromise: The dream is not just an equivalent of a neurotic symptom, dream work is also part of the psychic work of working through. Hence, the analyst's satisfaction when, in the course of analysis, "good" dreams appear.

The classical theory of dream function takes for granted an ego capable of adequate repression and of performing the psychic work of dreaming, which, to my mind, implies a certain amount of working through of internal problems. It also takes for granted the capacity for symbolisation. Now, when we extend our psychoanalytical researches, we come more and more across patients in whom those functions, on which dreaming depends, are disturbed or inadequate. The function of symbolisation should be investigated further. Freud took the existence of symbols as given and universal and, I think, unchangeable phenomena. This, of course, was particularly so before he broke with Jung and the Swiss School of analysts. Jones, in his paper on symbolism, which denotes the main break with the Swiss School, implies already, though he does not explicitly state it, that symbolisation involves psychic work connected with repression—"Only the repressed is symbolised —only the repressed needs to be symbolised" (Jones 1916). Melanie Klein made the next big step forward. In the analysis of an autistic little boy described in her paper 'Symbol Formation and its Importance for the Development of the Ego' (Klein 1930), she gives an account of the analysis of a child who was incapable of forming or using symbols. In her view, symbolisation occurs by a repression and displacement of interest in the mother's body so that objects in the external world are endowed with symbolic meaning. In the case of Dick, the autistic child, a phantasised, sadistic and projective attack on to his mother's body gave rise to a paralysing degree of anxiety so that the process came to a stand-still and no symbol formation occurred. The child did not speak or play or form relationships. I investigated further those phenomena describing the psychic dynamics of the formation of what I called the symbolic equation or the concrete symbol characteristic of psychoses and the symbol proper suitable for purposes of sublimation and communication (Segal 1957). Briefly stated, in my view, when projective identification is in ascendance and the ego is identified and confused with the object, then the symbol, a creation of the ego, becomes identified and confused with the thing symbolised. The symbol and the object symbolised become the same, giving rise to concrete thinking. Only when separation and separateness are accepted and worked through does the symbol become, not equated with the object, but a representative of the object. This, in my view, implies a full depressive elaboration; the symbol becoming a precipitate of a process of mourning. The disturbance of the relationship between the self and the object is reflected in a disturbance in the relationship between the self, the object symbolised and the symbol. I define the term 'symbolic equation and symbol' in the following way: "In the symbolic equation, the symbol substitute is felt to be the original object. The substitute's own properties are not recognized or admitted . . . the symbol proper available for sublimation and furthering the development of the ego is felt to represent the object. Its own characteristics are recognized, respected and used. It arises when depressive feelings predominate over the paranoid-schizoid ones, when separation from the object, ambivalence, guilt and loss can be experienced and tolerated. The symbol is used, not to deny, but to overcome loss. When the mechanism of projective identification is used massively as a defense against depressive anxieties, symbols already formed and functioning as symbols may revert to symbolic equations"—as, for instance, in a psychotic breakdown.

To Jones'—'only what is repressed needs to be symbolised,' I added, 'only what can be adequately mourned can be adequately symbolised.' Thus, the capacity for non-concrete symbol formation is in itself an achievement of the ego—an achievement necessary for the formation of the kind of dreams covered by Freud's theory.

We know that in the psychotic, the borderline, and the psychopathic dreams do not function in this way. In the acute psychotic, often, if not always, there is no distinction between hallucinations and dreams. Indeed, no clear distinction occurs between states of being asleep or awake, delusion, hallucination, night-time events, which could go by the name of dreams, and they often have the same psychic value. In nonchronic states, but when psychotic processes are in ascendance, dreams may be experienced as real and concrete events. Bion reports on a patient who was terrified by the appearance of his analyst in the dream, as he took it as evidence of having actually devoured the analyst (Bion 1958). Dreams may be equated with faeces and used for purposes of evacuation or when minute, internal fragmentation occurs, they may be felt like a stream of urine and the patient may react to having bad dreams as to incidents of incontinence (Bion 1958). A patient can use dreams for getting rid of rather than working through unwanted parts of the self and objects and he can use them in analysis for projective identification. We are all familiar with patients who come and flood us, fill us, with dreams in a way disruptive to the relationship and to the analysis.

I had the opportunity of observing this type of function of the dreams particularly in two borderline psychotic patients both of whom dreamt profusely, but in whom it was the function rather than the content of the dreams that had to be paid attention to. In these patients, often dreams were experienced as concrete happenings. This was particularly clear with my woman patient. This woman, who is very quarrelsome in a paranoid way, can bring a dream in which she was attacked by X or Y, or sometimes myself, and if one attempts to understand some aspect of the dream, she will say indignantly "But it is X or Y or you who have attacked me," treating the event in the dream as a completely real event. There is apparently no awareness that *she dreamt* the dream. Similarly, an erotic dream in which, say, a man pursues her, is felt practically as a proof of his love. In fact, her dreams, although she calls them dreams, are not dreams to her but a reality, and in this they parallel another mental phenomenon in her life, in which she uses a similarly misleading word. She experiences most weird and bizarre sexual phantasies and she freely speaks of them as 'phantasies,' but if one enquires into them more closely, it becomes apparent that these are not phantasies but hallucinations. They are felt as real experiences. For instance, she walks very awkwardly because she feels she has a penis stuck in her vagina; and mentally, when she phantasises a sexual relationship with someone, she uses the word 'phantasy,' but in fact, she believes and behaves as if it were a reality. For instance, she accuses me of being jealous of her sexual life, busting her relationships, etc., when, in fact, she has no sexual life or relationships. So what she calls phantasy and what she calls a dream are, in fact, experienced as a reality though she thinly denies it. These so-called dreams constantly invade the external reality situation. For instance, she will complain about the smell of gas in my room and it will transpire later that she dreamt of bursting a balloon or exploding a bomb. The evacuation that happens in the dream seems to invade the perception of the reality.

These concretized dreams lend themselves particularly for purposes of expulsion. This was especially clear in my male patient, who used to write his dreams extensively in a little notebook. He had volumes and volumes of them. For instance, following his mother's death, he had dreams of triumph over her, aggression, guilt, loss, but in his conscious life, the mourning of his mother was conspicuous by its absence. It was interpretations of the kind — 'you have got rid of your feelings for your mother in your dream' — that were more effective in bringing about some conscious experience of his affect than any detailed analysis of the dream. He was using the dream to get rid of that part of his mind which was giving him pain and later discharged the dream into his notebook. He deals similarly with insight. An insightful session is often followed by a dream which seems to be closely related to it. In other patients, this kind of dream is usually a step in the working-through. In his case, however, more often than not, such a dream means that he got rid of all feeling about the previous session by making it into a dream and getting rid of it from his mind.

In the woman patient, similarly, the dream is part of an expulsive process. For instance, when she complains about the smell of gas in my room, she mentally expels the gas into the room.

Their dreams were characterised by very poor and crude symbolisation and one was struck both by the concreteness of the experience and the invasion of reality, as though there was no differention between their mind and the outside world. They had no internal mental sphere in which the dream could be contained. Khan, elaborating Winnicott's concept of transitional space, describes it in terms of dream space (Khan 1974). For myself, I found most helpful in understanding those phenomena, Bion's model of mental functioning, particularly, his concept of the alpha and beta elements and his concept of a mother capable of containing projective identification (Bion 1963).

Bion distinguishes between alpha and beta elements of mental functioning. Beta elements are raw perceptions and emotions suitable only for projective identification—raw elements of experience to be gotten rid of. Beta elements are transformed into alpha elements by the alpha function. Those are elements which can be stored in memory, which can be repressed and elaborated further. They are suitable for symbolisation and formation of dream thoughts. It is the beta elements which can become bizarre objects or concrete symbols, in my sense of the word, that I think are elements of the psychotic-type dream, and alpha elements, which are the material of the neurotic and normal dream. This elaboration is also linked with mental space. In Bion's model, the infant's first mode of functioning is by projective identification (an elaboration of Freud's idea of the original deflection of the death instinct and Klein's concept of projective identification). The infant deals with discomfort and anxiety by projecting it into mother. This is not only a phantasy operation. A good enough mother responds to the infant's anxiety. A mother capable of containing projective identifications can elaborate the projections in her own unconscious and respond appropriately, thereby lessening the anxiety and giving meaning to it. If this condition obtains, the infant introjects the maternal object as a container capable of containing anxiety, conflict, etc., and elaborating them meaningfully. This internalized container provides a mental space and in this space alpha function can be performed. Another way of looking at it would be that it is in this container in which alpha functioning can occur that primary processes begin to be elaborated into secondary ones. The failure of the container and alpha functioning results in the inability to perform the dream work and therefore, the appearance of psychotic, concrete dreams.

I would like to give an example which shows, I think, the function of dreaming and its failure, resulting in concretization. The material comes from an unusually gifted and able man who has a constant struggle with psychotic parts of his personality. We ended a Friday session with the patient expressing enormous relief and telling me that everything in that session had a good resonance in him. On Monday, he came to his session very disturbed. He said he had a very good afternoon's work on Friday and Saturday morning, but he had a dream on Saturday which had disturbed him very much. In the first part of the dream, he was with Mrs. Small. She was in bed and he was either teaching or treating her. There was also a little girl (here he became rather evasive)—well, maybe a young girl. She was very pleasant with him—maybe a little sexy. And then quite suddenly, someone removed from the room a food trolley and a big cello. He woke up frightened. He said it was not the first part of the dream that frightened him, but the second. He felt it had something to do with a loss of internal structure. On Sunday he could still work, but he felt his work lacked depth and resonance and he felt something was going very wrong. In the middle of Sunday night he woke up with a dream, but he could not hold on to it and instead he became aware of a backache low in his back—maybe the small of his back.

He said the "Mrs. Small" part of the dream did not disturb him because he could quickly see through it. In the past, Mrs. Small, whom he does not think much of, represented a belittling of Mrs. Klein (Klein-Small) and he understood that and he supposed she represented me changed into a patient and also into a sexy little girl. He supposed it was an envious attack, because on Friday he felt so helped by me. He then had some associations to the cello —his niece having one, his admiration for Casals and a few other associations which led me to suggest tentatively that it seemed to be a very bisexual instrument; but that interpretation fell rather flat. What struck him more he said was that it is one of the biggest musical instruments around. He then said that I had a very deep voice and another thing that frightened him was that when he woke up from the dream, he could not remember what we were talking about in the session.

It seems to me that the whole situation, which in the first night is represented by the dream, in the second night, happens concretely. By changing me into Mrs. Small, he had lost me as the internalised organ with deep resonance. The cello represents the mother with deep resonance, the mother who can contain the patient's projections and give a good resonance; but with the loss of this organ, there is an immediate concretization of the situation. In his dream on Saturday night he belittles me by changing me into Mrs. Small. This leads to the loss of the cello—"one of the biggest musical instruments there are." He wakes up anxious. The function of the dream to contain and elaborate anxiety begins to fail. The next night, instead of a dream, he has a pain in the small of the back. Hypochondriasis, much lessened now, had at one time been a leading psychotic-flavoured symptom. The attack on the containing functions of the analyst represented as an organ with the resonance resulted in the patient losing his own resonance (his depth of understanding), and his memory—he cannot remember the session. When this happens, he can only experience concrete physical symptoms. The belittled analyst, who, in the dream, was represented by Mrs. Small becomes a concrete pain in the small of his back.

My attention has been drawn recently to a borderline phenomenon exhibited markedly by the two borderline patients whom I have mentioned earlier. They both frequently presented what I have come to think of as predictive dreams. That is, their dreams predicted their action—what has been dreamt, had to be acted out. Of course, up to a point, all dreams are acted out, as the dream expresses problems and solutions carried out also by similar means in life, but in these patients the acting out of the dream was extraordinarily literal and carried out in complete detail. For instance, my male patient is often late and, not surprisingly, often dreams of being late. What drew my attention to the predictive character of his dreams was the extraordinary precision with which a dream predicts his lateness to the minute. For instance, he will come 2, 6 or 45 minutes late and give me a plausible, to himself, reason, but later in the session he will report a dream in which he was late for a meal or a meeting for exactly the number of minutes which he actually was late on that day. I do not think it is a post hoc interpretation he puts on his dreams since he writes them down carefully first thing in the morning. I have also become aware that a Thursday or Friday dream containing phantasies of acting out at the weekend, is by no means a dream *instead* of the acting out but often a dream containing a plan for acting out, which is often then carried out in precise detail. This, of course, could be a failure of my analysis of the dream preceding the weekend. Other patients sometimes bring a similar plan for acting out in order to warn the analyst and get help and effective analysis obviates the need to act out, but I have a feeling that there is something so powerfully automatic in this patient's compulsion to act out the dream that analysis seldom moves it. Often he would not report the dream until the weekend.

In the woman, these predictive dreams particularly relate to paranoid dreams. There is a kind of row that I have become familiar with now that is characterised by an extra-ordinary automatic progression, apparently totally unaffected by my response. The session can go something like this—she will say in an accusing voice "You frowned at me." There can be any number of responses and I have tried various ones at different times. For instance, I could interpret "You are afraid that I am frowning at you because you slammed the door yesterday"; or I could say "What do you think I am frowning about?"; and here she might answer "You frowned at me because I slammed the door"; or I can be silent and wait for developments, but my silence is taken as a confirmation that I am terribly angry with her. Then it will be, "not only do you frown, but now you are silent, which is worse." I never say, "I did not frown," but I did try pointing out to her that it did not occur to her that she may have been mistaken in her perception. This could only make the row worse, because now, not only do I frown, but I accuse her of being mad. In either case, I have a feeling that my response is completely irrelevant and the row, the quarrel in which certain roles are assigned to me, will continue in a completely automatic fashion. At some point, however, usually when an interpretation touches on some fundamental anxiety, she will tell me a dream and then it will appear that the row we were supposed to be having in the session, is an almost word-for-word repetition of the row she has actually had in the dream, either with me or her mother or father or some thinly veiled transference figure like a teacher. This response to an interpretation—telling me a dream—only happens, however, when the row has run its course, at least for a time. Other similar interpretation, given earlier in the session, would be ignored or woven into the row. Now, I have come to recognise the particular feeling in the counter-transference. It is like being a puppet caught in someone else's nightmare and totally unable to do anything else but to play the allotted role, usually the one of the persecutor. So now, when the row begins in this particular way, I sometimes simply say "you have had a quarrel with me or someone like me in the dream" and sometimes this obviates her need to act out in the session. It is as though in those predictive dreams of both patients, dreams act as what Bion calls a "definitory hypothesis" (Bion 1963). They define in detail how the session is to happen.

I was wondering in what ways the predictive dreams differed from the evacuative dreams, whether of the kind I described that my male patient experiences, or the kind that the woman patient experiences as happening, when they spill over, as it were, into reality. I think they are somewhat different. I think that the evacuating dream actually successfully evacuates something from the patient's inner perception. Thus, when my patient dreams of mourning his mother, he does not need to mourn her. The predictive dreams, however, seem to be dreams which do not entirely succeed in the evacuation and they seem to remain in the patient's psyche like a bad object which then the patient has to dispose of by acting the dream out. The evacuation does not seem to be completed until the dream has been both dreamt *and* acted out. This is very marked with the woman patient: going through the row, telling me the dream, getting the interpretation, gives her enormous relief, but I am seldom convinced that the relief is actually due to an acquired insight. It seems more to be due to a feeling of completed evacuation.

In conclusion: We can say that we are far from having exhausted the possibilities of understanding the world of dreams opened up by Freud, but our attention is increasingly drawn to the form and function of dreaming rather than to the dreams' content. It is the form and the function which reflects and helps to illuminate the disturbances in the functioning of the ego.

REFERENCES

Bion, W. R. (1957). The differentiation between the psychotic and non-psychotic personalities. *Int. J. Psycho-Anal.* 38, 266–275.

—— (1958). On hallucination. *Int. J. Psycho-Anal.* 39, 341–349.

—— (1963). *Elements of Psycho-Analysis.* London: Heinemann.

Jones, E. (1916). The theory of symbolism. IN: *Papers on Psycho-Analysis.* Boston: Beacon Press, 1961, 87–144.

Khan, M. (1974). The Privacy of the Self. IN: *Papers on Psychoanalytic Theory and Technique.* New York: IUP, 306ff. ALSO IN: *Int. J. Psa. Psychother.* 1972, Vol. 1, 31–35.

Klein, M. (1930). The importance of symbol formation in the development of the ego. *Int. J. Psycho-Anal.* 11, 24–39.

Segal, H. (1957). Notes on symbol formation. *Int. J. Psycho-Anal.* 38, 391–397.

11. The Psychological Function of Dreams: A Revised Psychoanalytic Perspective

James L. Fosshage

The psychological function that dreams serve is, as with all clinical data, the pivotal theoretical dimension that structures and guides our clinical understanding and interpretations. Within classical psychoanalytic psychology, Freud's (1900) conception of dreams as primarily energy discharging and wish fulfilling in function has undergone limited modification in theory and a comparatively greater change in its clinical use through the development of ego psychology, object-relations theory, and, more recently, self psychology. Despite proposed theoretical modifications, dream theory has not kept pace with contemporary changes in psychoanalytic theory, and Freud's wish-fulfillment hypothesis still remains central in discussion of dreams. At a symposium on dreams at the International Psycho-Analytic Congress in 1975, Chairman Jean-Bertrand Pontalis pointed out that "among the major theories of psychoanalysis, the theory of dreams has changed the least" (Curtis and Sachs, 1976). Some examples of the unchanging conception of dreams can be found in Altman (1969) who writes, "No dream can exist without the impetus of a wish representing the claim of an instinctual drive, which, although infantile in origin, retains an appetite for gratification throughout life" (p. 8), and who believes that "when dreams are carefully analyzed they can usually be seen as wish-fulfillment, hidden behind a variety of distortions" (Curtis and Sachs, 1976, p. 345); and in Blum (1976) who states,

Reprinted by permission of International Universities Press, Inc., from *Psychoanalysis and Contemporary Thought*, Vol. 6, 1983, pp. 641–69.

This paper was presented in June 1981 to the Long Island Association of Psychoanalytic Psychologists and in March 1982 to the Division of Psychoanalysis of the American Psychological Association.

I wish to express my gratitude to Drs. Frank Lachmann, Dale Mendell, Roland Moses, Lloyd Silverman, Robert Stolorow, and Montague Ullman for their critical reading of this paper and for their most constructive comments.

". . . Freud's masterful conceptions and insights into the dream have been so rich and relatively complete that new additions to dream theory have been very limited" (p. 315) (see also the Blancks, 1974, 1979; Garma, 1974, 1978; and Sloane, 1979, for further recapitulations of classical theory). Our unchanging theory of dreams is most probably contributing to the often-cited neglect of dream interpretation in contemporary psychoanalysis (Waldhorn, 1967; Altman, 1969; and Greenson, 1970).

The purpose of this paper is to contribute to a revised psychoanalytic theory of the psychological function of dreams based, in part, upon recent developments in psychoanalytic theory. Following a historical review of the theory of dreams as pertaining to their function, I will propose theoretical revisions and will present clinical data to illustrate and clarify the implications for dream interpretation. Regression, primary process, manifest and latent content, and dream function will serve as the major headings for the theoretical discussion.

DREAMS: A PRODUCT OF REGRESSION

Traditionally, psychoanalysts have viewed dreams as a product of regression to an infantile mode of thinking, called primary process, wherein drives are discharged through hallucinatory wish fulfillment. Since within the topographical model, primary process was ascribed to the Unconscious System, it required the assumption that dreams, expressions of the Unconscious System, were solely the product of primary-process activity. The dream, metapsychologically speaking, could not utilize secondary-process thinking and, accordingly, the latter's appearance was always viewed as a waking addition serving a defensive function. For example, Freud (1900) viewed the rather common dream statement, "This is only a dream," as a secondary-process thought defensively added upon waking in order to alleviate anxiety (5:488–489). Hence, the later developed and more complex modes of cognition were theoretically excluded from dreaming activity.

Within the topographical model, instinctual drives are discharged through hallucinatory wish fulfillment and are defensively disguised through the dream-work mechanisms in order to provide a sleep-guardian function for the dreamer. Freud wavered as to whether the dream-work mechanisms were intrinsic organizational properties of primary process or were defenses provided by the censorship (Gill, 1967; Holt, 1967). Regardless, the appearance of the disguise—namely, the transformation of the latent into manifest content, viewed as an inherent part of the dreaming process—could not be attributed to the Unconscious System within the topographical theory and served as a partial impetus for Freud (1923a) to develop the structural model.

Within the tripartite structural model, dreams are again viewed as a product of a regression, but now a regression in ego and superego systems which allows for a preponderance of id material (Arlow and Brenner, 1964). For the first time in psychoanalytic theory, both primary and secondary processes, as well as unconscious ego and superego functions, are considered to be operational in dreaming. Most significantly, the regression in mental functioning is viewed no longer as total, but as varied for each system within a dream and from one dream to another (Freud, 1917; Fenichel, 1945; Arlow and Brenner, 1964). Our observations that dreams, at times, involve highly developed problem-solving secondary-process activity can now be explained as a momentary expression of nonregressed ego functioning (see Hartmann, 1973, 1976). Within this paradigm, the dream statement, "This is only a dream," is accepted as part of the dream and is understood on the manifest level as a function of the observing ego which may or may not be serving a defensive purpose (Arlow and Brenner, 1964).

However, despite the theoretical possibility of fluctuations in the degree of regression in ego and superego systems and the operative potential for higher-level functions in dreams, dreaming has continued to be viewed as a predominantly regressive process in which higher-level functions participate minimally. For example, Arlow and Brenner (1964) maintain that ". . . during dreaming the mind functions in a more primitive and infantile way than during waking life, i.e. that during the dream there occurs a profound regression in mental functioning" (p. 135); and Greenson (1970) concurs: "Occasionally one can observe more mature ego functions, but they are rarely dominant" (p. 524). Dreaming activity is so identified with regression that the Blancks (1979) include regression in the definition of a dream: "Every dream is, by definition, a regression" (p. 166).

This prevailing view that dreams are predominantly a product of regression is theoretically linked to or dependent upon the traditional conceptualization of primary process. Since primary process, still viewed as the predominant mode of mental functioning in dreams, is conceptualized as a primitive and infantile mode of functioning which does not change or develop, the dream necessarily becomes, theoretically speaking, a predominantly primitive, regressed product.

The psychoanalytic conception of dreams as a product of predominantly regressive modes of mental functioning profoundly affects our understanding of the psychological functions of dreams and their clinical use. It is my thesis that this metapsychological view of dreams as predominantly a product of regression to primitive-infantile levels of functioning and organization has tended to preclude the recognition of the organizational or synthesizing purposes of the dream, the manifestation of varying levels of organization in dreams, and the use of dreams for the assessment of object-relational development or the level of differentiation and structuralization of self and object representations.

PRIMARY PROCESS

Since the concept of primary process is so closely interrelated to the theory of dream formation, I will review briefly the historical changes in its conceptualization (refer to Noy, 1969, 1979, for a thorough review) and will propose theoretical revisions.

Freud (1900) discovered that unconscious processes as manifested in dreams and symptom formation were ruled by a mode of mental organization different from that mode used in our conscious mental activity which he called primary process and secondary process, respectively. His theoretical distinction was based primarily on an economic point of view. The primary process referred to a mode of energy discharge wherein the mobile cathexis pushes for immediate discharge according to the pleasure principle. The energy in the secondary process is bound, and its discharge is delayed in accordance with the reality principle. Freud viewed primary process as the original infantile mode of mental functioning and secondary process as a later development. This original formulation based on economic theory remains with us today, although primary and secondary processes tend to be viewed as the two poles on a continuum of energy mobility (see Arlow and Brenner, 1964; and Beres, 1965).

The conceptualization of primary process, as with many psychoanalytic terms, has led to considerable confusion. Freud varied in his conception of primary process from the more metapsychological description, "a chaos, a cauldron full of seething excitations" (Freud, 1933, p. 73), to the more clinically induced organization principles of condensation, displacement, and symbolization (Freud, 1900; Holt, 1967). While the economic definition of primary process, i.e., mobile cathexes, leads logically to the picture of "seething excitations," the principles of condensation, displacement, and symbolization (despite their comparative fluidity) imply organization and structure. Indeed, the economic definition of primary process ran counter to Freud's great discovery that dreams and forms of pathological cognition, previously viewed as random and meaningless events, were organized, structured, and meaningful. Shifting from the economic to a structural vantage point, Holt (1967), in a significant contribution, emphasized the organizational properties of the primary process and concluded that it is "a special system of processing information in the service of a synthetic necessity" (p. 383).[1] Hence, from this vantage point, primary and secondary processes become two different systems or modes of processing information, both serving an integrative, synthetic function. However, Holt continued to view the primary process as a comparatively primitive system. This revised conceptualization of primary process implied that dreaming *could* be conceived as a primitive organizational attempt at integrating and synthesizing information.

The primitiveness of the primary process again is an assumption based on economic theory. Ideation dominated by mobile cathexes precludes organization and structure and, therefore, conveys a primitiveness. The notion of mobile cathexes also precludes theoretically any possible change or development of primary-process ideation, for psychological development implies increased levels of organization. Hence, when primary process is operative, regression to early primitive-infantile (unorganized) forms of mentation is always implied. Within this context, the observed sequential development of images from dream to dream is explained in terms of alterations in the ego and superego systems, e.g., defensive processes such as secondary revision.[2]

1. In a similar departure from economic theory, Loewald (1978) redefines cathexis as ". . . a concept for organizing activity (in contrast to what might somewhat facetiously be described as a fuel-injection notion). Applied to object-cathexis . . . this means: object-cathexis is not the investment of an object with some energy charge, but an organizing mental act (instinctual in origin) that structures available material as an object, i.e., as an entity differentiated and relatively distant from the organizing agent" (p. 195).

2. In a recent study (Fosshage and Loew, 1978), we presented to five psychoanalysts of various theoretical persuasions six dreams from a four-year period in the analytic treatment of a young woman. All the analysts, with comparatively little contextual material, noted personality

However, because primary process is the predominant mode of mentation in dreaming, a more cogent explanation of sequential changes in dream images is the development of primary process itself. This explanation corresponds with Loewald's (1971) conceptualization of the development of the id wherein the id both remains within the personality as the original motive force with its corresponding structures and is also transformed into "higher, more individually centered order of motivational energy and structuralization of such energy" (p. 113).

However, because our theory has been primarily energy-based, the notion of the development of primary-process mentation has all but been absent in the psychoanalytic literature (Holt, 1967, and Noy, 1969, are notable exceptions). The structural viewpoint introduces the possibility of developmental changes in levels of organization as primary process carries out its integrative and synthetic function. In this vein, Holt (1967) did not assume that the primary process is a constitutional given, but described its emergence during infancy and considered it to be a developmental achievement requiring considerable structuralization. Noy (1969 and 1979) extended the developmental schema for the primary process so that it, too (like the secondary process), changes in the complexity of its organizational structure throughout life. Using dreams and art to support his thesis, he concludes:

. . . it seems that there is really no difference between the primary process and any other mental function: the processes remain the same, but their level of organization and performance changes, develops and improves constantly, along with general cognitive development. For instance, in logical language, which is a secondary-process function, the processes themselves also remain constant, but their level of functioning changes. For example, the processes of causal thinking or concept formation remain forever as basic constituents of logical thinking, but there is a clear development from childhood causal thinking and concept formation to the same functions in the adult and we cannot compare childish thoughts to adult ones. Why not apply this knowledge to our theory of the primary processes? It means that the basic processes of condensation, displacement and symbolization remain the same all through life, but their level of functioning and performance constantly develops and improves—and as expression of "concept formation" is not regarded as a regression

---

development in the patient's dreams. In order to avoid inserting a bias in our dream selection unconsciously, we chose as one of our criteria for selection of dreams the manifest appearance of a cockroach. All the analysts again noted in her dreams sequential change in this cockroach image. (It should be noted, however, that a more rigorous research design would be needed to exclude the possible effect of the judges' expectations. The dreams would need to be presented in a randomized order, while requesting the judges to order them according to their sequential development.)

to a childish kind of thinking, even though this process stems from childhood, so also expression of displacement need not be regarded as "regression" [1969, p. 158].

Hence, while the principles or processes of organization (themselves a product of development) remain basic to the primary-process and secondary-process modes of ideation, the level of functioning and the complexity of organization in both the primary and secondary processes develop or increase more or less throughout one's lifetime. Within this paradigm, regression refers to the reemergence of developmentally earlier ("temporal regression") and less complex (structural regression) levels of primary-process organization, not to a primitive, unorganized mode of mentation ("formal regression").

If both primary and secondary processes develop organizationally in overall service of a synthetic function, what distinguishes one mode of mental activity from the other? I propose that we define *primary process as that mode of mental functioning which uses visual and other sensory images with intense affective colorations in serving an over-all integrative and synthetic function.*[3] Secondary process, on the other hand, is a conceptual and logical mode that makes use of linguistic symbols in serving an integrative and synthetic function. These processes may be described as different but complementary modes of apprehending, responding to, and organizing the external and internal worlds. The right-left-brain-hemisphere research that has established the functional asymmetry of the cerebral hemispheres may support this structural division (Ornstein, 1973; Dimond and Beaumont, 1974; Kinsbourne and Smith, 1974; Hoppe, 1977; and Bakan, 1978). Summarizing this extensive research, Bakan (1978) describes:

There is evidence of left hemisphere superiority in tasks involving grammatically organized word sequences over time, and motor coordination. Right hemisphere function seems dominant in tasks involving imagery, certain visual and constructive activities such as drawing, copying, assembling block designs, perception and manip-

3. The use of visual and other sensory imagery in primary-process mentation was, of course, well delineated by Freud (1900); but, in addition to this imagery serving a wish-fulfilling function (using the clinical theory while extricating it from the biologically based energy-discharge model), I am, following Holt and Noy, postulating that this imagery is used in the over-all service of an integrative and synthetic function and has a developmental history in organizational complexity.

To define primary process as imagistic or representational thinking also corresponds with Piaget's description of the sixth and final stage of sensorimotor intelligence, as compared to conceptual intelligence, in which the 18-month-old child develops a capacity to perform tasks requiring imagined representation (Flavell, 1963).

ulation of spatial relations of and between objects or configurations, and the simultaneous grasping of fragments or particulars as a meaningful whole [p. 163].

Despite the specialization of function, both hemispheres process not independently, but complementarily (Kinsbourne, 1982). Similarly, both primary and secondary processes are operative and complementarily interwoven in all mental activity (i.e., in waking and sleeping cognition), but their proportional balance may vary from moment to moment and from person to person (i.e., personality stylistic differences). Clearly, both modes are operative in self and in reality concerns as is evident in patients' use of both modes to describe their inner experiences and reality problems. Those patients who logically and methodically describe their experiences in contrast to those who use vivid images and feelings in their communications convey, in part, the stylistic differences in the proportional balance of these two modes.

In view of the revised conception of primary process, our conceptualizations of how primary process utilizes the principles of condensation, displacement, and symbolization also require revision. Instead of an energy-based definition of condensation as a concentration of energies related to different chains of thought, made use of by the censorship to serve a defensive function (Freud, 1916–1917, p. 173), condensation is viewed as a process of organization of mental events, i.e., experiences and memories, through the combination of imagistic mental elements involving similar thematic experiences.[4] If the primary-process mode is an attempt to synthesize psychic phenomena, the notion that displacement is only a form of concealment whereby the cathectic intensities are transferred to ideas of lesser importance is no longer applicable.[5] Displacement is conceived of here as an organizing principle in which experiences generating the same affective reaction (the associative connection) are all nodal points or cues for a particular thematic experience. The nodal point, in serving an over-all organizational function, is selected at times for defensive purposes and much more frequently to express a most poignantly affective thematic experience. Symbolization,

4. Using information-processing theory, Palombo (1978a, 1978b) refers to condensation as a matching process through the superimposition of memories.

5. As explicated later in the text, representational ideation, like secondary-process thinking, can be used for, but is by no means limited to, the service of a defensive function. Through the revision of the concept of primary process, extricating it from the physicalistic-energy model, I am attempting to redefine the major principles of primary-process mentation in which these principles are serving an organizational and synthetic function (which may, in turn, involve certain defensive processes, e.g., regression to earlier levels of organization) in contrast to an exclusively sleep-preservative defensive (disguising) function.

likewise, refers within this framework to a process of organization whereby a particular image expresses a thematic pattern of experiences and memories. Instead of a disguised representation of or substitution for instinctual wishes, ideas, and conflict, a symbol is a particular imagistic configuration that captures and expresses thematic and affective meaning. In other words, in contrast to the energy-based definitions of condensation, displacement, and symbolization which emphasize an exclusively defensive (disguising) function, these terms are conceptualized here as the organizing principles of the primary-process mode of mentation which serve to further the internal process of integration and organization of experiences and memories (which includes, but is not limited to a defensive function).

The thesis that the basic function of primary process is to organize and synthesize mental phenomena also has implications for the manifest-latent content distinction.

MANIFEST-LATENT CONTENT

Freud's differentiation of manifest and latent content was again based on drive theory in which the original latent impulses or wishes are disguised and transformed into the manifest dream, i.e., the reported dream, as a compromise between drive discharge and the work of the censor for the purpose of sleep preservation. Within the tripartite structural model, the omnipresent discrepancy between manifest and latent content is the result of intersystemic conflict wherein the ego's defense mechanisms disguise id impulses in keeping with superego prohibitions, once again for the preservation of sleep.

However, if from a structural, rather than an economic viewpoint, primary process and, therefore, dreams serve an organizing and synthetic function, *there is no theoretical necessity to posit the ubiquitous operation of disguise and transformation of latent into manifest content.* Indeed, object-relational processes (Fairbairn, 1944), self-esteem regulation (Kohut, 1977), the individualized ego modes of experiencing and relating (Erikson, 1954), and the developmental, organizational and regulatory processes, posited in this paper, are all manifestly observable in dreams. This thesis is additionally supported by the well-replicated dream content and REM research finding that emotionally stimulating and meaningful experiences are directly incorporated into the manifest content of dreams (Witkin, 1969; Breger, Hunter, and Lane, 1971; Whitman, Kramer, and Baldridge, 1967; and Greenberg and Perlman, 1975). When psychic conflict is involved, however, the utilization of defensive processes during dreaming potentially increases the discrepancy between the manifest defensive content and the underlying latent content, just as in waking mentation. When conflicting intrapsychic forces are operative, the intensity and, therefore, the psychological priority of these conflictual forces, as compared to other developmental, organizational, and regulatory processes, vary considerably and result in the observed variability of the discrepancy in the manifest and latent content in dreams. In addition, the degree of the dreamer's internal recognition, clarity, and acceptance of the conflict in conjunction with the particular defensive processes utilized and the degree of success of the mastery processes affect the manifest-latent discrepancy. Thus, even when psychic conflict is involved, the manifest-latent discrepancy in dreaming, as in waking mentation, varies according to the level of intensity and priority of the conflictual forces, the degree of recognition and clarity, and the specific mastery and defensive processes. Within this paradigm, we can explain, therefore, the frequently observed phenomenon that as the analysis progresses, "the manifest dreams tend to become clearer and less distorted" (Sloane, 1979, p. 241).

DREAM FUNCTIONS

To reiterate, within the topographical model Freud posited that the primary function of the dream was to provide discharge for unconscious impulses and thereby, secondarily, to serve as the "guardian of sleep." The unconscious impulse is experienced as a wish, infantile in origin, which is fulfilled in the dream through a hallucinatory process, a primitive mode of mental functioning.

With the advent of the tripartite structural model, the dream's scope enlarged to include intersystemic conflict. The specific functions of energy discharge and sleep protection remained unaltered, but the inclusion of defensive processes and intersystemic conflictual forces characterized dreaming activity as potentially more similar to waking mental activity than previously conceptualized.[6] The tripartite model theoretically made possible the participation of later-developed, comparatively nonregressed ego functions in dream formation, e.g., the functions of observation, reality testing, integration, and

---

6. Freud suggested this correspondence between waking and dreaming ideation when in 1923(b) he was deprecating an exaggerated respect for the "mysterious unconscious" and stated: "It is only too easy to forget that a dream is as a rule merely a thought like any other . . ." (p. 112).

synthesis. Clinically, psychoanalysts looked less for the latent wish and more for the intersystemic conflictual forces in the dream. Moreover, the nonregressed ego functions were often implicitly operative in the clinical understanding of dreams.[7] However, the continual emphases on regression, drive discharge, and the economically based conceptualization of the primary process as primitive unbound energy have theoretically tended to exclude from dream construction these more highly developed ego functions.

Other theoretical developments have highlighted the operation of the full developmental spectrum of ego functions in dreams and have implicitly moved us toward a major revision of our conceptualization of the psychological function of dreams. For example, Fairbairn (1944) in his development of object-relations theory posited that "dreams are representations of endopsychic situations over which the dreamer has got stuck (fixation points) and *often includes some attempt to move beyond that situation* (Padel, 1978, p. 133; my italics). Hence, the dream's function is to work through and master object-relational struggles, in sharp contrast to Garma's (1978) position in which all dream solutions are "fictitious" and serve a defensive function. Fairbairn's conceptualization of the dream function substantially differs from the energy-discharge and intersystemic-conflict models in that the synthetic, organizing, or mastery-competence function (Nunberg, 1931; Hartmann, 1950; Bellak, Hurvich, and Gediman, 1973), a function which has been traditionally ascribed to the ego, predominates in establishing the purposeful direction of the dream. Within the developments of ego psychology, Erikson (1954) introduced, and Jones (1962, 1970) and De Monchaux (1978) extensively elaborated on, the operation in dreams of the ego's organizing or synthetic function. De Monchaux, for example, explained post-traumatic dream repetition as an attempt to synthesize or integrate the trauma into a whole self rather than to leave it as a dissociated fragment and, therefore, as a split in the self. Similarly, psychoanalysts with an interpersonal orientation have frequently noted the synthetic, integrative, and mastery functions of dreams

7. A clinical example of the operation of more highly developed ego functions can be found in the following dream reported during a Kleinian analysis (Greenson, 1970, p. 531): ". . . red spiders were crawling in and out of the patient's anus. A doctor examined him and told the patient that he was unable to see anything wrong with him. The patient replied, 'Doctor, you may not see anything, but they are there just the same'." In his interpretation Greenson suggests that the dreamer may have justifiably reproached the analyst for really missing something. His interpretation is based on manifestly evident material, i.e., there is no discrepancy between the manifest and latent meaning, and implies the functioning of "nonregressed" reality testing in the dream.

in their attempts to resolve focal conflicts (Ullman, 1959; Bonime, 1962; French and Fromm, 1964; Ullman and Zimmerman, 1979).

The attempt in dreams to rectify problematic endopsychic situations is described also in what Kohut (1977) calls "self-state dreams." In these dreams, the healthy sectors of the personality are manifestly reacting to and attempting to deal with an "uncontrollable tension-increase" or "a dread of the dissolution of the self" (p. 109). Rather than a regression to a primitive mode of drive discharge, the organizing and internally regulating personality sectors predominate in these dreams in the service of the restoration and maintenance of a cohesive self structure.

Recently, within information-processing models, the adaptive function of dreams has also been described (Breger, 1977; Palombo, 1978a, 1978b). According to Breger, ". . . dreams serve to integrate affectively aroused material into structures within the memory systems that have previously proved satisfactory in dealing with similar material" (p. 24). Palombo (1978a) similarly views dreams as adaptively matching new perceptions and experiences with permanent memories and solutions in a continual "reordering and enriching of the associative structure of the permanent memory" (p. 468). Extrapolating from the physiological research finding that REM quantitatively decreases during our life span, Meissner (1968) and Breger (1977) posit that dreaming fosters structuralization of the nervous system which is the physiological analogue to Holt's thesis that primary process serves a synthetic function and, thereby, increases psychic structuralization. Additionally, the facts well established in the sleep laboratory—that sleep and dream deprivation produce psychological disturbances and disorganization and that sleep and dreaming in turn are rehabilitative—indicate again the organizational function of these two activities (Meissner, 1968; Cartwright, 1981; Hartmann, 1981). Certain properties of dreaming, Breger notes, facilitate the mastery-adaptive or synthetic functioning in dreaming. For example, the relative absence of external stimulation makes dreaming especially suited for "internal transformations of stored material." A greater number of programs (including what we can now refer to as various developmental levels of primary-process and secondary-process programs), as well as considerably more memory content are available. The substantially increased use of visual representations as well as language broadens the range of information-processing methods. And finally, the processing of information is not as limited by the rules of logic and social acceptability which constrain the output of our waking state. Within an information-process paradigm, dreaming is viewed as a creative act in which problem solving is facilitated by the availability of an increased number of psychological elements and a greater flexibility and means of combining these elements.

Despite the clinical and sleep-laboratory evidence in support of a mastery-adaptive model of dream function, and despite the fact that this model is significantly different from those of drive discharge and intersystemic conflict, the classical models continue to be reiterated in direct opposition to the newer ones. For example, Blum (1976) stated: "Dreaming is an archaic process which is not suited to considerations of logic or reality and does not have a primary function of information process, problem-solving, or adaptation" (p. 321).

A REVISED MODEL

To summarize and synthesize, the classical theory of dream formation—namely, dreaming is a predominantly regressed, primitive, primary-process mode of mentation directed toward fulfillment of wishes as an avenue of energy discharge and disguised by the dream-work mechanisms for the preservation of sleep—is often reiterated as a "given" in psychoanalytic discussion of dreams. Even the tripartite structural model, which theoretically made possible the participation of the broad range of ego functions in dream construction, has continued to neglect the integrative, synthetic, and mastery function of dreams due to the repeated emphasis on the predominance of regression and the continued inclusion of the drive-discharge function within the intersystemic-conflict model.

However, new models of dream formation which have emerged in object-relations theory, self psychology, and information-process theory have emphasized the function of integration, synthesis, and mastery. Similarly, a structural view of the primary process emphasizes its synthetic function (similar to that of the secondary process) as well as a developmental schema in which the primary process (like the secondary process) increases in its complexity of structural organization. I have schematically characterized primary process as the affect-laden imagistic, sensory mode of apprehension and cognition and the secondary process as the conceptual, logical, and linguistically dominated mode of apprehension and cognition. Both develop in organizational complexity (e.g., compare the intricacy of the artist's imagery to that of the lawyer and the lawyer's conceptual complexity to that of the artist), and both function to bring about integration, synthesis, and mastery. Implicit is a fundamental principle based on evolutionary and developmental theory that all psychic activity, i.e., waking and dreaming mentation, evolves or moves fundamentally toward higher, more complex levels of organization. Loewald (1973) posits just such a direction: "... a force must be assumed to operate in mental processes . . . that favors the tensions of mental life, works in opposition to as well as in fusion with the motivating power of the death instinct, and which promotes higher or more complex organization of the psychic structures resulting from, and transforming in their turn, psychic processes" (pp. 79–80).

Hence, my thesis is that *the supraordinate function of dreams is the development, maintenance (regulation), and, when necessary, restoration of psychic processes, structure, and organization.*[8] Dreams, utilizing predominantly but, by no means exclusively, the representational (primary-process) mode, serve this developmental, regulatory, and restorative function in three major ways. *First,* dreams participate in the development of internal organization through the representational consolidation of newly emergent psychic configurations. Examples are modification of self and object representations and the emergence of unformed and undeveloped psychological processes and configurations. *Second,* dreams maintain, regulate, and restore current psychic configurations and processes, including the maintenance, regulation, and internal balancing of self-esteem ("self-state dreams"), sexual and aggressive processes (including wish fulfillment, which can regulate sexual, aggressive, and narcissistic processes). An example is the reinforcement of current self and object representations, particularly when these configurations are threatened by anxiety-producing, disorganizing change (e.g., when the intrapsychic image of the analyst is shifting from a negative to a positive valence, the dreamer may resurrect the negative, rejecting image of the analyst to restore the prior, and therefore less anxiety-producing, object configuration and level of organization). *Third,* dreams continue the unconscious and conscious waking efforts to resolve intrapsychic conflicts through the utilization of defensive processes, through an internal balancing or through a creative, newly emergent reorganization (this thesis includes the intersys-

---

8. Stolorow and Atwood (1982) independently arrived at a similar formulation. Jung (1916) was the first to view dreams as regulatory and developmental ("compensating" and "prospective") in function. Recently, Jones's (1980) metaphor of the dream poet, referring to an adaptive and a creative function, implies a developmental function. However, in classical psychoanalysis, because of the dominance of the energy model and the postulated discharge function of dreams, the psychological-developmental function of dreams has been seriously neglected.

temic conflict model, but adds the function of resolution through a creative reorganizational process). This latter reorganization may be contributed to by the introduction of new elements previously either unformed or unavailable to consciousness. For example, when confronting sexual or aggressive feelings the dreamer may defend through a regression to an earlier developmental stage or may modify opposing attitudes and frightening feelings through the use of newly emergent, previously unformed, and/or repressed, perceptions of self and object.[9]

With reduced attention and need to cope with the external world, sleep appears to be a time when the organism through the dreaming process, an altered state of consciousness, monitors and regulates, primarily but by no means exclusively through the use of representational ideation, the aroused affects and thoughts of the day which are intricately interwoven with the complex motivational, memory and self- and object-representational network. The reduced demand to deal directly with the external world provides the organism with a necessary and potent time for the development, maintenance, and restoration of internal organization.

Because of the organizational function of dreams, psychological development in terms of the achievement of new levels of psychic organization is observable in dreams. As with waking mental activity (Loewald, 1957), the

9. The functional thesis presented herein and its implications for interpretation should in no way be construed as equivalent with the so-called anagogic interpretation, as one reviewer suggested. Silberer proposed that all dreams required two interpretations, the psychoanalytic with its emphasis on infantile-sexual wishes and the anagogic with the focus on what he considered to be the more serious and important thoughts. Freud (1900) assessed anagogic interpretations to be invalid while viewing them as the more "abstract" and intellectualized interpretations "given by the dreamer without difficulty" (p. 524). Following Freud, classical analysts use the term, "anagogic interpretation," pejoratively, but its meaning remains elusive. In a recent paper, Stein (1982) implies that any interpretation (including even the supernatural or those based on "the view that dreams are generated outside the psychic apparatus" [p. 4]) which does not include the expression of wish fulfillment and the notion of distortion is anagogic and, therefore, is invalid (pp. 4–6). Accordingly, Kohut's interpretations of the "self-state" dreams are viewed as anagogic (including neither wish fulfillment nor distortion) despite the fact that this type of dream or these interpretations could scarcely be characterized as "abstract" or intellectualized. And what should we do with the frequently observed phenomenon of the increase in manifest clarity of dreams and in the dreamer's case of understanding as analysis progresses? To assume the operation of ubiquitous distortion in dreams is unnecessary and misrepresents the facts. I believe it is clear that my thesis of the function of dreams, and implicitly the corresponding interpretations, includes, but is not limited to, the operation of wish fulfillments and defensive functions. And, as I have stated, dreams vary in the degree of obscurity—i.e., manifest-latent discrepancy—which is related to defensive functioning and/or to newly emergent and therefore unclear psychic processes.

most recently established levels of organization are also most subject to change, whether due to an instability and regression to an earlier organization or due to a process of a new progressive reorganization, which accounts for the progressive and regressive movements and the degree of dramatic cohesiveness of dream imagery.

CLINICAL IMPLICATIONS

To view dreams as serving to develop, regulate, and restore psychic organization is to accord dreaming a profound role in psychic life. Within classical psychoanalytic theory dreams have been portrayed as the "royal road" to the latent wishes and as the expression of intersystemic conflicts, but they have been insufficiently recognized for their primary developmental, regulatory, conflict-resolving, and reorganizational functions, a role of even greater import than previously conceived. In contrast to the consistent metapsychological portrayal of dreams as predominantly a product of a primitive and undeveloped mode of mentation, dreaming can now be conceptualized as an extremely complex mode of mentation, predominantly representational in form, which closely corresponds with the deepest emotional levels of conscious and unconscious waking mentation and continues the many regressions and progressions of waking mentation in experiencing, differentiating, and integrating the self and object world.

This revised conceptualization expands the possible meanings of dreams and the contribution of dreams in the internal developmental efforts of the dreamer. In addition to latent wishes and intersystemic conflict or, more generally intrapsychic conflict, new developments in self and object representations involving previously unformed as well as repressed elements and perceptions may emerge in dreams. Regulatory processes and new developmental movements in the narcissistic, psychosexual, and object-relational arenas may also be expressed in dreams. This revised conceptualization potentially enhances our clinical use of dreams, for dream images that are accompanied by and evoke intense affects may portray not only intersystemic conflict, but also new internal developments (of which the dreamer may be scarcely, if at all, aware), the conscious consideration of which will further the analytic and developmental processes.

To view the manifest level of the dream as the product of defensive processes (increasing the manifest-latent content discrepancy) only when intrapsychic conflict is involved diminishes the possibility of facile translations of dream imagery (e.g., the frequent and persistent translations of dream personages as transferential stand-ins for the analyst) and allows us to remain with and understand the poignant dream imagery at the phenomenological level.[10] To work with dreams, as with all clinical material, at the phenomenological level facilitates the dreamer's participation and conviction in understanding dreams and, thereby, increases the potency of dream work. For example, at the phenomenological level a dream's vagueness and incomprehensibility is not attributed necessarily to defensive processes, but possibly to yet unformed and, therefore, unclear intrapsychic processes (just as in secondary-process thinking conceptual clarity is a product of incremental developmental steps). Also, at the phenomenological level it is clear that dreams vary considerably as to their significance or intensity of meaning and impact the dreamer. This corresponds with our revised theory, namely: dreams vary according to the developmental, regulatory, and restorative needs of the dreamer.

CLINICAL ILLUSTRATIONS

Let us turn to clinical illustrations with the specific focus on the psychological function that the dreams served for the dreamer. The interpretations are by no means complete, a task often not possible or therapeutically useful, but rather the most salient molar themes (Stolorow, 1978) are examined.

I have selected two dreams which Susan reported during the fourth and sixth years of her analytic treatment. Susan was a bright, attractive, and generally well-functioning young woman who entered treatment following graduate school because of dissociation from feelings, low self-esteem, emo-

10. To begin investigation and description at the phenomenological level (see Spiegelberg, 1965, and Boss and Kenny, 1978) is central to the empirical foundation of the clinical theory and practice of psychoanalysis. For purposes of explanation, the pooling of data into general patterns, of course, requires higher, more general levels of inference and abstraction farther removed from the observed and experienced phenomena. All sciences move back and forth between the observed data and the higher-level (theoretical) inferences. However, perhaps because of an overemphasis on the manifest-latent content discrepancy, as well as the predominant functioning of a different mode of cognition in dreaming, patients' dreams, more frequently than other clinical material, seem often to engender in us leaps into theoretically dominated translations of dream imagery. I am re-emphasizing the importance of not straying too far from the observed and experiential level of the dream and believe that the revisions, set forth in this paper, of the functions of primary process and dreaming encourage in the clinical setting elaboration of, rather than the translation of—and thereby, the close adherence to—the observed dream imagery.

tional constriction, and difficulties in establishing a satisfying heterosexual relationship. In a session after a date with a man whom she had recently met and liked, she reported the following dream:

I was in a nice hotel and getting ready to go someplace or go to bed. There were two other people, Ann, whom I work with, and Joan, my ex-roommate. I looked down on the floor and there was a beautiful gold necklace. It had mythological characters —Poseidon and sea horses—like an Egyptian necklace—like a collar. It was very valuable and very pretty. I picked it up and said, ''Isn't this beautiful. Ann has some really pretty jewelry.'' It belonged to her.

In her associations Susan described Ann as a ''super-feminist, angry, but also something kind of attractive about her; I'm more connected to her.''Joan has a lot of potential, but keeps it down, is super nice, and doesn't dress in an attractive way.'' In the ensuing discussion it became clear that Susan, who was overly compliant and sexually repressed, similar to her associations of Joan, was in process (i.e., the necklace still belonged to Ann) of recognition, appreciation, and integration of her sexuality, femininity, and assertiveness (poignantly imaged respectively in the sea and horses of the Egyptian necklace). The beautiful gold necklace appeared to be a new symbolic configuration which unified partially unformed and partially repressed sexual, feminine, and assertive elements. The dreamer's discovery and appreciation of this gold necklace appeared to serve the function of integration and movement toward more complex levels of organization. These elements also emerged in her waking perceptions of others and in the experience of her self both while she was with the new man and in the transference. The latter was indicated when she said for the first time in the session, ''I feel you're feeling positive about me, seeing beauty in me.''

Clinically, this is not an unusual dream and, perhaps, would be understood similarly by many analysts. However, this understanding is not based on and could not be derived solely from the classical theories of simple wish fulfillment or intersystemic conflict. To view this dream solely as a wish fulfillment, in my judgment, undermines its meaning and its usefulness to the dreamer for the process of integration. The formulation of an oedipal wish, a disguised gratification of sexual impulses, or even an ego wish does not sufficiently incorporate the dreamer's developmental attempt to integrate her feminine sexuality. To view this dream solely in terms of intersystemic conflict is strained, for phenomenologically no conflictual forces appear. The emergence of partially repressed elements indicates the presence of intersystemic conflict, and the fact that the necklace still belongs to Ann suggests the operation of defensive (as well as developmental) processes; but, because the intensity of the conflictual forces is not sufficient to make their phenomenological appearance in the dream, the interpretive emphasis is placed on the developmental movement. The self-state model of dream function also appears to be inapplicable, for the dreamer, as far as my exploration could determine, was not experiencing an immediate vulnerability or a possible threat of dissolution to her self. Instead, with the recognition and appreciation of the gold necklace, the dreamer appears to be attempting to integrate a new configuration which will enhance her self organization. Through the dreamer's associations, we attempted to understand aspects of the symbolic configuration, i.e., the gold necklace, and, in addition, continued to use the image with its powerful affect in its representational mode (rather than solely translating it into the logical, verbal mode) to further the process of integration. Rather than a regression to a more primitive level of organization, the dreamer appears to be moving toward higher levels of organization through the integrative and synthetic efforts in dreaming. Recognizing and understanding this function of the dream, in my opinion, promoted this process of integration and self reorganization.

The second dream was in response to the emergence of intense sexual feelings and fantasies in the transference. The dream is as follows:

I was in a big park in a nice setting. I was with Ted, walking along a path, talking about whether to have sex or not. I was for it. We had known each other all this time —why not? We started. Then he started getting freaked out, going psychotic—it was like a psychotic transformation. I was going, "Oh my God, no wonder he didn't want to have sex." I was scared of him. He was terrified. I left him. I went off to the park to enjoy my mother and brother.

Following the dream report, Susan described Ted, her high-school boyfriend, as brilliant, rigid, controlled, and extremely afraid of sexual involvement. She recalled a painful experience in which Ted had verbally denigrated and rejected her upon discovery of a prior minor affectionate involvement with another young man. This experience exacerbated her fear of sexuality and men, which was gentically related to her father's unpredictable alternations between seductive behavior and prohibitions.

On the manifest level of the dream, Susan first expresses her desire for sexual involvement. The dream, thus far, approximates the dreamer's current articulated waking level of organization (i.e., her recent expression of sexual wishes toward the analyst) with no evidence of a structural regression to a lower organizational level. The appearance of Ted instead of the therapist in the dream is viewed in this instance not as a defensive disguise, but rather as the utilization of a poignant experience in memory which serves as an organizational nodal point for all such similar thematic experiences (displacement, condensation, and symbolization as redefined in this paper). However, as the dreamer begins to engage in sexual intercourse, a momentarily profound disorganizing and frightening regression to a more primitive and archaic level of organization occurs, again manifestly portrayed in the dream. In order to reestablish a sufficiently nonthreatening level of organization, the dreamer leaves the man to rejoin her mother and brother (a regressive defensive solution in the face of genital sexuality). The emergence of intense sexual feelings in the dream (precipitated by the same in the transference) was a movement in the direction of integration of her sexuality, but precipitated a profound anxiety about a disorganizing loss of control on the part of the man, which threatened to overwhelm her. The dreamer momentarily resolves this disorganizing encounter with a frightening object representation by moving toward a more secure and more tranquil level of organization, but without, momentarily, the achievement of the increased integration of her sexuality. Thus, the dream portrays intrapsychic conflict in the form of the emergence of a frightening repressed object representation associated with sexual feelings and provides a reorganizing function by regressively restoring an old psychic configuration with excludes the frightening object image and the sexual feelings. Despite the terrifying intensity of this conflict, both the conflict and its momentary regressive resolution are manifestly portrayed in the dream, suggestive of the dreamer's lucidity and comparative nondefensiveness (lack of disguise) in her intrapsychic encounter.

SUMMARY

In an attempt to extricate the dream from the biologically based drive-discharge model, a revised psychoanalytic model of the psychological function of dreams has been presented. It is posited that the supraordinate function of dreams is the development, regulation, and restoration of psychic processes, structure, and organization. Dreams attempt to integrate and organize current cognitive-affective experiences through the development and consolidation of new structures, the maintenance of current structures, and conflict resolution. The dual purpose in dreaming, as with all mental activity, is the maintenance of current structure while concurrently moving progressively toward more complex levels of organization.

REFERENCES

Altman, L. (1969), *The Dream in Psychoanalysis*. New York: International Universities Press.

Arlow, J., & Brenner, C. (1964), *Psychoanalytic Concepts & the Structural Theory*. New York: International Universities Press.

Bakan, P. (1978), Two Streams of Consciousness: A Typological Approach. In: *The Stream of Consciousness*, ed. K. S. Pope & J. L. Singer. New York: Plenum Press, pp. 159–184.

Bellak, L., Hurvich, M., & Gediman, H. (1973), *Ego Functions in Schizophrenics, Neurotics and Normals*. New York: Wiley.

Beres, D. (1965), Structure and Function in Psychoanalysis. *Internat. J. Psycho-Anal.*, 46:53–63.

Blanck, G. & Blanck, R. (1974), *Ego Psychology*. New York: Columbia University Press.

——— & ——— (1979), *Ego Psychology II*. New York: Columbia University Press.

Blum, H. (1976), The Changing Use of Dreams in Psychoanalytic Practice. *Internat. J. Psycho-Anal.*, 57:315–324.

Bonime, W. (1962), *The Clinical Use of Dreams*. New York: Basic Books.

Boss, M., & Kenny, B. (1978), Phenomenological or Daseinsanalytic Approach. In: *Dream Interpretation: A Comparative Study*, ed. J. Fosshage & C. Loew. New York: Spectrum, pp. 149–189.

Breger, L. (1977), Function of Dreams. *J. Abnorm. Psychol.*, 72:1–28.

———, Hunter, I., & Lane, R. (1971), *The Effects of Stress on Dreams*. New York: International Universities Press.

Cartwright, R. D. (1981), The Contribution of Research on memory and dreaming to a 24-hour Model of Cognitive Behavior. In: *Sleep, Dreams and Memory*, ed. W. Fishbein. New York: Spectrum, pp. 239–247.

Curtis, H., & Sachs, D. (1976), Dialogue on ''The Changing Use of Dreams in Psychoanalytic Practice.'' *Internat. J. Psycho-Anal.*, 57:343–354.

De Monchaux, C. (1978), Dreaming and the Organizing Function of the Ego. *Internat. J. Psycho-Anal.*, 59:443–453.

Dimond, S., & Beaumont, J. (eds.) (1974), *Hemisphere Function in the Human Brain*. New York: Halstead Press.

Erikson, E. (1954), The Dream Specimen of Psychoanalysis. *J. Amer. Psychoanal. Assn.*, 2:5–56.

Fairbairn, W. R. D. (1944), Endopsychic Structure Considered in Terms of Object-Relationships. In: *An Object-Relations Theory of the Personality*. New York: Basic Books, 1951.

Fenichel, O. (1945), *The Psychoanalytic Theory of Neurosis*. New York: Norton.

Flavell, J. (1963), *The Developmental Psychology of Jean Piaget*. Princeton, N.J.: Van Nostrand.

Fosshage, J., & Loew, C. (eds.) (1978), *Dream Interpretation: A Comparative Study*, New York: Spectrum.

French, T., & Fromm, E. (1964), *Dream Interpretation: A New Approach*. New York: Basic Books.

Freud, S. (1900), The Interpretation of Dreams. *Standard Edition*, 4 & 5. London: Hogarth Press, 1953.
——— (1916–1917), Introductory Lectures on Psychoanalysis. *Standard Edition*, 15 & 16. London: Hogarth Press, 1963.
——— (1917), A Metapsychological Supplement to the Theory of Dreams. *Standard Edition*, 14:219–222. London: Hogarth Press, 1957.
——— (1923a), The Ego and the Id. *Standard Edition*, 19:3–66. London: Hogarth Press, 1961.
——— (1923b), Remarks on the Theory and Practice of Dream Interpretation. *Standard Edition*, 19:109–121. London: Hogarth Press, 1961.
——— (1933), New Introductory Lectures on Psychoanalysis. *Standard Edition*, 22:3–184. London: Hogarth Press, 1964.
Garma, A. (1974), *The Psychoanalysis of Dreams*. New York: Jason Aronson.
——— (1978), Freudian Approach. In: *Dream Interpretation: A Comparative Study*, ed. J. Fosshage & C. Loew. New York: Spectrum, pp. 15–51.
Gill, M. (1967), The Primary Process. In: *Motives and Thought: Psychoanalytic Essays in Honor of David Rapaport*, ed. R. R. Holt [*Psychological Issues*, Monogr. 18/19]. New York: International Universities Press, pp. 259–298.
Greenberg, R. & Perlman, C. (1975), A Psychoanalytic Dream Continuum: The Source and Function of Dreams, *Internat. Rev. Psycho-Anal.*, 2:441–448.
Greenson, R. (1970), The Exceptional Position of the Dream in Clinical Psychoanalytic Practice. *Psychoanal. Quart.*, 39:519–549.
Hartmann, E. (1973), *The Functions of Sleep*. New Haven, Conn.: Yale University Press.
——— (1976), Discussion of "The Changing Use of Dreams in Psychoanalytic Practice." *Internat. J. Psycho-Anal.*, 57:331–334.
——— (1981), The Functions of Sleep and Memory Processing. In: *Sleep, Dreams and Memory*, ed. W. Fishbein. New York: Spectrum, pp. 111–124.
Hartmann, H (1950), Comments on the Psychoanalytic Theory of the Ego. In: *Essays on Ego Psychology*. New York: International Universities Press, 1964, pp. 113–141.
Holt, R. R. (1967), The Development of the Primary Process: A Structural View. In: *Motives & Thought: Psychoanalytic Essays in Honor of David Rapaport*, ed. R. R. Holt [*Psychological Issues*, Monogr. 18/19]. New York: International Universities Press, pp. 345–383.
Hoppe, K. (1977), Split Brains and Psychoanalysis. *Psychoanal. Quart.*, 46:220–244.
Jones, R. M. (1962), *Ego Synthesis in Dreams*. Cambridge, Mass.: Schenkman.
——— (1970), *The New Psychology of Dreaming*. New York: Grune & Stratton.
——— (1980), *The Dream Poet*. Cambridge, Mass.: Schenkman.
Jung, C. G. (1916), General Aspects of Dream Psychology. In: *The Structure and Dynamics of the Psyche. Collected Works*, vol. 8. New York: Pantheon, 1960, pp. 237–280.
Kinsbourne, M. (1982), Hemispheric Specialization and the Growth of Human Understanding. *Amer. Psycholog.*, 37:4, 411–420.
——— & Smith, W. (eds.) (1974), *Hemispheric Disconnection and Cerebral Function*. Springfield, Ill.: Charles C. Thomas.
Kohut, H. (1977), *The Restoration of the Self*. New York: International Universities Press.
Loewald, H. (1957), On the Therapeutic Action of Psychoanalysis. In: *Papers on Psychoanalysis*. New Haven, Conn.: Yale University Press, 1980, pp. 221–256.
——— (1971), On Motivation and Instinct Theory. In: *Papers on Psychoanalysis*. New Haven, Conn.: Yale University Press, 1980, pp. 102–137.
——— (1973), On Internalization. In: *Papers on Psychoanalysis*. New Haven, Conn.: Yale University Press, 1980, pp. 69–86.

—— (1978), Primary Process, Secondary Process, and Language. In: *Papers on Psychoanalysis*. New Haven, Conn.: Yale University Press, 1980, pp. 178–206.

Meissner, W. (1968), Dreaming as Process. *Internat. J. Psycho-Anal.*, 49:63–79.

Noy, P. (1969), A Revision of the Psychoanalytic Theory of the Primary Process. *Internat. J. Psycho-Anal.*, 50:155–178.

—— (1979), The Psychoanalytic Theory of Cognitive Development. *The Psychoanalytic Study of the Child*, 34:169–216. New Haven, Conn.: Yale University Press.

Nunberg, H. (1931), The Synthetic Function of the Ego. *Internat. J. Psycho-Anal.*, 12:123–140.

Ornstein, R. (ed.) (1973), *The Nature of Human Consciousness*. New York: Viking.

Padel, J. (1978), Object Relational Approach. In: *Dream Interpretation: A Comparative Study*, ed. J. Fosshage & C. Loew. New York: Spectrum, pp. 125–148.

Palombo, S. (1978a), The Adaptive Function of Dreams. *Internat. J. Psycho-Anal.*, 1:443–476.

—— (1978b), *Dreaming & Memory*. New York: Basic Books.

Sloane, P. (1979), *Psychoanalytic Understanding of the Dream*. New York: Jason Aronson.

Spiegelberg, H. (1965), The Essentials of the Phenomenological Method. In: *The Phenomenological Movement: A Historical Introduction*. The Hague: Nijhoff, pp. 653–701.

Stein, M. (1982), Rational vs. Anagogic Interpretation—Xenophon's Dream and Others. Unpublished.

Stolorow, R. (1978), Themes in Dreams: A Brief Contribution to Therapeutic Technique. *Internat. J. Psycho-Anal.*, 59:473–475.

—— & Atwood, G. (1982), The Psychoanalytic Phenomenology of the Dream. *Annual of Psychoanalysis*, 10:205–220.

Ullman, M. (1959), The Adaptive Significance of the Dreams. *J. Nerv. Ment. Dis.*, 129:144–149.

—— & Zimmerman, N. (1979), *Working with Dreams*. New York: Delacorte Press.

Waldhorn, H. (1967), *Indications for Psychoanalysis: The Place of the Dream in Clinical Psychoanalysis* (Monograph II of the Kris Study Group of the New York Psychoanalytic Institute), ed. E. D. Joseph. New York: International Universities Press.

Whitman, R., Kramer, M. & Baldridge, B. (1967), The Physiology, Psychology, and Utilization of Dreams. *Amer. J. Psychiat.*, 124:287–302.

Witkin, A. (1969), Influencing Dream Content. In: *Dream Psychology and the New Biology of Dreaming*, ed. M. Kramer. Springfield, Ill.: Charles C. Thomas, pp. 285–343.

12. Dreams and the Subjective World

Robert D. Stolorow and George E. Atwood

In our ongoing attempts to rethink the conceptual and methodological foundations of psychoanalysis (Atwood and Stolorow 1984; Stolorow, Brandchaft, and Atwood 1987), we have proposed that psychoanalysis should be reframed as an autonomous science of human experience, a depth psychology of human subjectivity. To that end, we have fashioned theoretical ideas designed to illuminate the nature, origins, and transformations of personal subjective worlds. In this chapter we apply this framework to the understanding and interpretation of dreams.

As our approach to dreams will show, our framework incorporates central ideas from Kohut's (1977) psychoanalytic psychology of the self, but is broader and more inclusive. Our basic units of analysis are *structures of experience*—the distinctive configurations of self and other that shape and organize a person's subjective world. We conceptualize these structures as systems of ordering or organizing principles—cognitive/affective schemata (Piaget 1970; Klein 1976; Stolorow 1978a; Slap and Saykin 1983) through which a person's experiences assume their characteristic forms and meanings. Such structures of subjectivity are disclosed in the thematic patterning of a person's subjective life. Other theoretical ideas that will be shown to have important implications for the analysis of dreams are our revised conception of the unconscious and our concepts of concrete symbolization and intersubjective context.

THE UNCONSCIOUS IN DREAMS

Historically, the psychoanalytic concept of the unconscious evolved in concert with the interpretation of dreams (Freud 1900). Hence, any significant

Portions of this chapter are reprinted by permission of The Analytic Press, Inc., from *Structures of Subjectivity*, by G. Atwood and R. Stolorow, Hillsdale, N.J., 1984.

This chapter is a synthesis of material previously published in Stolorow (1978b; 1989), Stolorow and Atwood (1982; 1989), and Atwood and Stolorow (1984, chapter 4).

alteration of the concept of the unconscious should bear directly on the psychoanalytic approach to dreams. In our reconsideration of the *dynamic* unconscious, we (Atwood and Stolorow 1984) first attempted to formulate its essence in experience-near terms, stripped of mechanistic metapsychological encumbrances:

[R]epression is understood as a process whereby particular configurations of self and object are prevented from crystallizing in awareness. . . . The "dynamic unconscious," from this point of view, consists in that set of configurations that consciousness is not permitted to assume, because of their association with emotional conflict and subjective danger. Particular memories, fantasies, feelings, and other experiential contents are repressed because they threaten to actualize these configurations. (35)

Later (Stolorow, Brandchaft, and Atwood 1987), we proposed that the psychological phenomena traditionally encompassed by the concept of the dynamic unconscious derive specifically from the realm of intersubjective transaction that Stern (1985) refers to as "interaffectivity"—the mutual regulation of affective experience within the developmental system. We wrote:

The specific intersubjective contexts[1] in which conflict takes form are those in which central affect states of the child cannot be integrated because they fail to evoke the requisite attuned responsiveness from the caregiving surround. Such integrated affect states become the source of lifelong inner conflict, because they are experienced as threats both to the person's established psychological organization and to the maintenance of vitally needed ties. Thus affect-dissociating defensive operations are called into play, which reappear in the analytic situation in the form of resistance. . . . It is in the defensive walling off of central affect states, rooted in early derailments of affect integration, that the origins of what has traditionally been called the "dynamic unconscious" can be found. (91–92)

From this perspective, the dynamic unconscious is seen to consist not of instinctual drive derivatives, but of disavowed central affect states and repressed developmental longings, defensively walled off because they failed to evoke attuned responsiveness from the early surround. This defensive sequestering of central emotional states and developmental yearnings, which attempts to protect against retraumatization, is the principal source of resistance in psychoanalytic treatment, and also of the *necessity for disguise when such states and yearnings are represented in dreams.*

In reaffirming the importance of defensive aims and disguise in the for-

1. The term "intersubjective context" refers here to the psychological field created by the interacting subjective worlds of child and caregiver.

mation of some dream imagery, our views differ from those of other authors who have been influenced, as we have, by the theory of self psychology (e.g., Fiss 1989; Fosshage 1989; Greenberg 1989). From our perspective, disguise in dreams cannot be seen as a product of isolated intrapsychic mechanisms. During treatment, such disguise, like the resistance from which it arises, must be understood as taking form within an intersubjective system —that is, at the interface of the interacting subjectivities of patient and analyst. Specifically, disguise becomes a prominent feature in a patient's dreams when aspects of the analyst's activity lend themselves to the patient's anticipation that exposure of emerging feelings and longings to the analyst will evoke a transference repetition of early developmental trauma. When disguise is prominent, associations to dream elements can assist in the investigation of the dream's intersubjective context of origin. Such investigation, in our view, is essential to analytic progress, as the following clinical vignette illustrates.

Clinical Illustration

A male therapist, a candidate in psychoanalytic training, had been working psychotherapeutically with a young woman for about a year, during which they seemed to make little progress in establishing a therapeutic bond. At this juncture she suffered what was for her a severe trauma—she was mugged and robbed while trying to enter her apartment house after returning home from a therapy session. Shortly thereafter she told the therapist she had decided to leave treatment. During what was to be their last session, she reported a dream.

In the dream, she was in a session with her therapist, a black woman. A robber broke into the consulting room as the therapist sat helplessly and did nothing. The patient's feeling in the dream was one off disparagement of the therapist. Her only associations were to the mugging and to a joke she had recently heard, the punch line of which described God as a black woman. Putting together the trauma of the mugging and the patient's manifestly disparaging feelings in the dream, the therapist commented that perhaps she felt disappointed that he had not been able to protect her from the assault. The patient was untouched by his interpretation and terminated, with no apparent understanding of her reason for doing so.

With hindsight it seems clear that the patient's association to the joke about God pointed to a powerful, walled-off, archaic idealizing longing, mobilized in the transference by the trauma of the mugging. The therapist's interpretation of her disappointment failed to take into account that this longing was *highly disguised* in the dream's manifest content, because it was being deeply resisted, as it had been from the outset of treatment. What the patient needed was for the therapist to investigate her *fears* of reexposing her idealizing yearnings to a transference repetition of crushing childhood disappointments and to extend empathic inquiry to her perceptions of qualities in the therapist that lent themselves to her expectations of retraumatization. Only by fully exploring this intersubjective situation could her dream, and the resistance it encoded, have been comprehended.

In addition to the dynamic unconscious, another form of unconsciousness has increasingly assumed a position of importance in our general theoretical framework as well as in our thinking about dreams:

The organizing principles of a person's subjective world, whether operating positively (giving rise to certain configurations in awareness), or negatively (preventing certain configurations from arising), are themselves unconscious. A person's experiences are shaped by his psychological structures without this shaping becoming the focus of awareness and reflection. We have therefore characterized the structure of a subjective world as *prereflectively unconscious.* (Atwood and Stolorow 1984, 36)

This form of unconsciousness is not the product of defensive activity, even though great effort is required to overcome it. It results from the person's inability to recognize his or her role as a constitutive subject in constructing his or her personal reality. The defenses themselves, when operating outside a person's awareness, can be seen as merely a special instance of organizing activity that is prereflectively unconscious.

It is our contention that an understanding of the form of unconsciousness that we have designated as ''prereflective'' sheds new light on the unique importance of dreams for psychoanalytic theory and practice. The prereflective structures of a person's subjective world are most readily discernible in his or her relatively unfettered, spontaneous productions, and there is probably no psychological product that is less fettered or more spontaneous than the dream. As human subjectivity in purest culture, the dream constitutes a *royal road to the prereflective unconscious*—to the organizing principles and dominant leitmotivs that unconsciously pattern and thematize a person's psychological life. We turn now to some technical implications of this close proximity of the dream to the unconscious structures of experience.

THEMES IN DREAMS

In classical psychoanalysis, the technical procedure for arriving at the meaning of a dream is to decompose the dream into discrete elements and then to collect the dreamer's associations to each of these elements. The rationale for this procedure is found in the theoretical idea that the associative chains provided by the dreamer, supplemented by certain connections and additions suggested by the analyst, will retrace the mental processes that gave rise to the dream and will lead the way back to the dream's latent content or unconscious meaning. It is assumed that the meaning of a dream, as determined by this method, is identical to the dream's causal origin; that is, the latent thoughts and wishes disclosed by the analysis are regarded as having been the elemental starting points of the dream's formation.

A hallmark of Freud's (1900) approach to the dream was his derogation of its manifest content as a beguiling, obfuscating facade, designed to conceal, rather than to disclose, the inner psychological life of the dreamer. It is our view, by contrast, that the thematic structure of the dream's manifest content can provide access to the prereflectively unconscious principles organizing the dreamer's subjective world. We have found that in addition to the discrete elements of a manifest dream, the distinctive thematic configurations of self and other that structure the dream narrative may also serve as useful points of departure for associative elaboration. Such themes, when abstracted from the concrete details of the dream and presented to the dreamer, can substantially enrich the associations that are produced and represent an important source of insight into the unconscious structures of a person's experience.

Clinical Illustration

As one of many possible illustrations of this approach, we have selected a vignette from the treatment of a woman who had sought therapeutic help at age thirty for multiple, severe agoraphobic symptoms. In the fifth year of her analysis she was experiencing wrenching conflicts in the context of a fully blossoming oedipal transference. During the last session before she was to leave for an extended vacation, she reported a dream from the previous night. She dreamed that she had dropped something in the toilet bowl—a tooth with a cavity in it. She did not want to put her hand in to get it. She said to herself, "The water is clean," and she closed her eyes and put her hand in and took it.

The patient was able to produce associations to only two of the discrete elements in the dream. First, the toilet reminded her that the toilet in her home had recently become clogged and had "backed up," and that the faecal material that remained in the bowl had been extremely disgusting to her. Second, the tooth reminded her that her father had recently had some dental work performed. The analysis of the dream remained at an impasse until the analyst was able to abstract for the patient the thematic configuration that he believed was represented therein.

He said that the dream's theme seemed to involve something being lost or separated from her, along with an acute conflict about reaching out to grasp or hold on to what was becoming lost. In the course of her associations to this theme, she remembered a romantically and sexually tinged fantasy involving how she wished to say good-bye to the analyst on this, their last, session before the vacation separation. She said she had resolved to keep the fantasy secret, because it was so shameful and embarrassing to her, and indicated that some of its details were represented in the dream. Respecting her "secret," the analyst was now able to show her, with the aid of her association to the toilet, that she was treating her romantic and sexual feelings toward him as if they were disgusting faecal substances that should be flushed away and kept hidden from view. Her association to the tooth provided the link to her father, who, in her memories at this time, had reacted to her romantic emotionality and oedipal sexuality as if they were utterly repulsive to him—an attitude she had expected the analyst to replicate. Indeed, she said she experienced the analyst's reserve—his tendency to explore rather than to respond emotionally—as a confirmation of her belief that her feelings would repel him. The dropped tooth as belonging not only to herself but also to her father pointed to her longing to share in idealized qualities of the analyst in order to repair the sense of defectiveness (the cavity) that was the legacy of her tie to her father, and also to her experience of the loss of these needed qualities in consequence of the impending vacation.

The analysis of this dream, while neither complete nor remarkable, demonstrates the fruitfulness of the mutually enhancing interplay between associations to discrete elements and associations to a manifest dream theme in facilitating the elucidation of the nature, origins, and purposes of the pattern dominating the transference at the time. The genetic and current contexts of the dream were shown to be united by their embeddedness in a common thematic structure that was becoming revealed as a red thread running through the patient's subjective life history.

At the heart of our psychoanalytic framework is a set of interpretive principles for elucidating psychological phenomena in their personal contexts. With regard to dreams, these principles provide ways of viewing dream imagery against the background of the dreamer's subjective universe. Many such interpretive principles are implicit in the classical Freudian theory of how dreams are formed. We believe this theory is most profitably viewed as a hermeneutic system of rules of interpretation rather than as a causal-mechanistic account of the processes of dream generation. Freud (1900) argued that interpretation reverses the dream work—that the activity of dream analysis moves backward along the paths of dream formation. It would be more accurate to say that the *theory* of the dream work reverses the pathways followed by psychoanalytic interpretation. The dream-work "mechanism" of condensation, for example, is the theoretical reverse of the interpretive principle that a single element in the dream text may be related to a multiplicity of subjective contexts in the dreamer's psychological life. Similarly, the mechanism of displacement inverts the principle that one may transpose and interchange the affective accents on various elements in the dream narrative in order to identify subjectively dangerous or conflictual configurations of images that the dreamer may be attempting to prevent from crystallizing in awareness.

The classical notion that dreams represent (attempted) wish fulfillments can also be viewed as an interpretive principle guiding the quest for a dream's connection to the subjective concerns of the dreamer. By giving the analyst an initial bearing in confronting the complexity of a particular dream narrative, this premise provides an orienting focus in relating the dream to emotionally significant issues in the dreamer's life. We would expand the classical conception of the centrality of wish fulfillment in dreams into a more general and inclusive proposition that dreams always embody one or more of the dreamer's *personal purposes*. Such purposes include the fulfillment of wishes as discussed by Freud, but also a number of other important psychological purposes (self-guiding and self-punishing, adaptive, restitutive-reparative, defensive) as well. Any or all such personal motivations can contribute to the construction of a dream, and it is essential to the therapeutic use of dream interpretation to determine the relative motivational salience or priority of the multiple purposes that the dream has served.

The interpretive principles of psychoanalysis as applied to dreams operate as aids to the interpreter in approaching the content of a manifest dream and its associations. They enable the analyst to construct a complex map of the various lines of symbolic expression that connect a dream to the personal world of the dreamer. The utility of these principles for examining a particular dream lies in the degree to which they lead to an interpretation that convincingly illuminates the various features of the dream text as embodiments of the issues and concerns having salience in the dreamer's subjective life. The correctness or adequacy of a particular dream interpretation, in turn, is assessed by the same hermeneutic criteria that govern the assessment of the validity of psychoanalytic interpretation in general—the logical coherence of the argument, the compatibility of the interpretation with one's general knowledge of the dreamer's psychological life, the comprehensiveness of the explanation in rendering the various details of the dream text transparent, and the aesthetic beauty of the analysis in illuminating previously hidden patterns of order in the dream narrative and in connecting these patterns to the background structures of the dreamer's personal subjectivity.

Let us now return from this general discussion of dream interpretation to a consideration of the central attribute of the dream experience—concrete symbolization.

CONCRETE SYMBOLIZATION IN DREAMS

Among recent critiques of Freudian theory, some of the most constructive have been those that rest upon George Klein's (1976) clarifying distinction between the metapsychology and the clinical theory of psychoanalysis. Metapsychology and clinical theory, Klein held, derive from two completely different universes of discourse. Metapsychology deals with the presumed material substrate of human experience, and is thus couched in the natural science framework of impersonal mechanisms, discharge apparatuses, and drive energies. In contrast, clinical theory, which derives from the psychoanalytic situation and guides psychoanalytic practice, deals with intentionality, conscious and unconscious purposes, and the personal meaning of subjective experiences. Klein wished to disentangle metapsychological and clinical concepts, and to retain only the latter as the legitimate content of psychoanalytic theory.

In this section we first comment briefly on Freud's two theories of the dream work—the metapsychological and the clinical. We then offer a clinical psychoanalytic theory of the purpose of concrete symbolization in dreams.

Freud's metapsychological theory of the dream work finds its clearest expression in chapter 7 of *The Interpretation of Dreams* (1900). There the dream work (with the exception of secondary revision) is conceptualized as a nonpurposeful, mechanical consequence of a process whereby preconscious thoughts receive an energic charge from an unconscious wish "striving to find an outlet" (605). The dream work occurs as the preconscious thoughts are "drawn into the unconscious" (594) and thereby automatically "become subject to the primary psychical process' (603).

In contrast with this mechanistic view of the dream work, germs of a clinical theory emphasizing its intentional and purposeful quality appear in an earlier chapter on "Distortion in Dreams." There the dream work is seen "to be deliberate and to be a means of dissimulation" (141) and disguise, serving the purpose of defense. In these passages, we can readily recognize the dream censor as being the dreamer himself, actively transforming the content and meaning of his experiences in order to protect himself from direct awareness of forbidden wishes.

This germinal clinical theory of the dream work, emphasizing its defensive purpose, applies principally to the process of displacement, and perhaps also to condensation. It does not shed a great deal of light on what we regard as the most distinctive and central feature of the dream experience—the use of concrete perceptual images endowed with hallucinatory vividness to symbolize abstract thoughts, feelings, and subjective states. Freud's explanation of this feature of dreams was an entirely metapsychological one: A "topographical regression" (548) of excitation from the motor to the sensory end of the psychic apparatus was thought to result in"a hallucinatory revival of . . . perceptual images" (543). Thus, in Freud's view, the pictorial and hallucinatory quality of dreams was a nonpurposeful, mechanical consequence of the discharge path followed by psychic energy during sleep. In contrast, we are proposing that concrete symbolization in dreams and their resulting hallucinatory vividness serve a vital psychological purpose for the dreamer, and that an understanding of this purpose can illuminate the importance and necessity of dreaming.

In order to develop this thesis, it is necessary first to touch briefly on the problem of human motivation. Our framework does not postulate a theory of the nature of personality as an "objective entity." Instead, it consists in a methodological system of interpretive principles to guide the study of meaning in human experience and conduct. Its explanatory concepts thus emphasize not "psychic determinism" and a natural science view of causality, but rather a *subjective contextualism* that brings to focus the nexus of personal meanings in which a person's experience and conduct are embedded. Rather than formulating impersonal prime movers of a mental apparatus, it seeks to illuminate the multiple conscious and unconscious purposes (Klein 1976) or personal reasons (Schafer 1976) that lead a person to strive to actualize his or her psychological structures.

The evolution of our framework has led us to propose an additional, more general, supraordinate motivational principle: that the *need to maintain the organization of experience* is a central motive in the patterning of human action. It is here that we can discover the fundamental purpose of concrete symbolization in dreams. When configurations of experience of self and other find symbolization in concrete perceptual images and are thereby articulated with hallucinatory vividness, the dreamer's feeling of conviction about the validity and reality of these configurations receives a powerful reinforcement. Perceiving, after all, is believing. By reviving during sleep the most basic and emotionally compelling form of knowing—through sensory perception—the dream affirms and solidifies the nuclear organizing structures of the dreamer's subjective life. Dreams, we are contending, are the *guardians of psychological structure,* and they fulfill this vital purpose by means of concrete symbolization (see also Fosshage 1983).

Dream symbolization may serve to maintain the organization of experience in two different senses, frequently within the same dream. On one hand, dream symbols may actualize a *particular* organization of experience in which specific configurations of self and other, required for multiple reasons, are dramatized and affirmed. Dream images of this first type often appear in the context of firmly structured inner conflict. In such instances, as was seen in our first two clinical illustrations, there is usually a significant gap between the manifest dream imagery and its latent meaning, because the aims of defense and disguise have been prominent. Our approach to such dream images incorporates Freud's clinical theory of the dream work, updated to include the principle of multiple function (Waelder 1936; Arlow and Brenner 1964). As we described earlier, we also supplement the classical technique with a focus on dream themes and their associative elaboration, as a further means of discovering the specific configurations of self and other that the dream symbolism has both actualized and disguised.

On the other hand, dream symbols may serve not so much to actualize particular configurations of experience as to maintain *psychological organization per se.* Dream images of this second type occur in the context of developmental interferences and arrests, whereby structuralization of the subjective world has remained incomplete, precarious, and vulnerable to dissolution (Stolorow and Lachmann 1980). With these dream images, the distinction between manifest and latent content is less germane, because the aim of disguise has not been prominent. Instead, the vivid perceptual images serve directly to restore or sustain the structural integrity and stability of a subjective world menaced with disintegration. For persons with severe deficits in psychological structure formation, concretization may serve a similar purpose in their waking lives as well, in the form of delusions, hallucinations, or concrete behavioral enactments that attempt to sustain the cohesion and continuity of a fragmenting sense of self or other. The organization-maintaining function of dream symbolization can be observed not only when existing structures are threatened, but also when *new* organizing principles are beginning to crystallize and are in need of consolidation (see Fosshage 1989).

"SELF-STATE DREAMS"

Important examples of this second type of dream imagery, in which concrete symbols serve to maintain psychological organization per se, can be found in the "self-state dreams" discussed by Kohut (1977). These dreams portray in their manifest imagery "the dreamer's dread vis-a-vis some uncontrollable tension-increase or his dread of the dissolution of the self" (109). Kohut suggests that the very act of portraying these archaic self-states in the dream in a minimally disguised form "constitutes an attempt to deal with the psychological danger by covering frightening nameless processes with namable visual imagery" (109). Socarides (1980) has discovered a similar purpose fulfilled by dreams that directly depict perverse sexual enactments similar to those performed by the dreamer in his or her waking life. The hallucinatory visualization of the perversion during sleep, like the perverse enactment itself, shores up an imperiled sense of self and protects against the danger of its dissolution.

The principal purpose of the perceptual imagery of self-state dreams is not, in our view, to render nameless psychological processes namable. By vividly reifying the experience of self-fragmentation, the dream symbols bring the state of the self into focal awareness with a feeling of conviction and reality that can only accompany sensory perceptions. The dream images, like sexual enactments, both encapsulate the danger to the self and reflect a concretizing effort at self-restoration.

A number of authors (Tolpin 1983; Fiss 1989; Greenberg 1989) have suggested that the theory of the self-state dream should be broadened to encompass the depiction in dreams of self-experience other than fragmentation. It is our view that the concept of concrete symbolization obviates the need for the distinction between self-state dreams and other dreams. Dream imagery concretizes the principles organizing the dreamer's experience, at whatever level of structuralization these principles may be operating, including situations in which organization is breaking down or fragmenting. We picture an *experiential continuum* of varying degrees of cohesion and continuity, with dream imagery concretizing the state of the subjective world, including the self, at any of the points along this continuum. For example, in the dreams discussed in the two earlier clinical illustrations, the imagery depicted states in which the self was more or less firmly integrated, although, in the first vignette, intensely endangered, and, in the second, highly devalued. In the following more extensive clinical material, the imagery of the first dream portrays an extreme state of self-disintegration, whereas the images of a second dream dramatize a unified sense of self in the process of becoming established and consolidated.

Clinical Illustration

The case we have chosen to illustrate our conception of the structure-maintaining function of concrete symbolization in dreams is that of a young woman whose sense of self had become fragmented into a set of separate, quasi-autonomous personalities. The dreams discussed reflect various aspects of her lifelong struggle to maintain the organization of her subjective world and achieve unity and cohesion in her self-experience. A feature of this case making it especially well suited for this discussion is that the patient engaged in specific concrete behavioral enactments that served a purpose closely paralleling that of her dreams. Viewing her dreams in the context of these enactments will bring the organization-maintaining function of her dream imagery into sharp focus.

The family environment in which the patient grew up was one of extreme physical and emotional abuse. Both parents treated her as an extension of themselves and as a scapegoat for their frustrations and disappointments in life. Violent physical beatings represented a frequent form of interaction with the parents, and throughout her early childhood she thought they wished her dead. A sense of profound personal disunity had haunted the patient all her life, appearing even in her earliest recollections. For example, she recalled from her fourth year an obsession with the issue of how it could be that her mind controlled the movements of her body. A disturbance in mind-body unity was also indicated by quasi-delusional journeys outside of her body, which began during that same year. These journeys commenced on the occasion when she was visited by the benevolent ghosts of two deceased grandparents. The ghosts taught her to leave her body and fly to a place she called "the field," a peaceful expanse of grass and trees somewhere far removed from human society. She felt safe in the field because she was alone there and no one could find her.

The psychological disintegration implicit in the patient's out-of-the-body journeys was embedded in a broader context of self-division resulting from the violent abuse and rejection she had received in her family. Beginning at the age of two and one-half, when her parents abruptly ceased all affectionate bodily contact with her, and continuing through a series of pivotal traumatic episodes over the next several years, she was successively divided into a total of six fragmentary selves. Each of these fragments crystallized as a distinct personality, possessing its own individual name and unique personal attributes.

When the patient was seven years old she developed a renal tumor, causing agonizing pain. The need to escape the suffering generated by her condition became an additional motive underlying the journeys outside of her body. It was more than one full year before her illness was correctly diagnosed and the tumor finally removed. The surgery itself was handled with brutal insensitivity by her parents and doctors, and she experienced it as an overwhelming trauma. The impact of all these circumstances on her precarious selfhood was symbolized in a set of recurring nightmares that began during her recuperation from surgery and continued throughout her life thereafter. In these dreams she stood alone in the small train station of her town as flames sprang up all around her. Soon the whole building was engulfed in fire. After the station had burned to the ground, two eyeballs lay quietly in the smoking ashes and then began to quiver and roll about, conversing with each other by means of movements and glances. This dream of burning down to small fragments concretely depicted the disintegrating impact of a world persecuting her both from without and from within.

What psychological function can be ascribed to the patient's recurring dream of being burned down to isolated fragments? The repeated transformation of the experience of self-disintegration into an image of the physical incineration of her body enabled her to maintain the state of her self in focal awareness and encapsulated her effort to retain psychological integrity in the face of the threat of total self-dissolution. By utilizing concrete anatomical imagery, she was giving her disintegrating existence tangible form, replacing a precarious and vanishing sense of selfhood with the permanence and substantiality of physical matter. The image of the interaction and communication between the eyeballs at the end of the dream symbolized a further restitutive effort to reconnect the broken fragments and restore a measure of coherence to her splintered self. The specific symbol of the eyeballs captured an essential feature of what became her principal mode of relating to her social milieu. She assumed the role of an ever-watchful, often disembodied spectator, perpetually scanning her environment for desirable qualities in others that she hoped to appropriate and assemble into a rebuilt self. Thus, both her self-restorative efforts and what remained of her vanishing self became crystallized in her waking life in the act of looking and in her recurring dreams in the imagery of the eyes.

The central salience in the patient's subjective world of the need to maintain selfhood and recover a sense of personal unity was also indicated by an array of bizarre enactments that appeared concurrently with the onset of the recurring dream of being burned. These enactments included the self-administration of severe whippings with a leather belt, delicate cutting and puncturing of the surface of the skin on her wrists and arms, gazing tirelessly at the reflected image of her face in pools of water, fondling and staring into translucent pieces of glass, scratching and rubbing at cracks and crevices in hard physical surfaces such as walls and sidewalks, and stitching the skin of her separate fingers together with needle and thread. Since the appearance of the enactments coincided precisely with the onset of the recurrent nightmare, we have regarded the enactments as "associations" embedded in the same contexts of meaning in which the dream imagery took form.

The self-whipping ritual arose initially as an internalization of the punishing treatment the patient had received during her earlier childhood. She tended at first to whip herself in response to acts that previously would have evoked her parents' wrath—for example, acts of asserting her needs, seeking attention, or expressing unhappiness. The function of the self-punishments at this stage was primarily to master a sense of helplessness and counteract the dreaded feeling of being vulnerable to attack from the outside world. The ritual also came to include a wishfulfilling and restitutive element in the form of a sequel to the actual whipping. After first violently beating herself on the back and buttocks, she would adopt the role of loving parent and say to herself in a soft voice, "It's all right honey, now there will be no more pain." Then assuming the role of comforted child, she would fall blissfully asleep. This hard-won feeling of peacefulness, however, was rudely shattered when she later awoke and found herself still entirely alone.

In addition to helping her master persecution anxiety and maintain needed images of herself being cared for, the whipping ritual also began to serve a more fundamental purpose in the patient's subjective life. One of the consequences of her profound and enduring emotional isolation was a feeling of being unreal, unalive, and insubstantial. This feeling was magnified by the continuing out-of-the-body journeys to the field. The increasing frequency of these journeys came to pose a new and even more menacing danger to her safety—namely, the severing of all connection to physical reality and the final obliteration of her psychic self. The terror that she might permanently lose her physical form and somehow evaporate into thin air led her to return to the whipping ritual with redoubled intensity. The strong sensations of pain distributed on the surface of her skin were used to provide reassurance of her continuing embodiment and survival in the real physical world.

Essentially parallel functions were served by the patient's ritualistic cutting and puncturing of the skin on her wrists and arms. These behaviors seemed to originate as a restaging of the traumatically impinging medical procedures associated with her renal surgery. In addition to the operation itself, the procedures included a spinal tap, numerous injections, catheterization, intravenous administration of medications and fluids, etc. By cutting and puncturing her skin, she actively relived a passively endured trauma and sought mastery over her feelings of unbearable helplessness. Like the ritualized whipping, the cutting and puncturing activity also began to serve the function of strengthening the patient's conviction that she was substantial and real. By violating the physical boundary of her body with a needle or a knife, she dramatized the very existence of that boundary and reestablished a sense of her own embodied selfhood. In addition, the stinging sensations and the droplets of blood produced by the delicate cutting provided her with concrete sensory evidence of her continuing aliveness.

The enactments involving water and glass were more complex, but also related to struggles with a precarious self-structure and a deep sense of helpless vulnerability. The water ritual began when she gazed at her reflection in ponds and pools of rainwater. She recalled becoming fascinated by how the image of her face would disappear and then magically reappear when she disturbed the water's reflecting surface. One meaning of this activity pertained again to her need for mastery over passively experienced traumata —by actively being the cause of the disappearance of her image she was seeking to overcome the shattering impact on her sense of selfhood of her whole earlier history of victimization and abuse. In addition, in eliminating her reflected image she thought of herself as actually ceasing to exist and becoming nothing, which provided a feeling of safety because what does not exist cannot be made a target by a persecuting world. The water also seemed to function to give reassurance that while her sense of self (concretized in a visual reflection) might be made to vanish on a temporary basis, it could not be annihilated permanently. A sense of self-continuity was thus tenuously achieved. A final significance of water to the patient was associated with its paradoxical quality of being both *transparent* and *reflecting*. There was something in the conjoining of these two properties with which she wishfully identified, and this identification was even more pronounced in her involvement with objects of glass.

The patient began to collect small glass objects during her early adolescence. The reflecting and refracting properties of crystal prisms and spheres particularly fascinated her. Acts of fondling and staring into such objects developed into a ritual behavior pattern duplicating and sometimes blending into her relationship with water. On occasion she would fill a crystal container with water and place it in a window where she could observe its interaction with the sun's rays. This ritual was enacted several times during the psychotherapeutic sessions. As she studied the interplay between the light, the water, and the glass, she would softly chant, "water . . . glass . . . water . . . glass." Her consciousness could become wholly absorbed in this preoccupation, which she seemed to experience as a refuge from the social environment. The psychological sources of the patient's attraction to glass were bound up with her difficulties in maintaining a feeling of her own personal selfhood. She was excessively vulnerable to the expectations and perceptions of others, and tended to feel that she became whomever she was seen as being. For instance, when a grandfather told her wistfully how much she reminded him of his long-dead beloved wife, the patient felt the departed soul of the wife invading and assuming command over her body. Such episodes drastically affected her sense of being in possession of her own identity, and she responded to them by cultivating secret realms of herself protected from the annihilating potential of others' perceptions and definitions. Included in the elaboration of these hidden sectors of her subjective life was the development of her alternative personalities, each christened with its own secret name. The fact that no one knew her secret names made her feel safe from the engulfing potential of others' experiences of her. A consequence of the patient's defensive secrecy, however, was a further intensification of her feeings of estrangement. She was driven into isolation in order to protect herself from self-loss in relationships; but the isolation itself presented the danger of self-extinction through unendurable loneliness. Her preoccupation with glass sprang directly from the conflict between her need to retreat from others into a world of secrecy and her need to break out of isolation and reestablish bonds to the social environment. The glass concretized a wishful solution to this conflict by embodying the twin properties of translucency on the one hand and reflectivity on the other. The translucency of the glass meant that it was open to the passage of light from the outside, which served to lessen the patient's fear of isolation and entombment within her own secret world. The reflectivity of the glass objects, their solidity, and their firm boundaries, by contrast, meant that they were real and substantial, which made her feel safe from the dangers posed by involvement with her social milieu. A fusion of these properties also appeared in a recurring fantasy concerning a house she wished to build in the field she had been visiting in the out-of-the-body projections. She pictured this house as a beautiful construction of one-way glass, so that from the outside it would be a mirror, but from the inside transparent.

The remaining enactments to be considered were those in which the patient scratched and rubbed at cracks in solid surfaces and stitched her fingers together with thread. These enactments pertained to the patient's experience of being an assembly of disjointed parts. With regard to the scratching pattern, she explained that crevices and cracks in the external environment "itched" unbearably and compelled her to scratch them. The locating of the subjective sensation of itching in physical objects represented a transposition onto the plane of material reality of her feeling of inner fragmentation. She described herself as being like a jar filled with small spheres or cubes with concave surfaces, and as a checkerboard filled with round checkers; even though the constituent elements might be packed together very tightly, they still would not form an integrated and smoothly continuous whole. The itching cracks and crevices in the external environment corresponded to the subjective interstices between the various fragmentary entities comprising her self-experience, and the scratching represented her effort to find relief from her distressing lack of inner cohesion.

Closely similar was the function of her pattern of sewing her fingers together with needle and thread. This ritual began with holding her hand up to the light and gazing at the spaces between her separate fingers. Then she would push a needle and thread just under the skin of her little finger, then under the skin of the next one, and the next, etc., and then back and forth several times until they were all tightly interconnected and pressed together. The act of weaving the fingers together was one in which separate parts of her physical self were literally joined and made to appear whole and continuous, concretizing her effort to fashion an internally integrated identity out of the collection of part-selves into which she had divided during the course of her traumatic early history.

The enactments in which the patient engaged are functionally parallel to her recurring dreams of being burned to fragments. The essential feature the two sets of phenomena share in common is the reparative use of concretization to given an experience of self-disintegration a material and substantial form. In the dreams the emphasis appears on the concrete symbolization of the experience of self-dissolution, and the additional reparative trend of reassembling the broken pieces is hinted at in the image of the communication that develops between the eyeballs. In the enactments one finds analogous symbolizations and also the vivid expression of the patient's need to mend her broken self by reconnecting the separate fragments into which she had disintegrated.

Each of the patterns of behavior discussed here was repeatedly enacted during the psychotherapeutic sessions. Some of these performances were extremely difficult for the therapist to witness, especially those in which she slapped, whipped, and cut herself. For the first year and a half of treatment she brought knives, needles, pieces of broken glass, and a leather belt to the sessions on a regular basis and frequently used one or more of these objects against herself. When the therapist attempted to prevent this behavior by taking her objects away, she would scratch, slap, and beat herself with her hands and fingernails. The only means of ensuring that the patient would not engage in self-abuse was to physically restrain her until the self-destructive urges had passed. This physical restraining occupied a significant portion of many sessions during the early phases of the psychotherapeutic work and proved to be critically important in solidifying the therapeutic bond. In addition to the restraint required to prevent the patient from harming herself, there were a number of times when she approached her therapist and grasped him tightly, pressing her face against his body. After the first occasion of such an approach she explained she had needed the physical contact to prove he was not an unreal apparition or hallucination she had conjured up. She reported having been shocked and surprised when her arms met the solid resistance of his flesh, for she had expected them to pass right through him as though he were made of mist. Contact with her therapist's physical being served to differentiate him from the ghosts and other imaginary entities on whom she had previously depended. This contact also provided an anchoring point for the beginning stabilization of her own physical embodiment. It emerged in discussions of the meaning and significance of holding and being held that the patient had not experienced affectionate bodily contact with another human being since the age of two and one-half, when her parents ended all such interaction with her.

The first year and a half of the patient's treatment were devoted primarily to establishing a therapeutic relationship that would give her some relief from her estrangement and loneliness while at the same time strengthening her sense of individuality and separateness as a person. She oscillated during this period between expressions of suicidal despair and a mergerlike closeness in which she seemed to want nothing but physical proximity to the therapist. The actual physical contact, together with the symbolic holding (Winnicott 1965) implicit in the therapist's consistent provision of acceptance, concern, and understanding, established a nexus of archaic relatedness in which the patient's aborted psychological development could move forward once again. Very gradually the functions inhering in the enactments we have described passed over to the empathic bond that was becoming established. The nature of the patient's evolving reliance on her analyst at the beginning of this process was shown by her reactions to his periodic failures to comprehend or appropriately respond to what she tried to communicate. Such misunderstandings tended to be followed by a resurgence of one or more of the enactments, which then continued until the disrupted empathic bond could be reestablished. As she increasingly came to rely on the therapist for the maintenance of her psychological organization, the ritualized enactments (and the out-of-the-body projections), which she had formerly needed for this purpose, lessened and finally disappeared. The repeating nightmares of being burned to fragments came to an end simultaneously.

The function of dreams in maintaining the organization of a person's subjective world is to be seen not only in situations wherein structures are breaking down, as was the case with the patient at the time of the onset of her nightmares; dreams may also play an important role in consolidating and stabilizing new structures of subjectivity that are in the process of coming into being. Let us turn now to a consideration of another dream of the patient we have been discussing, this one having occurred midway through the long course of her psychotherapy. The context of this dream in the treatment was one of intense conflict and struggle over the issue of self-unification. Two of the initial six part-selves had at this point been assimilated into the remaining four, but the next steps of integration were being approached by the patient with trepidation and reluctance. Specifically, she feared that becoming one would render her vulnerable to being destroyed, either by attack from the outside world or by unendurable loneliness. At the same time, however, she had come to abhor the prospect of a life spent in continuing disunity.

In her dream she walked into the living room of her house and saw on the mantel above the fireplace four cement boxes resting side by side. There seemed to be bodies inside the boxes. The scene terrified her and she awoke, but then fell back asleep and the dream continued. Now the four boxes were replaced by just one box, with four bodies arranged inside with their backs against the cement walls and facing inward toward a central point. The box seemed to be a coffin. In discussing this dream with the therapist, the patient spontaneously associated the four boxes with the four remaining part-selves still requiring integration. A great deal of progress toward this goal had already been achieved, principally through the four parts growing less and less distinct from each other in the facilitating medium of the therapeutic relationship. The patient was oscillating, however, between experiencing herself as a single person with multiple facets, on the one hand, and as a collection of separate persons who happened to resemble each other and share the same body, on the other.

The dream concretizes one phase of this oscillation by replacing the image of four separate boxes with the image of just one that contains four bodies. The patient spontaneously offered the interpretation that the shift from four to one could be understood as a prelude to the integration of her personality, with the exterior boundaries of the final box representing the developing structure of a unitary self. The danger felt to be associated with her impending integration is also concretely symbolized in the dream, by the identification of the box as a coffin. The patient frequently expressed deep anxiety that becoming one would end her life, and she once even suggested that she was coming together as something dead.

The image of the box containing four bodies may also be understood as a symbol of her experience of the therapeutic relationship. The empathic bond, which by this time had become well established, was exercising a holding, containing, and integrating function in the patient's efforts to achieve psychological wholeness. Her ambivalence regarding this task emerged quite clearly in the transference, wherein she alternated between embracing her therapist's unifying comprehension and rejecting it as a deadly threat to the survival of the selves. These alternations arose most fundamentally from the patient's deep conviction that she could never fully trust another human being, a conviction that was gradually overcome in stages closely paralleling the integration of her personality.

The dream of the transformation of four boxes into one box buttressed the patient's evolving self-integration by giving her developing unity a concrete form. In the same way that the earlier dream of being burned encapsulated her need to maintain her self-experience as she underwent psychological dissolution, this second dream expressed her need to maintain and consolidate the new but still unsteady structure of integrated self-experience that was gradually crystallizing. An enactment sharing this later function appeared some nine months after the dream of the boxes. During the interim the patient had continued to wrestle with the problem of unifying herself, with each of the residual fragmentary personalities making a common commitment to a shared future as one individual.

In the subsequent context of such statements as "We are me!" and "I am one now—we voted last night and we all agree," the patient began a therapy session by bringing out twelve small pieces of paper. On six of the slips were written the six names of the part-selves, and on the other six were short phrases designating the pivotal trauma she considered responsible for each of the self-divisions. After asking the therapist whether he thought he could match the selves with their appropriate traumas, she cleared off his desk and assembled out of the twelve pieces of paper two closely juxtaposed columns displaying the temporal sequence of her shattering psychological history. The act of arranging the names and experiences into a single ordered structure clearly concretized the patient's increasingly successful efforts to synthesize an internally integrated, temporally continuous self. By giving the newborn self a tangible form and demonstrating its unity and historical continuity to the therapist, she consolidated the structure of her experience more firmly than had been possible heretofore. Following the integrating enactment involving the twelve pieces of paper, the patient came to feel her own subjective integrity on a consistent basis, and the focus of the therapeutic work shifted to issues other than that of mending her self-fragmentation.

REFERENCES

Arlow, J., & Brenner, C. (1964) *Psychoanalytic Concepts and the Structural Theory*. Madison, CT: International Universities Press.

Atwood, G., & Stolorow, R. (1984) *Structures of Subjectivity: Explorations in Psychoanalytic Phenomenology*. Hillsdale, NJ: Analytic Press.

Fiss, H. (1989) An experimental self psychology of dreaming: Clinical and theoretical applications. In *Dimensions of Self Experience*, ed. A. Goldberg. Hillsdale, NJ: Analytic Press. 13–23.

Fosshage, J. (1983) The psychological function of dreams: A revised psychoanalytic perspective. *Psychoanal. & Contemp. Thought* 6:641–69.

——— (1989) The developmental function of dreaming mentation: Clinical implications. In *Dimensions of Self Experience*, ed. A. Goldberg. Hillsdale, NJ: Analytic Press. 3–11.

Freud, S. (1900) *The Interpretation of Dreams*. Standard Edition, vols. 4 & 5. London: Hogarth Press, 1953.

Greenberg, R. (1989) The concept of the self-state dream, revisited: Contributions from sleep research. In *Dimensions of Self Experience*, ed. A. Goldberg. Hillsdale, NJ: Analytic Press. 25–32.

Klein, G. (1976) *Psychoanalytic Theory*. Madison, CT: International Universities Press.

Kohut, H. (1977) *The Restoration of the Self*. Madison, CT: International Universities Press.

Piaget, J. (1970) *Structuralism*. New York: Basic Books.

Schafer, R. (1976) *A New Language for Psychoanalysis*. New Haven: Yale University Press.

Slap, J, & Saykin, A. (1983) The schema: Basic concept in a nonmetapsychological model of the mind. *Psychoanal. & Contemp. Thought* 6:305–25.

Socarides, C. (1980) Perverse symptoms and the manifest dream of perversion. In *The Dream in Clinical Practice*, ed. J. Natterson. Northvale, NJ: Jason Aronson. 237–56.

Stern, D. (1985) *The Interpersonal World of the Infant*. New York: Basic Books.

Stolorow, R. (1978a) The concept of psychic structure: Its metapsychological and clinical psychoanalytic meanings. *Internat. Rev. Psycho-Anal.* 5:313–20.

——— (1987b) Themes in dreams: A brief contribution to therapeutic technique. *Internat. J. Psycho-Anal.* 59:473–75.

——— (1989) The dream in context. In *Dimensions of Self Experience*, ed. A. Goldberg. Hillsdale, NJ: Analytic Press. 33–39.

———, & Atwood, G. (1982) Psychoanalytic phenomenology of the dream. *Ann. Psychoanal.* 10:205–20.

———, & Atwood, G. (1989) The unconscious and unconscious fantasy: An intersubjective-developmental perspective. *Psychoanal. Inq.* 9:364–74.

———, Brandchaft, B., & Atwood, G. (1987) *Psychoanalytic Treatment: An Intersubjective Approach*. Hillsdale, NJ: Analytic Press.

————, & Lachmann, F. (1980) *Psychoanalysis of Developmental Arrests:.Theory and Treatment*. Madison, CT: International Universities Press.

Tolpin, P. (1983) Self psychology and the interpretation of dreams. In *The Future of Psychoanalysis*, ed. A. Goldberg. Madison, CT: International Universities Press. 255–71.

Waelder, R. (1936) The principle of multiple function: Observations on over-determination. *Psychoanal. Quart.* 5:45–62.

Winnicott, D. (1965) *The Maturational Processes and the Facilitating Environment*. Madison, CT: International Universities Press.

PART III

SPECIAL TOPICS

A. Trauma and Pathology

13. Emergence of Hidden Ego Tendencies during Dream Analysis

N. Lionel Blitzsten, Ruth S. Eissler, and K. R. Eissler

From the early days of psycho-analysis dreams have been one of the main roads to uncovering the unconscious, and no other system of psychotherapy or psychology has given them the same emphasis or put them to such constructive use.

It became apparent to Freud that the complex configuration of a dream is not a static phenomenon but the end product of various forces striving towards partly identical and partly disparate goals. His disentanglement of these forces, his ability to use the dream as a phenomenon to deduce and describe the forces which must be at work in its production and his reconstruction of what must be the structure of the apparatus which is endowed with the faculty of producing dreams is one of the greatest intellectual achievements. Rarely was so much concluded from so little by succinct ratiocination and empirical observation. It would seem that little could be added after Freud's exhaustive analysis. And actually, as Freud himself mentioned, little new has been added, although he seems to have thought that our knowledge of dreams and particularly of the dream work is far from complete. With the shift of psycho-analytic interest to ego psychology it was logical that some analysts should scrutinize anew the dream contents for clues to the unconscious structure of the ego. In Freud's first publication, the ego's contribution to dreams was limited to its wish to sleep, to the censoring function, and to the secondary elaboration. In 1923, however, Freud distinguished between 'dreams *from above* and dreams *from below*'[1] and in 1938 he wrote: 'dreams may arise either from the id or from the ego',[2] thus enlarging the ego's contribution to dreams. Yet from the beginning of the

Reprinted by permission of the authors and the *International Journal of Psycho-analysis*, from Vol. 31, 1950, pp. 12–17. Copyright © Institute of Psycho-analysis.

Paper read at the 16th International Psycho-Analytical Congress, Zürich, August, 1949.

psycho-analytic interest in dreams, attention was paid to another series of dream problems albeit of minor importance, namely the vicissitudes of the dream after awakening. There are two main alternatives. The dream is either forgotten or distorted. Distortion is the engrossment or continuation of that work which had been initiated prior to the dream's appearance in the conscious. The forgetting is the manifest victory of those forces which are called by the general term 'resistance' but which are also actively engaged in dream work.

A composite of all these forces was found in a clinical observation in regard to those patients who occasionally or habitually write down the dream immediately after its occurrence in order to rescue it from obliteration and to preserve it for psycho-analytic interpretation. There seems to have been a general agreement that this is a camouflaged form of resistance. Dreams thus preserved, it is said, cannot be analysed because the resistance which necessitated the written record will continue to obstruct its interpretation after the dream record has been brought to the analyst's notice, and the patient ought to give his associations. But this does not seem to be consistently correct. There are patients who are successful in counteracting their resistances by writing down their dreams. It is true that such dreams are always loaded with particularly heavy resistances and that the patient's need to write down his dreams must also be analysed. But under certain circumstances the written record may be an important contribution, and it may be of help to the analyst in steering the patient through a period of increased resistance by consistently providing him with a record of the patient's current dreams.

The subject-matter of this study is related to the type of problem just mentioned. It asks what can be learned from the patient's attitude toward his dreams once they have been dreamed and reported in his analysis. Our interest in this study does not concern the patient's affective and emotional reactions to the manifest dream content, nor his emotional attitudes towards the latent dream thoughts, but the manner in which his wakeful personality, his ego, deals with the manifest dream in analysis. The patient may, for example, say after having reported the dream that nothing comes to his mind. If it does not concern a symbolic dream, this is the sign that he is in resistance. The ego refuses co-operation in the process of establishing the true meaning of a dream. If this reaction occurs repeatedly or habitually, however, it may be the result of a character trait. It may be due to stubbornness that the patient consistently refuses co-operation.

There is also the type of patient who fears being suddenly confronted with a content which up to then he had successfully repressed. Or the patient may be competitive, and therefore not want the analyst to make a discovery before he himself can ascertain the possible background of the dream. Thus we see that a simple lack of associations may be indicative of a variety of character traits. Silence or claiming a blank mind after reporting a dream is an unspecific reaction, and its particular meaning in terms of character traits must be derived from other sources. Yet sometimes a patient will show attitudes which permit more specific conclusions.

There are patients who always produce associations to every last element of the manifest dream. Others pick out one little detail and associate to that exclusively, thus presenting a particular facet of their compulsive characters.

One of the authors had occasion to observe a patient, an obsessional character, whose technique of handling dreams distinctly repeated a basic pattern of his life history. His associations would go to a certain point and then he would drop the entire subject. His behaviour in other pursuits followed this same pattern. He practised coitus interruptus in spite of having been advised against it. In his medical practice he changed to four different specialties one after the other. He had moved five times from one city to another in the course of his professional life. In the army he submitted obsequiously to his superiors, only soon to become a source of such irritation that he was in danger of being court-martialled.

The behaviour of the patients so far mentioned did not differ during dream analysis from that in many other of their life situations which were known to the analyst. Since not only the unconscious but also character continuously reveals itself, it is not surprising to find general features of a patient's character structure delineated in the particular situation of associating to a dream. In this study, however, we wish to go a step further and show that in some instances, by his way of manipulating the dream, the patient may usher in certain fundamental particularities of his ego structure which are brought into full light only after prolonged analysis, but made their appearance in the initial phases of the treatment in no other situation but that of dream analysis. Three clinical instances will be reported here. In all of them it became quite evident in the course of analysis that the most important disturbance of the ego had become accessible to the analyst's observation for the first time during dream analysis.

A thirty-nine-year-old woman sought analysis because of maladjustment to almost every sector of life. She suffered from anxiety, inhibitions, feelings of isolation, depression, feelings of rejection by her environment, and was incapable of getting enjoyment from love or work. Emotionally she was almost completely dependent on the members of her family and on a few women friends to whom she attached herself in a leech-like fashion. Although she held several degrees in art, she worked in an inferior position and even there had difficulty in maintaining her job because of her character disturbance. Her appearance was a mixture of old-maidishness and early adolescence. Her manners were affected and her shyness histrionic. Her heterosexual relationships had been confined to an incestuous experience. Although she never had any overt homosexual relationship, she always found some woman to whom she attached herself and whom she tried to dominate as much as the victim permitted. Her desire to dominate led her to pry into the private affairs of her victim, misinterpreting whatever the other person did or said and constantly referring to herself everything that the other person did. Whenever her victims defended themselves against her by withdrawal she felt unloved and rejected and indulged in elaborate phantasies of a masochistic colouring.

She came from a rigidly puritanical middle-class family. Her mother was a socially active, attractive, and domineering woman; her father, a shy, withdrawn man, entertained no contacts outside his family and showed the traits of a compulsive character. Of her two older sisters, one had gone through a stormy schizophrenic episode which was arrested by psycho-analytic therapy; the second sister did not show any overt schizophrenic condition, but had suffered a bland character change during adulthood. All three sisters were talented above the average, and the two older ones held responsible positions commensurate with their abilities.

Although it was clear from the beginning that this patient was at least a borderline case, the definite diagnosis of a paranoid condition could not be made with certainty. Her analysis centred for a long period essentially round her pre-genital fixations of a scoptophilic and sadomasochistic nature. We did not understand until very late that behind the scoptophilic impulse was a phantasy of destroying the object by the magic of her eyes.

From the beginning of her analysis the patient showed a specific, well-circumscribed attitude towards her dreams. Although she had an active and elaborate dream-life which she usually presented without marked inhibition, she never spontaneously commented upon her dreams, but resisted any attempt at working with the dream material. We are not referring here to those periods during her analysis in which she used the reporting of her dreams for specific gratification of sado-masochistic impulses in the transference relationship, but to a reaction of panic and extreme rage which always occurred whenever her attention was drawn to her dreams and she was asked to associate to them. The violence of her objection was so great that she even sometimes jumped up from the couch, and huddled in a corner. This attitude, although extreme, may give the impression of the well-known features in anal characters which, valuing every production of their own as something precious, obstinately refuse to co-operate in analysing their dreams for fear of devaluation. This mistake of classifying her attitude towards her dreams as part of an anal character was made in the beginning of her analysis. Looking back at those initial stages we believe that this mistake could have been avoided and that a correct understanding of this attitude would have led directly to the patient's most important and essential disturbances. As it turned out, her specific reaction expressed an intolerable fear least she destroy a part of herself by looking at the dream and lest simultaneously, by being looked at and discussed, the dream might come alive and destroy her. Her disturbance took place on a level which was not far from that of primary narcissism where the ego cannot diffferentiate between external and psychic reality. In the early stage of her analysis this core of a paranoid mechanism could not be seen in any other clinical manifestation but only in this regular, specific reaction to her dreams. Later in her analysis this conflict became evident in other manifestations also, and was confirmed as the central issue of her latent psychosis. In the course of her treatment a remarkable upswing of her artistic creativity took place. She became quantitatively more productive and her creations met with public recognition and acceptance. But whenever she had to show her creations to her agent she produced the identical reaction of panic and rage which she showed toward her dreams. At first she could draw only series of human figures which looked identical and were expressionless and lifeless. These two features of serialization and lifelessness served to deny the individuality of her creations, i.e., the defence against her fear lest any of the drawn figures might come alive. At a later stage the series of identical figures was broken up into recognizably different characters; nevertheless, each single figure continued to preserve a character of pure formality and lifelessness.

During one period of her analysis she produced delusional ideas; once, for instance, she angrily reported that in walking to the analyst's office she saw a soiled sanitary towel on the street and was convinced that it had been put there for the purpose of forcing her to look at it. At other times she would spend her analytical hour in just staring at the analyst in order to express destructive impulses. A great deal of the material elicited during the analysis justified the assumption that at some time during the patient's childhood her mother had been pregnant and had miscarried. Only after the termination of her analysis was this reconstruction verified from an external source. It is likely that the patient's fears of destroying a part of herself by looking at her dreams, or her fears that these dreams might come alive and destroy her, were intimately connected with that particular incident in her life.

We believe that though the patient's behaviour in connection with her dreams during the initial phases of her analysis served the purpose of resistance it sporadically brought the central issue of a latent psychosis to the surface. This issue later became the stumbling-block of her analysis, but initially it was clinically mute and at that time manifested itself only in the manner aforementioned. Subsequent analysis revealed some of the reasons for the dislocation and restriction, as Freud called it, which her ego had suffered. Yet we want to re-emphasize that in the beginning of her analysis, at a time when one could not have guessed its historical foundation, her ego modification became discernible only in her reactions to her dreams.

The second case concerns a twenty-eight-year-old woman who came to analysis because of erythrophobia. She complained about the fear of blushing which had made it impossible for her to continue work as a nurse. She hoped to avoid her anxieties by taking a job as a secretary in a business office, but was utterly dissatisfied with her professional life. Socially, too, she felt handicapped by her symptoms, and in general had the feeling that the symptom interfered with any achievements in her life, although she was good-looking and intelligent. Coming from a puritanical family she tried rigidly to fulfil her duties and to comply with traditional standards. Since her adolescence she had scarcely had any heterosexual contacts, and her emotional life centred around the members of her family. She had lost her father when she was about twelve years old. From the beginning of her analysis this patient showed a very striking attitude toward her own dreams. She either introduced her dream report by saying 'I had a peculiar dream' or she ended the account with the sentence 'That's all there is to it.' The remark 'I had a peculiar dream' could have been taken as still belonging to the dream thoughts. The same might have been true for the ending remark. However, since it soon appeared that these sentences were stereotyped, it did not seem likely that they were actually a part of the dream or referable to the latent dream content. The first sentence especially was pronounced in a way which conveyed the patient's feeling that she actually had no part in the production of the dream, that it was foreign to her almost as if imposed on her from the outside. Once, for instance, she dreamed about her mother being drunk. She showed a very indignant attitude about the contents of this dream, commenting that she did not know why her mother should behave in such a way since she never drank, and apparently at that moment lacked the capacity to distinguish between reality and dream, thus overlooking that the dream was a creation of her own. The ending sentence 'That's all there is to it' cut off any possible further associations to the dream elements. It was almost as if she showed some part of herself and then decided not to proceed any further with the exposure. Altogether she usually responded to the content of her dream with a feeling of suspicion, as though it were put in her way in order to irritate and annoy her. These stereotyped reactions towards her own dreams roused the suspicion that a paranoid condition underlay the seemingly hysterical erythrophobia. The subsequent course of her analysis justified this assumption and made the meaning of the two sentences more understandable.

Between the age of eight and ten she had been a rather delicate child, easily fatigued, and her parents used to insist on her taking a nap after school. She interpreted this regimen as a punishment inflicted upon her by her mother, whom she thought to be hostile towards her. One day when her mother gave her a jumper as a present she concluded that her mother wanted to indicate by means of the gift that she was no longer hostile towards her. But the next day, when her mother still insisted that she should go to bed after school, she was convinced that her mother had given her the present in order to make her feel secure so that by punishing her the patient would feel even more humiliated and crushed than before and the mother could feel she had triumphed over her. These paranoid ideas concerning her mother persisted in all kinds of phantasies. However, she also transferred her suspicious phantasies towards other female persons, and although during her analysis she claimed that she was aware of the unrealistic character of the phantasies, one still had the impression that she was not completely convinced of this statement. When, for instance, during her analysis she was able to change her position back to being a nurse, she very soon developed the idea that the other nurses stared at her in order to make her blush and thus to humiliate her.

The history of her erythrophobia was intimately connected with certain sexual activities of her childhood. From an early age on up to the age of thirteen she and a male cousin of hers used to undress in front of each other in order to look at each other when urinating. At about the age of seventeen, she had a date with a boy who tried to kiss her in his car. By that time the patient had become sexually rather inhibited. The next day when she, the boy, and a brother of the cousin with whom she had shared her childhood sexual games, were together, the boy made some comment about kissing and necking. The patient suddenly had the conviction that the cousin knew that the remark referred to her. She blushed, and from that moment on the symptom of erythrophobia was established. She avoided contact with men, isolated herself, but always was able to use some superficially convincing rationalization. In this way she never became conspicuous. During her analysis she was very reluctant to present material about herself that would show her at a disadvantage. Behind an attitude of seeming modesty one could guess at inflated ideas about herself and at extreme arrogance. It was hard for her to accept any criticism, and she denied responsibility for any actions which were not ego-acceptable, just as she denied responsibility for her dreams. Her attitude toward her dreams suggested that for her they were a repetition of her early exhibitionistic activities as well as a denial of any responsibility for them. The end sentence seemed to express both stubborness and the specific hostility of teasing by exposing herself and withdrawing, thus preventing any further approach.

Again, it is striking that the paranoid part of her personality first became visible in a trivial remark about her dreams. This particular remark is often made by patients, and frequently refers to a normal response to dreams. It was the patient's voice among other signs which gave the impression of a paranoid attitude. Moreover, the reaction of indignation as if someone were out to tease or irritate her appeared significant. In spite of an extensive phase of paranoid ideas during the late latency and early adolescent period, it is noteworthy that the history she gave and her general behavior and reports during the early phases of the treatment did not show any other trace of this hidden ego pathology.

The third patient, a woman in her middle thirties, came to analysis because she suffered from depression and anxiety and was unable to form any lasting relationships. She showed certain compulsive character traits, but did not present the picture of a clearly defined obsessional neurosis. Early in her analysis her attitude towards her dreams gave an indication of the severity of a condition which later showed itself to its full extent, and led to almost unconquerable difficulties in her analysis. Instead of associating to her dreams, she did nothing but repeat the manifest dream content in a stereotyped way without being fully aware of doing so. This repetition, which she would continue endlessly if not stopped, served as negation of the dream altogether, much like a mechanism that one frequently finds in children who repeat a word or a sentence endlessly until it becomes meaningless. Usually a feeling of depersonalization accompanies this procedure. Much later in her analysis this patient remembered an incident of her early schooldays when she was supposed to recite a poem at school assembly. After reciting the first verse, instead of going on to the second, she compulsively repeated the first and suffered great embarrassment. From her associations it could be assumed that this incident was intimately connected with earlier exhibitionistic experiences which she had every reason to negate, because they had been connected with an unbearably humiliating experience at that time. Her attitude towards her dreams was a warning of what was to be expected in the course of her analysis. She actually showed the same mechanism of defence in using repetitiveness in order to deny and negate and depersonalize throughout her analysis. At the same time the constant repetition of the dream had the opposite meaning too, namely the preservation of the object and a defence against mutilation. This was borne out by the memory of early masturbatory phantasies consisting of mutilation of women, children and animals. This impulse to mutilate and to cut into pieces showed up in the mechanism of isolating which she employed freely in phases of resistance. In the course of her analysis, repetition, isolation and depersonalization became so strong that her treatment came to a complete standstill in spite of her continuous talking. Her discourse became empty chatter. It is noteworthy that the patient was informed by her mother that at the age of eleven months she had witnessed her mother's miscarriage. The child was standing in her crib greatly excited and babbling incessantly. This ancient defence mechanism had been overlaid by others, but became clinically visible in her analysis for the first time in her reactions to her dreams.

We believe that in the three instances here briefly described, the patient's attitude during the process of dream analysis revealed an ego level which was effectively hidden in all other life situations. The remarkable feature was that this particular ego structure became in the further course of the treatment a real stumbling-block, and it appeared questionable whether that particular ego deformation could be overcome at all by our ordinary psycho-analytic techniques.

Assuming that our observation was correct, two questions which cannot be answered immediately arise. Firstly, why did this hidden structure come to the fore just in the process of dream analysis? Is this due to personality peculiarities on the part of these patients, or is there perhaps something in the dream which provokes the waking ego when dealing with dreams to regress to an archaic, but still living, mode of dealing with the internal and external world? Secondly, we must ask, what is that new structure which came to the fore in these clinical instances? We believe that we are dealing here with what Freud called the ego-modification, to which, in *Analysis Terminable or Interminable,* he attributed such overwhelming importance. There he stressed that it was not the symptom *per se* that was the decisive factor regarding the prognosis of the psychoanalytic treatment, but its genesis. If the symptom was the result of trauma, the clinical evaluation must be quite different from what it would be if it is the result of a permanent modification which the ego has suffered in the course of its development. From this viewpoint our clinical observation may obtain some general importance. The patient's behaviour during dream analysis may become initially a particular source of information as to the degree of ego modification which might become revealed in the later course of analysis. In view of the decisive bearing the patient's ego modification has on the treatment, behaviour during dream analysis may become a clinically important guide for the analyst as to where to look for the battlefield on which the decisive analytic battle will be fought.

NOTES

1. *Int. J. Psycho-Anal.,* 24, 1943.
2. *Int. J. Psycho-Anal.,* 21, 1940.

14. Depersonalization and the Dream

Harold L. Levitan

Despite our detailed studies of the process active in depersonalization, we do not fully understand how symptoms develop. Our formulations seem inadequate to encompass the complex phenomena of depersonalization. Oberndorf (10) suggested that denial in fantasy of one half of a split self-representation plays a part; but this explanation seems incomplete without a more functional or topographic basis. Recently, however, our understanding has deepened with the recognition that the depersonalized patient is in an altered state of consciousness close to sleep. Blank (1, p. 36) and Lewin (7) have stated that depersonalization is a compromise between dreaming and waking. 'The patient experiences depersonalization in an attempt to maintain control (wakefulness) and simultaneously eliminate the pain (unlust), the latter result being ordinarily attained through the anesthesia of sleep'. Their argument supposes that these states are divisible into several components so that some components of either state may be retained while others are lost. Stamm (13) has also stressed the relationship of depersonalization phenomena to hypnagogic states with the important additional suggestion that regression to these states results in some way from the oral triad and especially the wish to sleep. However the evidence these authors offer from the dreamy condition of their depersonalized patients is often inferred or else is taken from states of wakefulness or partial wakefulness rather than from sleep. For this reason they suppose that their patients are regressing into the depersonalized state.

In this note I will offer some data from the dreams of a young woman with depersonalization. These data supplement those of Stamm by enabling us to observe the contrary process: the patient appears to progress from sleeping and dreaming into depersonalization. This approach has heuristic advantages and it illustrates that sleep and dream play an important part in the compromise-formation. Jacobson (6) offered us another example of this progression from sleep to sleep derivative (though she did not say so) when

Reprinted by permission of the author and *The Psychoanalytic Quarterly*, Vol. 36, 1967.

she noted that the depersonalized political prisoners studied by her would 'wake at night with feelings that their limbs and their face did not belong to them. They would anxiously touch the estranged body parts trying to recover the feeling of intactness of their body self.' As will be shown, however, before progression into depersonalization there is regression into deeper sleep within the dreaming state itself.

My patient, a young married secretary, had a most unusual dream life. Each night over a period of years she experienced traumatic dreams which seemed very real to her but which did not awaken her (in contrast to Jacobson's subjects) and each morning she again became depersonalized. I propose that this patient's full-blown depersonalization was a continuation into the next day of the complex response to the traumas occurring in her dreams.

André Gide writes in his Journal: '. . . I used to have frightful nightmares from which I would awaken bathed in sweat. . . . Suddenly the gland ceased to function. At present I can have horrible dreams, see myself pursued by monsters, knifed, cut into bits . . . but it never becomes a nightmare' (3). This experience is of great interest. It is one of the few reported examples of failure to waken from traumatic dreams because of disappearance of affect in their manifest content. Moreover it is associated with depersonalization from which, as he explains earlier in the same paragraph, Gide suffered rather severely.

My patient's depersonalization became chronic three years before treatment began. It came after the beginning of a secret love affair with her high school teacher whom she later married. Though the affair was secret she knew that her father would 'murder' her if he found out. We can assume that the 'murder' took place, since her father continued to be strongly against their marriage even after it had occurred, and in this fact we see a motive for her depersonalization. Indeed she complained that life was passing her by because she was 'not with it' and was in effect 'dead'. For example, she 'wasn't at her own wedding because she felt so much detached by being 'not with it'.

This detachment resulted from splitting of her ego into an observing or mental half and a participating or bodily half. Her bodily half became so alienated from her mental half that as she stepped off a subway train she imagined her body continuing on the train while she remained on the platform. The sudden change from the constant motion of the train to the solid ground of the platform provoked anew her awareness of the separation of her mind and body. Sometimes too she had vague pains or itches which she could not localize or 'contact', as if she were scratching 'in a void' instead of on a familiar surface of the body. In the same way she did not know when she was hungry or when she was satiated. Suddenly she would get mad or cry without knowing why; she would then ask: "Where did that come from?'. 'Sometimes', she said, 'I have the feeling without the pictures'. This separation of affect and ideation was the reverse of her dreams, in which the picture was often present without the feeling.

She was not only in a dreamlike state described as 'on a cloud', 'floating', or 'insulated', but felt as if she were dominated by the content of the dream of the night before, which appeared to her more real than her daytime life. Since she could not distinguish very well between what had happened at night in her dreams and what was happening during the day, she was often confused and made remarks appropriate to the context of her dreams, regarding which, of course, only she was aware. Also because she was so much in her dreams she could not well distinguish fact from fancy and was very gullible despite her high intelligence. In this as in so many other ways she resembled Stein's patients who suffered from altered states of consciousness (14). My patient could become terrified, for example, as in years gone by, upon hearing the story of The Three Bears and once her husband convinced her there was a whale in their swimming pool. She possessed a large store of early memories in which she could become remarkably absorbed. Many of these memories appeared in her dreams and may in that way have been refreshed.

She complained constantly of a hallucination of semitransparent grey fog before her eyes through which she had to strain to perceive objects. She said too that because of the proximity of the fog she had an annoying awareness of the edges of her own eye sockets and the bridge of her nose. Often even when she could perceive objects through the fog they did not appear as discrete objects but as planes of light and shadow. Her Sunday paintings were, as might be expected, in the cubist style. Both Stewart (16) and Glauber (4) have reported difficulties in perception in their depersonalized patients. Glauber emphasized the interruption of automatic perceptual processes. My patient's difficulties in ordinary perception as well as her artistic vision are excellent examples of this failure.

Innumerable times each day when confronted with rather ordinary as well as remarkable events she would exclaim, 'I can't believe it!'. This denial, which is of course part of her naïveté, may be related to the intense sense of realness of her dreams and their persistence into the next day as though she were saying, 'Only my dreams are real and I know I can't believe them!'. Stein (14) has recently suggested that repetition of traumatic events in dreams is a consequence of the wish to turn real traumas into dreams which can then be denied. Indeed if we include in the manifest dream the 'anesthesia' or blackness afforded by sleep, then the entire portion of the manifest dream retained in waking life as depersonalization may be considered a massive screen memory. The seeming reality of dreams has usually been explained as referring either to the reality of events in the latent content or to the lack of judgment possessed by the sleeping ego. I explain it by the wish to form a screen memory that seems real, more real in fact than the dreamer's actual life. This wish for realness is more easily understood if the content of the dream is obviously pleasant than if it is traumatic. In fact my patient's memory for current events was, as she said, 'choppy'. Thus she often forgot the beginning of a sentence before she got to the end because of the intrusion of dream elements including blankness. The process at work here is close to ordinary repression, the investigation of which in relation to states of consciousness even in waking life has just been begun (Cf. *14*).

The invasion of waking life by manifest dream content suggests the similar process which occurs in mania as described by Lewin (8). In Blank's case study depersonalization seemed to occur when the manic defense had failed (1). My patient too had hypomanic episodes in years gone by though not during the period of my observation of her. They occurred, for example, when she experienced intense excitement and hyperactivity and was at such times capable of performing outstanding gymnastic feats and high dives. Also the grandiose but successful wooing of her teacher had many manic aspects.

Here, to choose among scores of them, is the first dream that alerted me to her remarkable nightly experience.

I am climbing the side of a mountain in the company of my husband and mother [who was actually visiting at her new home that night]. I call out: 'Be careful because the rocks are slippery!'. Then I lose my footing and fall into space. I am horrified and screaming all the way down. I can't believe it is really happening [her usual daytime remark]. I see the bottom and then hit with a thud [but without pain] and my body splatters in several directions. I feel foggy and lightheaded as if walking on air [all concomitants of her daytime state of depersonalization]—but I do not awaken.

Ordinarily, of course, the intense stimulation of falling and crashing would lead to awakening of the body ego and then the body itself. She explains that she did not awaken because in view of the intense reality of the dream 'there was nothing to awaken from'. Under these apparently realistic and traumatic circumstances which proceed so far without awakening, depersonalization is as automatic and appropriate a last-ditch response as it would be during a similar daytime crisis. However, and this is central to my thesis, because of the lability of the mechanism of sleep and the partial depersonalization already prevailing in sleep and dreaming, the process of further depersonalization is considerably facilitated. Here is another traumatic dream experience, this time following intercourse.

I am dancing at a wedding, but it is a peculiar kind of dancing because I am on my husband's back [a game she and her father had played frequently in past years]. While we are twirling very rapidly, I put my hands over his eyes so that we crash into the wall. There is a thud which I hear, but there is no pain and no waking up. People rush over to see if we are hurt, but we get up and continue to dance.

The moment when she was aware of the crash but did not feel it was the prototypical moment of full depersonalization. It is interesting to note that both these dreams contain considerable vestibular stimulation which, as noted by Stein, Schilder, and Stern (14, 12, 15) may be a necessary predecessor, at least in waking states, of a change in level of consciousness.

Depersonalization occurs to various degrees and involves several levels of psychological functions. It may be defined essentially as a condition in which the body ego is maintained mainly as an ideational representation with only limited access to affective sources within the body itself. The alienation from the representations of self and object (derealization) in this condition seem to be secondary to the alienation of the body representation. To put it another way, the bodily reverberations which form the basis of the affectively valid and thus 'real' experience are, in large degree, absent in depersonalization. And perhaps even ordinary denial of waking reality begins with a mechanism like that of depersonalization—at least to the extent that affect must be withdrawn from an idea before the idea can be altered. Because the usual state of dreaming precisely fits this description, there may be some difficulty in conceiving of further changes of this kind within the dreaming state. But in most dreams there is at least minimal sensory participation which, under certain circumstances, can be further diminished. This increasing loss seems to take place through a temporary deepening of sleep within the dreaming state itself. In other words, even REM sleep is not a uniform state but a fluctuating one, which is subject to change under predictable conditions.

Most importantly, in my patient this deepening of sleep always occurred at the moment one would have expected the intense stimulation to have awakened her. For example, several experiences of 'anesthesia' in the manifest content of her dreams occurred in response to intense pain in the dream itself.

Somebody, myself or my grandfather, is on the operating table, having a skull flap sewed on. . . . suddenly it begins to hurt, and because of insufficient anesthesia, he wakes up and grabs the surgeon's knife. . . . there is running. . . .

This example is a good one because the mechanism of anesthesia nearly failed and partial awakening occurred. This type of dream mechanism may also cast some light on the pavor nocturnus of children in which full awakening does not take place. In another instance the anesthesia, through deeper sleep, occurred in the manifest content as an afterthought in a rather *ad hoc* fashion after the onset of the operation in response to pain, rather than at the beginning of the operation as one would have expected.

My teeth are being pulled with a new type of machine. . . . I feel every bit of pain. . . . This new machine also sprays gas and hypnotizes you. The dentist said, 'Now you won't feel anything'. I could feel myself fighting the sleep, while saying at the same time, 'I know this will never work and I'll suffer again'.

Or,

I am having trouble breathing. . . . I am having an operation which has slight chance. . . . They put me to sleep and I died for a few seconds. . . .

Very probably, dying in the manifest content of this last dream meant a sleep so deep that not even ideational representations were present. It is interesting to note with regard to this dream that, in fact, in childhood she did have rather similar dental work done, to her great distress, without anesthesia so the anesthesia in this dream may represent fulfilment of the wish to be rid of the pain at the time of the operation itself.

Indeed many of her dreams originated in just this way—in repetition of painful events from her past before she was subject to depersonalization, but now without the experience of pain. This process illustrates the formation of the screen memory mentioned earlier and may suggest an additional explanation for the phenomenon of repetition in dreams of traumatic daytime events as in traumatic neurosis. Perhaps we have overlooked the anesthesia in this type of dreaming because of the more usual failure of the process which allows intense anxiety to break out, with subsequent awakening. Nonetheless, because her experience of affect in dreams, before the anesthesia sets in, is so much more genuine and full than that in her depersonalized awake state, she tries (and often fails) to re-experience at night events and affects, some of them, perhaps pleasant, that she missed during the day because of her depersonalization. Here is a fragment which revives a true traumatic scene of several years earlier, but in which she fails again to undergo the full experience.

Grandma is very sick and dying. . . . I am crying. . . . Grandma is in pain—but I couldn't make myself feel pain. . . . I wondered how my aunts could stand the sorrow. . . .

We see that the anesthesia works even when there is a contrary wish to experience affect.

Here is another fragment which contained some positive affect for a brief period before it too was extinguished.

I am waiting for Karl, my old boyfriend. . . . I am taking a shower—I have the old, good, excited feeling . . . lovey-dovey . . . the real thing . . . but then the fog comes and I can't feel anything.

Apparently when the depersonalization or anesthesia works, it works completely, without discrimination between negative and positive affect.

Several dreams, examined in combination with data from the daytime depersonalized state, indicate more about the actual mechanism by which sleep is deepened and the sensory pathways abolished. This mechanism seems to be identical to the dream screen and associated oral triad as described by Lewin (8) and discussed by Stamm (13). Indeed, so many of the patient's dreams showed this phenomenon that they offer much data on this apparently rare occurrence. However, I have seen in the literature only one example, reported by Stern (15) and to be quoted directly, in which the dream screen became part of the manifest content in response to obvious trauma, and there has been no mention of the fact that the phenomenon may occur as an alternative to awakening. Stern's patient dreamed,

. . . the car skidded and fell down a precipice, crashing the windshield and obscuring my vision. . . .

This example is very similar to the first one quoted from my patient, except that the screen is deftly woven into the manifest content of the dream as the crushed windshield.

If Lewin is correct, as I believe he is, regarding the significance of the manifest dream screen as representing the wish to sleep, then this wish may, in moments of trauma, overcome the more usual tendency to wake. In these circumstances the wish is not so much to sleep as to gain the benefit of some of the components of sleep which include the abolition of affect. Here is an interesting example of my patient's manifest screen.

President Johnson is giving an angry—and to me unpleasant—speech about patriotism. . . . suddenly, my field of vision is filled by a huge butter cookie [her favorite cookie which she had been consuming by the dozen on the day of the dream] which has moved in from the upper left corner. . . . it just stayed there for several seconds. . . .

Butter cookies, with their raised center and brown edges, resemble the breast very closely. It is significant here that a favorite food was transformed into a type of manifest screen. In other dreams, the screen and its near derivative were much less stable, and did not remain easily in the field of vision.

I am trying to balance a huge glaring white structure on three legs which filled the field of vision. . . . all night I tried to keep it in front of me. . . .
. . . Some huge potato chips [another of her favorite foods] are standing upright. . . . They seem as if they would fall at any minute. . . .

These balancing dreams may reflect her difficulty in maintaining the screen derivative, and therefore in staying asleep.

In the following fragment a vivid hallucination of fog, which was a principal feature of her daytime depersonalized state, appeared in the manifest dream content. (One is reminded of Lewin's case in which a photograph, though apparently innocuous, was also obscured by fog [9].)

I am madly in love with my boss. . . . He calls me while I am in the bathroom to say, 'Mother and I are queer'. . . . Then he is in the bathroom doing something mysterious and horrible . . . eating something, . . . suddenly, fog obscures the picture—and I feel foggy as during the day. . . .

Other examples of dream scenes obscured by fog include a frankly incestuous scene between herself and her brother, as well as the positively toned dream quoted earlier in which she was waiting for her boyfriend.

In both mania and depersonalization, dream content invades waking life and in both conditions there is an important alteration of the affect. In mania, as in the manifest content of many dreams, unpleasant affect is denied by converting it into its opposite to the accompaniment of ideation close in style to that of manifest dream content. In depersonalization the affect is not converted but abolished at its source, as in the second stage of dreaming described. The differences between the two conditions may reflect the differences between the stages of dreaming observed in this patient. Which of the two conditions is present may be determined by which stage or combination of stages of the dreaming state is retained in waking life. We can understand too, if this is correct, how depersonalization may come into operation, after failure of the manic attempt, by a process of further regression. It is possible that the stage of dreaming I have called the stage of anesthesia may be very close to or identical with the blank dream (pure sleep, complete fusion) as described by Lewin (7). In Lewin's case such a dream occurred in isolation, but here it may be seen in relation to the manifest content that precedes it. However in Lewin's reported case of mania the blank dream occurred at night and was followed during the next day by belated manifest content in the form of the manic episode. In my patient the sequence was reversed, in that the manifest content occurred at night and was followed the next day by a continuation of the manifest content along with the belated blank dream in the form of fog. Lewin believed that in his case the manic attack denied the dangerous homosexual wish fulfilled by the blank dream. In my patient we have seen, possibly again in reverse, the blank dream defending against the affect associated with the traumatic manifest dream.

In other dreams, and during incredibly long periods of hypersomnia that lasted around the clock, my patient experienced what seemed to be the tactile equivalent of fog or of the visual dream screen: she felt wrapped in a soft styrofoamlike substance. Sometimes this occurred in combination with a perception of fog. We must suppose that the dream screen appears in the visual field as only one component of a total mental state. If it is maintained as fog into the waking state, then what we call depersonalization may reflect other components of that state, including blocking of the sensory pathways from the interior of the body. Or as mentioned by Isakower (5), absorption in the dream screen phenomenon as in dreams themselves may be so great that it and sensory representation from within the body are mutually exclusive. This concept bears very much on our theories of identification, and at present remains unexplored, especially as regards the mutual relationship between the shifting of identifications and alterations in states of consciousness. For example, it is possible that a change of identification requires an alteration in consciousness in order to occur. Another indication of absorption in the dream phenomena at the expense of the outer world in my patient, as in all depersonalized patients, is the marked effect of a minor change in locale, which may either initiate the episode of depersonalization or deepen it if it is already present. In like manner the effects of drugs such as tranquilizers and alcohol are inordinately great because they facilitate the sleeping half of the compromise formation. This is an important practical point not emphasized in the literature.

However, these protective components of the sleeping and dreaming state are unlikely to be stable, especially in the transition from sleeping to waking. Thus after a 'horrible' dream—without anxiety—my patient often experienced upon awakening in the morning a few extremely anxious seconds, after which the protection of the fog and the full-blown depersonalization supervened. One is reminded here of Oberndorf's thoughts about sequestration of anxiety in depersonalization (11). Perhaps the sleeping state by abolishing the sensory pathways from within can accomplish this feat of sequestration, even when the manifest content would warrant affect. I stress this point regarding manifest content because French's earlier theories of absorption of affect by sleep involved primarily an alteration away from pain and anxiety in latent thoughts, rather than in manifest content (2).

The patient herself described this absorption of affect in her dreams as a blanketing of feeling, through which (as mentioned earlier) she tried to break in order to reach sensory awareness, sometimes going to great lengths as in the following dream.

I am jumping from a high tower into a narrow tub of water. . . . I am terribly frightened while in the air, but as soon as I reach the water, the feeling changes. . . . I do this repeatedly . . . perhaps twenty times. . . .

She referred to the feeling underwater as 'a kind of calm, slow-motion feeling', which she often used to describe her daytime depersonalized state. This was in sharp contrast to the frightened feeling while falling. She recalled actually jumping as a youngster from a high stoop 'to see what it felt like' or more likely to see what it did not feel like. And while at the bottom of the ferris wheel, she always forgot how scary it was split seconds earlier while falling from the top, thus indicating the rapidity with which anxiety could disappear. One is reminded again of Stein's patients in whom such remarkable and sudden transformations occurred. Often she felt as if her dream, or herself in her depersonalized state, was enclosed in a cellophane bag, which I suppose to be a screen derivative, much like the Wolf-man's caul. Significantly one of the dreams reported to Stamm by a patient with depersonalization contained a cellophane bag in its manifest content (13). In the attempt to break out of the cellophane bag, many of my patient's dreams seemed to her repetitious throughout the night, even when there was frequent change of scene in the manifest content. It seemed, in short, as though she were trying and failing to experience particular feelings.

This process recurred each night, and lasted into the next day. May not this defensive process which uses varying depths of consciousness within stage one of consciousness involve regression in a historical sense as well? Acute traumas which occur in the crucial stages when a very young child is beginning to emerge into consciousness may cause him to lapse back into the deeper sleep of the first days after birth. This patient's early and late childhood was punctuated by a series of astounding traumas inflicted by a father who apparently had no appreciation of the child's sensibilities. His manner was suddenly to shock her into a state of terror and, as noted earlier, her dreams were taken up with these situations and their consequences. To cite one of many examples, he would begin by speaking softly and then break out into a loud attack on her. Or in teaching her how to swim, he would suddenly throw her into the water without warning. It was well known in the family that in the first weeks after her birth, he would throw her in the air as high as possible, catching her only at the last moment. Stimulation of this type and degree, including vestibular activation occurring at a time when regression was the sole defense available, may have set a pattern for dealing with later traumas as well.

SUMMARY

The traumatic dreams of a patient suffering from periods of depersonalization, peculiar in that they did not progress to intense affect and awakening, are presented in support of the hypothesis that depersonalization is a compromise state between dreaming and waking. Some theories about varying levels of sleep within the process of dreaming are suggested to explain this abrogation of affect. The depersonalization itself seemed to be a night residue of this dream mechanism which persisted into the next day as a type of screen memory. The 'dream screen' seemed to play an important part in this mechanism. A tentative hypothesis relates mania and depersonalization to the successive stages within the process of dreaming.

REFERENCES

1. Blank, H. Robert: *Depression, Hypomania, and Depersonalization.* Psychoanalytic Quarterly, XXIII, 1954, pp. 20–37.
2. French, Thomas M.: *Reality Testing in Dreams.* Psychoanalytic Quarterly, VI, 1937, pp. 62–77.
3. Gide, André: *Journal, 20 December, 1924.* New York: Vintage Books, Inc., 1956.
4. Glauber, I. Peter: Scientific Proceedings. Panel Report. *Depersonalization.* Reported by Walter A. Stewart. J. Amer. Psa. Assn., XII, 1964, pp. 182–183.
5. Isakower, Otto: *A Contribution to the Pathopsychology of Phenomena Associated with Falling Asleep.* Int. J. Psa., XIX, 1938, pp. 331–345.
6. Jacobson, Edith: *Depersonalization.* J. Amer. Psa. Assn., VII, 1959, pp. 581–610.
7. Lewin, Bertram D.: *The Psychoanalysis of Elation.* New York: W. W. Norton & Co., Inc., 1950. Reprinted by The Psychoanalytic Quarterly, Inc., 1961.
8. ———: *Reconsideration of the Dream Screen.* Psychoanalytic Quarterly, XXII, 1953, pp. 174–197.
9. ———: The Forgetting of Dreams. In: *Drives, Affects, and Behavior, Vol. I.* Edited by Rudolph M. Loewenstein. New York: International Universities Press, Inc., 1953.
10. Oberndorf, C. P.: *Depersonalization in Relation to Erotization of Thought.* Int. J. Psa., XV, 1934, pp. 271–295.
11. ———: *Role of Anxiety in Depersonalization. Op. cit.,* XXXI, 1950, pp. 1–5.
12. Schilder, Paul: *Mind: Perception and Thought in Their Constructive Aspects.* New York: Columbia University Press, 1942.
13. Stamm, Julian: *Altered Ego States Allied to Depersonalization.* J. Amer. Psa. Assn., X, 1962, pp. 762–783.
14. Stein, Martin: States of Consciousness. In: *Drives, Affects, and Behavior, Vol. 2. Essays in Memory of Marie Bonaparte.* Edited by Max Schur. New York: International Universities Press, Inc., 1965.
15. Stern, Max M.: *Blank Hallucinations: Remarks about Trauma and Perceptual Disturbances.* Int. J. Psa., XLII, 1961, pp. 205–215.
16. Stewart, Walter A., Reporter: Scientific Proceedings. Panel Report. *Depersonalization.* J. Amer. Psa. Assn. XII, 1964, pp. 171–186.

B. Nightmares

15. Nightmares and the Combat Neuroses

Theodore Lidz

A study of the ætiology and significance of repetitive nightmares of combat was undertaken because the symptom was a major complication to the treatment of the war neuroses in the South Pacific. The search after the meaning of the nightmares led to a clearer understanding of the combat neuroses of which they were a symptom. Eventually the nightmares became a guide rather than a hindrance to therapy. This paper summarizes the views gained from the observation and treatment of a few hundred patients who suffered from recurrent nightmares, and particularly from an analysis of 25 case histories in which nightmares were particularly striking.

Mass startle reactions to sudden stimuli and repetitive nightmares are two of the outstanding features which distinguish the behavior of patients who have suffered panic or severe anxiety in battle from the general run of civilian neuroses. Both symptoms appear to be exaggerated defensive patterns acquired when the soldier had become attuned to constant alertness while helpless to combat the danger actively. The reactions appear comprehensible and there is a tendency to believe that recent stresses, capped by an unusually traumatic experience, explain the abnormal behavior pattern.

It may well be true that every soldier has his breaking point. Experience with casualties from the first months of the Guadalcanal campaign indicated that relatively few men emerged from the months of ordeal without some evidences of emotional instability. However, there is a wide variation among men in the severity of the conditions necessary to provoke neurotic behavior, in the extent of the incapacitation, and in the rapidity and degree of recovery. Without an understanding of what the experiences mean to the patient and to the continuity of his life, the combat traumata are an insufficient explanation. The study of recurrent nightmares, by clarifying the dynamics of a group of

Reprinted by permission of the author and *Psychiatry*, Vol. 19, 1946.

the war neuroses, has afforded a focal point for the study of the problem of why certain personalities are more susceptible than others to the trials of war.

The nightmares allow a fairly typical pattern. The soldier is helpless in the face of an attack. He is caught without shelter when planes strafe, as mortar fire draws closer and closer, as a wave of Japs comes over a ridge. Warships shell the coast. He is pursued by a Jap with a bayonet. He may feel rooted to the spot, unable to flee. If he attempts to defend himself, he is impotent for the bullets drop to the ground or the knife slips from his hand. He awakens with a terrified scream in an attempt at flight. The dreams carry a reflection of jungle warfare in which the soldier is forced to remain inactive in a foxhole throughout the night, ever alert for the infiltrating Jap but forbidden to shoot lest he disclose the position. The dream is sometimes the repetition of an actual experience, but a number of patients were certain that the episode had never occurred in reality. Indeed, similar nightmares were suffered by soldiers who had never experienced combat. In many patients the same dream was repeated nightly, but others varied the setting of the theme of helplessness.

The nightly recurrence of terrifying dreams binds the patient to the trauma of battle. The symptom becomes a complication. The soldier fears sleep, fights it, and when he finally succumbs soon awakens in a state of terror. Sedation often increases the torment by making the awakening difficult. The emotional pattern established in combat is reinforced nightly. The treatment of others is disturbed. A ward filled with psychiatric casualties from a severe campaign contains men who wreck the sleep of all by sudden screams and frantic lunges through the mosquito bars. The presence of a soldier with recurrent nightmares is even untenable in the camps of troops resting from combat and leads to the admission of patients with the primary complaint of nightmares. While the nightmares persist the soldier is incapacitated for jungle warfare as he is a menace to the general safety. Moreover, it has become clear that a soldier who suffers from repetitive nightmares is emotionally unsuited for further combat even though occasionally he may seem calm and sound by day.

In the majority of the psychiatric casualties the nightmares subsided as security was regained, but in some patients they continued with undiminished intensity. Other patients who had shown no overt instability in combat first suffered from nightmares in the rest area; and even after they had been removed from combat units because of physical disabilities. The subjects of this study were mainly chosen from among those patients in whom the intensity of nightmares was disproportionate to the remainder of the symptoms, or whose nightmares failed to subside, or in whom they first appeared long after combat.

A variety of therapeutic approaches based on several theoretical considerations were attempted before a satisfactory solution was reached. Efforts were made to uncover a traumatic episode which had been repressed. Detailed reminiscence and emotional abreaction were aided by barbiturates or hypnosis. The results were disappointing. Even when an actual episode provided the source of the dream it was found that the event had rarely been forgotten. Periods of amnesia were usually for happenings subsequent to the panic. Patients were encouraged to cease pushing the memories and fears of combat from consciousness during the daytime. They were helped to accept the experiences and emotional reactions by informal group discussions. Efforts were made to eradicate any need they might have to relive the terror nightly to justify the neurotic flight. Patients were assured of the security of noncombat duty, and when necessary, of return to the United States. These and other measures were beneficial but far from successful, and it was believed that the core of the problem had not been reached.

Eventually a general pattern was found to recur which had been masked by the plethora of traumatic occurrences. The understanding of the dynamics of the nightmares led to an appreciable improvement in therapy. The gist of the conclusions will be presented before the case material upon which they are based. The simple theme may be perceived more readily after it has been isolated from its numerous and complex variations.

The significance of the nightmares became apparent when it was understood that the dream expressed a type of wish fulfillment despite the terrifying content. Kardiner[1] has stated that the catastrophic dream contradicts the formula that dreams represent wish-fulfillment. Ernest Jones[2] regards the classical nightmare as an expression of a wish,—of an incestuous wish which must be disguised into horrifying forms to overcome the repression and to conceal the wishful nature of the dream. The dim awareness that the desire may overpower the will creates the panic-stricken terror. The combat nightmares are also concerned with a terrifying desire. They express the wish for death and the wish to escape death. They reflect the ambivalent state of the dreamer who has reason both to desire death and to be terrified by the desire. The psychiatrist who has treated casualties from unusually intense and disheartening campaigns learns that death is not undesirable to many patients. Suicidal thoughts are not uncommon. Soldiers have seen friends kill themselves or attempt a last heroic deed to end the intolerable suspense. Suicide rather than capture and torture is an accepted policy, and buddies make pacts not to let the other fall into Jap hands if wounded and helpless. Some fear permanent insanity and have considered death to be preferable. Some have reason to fear the results of uncontrollable hostility towards their own officers. Combat is a life situation in which life may readily come to seem scarcely worth the ordeal. Still, death may be more frightening, particularly to the immature and insecure personality. The thoughts are strange and frightening. They are repressed only to reappear in projected form during sleep. The danger from within the individual, from which he does not know how to defend himself, is turned into fear of the danger of the enemy, which is more obvious. In turn, the fear of the enemy is heightened.

It may be well to note that a similar situation existed in the only case of night terrors cited by Freud in his *Interpretation of Dreams*.[3] Freud emphasized the youth's struggle with masturbatory concerns, the threats of punishment, and the transformation of the suppressed libido into anxiety. However, it is to be remarked in the case history, which he has cited from Debacker, that the patient stated that he was so upset by his concerns that he had often thought of jumping from his bedroom window.

When the patient regains his equilibrium with security, the ambivalent attitude towards life and death vanishes and the nightmares cease. When nightmares persist the problem focuses on why the negative orientation towards living continues after physical safety has been assured. It will be seen that the profound hopelessness is generally concerned with problems which are relatively extraneous to the fighting. The emotional reactions surrounding combat have simply brought them to the fore. The combat situation alone does not usually provoke consideration of death as a solution.

With surprising frequency these patients had suffered a severe blow at the time of the onset of the neuroses by the disruption of the single important interpersonal relationship in their lives. The loss of a buddy, fiancée, or mother had left them feeling deserted and helpless, bereft of impetus towards survival, and with animosities which they could not handle. Their orientation towards the future had been disrupted beyond being reparable by the assurance of physical safety. Their security had rested upon a single relationship. They had lived in a symbiotic relationship with the buddy who had been killed; or he had been a guide and model. The fiancée's infidelity had shattered the plans which had been carrying the soldier through the months of lonely and terrifying existence. The mother had been the sole person who had given meaning to life. The insecurity provoked rage and despair for these were not any random soldiers who had been unfortunate, but a special type of person who had been sensitized throughout life.

The patients who had suffered from persistent nightmares had emerged from homes in which the family life had been distorted to an unusual degree. Experience with the war neuroses has led to the unequivocal affirmation of the statement of Henderson and Moore,[4] ''—mention has been made of the frequency with which these patients came from broken or distorted homes, and we reemphasize the opinion that this is the most important of all the predisposing factors that have been analyzed.'' The instability of the home was particularly severe among the sufferers from nightmares. Absence of affection, or insecurity of affection, had left a lasting scar. Hostility towards a parent had been a source of considerable guilt. The resultant of the unfortunate childhood was a youth or adult who still strived after an immature affectional relationship in which he was dependent upon another for support, and who reacted to deprivation of the relationship by regressing to a state of profound insecurity, hostility, and guilt. The adaptability of the soldier who had been prepared so poorly for living was almost certain to be inadequate for combat and prolonged separation from normal social existence.

The pattern of the dynamics which leads to recurrent nightmares of combat has been presented in outline. The soldier's development in an unstable family environment leaves him insecure in his interpersonal relationships and hostile when deprived of affection. He finally achieves a dependent relationship with a single person. When deprived of this bulwark of security when alone in a terrifying setting, he loses his desire to live. The suicidal thoughts are repressed and the danger from within the self is projected in the nightmares as an external threat. The variety and complexity of the pattern will become apparent from the clinical material. All of the factors are not to be found in every case. It is a matter of balance. For example, the entire past life of some men had been so unsatisfactory that they had often questioned the value of living; it required little more than the tribulations of combat to reawaken suicidal thoughts. In contrast, soldiers with relatively stable backgrounds might be so overwhelmed by the unexpected infidelity of a loved one at a time when the environment provided no compensations that life lost all value. However, all factors were usually present in the severe cases which form the topic of this study.

The importance of hostilities which provoked profound guilt feelings, and, perhaps, the need to sacrifice one's life in atonement will be discussed later when alternative formulations of the dynamics are offered. To avoid misunderstandings while the case material is being read, it is stated that it does not seem proper to seek causal connections between the hopelessness, insecurity, hostility, and guilt provoked by the circumstances. The connection between these emotions was formed in early childhood. The patient displays a personality configuration in which these emotional responses are interrelated. All are apt to appear simultaneously for the soldier is meeting the situation by regressing to an old emotional pattern.

CLINICAL MATERIAL

The general theory concerning the ætiology and significance of repetitive nightmares which has been presented in broad outlines will be given more concrete form by the presentation of abstracts of case histories. The first illustrations will show how it was possible, in occasional cases, to separate from the general mass of combat experiences to which the patients had been exposed the features which had particular pertinence to the nightmares. It was found that the dynamics thus isolated recurred in case after case. Twenty-five histories were then selected at random from among the records of patients in whom nightmares were a prominent symptom and reviewed carefully. The analysis of these histories broadened the understanding of the ætiology and provided statistical data concerning the frequency of the occurrence of the severe principal factors involved. Illustrative records will be offered in sufficient abundance to show how the same theme recurs with variations from case to case. All will be drawn from the 25 histories which were reviewed to avoid utilization of exceptional cases selected to demonstrate a theory.

The relationship between nightmares of combat and traumata which was unrelated to combat but produced suicidal ideas was suggested by a patient who first suffered from nightmares several months after removal from combat.

Case A: A 22 year old infantry man was admitted to a general hospital because of severe nightmares and stammering. He was suffering from anxiety attacks and was moderately depressed. Every night he had terrifying dreams of being caught on an open beach during a strafing attack. It was like reliving an actual episode he had experienced in combat. Anamnesis failed to relieve the nightmares, but the stammering was modified by suggestion.

The soldier had been moderately upset on several occasions during the fighting on Guadalcanal but had never lost control of himself. He had been considered to be as steady as most of the men in his company. Evacuated to a quiet island because of amoebic dysentery, he had not suffered from nightmares during the two months in the hospital. He left the hospital to rejoin his unit on Guadalcanal only to reach his regiment on the day it was being withdrawn to rest on another island. He was upset to learn that several good friends had been killed, but even more by the absence of mail from his fiancée. A close friend reluctantly informed him of news that the girl had become engaged to another man. The patient suffered from his first nightmare that night, almost falling overboard in his panic. The nightmare recurred several times a week until he learned that the girl had married. Thereafter, the patient became despondent and the nightmares occurred nightly. Several nights prior to his admission to the hospital, the soldier suffered a somnambulistic episode in which he carried on an imaginary telephone conversation with the girl. The stammering started on the following day.

In the hospital the patient told that his life had been shattered by the news of his girl's marriage. He had been buoyed by the thoughts of his future marriage during combat. There had been no other attachments. He had contemplated suicide on the day when his friend had informed him of her infidelity. The preoccupations had grown more intense after the news had been confirmed. Little is known about his early years. He had many siblings and had received little attention from his parents. There had been occasional episodes of somnambulism and nocturnal enuresis in early childhood.

The story of an onset of nightmares long after removal from combat was obtained from other patients. The precipitating factor was amatory disillusionment which overthrew their security, produced marked resentment towards the person they had loved, and made them feel that life wasn't worth living. Usually, hysterical stigmata were not present.

Case B: A medical corpsman who had been considered extremely stable and efficient during several months of active combat on Guadalcanal, had been resting from combat for several months when admitted to the hospital with a recurrence of tertian malaria. A psychiatric consultation was requested because his recurrent nightmares of combat upset the ward as well as the patient. The soldier told that he had been feeling very well until a medical officer to whom he had been very much attached had been returned to the United States because of emotional instability. Soon thereafter he had received news that his fiancée had married. He had been sending her money regularly to furnish the home they had planned, and he had bolstered himself during combat with daydreams of their future. He felt very bitter towards her, and became moderately despondent with thoughts that he might as well return to combat and get himself killed. The nightmares ceased soon after the situation was discussed and he managed to alter his attitude. Only one nightmare occurred in the ensuing weeks; after he had heard the song, *Somebody Stole My Gal*, shortly before going to sleep.

In contrast, a patient stated that the period during combat when he had suffered from nightmares had been when he had felt embittered and suicidal.

Case C: This patient was seen in psychiatric consultation long after combat because of a relatively minor psychosomatic complaint. During the interview he told that he had suffered from severe nightmares during a period of two weeks while fighting on Guadalcanal. The soldier had been very steady until he had received news that his fiancée had married. He then ceased to care whether he lived or not and performed a series of brave but foolhardy acts in the hope that he would be killed. His friends recognized his intent; they persuaded him to adopt a more charitable attitude towards the girl, and to take the blow less seriously. He again became reasonably cautious and the nightmares ceased.

Occasionally patients were seen who had never felt that life was worth the struggle and had suffered from nightmares during earlier periods of suicidal rumination when they had felt extremely hostile towards a parent.

Case D: This soldier was admitted to the hospital while resting from combat on a quiet island because of persistent nightmares of being caught by Japs. He had suffered an episode of acute panic while in combat but had managed to return to duty after a brief rest. He regarded the experiences of battle as little more than one of many disheartening influences in his life. His home life had been extremely disrupted and he had felt thoroughly neglected. He told that he had suffered from nightmares during discrete periods earlier in life. These always came when he felt antagonistic towards his brutal alcoholic father and when he had actively contemplated suicide. During combat he had spoken to his buddy of his desire to commit suicide rather than endure further suspense. When the buddy, upon whom the patient had been very dependent, was killed, the patient had gone to pieces.

In patients who had never been in combat, it was obvious that the nightmares were not residua of actual experience. The type of dream was identical to those of soldiers who had been actively engaged in battle. An extremely complicated record is presented briefly.

Case E: An infantry lieutenant was admitted to the hospital because of repeated nightmares of being pursued by Japs and being unable to defend himself or escape. He had joined his unit as a replacement after fighting had ceased on Guadalcanal. He was a well known athlete who was thought to be very stable by his fellow officers. However, there was a history of lifelong instability, including a phobia of being alone in the dark and a pathological fear of knives. While attending college he had contemplated suicide following an accident, supposedly because he felt himself a burden to his friends and family. Two minor fugues experienced during this time had been hidden because of his national reputation as an athlete. He had volunteered for overseas duty because of guilt feelings when a younger brother went into combat in North Africa. When he reached Guadalcanal he knew that it would be impossible for him to remain in the jungle at night. Certain that he would disgrace himself, he immediately made plans to die a heroic death as soon as possible, or to kill himself in a manner that would make it seem that he had been killed by the enemy. A reprieve was granted when his unit was withdrawn from the island without leaving the beach. When it became certain that the regiment would return to combat, the preoccupations with his plans for suicide recurred and the nightmares started. The patient had been raised in a home filled with strife between his parents and between the children and the father. His animosities towards his father were quite conscious.

The temporal relationship between suicidal urges, nightmares, and panic reactions stood out in bold relief in a patient who became a psychotic.

Case F: A regular army sergeant was admitted to the hospital from combat because of recurrent malaria and chronic gonorrhea. He had been in the hospital for several months without displaying emotional difficulties before he was seen by the psychiatrist under dramatic circumstances. He was lying in the mud in a tropical rainstorm, at night, acting as if in combat. He spoke disconnectedly of Japs, mortar fire, gas. He was fearful of the ward man who was trying to keep him from running away. He was quieted by suggestion but remained completely disoriented until given heavy sedation orally. Then, with considerable emotional stress, he told of an episode of panic during combat when he had fired at his own men and had been held in his foxhole for several hours by a friend. The episode had never been forgotten. He had feared to tell of it lest his officers remove him from his platoon. The panic had confirmed an old belief that he would become insane sooner or later. On the day following the acute episode in the hospital, the patient told that he had been considering suicide for his life was a hopeless muddle, and because death was preferable to insanity. The decision had finally been reached on the preceding night and he had left his bed to seek some poison when there was a peal of thunder. The subsequent events of the evening could not be recalled. Nightmares had started several nights before when contemplation of suicide had become marked. They continued for several days until he told that suicide was still a frequent preoccupation and explained the reasons.

His father and an older brother had been men of violent tempers who had died in insane asylums. The patient had feared the same fate. The father had been a cruel man who had mistreated the mother and children, and the patient had hated him. The patient had supported his mother but had resented the restriction. He married impulsively and immediately felt very guilty for having deserted his mother. Vague feelings that his family had turned against him, and that the townspeople thought ill of him, became so intense that he deserted his wife and fradulently enlisted for Hawaiian service. In Hawaii he felt guilty for deserting his wife. He contemplated suicide at times and suffered from sporadic nightmares. After reaching Guadalcanal where he felt that it would be years until the harm he had done could be repaired, he felt more worthless and hopeless.

It was possible to inject some hope into the situation by promising rapid return to the United States, where, judging from his mail, circumstances were not beyond repair. The depression subsided and nightmares ceased. When a ship finally arrived after a prolonged wait it was not possible to transport the patient, who was considered to be a suicidal risk. Despite careful explanations the patient lost faith in the hospital, insisted that he couldn't wait longer, and made an impulsive suicidal attempt. Nightmares recurred. His condition became markedly aggravated and he was actively delusional for a brief period. He remained depressed and actively suicidal during the ensuing months.

The illustrations given thus far show that the recurrent nightmares do not bear a simple relationship to combat experiences. They may not start until after other profound discouragements have intervened, and may appear in soldiers who have never been in combat. The common denominator appears to be the hopeless attitude towards the future which has stirred up considerations of suicide, perhaps aided by the hostile thoughts which have come to the fore. The presence of this danger from the self will also be apparent in the cases which will be cited for other purposes.

An understanding of the origin and persistence of nightmares is not reached by relating them to the desire for, and the fear of, suicide. The dangers and terrors of combat provoke a preference for death only under the most extreme conditions unless other factors have contributed to the negative orientation towards living. In most of the cases reviewed it was found that the patient found difficulty in facing the future because of a sudden withdrawal of a source of protection or affection. This has been illustrated by the histories of patients in whom nightmares appeared immediately after the loss of a fiancée or buddy. The despair engendered by such disappointments is greater than at home. The soldier, living in the jungle and anticipating years of further lonely existence, is bereft of opportunities for compensation. Social life exists only in fantasy of the past and of a future based on that past. The frustration and bitterness of the soldier can be intense even when the letter he receives is not worded as bluntly as the one which read, "I have just heard that you are on Guadalcanal and have little chance of coming home alive. I cannot take the chance and so am marrying—." It seems understandable that the loss of a buddy, the only person to whom the patient seemed to mean anything, can arouse hostility that requires a scapegoat among the command, or can provoke feelings of guilt because the worthy friend rather than the worthless self was killed. However, such experiences come to many, and in relatively few lead to feelings of complete futility.

The reason the loss of the only significant interpersonal relationship leads to the loss of hope for the future may be understood when it is learned why the relationship was so important to the patient. The patient had been sensitized early in life. The meaning of these blows to the soldier's stability will be shown by presenting them against the background provided by the family life. The lost relationship had finally provided these men with the needed affection they had been seeking since childhood. The loss of it renewed a pattern of insecurity, resentment, and guilt that had been established by the inconstancy or absence of parental affections.

An involved picture of a confused emotional life is presented in outline to show how the loss of a buddy had catastrophic results because of the frustration and hostility in the home.

Case G: A 20 year old infantryman was evacuated from combat following several episodes of panic accompanied by seizures. In the hospital it became apparent that he suffered from hyperventilation tetany during attacks of acute anxiety. Severe nightmares terrified him every night and made him try to avoid sleep. He was extremely bitter, quick-tempered, and easily discouraged. There were repeated threats of suicide as the only escape from a hapless life. He believed that he would never recover and did not wish to live as a shellshocked veteran. His sole desire was to return to combat and sacrifice his life while killing Japs. He rapidly formed an attachment to a ward man and became dependent upon him for daily guidance. When a nurse was forced to reprimand the ward man, the patient became sullen, anxious, and actively suicidal.

The patient's father had been "shellshocked" in the last war. He had returned a useless and cruel man who had kept the home in a turmoil, and, at times was "out of his mind." He had disappeared when the patient was eleven years old, but the hatred engendered had not diminished with time. The soldier also deeply resented his mother whom he felt had neglected him. He had left home after finishing high school following a fight with his mother. He had felt hurt that she had not tried to persuade him to return home. They had become reconciled after his induction but the soldier believed that she was interested in the allotment rather than in him.

The soldier's accounts of his combat experiences were muddled at first because of his failure to mention his "buddy." Far from forgotten, the topic was too painful to discuss. The attempt at repression had obliterated or obfuscated the memory of several days of fighting. Under heavy oral sedation the continuity of events was recovered. The soldier had formed a very close friendship with a corporal whom he had regarded as a model of perfection. he had listened to his advice and started to remodel his disposition and life after the friend's pattern. The friend had assumed a parental attitude. Although the patient had been shaken during the first days of combat, he had remained calm in his friend's company. Then, in a harrowing engagement in which the platoon was isolated for a few days, the friend was killed. The soldier continued to fight in desperate fashion, seeking to avenge his friend, but he was dazed and scarcely knew what was happening. He felt that all of the Japs on the island could not pay for his friend's life. His hostility was also directed against his own officers who had ordered the platoon into the exposed position. The desire to sacrifice his own life to gain vengeance on the Japs and his marked insecurity conflicted. He became agitated, developed seizures, and had to be evacuated.

The treatment involved having the soldier relinquish his plans for revenge and constructing hope that a decent civilian life would be possible despite the handicaps of his family background.

The story recurs with countless variations. A few will be given very briefly. The patients were often aware of the importance of the family background as a source of their instability.

Case H: An 18 year old Marine was evacuated from Guadalcanal because of repeated episodes of panic. Panic occurred for the first time shortly after bayoneting a Jap. He had managed moderately well for about two months of fighting until long awaited mail from home arrived. It told that he had impregnated a girl shortly before embarkation. The girl was almost a stranger, but his mother had taken her into the home and had told everyone that they had been married. He felt trapped. There was as little desire to return home as to remain in combat. He might as well get killed as face the responsibility. He couldn't conceive of himself as a married man and a father. He had never been able to care for himself, and joined the Marines to escape the family who hounded him to support himself. The parents had been grossly incompatible. The mother was a highly emotional woman and the alcoholic father was unable to support the family, which lived on relief. The patient had felt unwanted about the home. He had been sent to live with a relative where he was supposed to support himself. His severe temper had led to predictions of an eventual end in an institution. In the hospital the soldier made frequent threats of suicide in rather childish fashion. The nightmares continued long after he was assured that he would not be returned to combat. They began to subside only after he faced his problem and began to understand that it might be possible to accept the responsibility of a family.

A more mature soldier became extremely insecure when he began to doubt the fundamentals of his orientation in life. He had been conscious of extreme hostility towards his father, and in combat identified himself with his father.

Case I: this soldier was admitted to the hospital from a rest area because of anxiety attacks and recurrent nightmares. He was depressed and extremely tense. It had been necessary to remove him as operations sergeant during combat because of his indecisiveness, and he felt disgraced. The first upset came after he had sent out two patrols in which good friends were killed. Having altered the route of one patrol on his own initiative to lessen the danger, there was reason to feel guilty. He felt that a person of superior education should be above emotional upsets and that his entire education, which had been gained despite great difficulty, was valueless.

The father had marred the home by his violent temper. The soldier had considered him to be an ignorant immigrant. He had determinedly obtained a college education despite his father's opposition. A leading motive in his life had been the effort to differentiate himself from the despised father. The belief had been constructed that through education he had conquered everything he disliked in his father. They had not spoken to one another in five years. In the hospital the patient constantly expressed his feelings of worthlessness and intimated that he did not care to continue living for his education had failed him. Fortunately, the patient was happily married, but he had to rid himself of resentment towards his wife who had concealed the fact that she was epileptic until after the marriage.

In one patient, the content of the nightmares showed the relationship between the experiences of combat and the hostility towards a parent.

Case J: A 22 year old infantryman first began to suffer from nightmares several months after leaving combat, but immediately after the suicide of a friend had reawakened his own suicidal preoccupations. His dreams were of particular interest. At times, the dream of being chased by a Jap would change into a dream in which he chased his mother to kill her; or the threatening Jap might turn into a threatening and hostile mother.

He had been badly frightened during combat but had only become overtly upset after receiving a letter from his father stating that his mother had once again run off with another man. He then felt life to be so futile that only his strict religious beliefs restrained him from committing suicide. His great desire in life had been to establish a decent home. He had been hoping that the reconciliation between his parents, arranged after his induction, would be lasting. The family had spent a homeless existence as carnival and circus followers. His father was an inadequate person who peddled trinkets. The mother had run off with other men on several occasions. She had attempted to place the patient in an institution for the feeble-minded to be rid of him several times. Actually the soldier was quite intelligent though virtually illiterate. His fantasies had always centered on having a happy home, and he had sought constantly to keep his parents together despite his antipathy for his mother. After his friend killed himself he became preoccupied with the notion that suicide was the proper solution as life held nothing for unfortunates such as he.

Although the involved histories have been presented in meager outlines, the sketches seem sufficient to indicate why the deprivation of affectional ties was catastrophic to patients who suffered from nightmares. Insecurity, hostility, and guilt reactions had been an integral part of the relationship with the parents. The pattern of emotional response to the withdrawal of affection resulted in feelings of profound futility and worthlessness. During combat these persons needed the assurance of affection more than ever, and it was precisely at this critical time that they were deprived of it.

In the review of the 25 cases the relationship between the home background and the recent experiences could not always be traced. Most of the cases had been seen before the various factors outlined in the paper were sought after specifically; and due to the press of work, histories were sometimes fragmentary. However, the story of insecurity in the home and hostility towards parents is noted in almost all of the records. A few examples of variants will be given briefly.

Case K: This patient spontaneously submitted a written account of his family life on the day following admission. He believed it essential to the understanding of why he had broken in combat. His father had been a brutal alcoholic who had kept the home in a turmoil until he died when the patient was still young. His mother had been adjudged incapable of raising the patient when she had an illegitimate child. An older sister who was charged with his care was disinterested and her gross negligence had fostered hatred for her. Social agencies had kept shifting the patient between orphanages and the homes of relatives.

Case L: A soldier told reluctantly of his animosity towards his alcoholic father who had disgraced the family by being sent to jail for rape. The patient had become socially seclusive because of the shame.

Case M: This man entered battle harassed by his father's prediction that everyone involved in the war would be killed. The father had been a religious fanatic since the last war. The soldier had left home because his father had thwarted his ambitions for an education, and he blamed his inability to gain a commission on his father.

Case N: A 22 year old soldier had married for the third time while stationed in Hawaii. His first two marriages had been to women who were many years his senior. He believed that his life was disorganized beyond repair and that his third wife would be happier without him. His mother had deserted him when he was an infant. His father had been a worthless alcoholic, and his step-mother had driven him from the home by her harshness and her favoritism for her own children.

A sufficient number of examples from the 25 cases surveyed have been given to illustrate the nature of the parental influences. The illustrations do not deal with traumatic experiences of childhood but with symbols of the constant emotional environment in which the patients had been raised. It is believed that they are adequate to lead the reader to an expectation of the formation of personalities which might well be extremely insecure in interpersonal relationships, subject to the arousal of resentment by the withdrawal of security, and to the display of hostility towards parental substitutes.

STATISTICAL SURVEY

The case histories lend meaning to the statistical data collected from the 25 histories which were analyzed. They show that minor matters have not been made a focus of attention. The figures which will be given represent the minimal occurrence of the factors analyzed for doubtful material will not be included. They indicate that the case histories are not exceptions, extracted to provide striking illustrations, but are typical of the group.

Suicidal Ideas: Nineteen of the 25 patients discussed the contemplation or the fear of suicide. Several others may well have had similar concerns. The remaining six patients had the feeling, at least, that return to combat was impossible for them and would lead to insanity, courtmartial, or irrevocable disgrace.

Family Background: The parents of 13 of the 25 patients had been divorced or permanently separated. Another four had been brought up by parents who were so markedly incompatible that there was little semblance of home life. Thus, 17 of 25, or 68%, had parents who had been grossly incompatible.

Five patients had lost parents in early childhood through death, and of these two had been divorced. Thus, in 20 of the 25 cases there had been a disruption of the usual pattern of parental guidance. Serious sibling rivalry is known to have existed in two of the other five cases.

It is difficult to obtain data for comparison. Similar information was sought by the writer in a survey of 50 soldiers who suffered from chronically recurring malaria;[5] a group which was not considered superior to the average in emotional stability. Of the malaria group but 12% came from homes in which parents were grossly incompatible as contrasted to 68% of the nightmare group. Only 8% of the malaria group came from homes broken by separation, as contrasted to 52% of the subjects of this study. Whereas 28% of the malaria group had a parent who might be termed unstable, 56% of the nightmare series had a parent who was obviously unstable.

Hostility Towards a Parent: The hostility towards a parent which seemed prominent in the case histories was recognized by 11 or 12 of the 25 patients. The proportion seems to be very high as such antagonisms are not apt to be recognized, and if recognized are not likely to be admitted readily. The home situations had been so unsatisfactory that these soldiers felt little loyalty towards the parent. In all but three or four instances, the hostility was focused predominantly on the father.

Extraneous Traumata: Sources of insecurity and hostility which were relatively unrelated to combat, or to the situation in the army, have been noted as significant precipitants of feelings of hopelessness. Sixteen patients gave a clear history of some such specific traumatic occurrence. Seven soldiers had lost "buddies" with whom they had been inseparable, and who had been closer to them than any other person. Five patients had received word that their fiancées had married, and only relationships which had been considered as final by the soldier are counted. Two soldiers had been upset while in combat by the news that they had impregnated a girl prior to embarkation. Two learned that their mothers had died, and one that his wife was seriously ill. Several others had lost parents while overseas but the loss was not connected with the onset of symptoms directly and did not seem a vital factor in the onset of the illness. Still other reasons for increased insecurity which cannot be classified readily will have been noted among the case histories which have been presented.

In summary of the 25 case histories, it is found that 19 had suicidal ideas; 16 had suffered some specific blow to the stability of their interpersonal relationships at the time the nightmares started; 20 had been raised in families which showed some gross disruption of the usual pattern of parental guidance; 11 or 12 expressed overt hostility towards one or both parents. These figures, even without case illustrations, suggest that attempts to relate the recurrent nightmares to the experiences of combat alone would miss material pertinent to the understanding of the reaction.

DISCUSSION

The repetitive nightmares of combat are to be regarded as wish-fulfillment dreams despite the terror which accompanies them. The dreams are projections of suicidal wishes provoked because life no longer seems worth living. The patient is in an ambivalent state for he fears death as much as he desires it. Life does not seem worth continuing largely because of his extreme insecurity; but death frightens because it means final separation from sources of affection. The nightmare is a projection of this danger of the self onto the obvious danger in the surroundings; and the terror and impotent attempts at defense in the dream express the fear of death.

The reasons for the profound hopelessness are not to be found in the combat situation alone. Usually it is found that the soldier's entire orientation in life has been shattered by the loss of the single important interpersonal relationship in his life. The patients, as a group, were found to be persons who had needed someone upon whom they could be dependent. Their lives had been devoid of satisfactory affectional relationships. They had emerged from families that had been disorganized or disrupted, and had never provided security of affection. Frequently, they had been markedly hostile to a parent with resultant insecurity and guilt. They had sought to fill the void left by the lack of affection in the home. When in adult life, the source of affection and security was removed, they regressed into the old pattern of insecurity, hostility, guilt and hopelessness.

The patients studied were soldiers in whom the nightmares persisted long after combat or first arose while resting from combat. In most patients the nightmares subsided gradually as security was regained, for life was considered untenable only during the extreme conditions of jungle combat. When withdrawn to safety, the desire to live returns and is free from obsessive concern that death is a preferable alternative. When the nightmares continue, it is an indication that the attitude towards the future is still one of despair.

The material may be put together differently. The nightmare may be considered a projection of the soldier's wish for punishment rather than the projection of an ambivalent wish for death. The total situation, combat and extraneous frustrations, provokes overwhelming aggressive hostility in individuals in whom hostility is accompanied by feelings of worthlessness and guilt. The guilt requires punishment. The nightmares, as well as the suicidal thoughts, reflect the need and wish for final punishment to atone for death wishes towards others. This interpretation is more acceptable to some schools of thought, but it does not appear to fit the facts as well. Although the question cannot be decided without more prolonged study of patients than was feasible overseas, the suicidal thoughts seemed more clearly the result of the hopeless insecurity aroused by deprivation of a source of affection than the consequence of a need for punishment for overwhelming hostility.

There is no need to attempt a clear-cut decision. Both hypotheses lead to emphasis on the same factors. The nightmares are not simple residua of combat experiences to be eradicated by emotional abreaction. They are concerned with suicidal thoughts in persons who are markedly unstable in their interpersonal relationships, and who are prone to be overwhelmed by hostility, insecurity, and feelings of hopelessness in a repetition of a pattern that arose in childhood. However the pieces are fitted together, it becomes apparent that the anxiety and nightmares are concerned with the future and not the past. The future is cut off, and, without direction or support, the patient is without direction or support, the patient is foundering in bitterness and frustration.

The treatment then, requires the opening of a path into the future for the patient. The catharsis of the experience of battle is insufficient. There is a need for reorientation towards the worth of living and guidance towards realization that a happy life is possible despite emotional handicaps and the frustrations of the past. The therapy may take a wide variety of forms and requires as much individualization as in civilian practice. The apparent similarity of the precipitant of combat in all cases does not permit the belief that treatment can be formalized into a definite pattern. The soldier may simply require help in overcoming the frustration and rage at the infidelity of a loved one at home. He may only need aid in his mourning for a dead buddy. However, as has become clear from the case histories, when the patient suffers from repetitive nightmares the therapeutic problems may be extremely involved because of the lifelong personality difficulties.

Here, as in a civilian neuroses, the dream may lead to the core of the conflict. Recurrent nightmares are not a problem in themselves. They are a symptom of a type of severe combat neuroses. The attempt to gain an understanding of the ætiology of the nightmares has been a study of the dynamics of a group of the war neuroses. The features which have been noted and isolated form the histories of these severe cases are found in a large number of psychiatric casualties emerging from severe combat. The factors may not appear with such flagrance but the configuration of significant dynamic features in both events and personality recurs with surprising frequency. The soldier loses himself in panic after a long series of stresses culminates in the feeling that life can no longer be endured under such tension. He considers death as a means of escape from either unendurable suspense or insanity and then his danger is heightened by the fear of being overwhelmed by his desire to die. The fear of the self is repressed and projected onto the fearsome surroundings. The soldier is then battling against a foe whose proportions are magnified, and he is struggling with opposing desires within himself that are insoluble. Without means of escape from the dilemma, panic results. It is more than extreme fear. It is the whirlpool of opposing forces of utmost moment to the patient.

SUMMARY

Repetitive nightmares of combat became a focus of attention because they presented a major problem in therapy. Occasional observations concerning the dynamics were broadened by a review of 25 case histories selected at random from a very large series. It is concluded that recurrent nightmares express conflict concerning ambivalent suicidal thoughts provoked by extreme hopelessness. They occur in patients who, having been sensitized early in life by faulty family relationships, are particularly incapable of withstanding withdrawal of affection and feelings of hostility. A pattern of dynamics is presented which recurs with surprising frequency from case to case. The study of nightmares, a symptom of the severe war neuroses, has pertinence to the topic of the ætiology of combat neurosis in general.

NOTES

1. Kardiner, Abram, *The Traumatic Neuroses War*, Paul B. Hoeber, Inc. N. Y. 1941, p. 185.
2. Jones, Ernest, *On the Nightmare*, The Hogarth Press, London, 1931, pp. 43–44.
3. Freud, Sigmund, *The Interpretation of Dreams*, Translation of 3rd Ed. by A.A. Brill, New York, The Macmillan Company, 1915, p. 463.
4. Hendesson, J. L., and Moore, M., The Psychoneuroses of War, *New England J. of Medicine*, 230:273, March 9, 1944.
5. Turnulty, P., Nichols, E., Singewald, M., and Lidz, T., An Investigation of the Effects of Recurrent Malaria: An Organic and Psychological' Analysis of Fifty Soldiers, *Medicine*, 25:17-75, Feb. 46.

16. Toward a Theory of Nightmares

John Mack

Severe anxiety dreams or nightmares contain in themselves, or are related to, so many fundamentally important clinical phenomena that they present a unique challenge and opportunity for the kind of investigation that can lead to the development of psychoanalytic and other psychological theories. The psychology and physiology of dreaming, the problem of anxiety, the adaptation to external threat or trauma, the relation of nightmare to psychosis, the development of early ego functions and mental structures, the psychic handling of aggression, the relationship between erotism and destruction, and the various forms of regression with which such dreams are associated—all are among the major topics that come under consideration when one attempts to achieve a comprehensive view of the nightmare.

Our review and analysis of nightmares up to this point has placed certain demands as well as restrictions upon any theory that might be proposed. Such as theory must, for example, take into account the fact that nightmares —or at least awakening from an apparently fearful hallucinatory experience —can occur in children of about one year of age in whom the development of psychic structure has advanced very little. Also, it must explain how such severely disturbing dreams can take place, not only in emotionally disturbed individuals, but also in persons who otherwise appear to function well or give little or no evidence of being anxious, troubled, or especially "neurotic" during waking life. The theory must be consistent with the widespread occurrence of nightmares and therefore be applicable to persons of other cultures, including primitive societies, who seem to have no immunity from such disturbing dreams. We need also to consider the fact that, unlike other dreams or mental phenomena that occur during sleep, the most severe night-

All cross references in this contribution refer to the chapters of the original book from which it has been excerpted.

Reprinted by permission of the author and Russell & Volkening, Inc., from *Nightmares and Human Conflicts*, Little Brown, Boston, 1970. Copyright © 1970 by John Mack.

mares seem to take place in non-REM periods rather than during REM periods, of which dreaming is regarded as more characteristic. Finally, our explanations must account for the fundamental clinical characteristics shared by nightmares at any age: the feelings of helpessness and powerlessness, the perception of severe danger, the overwhelming or life-and-death quality of anxiety and, finally, the threat or actual presence in the dream of violence and destructiveness.

THE SITUATION OF THE DREAMER

Before trying to approach the particular experience of the nightmare further, it may be useful to look once again at the situation of the dreamer. To begin with, he is usually alone and in the dark. If anyone doubts that such a situation can cause concern for small children, he has only to recall the vigorous efforts with which they resist the inevitable nighttime separation, complain about being left alone in their rooms, seek out the parents repeatedly before finally allowing themselves to be retired for the night, and fortify themselves for the hours ahead through pre-sleep rituals and the gathering of bedtime companions, both real and imaginary. Many children have nightmares when they sleep alone; these usually cease when they have in the same room a sibling or any other person—it often matters little who it is. These fears of being separated and alone at night persist in varying degrees in persons of all ages. In addition, many children and adults struggle against the act of falling asleep, as if this helpless surrender were itself dangerous, apart from the anxieties that may be encountered during sleep. The danger associated with relinquishing reality and withdrawing from the outside world, especially from love objects, also contributes to this fear of surrendering to sleep. Total darkness makes the absence of the parents more complete, deprives the child of the familiarity of his surroundings and of external cues that could aid in reality judgment, and makes more difficult the realistic assessment of anxiety-provoking fantasies before the onset of sleep. These frightening fantasies may then contribute to the content of subsequent nightmares. For example, frightening illusions, that is, distorted perception of objects in the environment, are commonplace for children going to sleep in the dark; the biting monster the child creates from a familiar chair may also find its way into a nightmare. Furthermore, when a child—or an occasional adult, as well—awakens from a severe anxiety dream, the restoration of reality is usually more difficult than is the case in most dreams; conversely, the persecutory images of the dream persist much longer, especially in total darkness. Thus, the helplessness that accompanies separation and the sense of isolation and anxiety that accompany surrender to sleep may all contribute to the intensity of such feelings as occur in the nightmares themselves.

The anxiety associated with this surrender may relate also to the regression with which sleep is associated, especially the revival of infantile dependent longings and fears that replicate in many ways the conflicts that grow out of the early mother-infant relationship. The anxieties evoked by the regressive cloistral aspect of the sleep situation may also contribute to the revival in the dreams of early conflicts related to infantile dependent desires and fears.

In Chapter 2 we saw how many of the features that characterize dreaming and distinguish dreams from ordinary thinking may be considered in relation to the concept of regression. Topographical regression refers to the revival in dreaming of forms of thought that rely upon concrete imagery and the representation of ideas and wishes in visual and other concrete sensory modes. In addition, the traces of early thoughts and memories are revived. In dreams there also occurs a libidinal regression, accompanied by a return, not only to wishes for earlier forms of sensual gratification, but to the dependent and more helpless qualities of the small child's relationships with other persons, especially the parents. In these relationships he feels, and in dreams may appear, very small in relation to larger, more powerful creatures. The narcissistic regression of dreams also contributes to the abandonment of persons in the outside world as the dreamer becomes totally invested in his own feelings and mental productions.

Although certain ego functions continue to be active during sleep—as demonstrated, for example, in the capacity of some persons to monitor the time for their awakening or of sleeping mothers to discriminate faint sounds of the nursery from louder but more neutral noises—ego functioning also succumbs to the regression that accompanies sleep and dreaming. Primitive, childlike forms of thinking predominate, and dreams reflect the symbolization, distortion, displacement, and projection mechanisms that characterize the thinking of early childhood. Although many ego functions remain intact within dreams, the individual's capacity to judge the dream phenomena by the measures that he applies to reality during the waking hours suffers most. It is as though one portion of the ego has split off and can carry on in the dream as if it were dealing with life as usual, while another portion—the part that is ordinarily busy in the daytime deciding what is possible and what is real, discriminating what is a thought from what is happening in the outside

world, and distinguishing a mere wish from an accomplished deed—is
largely unavailable. Dostoevsky, in a passage in *The Idiot*, revealed his
understanding of this split in the ego during dreaming, as well as the active
part played by unconscious wishes and desires not revealed in the dream's
manifest content [1]:

> You remember first of all that your reason did not desert you throughout the dream;
> you remember even that you acted very cunningly and logically through all that long,
> long time, while you were surrounded by murderers who deceived you, hid their
> intentions, behaved amicably to you while they had a weapon in readiness, and were
> only waiting for some signal; you remember how cleverly you deceived them at last,
> hiding from them; then you guessed that they'd seen through your deception and were
> only pretending not to know where you were hidden; but you were sly then and
> deceived them again; all this you remember clearly. But how was it that you could at
> the same time reconcile your reason to the obvious absurdities and impossibilities
> with which your dream was overflowing? One of your murderers turned into a woman
> before your eyes, and the woman into a little, sly, loathsome dwarf—and you
> accepted it all at once as an accomplished fact, almost without the slightest surprise,
> at the very time when, on another side, your reason is at its highest tension and
> showed extraordinary power, cunning, sagacity and logic? And why, too, one waking
> up and fully returning to reality, do you feel almost every time, and sometimes with
> extraordinary intensity, that you have left something unexplained behind with the
> dream? You laugh at the absurdities of your dream, and at the same time you feel that
> interwoven with those absurdities some thought lies hidden, and a thought that is real,
> something belonging to your actual life, something that exists and has always existed
> in your head.

In summary, our sleeping nightmare victim is likely to be alone in darkness, separated from those he loves and upon whom he may still be dependent; he may be in a regressive state and withdrawn from reality. We have
only set the stage and described the situation of any dreamer. We have set
forth some elements in his vulnerability to nightmares, but have said nothing
that distinguishes the nightmare from an ordinary dream or the nightmare
victim from any person asleep. We shall now turn to these considerations.

NIGHTMARES AND THE PROBLEM OF ANXIETY

I have defined the nightmare as a type of severe anxiety dream in which the
level of anxiety reaches overwhelming proportions. The principal problem
this definition raises is one that Freud posed in 1925. "Again," Freud wrote,
"it is not to be expected that the explanation of anxiety dreams will be found
in the theory of dreams. Anxiety is a problem rather of neurosis, and all that

remains to be discussed is how it comes about that anxiety can arise under dream conditions'' [2]. I would amend this statement of the problem and suggest that the explanation will not be found *solely* in the theory of dreams or in the theory of neurosis or anxiety. Rather, the problem belongs both to the theory of dreams and the theory of anxiety and love, above all, involves the relationship between the two.

A number of authors have pointed out that the ego must undergo some development before true anxiety can develop in infancy [3–6]. Above all, there must be sufficient cognitive development to give structure to perceptions, to represent them internally, and to assign meaning to them. According to Spitz, the earliest anxiety occurs in the second half of the first year as stranger anxiety, the shock the infant experiences upon seeing some unfamiliar face, not his mother's. Benjamin has distinguished a second form, separation anxiety, from stranger anxiety, documenting its onset in the sixteen to eighteen month period. According to Benjamin, separation fear, in contrast to stranger anxiety, requires a more complete mental representation of the mother and thus demands an appreciation of the significance and danger that attend her departure or absence. Fears occurring after onset of sleep are among the earliest clear manifestations of anxiety that parents note in their infants; some of the earliest nightmares that have been described occurred either in relation to confrontation with strangers, separation situations, or the child's fear of some destructive or ''devouring'' agency or a machine such as a vacuum cleaner [35].

Two observations in Freud's later theory of anxiety are particularly relevant for the study of severe anxiety in dreams. First, Freud noted that each phase in the child's development had its characteristic danger situation and associated form of anxiety. Thus, according to Freud, the earliest danger, arising when the child is psychologically and biologically most immature, is fear of loss of the person who cares for him and, later, loss of that person's love. In later phases of development, fear of the loss of a valued part of the body—castration anxiety—takes precedence, and this is followed by fear of disapproval by an internal self-judging agency or superego. Anna Freud has added to this list fear of the intensity of one's instincts, the fear of being overwhelmed by uncontrollable forces from within [9], and Waelder has stressed the danger some individuals experience of masochistic surrender [10]. Each of the danger situations, Freud noted, could exist side by side, and the ego could react at a later period with anxiety that was originally appropriate to an earlier one. As we have seen, adulthood also has its characteristic danger situations, such as the possibility of failure or the various risks and dangers associated with commitment to the adult responsibilities of marriage and parenthood. The analysis of these adult fear situations often shows that they are intimately linked with unresolved childhood anxieties.

The second observation of Freud, particularly important for our understanding of nightmares, is that small amounts of anxiety under the control of the ego may act as a signal to prevent the development of a traumatic situation, in which there occurs anxiety of overwhelming proportions. In a recent attempt to amplify Freud's theory, Rangell has viewed anxiety of varying intensities as a kind of sampling of a traumatic state that has the function of preventing the occurrence of a more severe traumatic situation [11]. This signal or sample anxiety gives the ego the opportunity to avoid the danger situation or to bring into play judgment, reality-testing, and various psychological defenses that may help to prevent anxiety of overwhelming intensity from arising.

How can these two observations of Freud be applied to our understanding of the intense anxiety that occurs in nightmares? In our case examples, we have seen repeatedly that, in each phase of development, nightmares occur in association with the external danger situations that are characteristic of the period. The two-year-old Sam, for example (see Chapter 2), who faces the danger of loss of love because of his destructive impulses, has nightmares in which a lion threatens to bite him. Rachel at age four (Chapter 2), feared grabby monsters that might take her away or cause genital injury. Carol at nine (Chapter 4) was struggling with powerful feelings of love and hatred toward both her mother and father that caused her intenses feelings of guilt. Her guilt precipitated a complex nightmare in which she engaged in a terror-filled struggle to ward off a blood bath brought about by monstrous figures that would destroy her and her sister. The young father (Chapter 2) who struggles with his ambivalent feelings toward his baby son has a nightmare about a threat to the infant and violent feelings toward those who would neglect it. Many other examples could be cited.

In each instance in which it has been possible to obtain detailed information regarding the dream and its associated material, we have seen that in the nightmare the anxiety related not only to the current danger situation that confronted the dreamer during his waking hours; in the regressive sleep dream situation, the current danger became linked with earlier dangers, the current anxiety with earlier anxieties. Thus, in the nightmare of five-year-old

Timmy, precipitated by his father's assignment to an overseas war zone, we find both fear of retaliation for his hostile wishes toward his father and fear, stemming from an earlier period of childhood, of being abandoned by his mother and separated from her with no one to take care of him. Similarly, the seduction nightmare of the thirty-year-old woman described in Chapter 2 was precipitated by the revival in analytic treatment of her conflicts over forbidden childhood sexual curiosity. The analysis of the determinants of the overwhelming anxiety of the nightmare revealed that it was linked with many childhood fears extending back to the early danger of loss of her mother's love at the time of her brother's birth when she was twenty months old. Thus, the intensity of anxiety in nightmares may occur in part as a result of the regressive linking or coalescence of current anxieties with those of earlier periods, especially in the second year of life when abandonment and loss of love are such critical dangers for the child. This regressive revival of early fears and wishes in nightmares may account for the frequency with which cannibalistic experiences of being bitten or devoured occur, not only in the nightmares of early childhood, but in those of older children and adults, as well.

Ego regression may also contribute to the intensity of anxiety in nightmares and especially to the quality of utter helplessness that is usually experienced in these dreams. It appears as if, in the nightmare, the ego state that once accompanied childhood fears is revived along with the fears themselves. Thus, even the adult nightmare victim confronts his nemesis, not as the competent person he may actually have become, but as the small and helpless child surrounded by a world of large people and dangerous forces that he perceives in much the same way as he did in the earlier period when they confronted him daily with his powerlessness. This factor of ego regression and helplessness seems also to contribute to a certain uniformity among nightmares in the various developmental phases.

The second factor that contributes to the occurrence of such overwhelming anxiety in dreams is the failure of the signal function to prevent the development of more intense anxiety. The ego in the dream situation is unable, if we may use Rangell's terminology, to ''sample'' a traumatic situation in the dream or to regulate effectively the amount of anxiety that is experienced. One factor that accounts for this inability has already been discussed, namely, the power of the regressive pull in the dream situation that leads to ego regression and the revival of earlier anxieties. In addition, however, as discussed earlier in this chapter, there are unavailable to the dreamer certain ego functions that ordinarily serve to limit the intensity of anxiety during the waking hours. Ego defenses such as repression and intellectualization do not function effectively in dreams; above all, the capacity to judge danger situations and avoid them, to evaluate reality, and to distinguish frightening thoughts from genuinely threatening situations, is impaired. Furthermore, during the dream other persons are unavailable to provide reassurance or love or even to aid in reality-testing, a service among human beings whose importance even in everyday waking life is often underestimated. Thus, in the dream all threatening objects or perceptions are regarded as if they were external or real, as if the danger were actual. The struggle to remedy this troublesome situation is demonstrated by the dreamer's effort to assure himself that what he is undergoing is "nothing but a dream." The ego regression within the nightmare compounds an already difficult situation for the dreamer, who is in any event little able to judge the status in reality of his dream images. Once massive anxiety has developed, the nightmare victim has only one available option: to wake up. In so doing, he reestablishes a sense of reality and judgment and regains his perspective. Adults can usually accomplish this task by using only their own ego functions. Small children, however, require reunion with the parental love object in order to receive help with these difficult tasks. As Kanzer has written, "nightmares pass directly into communication when the child cries for his mother, or reflect the paralyzing fear of being unable to establish such communications" [12]. If the individual is unable, soon after awakening, to reverse this appraisal of the dream dangers as actual, we are dealing not with a nightmare, but with a psychosis. The nightmare, as the patient described in Chapter 5 stated, would then have become "a continuing fact in time."

In addition to their occurrence in response to obvious danger situations, nightmares seem also to take place in association with developmental shifts or advances in childhood or critical periods in adult life. Learning to walk and explore, toilet training, the heightening of phallic interests, puberty, marriage, parenthood, and increased career responsibilities are a few such milestones that seem frequently to be associated with nightmares. One possible explanation has already been mentioned: that the assertiveness that produces the advance or shift is associated with destructive wishes or intentions. Another factor may be operating as well. Throughout this book we have stressed the fundamental importance in nightmares of feelings of helplessness, of the sense of vulnerability. The earliest helplessness, an attitude that seems to underlie the anxiety in nightmares at all ages, resembles that of the very small child who feels powerless to control the coming and going of the mothering person upon whom he is totally dependent. This feeling of powerlessness and the anxiety with which it is accompanied may recur each time a major new task is attempted, until skills that will lead to mastery and a reduction of anxiety are attained. Nightmares are often a sensitive indicator of the presence of anxiety and may reflect this feeling of helplessness that occurs when major new tasks are undertaken before the motor skills, cognitive capacities, defenses, or other ego functions necessary for such mastery have developed. The content of the dreams may be of the usual "raw-head and bloody-bones" variety, but the ego factor of powerlessness, which makes the dreamer feel subject to danger and attack, maybe of greater importance than the instinctual elements that are suggested by the dream's content.

NIGHTMARES AND THE CONCEPT OF TRAUMA

A nightmare can be traumatic in two senses. First, as will be discussed shortly, it is by definition a traumatic response to external or internal events or stimuli. Second, the frightening dream can produce a further traumatic effect through the persistence during the waking hours of its powerfully disturbing affects.

A recent book devoted to the subject of psychic trauma has demonstrated that it is easier to write about the clinical effects of traumatic events than to define trauma [13]. Freud used the term originally in relation to a hypothetical stimulus barrier that, under ordinary circumstances, protected the organism from psychic injury. Stimuli of too great intensity arising from outside or inside the organism could potentially overwhelm this barrier, leading to a state of helplessness and an accumulation of excitation with which the organism was incapable of dealing. In recent psychoanalytic literature, Freud's stimulus barrier has come to be regarded as a kind of precursor of ego defense functions; the concept of trauma has been approached in terms of ego's capacity to deal with a variety of potentially noxious or injurious conditions [14].

The principal difficulty in the use of the term *trauma* has been the uncertainty as to whether to emphasize the events or threats that give rise to a disturbing state or to stress this traumatic state itself, the *response* of the individual. Nightmares can be helpful in clarifying the problem of trauma, since they dramatize the lack of correspondence between the objectively disturbing or dangerous quality of outside events and the intense response of the nightmare victim, which may be out of all proportion to these threats. The nightmare is a *traumatic response* inasmuch as the ego is overwhelmed with anxiety, and the dreamer experiences an acute feeling of helplessness, criteria cited in virtually all definitions of trauma. The nightmare gives evidence that the organism has been "traumatized." However, if the traumatic response is limited to the sleep situation in the form of a nightmare, does not invade waking consciousness, and is not accompanied by other symptoms, signs of ego regression, or developmental difficulties, it is reasonable to say either that this is a "successful" handling of the traumatic situation or that the traumatic experience has been well circumscribed. In any discussion, the term trauma will refer to this *response* of the individual.

The question then arises: a traumatic response to what? The case examples make clear that this question can be approached only in terms of the interplay between external events and the internal meaning these have for the dreamer. Clearly, there is no direct relationship between the magnitude of an outside threat or potential danger and the intensity of a nightmare or other traumatic response. In the case of the traumatic war neuroses, in which repetitive nightmares are the most characteristic symptom, the external threat to the life of the soldier has often been constant and severe.[1] Similarly, children and adults have frequent night terrors and nightmares following or during a period of surgery. By contrast, often the event that precipitates a nightmare is manifestly anything but threatening and may even appear to be a source of gratification, as in the case of the young father described in Chapter 2 which had a severe nightmare the night after he had proudly shown his eight-month-old son to his in-laws. Alternatively, as in the case of eight-year-old Laura's

---

1. G. W. Crile has given a vivid description of the battle nightmares of men in the trenches in World War I: "The dream is always the same, always of the enemy. It is never a pleasant pastoral dream, or a dream of home, but a dream of the charge, of the bursting shell, of the bayonet thrust! Again and again in camp and in hospital wards, in spite of the great desire to sleep, a desire so great that the dressing of a compound fracture would not be felt, men sprang up with a battle cry, and reached for their rifles, the dream outcry startling their comrades, whose thresholds were excessively low to the stimuli of attack.

"In the hospital wards, battle nightmares were common, and severely wounded men would often spring out of their beds. An unexpected analogy to this battle nightmare was found in anesthetic dreams. Precisely the same battle nightmare, that occurred in sleep, occurred when soldiers were going under or coming out of anesthesia, when they would often struggle valiantly, —for the anesthetic dream like the sleep dream related not to a home scene, not to some dominating activation of peaceful days, but always to the enemy, and usually to a surprise attack" [15].

nightmare (see Chapter 2) soon after a trip to the planetarium, the traumatizing event may give no indication at the time of being disturbing; the reason it precipitated a nightmare will be unclear unless the specific meaning of the incident or series of events leading up to the dream is understood. In Laura's nightmare of the yellow monster, for example, it was important to know the relationship between the scientific demonstration at the planetarium (that the sun might collide with and consume the earth) and Laura's anxiety about being too close to her mother or being swallowed up in this troublesomely intimate relationship.

The power of an event or series of events to bring about a traumatic response depends upon their confirmation of the fears that are currently active for the child or adult or the capacity of such events to revive the memories of incidents that were previously disturbing, often in association with the anxieties of earlier developmental phases. A child between one and two, for example, who fears being abandoned as a consequence of his aggression is likely to have nightmares following even brief separations from the parents because these departures confirm the possibility he fears most. Sara's frightening hallucination of a biting snake was precipitated by the conflicts surrounding her exaggeratedly erotic oedipal situation. However, the anxiety related to her destructive wishes toward her mother in the oedipal rivalry reevoked in the sleep situation the fears associated with multiple *actual* separations from the mother from the time she was one-and-a-half; these corresponded to what she most dreaded and possibly also revived a memory of having been frightened by a rat in her bed at age one. It was the coalescence of the current fears with anxieties from earlier developmental phases that gave the nightmare its overwhelming traumatic quality. Many similar examples have been provided. Freud may have had something similar in mind when he wrote, "Affective states have become incorporated in the mind as precipitates of primaeval traumatic experiences, and when a similar situation occurs they are revived like mnemic symbols" [16].

Although the overwhelming character of anxiety in nightmares and the sense of powerlessness and helplessness that characterize these dreams lead us to define them as traumatic, under ordinary circumstances this is a very limited sort of trauma. As Sandler has recently pointed out, early childhood is filled with traumatic situations, with many "silent traumas" [17]. The only "noise" these give off may be an occasional nightmare. To fall repeatedly while learning to walk, to give up the stool, to observe that living things can be destroyed—these are but a few of the many experiences whose threat to the child and whose traumatic impact may become evident only in a nightmare that can pass virtually unnoticed. Usually the dreamer awakens and, if he cannot restore reality by himself, calls the parents, who provide comfort and reassurance and turn on the light. Perhaps this is as it should be, for nightmares are a small price to pay for the achievement of important developmental strides. In the case of older children and adults, simply waking up is usually sufficient to restore reality and terminate in a short time the traumatic effects of a nightmare, although the tendency of nightmarish affect to persist for many hours after waking is well known.

However, there are several situations in which the traumatic effects of the nightmare are more extensive. The simplest of these is the case of the childhood nightmare or night terror, the frightening power of which pervades the waking hours, requiring further parental or even professional intervention. The child's immature ego is unable to offset or defend itself adequately against the powerful affects carried over from the dream or, as in the cases of several three- and four-year-old children described earlier, to distinguish persisting dream images from perceptions emanating from the outside world. When severe, such states can progress to a childhood hallucinatory psychosis. In these instances, the history often reveals that there have been repeated severe threats to the child's body or to his or her very existence preceding the nightmare. In older children or adults a nightmare may become more severely traumatic when it persists into the waking hours as, for example, in states of febrile delirium or when, as in the case of alcoholics, it erupts into delirium tremens. Even in normal adults, the emotions and disturbing scenes of a nightmare may carry over into the waking hours, sometimes affecting the individual's mood throughout the day. Acute schizophrenics may find their nightmares—even ordinary dreams—severely traumatic when they have lost the capacity to distinguish where dreams leave off and waking reality begins. Finally, by the very intensity of its terrifying content a nightmare may become traumatic, even for an adult, if the individual has difficulty integrating its disturbing content. This is illustrated by the case Levitan has described of a forty-five-year-old woman who reexperienced as a blinding flash of light in a nightmare the devastating impact of the news she had received earlier that day of the sudden death of her husband [18]. In this instance the nightmare was experienced as a kind of second traumatic event.

Repetitive nightmares are one of the principal indications of traumatization and one of the most prominent symptoms of traumatic neuroses. The nightmare represents, with varying amounts of symbolic distortion and condensation with earlier traumata, a repetition or reliving of the disturbing experience that precipitates the disorder. The war or battle neurosis is the best-known example of a traumatic neurosis; sufferers from these disorders very frequently experience repeated severe nightmares that may persist for many years after the individual is removed from the stressful situation [19]. Although war neuroses are the best described of such disorders, frequently nightmares can also occur following accidents, injuries, hospitalization or surgery, unusual cruelty, brutalization of children by parents, or loss of important persons upon whom the individual is dependent. The common feature in all of these situations is an external event that is perceived as threatening to the life or person of the individual and that cannot be integrated with the psychological resources available to him. Such a situation, as we have seen repeatedly in this book, is particularly common in early childhood when the ego is immature, when the threatening significance of environmental threats tends to be exaggerated, when reality-testing is fragile, and when dependency upon others is extreme.

The observation of the existence of these disorders caused Freud and his associates to revise their theory of the sexual etiology of neurotic disturbances [20, 21]. They did not abandon the role of sexuality, but recognized that symptoms could arise as a result of conflict within the ego itself on the basis of narcissism, that is, the investment of libido in the subject's own ego. In the traumatic disorders the ego experiences a threat to itself, a fear of annihilation. Such symptoms of the traumatic neurosis as anxiety dreams reflect the ego's struggle to guard itself, to "protect its investment," to survive. Thus, these disorders require a reconsideration of the role of self preservation in human motivation and the reintroduction of concepts closely allied to Freud's earlier concept of "ego instincts."

The repeated nightmares and other symptoms that occur in the traumatic disorders are not the result simply of a current reality experience. Rather, the current traumatic events become regressively linked with earlier traumatic situations, dating back to early childhood, the common feature of which is the ego's experience of helplessness in the face of overwhelming danger. For example, Lidz has shown that, even in the nightmares associated with combat neuroses, the men often had long histories of unstable relationships in which early terror and insecurity were common [19].

One view of repetitive nightmares, as well as of other phenomena that the individual seems compelled to repeat in a seemingly irrational fashion, is that they represent an effort to transform a traumatic experience, in which the individual was passive and painfully helpless, into one of active mastery. For example, Freud suggested that, in the traumatic neuroses, the frightening dreams are "endeavoring to master the stimulus retrospectively, by developing the anxiety whose omission was the cause of the traumatic neurosis" [22]. In fact, Simmel developed for these disorders a treatment in which he encouraged the nightmare victim to convert his terror of death into fierce outbursts or rage against his imaginary dream adversaries, who presumably represented the attacking enemy, or against the superiors who had put the soldier in such a helpless position, demonstrating once again the close association between nightmares and violent aggression [23].

Since Freud made his famous statement about mastering a stimulus retrospectively, debate has persisted as to whether such repeated nightmares actually represent an effort at mastery and adaptation or are merely the result of nightly regression in which, to use a later expression of Freud, the "upward pressure of traumatic fixation" is irresistible. In my own view, there is no contradiction as long as one does not limit mastery and adaptation to conscious or deliberate processes. The mind does turn back to the past in sleep; memories that can be kept out of awareness during the waking hours, when the individual is in contact with other people and has a full range of defenses available to him, inevitably force themselves upon the ego during sleep and dreaming. Recent and past memories of events that have had a traumatic effect are reevoked in sleep in what may be regarded as an obligatory regression. At the same time, however, through dream-formation and elaboration, the individual may struggle to limit and confine to the sleep situation the anxiety associated with memories of the traumatic situation; the experience does not therefore necessarily pervade the individual's waking consciousness and overwhelm the ego and its functions as it originally did.

Interestingly, Simmel felt that the symptoms of war neuroses served to protect soldiers against a more serious regression, that is, from psychosis. "The war neuroses," Simmel wrote, "are essentially interposed guarantees, the object of which is to protect the soldier against psychosis. Anyone who has examined a great number of patients for eighteen months with perception that has been analytically sharpened must recognize that the proportionately small number of war psychoses is only to be explained by the proportionately large number of war neuroses" [24]. Inasmuch as some psychoses begin at night in association with the regressive experiences of sleep and dreaming, it would be of particular interest to study further how the ego's defensive and adaptive mechanisms operate in sleep and dreaming and how, in a nightmare,

they circumscribe a disorder that otherwise contains the ingredients or poten-
tiality for becoming a psychosis. It should be stressed once more that these
are not deliberate or conscious processes. Rather, we are concerned with
fundamental early ego defenses and adaptations—and perhaps also with
physiological homeostatic mechanisms—that function to maintain the equilibrium and integrity of the organism as a whole during sleep and waking.

NIGHTMARES AND INSTINCTUAL DRIVES

In psychoanalytic theory, sexuality and aggression are regarded as instinctual
drives that are believed to underlie most conflicts. However, extensive research, including numerous studies of animal behavior, has failed to find
evidence in either animals or man to support a view that either libido or
aggression necessarily builds up or accumulates as a result of deprivation or
the absence of opportunities for drive discharge or gratification [25]. On the
contrary, the available evidence, reviewed recently by Holt, indicates that
both sexual and aggressive drives arising from within the organism function
in a continuous ongoing relationship with external forces that stimulate,
arouse, provoke, frustrate, or otherwise act to call forth the expression of one
drive or another [26].

Similarly, in the case of nightmares, which have traditionally been conceived of as a kind of massive discharge phenomenon for accumulated
instinctual tensions [27, 28], there is little evidence to support the view that
these terrifying dreams occur in association with a buildup of instinctual
forces. Indeed, the work of Fisher et al. and of Broughton has demonstrated
that the most severe nightmares can arouse the dreamer spontaneously from
the state of non-REM sleep [29, 30], in which the physiological activity of
the organism is generally less intense than during the REM periods with
which dreaming is more regularly associated. Nevertheless, in our case
examples we have seen repeatedly that nightmares do occur in situations in
which the dreamer has been undergoing severe conflict over sexual and
aggressive impulses or drives and that these dreams are filled with aggressive
content (see Chapter 4).

There is really no contradiction in these observations if one is willing to
abandon a physical energy-discharge model in conceiving of these dreams
and to consider the possibility that the motives, desires, or wishes that have
given rise to the conflicts reflected in nightmares are not active during sleep
in the same way as they are in the daytime. Let us assume that the individual

during his waking hours, including both the recent and distant past, has accumulated or "internalized" countless mental representations, stored in his mind as memories, of the possible consequences of particular wishes or intended actions. Let us assume also—as recent research in the sleep-dream field strongly suggests—that the mind is active during a large proportion of the sleeping hours, or at least that ideas occur in the mind, even though we cannot observe how this comes about or know the content of these thoughts. The danger for the child or adult from his impulses or wishes could then be represented in nightmares by thoughts without necessarily assuming the accumulation or discharge of drive energies during sleep.

Let us say, for example, that a four-year-old boy has had an intense interest before going to sleep in visiting his parents' room and climbing in bed with his mother. He has made such a nuisance of himself that his father has yelled at him angrily and even threatened punishment. Reluctantly, the boy dozes off to sleep, only to be awakened two hours later by a nightmare in which he is being chased by a horrid monster that threatens to eat him. How could the nightmare have come about? A possible answer is that it could have been precipitated by thoughts that arose in the sleep situation. Enraged by his father's authority, he has had thoughts of murdering him before going to sleep, and these may have continued to form in his mind once he is asleep. However, these thoughts are potentially very dangerous, not only because his father might retaliate if he tried to kill him, but also because he is likely to conceive of the deed as accomplished; his still fragile ability to distinguish the difference between thoughts and deeds may lead him to equate the wish or thought with the deed, and he does not want to lose his father. This conflict may then be carried over into sleep, with the murderous thoughts and their anticipated consequences finding representation in dreams or nightmares. Furthermore, the danger associated with the current situation becomes linked with the mental representations of earlier dangers, for example, the possibility of being left by the mother or of being eaten. The regression in thinking that occurs in dreams may also contribute to the form of the manifest dream thoughts, giving rise to images of devouring monsters and the like. Finally, as discussed previously, the terror is intensified by the dreamer's difficulty in applying a realistic judgment to the dream's content. Thus, the conflict over sexual and aggressive wishes may actively give rise to the dream and be represented in its symbolic content. This does not necessarily mean, however, that sexual and aggressive drives are directly active in the nightmare in the same sense that they may be when the child is engaged with objects during the waking hours.

The problem is complicated by the fact that, in dreams, thoughts can give rise to a direct biological sexual response, as in a nocturnal emission. There is little evidence, however, that nightmares are related to eroticism in this direct sense. When it occurs in dreams, anxiety seems actually to inhibit eroticism [31]. In the case of aggression, there seems to be even less likelihood that physiologically active destructiveness gives rise to nightmares. All-night sleep recordings furnish no physiological evidence that accumulated signs of rage, for example, precede the onset of nightmares [29, 30, 32]. In the instances described in the literature in which nightmares were followed by actual murders, the killing occurred because the dreamer interpreted the nightmare images to mean that he was in mortal danger; an anticipated assailant in the outside world whom he confused with his dream attacker [33].

In conclusion, conflicts over sexual and aggressive impulses probably lead to nightmares, not through the biological expression of these drives during sleep, but through the danger experienced in relation to the mental representations of the conflict as these confront the dreamer in more or less distorted form in the dream. This view is based on the assumption that the mental representations of the elements of conflict can give rise to anxiety apart from the biological activity of the drives that originally may have played a part in the conflict.

NIGHTMARES, CONFLICT, AND THE DEVELOPMENT OF PSYCHIC STRUCTURE

Nightmares occur in response to the characteristic danger situations that human beings confront in the course of development, beginning with the fear of strangers and the dread of abandonment in infancy and the fear of bodily injury in early childhood, and ending with the fears of failure, death, and loss of function in adulthood and old age. Frequently the anxiety that may accompany these dangers is not evident in the lives of healthy individuals during waking hours; it may emerge only during sleep in an anxiety dream at a time when the individual does not have available the psychological defenses he normally employs during the daytime. William James actually stated, evidently with confidence: "In civilized life, in particular, it has at last become possible for large numbers of people to pass from the cradle to the grave without ever having had a pang of genuine fear. Many of us need an attack of mental disease to teach us the meaning of the word" [34]. He might have added to "mental disease" the more frequent experience of a nightmare. Nightmares may become the prototype expression of the anxieties that characterize each period of development.

From the neurophysiological standpoint, the apparatus essential for dreaming, or at least for the occurrence of the various sleep stages and the REM-non-REM sleep cycle that is associated with dreaming, exists at birth. However, if nightmares are to take place, the capacity to experience anxiety, for the ego to anticipate danger, must be present. The object of outside danger must be perceived, represented internally, and then feared, a mental operation requiring the formation of psychic structure. According to Benjamin, the development of this capacity coincides with the first clearly defined infantile anxiety, the fear of strangers, which develops in the second half of the first year. In Benjamin's view, this anxiety depends not only upon the infant's libidinal attachment to the mother: "To this must be added what is at least a highly *contributory,* and possibly a *necessary condition* for these particular anxiety manifestations: the maturational organization of aggression as such into *object-directed* hostility and anger, with the resultant marked increase in fear of object loss" [35]. We have seen how this fear of the consequences of hostility directed at other persons continues to play an important role in the occurrence of nightmares at later stages of development, as well; it may be obvious in the dreams of adults, as well as those of children. The complexity and structure of nightmares advance greatly as development proceeds, but the fear of hostility toward other persons may usually be detected.

The increase in the complexity of nightmares seems to occur largely as a result of various identifications with parental objects and through the elaboration of symbolic structures. Internalization of the qualities of persons who threaten the child, "identification with the aggressor," is a prominent defense mechanism through which the individual seeks to avoid danger from another person's wrath or disapproval by merging with the object or by taking its threatening qualities into the self. However, this incorporation of aspects of other persons who are perceived as threatening or dangerous sets up in the ego potentially destructive elements that may emerge in nightmares as angry voices, noises, or threatening creatures but endanger the dreamer once again. A simple example is provided by a girl between three and four who had, after a great deal of screaming and resistance, reluctantly submitted to shots and other pediatric procedures and examinations. In her subsequent play she angrily identified with the doctor who gave shots, viciously sticking a toy needle into the chest and ears of a recalcitrant child, represented by a small doll. That night she awoke from a nightmare screaming, evidently suffering from hallucinations in which aspects of the menacing pediatric personnel had become associated with other threats. "Don't let them get my nose," she wailed.

After age four or five, through the extension of these and more positively acquired identifications, superego structures form; these regulate the child or adult's behavior from within. As discussed in detail in Chapter 2, the qualities of objects that were internalized in the course of development to form the superego and other stable psychic agencies or structures may become reseparated into discrete voices or visages in nightmares and confront the dreamer once more in the hostile form in which they appeared to the child in the earlier developmental period.

The distinction between punishment and anxiety dreams or nightmares may depend on the depth of regression involved, that is, upon the degree to which previously internalized aspects of objects become "separated out" and externalized in the dream in the destructive form they assumed for the child in an earlier period. In a simple punishment dream, for example, a critical voice or attitude of a teacher or parent figure may confront the dreamer, inspiring merely feelings of guilt and moderate anxiety. The deeper regression of nightmare, however, may additionally include the emergence of more primitive superego precursors that are perceived in the dream, as they were by the child in an earlier time, as potentially annihilating or devouring. The processes of condensation, segregation, and displacement that occur in dream production result, of course, in the formation of *new* combinations of percepts and images from the present and from the recent and distant past; consequently, the manifest content of the dream tends to be unique or original, that is, not simply a reproduction of the qualities of the objects that have been internalized in the course of development.

An endlessly fascinating subject that remains unsettled is the degree to which anxiety promotes the development of psychic structure. In Kris' formulation, "comfort serves to build object relationships, discomfort stimulates the differentiation, i.e., structure formation in the psychic apparatus" [36]. We may well ask how much discomfort promotes differentiation as opposed, for example, to disintegration? When one studies the elaborate structure of some children's nightmares—for example, those of Laura (Chapter

2), Carl (Chapter 3), or Carol (Chapter 4)—one cannot help but be impressed by the dream's rich and creative unfolding and elaboration in response to the anxiety situation. Whereas some nightmares seem to have no content other than a menacing sight, sound, or voice, others resemble works of art, pieces of desperate creativity, remarkably rich in form and meaning that have occurred in response to the traumatic situation. This creative elaboration does not cease with the dream work, but proceeds during the telling of the dream in further imaginative embellishments, a process related to but extending beyond Freud's "secondary revision." Some writers (see Chapter 3) have put the creative elaboration associated with dreams and their subsequent embellishment into the service of their art, or at least have claimed to do so. More research is needed regarding the various relationships between anxiety, dream formation, creativity, mastery, and the development of psychic structure.

NIGHTMARES, HALLUCINATIONS, AND THE DEVELOPMENT OF REALITY-TESTING

There is a period in early childhood in which dreams are regarded as real and in which the events, transformations, gratifications, and threats of which they are composed are regarded by the child as if they were as much a part of his actual daily life as his daytime experiences. The capacity to establish and maintain clear distinctions between the life of dreams and life in the outside world is hard-won and requires several years to accomplish, not being completed even in normal children before ages eight to ten. Nightmares, because of their vividness and compelling affective intensity, are particularly difficult for the child to judge realistically; the various regressions of ego functioning that accompany them may also contribute to the child's problem in knowing that such dreams are not in fact disaster or danger situations.

Four seems to be a critical age in the development of the capacity to reality-test dreams. Some four-year-olds treat their dreams, and their nightmares in particular, as they would any important part of their lives. We may recall how the four-year-old girl Rachel, described in Chapter 1, suffered from nightmares that were so troubling to her that only her mother's actual presence at night could comfort her. During the day, she continued to think about the dream's monsters and became increasingly anxious as night approached, for she knew that she was likely to encounter the monsters once more after falling asleep. Even after she awoke, the nightmare monsters seemed as real as any part of her life. Another four-year-old described elsewhere had begun to achieve a compromise in his judgment of his dream attackers, concluding that lobsters that bit his toes at night were not really in his room, but were images of lobsters transmitted from somewhere else by television [37].

The development of the capacity to reality-test the nightmare experience seems to depend on several factors. Among the most important of these is the attitude that the parents take toward the dream experiences as the child reports them. The very early role of the parents in helping the child to distinguish fantasy and reality in relation to nightmares and to master the anxiety contained in them is illustrated by the experience of a twenty-seven-month-old boy whose father took him to the zoo. Two weeks before this outing, the child had developed a viral infection with high fever lasting several days, after which the parents went away for four days. The boy endured the separation uneventfully, but for a week thereafter was unusually fearful. He was afraid to let his mother leave him during the day, had great difficulty sleeping at night, and refused to let his mother leave the room before he went to sleep at night. This was the situation when the trip to the zoo took place.

At the elephant house, the father reached out his hand toward one of the elephants, who obliged him by holding out his trunk to be petted. The child, who had been watching this somewhat apprehensively from a considerable distance, suddenly burst into tears, evidently fearful that something would happen to his father. He was inconsolable and had to be taken home. After this he began to awake each night from terrifying dreams in which he cried out, "Elephant scare you." His mother was forced to awaken him fully, assure him that he need not fear elephants, and show him that there were no elephants in his room. At first, the mother could not leave the child's room after he awoke from a nightmare until she had given him milk and rocked him to sleep. After several nights, he was sufficiently reassured if his parents called out to him from their room when he awoke from frightening dreams; they also provided him with a night light. The nightmares soon ceased altogether. Shortly thereafter, the child developed the habit of talking in his crib for several minutes before going to sleep, as if preparing himself for the night ahead. One night his mother listened outside his door and overheard him muttering, "Elephants scare me. Monkeys scare me." This was followed by a brief period of silence; then, in his mother's tone of voice and using her inflection, he declared, "Oh, come on. Elephants don't scare you." Then he was quiet and went to sleep.

This little boy was able to internalize his mother's reassuring voice and attitude and to make use of the clarification she provided in order to dispel the terror of his nightmares. The compassionate parental intervention enabled him to make these reassurances a part of his own ego functioning and thereby to master the anxiety he experienced in his dreams.

Not all parental intervention following nightmares is so compassionate, skillful, and constructive. A nursery school teacher who worked with disadvantaged children in a large city found that virtually all of her four- and five-year-old pupils reported obvious nightmare experiences as real; many of these children continued to be haunted by their nighttime attackers throughout the day, often requiring that she contend with these distortions during the class [38]. As she interviewed the parents of these children, she found that the child's conflicts corresponded with theirs; alternatively, the child's fear at night revived the parent's fears with such intensity that they themselves had difficulty offering comfort or reality-oriented corrections of the hallucinatory distortions reported by the child. The parent might even confirm the child's apprehensions by treating the nightmare content as a reality. Some parents were so uncomprehending or angered by the child's screaming that they chastised the child for making a disturbance. Other parents employed the hallucinated attakers described by their children to manipulate and control them, threatening that the monsters or ghosts would return in the night if they did not behave. This pathological handling of nightmare content by parents reminds us of the way in which members of primitive cultures treat the events and perceptions of dreams as real and manipulate the situation accordingly (see Chapter 1). However, in these cultures the implications for later development are not so severe because the distortion is a "shared delusion" in which the dreamer may participate in the other supports that the society provides. Furthermore, in these cultures the distorted handling of the dream experience does not reflect a disturbed relationship between the parent and the child. In our society, however, such handling of the dream experience has grave implications for the future ego development of a particular child. The parents have a vital role, not only in comforting the child at night and in allaying fear, but also in aiding the child's cognitive development with respect to dreaming and dream-reality distinctions. As discussed in Chapter 5, the failure to reality-test the nightmare experience, as well as the undermining by the parents of the child's early efforts to establish boundaries between dream and reality, may be of profound importance in predisposing the individual to the later development of psychosis.

The daily environmental realities with which the child must deal constitute another important element affecting the development of the capacity to reality-test or integrate the nightmare experience. If, for example, the child's actual experience is of a world filled with violence in which his parents attack each other or himself or in which he is subjected to frequent losses, abuses, and actual abandonments, the terrifying nightmare-hallucinations may be particularly difficult for the child to distinguish from the experience of his waking life. It may be true that the nightmare images are distorted as a result of the child's conflicts and by the dream process; he may never literally have encountered monsters such as those that populate his dreams; nevertheless, the ego state of helplessness in the dream and the terror experienced in the face of powerful external forces that threaten to destroy or overwhelm him may differ little qualitatively or even quantitatively from his waking experience of outside reality. Furthermore, since these daytime realities, including such violence or threats, constitute the day residues that the child attempts to integrate each night in his dreams, he is additionally burdened by their intensity and threatening qualities. Serious sleep disturbances are commonplace among children who live in a continuously threatening environment. They are awakened by frequent nightmares that overwhelm them, both as a result of the dream's intensity and because of their inability after waking to offset the disturbing quality of dream experiences through reality judgments and by obtaining external comfort. If one adds to all this the previous observation of how parents may foster deficiencies in reality-testing rather than its growth, then one can readily see how the combined effect of all these factors may seriously impede the development of these functions. Although a situation such as this is more common in lower-class families that live more continuously with violence and loss or in an atmosphere of jeopardy and danger affecting the whole family, these same circumstances arise in middle- or upper-class families, as well.

NIGHTMARES: SYMPTOM OR ADAPTATION?

As Fisher et al. have recently pointed out, the nightmare may be regarded as a symptom, a compromise between instinctual wishes or forces and the demands of the ego or superego [29]. Looked at from this point of view, the nightmare becomes a pathological structure, disrupting sleep and terrorizing its helpless victim. Fisher et al. conclude that "if the function of the nightmare is to master traumatic anxiety it cannot be said that it is very efficient," and Fisher observed that several of their subjects had continuous repetitive nightmares for over twenty years. How, then, can the nightmare be regarded as adaptive or as aiding in the mastery of anxiety? Surely, the experience of such intensely disruptive anxiety must be considered a failure of ego functioning, a failure to master anxiety.

Success and failure with respect to ego functioning are not absolute concepts; if they have any value, they must be considered in relation to the task or challenges at hand and the maturity of the ego or in relation to other possible outcomes. Let us consider, for example, the five-year-old child Timmy described in Chapter 4, who developed nightmares when his father went to an overseas war zone. Terrifying dreams in which his father was in grave danger interrupted his sleep about twice each week; if one judges his dreams from the standpoint of their function in preserving sleep—an early hypothesis of Freud that has been seriously questioned in recent years—the nightmares reflect failure. However, this boy was living in a situation of daily fear, which his mother was also experiencing, in which the possibility of the father's death and loss was a continuous threat. Although the boy suffered from nightmares, his functioning in school and in his relationships with others was unimpaired, and he had no unusual fears during the daytime. If the nightmares may be looked upon as limited, circumscribed expressions of intense anxiety occurring specifically under the regressive conditions of sleep, they could hardly be regarded as a "failure." Furthermore, by forcing the child to wake and cry out, they may enable a child to be reunited with his mother in order to allay the anxiety. This particular boy became able to manage the dream anxiety by turning on his own light, and after a time he did not need to call for his mother. In the case of a child whose nightmare becomes a severely disturbing experience or continues during the remainder of the day as a terrifying hallucination, or of an adult who becomes disorganized or psychotic following a nightmare, we are dealing with a different situation, one in which reality-testing and other ego functions continue to be overwhelmed even after waking from the dream. In these situations we find it more difficult to see the nightmare as serving an adaptive or integrative function. Surely, here we may say that the nightmare has "failed" to achieve any adaptive or integrative purpose. Nevertheless, even in these situations we need to ask, for example, what the situation of the dreamer was preceding the dream; how long he had had nightmares before becoming psychotic; what threats to life, losses, or separations he had undergone; what drugs he might have taken; and whether he had a fever. Here again the nightmare may have served as an "attempt" at psychological integration, not in a conscious or purposive way, but in the employment of fundamental mechanisms available to the organism during sleep for the handling of anxiety and conflict. The fact that hallucinations or psychoses eventuates does not, therefore, necessarily mean that the nightmare did not function adaptively. The dream in this instance may reflect the individual's efforts to master anxiety and conflict and represent an intermediate handling of conflict that was unsuccessful and was therefore followed by a psychotic regression.

Freud repeatedly stated his view that the anxiety dream represented a failure of censorship, a threatened breakthrough of instinctual wishes in which the dream content has undergone little distortion. Although this view had been generally accepted by psychoanalysts, there is little evidence to support it. There is actually great variation in the amount of disguise or distortion that occurs in anxiety dreams or nightmares; when distortion is absent, it seems more often to be the threatening force in the outside world that appears undisguised or that appears in combination with a projected impulse of the dreamer, rather than an instinctual wish. In other anxiety dreams there is marked distortion of content, with some nightmares containing bizarre transformations and elaborate disguises; in the case of small children, these dreams demonstrate some of the most precocious examples of symbolic representation. Because nightmares so frequently reflect conflict over primitive destructive impulses, the disguises that occur therein follow the mode of early ego defenses against aggression, especially projection, externalization, and displacement. As we have seen repeatedly in case examples, however, even in the case of violent aggression the subject's own wishes are rarely directly expressed as he falls victim in the nightmare to imaginary external creatures or forces. By definition, there is a failure to contain anxiety in nightmares, but direct expression of libidinal or aggressive wishes is uncommon.

The fact that an individual may have repetitive nightmares throughout his lifetime does not in itself mean that the nightmare fails to master anxiety, for we do not know what the alternative might be. In this situation, the nightmare could serve to compartmentalize a conflict related to highly disturbing unconscious memories, the disruptive potential of which might become evident only during sleep. For example, it is possible that, were it not for the nightmares, the individual might be even more burdened with anxiety during the daytime, perhaps even unable to function effectively. It should be pointed out, however, that stating the possibility that nightmares may serve an adaptive function does not constitute evidence that this is so. To obtain positive evidence that any kind of dream serves adaptation is very difficult, indeed, as will be discussed further.

From a psychological standpoint, it is perhaps more useful theoretically to look upon the nightmare as a kind of end product, reflecting a great variety of other forces, some of which foster adaptation and integration, while others tend to bring about disintegration or disorganization. For any child or adult, dangerous environmental threats, loss and separation, unstable object relations, ego immaturity or disturbances of function, inner hatred and aggression, unassimilable sexual stimulation, certain drugs or fever, and the store of traumatic memories from the past might all operate in the direction of disintegration. At the same time, the availability and stability of other human relationships, the ego defenses of the individual, including the capacity to limit and control the extent of regression, and internalized positive object representations may operate in the direction of integration. Nightmares, as we have seen, arise in the context of environmental threat, the revival of traumatic memories, or the thrust of developmental advance, but the *outcome* of the dream, whether or not it is followed by integration and mastery or disintegration and further regression, depends upon the complex interplay of *all* of the above forces as they interrelate uniquely in any given instance or individual situation. Such an approach does not greatly emphasize the adaptive or integrative potential of the dream itself, which may be a problem of neurophysiology as well as psychology; rather, it would see the dream or nightmare in relation to all the forces that impinge upon the ego and act together to produce the dream and the changes that follow.

This complexity—the great number of determinants of nightmares—may account for the difficulty of anticipating on any given night whether a particular child or adult will have a nightmare or of explaining why some individuals seem to be especially prone to express conflict through nightmares. I have described situations such as loss, separation, certain spontaneous developmental changes, and hospitalization or surgery, which seem regularly to lead to nightmares in children; we have seen examples of characteristic danger situations, such as war, failure, professional advancement or disappointment, and loss of body function, which often precipitate nightmares in adults. However, to which kinds of external situations different individuals will respond is highly idiosyncratic and often difficult to predict. Furthermore, even if we suspect which external situations are likely to be especially threatening, it is difficult to ascertain the multitude of internal factors that must operate in relation to them in order to produce a nightmare. Furthermore, if a given combination seems to have led to a nightmare in one instance, we cannot be certain that the same coexistence of factors will do so in the next. Neither can we explain why similar conflicts may produce nightmares without neurotic symptoms in the daytime for one person, while another equally troubled individual may suffer from phobias or other fears without having nightmares.

"A dream, a nightmare, a madness"—Dostoevsky's phrase describes a hierarchy, possible levels of personality disorganization. In Chapter 5 I had noted how we may think of "ordinary dreaming," nightmares—we might insert here as another "level" repetitive, unusually severe, or disorganizing nightmares—and acute psychoses as functioning on a continuum in the maintenance of personality integration. Perhaps the word "maintain" is inappropriate, implying a more explicit or active functional role for the nightmare than is actually the case. We are on surer ground if we observe that these different levels of organization exist and reserve judgment as to how they are maintained. Many of the same mechanisms, such as distortion, symbolization, externalization, projection, and regression, operate in the dream, nightmares, and psychoses. However, in nightmares ego defenses against disorganizing anxiety begin to fail, projection is employed intensively with respect to destructive aggression, and return to reality after waking is more difficult. In the acute psychosis, externalization and projection continue during the daytime, object relations are severely disturbed, and thinking may become chaotic or confused, while the establishment of reality contact and judgments becomes impaired. The clinical sequence dream–nightmare–disorganizing nightmare–frank psychosis is often observed and frequently occurs in reverse order during recovery.

Lesse studied 1,000 dreams of 130 adult patients with a variety of clinical diagnoses [39]. He found that the degree of terror, violence, and rage in nightmares was one of the best indicators of the overall course of the patient's treatment and his general level of anxiety. As anxiety in dreams mounted, other clinical symptoms appeared, and vice versa. In certain patients, greater amounts of anxiety led to the disorganization of manifest dream content and to the occurrence of hallucinations in the waking state. Lesse regarded hallucinations and other psychotic symptoms as primitive structuring, "the

last of a succession of secondary defense mechanisms to be called into play
—the last line of defense before the ego is completely overwhelmed and
psychic anarchy prevails'' [40]. In Lesse's view, the primary function of
both dreams and hallucinations is as a "secondary defense mechanism against
mounting anxiety,'' with the psychotic symptom serving as a kind of last
effort to maintain integration. My own view has points in common with
Lesse's, although I would see the dream, the nightmare, and the psychosis
more as basic psychic and physiological processes reflecting the state of the
organism as a whole rather than as serving as such active instruments of
adaptation.

NIGHTMARES AND THE PROBLEM OF SURVIVAL

Our point of departure in this consideration of severe anxiety dreams or
nightmares has been the quality, manifest in all such dreams, of danger or
jeopardy, by reason of which the dreamer feels helpless and especially
vulnerable in the face of powerful forces that threaten to destroy him. I have
suggested that this quality of helplessness relates to the sense of powerlessness of his existence—and the possibility that he, like the objects around
him, might disappear or be destroyed—is incorporated into his earliest
dreams and finds expression in nightmares. I have suggested also that this
early ego state is regressively revived in the nightmares of older children and
adults and accounts for the tendency of nightmares in individuals of various
ages or periods of development to resemble one another, not only in the
affective state of terror they possess, but in the threatening content of the
dream images, as well. It is to this matter of danger and survival that I will
devote the concluding paragraphs.

The neurophysiological findings of the past fifteen years in the fields of
sleep and dreaming, especially the discovery that we probably dream for a
considerable portion of the night, have shifted the attention of many workers
in this field, including a number of psychoanalysts, away from the consideration of the meaning of individual dreams toward the study of the functions of
dreaming itself or of the sleep phases with which it is associated. In addition
to this discovery, several other findings have led to considerable theorizing
regarding the importance of the REM periods, with which dreaming is
particularly associated, in promoting central nervous system growth and
development and of REM and non-REM periods in maintaining physiological
and psychic integration. These include (1) the surprising activity of the

central nervous system during REM periods in which limbic-hippocampal and other subcortical and cortical structures are undergoing a high degree of activation and excitability, (2) the discovery that infants spend a particularly high proportion of sleep in the REM state, and (3) the finding that REM deprivation can produce anxiety, instability, illusions, hallucinations, and a variety of other symptoms or evidences of psychic disorganization.

These and related findings have inspired a number of useful theoretical papers concerned with the role of the various sleep phases and of dreaming in maintaining the integrity of the organism, not only during sleep, but throughout the twenty-four-hour sleep-waking cycle. Excellent papers by Breger, by Ephron and Carrington, by Hawkins, and by Meissner present the range of evidence and arguments that support these views [41–44].

The terms *integrity* and *integration* are used in several ways, and it is important to keep these various meanings clear before proceeding further. For example, *integrity* is used to designate intactness of ego function, especially the maintenance of psychic defenses. This is essentially a psychological or psychoanalytical usage. The term is also used in a physiological sense with a meaning close to that of homeostasis. Ephron and Carrington, for example, suggest that the REM period "serves a homeostatic function of periodically restoring 'cortical tonus,' thereby promoting cortical efficiency or a readiness for adaptive responses while sleep is permitted to continue" [45]. It may or may not be possible to correlate this theorizing on a physiological level with concepts derived from psychoanalytic ego psychology. When these same authors, for example, speak later of the "ego reintegrative process in the dreams" that "mobilizes emotional responses and memories and integrates them into images of special meaning for the dreamer" [46], they are pursuing a discourse on an entirely different level. It is important to avoid the pitfalls of shifting too readily from the use of terms such as *adaptation* and *integrity* in their physiological sense to applying them in a psychoanalytic or metapsychological theoretical framework. For example, if the REM state promotes growth and development of cerebral structures in early childhood or maintains cortical activation during sleep when sensory input to CNS structures from outside sources is cut off or greatly reduced, it does not follow that dreams necessarily solve problems or maintain intact ego functioning. Either one of these possibilities or both or neither might be true, depending on additional evidence.

With these cautions in mind, we can turn to the possible functions of nightmares from these two points of view. From the physiological standpoint, the individual who is having a severe nightmare is reacting, like an animal in mortal danger, with bloodcurdling screaming, intense autonomic discharge, rapid heart rate, and rapid, irregular respiration, terminating in arousal [29, 30, 32]. The psychic content that accompanies both these and less severe nightmares is also related to intense and immediate dangers to the dreamer, often with the imminent threat of annihilation. As Broughton and Fisher et al. have pointed out, however, there is as yet no method available for determining whether the terrifying dream occurs in response to a spontaneous physiological arousal phenomenon or to a terrifying thought that has arisen during sleep. Although a primary physiological "arousal response"—one occurring without any particular relationship to preceding mental content— to which the subject then reacts by dream elaboration cannot be ruled out, the analysis of many examples of nightmares in this book has shown that they occur principally in relation to conflicts in the individual's life that he experiences as life-threatening or in which the memories of earlier conflicts involving the danger of annihilation were regressively revived in the sleep situation.

Although the most catastrophic nightmares or night terror attacks seem to occur during non-REM periods, especially the first one of the night, the more common, less severe nightmares usually seem to occur during REM periods. I have suggested earlier (see Chapter 6) that the lesser intensity of anxiety during REM periods may be related to the greater availability and flexibilty of symbol formation, displacement, and other primary process mechanisms for transforming threatening dream content in accordance with the defensive requirements of the sleeping ego and for bringing such content into some degree of equilibrium with earlier memories and conflicts. Conversely, such modification or transformation of dream content seems to be less possible during non-REM periods, which tend to be limited to more literal, less symbolic forms of thinking; this is true, whether this content is a direct representation of an immediately threatening event in the individual's life, as in Levitan's case described on page 354, or is heavily influenced by earlier traumatic memories.

In both non-REM and REM nightmares, the dreamer experiences himself as being in situations of grave danger; waking and arousal occur from both states in order to avoid these perils. Thus, the nightmare is manifestly concerned with danger; in the case of most children and many adults follow- ing the experience, the reestablishment of contact with a protective person indicates that a critical function of awakening from the nightmare is to ensure survival and safety. I have tried to show that the deeper latent or unconscious content of nightmares is also involved with conflicts and fears concerning destructive aggression, sexuality that is linked with annihilation, devouring, and being devoured, and loss of the protecting, or need-satisfying object, in all of which the survival of the individual himself is at stake. Although the immediate precipitating stress for a nightmare may relate to a problem at a more mature developmental level, the various forms of regression that accompany sleep result in the revival of these earlier infantile conflicts, accounting for the similarities of nightmares at various ages.

In the sleep situation the dreamer, cut off from reality and unable to distinguish between real and imaginary attackers, seems to revert to self-preservative mechanisms similar to those that would be brought to bear were the subject in an objective danger situation. Arousal, reestablishment of motility, action and even preparation for counterattack, flight, and turning to a mothering person for protection are among the self-preservative mechanisms that occur in association with nightmares.

In recent years interest has been growing in the possible functions of the various sleep phases in maintaining psychic vigilance during sleep, in alerting the organism to possible dangers in the environment, or in mobilizing orienting mechanisms or impulses that might enhance survival [42, 47, 48]. These mechanisms may be grounded in the phylogeny of mammalian species that must ensure some protection, even while asleep, from predators and other possible dangers in the environment. In nightmares, the dreamer reacts to dangers, the origin of which may be in large part internal or at least the result of the interplay of external and internal factors. However, he reacts entirely as if he were confronted with an external danger. Such a reaction may be influenced by phylogenetically transmitted mechanisms that originally had the function of aterting and protecting the organism from real external danger. In the nightmare such mechanisms may be exaggeratedly or even unnecessarily triggered by minimal environmental threats recalled in the sleep situation or by disturbing impulses arising internally; these may be mistaken for external threats, particularly when given visual, externalized representation through the processes that lead to the formation of dream images. In this way the nightmare may not only be made up of memories and other aspects of mental functioning that originated in early childhood, but may be linked with neurophysiological mechanisms subserving self-preservation and sur-

vival that are phylogenetically older than those that are the exclusive possession of the human species.

REFERENCES

1. Dostoevsky, F. *The Idiot.* (Trans. by Constance Garnett.) New York: Bantam Books, 1963. Pp. 438–439.
2. Freud, S. Some Additional Notes on Dream-Interpretation as a Whole (1925). In *The Standard Edition of the Complete Psychological Works of Sigmund Freud,* tr. and ed. by J. Strachey with others. London: Hogarth and the Institute of Psycho-analysis, 1961. Vol. XIX, p. 135.
3. Benjamin, J. D. Some developmental observations relating to the theory of anxiety. *J. Amer. Psychoanal. Ass.* 9:652–668, 1961.
4. Brenner, C. An addendum to Freud's theory of anxiety. *Int. J. Psychoanal.* 34:18–24. 1953.
5. Schafer, R. Contributions of longitudinal studies to psychoanalytic theory. Panel report. *J. Amer. Psychoanal. Ass.* 13:605–618, 1965.
6. Spitz, R. Anxiety in infancy: A study of its manifestations in the first year of life. *Int. J. Psychoanal.* 31:138–143, 1950.
7. Fraiberg, S. *The Magic Years.* New York: Scribner, 1959.
8. Mack, J. E. Nightmares, conflict and ego development in childhood. *Int. J. Psychoanal.* 46:403–428, 1965.
9. Freud, A. *The Ego and the Mechanisms of Defense.* New York: International Universities Press, 1946.
10. Waelder, R. *Basic Theory of Psychoanalysis.* New York: International Universities Press, 1960.
11. Rangell, L. A further attempt to resolve the "Problem of Anxiety." *J. Amer. Psychoanal. Ass.* 16:371–404, 1968.
12. Kanzer, M. The communicative function of the dream, *Int. J. Psychoanal.* 36:260–266, 1955.
13. Furst. S. S. *Psychic Trauma.* New York: Basic Books, 1967.
14. Greenacre, P. The Influence of Infantile Trauma on Genetic Patterns. In Furst, S. S. (Ed.), *Psychic Trauma.* New York: Basic Books, 1967.
15. Crile, C. W. *A Mechanistic View of War and Peace.* New York: Macmillan, 1915. P. 27.
16. Freud, S. Inhibitions, Symptoms and Anxiety (1926 [1925]). *Standard Edition.* 1959. Vol. XX, p. 93.
17. Sandler, J. Trauma Strain and Development. In Furst, S. S. (Ed.), *Psychic Trauma.* New York: Basic Books, 1967.
18. Levitan, H. I. A traumatic dream. *Psychoanal. Quant.* 34:265–267, 1965.
19. Lidz, T. Nightmares and the combat neuroses. *Psychiatry* 9:37–49, 1946.
20. Freud, S. Introduction to Psychoanalysis and the War Neuroses (1919). *Standard Edition.* 1955. Vol. XVII, pp. 207–210.
21. Jones, E. War Shock and Freud's Theory of the Neuroses. In Ferenczi, S., Abraham, K., Simmel E., and Jones E., *Psychoanalysis and the War Neuroses.* London: International Psychoanalytical Press, 1921. Pp. 44–59.
22. Freud. S. Beyond the Pleasure Principle (1920). *Standard Edition.* 1955. Vol. XVIII, p. 32.

23. Simmel E. In Ferenczi, S., Abraham, K., Simmel E., and Jones E., *Psychoanalysis and the War Neuroses*. London: International Psychoanalytical Press, 1921. Pp. 30–43.

24. Ibid. P. 32.

25. Dahl, H. Psychoanalytic theory of the instinctual drives in relation to recent developments. Panel report. *J. Amer. Psychoanal. Ass.* 16:613–637, 1968.

26. Holt, R. H. On the Insufficiency of Drive as a Motivational Concept, in the Light of Evidence from Experimental Psychology. Paper presented at the meetings of the American Psychoanalytic Assn., Dec. 15, 1967.

27. Stern, M. Pavor nocturnus, *Int. J. Psychoanal.* 32:302–309, 1951.

28. Hadfield, J. A. *Dreams and Nightmares*. Baltimore, Md.: Penguin Books, 1954.

29. Fisher, C., Byrne, J., and Edwards, A. REM and NREM Nightmares and their Interrelationships. Lecture delivered to the Department of Psychiatry, The Mount Sinai Hospital, New York, April 10, 1968.

30. Broughton, R. Sleep disorders: Disorders or Arousal? *Science* 159:1070–1078, 1968.

31. Karacan, I., Goodenough, D. R., Shapiro, A., and Starker, S. Erection cycle during sleep in relation to dream anxiety. *Arch. Gen. Psychiat.* (Chicago) 15:183–189, 1966.

32. Gastant, H., and Broughton. R. A Clinical and Polygraphic Study of Episodic Phenomena During Sleep. In Wortis, J. (Ed.), *Recent Advances in Biological Psychiatry*. New York: Plenum Press, 1965. Vol. VII, pp. 197–221.

33. Macnish, R. *The Philosophy of Sleep*. New York: Appleton, 1834.

34. James W. *The Principles of Psychology*. New York: Holt, 1890. Vol. II, pp. 415–416.

35. Benjamin, J. O. Some developmental observations relating to the theory of anxiety. *J. Amer. Psychoanal. Assn.* 9:662, 1961.

36. Kris, E. Data in psychoanalytic perspective on the mother-child relationship. *Psychoanal. Stud. Child.* 17:175–215, 1962.

37. Mack, J. E. Nightmares, conflict and ego development in childhood. *Int. J. Psychoanal.* 46:425, 1965.

38. Berman, D. Personal communication, March 1969.

39. Lesse S. Experimental studies on the relationship between anxiety, dreams and dream-like states. *Amer. J. Psychother.* 13:440–455, 1959.

40. Ibid. P. 451.

41. Breger, L. Function of dreams. *J. Abnor. Soc. Psychol.* 72:1–28, 1967.

42. Ephron, H. S., and Carrington, P. Ego Functioning in Rapid Eye Movement Sleep: Implications for Dream Theory. In Masserman, J. (Ed.), *Science and Psychoanalysis*. New York: Grune & Stratton, 1967. Vol. XI, pp. 75–102.

43. Hawkins, D. R. A review of psychoanalytic dream theory in the light of recent psychophysiological studies of sleep and dreaming. *Brit. J. Med. Psychol.* 39:85–104, 1966.

44. Meissner, W. Dreaming as process. *Int. J. Psychoanal.* 49:63–79, 1968.

45. Ephron, H. S., and Carrington, P. Ego Functioning in Rapid Eye Movement Sleep: Implications for Dream Theory. In Masserman J. (Ed.), *Science and Psychoanalysis*. New York: Grune & Stratton, 1967, Vol. XI, p. 79.

46. Ibid. P. 89.

47. Ullman, M. Dreaming, altered states of consciousness and the problem of vigilance. *J. Nerv. Ment. Dis.* 133:529–535, 1961.

48. Snyder, F. Toward an evolutionary theory of dreaming. *Amer. J. Psychiat.* 123:121–142, 1966.

17. Nightmares and Boundaries in the Mind

Ernest Hartmann

In the previous chapters, I suggested that artists, on the one hand, and schizophrenics, on the other, have thin boundaries and that persons with frequent nightmares can be characterized as persons having unusually thin boundaries in a number of senses. In this chapter, I shall discuss in more detail what I mean by boundaries in the mind, and the ways thin boundaries are found in people with nightmares; I shall investigate what insights we can gain into boundaries in general from the data acquired from studies of persons with nightmares.

The formation of boundaries is part of a child's development of mental structures. Partly as a simple matter of neurological maturation and partly as a result of interaction with the environment, a child learns to distinguish between himself and others, between fantasy and reality, between dreaming and waking, between men and women and so on. Each of these distinctions implies mental realms with boundaries around them. Boundaries of many kinds are built up and all of them can vary from very "thin," "fluid," or "permeable," to "thick," "solid," or "rigid." In every sense, as we shall see, people with frequent nightmares appear to me to have "thin" or "permeable" boundaries.

I am using the term "boundary" in a very inclusive form. I include straightforward boundaries such as those between sleeping and waking. But I also mean to include among others the *Reitzschutz* (or boundary protection against irritation) described by Freud (1920), the conceptual boundaries discussed by Eugen Bleuler (1950), the topological boundaries around the self of Kurt Lewin (1936), ego boundaries discussed by many psychoanalysts such as Paul Federn (1952a, 1952b) and more recently by Bernard Landis

Reprinted by permission of Basic Books, Inc., Publishers, New York, from *The Nightmare: The Psychology and Biology of Terrifying Dreams*, by Ernest Hartmann. Copyright ©1984 by Ernest Hartmann.

(1970), heavy boundaries called "character armor" described by Wilhelm Reich (1933), and the "boundary-related" measures derived from projective tests—usually Rorschach responses involving contaminations, confabulation, and fabulized combination (Zucker 1958, Jortner 1966, Blatt and Ritzler 1974, Blatt et al. 1976). My assumption is that these many uses of the term boundary are not simply unrelated analogies but that there is an important structural-developmental concept underlying the term's many uses. Obviously, we do not yet know much about such an underlying basic boundary structure. The present discussion is a preliminary exploration, undertaken because empirical data, such as that persons reporting frequent nightmares appeared to have problems touching on *all* these types of boundaries, pointed to the legitimacy of a search for a basic boundary structure embracing diverse types of mental demarcations.

TYPES OF BOUNDARIES

The term boundary has been used in a variety of ways (see table 17.1). Clearly, many boundaries are interrelated and some could be called subtypes of others. I have not attempted a complete systematic classification but I have listed the types separately to emphasize their great number, their diversity, and their ubiquity in our lives.

Waking versus Sleep

This is one of the simpler uses of the term since we tend to divide our lives into waking versus sleep, and there is for most of us a clear boundary between them; we are either in one state or the other. However, for the nightmare subjects, boundaries are less firm even in this simple sense. Many of us sometimes spend a few seconds or even minutes not quite certain if we are awake, but among the nightmare subjects, this indeterminate period often lasted half an hour or an hour, or longer. Especially after a vivid dream, not necessarily a nightmare, they were often unsure whether they were awake or asleep for a considerable amount of time.

Waking versus Dreaming

Most people wake up from a dream and know they are clearly awake. The nightmare subjects—more than half of them—report sometimes waking

Table 17.1
Some Major Types of Boundaries

Waking versus Sleep
Waking versus Dreaming
Waking Reality versus Dream Reality
Fantasy versus Reality: Daydreams
Play versus Reality
Interpersonal boundaries
• open versus closed
• sharing versus not sharing
• unguarded versus guarded
• topological boundaries
Territorial Boundaries
• group, community, nation
Sexual Identity
Sexual Preference
Adult versus Child
Human versus Animal
Animate versus Inanimate
Body Surface
Self in the World
Memory
• familiar versus unfamiliar
• primal repression
Physical Dimensions
• size constancy
Temporality (Sense of Time)
Ego Boundaries (Ego versus Id)
Defense Mechanisms
• isolation
• character armor
Ordinary Sensory versus Extrasensory Experience

---

from a dream into another dream. They are having a dream—perhaps a nightmare; they wake up; or rather they have the experience of waking up, apparently getting out of bed, doing something else, and then notice that they are still in a dream and that they have to wake up again. In other words, they have dreams within dreams.

Waking Reality versus Dream Reality

Many people do not remember dreams clearly and remember them as a bit vague, indistinct, and different from waking perception. Even those who dream clearly and consider them important nonetheless place a kind of boundary around them—"It was powerful, but it was just a dream." Dreams are kept separate from waking reality, and there is an emphasis made of their difference from waking reality. The nightmare subjects in many cases describe all their dreams, not just their nightmares, as "extremely real," "just as real as waking."

Fantasy versus Reality: Daydreams

Most people have daydreams to a varying extent, but these are usually very much under the person's control. Frequently our daydreams are simple, undisguised wish fulfillments—we're rich, we're famous, we're making love to our favorite movie stars. We daydream of things the way we would like them to be, but we are aware it's "only a daydream." The nightmare subjects, much more than most of us, get lost and caught up in their daydreams to such a degree that sometimes they are not sure whether the daydreams are real or not. And related to this, the daydreams sometimes run away with them, go out of control and turn into "daymares." When I asked the ordinary dreamers or vivid dreamers whether they had "daymares," they said without exception either, "no" or more frequently "I don't know what you mean." The nightmare sufferers always knew what I meant and some of them described vivid "daymares."

Play versus Reality

Children differ a great deal in the degree to which they get caught up in play, lose themselves in play, and have trouble coming out of it into ordinary reality. Among adults, too, some completely "lose themselves" in a book or a piece of music much more than others. The subjects with frequent nightmares were definitely at the high end of the continuum on this measure of "losing oneself in play" and had been that way as children, too. This characteristic or ability is obviously found in other groups, especially creative people.

Interpersonal Boundaries

We differ greatly in the extent to which we are willing to open up, share with others, share secrets with friends, fall in love, and, in general, let others into our lives. The nightmare sufferers were extremely open and tended to let others in and to merge with others very easily. This was clear in their relationships where often they rapidly became intimate and very involved and sometimes found themselves enmeshed in disturbing relationships from which they had problems extricating themselves.

In interviews, the nightmare subjects were unusually open and unguarded in many senses. What I mean is this: a patient in psychoanalysis is specifically asked to say whatever comes to mind and is highly motivated to do so, or to try his best. Even under these conditions, this is not an easy task. It often takes patients a long time to be willing to share shameful secrets— material consciously suppressed—not to mention material that is not accessible to the patient because it is repressed by various unconscious mechanisms. A subject volunteering for a research study is in a very different position. He expects to be asked questions and, generally speaking, is prepared to answer honestly. At the same time, most subjects maintain a certain guardedness. Their position is, "All right, I'm in this study; I'm interested; I'm helping science; maybe I'll learn something about myself; I'm being paid for it; I want to cooperate and I'll try to answer questions; however, I am certainly not going to bare every dark secret, and I am not going to volunteer really painful or embarrassing information unless it is specifically asked for, or it seems essential." The subjects with nightmares were extreme in that most of them did not maintain this guardedness. Within five or ten minutes into an interview, they were telling me intimate family problems, sexual problems, interpersonal problems. They pulled skeletons out of the closet in answering open-ended questions such as "What was your childhood like?" or "What important things have happened to you in the last few years?" There were a few exceptions that occurred among the two or three subjects who had paranoid features; but in these, I felt a tendency to openness, too—they would begin to open up and share a lot, and then become suspicious and "clam up." Those were the ones who had learned that it can be painful or dangerous to be too open or trusting; they suddenly and somewhat clumsily erected a wall. There was not the usual sense of modulated defense or guardedness, gradually decreasing as an interview progresses. These interpersonal boundaries form much of what Kurt Lewin (1936) meant by "topological boundaries" around the self.

Another related aspect is the boundary around one's family, a group of friends, one's now neighborhood group or ethnic group. Without thinking about it, most of us tend to share information and to be open with certain people, to be less open with others, to be much more guarded with strangers. The nightmare sufferers made little use of this sort of group boundary. They seldom saw themselves as firmly part of a group; they were "liberal" with their friendship and made little distinction between members of their group or neighborhood and others. The nightmare sufferers were not people who placed great emphasis on their being part of an ethnic or national group.

Territorial Boundaries ("Turf")

Most people who live in urban settings know that there are certain areas where they can feel safe and walk freely and other places where they have to be careful. There are places where they tend not to go at all, or to be very much on their guard if they do find themselves there. Again, the nightmare subjects did not have this sense of territorial boundary. They were overly trusting; they walked alone in parts of town where most others would fear to tread; they did not "put up their guard" when in potentially dangerous territory. This characteristic may help account for the high incidences of muggings and rapes reported by the nightmare sufferer group.

Sexual Identity

Some people have an extremely firm or rigid sense of themselves as male or female: "Men do things this way. Women do things that way. I am a man and I do things the man's way." Others are much more inclined to think of themselves as a mixture of masculine and feminine. The nightmare subjects were clearly in the latter group. Among the many men with nightmares I have interviewed, there was not a single one who came anywhere near the typical macho male image. Among the women there were none who adopted the stereotyped feminine role. Several women in the nightmare group reported they often had dreams in which they were men; this did not occur in the other groups.

Sexual Preference

Most people draw a very firm boundary line around their sexual preferences. They are heterosexual and do not allow themselves the least hint of homosexual behavior or even homosexual fantasy or thought. Some homosexuals are equally strict about their preference. The nightmare subjects were much less strict. A few were actively homosexual, most were heterosexual, but several had had sexual relations with both sexes and most experienced fantasies or thoughts about sexual relations with both sexes.

Adult versus Child

Some persons maintain this kind of boundary with great rigidity. "I was a child. Now I am grown up. Certain things are appropriate for children. other things are appropriate for adults, and that's it." Again, there is a great variation in the extent to which people maintain this "generational" boundary, but the nightmare sufferers were definitely on the side of fluid boundaries. Many of them, although young adults, thought of themselves in some ways as children. They spoke with pride of not having lost their childhood wonder and naiveté, which they felt most adults had lost. Several were acutely aware of the loss of wonder and magic involved in no longer being a child and seemed to be fighting against it. Their statements about childhood were paraphrases of Wordsworth's "Intimations of Immortality." [1] Two who were teachers felt that an especially important part of their job was to maintain in their pupils a childhood wonder and excitement about the world

1. Especially stanzas 1 and 2:

1
There was a time when meadow, grove, and stream,
The earth, and every common sight
To me did seem
Apparelled in celestial light,
The glory and the freshness of a dream.
It is not now as it hath been of yore;—
Turn wheresoe'er I may,
By night or day,
The things which I have seen I now can see no more.

2
The Rainbow comes and goes,
And lovely is the Rose,
The Moon doth with delight
Look round her when the heavens are bare,
Waters on a starry night
Are beautiful and fair;
The sunshine is a glorious birth;
But yet I know, where'er I go,
That there hath past away a glory from the earth.

and not allow them to be pigeonholed or their feelings to be blunted by society.

Human versus Animal and Animate versus Inanimate

Most people maintain very strict boundaries between these categories. Again, the nightmare subjects seemed to be more flexible or loose in this way, at least in their dreams and fantasies. Several reported dreams in which they were dogs or other animals. One reported a dream in which she was a butterfly; one reported being a leaf floating in the wind. These sorts of images sometimes occurred in their daydreams as well. Most people may be capable of this sort of fantasy; for instance, creative writing teachers (who presumably can do it themselves) sometimes assign themes in which the student is supposed to imagine himself to be a dog or a butterfly. For many people this is not an easy task and for some with rigid boundaries the task may be impossible. The nightmare subjects have no trouble with such an assignment; they find it easy and enjoyable.

Body Surface

Most of us think of our bodies as a whole. In our dreams and daydreams, as well as in our thoughts, our bodies are intact. The body surface—our skin—is an important boundary. For many it is not only painful but actually difficult to imagine their body torn, or to imagine isolated fragments of a body. The nightmare sufferers in their nightmares, in their other dreams, in their daydreams, and in Rorschach tests, saw their own bodies and other bodies as torn, broken, or penetrated. A frequent nightmare theme involved being cut, or stabbed, or something of the kind. Pieces of flesh, or whole arms, legs, and lips were described as cut off. The Rorschach responses which led to the high "boundary deficit" scores (chapter 4) are responses involving thin or torn clothing, torn skin, stab wounds, etc.

Self in the World

Along related lines, there is the background sense most people have of being a solid self in a solid world. This sense was less firm in the nightmare subjects, who experienced episodes of depersonalization—not quite feeling themselves, not knowing who they were, not feeling their body was their own—and derealization—not being sure the world was real, not feeling it was solid. Again, there was a continuum; many people have such experiences occasionally, especially with the assistance of alcohol or marijuana, but many of the nightmare subjects appeared to have these experiences relatively often and without chemical help.

Memory

Most of us maintain a more or less clear boundary around our memories. We make our way through the world dividing it smoothly into familiar places— "Yes, I've been here before"—and unfamiliar, new places; likewise, people we know and people we don't know, familiar and unfamiliar faces. Once in a long while, we are struck by an odd experience such as *déjà vu,* in which we feel certain we have been here before, although we know we haven't; or *jamais vu,* in which a place we knew well suddenly seems unfamiliar. The nightmare subjects had frequently episodes of *déjà vu* and *jamais vu.* For some of them, these experiences were not just isolated instances; they did not appear to have the usual reassuring division of the world into "familiar" and "unfamiliar."

There is another kind of memory boundary. The average person remembers almost nothing of the first three or four years of his or her life and only isolated bits and pieces of the subsequent two or three years. Freud suggested an active repression of early material, and called it "primal repression." Others explain the same facts by suggesting that early memories are not stored, or stored in poorly retrievable ways by an immature nervous system. In any case, there is a boundary between this childhood period of no memory or isolated memory and the later period of clear and connected memory. In some persons this forgetting or repression is especially massive and they can remember nothing of their first eight or ten years. The nightmare sufferers were at the other extreme: they remembered a great deal from before the age of three, sometimes even from before the age of two.

Physical Dimensions

Most people without really thinking about it keep things in their proper size. Our bodies are a certain size; our houses are a certain size; objects and people generally maintain their size even in our fantasies and dreams, though there are occasional exceptions. However, again, the nightmare subjects shifted sizes more; they reported many dreams and daydreams in which objects, people, faces became larger and smaller and their own bodies lengthened and shortened. This is somewhat similar to what often occurs in an LSD experience.

I have heard dream reports from quite a few patients and others involving faces that become larger or frightening; usually, there were no associations to recent events. I suspect that these images may have been related to very early memories of being a child, perhaps still in the crib, and having an adult face suddenly come close. This sort of report was found to a varying degree among many persons, but was especially frequent among the nightmare subjects.

Temporality (Sense of Time)

Everyone organizes his life in time, but there are great differences in the degree of rigidity versus flexibility. Some maintain a rigid schedule throughout their day; some have a definite exact sense of how long any given task should take. Others, including the nightmare subjects, are looser or more casual about time. This was especially striking in the interviews. Most subjects, when asked a specific question such as, "How long do you usually sleep?" gave an answer lasting only a few seconds. When asked an open-ended question such as: "What were things like in high school?" gave a longer answer lasting perhaps up to two minutes; they had a sense of social time limits. The nightmare subjects did not have such boundaries—they frequently went on for five or ten minutes or more answering a single question. Also, in terms of longer epochs of time, the nightmare subjects did not tend to put their plans in terms of specific time frames. Thus, they hardly ever said, "I am planning to go to graduate school for the next two years and then I'll take a job in such and such a field for the next year or two."

Ego Boundaries (Ego versus Id)

Ego boundaries[2] are thinner in nightmare sufferers. Most people have quite firm boundaries between their ego and their id—the impersonal, often rejected "It" consisting of those forces, impulses, desires which they do not

2. I refer here to ego boundaries in the narrow sense, between ego and id. The term ego boundaries is sometimes enlarged to include many of the other boundaries discussed. See, for instance, Landis (1970).

really acknowledge as being part of themselves. Usually, the sexual and aggressive wishes of the id are kept out of awareness or are dimly, indirectly perceived. In fact, in a typical psychoanalysis of a neurotic patient, the patient's ego boundaries are often seen as too tight or too rigid; during a successful analysis the boundaries of the ego loosen and expand so that more and more of the dangerous id material is eventually taken in by the ego. "Where id was, ego shall be" (Freud 1939). This neurotic problem clearly was not the problem of the nightmare sufferers. On the contrary, they were very aware of id impulses; they seemed to either accept them or sometimes used primitive coping mechanisms such as projection, attributing their feelings or wishes to someone else.

Defense Mechanisms

I have already mentioned repression. Some of the other well-known mechanisms of defense can also be seen in terms of boundaries—for instance, the mechanism of isolation. Basically, isolation consists of not allowing a thought and its associated emotion to come into consciousness at the same time. Some people are very adept at thinking about something disturbing, but protecting themselves by keeping the emotion out of consciousness. A very obsessional person who likes to keep things pigeonholed (bounded) and not let anything get out of hand often employs the mechanism of isolation. Again, the nightmare subjects tended *not* to do this. In fact, in many senses, the nightmare subjects had characteristics opposite to those of the obsessional character.

Related to this is the heavy boundary known as character armor (Reich 1933). This implies a use of some characteristic pattern of behavior and defense in a solid, constant manner that prevents any change or any influence from outside. I was struck by how little such defense or armor the nightmare subjects had. Again, there is a continuum; but with a few exceptions (those with paranoid features), the nightmare subjects were among those who did not armor themselves against the world.

Ordinary Sensory versus Extrasensory Experience

Almost half of the nightmare sufferers interviewed reported some unusual or paranormal experiences such as telepathy, out-of-the-body experiences, clairvoyance, or precognition. Again, many persons who are not frequent nightmare sufferers have some such experiences. In our study the nightmare sufferers had these experiences much more frequently and dramatically, although several of the twenty-four vivid dreamers and ordinary dreamers also reported such experiences. However, the nightmare sufferers were not firm believers in the occult. None that I spoke to felt absolutely convinced that he or she had special powers; none had put on shows or demonstrations or tried to make use of such powers commercially. Usually, they took a noncommittal attitude—they believed they were different and more sensitive than most people, and they more-or-less believed in extrasensory phenomena. Some believed that there are unknown energies and influences around and that they were just a bit more sensitive than most people to such "influences." However they were not certain; and some had a very reasonable scientific scepticism about their experiences.

This is an intriguing area that deserves further investigation, but is almost impossible to study. The most parsimonious explanation is that the nightmare sufferers are sensitive in many ways, often have vivid imaginations, and are not too concerned with boundaries of reality. Thus they may interpret some of their vivid memories or daydreams, or feelings of depersonalization, as extra-sensory or parapsychological. On the other hand, it is possible that forces or forms of energy exist that science does not yet fully understand. For that matter, there are well-understood forces for which we have no recognized sensory receptors; for instance, we live in a network of magnetic fields including the earth's but apparently are unable to sense these fields. Yet recently some animals have been shown to have a kind of receptor for magnetic fields and to be able to use the information in guiding their travels. It is conceivable that humans have some form of rudimentary receptors for such forces or others, and there might be great variation in the degree to which people have any awareness of such dim sensations. If so, it might not be surprising that the nightmare sufferers who are sensitive in so many other ways might also be sensitive to such unusual sensations and be more aware of them than most.

Under either assumption, we are dealing with an aspect of thin or permeable boundaries. If the phenomena are nothing other than ordinary psychological ones, the nightmare subjects demonstrate poor reality testing—indistinct boundaries between what is coming from inside themselves and from outside. Alternatively, if there are indeed forces or receptors yet to be understood, these persons have a thin boundary or thin skin in a very interesting new sense.

BOUNDARIES IN SCHIZOPHRENIA AND OTHER CONDITIONS

The list of boundaries just summarized is not complete, and the types of boundaries have not been organized and classified in a systematic manner. Rather, the list is meant primarily to emphasize the multiplicity of boundaries in the mind and the fact that the nightmare sufferers appear to have thin boundaries in all the categories we considered. It is important to note, however, that thin boundaries are not unique to our group. A number of the aspects of thin boundaries we have discussed can be found in schizophrenic patients. Indeed, boundary disturbances may be an important aspect of the pathology of schizophrenia especially as they relate to problems in ego boundaries and boundaries between fantasy and reality. Bleuler (1950) and others were especially struck by differences in concept boundaries, leading to studies of overinclusiveness—including too many items within a given conceptual category (see, for instance, Cameron and Margaret 1951; Chapman 1961). David Shakow's (1963) well-known formulation of the cognitive problem in schizophrenia as "inability to maintain a major segmental set" is a boundary concept; Harold Searles (1960) emphasized the schizophrenic's problem with the boundaries between human and nonhuman, and between animate and inanimate. In some schizophrenics the boundary problems are prominent features, in others less so. There is no question but that we can find evidence of thin or permeable boundaries in many patients with schizophrenia, but often the boundary problems are not so apparent because there is so much flagrant symptomatology. In the nightmare subjects, who are not psychotic, we were looking at boundary problems without being distracted by other associated problems and issues.

Is this thin boundary condition found also in persons with a variety of psychiatric illnesses, or persons with sleep problems other than nightmares? Clinical experience and research studies of depressed patients, anxious patients, patients with insomnia, narcolepsy, sleepwalking, or night terrors do not reveal, in any of them, the boundary problems or the personality characteristics of the frequent nightmare group. For instance, patients with various kinds of insomnia have been studied in some detail in my laboratory and others. It turns out that there are many medical causes for insomnia; some insomniacs have painful medical or surgical conditions; some have sleep apnea, nocturnal myoclonus, or other sleep-related illnesses.[3] But even among those who do not have clear medical reasons for their insomnia—those who have "psychophysiological" types of insomnia—MMPI profiles and other test results are quite different from those of the nightmare sufferers (Coursey 1975; Kales et al. 1976; Beutler, Thornby, and Karacan 1978). Insomniacs tend to have elevations in depression, hypochondriasis, and hysteria on the MMPI—the so-called neurotic scales—more than on the psychotic scales that are elevated in the nightmare subjects. Also, my hundreds of interviews with such patients do not reveal the thin-boundary characteristics of the nightmare sufferers.

As we said before, night terrors are severe, and sometimes extremely disturbing phenomena and had previously been thought of as being simply worse forms of nightmares. However, I have studied many subjects with severe night terrors in pure culture and their MMPI profiles do not show the elevated psychotic scales of the nightmare subjects (Hartmann, Greenwald, and Brune 1982); most had quite normal profiles (table 17.2). In fact, the two patients with the most severe night terror conditions I have seen—one of them caused several deaths during a night terror episode—were totally different from the nightmare sufferers. Neither of these men had any of the aspects of thin boundaries we have listed. Both were solid citizens with no hint of schizophrenia or artistic tendencies. Both were somewhat rigid, obsessional, and well defended; in most senses discussed, they were characterized by very thick boundaries. These are obviously very different people from the nightmare sufferers.

Scanning MMPI profiles of groups with a wide variety of medical and psychiatric illnesses and problems (Lanyon 1968) leads to the same conclusion: there are no groups with mean profiles similar to those of nightmare sufferers except for a few patient groups with schizophrenic and related conditions, and possibly groups of artists. Individual patients who do have similar profiles are usually schizophrenic patients or persons who may be diagnosed as "schizoid," "schizotypal," or "borderline." These are individuals who may be considered vulnerable to schizophrenia. I believe there is a true relationship between these groups and the nightmare sufferers; and that persons with frequent nightmares form part of the population of persons vulnerable to schizophrenia. Conversely, we have noted that persons who

3. Sleep apnea refers to a serious condition in which breathing (air flow) ceases numerous times each night. Nocturnal myoclonus is a condition characterized by frequent muscle jerks during sleep.

Table 17.2
MMPI Scores in Night Terror Sufferers
Compared to Nightmare Sufferers

	MMPI T-scores (mean values)											
	L	F	K	Hs	D	Hy	Pd	Pa	Pt	Sc	Ma	Si
Night Terrors												
Males												
N = 7	48	58	53	59	56	59	67	58	64	63	69	52
Females												
N = 11	49	55	58	54	51	58	59	60	53	57	55	48
All Subjects												
N = 18	48	56	56	56	53	58	62	59	57	59	60	49
Nightmares												
Male and												
Female												
N = 12	46	73	48	57	63	60	72	70	69	77	74	52

NOTE: The MMPI scales are as described in chapter 4. T-scores refer to standardized scores such that for each scale the population mean is 50 and the standard deviation is 10. Thus, a score of 70 is two standard deviations above the mean.

have demonstrated such a vulnerability by actually becoming schizophrenic have a history of nightmares far more commonly than has been thought.

DEVELOPMENT OF THIN BOUNDARIES

If thin boundaries are a basic structural characteristic in persons with frequent nightmares, it is crucial to our understanding of nightmares to know how these thin boundaries come about. Since nightmares are already present in childhood, we are not dealing with boundaries somehow being torn by a traumatic event in adolescence or adulthood: obviously, the condition (of thin boundaries) started very early. As I said earlier, we failed to find evidence of obvious traumatic events in early life. We even asked about traumatic births or obstetrical complications without finding anything striking. Yet, the possibility of undetected perinatal trauma or even intrauterine trauma cannot be completely ruled out. On the basis of the data we have discussed, I suggest that a predisposition to thin boundaries may well be present from birth, perhaps on a genetic basis.

Persons with this biological predisposition can be seen as having a vulnerability to later developing schizophrenia, developing in an artistic direction if they have appropriate talents, having frequent nightmares, or various combinations of these tendencies. Environmental factors probably determine the path followed, and presumably particular environmental factors may induce longterm frequent nightmares in some children with thin-boundary conditions. If there is such an environmental component, I suspect from data on a few subjects that it may be related to a lack of support by the mother in the first two years of life. In a few cases, though there was no clear trauma, the mother was definitely depressed and unavailable to the child; in others, although the mother was not obviously depressed or physically unavailable, the child was not given support and encouragement to master age-appropriate tasks and to overcome the fears and terrors associated with early development. In some the birth of a younger sibling at age one to two, accompanied by the relative unavailability of the mother for a time, appeared to be especially traumatic and they later developed lifelong nightmares. In all these situations the child was left alone with his or her impulses and fears, with insufficient support, or insufficient amounts of what Gerald Adler and Daniel Buie (1979) have called "soothing."

If persons with frequent nightmares are born with a genetic/biologic tendency to thin boundaries, perhaps compounded by lack of early support, how does this thin-boundary condition affect their development? The tendency to form thin boundaries probably has a pervasive effect: they may form less firm ego boundaries, less solid boundaries around their feeling of self, and less firm interpersonal boundaries among others. These people are painfully sensitive to, and in danger from, their own wishes and impulses as well as demands or threats from the world outside. Indeed, the childhood histories obtained from the nightmare sufferers are those of persons who were always unusually sensitive, unusually open and vulnerable, and thus to some extent felt different from others. They often have had a painful and sometimes lonely childhood followed by a stormy and difficult adolescence. As they became adults, some of them—and this is more true of women—were able to maintain the openness inherent in a thin-boundary condition and were able to apply it in their work as artists, teachers, or therapists, but it was a difficult state to maintain and they were sometimes vulnerable to psychosis and also to physical injury, as we have seen. Some of them (often males), as they became older, found they could not live in this open way and desperately tried to develop boundaries, defenses against the world outside. But, deficient in the ability to develop the usual firm and sometimes flexible boundaries, they then tended to develop a massive sense of alienation from the world, and paranoid tendencies. If we look at these paranoid tendencies in terms of boundaries, we see a desperate effort to escape the vulnerable thin-boundary condition by differentiating "I" firmly from "you people," "them," and "society." In this effort, the "others" of course are given negative qualities. Persons who take this path can be considered to have belatedly built themselves a thick boundary or armor. But it is hastily constructed, cumbersome, and interferes with their lives as much as it protects them.

THIN BOUNDARIES AND ALTERNATIVE CONCEPTS IN NIGHTMARE SUFFERERS

I have found that the term thin or permeable boundaries is the clearest and most basic way to describe the mental structure of persons with frequent nightmares; it fits my clinical experience in psychotherapy and psychoanalysis with patients who have occasional nightmares as well with those who have frequent nightmares. However, it will be worthwhile to examine some alternative formulations that have been proposed or may be proposed on the basis of the facts and theories discussed.

Are persons with nightmares anxiety neurotics or phobic patients? In other words, are they persons in whom intrapsychic conflicts, fear of their own wishes or fear of their own conscience, produce these nighttime symptoms? It would not be unreasonable to suppose that someone constantly frightened at night by nightmares might have a variety of daytime fears as well; and we have discussed the role of guilt in at least some nightmares. However, the nightmare sufferers definitely did not appear to be phobic or anxiety neurotics, on the basis of clinical interviews or psychological tests as discussed in chapter 4. They scored high in psychotic rather than neurotic scales of the MMPI. They did not describe especially many fears on the Fear Survey Schedule. They did not appear to have the well-formed psychic structures, good reality perception, and definite intrapsychic conflicts characteristic of neurotic patients, but rather had problems with reality and structure formation. Also, they were not, as far as we could determine, persons who had a powerful sexual wish met by a powerful inhibition, in Jones's phrase. There was little evidence that sexuality and sexual conflicts played an unusually important part in their symptoms or in their lives, although many of them certainly had problems with sexual identity and sexual relationships.[4]

Another formulation, already discussed, is that these are persons who had had terrible traumatic experiences early in childhood and were now suffering from long-term, post-traumatic nightmares. As we have seen, there was little or no evidence for severe early trauma in the usual sense. However, it is difficult to disprove the presence of trauma completely; and I have discussed the possibility that certain environmental events not usually thought of as traumas, such as a depressed or unavailable mother, may have played a role.

Some psychiatrists have suggested that people with frequent nightmares involving violence, mutilation, and death must be unusually hostile, angry people. I found little evidence to support this idea. Most of our subjects could not be described as hostile in psychiatric interviews, either with a male or a female interviewer, or in Rorschach tests or TATs: the nightmare subjects did not have higher scores than the controls on a scale specifically designed to measure aggressive fantasy. Our impression in the interviews was that more anger and hostile feelings, like other emotions and experiences, "got through" and were perceived more readily by these people than by most (an aspect of thin boundaries). In other words, I see the problem not as an excess of hostility, fear, or anger but as an excess of awareness or perception. The nightmare sufferer is more intensely aware of fears and rages that we all possess that in most persons are more walled off, perhaps, or differently handled. The fact that nightmare content seldom refers to a particular traumatic or frightening event, but more to a general sense that something is dangerous, something is chasing him or her, etc. suggests that persons with nightmares are especially sensitive to or aware of their helplessness in childhood—a helplessness that is part of reality for all of us.

Another possible formulation, relating to Freud's view of superego wishes and punishment dreams, is that persons with frequent nightmares might be persons with unusually strong and punitive superegoes. However, I saw no evidence for this supposition based on interviews with the frequent nightmare sufferer subjects and clinical experience with patients. The nightmare suffer-

4. It can be argued that the tests and the two or three hours of interview time spent with the fifty subjects of the frequent nightmare study may not have been sufficient to uncover powerfully repressed wishes. However, I reached the same conclusion from patients with whom I have spent hundreds of hours in psychoanalysis and psychotherapy; admittedly, the latter group had a less severe history of nightmares.

ers did not appear to be feeling especially guilty in the daytime; they did not "undo" or take back their actions or words on the basis of conscious or unconscious guilt as many patients do; they did not have an inappropriately poor opinion of themselves or their abilities; they did not enter into a project (or relationship) and then unconsciously sabotage the project and make it collapse. Some of them described guilt feelings, but fairly appropriately, not in a hidden, distorted way. They seemed often quite open and conscious of guilty feelings, as of so much else. Their superego functions related to moral or ethical beliefs were certainly not powerful and punitive. The nightmare sufferers were quite flexible and relativistic in terms of their value judgments and ethical beliefs. In other words, if they had an excessively punitive superego, it was strangely selective, punishing them only during their dreams.

A number of other formulations or descriptions were considered as we worked with the frequent nightmare sufferers. For instance, we often spoke of them as basically "open" and this is still my impression; it is true of many of the patients I have seen, as well as the research subjects. But as I have discussed, I would consider this "openness" part of the thin boundary condition. Likewise, we often have spoken of frequent nightmare sufferers as being "defenseless." This is true in the sense that they did not have well-developed neurotic or mature defenses. They were either defenseless, excessively open, or used relatively primitive defense mechanisms such as projection. Again, I believe "defenseless" is a valid description, but it is one way of saying that they did not have ordinary, carefully formed, or bounded psychic structures, but rather were too open and perhaps let too much in.

I have been asked by some associates whether the persons with nightmares I am talking about were not simply "a little crazy": were they simply pre-schizophrenic patients, some of whom had not yet become manifestly ill? A few could have been described in this way, as we have seen, but I would insist that many could not have been. I believe they may have had a vulnerability to schizophrenia, which I see as a lack of boundaries, including defenselessness, making it possible for them to develop schizophrenia. But many were obviously improving at the time I saw them, usually in the direction of developing a life based on their artistic or empathic talents; they could have been called "a little unusual" in that they were so open, empathic, sensitive or artistic, but they were certainly not "crazy" in the sense of being headed for a life of constant or intermittent hospitalization for mental illness.

AWARENESS OF THIN BOUNDARIES

Did the concept of thin boundaries make sense to the nightmare sufferers themselves? Were they aware that they had thin boundaries along the lines discussed? In many ways I believe they were. They did not think of themselves as violent people, but as being fragile or sensitive, often as teachers and artists having special abilities in terms of insight and communication. They had insight into the fact that they were somewhat unusual people and many accepted that they perhaps were unusually vulnerable to mental illness or at least to unhappiness and difficulty though they may not have thought of it as mental illness. One of them expressed it as "if you remain alive and open, the way I am, you eventually get hurt." Many of them had sought help in the form of various kinds of therapy or counseling. Interestingly, they had seldom sought psychotherapy specifically for their nightmare problem. Their nightmares had been accepted as being part of the way they were, perhaps even as being helpful at some time along the way. Most recognized that they had unusual perceptions and often unusual reactions: for instance, most had experimented with street drugs but almost all had given them up. They either had experienced some disturbing effects—perhaps further loosening or paranoid reactions—or expressed the feeling that they had not "needed" psychedelic drugs such as LSD as other people did. Several of them said something like this: "I have had people describe LSD trips to me, how vivid and bright the colors are, how meaningful everything is, etc., but for me it's that way all the time. I don't need LSD."

THICK AND THIN BOUNDARIES

If one accepts the concept of boundaries, one cannot help being struck by the fact that the nightmare group has thin boundaries in a great many senses. There may be others who have thick boundaries in all senses. I believe these would be persons such as severe obsessional characters who "pigeonhole everything" and keep feelings and thoughts, as well as material objects, clearly in their places; but there may be a number of other "thick-boundary" types as well.

There are many kinds of boundaries and it is not necessary that any one person have totally thin or totally thick boundaries. In fact, we have discussed some possible combinations. Thus, someone who initially has very thin ego boundaries and is very open to and perhaps scared of his own impulses and desires may sometimes become suspicious and paranoid, and thus secondarily develops thick boundaries or armor. In an extreme case, a person who develops a definite paranoid system takes one section of reality and projects onto it his own unacceptable impulses; certain persons become the "persecutors"; this part of reality is strikingly impermeable to any change or to connections with the rest of reality; it is walled off. In this way, a person who has very thin boundaries "inside" may have one very thick boundary of this kind for protection; I have seen this developing in two of the male subjects with nightmares as they became older.

Some neuroses can be conceptualized in terms of boundaries where only a specific boundary is thickened, corresponding to a specific defense. Repression is a kind of walling off. Thus, a person with a hysterical character may have walled off a whole region of the mind relating to frightening sexual thoughts, impulses, or experiences so that they became inaccessible to ordinary consciousness. However, this same person, once he or she has walled off these dangerous areas, may be open and unguarded and have apparently very thin boundaries in interpersonal relations or in other areas. Or an obsessional neurotic, who uses the defense mechanism of isolation of thought from emotion, may appear to have a very thick boundary or wall in this one area. When something happens that might be expected to make him or her angry, sad, or happy, thoughts are readily forthcoming, but the emotional aspect is walled off and inaccessible. However, despite this specific thick boundary, the same person may have thin boundaries in other senses.

A CLINICAL VIEW OF THIN BOUNDARIES

The concept of thin boundaries has many clinical implications. For example, because persons with thin boundaries are unusually sensitive to the pains of life and feel their own impulses and fears unusually intensely, we might suspect that they would be unusually prone to suicidal thoughts and to suicide itself. With this concern in mind, I reread the records of ten patients with nightmares I had treated clinically. In each patient, there was a record of suicide attempts or at least suicidal thoughts, though none had actually killed him- or herself. This led me to review once more the records of these subjects. Even though these subjects had been seen only a few hours each, and thus there had been less opportunity to talk of suicide, twenty-one of the fifty subjects mentioned that they had thought seriously of suicide at some

Table 17.3
Number of Subjects Answering Two Suicide-Related MMPI Questions "True"
(Suicide-prone Direction)

	Question 139[a]	Question 339[b]
Ordinary Dreamers (N = 12)	0	0
Vivid Dreamers (N = 12)	2	0
Nightmare Sufferers (N = 12)	5	1
Nightmare Sufferers from the earlier study (N = 38)	14	5
Or, considering all nightmare versus all non-nightmare subjects:		
Non-Nightmare Subjects (N = 24)	2 (8%)	0 (0%)
Nightmare Subjects (N = 50)	19 (38%)	6 (12%)

[a]Question 139: "Sometimes I feel as if I must injure either myself or someone else."
[b]Question 339: "Most of the time I wish I were dead."

time, and eleven had attempted it. I also re-examined the MMPI data looking especially at the answers to two items sometimes considered to be suicide warnings.[5] I found the two questions answered in the suicide-prone direction far more frequently in the nightmare group than in the other group (table 17.3). I then attempted to find as many of the subjects as possible for a follow-up study; unfortunately, the population had been a transient one and I was able to locate only a very few. Those I was able to locate—about one-fourth of the total—were on the whole doing better than they had been at the time of the original study several years before. But this was only partly reassuring. Facilities not having been available for a more thorough follow-up study, I could not know of any actual deaths in the group. But I cannot help being concerned that a number of them may have encountered too much pain or too little support and may have killed themselves.

Our studies also suggest that those who have continuing nightmares, or other signs of thin boundaries in childhood, may be vulnerable to developing schizophrenia. If we can identify these at-risk people, we may be able to help them—in structuring reality, in developing a particular artistic talent, in bearing pain without losing touch with reality and people, and perhaps help in the form of medication. Help in these various forms may prevent a schizophrenic outcome and allow positive potential to emerge.

5. These are item 139—"Sometimes I feel as if I must injure either myself or someone else"; and item 339—"Most of the time I wish I were dead."

Thin boundaries can be a valuable and useful characteristic if associated with the right combination of intelligence, talent in some particular direction, and interpersonal support. Having thin boundaries can be an advantage in allowing insight into one's own mental content and mental processes, and presumably those of others, making one a better writer, painter, teacher, therapist, negotiator. Scientific as well as artistic creativity requires "regression in the service of the ego" implying an ability to regress to a point where different realms of thought are merged, to temporarily ignore boundaries in order to put things together in a new way. This regression may be easier for people with a tendency to thin boundaries. On the other hand, keeping regression in the service of the ego may be more difficult for them than it is for others.

THE BIOLOGY OF BOUNDARIES

Finally, if we accept that thin boundaries may be a useful psychological concept, can we say anything about the underlying biology—about what aspects of brain function or structure underlie thin boundaries? Nothing is conclusively established. However, in chapter 10 we discuss in detail the biology and especially the chemistry of the nightmare. If nightmares are an indication of thin boundaries, and an indication of a certain kind of vulnerability, as we have suggested, perhaps the chemistry of the nightmare also forms part of the chemistry of thin boundaries in the mind and the chemistry of these vulnerabilities. I propose that there is a basic structural concept of thin or thick boundaries underlying our many uses of the word and that this structure must have a brain biology. Furthermore, I believe a concept such as boundaries may be one psychological concept that lends itself especially readily to a search for an underlying biology. For instance, it is not impossible that thickness of boundary could refer to "insulation" or resistance to spread of excitation from one part of the forebrain to another, though the situation will probably turn out not to be quite so simple. There is already evidence that some of the brain substances—serotonin, norepinephrine, and dopamine—are involved in the chemistry underlying dreams and nightmares, can act as "neuromodulators" increasing or decreasing the conductivity or resistance to conductivity of certain synapses in the brain (Weight and Swenberg 1981; Descarries, Watkins, and Lapierre 1977).

CONCLUSION

In any case, whether or not it leads to a relevant biology, I am suggesting that boundaries in the mind, the ability to form boundaries, and the types of boundaries formed are among the most important human psychological variables. And persons who have frequent nightmares, continuing since childhood, appear to be among those who have thin boundaries in a great many senses.

I have now completed my attempt to answer the question "Who has nightmares?" This issue, along with the relation of nightmares to schizophrenia and creativity, and the development of the concept of thin boundaries, represents the principal conclusions of this book. In my focus on the development of this thesis, I have necessarily omitted a number of important aspects of the study of nightmares that have practical as well as theoretical importance. Later I consider the more clinical aspects of the nightmare that lead us in several new directions but also lead us back a number of times to the material just discussed.

REFERENCES

Adler, G., and Buie, D. 1979. Aloneness and borderline psychopathology; the possible relevance of childhood development issues. *International Journal of Psychoanalysis* 60:83–96.

Beutler, L. E., Thornby, J. I., and Karacan, I. 1978. Psychological variables in the diagnosis of insomnia. In Williams, R. L., and Karacan, I., eds., *Sleep Disorders: Diagnosis and Treatment*, New York: John Wiley & Sons.

Blatt, S., and Ritzler, B. 1974. Thought disorder and boundary disturbance in psychosis. *Journal of Consulting and Clinical Psychology* 42:370–81.

Blatt, S. J., Brenneis, C. B., Schimek, J. G., and Glick, M. 1976. The normal developmental and psychopathological impairment of the concept of the object on the Rorschach. *Journal of Abnormal Psychology* 85:304–73.

Bleuler, E. 1950. *Dementia Praecox or the Group of Schizophrenics*. New York: International Universities Press.

Cameron, N., and Margaret, A. 1951. *Behavior Pathology*. Boston: Houghton Mifflin.

Chapman, L. J. 1961. A reinterpretation of some pathological disturbances in conceptual breadth. *Journal of Abnormal Social Psychology* 62:514–19.

Coursey, R. D. 1975. Personality measures and evoked responses in chronic insomniacs. *Journal of Abnormal Psychology* 84:239–49.

Descarries, L., Watkins, K., and Lapierre, Y. 1977. Noradrenergic axon terminals in the cerebral cortex of rat. III. Topometric ultrastructural analysis. *Brain Research* 133:197–222.

Federn, P. 1952a. The ego as subject and object in narcissism. In *Ego Psychology and the Psychoses*, pp. 283–322. New York: Basic Books.

Federn, P. 1952*b*. On the distinction between healthy and pathological narcissism. In *Ego Psychology and the Psychoses,* pp. 323–64. New York: Basic Books.

Freud, S. 1920. *Beyond the Pleasure Principle.* Leipzig, Vienna, and Zurich: Internationales psychoanalytischer Verlag.

Freud, S. 1939. *New Introductory Lectures to Psychoanalysis.* In *Standard Edition of the Complete Psychological Works of Sigmund Freud,* vol. 22, p. 80. London: Hogarth Press.

Hartmann, E., Greenwald, D., and Brune, P. 1982. Night terrors-sleep walking: Personality characteristics. *Sleep Research* 11:121.

Hobson, J. A., McCarley, R. W., and Wyzinski, P. W. 1975. Sleep cycle oscillation: Reciprocal discharge by two brainstem neuronal groups. *Science* 189:55–58.

Jortner, S. 1966. An investigation of certain cognitive aspects of schizophrenia. *Journal of Projective Techniques* 30:554–68.

Kales, A., Caldwell, A. B., Preston, T. A., Healey, S., and Kales, J. D. 1976. Personality patterns in insomnia. *Archives of General Psychiatry* 33:1128–34.

Landis, B. 1970. Ego boundaries. *Psychological Issues* 6 (Monograph 24):1–177.

Lanyon, R. I. 1968. *A Handbook of MMPI Group Profiles.* Minneapolis: University of Minnesota Press.

Lewin, K. 1936. *Principles of Topological Psychology.* New York: McGraw-Hill.

Reich, W. 1933. *Charakter Analyse.* Vienna: Sexpol Verlag.

Searles, H. F. 1960. *The Nonhuman Environment.* New York: International Universities Press.

Shakow, D. 1963. Psychological deficit in schizophrenia. *Behavioral Science* 8:275–305.

Weight, F. F., and Swenberg, C. E. 1981. Serotonin and synaptic mechanisms in sympathetic neurons. In Jacobs, B. L., and Gelperin, A., eds., *Serotonin Neurotransmission and Behavior,* pp. 131–55. Cambridge, Mass.: MIT Press.

Zucker, L. 1958. *Ego Structure in Paranoid Schizophrenia.* Springfield, Ill.: Charles C. Thomas.

18. The Screening Function of Post-Traumatic Nightmares

Melvin R. Lansky

I

Nightmares, especially post-traumatic nightmares, have posed major problems for the theory of dreams. If it is presumed that the manifest dream is a virtually unmodified representation of the traumatic event—something like a vivid, affect-laden night-time memory—then it would seem that the manifest and latent 'content' of the dream are identical, and there is neither dream work nor the representation of unconscious wishes as fulfilled, nor the need for distortion and disguise that accompanies the expression of unconscious wishes. Furthermore, since nightmares are anxiety dreams which wake the sleeper, the function of dreams as guardians of sleep is not in evidence. Affects in dreams are presumably dampened but certainly not amplified (Freud 1900, p. 467). Accordingly, the enormity of affect—which has made the word 'nightmare' paradigmatic for overwhelmingly frightful experience in the face of which one is helpless—seems to belie the stimulus modulating function of dreams.

Perhaps the most perplexing feature of the nightmare revolves around the issue of wish fulfilment. If a dream is the disguised expression of an unconscious wish represented as fulfilled, how is one to account for the generation in dream life of an unmodified replay of an experience of sudden and overwhelming trauma? The dream, in recreating the terrifying experience, seems to act in ways utterly different from that in which stimuli or wishes are represented as fulfilled by the consummatory act of hallucination that we call dreaming.

These issues, of course, have a prominent place in the history of psycho-

Reprinted by permission of the *British Journal of Psychotherapy*, Vol. 6, 1990, pp. 384–400.
The author gratefully acknowledges Dr. Allan Compton for helpful commentaries on an earlier draft of this paper.

analysis. Writing of anxiety dreams, Freud (1900) was careful to demonstrate that such dreams were only apparent contradictions of the theory of wish fulfilment. The anxiety, he took great pains to point out, belonged not to the manifest dream scene which appeared to generate them, but rather to the latent dream's thoughts (p. 580), and were reflective of the conflict (either libidinal stasis, or later a signal of danger) between the unconscious wish and the forces of censorship.

But the problem of post-traumatic dreams does not seem explicable in these terms. If the manifest dream is presumed to be an exact replay of the traumatic situation, then there is no evidence of the existence of latent content, unconscious wish, or anxiety stemming from an intrapsychic conflict. The very notion that dreams have the function of keeping the sleeping psyche from being disequilibrated by sleep-threatening stimuli seems not to apply to the case of post-traumatic nightmares.

Freud did pay considerable attention to these phenomena. In the wake of World War I experiences with combat nightmares, and with the evolving of psychoanalytic theory and clinical experience, he postulated in 1920 the compulsion to repeat. This compulsion to repeat can be seen as a wish *from the ego,* originally overwhelmed, but preparing itself in both dreams and repetitive acts to replay and eventually to master overwhelming traumatic experience. Post-traumatic dreams then were 'beyond the pleasure principle', that is, attempts of the once overwhelmed ego at mastery. In these anxiety-laden repetitions, the psyche amplified rather than diminished threats to its equilibrium. In later works Freud remained sceptical that traumatic dreams really go beyond the pleasure principle (Freud 1933). The subsequent history of psychoanalysis has seen a movement toward considering nightmares through frames of reference that are not exclusively psychoanalytic nor even clinical. The tendency even among psychoanalytic investigators has been to consider nightmares in the light of recent laboratory findings from sleep and dream research (Fisher *et al.* 1970, Hartmann 1984).

This communication concerns *chronic* post-traumatic nightmares in an inpatient psychiatric population. The sample, therefore, is limited to patients sufficiently impaired to require at least one, and usually more, psychiatric hospitalisations. The investigation was phenomenologically based, clinically rich, psychoanalytically informed and psychodynamic, but it does not derive from the psychoanalytic nor even from the psychotherapeutic situation itself. The study of chronic post-traumatic nightmares is part of an effort to study all nightmare experiences of that inpatient psychiatric population over a period of time. The overall project included nightmares that were non-traumatic and those that were acute. In the overall study from which the current communication was derived, most post-traumatic nightmares were chronic, having occurred for the most part more than a decade later than the trauma represented in the nightmare scenario. Thus I cannot assume that the sample of nightmares, the chronic ones in particular, are the same phenomena as the type of nightmare that follows shortly after a traumatic event and in persons otherwise free of psychiatric disorder. The fact that the entire study was drawn from an inpatient psychiatric population provides a stern cautionary against generalisation of these findings to nightmare sufferers outside of the specific type of population and type of nightmare represented in this study.

Post-traumatic nightmares are usually described in the literature, even psychoanalytic literature, as though they were unmodified reproductions of the traumatic scene replayed in exact or almost exact detail. That is also the way the dreamer experiences them. Such dreams appear to have a somewhat different biological substrate from that of nightmares of lifelong nightmare sufferers (Hartmann 1984). Traumatic nightmares usually occur in NREM sleep, in the middle of the night. Those of lifelong nightmare sufferers occur in REM sleep, and more towards morning. Much of the recent literature on nightmares tends to view these dreams as markers of stress response, not as products of the imagination, deriving from an excess of stimulation and functioning to keep the psyche in more modulated equilibrium; not as freshly woven ideational product revealing details of the patient's history and psychic disequilibrium and woven from the pattern of personal experience making use of recent and indifferent materials for the dream collage. That is to say, nightmares tend to be overlooked as true dreams in the psychodynamic sense, having *meaning* not just in relation to trauma but also to the dreamer's entire psychic continuity, and having the *function* of modulating excessive disrupting stimuli by representing them in a less disturbing way, as fulfilled wishes.

Most patients in our sample were interviewed one or more decades after the trauma occurred. Accordingly, the study throws rather limited light (two patients in a sample of 40 nightmare sufferers, 15 of whom had post-traumatic nightmares) on acute post-traumatic nightmares. Such nightmares often, but not always, seem to the dreamer to be simple replays of the traumatic event. Most patients in this sample suffered traumata one to four or more decades before the most recent nightmare about which they were questioned. It has been observed (Hartmann 1984) that within a few weeks or months post-traumatic nightmares begin to blend with other dream elements and eventually to disappear. One would expect that acute post-traumatic nightmares as stress-response imagery would have a relatively short natural history. Nonetheless, clinical experience, as well as experience in the literature, point to the chronicity of nightmares. Although there is mention in the literature (Van der Kolk 1984) of chronic nightmares, I could find nothing in the literature attempting to explain the chronicity of these nightmares nor what factors would tend to support the continuation of repetitive nightmares occurring over a period of years to many decades. Why do some blend with other dream elements after a few weeks to months and cease to be nightmares, while others persist for years or even decades? I attempt to illustrate with clinical material factors which bear on the chronicity of post-traumatic nightmares.

II

The investigation took place in a 20-bed inpatient unit at the Brentwood Division, West Los Angeles VA Medical Center. The ward, a centre for psychiatric residency training, has both a psychodynamic approach to the patient and a commitment to an exploration of, and involvement with, that patient's family system present and past.

The interest in nightmares was given impetus by psychotherapeutic contact with combat veterans and with patients who had suffered physical or sexual abuse as children. Both of these groups of traumatised patients tended to have a high prevalence of chronic nightmares. The ward did not select its admissions based on an interest in such patients.

On admission every patient was asked if he or she had nightmares (Lansky & Karger, 1989). There were no pre-established criteria for what was and what was not a nightmare. The patients were later asked why they had called the dream experience a 'nightmare', and there was enough uniformity in the answers to give a reasonable working model. All had awakened from sleep out of fear, most felt helpless, some even tried to escape the dream scene. The method of study was to combine clinical knowledge of the patient with an open-ended written questionnaire. That questionnaire was filled out prior to an interview of 30 to 60 minutes which covered and amplified what was written by the patient. The interview was tape recorded.

It is noteworthy that all 40 patients who acknowledged having nightmares consented to fill out the questionnaire and to participate in the taped interview. There were follow-up interviews with some patients. Most were eager to pursue the topic once it was open and wanted to talk more.

The questionnaire was deliberately open ended and left room for a detailed account of the patient's most recent nightmare, details of events and emotional states surrounding the nightmare experience, and the psychic and bodily feelings experienced after awakening. The patients were asked about their first and other nightmares. Patients were asked for their views about the relationship of any of these to the experiences of trauma, to childhood experiences, to the current family situation and to the treatment setting. The last section of the questionnaire covered details of the current family situation and the family of origin. These data are certainly not equivalent to an associative anamnesis, particularly one that takes place in the context of an ongoing treatment relationship. Nevertheless, an astonishingly reflective mode of self-inquiry was established rapidly with most patients, even those whose treatment alliance and observing ego had seemed minimal or even absent prior to the investigation. This heightened reflectiveness made possible a limited but significant use of the associative method, and even brief forays into interpretive synthesis that was useful to the treatment enterprise. The purely investigative data co-mingled with the knowledge of the patient's current situation, based on 24-hour ward observation and data for supervision of meetings with patient and family.

This blend of investigative data, clinical material and results of intensive family study gave a uniquely rich perspective on infantile (familial) trauma, on current familial dysfunction, and on specific current difficulties viewed in the treatment setting and the patient's current life setting. The comprehensiveness of clinical immersion provided an unusually rich perspective on to the day residues, i.e. the preconscious preoccupations with which the dreamer dealt. This perspective was far more detailed than that in any study I have come across in the published literature, the majority having relied on volunteer respondents seen outside of a treatment context (Hartmann 1984, Hersen 1971, Van der Kolk 1984).

For purpose of the present investigation of chronic post-traumatic nightmares, I am calling *chronic* any nightmare occurring more than two years after the initial trauma, and *post-traumatic* any nightmare identified by the dreamer as being *about* a traumatic experience that actually happened. Hence, even if a dream scenario, on detailed examination, proved not to be about, e.g., a battlefield experience, that nightmare was designated 'post-traumatic' if the patient identified it as replaying a traumatic event. 15 of the 40 nightmare sufferers were post-traumatic using the above criterion.

III

These nightmare sufferers had chronic post-traumatic nightmares containing a recognisable traumatic event that had occurred years, usually decades, previously. Most, but not all of the patients, were non-psychotic. Virtually every one of the traumatic nightmare sufferers had easily identifiable, gross and continued dysfunction in the families in which they grew up. The vast majority of those who were combat veterans with post-traumatic nightmares had volunteered for combat. There was also gross dysfunction in the current familial relationships or alienation from current family or family of origin when the patient was an adult. The latter finding, of course, must be considered in the context of a patient population disturbed enough to require psychiatric hospitalisation, usually more than once.

I shall discuss the clinical material with emphasis on the processes of distortion involved (especially secondary revision), global familial dysfunction in these patients throughout the life cycle, chronicity of the nightmare, and the screening function of chronic post-traumatic nightmares.

Secondary Revision

Of particular note is the fact that the nightmares, though described by the dreamers themselves as a re-experiencing of specific traumatic situations — that is, almost as a charged night-time memory rather than a true dream — were, in this sample, never simple 'replays' of upsetting experiences. They were infiltrated with material from childhood or adolescence or with current concerns. They were usually so constructed that the patient was attacked rather than attacking in the dream scene, i.e., aggression was projected. In some instances, battlefield scenes were present in the nightmares even though the patient had not been in combat.

The fact that patients *experience* dreams as though they were flashbacks or simple memories of the trauma is noteworthy enough to warrant discussion. Patients would describe as re-experiencings of battlefield situations nightmares that had nothing to do with the battlefield. Some had obvious origins in the early familial situation. Some patients who were never in combat had dreams of battlefield situations. The patient's surprise at interview, on realising that these post-traumatic dreams were obviously much more complex products of the imagination, must be seen as an aspect of disguise, a type of *secondary revision* added on to the patient's recollection of his or her experience of the dream for the purpose of keeping the experience from being too troubling and too much a part of the patient's ongoing and disturbing psychic continuity.

Freud identifies secondary revision as part of the dream work done by preconscious, not unconscious processes (1900, p. 499). Secondary revision consists of an afterthought or judgement about the dream itself, for example, 'it's only a dream' or, in the sample here described, 'It's a replay of what happened to me.' Secondary revision is the line of defence used when distortion by displacement, condensation and symbol formation fail to dampen the disturbing impact of the dream. Such secondary revision '. . . appears in a dream when the censorship, which is never quite asleep, feels that it has been taken unawares by a dream which has already been allowed through. It is too late to suppress it, and accordingly the censorship uses these words to meet the anxiety or the distressing feeling aroused by it' (p. 489). 'Secondary revision' in the topographic theory of 1900 was an early conceptualisation of what would later be subsumed under the activities of the ego.

One patient regarded his nightmare as having nothing to do with upsetting experiences in his life.

Example 1. A 36-year-old man stated emphatically during the interview that his nightmares, suffered since adolescence, had nothing to do with upsetting experiences in his life. (Accordingly, by our narrow criteria for post-traumatic nightmares, his nightmares could not be classified as post-traumatic in our study.) He had been admitted for a host of problems which included spouse and child abuse. Nonetheless, he related a recent nightmare that had an obvious relationship to a traumatic event:

I went to sleep about 1.00 a.m. I dreamt I went to my front door to answer it. A man blew my head off and then my wife shot him. The man's face was like a blank page. I awakened sweaty with my heart beating fast. I was frightened.

Later in the interview, discussing his military experience, he described a horrifying event that he said had taken place in boot camp.

A fellow soldier, a homosexual, jumped into bed with me. I grabbed him by the neck and threw him out. I guess he was to be arrested. The next night he came back with a gun to get me. My (best) friend R pushed me out of the way. R was killed. We had enlisted together as buddies. I had amnesia for the whole war experience. I didn't even get to his funeral. I still have nightmares about it (18 years later).

The nightmare replayed the trauma in the barracks but with a number of striking modifications. The murder is relived but this time *the patient, rather than R, is killed*. The dream work deals with his guilt over his friend's death, over the physical abuse of his children, over his homosexuality and over his longstanding hatred of his parents stemming from his being abused during childhood. *The attacker had a blank face*. As was the case with his amnesia for events after R's death, he cannot allow himself to be specific concerning the traumatic scenario that would upset him too much. The dream emphasised that *he is married*, i.e., the dream work tries to obviate the issue of homosexuality in the barracks. *His wife kills his attacker*. This element deals in modified form with his reactions to the cruel beatings received by his father and his overly strong attachment to his mother, but also his own guilt feelings for abusing his children with the fatal act of justice accomplished on himself—as the man with the blank face—at his wife's hand. In the nightmare his propensity for violence is projected: *everyone is violent except himself*.

The patient's insistence that his nightmares had nothing to do with his life experiences is a quite striking example of secondary revision, that is, a conscious afterthought on the dream used to dissociate the dream experience from integration with the entire continuity of his life: his childhood, his military experience, and his current familial difficulties—all of which had to do with uncontrolled and sexualised aggression.

Another patient told himself that his nightmares were 'about the war.'

Example 2. A 41-year-old black man with a history of cocaine abuse and numerous prison sentences reported the following nightmare.

I was being held prisoner by a bunch of guys, I don't remember who exactly. I was chained to a wall while they prepared instruments of torture. The torture never took place as I realized it was a dream. I tried to escape from the dream and awoke.

He recalled having the same nightmare around 3:00 A.M. every few months since he returned from Vietnam at the age of 20. He had suffered from nightmares since the age of 12.

His view of the nightmare was that it was a dream of an actual scene of being held prisoner in a prisoner of war camp. He elaborated.

I'm always in this compound, either put in tiger cages or staked to the ground or carried on a pole with my hands and wrists tied. I got beaten. I always wonder how I could withstand the pain. I awakened yelling.

He had at first attributed the nightmare scenario to his combat experiences but, when questioned, he acknowledged that he had never been imprisoned in Vietnam. Questioned about his childhood, he gave an account replete with family strife: alcoholism, abusiveness and violence by his father. The father would drink himself into a fury so much so that the patient would feel terrified if he saw his father's car at home when he returned. Father, when in rages, beat his mother and all the children. At other times he would tie the patient and his brother to stakes, whipping them mercilessly. In the midst of these beatings, he would take breaks and calmly smoke a cigarette before picking up the whip and hitting the boys again. His mother did nothing to protect her children, and the patient realised only in high school that other families were not like this.

As the patient became aware of the obvious relationship of his nightmare to his early familial experiences, he became profoundly shaken. His cocksure and slick façade collapsed almost immediately, and he was visibly agitated and upset. The day following the interview, he requested a brief pass from the ward, claiming that he had an appointment with his parole officer. He did not return, and the ward received a phone call the next day from the parole office informing them that the patient had produced a urine specimen positive for cocaine and was imprisoned immediately. The insight provided by discussion of his nightmare about his eroticised childhood abuse made it clear that his engineering his own imprisonment on the day after the nightmare interview was an acting out in which he engineered an imprisonment, an experience very much like the one in the nightmare. This episode of acting out served to replace his devastating remembrances of childhood abuse with an actual imprisonment.

Dysfunctional Families

Lidz (1946), describing a sample of acute post-traumatic combat soldiers, reported the ubiquity of dysfunctional families, that is, predispositions to traumatic neuroses (see also Moses 1978) in the histories of his patients. He also noted hatred of the same sex parent and suicidal wishes, and observed considerable evidence of dream work in acute nightmares evidenced, for example, by the patient's wishes to attack portrayed in the dream scenarios as attack on the patient. Many of our patients (Lansky & Karger 1989) reported severe early familial dysfunction (13 of 15 or 86.6%) and upsets contemporaneous with the time at which the trauma occurred, e.g., death of a close buddy, 'Dear John' letters from a girlfriend (six of six questioned, 100%). (Questions about narcissistic wounding contemporaneous with battlefield trauma were begun after the study was under way. Hence the small proportion of the sample questioned.) These narcissistic wounds contributed to these persons' greater experience of traumatic damage compared to others exposed to the same battlefield trauma. Our sample, then, suggested a view of the origin and nature of post-traumatic nightmares similar to that of Lidz, i.e., that these nightmare experiences were very much dreams in the true psychodynamic sense.

The following case illustrates traumatic familial dysfunction, past and present, utilised by the dream work in nightmares involving combat situations.

Example 3. A 44-year-old man with dissociative states in which he crossdressed had the following nightmare after an angry exchange with his resident physician who had just set his discharge date.

It was as if somebody was telling me that they were going to get me or kill me if I didn't get them first. Vietnamese, two men and a woman, that I actually killed. Then I woke up and found myself cross-dressed.

Exploration of his early family life revealed a devastating pattern of abuse and traumatisation. His mother had brought home numerous lovers and had had intercourse with them with the patient present. He was not able to tell his father about mother's activities until she deserted the family when he was nine years old. He had felt disloyal to the father and unable to approach him. The patient's dissociative episodes in adulthood followed situations in which one might have expected him to feel anger. In the dream itself he felt no anger but only the persecutory fear that the Vietnamese might get him. The anger is, of course, implicit in the dream text; he had killed the people who, re-embodied in the dream, were seeking vengeance. When he awoke crossdressed, he felt rage at his doctor for setting a discharge date and fear of his anger. His current hospitalisation provided the first opportunity that he had ever had to feel anger in an environment that he saw as supportive enough to tolerate his emotional turbulence. His acknowledgment of rage in the therapy situation helped him to acknowledge his rage at his mother's sexual escapades, her involving him as a witness, and at his traumatic and neglectful upbringing in general. Soon the rage replaced the dissociative episodes during which he cross-dressed, and the anger became available for his work in psychotherapy.

This patient became extremely interested in his inner life following his therapy and the nightmare interviews. A second nightmare interview was held at his request about a month after the first. He reported the following nightmare.

I've gotten sprayed in the shoulder with shrapnel. We'd been evacuated out of a combat area, Vietnam or somewhere. Everybody got on the plane. After we took off, my daughter wasn't on the plane. She was in the nightmare. My wife was there too. So were several (he named three female) staff members. Other nurses. When we got ready to take off, one guy said, 'What about these wires?' I said, 'Yank them out.' Took all of the food out of the house. My daughter was locked out of the house trying to figure out how to get out. I got sprayed by shrapnel—face and parts of the shoulder. Then we were in some kind of a depot. I was taking in dirty linen—pajamas and linen. A short, petite girl had a pair of shower shoes on four sizes too big. More rounds came in on us. My daughter got him, then I jumped out of bed.

He had said that this was like a dream the week before. It also involved his daughter. He was able to identify his physical pains in the dreams as actual feelings from shrapnel wounds that he had received. He had several more nightmares in which his daughter was killed.

After an exploration of details in his current life circumstances, it became increasingly clear that after he had left the hospital and gone home there had been a good deal of tension in the family on his return. His 11-year-old daughter, who had had all of her mother's attention while the patient was hospitalised, became jealous. He went through a good many episodes of her appealing to her mother, interrupting intercourse, and in general attacking the couple's privacy. Although the patient did not feel conscious anger at this intrusiveness, he (as author of his dreams) included her in the battlefield scenes in the nightmare and killed her in several different nightmares. Discussion of the dream details enabled him to acknowledge his anger at his daughter without confusing that anger with the rage he felt in response to the early familial situation which had so overwhelmed him.

Chronicity

Some of our data served, however tentatively, to suggest some explanation of the *chronicity* of these nightmares. If the natural history of post-traumatic nightmares is such that these nightmares usually become diluted with other dream elements and disappear in a matter of weeks to months as true nightmares (Hartmann 1984), why do nightmares in these patients remain repetitive and chronic for decades?

It is likely that many factors contribute to the chronicity of these nightmares. In an attempt to approach the problem of chronicity, I draw upon the idea of a confluence of determinants other than the specific traumatic event portrayed in the nightmare. By determinants, I mean not only pre-existing concurrent and subsequent personality vulnerabilities that may have been traumata in themselves, but also co-existing traumata—usually from early life—find expression in the dream text (Examples 2–7).

The nightmares seemed clearly to have a screening function for infantile trauma and its residua. Most of these patients were raised in families in which marital strife, violence and alcoholism were rife. Frequently, the patient not only overtly hated his father or his mother's lovers, but attempted to attack or kill that person.

Example 4. A 38-year-old man was admitted rageful and depressed, claiming that wartime experiences had damaged him and that the government had not taken care of him and compensated him properly for the damage done. He reported several nightmares that were typical of those he had frequently since 1970 when he was 19.

He described one as follows.

A fire fight with a Viet Cong. A constant shooting and killing. I was running, falling on my belly, excited and scared of being killed. I woke up throwing up and sweating.

At a later point, when he described his family of origin, he recalled beatings by his father that occurred repeatedly and with no protection from his mother, who left the room when father went into a rage. Both parents were alcoholics. As he described these terrifying attacks in his early family, it became clear that he had experienced a virtually identical state of mind then as he had in the recurrent battlefield nightmare. He levied the same charges of being damaged and not cared for at the government as he did at his parents. Although it was clear that the battlefield trauma and the childhood trauma were indeed separate matters, the consciously felt rage at and demand for recompense from the government gave him the opportunity to express concretely his sense of being damaged, frightened, attacked, and to act on his fulminate sense of entitlement deriving from a sense of early life injury. He felt more convinced that he deserved better treatment from the government than he had felt in childhood about his parents' treatment of him. The nightmares served to concretise his state of mind, the helplessness and terror that were common to his childhood and the battlefield—the latter screening the former.

The same patient reported another recurrent nightmare, variants on a scenario that actually occurred.

I have an almost constant vision of a man that got killed in my place. He went on a mission I should have gone on. I see a floating head full of bullets or C being shot and being blown 15 feet in the air. In another scene he was calling for his mama. With the bullet holes, he looked like Jesus Christ with the crown of thorns. My pain (from a wound sustained at that time) was very evident. I was tough on him. He looked up to me.

The patient reported numerous variations on this nightmare and the feeling of intense guilt that the younger soldier whom he had disciplined harshly but who had idealised him died on a mission on which the patient felt he should have been sent.

The sense of guilt and determinants went back to his (conscious) childhood hatred of both parents, especially his father. In his current family situation, his guilt had a contemporary source that added to his childhood and young adult conflicts. His marriage had collapsed after his wife decided that his self-absorption, rage, and difficulty functioning in the family were intolerable. He became painfully aware that he could not tolerate his children getting close to him and he felt, to his horror, that he had become just like his father. The nightmare of the younger man's death and the sacrificial injury and subsequent feelings of guilt screened the sources of this sense of remorse by relocating it to the battlefield 18 years before and employing a recollection in which the actual injury done to the younger person was by enemy forces rather than by himself.

In addition to overt hatred of the father, there was terror at the father's violent methods of keeping tenuous control in a strife-ridden household, and also contempt felt for father's alcoholism and vocational failures. These factors combined to leave lifelong residua which served to generate further failures in interpersonal and vocational functioning. The lifelong (conscious) feeling of rage at father or mother's lovers was easily elicited by simple questioning. In addition to the rage, however, was a contempt for parents and a crushing sense of shame concerning the entire family. At an unconscious level was a shameful sense that the patient had of himself, resulting not only from his hatred of one or both parents, but also in large part from his unconscious identification with a man held in such contempt and only poorly captured by the phrase 'low self-esteem' (Greenson 1954).

Example 5. A 43-year-old man recalled the following nightmare experience. I have trouble knowing what my dreams are because they are multiple dreams. That night it was about my past. I was starting to awaken when the ward nurse checked on me. I woke up feeling very guilty, thinking this dream, like many, was about the fact that I miss a girlfriend that killed herself. I still take a lot of responsibility. The rest of my dream I felt very scared. I felt that I'm asleep, she's either next to me or trying to get in my apartment. It's so real, I'm fully carrying out a conversation with her. At the same time, there's a lot of anger. (He notes that a second girlfriend killed herself, too.) She's calling to me. Don't do this to her. I'm leading her on. She was asking me to help her. Why didn't I love her. In the dream, I was with the first one. (He recalled thinking about the losses a lot in the past.)

Curiously, he said that he had called this a nightmare because he wanted to kill himself. The events in the dream scenario actually happened. One girlfriend had committed suicide two years prior to the time of the nightmare and another three years before that. In the nightmare, a desperate scene is replayed concerning a girlfriend who subsequently killed herself. It is a small inferential step to presume that the action in the dream as well as the patient's feelings of guilt and anger derive from his murderous wishes toward the woman. But the nightmare, with its evident rage and deliberate destructiveness towards the women and his conscious guilt and rage, resonated also with his disruptive and traumatic childhood. He had been born into a chaotic family. His mother was in a psychiatric hospital when he was born. Both parents were alcoholics. His father had beat his mother repeatedly. His brother and mother had locked the patient up in a basement when he was very young, and the brother had molested him sexually. The father punished the patient sadistically with a phone cord and at one time abruptly sent him away to live with relatives in Mexico. The patient had had a sexual liaison with a housekeeper whom he later found out to be his half sister. He had spent some years as a homosexual prostitute. He carried with him (conscious) fury at both father and mother for the violence and chaos in the home.

Although this man clearly identified his nightmares as concerned with traumatic experiences, he felt that those experiences were the two women's suicides and did not, at first, recognise that the rage and guilt derived from his childhood, nor that the triumphant and sadistic conscious withholding of love was indeed a reversal of what was done to him.

The helplessness and fears of attack on the battlefield have strong reso-nances with early familial environment. Traumatic dreams screened these early experiences in many ways. Noteworthy among these is the actual staging of the dream setting on the battlefield (Examples 3, 4, 6, 7). While the nightmares *generated* terror—a manifest reaction to the attack—they *modulated* or diminished very powerful affects of shame and rage, very prominent in the patient's legacy from early familial traumata and con-sciously felt virtually all their lives. The patients not only felt these strong affects but also had continuing problems in life outside of the family with the sequelae of unacknowledged shame (Lewis 1971, 1987) and rage, either unexpressed or expressed with disastrous consequences in inappropriate places and in ways that made workable vocational and familial adaptation tenuous or unattainable. It seemed as though these patients' sense of shame derived in large part from their identifications with parents of the same sex who were not only the object of their hate but were also objects of contempt (Lansky 1985) and a major source of their contempt for themselves. While fear was the major (and even defining) affect in the nightmare, the shame and rage so operative in the patient's waking life are diminished (Examples 1,2,3,4,5). The setting of the nightmare, then, served the defensive function of revealing the basic childhood fears in a setting in which both unacknowledged shame and uncontrollable rage were neither operative nor problematic. The *justifi-cation* of fear and sense of attack provided by the battlefield scenario and the *elimination* of the patient's preoccupations with unacknowledged shame and uncontrolled rage—lived in the immediacy of the dream experience—can be looked at as a compromise formation that reveals fear and conceals shame and rage, and hence, as a representation of the unconscious wish to transpose these emotions as fulfilled.

This line of thinking gained support from a number of other findings. First, the vast majority of the post-traumatic nightmare sufferers (ten of eleven questioned) volunteered for combat. This selection of combat veterans was emphatic about wanting to serve in combat for personal, not for patriotic, reasons. That is to say, being in the combat situation was their *specific and conscious wish* prior to the experience of combat replayed in the dream. The reappearance of the battlefield scenarios may be presumed to represent *the same constellation of unconsious wishes that determined the conscious choice to volunteer for combat*, i.e., the handling of intense shame and uncontrolled rage by removing oneself to the battlefield where the sources of shame and rage are neutralised or rationalised by the battlefield situation. A high percentage of narcissistic wounds such as buddies dying in battle or 'Dear John' letters received from girlfriends has been pointed out by Fox (1974), who noted reactions of rage rather than grief in soldiers whose buddies died in combat, and by Lidz (1946). It was also high in our sample (100% of six patients questioned). Such narcissistic wounding is one source of shame and rage. The legacy of early familial trauma is undoubtedly a greater source of shame and rage. Examination of these patients' current familial functioning or lack of it opened up another confirmatory avenue of thinking; that is, that the nightmares also screen shame (often unacknowledged) and rage in current family or other relationships. Alienation from family of origin (thirteen of fifteen, 86.6%) or dysfunction in family of procreation (fourteen of fifteen, 93.3%) contemporaneous with our investigations was widespread. One patient (Example 4) reported his shame over the fact that he could not tolerate his children's approaching him. Another (Example 3) had a nightmare in which his 11-year-old daughter was killed in a raid.

One patient who was brutally abused as a child expressed suicidal wishes, first in nightmare, but later quite consciously, and related these to his horror and humiliation over his continual physical abuse of his wife and his children. His suicidal wishes were directly related not only to his guilt about the violence, but his shame at having become like his own father whom he had seen abuse his mother.

Example 6. A man in his late forties who was admitted for a combination of difficulties, including depression, alcoholism, spouse and child abuse, reported the following nightmare.

I was in the Marines, fighting in my hometown. There were gang members. In my dream, I was at my house (in a small town about 100 miles from Los Angeles). Across a big truck line. My adrenalin's really flowing. I'm back where I belong. There was this 17-year-old 'baby' who got shot. I laid him on a table. I said, 'My wife's a nurse'. He was shot in the groin on the right. I blanked out in a nervous state. I felt good. I was back in the military again. I was a platoon sergeant again. I'm important. After seeing this kid get shot, I felt I could have done more. I felt mad. I let him get shot. It could have been prevented.

He went on to discuss his fears in the dream with a sense of shame as though he were admitting cowardice in a real-life situation. In his account of another dream, in which he was having intercourse with a woman other than his wife, he talked as though he were discussing an actual act of adultery.

The relationship of the dream to this man's traumatic past and upsetting current familial situation was complex. He himself had come from an abusive family where he was neglected, beaten and deprived. He had felt that his mother had wanted to get close to him but his father would not allow that to happen. His mother would have wanted to have left if she could but she was afraid. In his own family, he ruled tyrannically and by force, orchestrating down to the last detail the conduct of his wife and five children. When he was employed, he worked as a trucker and was frequently away from home.

The dream dealt both with fear in his original familial situation and with reliving the fear that he had at the age of 17 when he enlisted in military service to escape the drudgery and depression of his adolescent existence for the exhilarations of the battlefield. This man was so unable to acknowledge fear that he felt he had to account for his cowardice when he felt helpless and afraid experiencing the nightmare. He could allow himself to feel fear for someone else's safety. The dream which took place in his current home town also expressed his death wishes toward his children (displaced onto the enemy) and his extreme guilt at being unable to prevent the harm he had done them. To his horror he had turned out very much like his abusive father. The dream also revealed the wish carried over from adolescence (i.e., with himself as the 17-year-old) to be killed and to make his father upset, sorry and wishing he had done more.

The nightmare, which he identified as one of many dreams related to upsetting experiences in his life, dealt in a complex way with his unacknowledged anxiety, his overwhelming guilt, and his feeling that he was unworthy to continue living both because of his early hatred of his parents and because of his current abusiveness to his family. The restoration of an exhilarated mood state, easily identified by the patient in the nightmare, had been an important motive for the patient's choosing a combat career in the first place. At the time of the interview, he voiced both the wish to return to the exhilaration of the battlefield—he wished he had the opportunity—and to be killed as a hopeless and unworthy head of his family.

These lifelong difficulties in interpersonal relationships, resulting from overwhelming shame as a legacy of family of origin and pathological identifications with the same sex parent felt to be contemptible, *generated further and almost continual psychic trauma in adult life.* Such trauma was further represented by terror and the feeling of helplessness and aloneness under attack, and explained by the battlefield situation and the justification and identity that comes with the combat soldier's role. Thus continuous and recurrent traumata resulted from the interplay of shame and rage in self amplifying spirals (Scheff 1987). These were evident from the ward observations and studies of current family and provided an almost continual day residue that was a further stimulus for the nightmares.

Screening

The function of the chronic nightmare in screening current familial difficulties was further confirmed by the manner in which these patients described their need for treatment. One patient (Example 4) appeared on the ward, rageful, demanding justice for his war injuries, and claiming that the government was unfair. His threats and demands and sense of entitlement were put forth with great bluster and self-righteousness. He demanded redress of unfairness received and damages done on the battlefield. Only later could he admit that his marriage had failed and that, despite his love for his children, he could not tolerate their approaching him. Even later he recalled shame and terror as a boy, watching scenes of brutality in which he saw his father beat his mother. The fact that his waking mind split off his battlefield experiences from his familial ones and intensified attention to the former at the expense of the latter again supports the presumption that the dream scenario directs attention from shame and rage in the familial settings past and present, and that the nightmare's placing of the patient back on the battlefield where shame and rage at love objects is replaced by (unacknowledged) fear is a representation of a wish as fulfilled.

In *this* sample, then, the chronicity of the nightmare seemed to be the result of an overdetermination by a lifetime of traumata. All this could be represented in the nightmare scenario, albeit at the cost of the generation of overwhelming fear and helplessness. The gain accomplished by the dream work was modulation of pervasive feelings of shame and the rationalising of the uncontrolled rage resulting from shame that is unacknowledged in the patient's current circumstances. What has the surface appearance of a simple replay of a scene to which intense helpless fear is an appropriate response (that is, an emotionally charged memory, a night-time flashback to the battlefield) *also* has the screening function of defensively distorting the continuous and perhaps more painful affective sequelae of infantile and adult traumata in such a way that shame and rage are dampened in an attempt to preserve the equilibrium of the psyche during the regressive relaxation of sleep.

These points are illustrated by the following example:

Example 7. A 32-year-old man was admitted 12 days after the murder of a friend who was sitting next to him in a car. The patient gave a somewhat evasive account of his connection with the deceased. He referred to him alternatively as 'my partner' and 'my friend' and described in a confusing way his efforts to locate this man in the weeks preceding the murder. His 'partner' was well to do but apparently was not regularly employed. The patient had recently been discharged from an alcohol rehabilitation program and was without funds or a place to stay. It seemed to the interviewers not unlikely that this person was a drug seller.

The patient's account of what happened was as follows: he and his friend were in a car going to get a drink when a car pulled up. There were three or four shots. The friend died instantly, slumped toward the patient who slid down in the seat, opened the door and ran. The patient apparently had a fugue state, awoke in a psychiatric hospital, left after a few days and was readmitted to another hospital.

He said his nightmares were exact repetitions of the upsetting event and that they had occurred every night since the shooting 12 days previously. He gave two versions.

He was in his friend's car. *A woman came up with a gun and called him by his first name* (a very unusual one). She shot his friend.

The second version:

He was in the friend's car. There were three or four shots. The friend slumped over. The patient got out of the car and ran (the actual event). He *stumbled*. He ran and fell. It was dark. He ran off a cliff or onto a body of water. The fear of falling woke him.

He recalled that he first started having nightmares at 14 when his baby half brother had just died. At the time when the child was terminally ill the father, running to telephone the doctor, *stumbled;* the baby was dead by the time the doctor arrived. The patient recalled conscious resentment of the new child who was the only child of his mother's and stepfather's union and hence (he felt) supplanted him. He recalled, 'I messed up to get attention', especially from his mother. The interviewer asked if he felt that his parents were angry at him. 'Yes', he replied, 'especially my mother'. The interviewer noted that the woman in the dream called him by his first name (a quite unusual one) and shot the other man. The patient added that only his mother calls him by that name. The interviewer noted that in both the recent situation and in the earliest nightmare when he was 14, there was reference to a male more favoured than himself who had died in his presence, a recollection of someone stumbling and running away. The patient then had recollections of his family: his mother was unfair to him; she blamed him for everything; he had carried around conscious rage at her since the age of four; he resented his half brother's birth; he was ashamed both of his resentment and his neediness; he lived in fear that he would be blamed for those angry feelings.

The dream then co-mingles the traumatic situation, the death of his accomplice, with the earlier death of his brother. The latter occurred right at the age his nightmares began. The dream work by substituting the mother for the unknown recent assailants brought his fear into the more predictable family situation. It was his mother's wrath over the feelings about his half brother's death that was to be dealt with rather than the more uncontrollable and incomprehensible shooting of his accomplice.

Despite numerous evidences of dream work linking the current trauma with the death of his half sibling at the age of 14, this patient thought that this recent post-traumatic nightmare was an exact repeat of the traumatic scenario.

The screening function that Freud (1899) first described for memories, screen memories, was described as memory in which unusual vividness accompanies a surprisingly bland content, the elements of which proved analysable, much like that of a dream into a latent content which was much more conflict-laden and upsetting. Freud's paper came near the end of the period where his central focus was on trauma and its reconstruction, so he did not elaborate the concept of screening further than these unusually vivid, but bland memories, that could screen experiences earlier or later. Nonetheless, the concept of screen memories remains a major aspect of psychoanalytic thinking. Glover (1929) pointed to the screening function of traumatic memories which may serve to express, but also to conceal, even greater traumata, citing a case of a traumatic circumcision screened by a hand injury.

The following case illustrates the screening of the experience of an emerging psychosis that was contemporaneous with a battlefield experience which was represented in a nightmare.

Example 8. A 33-year-old hospitalized schizophrenic combat veteran reported the following nightmare at age 20 in combat.

There were rocket attacks in Cam Rahn Bay. I was asleep. They rocket attacked the base. A room of four people. One got torn completely out of his boots. Pieces everywhere. Blood. I dream I find his face. In my bed. He's trying to talk to me. (Interviewer asks if he were close to this person.) yes. All four of us were real close.

This nightmare recurred three or four times monthly for 13 years up to the time of the interview. The actual scene did not occur as represented in the nightmare, but he did see people killed with pieces of their faces gone.

He described an uneventful childhood. In the military technical school in 1970, he received a 'Dear John' letter from his fiancée, became suicidal and volunteered for combat with the (conscious) hope of being killed. After several months of combat in which he saw a great deal of surprise attack, killing and dismemberment of close friends, he had an overt psychotic break and was hospitalised and evacuated back to the United States. Nightmares began after his return home.

When the events contemporaneous with his combat experience were explained, it seemed plausible that his recurrent nightmare chronicled and reworked not only his horrifying combat experiences but also—in allegorical fashion—his emerging shattered sense of self and unfolding psychosis.

I am here applying a line of thinking inputting the same screening functions to nightmares as Freud did to vivid memories. Explanation of their screening function may contribute to an understanding of the endurance of chronic post-traumatic nightmares as well as of their affect-regulating function. There were very few acute post-traumatic nightmares in the study. I assume that many acute nightmares may be more like flashbacks or nighttime intrusive memories, and that this screening function may have been superimposed on the acute nightmare. Further, these numerous sources of traumata—from earliest family of origin to the time of the inquiry—provided a rich overdetermination for which the original albeit modified scenario served as a screen. That is, the patient's regarding of the nightmare as though it were an upsetting but basically undistorted memory is in itself an aspect of secondary revision that is part of the dream work, a method of concealing the expression of conflicts resulting from adult and infantile traumata that resonate with the battlefield scenario.

Conclusions from these data should not be overgeneralised. They do not shed light on the problem of how or why certain traumata generate nightmares. The data concern the chronic, not the acute phase of the nightmare's natural history. Caveats regarding the specific sample are worth repeating: the sample is one of *chronically psychiatrically impaired inpatients*. This is an exceedingly disturbed population that differs greatly from populations used in other studies (Lidz 1946, Hersen 1971, Van der Kolk 1984, Hartmann 1984) and the traumatic scenario usually dated from one to more than four decades prior to the nightmares being studied.

Needless to say, noting the screening functions of the chronic nightmare is not meant to imply that the battlefield situation does not generate severe and lasting trauma. It has been my overall impression that the actual exposure to combat, the risk of attack, maiming and killing, having close comrades die and exercising one's own aggressiveness by deliberate attacks on others (no matter what the justification) exerted a permanent and virtually irreversible effect on these men's psyches. Detailed elaboration of the nature of battlefield trauma extends beyond the scope of this paper. Such experiences were perhaps more damaging in cases where inchoate and unmanageable rage at family members had been present prior to the combat experience.

The case material points convincingly to the usefulness of considering chronic post-traumatic nightmares to be dreams in the fullest psychoanalytic sense. Freud began *The Interpretation of Dreams* (1900, p. 1) with the claim that: 'Every dream reveals itself as a psychical structure which has a meaning, and which can be inserted in an assignable point in the mental activities of waking life'. The sample of post-traumatic nightmares provided a venue for the re-establishment of a sense of continuity in these patients' lives. Despite the terror, the unpleasantness represented and the fact that the patients' sleep was disturbed, these nightmares do not require a major revision of our understanding of dreams. Although the task of preserving sleep—a major function of dreams—has failed, an understanding of the specifics of the dream work points clearly to affect-modulating activities. If experiences of shame, isolation and rage can be thought of as more disturbing than the experiences of attack and comprehensible fear represented by the latter, serves to modulate affect and to attempt restoration of psychic equilibrium rather than to generate anxiety and promote disorganization of equilibrium. Patients' experiences after awakening were often of a sense of overwhelming shame and uncontrollable rage that became more accessible to psychotherapeutic amelioration when the dreams were utilised psychotherapeutically. In some way, the battlefield scenario embodied the wish to be out of their current (unmanageable) interpersonal circumstances and on the battlefield where their affective storms, paranoia, unmanageable rage and poor sense of their worth among intimates, made more sense than in their current families or relationship systems. The presumption of such an unconscious wish gained support from the fact that most of these patients made the conscious choice to volunteer for the combat situations that was represented in the nightmare. The dream work is evident in virtually every dream. Many features of the dream work are embodied in the screening function of the nightmare.

REFERENCE

Brenner, C. (1953) An addendum to Freud's theory of anxiety. In *International Journal of Psychoanalysis 34*, pp. 18–24.

Compton, A. (1972) A study of the Psychoanalytic theory of anxiety: II developments in the theory of anxiety since 1926. In *Journal of the American Psychoanalytic Association 20*, pp. 341–394.

Fisher, C., Byrne, J. V., Edwards, A. & Hahn, E. (1970) A psychophysiological study of nightmares. In *Journal of the American Psychoanalytic Association 18*, pp. 747–782.

Fox, R. (1974) Narcissistic rage and the problem of combat aggression. In *Archives of General Psychiatry 31*, pp. 807–811.

Freud, S. (1899) Screen memories. In *Standard Edition, Vol. 3*. London: Hogarth Press.

Freud, S. (1900) The interpretation of dreams. In *Standard Edition, Vols. 4 & 5*. London: Hogarth Press.

Freud, S. (1917) A metapsychological supplement to the theory of dreams. In *Standard Edition, Vol. 14*. London: Hogarth Press.

Freud, S. (1920) Beyond the pleasure principle. In *Standard Edition, Vol. 17*. London: Hogarth Press.

Freud, S. (1933) New introductory lectures. In *Standard Edition, Vol. 22*. London: Hogarth Press.

Glover, E. (1929) The screening function of traumatic memories. In *International Journal of Psychoanalysis 10*, pp. 90–93.

Greenson, R. (1954) The struggle against identification. In *Journal of the American Psychoanalytic Association 2*, pp. 200–217.

Hartmann, E. (1984) *The Nightmare*. New York: Basic Books.

Hersen, M. (1971) Personality characteristics of nightmare sufferers. In *Journal of Nervous and Mental Diseases 153*, pp. 27–31.

Lansky, M. (1985) Preoccupation and pathologic distance regulation. In *International Journal of Psychoanalytic Psychotherapy, 11*, pp. 409–426.

Lansky, M. & Karger, J. (1989) Posttraumatic nightmares and the family. In *Hillside Journal of Clinical Psychiatry, 11*, pp. 169–183.

Lewis, H. B. (1971) *Shame and Guilt in Neurosis*. New York: International Universities Press.

Lewis, H. B. (Ed.) (1987) *The Role of Shame in Symptom Formation*. Hillsdale, New Jersey: Erlbaum.

Lidz, T. (1946) Nightmares and the combat neurosis. In *Psychiatry 9*, pp. 37–49.

Moses, R. (1978) Adult psychic trauma: The question of early predisposition. In *International Journal of Psychoanalysis 59*, pp. 353–63.

Rangell, L. (1955) On the psychoanalytic theory of anxiety. In *Journal of the American Psychoanalytic Association 3*, pp. 384–414.

Rangell, L. (1963) The scope of intrapsychic conflict. In *Psychoanalytic Study of the Child 18*, pp. 75–102.

Rangell, L. (1967) The metapsychology of psychic trauma. In *Psychic Trauma* (Ed. S. Furst), pp. 51–84. New York: Basic Books.

Scheff, T. (1987) The shame rage spiral: A case study of an interminable quarrel. In *The Role of Shame in Symptom Formation* (Ed. H. B. Lewis), pp. 109–150.

Schur, M. (1953) The ego in anxiety. In *Drives, Affects and Behavior* (Ed. R. M. Lowenstein), pp. 67–103. New York: International Universities Press.

Schur, M. (1959) The ego and the id in anxiety. In *Psychoanalytic Study of the Child 13*, pp. 190–220.

Van der Kolk, B. *et al.* (1984) Nightmares and trauma: A comparison of nightmares after combat with lifelong nightmares. In *American Journal of Psychiatry 141*, p. 187.

C. Dreams and Current Research

19. Experimental and Clinical Approaches to the Mind-Body Problem through Recent Research in Sleep and Dreaming

Charles Fisher

The investigation of psychophysiological correlations during sleep holds great promise for making contributions toward the solution of the mind-body problems. As Rechtschaffen (1973) has indicated, there is generally greater physiological and psychological variability during sleep than during wakefulness, although this statement may be surprising. For example, the EEG of wakefulness is fairly uniform in amplitude while that of sleep can range from less than 10 to over 200 μv and from less than .5 to over 25 cycles per second. During wakefulness the eyes move intermittently depending on the task at hand, but throughout sleep there are well defined cyclic periods with a wealth of eye movement activity and other with little or no rapid eye movement. The enhanced variability of mental activity during sleep is even more apparent. On most days there is a fairly stable level of consciousness with few or no extended periods that we would describe as either completely blank or fantastically stimulating or exciting. By contrast, during each night of sleep we fluctuate many times between apparent mental voids and a sort of low-keyed mental idling, on the one hand, and the vivid highly emotional absorbing events of dreams, on the other. In addition, a vast array of sleep disturbances and disorders provides further opportunity for making psychophysiological correlations, and these conditions are accompanied by even more pronounced variability than occurs normally. The symptomatology of sleep ranges from nightmares, night terrors, somnambulism, sleeptalking, enuresis, to a whole series of motor phenomena, including tooth-grinding (bruxism), head banging, rocking, epileptic seizures, myoclonic jerks, sleep

Reprinted by permission of Human Sciences Press, Inc., from *Psychopharmacology and Psychotherapy: Synthesis, or Antithesis?* edited by Norman Rosenzweig and Hilda Griscom, New York, 1978.

Figure 19.1
Depth of Sleep

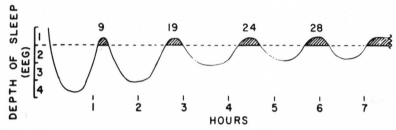

Schematic representation of the dream-sleep cycle in which EEG stages are plotted against hours of sleep. The shaded areas show the REMPs and the numbers above them the duration of the dream periods in minutes. The first REMP begins a little more than an hour after sleep onset. There are four dream periods in six hours.
REM—Rapid Eye Movements; REMP—Rapid Eye Movement Periods; NREMP—Non-Rapid Eye Movement Periods; EEG—electroencephalgram.

paralysis, etc. Sleep may be disturbed by a variety of nocturnal psychosomatic symptoms such as attacks of asthma, ulcer, and anginal pain.

An additional advantage of sleep studies is that they permit evaluation of psychophysiological correlations under conditions of reduced responsivity to external stimuli, thus decreasing variables contributed to non-experimental stimuli. Sleep permits observations to be carried out for hours under relatively constant conditions. Though the sleeper seems to be in an insensate coma, this is an illusion produced by the fact that there is an occlusion of incoming sensory input and a marked motor paralysis. Sealed off from the outer world the sleeping person may yet be in a state of intense psychological and physiological turmoil. The study of sleep has revealed new relationships and phenomena that could not have been anticipated from studies of wakefulness.

At this point I would like to review briefly a few of the new discoveries about sleep and dreaming. There are two types of sleep which along with waking constitute three major organismic states: REM or dreaming sleep, taking up 25 percent of sleep time, in which we spend about 1/16th of our entire lives, is distributed throughout the night in a 90 minute cycle, and NREM or orthodox sleep constitutes 75% of total sleep (Figure 19.1). Stage 3–4 delta sleep predominates in the first third of the night and REM sleep in the last third. REM sleep is associated with intense activation in both cortical and subcortical parts of the brain and in most physiological systems, and drive activation, as indicated by the cycle of penile erections synchronous

Figure 19.2
Combined Strain Gauge and Thermistors

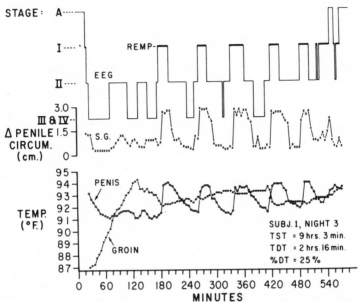

The upper graph shows the stages of the EEG plotted against time; the REMPs are indicated by the darker horizontal lines. Directly below is a graphic representation of the increases in penile circumference in cms, as measured by the strain gauge (S.G.); the increases are of an order of 2.5 cm or more, indicating full erection. These increases are sustained practically throughout the duration of the REMPs with very little fluctuation. The lower graph is a graphic representation of the penis and groin temperatures throughout the course of the night. With each REMP and synchronous with the increase in circumference, there were rises of penile skin temperature of 2.5° to 3°.

with REM periods (PREMs) (Fisher, 1965, 1966). Figure 19.2 is a graphic representation of this cycle recorded by strain gauge and thermistors.

In this paper I will briefly review work on several types of psychophysiological correlation. The most parsimonious hypothesis has been that very marked fluctuations in many physiological parameters during REM sleep represent correlates of the cognitive and affective activity of the concomitant dreaming. It has, however, been very difficult to demonstrate this. Although certain physiological changes can be shown to correlate with dream events at better than chance incidence, a complete one-to-one relationship has rarely

Figure 19.3

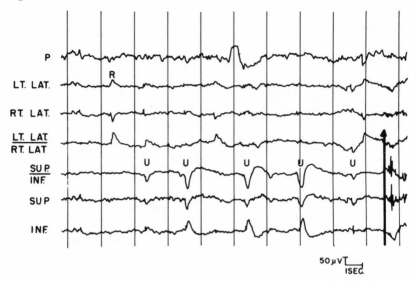

Five upward eye movements (U in the graph) in relation to a dream in which the dreamer walked up a flight of stairs lifting her eyes with each step upward. The upper line on the graph shows the EEG. The lower six lines represent tracings from different eye movement electrode placements. From Roffward et al. (1962), *Archives of General Psychiatry,* Vol. 4, pp. 235–58. Copyright 1962, American Medical Association.

been demonstrated. There appears to be a non-specific activation occurring in REM sleep that is not necessarily related to dream content. One of the most striking occurrences of REM sleep are the bursts of rapid eye movements. The so-called scanning hypothesis holds that there is a relationship between dream content and eye movements, that is, the eyes scan the objects and events of the dream (Figure 19.3) (Roffwarg et al., 1962).

There have been few attempts to make correlations between individual dreams and fluctuations in various physiological parameters. We have been able to demonstrate that anxiety dreams which awaken the dreamer may be associated with clearcut increases in heart and respiratory rates and the amount of eye movement (Figure 19.4) (Fisher et al., 1970). We have also been able to show that penile erections synchronous with REMPs show

Figure 19.4
Autonomic Change in Three Most Severe Nightmares

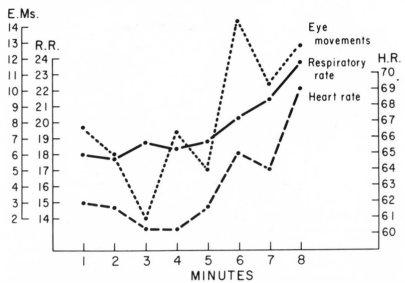

Increase in heart rate, respiratory rate and the number of eye movements during terminal anxiety of three severe REM nightmares. Graph shows the last 8 minutes of the REM period before arousal.

fluctuations in relation to dream content (Fisher, 1966). Thus anxiety dreams may bring about rapid detumescence of ongoing full erection (Figure 19.5) and dreams with manifest sexual content may stimulate rapid tumescence (Figure 19.6). Nocturnal emissions, rarely recorded, involve an additional excitation of the erections that normally accompany REMPs (Figure 19.7, Figure 19.8).

A second approach to the problem of psychophysiological correlation involves attempts to suppress a given sleep state with drugs or other methods and to investigate the psychological, physiological, and behavioral consequences. I will discuss two examples, one, involving suppression of night terrors by administering Valium, a drug which eliminates Stage 4 sleep out of which the night terror arises, and two, total and prolonged suppression of REM sleep by administration of the MAO inhibitor, Nardil. This latter investigation throws light on (a) the unresolved question of the function of

Figure 19.5
SUBJECT B.

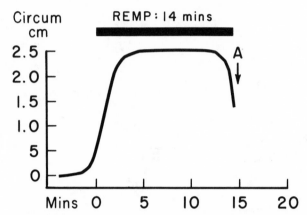

ONSET OF TUMESCENCE 1 MINUTE BEFORE ONSET OF REMP, FULL ERECTION (2.5 cm) ATTAINED 2 MINUTES AFTER, SUSTAINED FOR 11 MINUTES AND FOLLOWED BY A SUDDEN DETUMESCENCE OF 8 mm. A = AWAKENING

Figure 19.6
SUBJECT B.

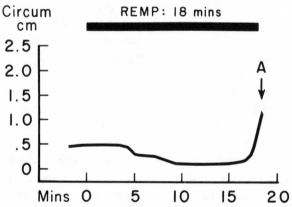

MARKED INHIBITION OF ERECTION FOR 17 MINUTES FOLLOWED BY ABRUPT TUMESCENCE OF 12 mm IN 1 MINUTE. A = AWAKENING

Figure 19.7
SUBJECT A.

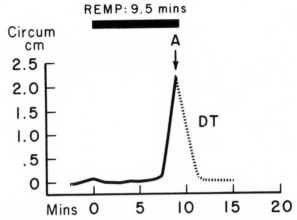

REMP: 9.5 mins

Circum cm

A

DT

Mins 0   5   IO   I5   20

REPRESENTATION OF NOCTURNAL EMISSION BEGINNING 7.5 MINUTES AFTER ONSET OF REMP. FULL ERECTION (2.1 cm CIRCUMFERENCE) WAS ATTAINED IN 1.5 MINUTES. NOTE RAPID DETUMESCENCE (DT). A = AWAKENING

Figure 19.8

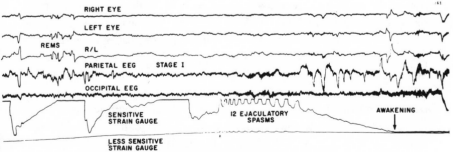

Sixty seconds of REM, EEG, and strain gauge recording during a nocturnal emission. Note the rapid rise of the strain gauge tracing and the 12 ejaculatory spasms.

Figure 19.9
Types of Nightmare in Relation to Sleep Stages

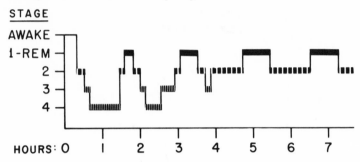

■■■ STAGE 1 - REM anxiety dream -nightmare. Majority of post-
traumatic nightmares

■■■■ STAGE 2 - Mild to moderate anxiety

▓▓▓▓ STAGE 3 and 4 - Night terrors of adults and children, minority of
night terrors of post -traumatic neurosis.

REM sleep, (b) the neglected problem of the relationship of physiological drives, sex, aggression, and hunger to the REM state, and (c) the connection between dreaming and psychosis.

Suppression of Night Terrors

It has been amply demonstrated that night terrors in children and adults, somnambulism, and most enuresis arise out of Stage 3–4 sleep in the early part of the night and are not associated with REM dreaming as has been traditionally assumed (Fisher et al. 1970, 1973). We have shown that spontaneous arousals associated with anxiety of varying degrees of intensity up to panic can arise from any stage of sleep (Figure 19.9). An important distinction needs to be made between the most intense, the Stage 4 night terror, which is relatively rare both in children and adults, and the much more frequent ordinary nightmare or REM anxiety dream, characterized by less intense anxiety and lower levels of autonomic discharge, motility, and vocalization.

In more than two-thirds of instances, night terrors occur in the first NREM period during which nearly two-thirds of Stage 4 also occurs, as early as 15 to 30 minutes after sleep onset. In its fully developed and most severe form, the Stage 4 night terror is a combination of extreme panic, fight-flight reactions in the form of gasps, moans, groans, verbalizations, cursing, and blood-curdling piercing screams. Although triggered out of Stage 4, the episode actually takes place as part of what Broughton (1968) calls, "the arousal response" characterized by a waking alpha pattern, body movement, and somnambulism (Figure 19.10). The subject may be hallucinating, delusional, and out of contact with the environment while he acts out the night terror which is accompanied by extreme autonomic discharge. The heart rate may reach levels up to 160–170/minute within 15–30 seconds, a rate of acceleration greater than in any other human response, including very strenuous exercise or orgasm. Respiratory rate is increased, but the most striking change is a tremendous increase in amplitude. The entire episode lasts only a minute or two, even when somnambulistic, and the subject returns to sleep rapidly. Amnesia for the experience may be present, but with immediate and careful interviews, in over 50 percent of arousals, some kind of content is reported, usually consisting of a single brief frightening image or thought, such as the idea of an intruder in the room. In contrast, the REM nightmare arises out of an ongoing lengthy dream (Figure 19.11).

Of special interest is the physiological state just prior to the explosive, catclysmic onset of the night terror. With rare exceptions, the night terror not only arises out of State 4, the most quiescent stage of sleep, but its intensity is correlated with the amount (in minutes) of this stage present just before the amount: the more Stage 4 the *more severe the episode*. That the sleep preceding onset of the night terror is quiescent is also shown by the fact the cardiorespiratory activity is normal or even slightly lower than normal. Thus, the night terror arises out of, and its occurence is contingent upon, the presence of a *specific physiological matrix*, Stage 4 sleep.

It occurred to us that if we could alter the physiological matrix out of which the night terror arises, we might be able to control the attacks. We were, however, hesitant to attempt this for two reasons: first, because removal of such a severe symptom might bring about displacement and substitute formation of a more serious nature, such as psychosis, and second, because suppression of Stage 4, considered to be a necessary stage of sleep, over prolonged periods might have some deleterious physiological consequence. However, it has been reported that chronic ingestion of diazepam, flurazepam, and phenobarbital produces marked suppresion of Stage 4 without harmful effects. We decided, therefore, to test the hypothesis that administration of diazepam would bring about a prolonged suppression of Stage 4,

Figure 19.10

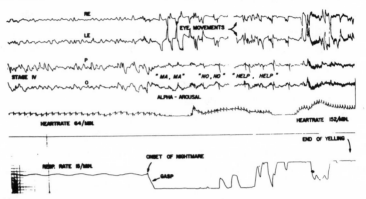

Severe Stage 4 night terror showing eye movements in the top two tracings, brain waves in the middle two tracings, and heart and respiratory rate recordings in the bottom two, just before, during, and after onset of the night terror. Note the large delta waves during Stage 4, the waking eye movements following arousal, the break in the respiratory rhythm associated with a gasp, initiating the nightmare, the normal heart and respiratory rates prior to onset, and the subsequent marked increase in heart rate to 152 per minute. The increases in respiratory rate and amplitude are distorted by artifacts caused by the screams to mother to help.

and, in so doing, eliminate the physiological matrix out of which the night terror arises, resulting in a decrease in its incidence or even total disapperance.

Diazepam (Valium) in doses from 5–20 mg was administered before bedtime to six subjects suffering from night terrors in nine experiments for periods from 26–98 days (Fisher *et al.*, 1973). Night terrors were reduced by an average of 80 percent, that is, from a mean incidence of about two per night to less than one-half per night. In some instances, we had 100 percent abolition. The decline in amount of Stage 4 was more marked than the incidence of night terror, amounting to about 90 percent (Figure 19.12).

Several subjects have been on Valium for more than two years and have been able to regulate dosage so as to virtually eliminate the night terrors they had been enduring for as long as 25 years. Although there do not appear to be any deleterious physiological consequences from prolonged suppresion of Stage 3–4, we are not absolutely certain that diazepam adminstration is without harmful psychological effect.

Figure 19.11

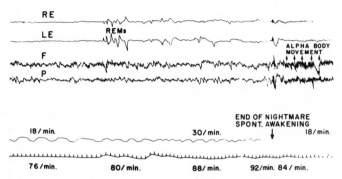

Recording of REM nightmare. RE and LE (Right and Left eyes) show REMs. F, frontal EEG; P, parietal EEG. Bottom two lines indicate respiration and heart rate recordings, showing increase in respiration from 18 to 30 per minute just before spontaneous awakening from nightmare, followed by immediate decrease in respiration to 18/minute, and heart rate increasing from 76 to 92/minute simultaneously with a decrease after awakening to 84. Note the fluttering type of respiration with decrease in amplitude.

PROLONGED SUPPRESSION OF REM SLEEP

In 1959 Dement and I carried out the first so-called dream deprivation experiment utilizing the method of awakening the subject whenever eye movements indicated onset of a REM period, thus bringing about a 75 percent suppression of REM sleep (Dement, 1960; Dement and Fisher, 1960a, 1960b). The subjects made progressively more attempts to dream on successive nights, as though they built up a pressure for REM sleep and/or dreaming which was like an irresistible force, spontaneous, peremptory, and obligatory. When subjects were allowed to sleep undisturbed, they showed a marked rebound increase in REM sleep partially compensating for that lost during the suppression period. The longest period of REMP deprivation carried out by the waking method in man has been 16 days (Dement *et al.*, 1967). Such prolonged periods of deprivation necessitate an enormous number of awakenings, more than 100 per night to prevent dreaming from occurring (Figure 19.13). The rebound increase in REM sleep after 15 or 16 nights of about 90 percent REMP suppression may be as high as 60 percent of total sleep and is associated with the appearance of a sleep onset REMP (Figure 19.14).

Figure 19.12

Effect of Valium on Number of Night Terrors, Number of Awakenings, and Amounts of Stages 3 and 4

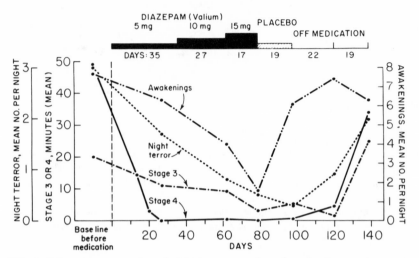

Effect of diazepam on number of night terrors, number of awakenings, and amounts of Stages 3 and 4, showing 90% reduction in night terrors and 100% reduction of Stage 4, with slow recovery on placebo and off medication. Note parallel course in Stage 3 and number of awakenings.

In the first flush of enthusiasm following these experiments, we became convinced that REM sleep and its associated dreaming were necessary psychobiological processes, that variations, deficits or excesses of this unique organismic state could be correlated with mental disorders and that severe and prolonged suppression would produce psychosis in man. These findings seemed to confirm certain psychoanalytic propositions about the relation of dreaming to psychosis.

Although Dement and I originally observed some mild disturbances of memory and other ego functions, extensive work in many laboratories has failed to show any universally agreed upon psychological and behavioral disturbances in man resulting from the relatively brief periods of two to seven days of REMP suppression generally utilized.

Some striking consequences of more prolonged and complete REMP suppression have been reported in cats, rats, and rabbits. Dement et al. (1967) found that even 70 days of nearly total REMP suppression in the cat were without fatal effects, but the animals developed a state of CNS hyper-

Figure 19.13

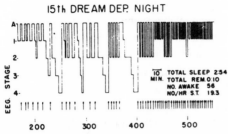

Continuous plot of the EEG stages for the 15th and last REM deprivation night (Subject #2). The arrows beneath the plot indicate the instances when the subject was awakened immediately following the disappearance of tonic EMG potentials. No dexedrine was given on this night. Note that REM sleep occurred at the initial sleep onset and that the early period of Stage 4 EEG was completely disrupted. After 4 o'clock, almost no non-REM sleep occurred. The subject had to be awakened almost as soon as he had returned to sleep. The recording was discontinued at about 5:30 o'clock because it was virtually impossible to allow the subject to sleep, so quickly did REM sleep intervene. From Dement *et al.* (1967), in *Sleep and Altered States of Consciousness,* ed. S. S. Kety *et al.,* Williams and Wilkins, Baltimore, 1967. © 1967 the Williams & Wilkins Co., Baltimore.

Figure 19.14

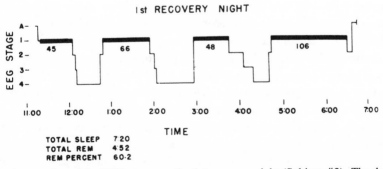

Continuous plot of the EEG stages on the 1st recovery night (Subject #2). The dark bars emphasize the periods of REM sleep. Note that REM sleep occurs at the initial sleep onset and that all periods are extremely long. The total amount of REM sleep was 4 hr. 52 min. which accounted for 60.2 percent of the total sleep time. The numbers below the bars show the length of the periods in minutes.

excitability during waking, characterized by the dramatic development of compulsive sexual behavior with persistent attempts by male cats to mount other males or females, and even anesthetized or dead animals. The deprived cats also developed increased hunger and rate of eating, would cross an electrified grill, and eat out of a dish with a burning candle in it. Rats showed significant increases in both aggressive and sexual behavior following deprivation. In contrast to the alteration of motivational behaviors, no consistent changes were observed in basic perceptual and motor functions, learning and memory, and even prolonged REMP deprivation did not elicit hallucinatory behavior, contrary to expectations. The association of REM sleep and dream activity demonstrated in humans had led to the expectation that something analogous to dreaming would ultimately erupt into the waking state in these animals. Dement concluded that prolonged REM sleep deprivation produces generalized CNS hyper-excitability reflecting an alteration in drive state or motivation, and increased probability that the animal will emit a stereotyped, drive-oriented response in the presence of the appropriate stimulus, or even without stimulation.

As noted earlier, another line of evidence pointing out the importance of drives to REM sleep and dreaming is the finding that 80–90 percent of REM periods are associated with partial or full penile erection. Preliminary findings suggesting equivalent sexual arousal, both clitoral and vaginal, during REM sleep in the female, have been reported (Karacan et al., 1970; Cohen et al., 1970a, 1970b). These developments seem to confirm certain psychoanalytic propositions about the importance of sexuality and drives generally in dreaming, but it must be said that the majority of the workers in the field of sleep research appear to regard them as epiphenomenal and they have played little role in theoretical considerations.

Although the early REM deprivation experiments in man suggested that the procedure might produce psychological disruption or even psychosis, later work threw doubt on this conclusion. It was believed that *during* prolonged REMP suppression a pressure to dream would reach such intensity that there would be a "breakthrough" of dreaming into the waking state. This has not been found to occur. Moreover, Vogel and Traub (1968) showed that seven days of REM deprivation carried out on chronic schizophrenics did not result in any aggravation of symptoms, as this notion would seem to call for.

Vogel hit on the remarkable notion that in certain conditions REM deprivation might even be helpful rather than harmful, e.g., might relieve the symptoms of depression (Vogel *et al.*, 1968). A number of lines of evidence led to this hypothesis: anti-depressants such as Elavil, or MAO inhibitors, such as Nardil, were potent REM suppressors; electro-shock also suppresses REM; and prolonged REM deprivation in animals is reported to intensify several functions which are retarded in depressive illness, that is, it results in increased psychomotor and drive activity. Vogel was, in fact, able to demonstrate that in severely depressed patients, both endogenous and reactive, periods of REM deprivation by the *waking method* brought about marked clinical improvement.

This surprising result has been confirmed through another approach. It has been discovered that only one class of drugs, namely, the anti-depressive MAO inhibitors, are capable of bringing about total suppression of REM sleep indefinitely (as long as three years) without increasing dosage. Both Wyatt *et al.* (1971a) and Akindele *et al.* (1970) treated a large number of severely depressed-anxious patients with phenelzine (Nardil) bringing about total suppression of REM sleep for periods up to 40–50 days without adverse effects. They observed that mood, appetite and anxiety improved coincidental with onset of total abolition of REM sleep (Figure 19.15). Thus, we are confronted with a complete turnabout and paradox. Whereas it had been feared that total suppression of REM sleep might eventuate in psychosis, this work indicates that such suppression for periods as long as a year or even more are without gross ill effects and, even more astonishing, large doses of Nardil have been shown to have a markedly therapeutic effect on severe anxious depressions, reactive or endogenous, improvement coinciding with the point at which total abolition of REM sleep is accomplished.

Although it is possible that MAO inhibitors bring about relief of depression, not because of suppression of REM sleep but due to independent biochemical action, Vogel's results which were similar to the waking method support the notion that it is the REM suppression itself that is somehow therapeutic.

Another point of great interest is that Wyatt and his co-workers did not systematically study dream recall but noted that following 160 nights of total REM suppression there were no reports of dreams in the morning, inferring that there may have been total elimination of dreaming.

I have had occasion to bring about nearly total suppression of REM sleep in three patients for as long as six or seven months by administering Nardil (Fisher *et al.*, 1972). Although given for therapeutic reasons, an opportunity was provided to investigate psychological and other effects of prolonged total

Figure 19.15

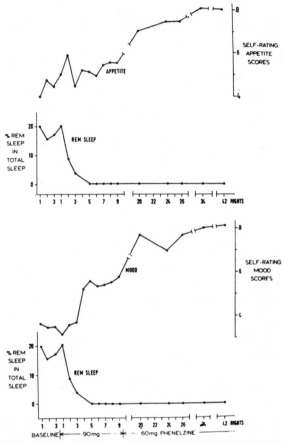

Showing increase in appetite and improvement in mood simultaneous with total suppression of REM sleep as a result of phenelzine administration. From Akindele *et al.* (1970), *Electroenceph. Clinical Neurophysiology,* Vol. 29, pp. 47–56. By permission of Elseveir Scientific Publishers Ireland Ltd.

REMP suppression and during rebound following discontinuation of the drug. I felt that prolonged REMP suppression would be more revealing about function or consequences than the usual 2–7 days of deprivation. Additionally, we did three things not done by previous investigators: (1) made all-night recordings of penile erection, (2) checked on frequency of dreaming or other mental content via appropriate awakenings during baseline, total REMP suppression and the post-drug rebound, and (3) administered a battery of psychological and projective tests before, during, and after total REMP suppression, and frequently checked on the subjects' mental state through clinical interviews.

A major contribution of sleep research has been the understanding brought to bear on narcolepsy. Classical or true narcolepsy consists of a group of four cardinal symptoms: sleep attacks, cataplexy, sleep paralysis, and hypnagogic hallucinations. It represents essentially a disturbance of REM sleep; all the symptoms can be explained on this basis. Thus, it has been shown that the diurnal sleep attacks are episodes of REM sleep associated with dreaming and loss of muscle tone. When narcoleptics have been observed around the clock (Figure 19.16), sleep attacks have been found to occur in a 90–100 minute cycle, suggesting that the REM cycle is latently present during the day (Passouant et al., 1968). In narcolepsy, due to failure of the waking system to keep it suppressed, the REM cycle manifests itself in the form of daytime sleep attacks.

In cataleptic attacks, the subject, under the stress of strong emotion or laughter, experiences sudden marked and total loss of muscle tone and falls down in a heap. It is assumed that these attacks represent the loss of muscle tone concomitant with REM sleep, dissociated from the sleep attack itself, since during cataplexy the subject is awake. One way of looking at the matter is that *mind sleep* is dissociated from *body sleep*. The nocturnal sleep of narcoleptics is normal except for the unusual occurrence of a sleep onset REM period. During this sleep onset REM period the subject may experience sleep paralysis, which is essentially a nocturnal cataplectic attack, and the initial dreaming is experienced as hypnagogic hallucinations.

This new understanding of narcolepsy as a disorder of REM sleep explains why amphetamines are useful therapeutically, namely, because they are partial REM suppressors, although often not very effective.

Because of the total and prolonged REM suppression effect of Nardil it occurred to Wyatt et al. (1971b) to test out the usefulness of this drug in narcolepsy especially in amphetamine-resistant patients. He treated seven such narcoleptics with Nardil and obtained a striking reduction in all four types of symptoms. There were, however, several important side effects. Most of the males became sexually impotent and orgastic females lost the capacity for orgasm. In both males and females sexual desire and interest disappeared. Weight gains up to 50 to 60 pounds due to excessive eating were a consistent problem for most patients. No apparent adverse psycho-

Figure 19.16

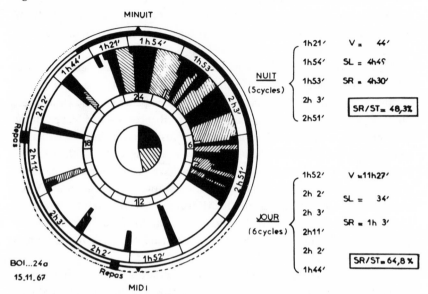

Twenty-four hour sleep study showing five REM periods during the night and six brief REM periods during the day, occurring approximately every two hours, the latter constituting the narcoleptic attacks. From Passouant *et al.* (1968).

logic effects resulted from total REMP suppression enduring as long as three years. None of the patients remembered dreaming in the morning and none indicated that the loss of dreaming was in any way detrimental.

Two patients, a 41 year-old female and a 58 year-old male, to whom I administered Nardil, suffered from narcolepsy. Both patients were given a battery of psychological and projective tests, including Rorschach Thematic Apperception Test (TAT), Figure Drawing, Wechsler Adult Intelligence Scale (WAIS), etc., and the narcoleptic female was given additional tests to assess "creativity" and visual memory and perceptual organization. These tests were administered during the baseline period before drug, during the prolonged period of Nardil administration and after drug withdrawal.[1] The findings in both subjects confirm and extend those of Wyatt (1971b) and Oswald (1969) and can be summarized as follows:

1. We were able to bring about a near complete disappearance of narcoleptic symptoms.

1. We wish to thank Dr. Melvin Sinowitz for administering these tests.

2. The male patient developed total erectile and ejaculatory impotence and the female lost sexual desire and capacity for orgasm but alleged that intercourse was still moderately pleasurable.

3. Through frequent spontaneous and elicted awakenings during prolonged periods of REMP suppression, it was ascertained that dreaming had in fact ceased, although previously both subjects were profuse dreamers with excellent recall. They no longer subjectively experienced dreaming and did not complain about the lack. The content of NREM awakenings showed no compensatory increase in dreamlike qualities, the reports obtained being either of brief thoughts or isolated images, e.g., "I was thinking about some chickens," "I was dicing an onion," or "I am the murderer."

4. Prolonged and total REMP suppression for more than six months did not produce psychosis *during* the suppression period and there were no obvious behavioral disturbances, but rather increased feelings of well being.

5. For both patients, psychological tests revealed that, as compared to baseline results, there was no increase in primary process thinking even after months of total REMP deprivation and no evidence that dreamlike activity had spilled over into the waking state. Reality testing, visual memory, and other ego functions were intact. The male narcoleptic, who, during baseline, showed a flooding of primary process thinking, reported the opposite while on the drug, namely, a predominance of secondary process with reduced fantasy production, increased affective constriction and control.

6. There was, however, one striking change in both patients, revealed by the WAIS. Although there was a slight falling off in verbal battery scores during periods of total REMP suppression, the so-called performance tests showed significant mean decreases up to 16–18 I.Q. points, and individual tests showed losses of 24–26 points.

7. I have stressed that *during* periods of total REMP suppression while the patient is on Nardil, psychosis does not develop nor is there evidence of other serious emotional disorder. But following rapid drug withdrawal, a toxic psychosis or delirium with hallucinations and delusions may develop *during* rebound (Figure 19.17). In our male narcoleptic, REM percent gradually increased, on the fourth withdrawal night attaining a level of 60 percent accompanied by a number of severe nightmares with verbalizations and cries for help. The following night, REM sleep reached a level of 69 percent and the patient entered into a drug withdrawal delirium. *There was a return of muscle tone resulting in a suspension of motor paralysis and in the subject's acting out his dreams* (Figure 19.18). Dreaming appeared to have *intruded*

Figure 19.17
Suppression of REM Sleep with Nardil in a Narcoleptic Followed by Withdrawal
Psychosis

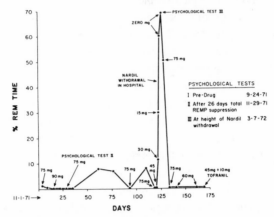

During three days of progressive drug withdrawal, REM percent rapidly increased.
On the 4th night, with 60% REM sleep and tremendous REMP pressure, the subject
had a number of severe nightmares with verbalization, cries for help, and motor
movements associated with dream content. The following day, the patient was given
his third battery of tests and that night REM sleep reached 69%, the subject entered
into a drug withdrawal delirium or psychosis. He appeared to be awake and hallucinating, though in actuality he was in REM sleep, dreaming having *intruded or spilled
over* in such a way that the motor paralysis normally accompanying REMPs was
suspended and he seemed to be acting out dreams in a motor fashion. That this was
occurring in REM sleep is indicated by the presence of saw-tooth waves. The subject
made running movements, got up, tried to open the door and gestured, these motions
being temporally associated with dream content and with a marked breakthrough of
muscle tone in the EMG (Figure 18).

or *spilled over* into the waking state and the motor barrier was breached. The
subject made running movements, actually got up and tried to open the door,
gestured and pointed and these movements were temporally associated with
dream content. He dreamed that he saw a clarinet lying on the floor and he
stood up to get it (actually he did get up). It was clear that he was hallucinating.

DISCUSSION

In conclusion I want to stress the following points:

1. There does not appear to exist a one-to-one correlation between dream

Figure 19.18

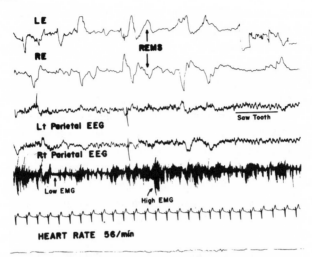

Subj. M BREAKTHROUGH OF MUSCLE TONE IN SLEEP ONSET REMP DURING REBOUND FOLLOWING NARDIL WITHDRAWAL. REM SLEEP = 69.0%

content and physiological fluctuations involving eye movement, autonomic functions, body movement, penile erection, etc., but there are partial correlations which occur more often than chance would allow. Some of the physiological fluctuations appear to be non-specific, part of the generalized activation of the REMPs.

2. Another type of psychophysiological correlation has been stressed. It is possible by suppressing, through drugs or other means, a particular stage of sleep, to simultaneously eliminate the mental activity normally associated with this the psychological and behavioral events occurring *during* total prolonged REMP suppression and the events associated with the rebound following withdrawal of the drug. The so-called REMP intrusion or spillover model does not appear to hold during prolonged periods of total REMP suppression. That is, the notion that during such periods REMP pressure develops, resulting in increased compensatory dreamlike activity, possibly producing psychosis, has turned out to be false. However, this theory appears to be applicable to the processes following rapid withdrawal of such drugs as Nardil, alcohol and barbiturates which result in marked rebound increases in

REM sleep. The threshold for REM intrusion into the waking state appears to be the point at which REM sleep reaches a level of 60 percent or more of total sleep time. When this occurs, muscle tone is regained, motor paralysis is breached and dreams are acted out. This state of affairs constitutes acute delirium or toxic pscyhosis, as in delirium tremens.

4. Not only does psychosis *not* develop during periods of prolonged REMP suppression but there is no evidence of increase in primary process thinking. There are currently two theories about the effects of REMP suppression. The first, the REMP intrusion model just described, holds that during REMP suppression, compensatory increases in dreamlike activity will occur during NREM sleep or during waking itself. The second theory (Arkin *et al.*, 1972) maintains that something quite different occurs, that is, that while REMP suppression is *ongoing*, compensatory increases in dreamlike activity to do occur in NREM sleep or waking but rather, there is a *disruption* of those cognitive processes having to do with dream formation and quite possibly a disruption of certain aspects of waking mentation that depend on these same cognitive processes. Thus, instead of compensatory activity, deficits develop.

5. The results reported support the second theory. The most striking finding was the marked decrease in the performance test scores of the WAIS. These tests of visual organization tap some highly complex cognitive processes, the ability to perceive, analyze and synthesize, involving spatial organization, the reproduction of abstract visual designs, and planning. The tests seem to indicate that our patients, while on the drug, showed defects in these abilities. Several of these performance tests seem to me to trench upon something that might be close to imaginative or creative thinking. They appear to require higher cognitive processes than the purely verbal tests involving information, comprehension, vocabulary, arithmetic, or digit span. It seems possible that the loss of efficiency in these tests, which have such a large visual component, may be related to the fact that visual processes involved in dreaming are disrupted during REMP suppression. It may be that a similar disruption goes on during the day associated with suppression of latent diurnal REMPs, for the existence of which there is considerable evidence (Friedman and Fisher, 1967). The sleep attacks of narcolepsy are in themselves proofs of this notion. That is, there may be some relationship between the visual-perceptual organizational processes of dreams and the capacity for visual, abstract, and synthetic functions demonstrated in the WAIS performance tests.

6. I have stressed the fact that in animals the most striking consquence of prolonged REMP suppression brought about by the waking method has been the development of CNS excitability with evidence of a hyperdrive state involving sexuality, eating, and aggression. When REMP suppression is brought about by the MAO inhibitor, Nardil, hypersexuality does not develop but the opposite, *hyposexuality*, impotence in males and the disappearance of orgastic capacity in females. It is not clear whether this represents a species difference due to the greater complexity of human sexual behavior or to differences in the biochemical consequences of REMP suppression by the two methods, waking and drug. I refer especially to the biochemical vicissitudes of the biogenic amine serotonin, importantly involved in both REM sleep and sexual behavior. It is known that serotonin depletion in the brain is associated with hypersexuality and the accumulation of serotonin with hyposexuality.

It is not certain at this point whether it is total REMP suppression that produces changes in sexual behavior or a biochemical action which simultaneously suppresses REM sleep and affects sexual behavior. This statement also holds for any other apparent effect of prolonged REMP suppression brought about by drugs. Hypersexuality has not been reported in man after REM deprivation for 15–16 nights. One final comment: most of Wyatt's patients treated with Nardil, and one of ours, developed marked weight gains due to hyperphagia. It is puzzling that Nardil has this differential effect on drives, decreasing sexuality but increasing eating behavior. At any rate, these results point out the importance of drives in relation to REM sleep and its deprivation.

7. There is good reason to believe that during REM sleep there is a release from inhibition of the drive centers and circuits within the limbic system. The removal during the REM state of the normal inhibitory and modulating influences of the hippocampus and amygdala on the hypothalamic drive areas are probably of prime importance. The functions regulated by the limbic system have in the broadest sense to do with self and species preservation, what neurophysiologists refer to as the four F's, namely, fight, flight, feeding and fornication, functions which Freud included in his all-encompassing dual instinctual drive theory of sex and aggression. What has not been sufficiently stressed is that, in addition to the marked physiological and physic activation that is the chief characteristic of the REM state, there is a concomitant activation of the drives. One important aspect of this is the arousal of sexuality in the broad psychoanalytic sense, including component instinctual

drives such as orality. Indeed, it may be suggested that REM periods represent one of the purest drive states we know of. Seminal emission in the male and orgasm in the female in association with an hallucinatory REM dream is a fact of singular importance. Amongst the physiological characteristics that make REMPs a special organismic state, these phenomena have not been sufficiently stressed. In fact, the REM state could be defined as that special state in which such astonishing processes can occur, since they are manifested in no other condition except in rare pathological instances in the waking state in man.

I want to conclude by suggesting that Freud's wish fulfillment theory of dreaming has been given a premature burial. I believe it is still a viable hypothesis that the unconscious wish (the cognitive format of the drive) is activated during REMPs and is raised to hallucinatory intensity in the form of a wish-fulfilling dream during a special organismic state that includes ongoing drive activity. In most recent theories, the conception of dreaming has become pallid and watered down in comparison to Freud's formulation in terms of the dream as an attempt to deal with those indestructible, especially repressed, unconscious infantile wishes, the mental representations of the great human passions, the instinctual drives. But it must be stated that however important all this has appeared to be when viewed from the chair behind the couch, the experiments reported suggest that human beings seem to be able to function fairly well for prolonged periods of time in the absence of dreaming. Thus, REM sleep and sleep generally become more mysterious the more we learn about them. It may be, as someone has said, "Sleep is to prevent us from wandering around in the dark and bumping into things" (Dement, 1972).

REFERENCES

Akindele, M. O., Evans, J. I. & Oswald, I. (1970), Mono-amine oxidase inhibitors, sleep and mood. *Electroenceph. Clin. Neurophysiol.* 29:47–56.

Arkin, A. M., Antrobus, J. S., Toth, M. & Sanders, K. (1972), The effects of REMP deprivation on sleep mentation. Progress Report No. 2. Association for the Psychophysiological Study of Sleep. Lake Minnewaska, New York.

Broughton, R. J. (1968), Sleep disorders: disorders of arousal? *Science,* 159:1070–1078.

Cohen, H. D. & Schapiro, A. (1970a), Vaginal blood flow during sleep. Paper presented at 10th Meeting of Association for the Psychophysiological Study of Sleep, Santa Fe, New Mexico.

——(1970b), A method for measuring sexual arousal in the female. Paper presented at Society for Psychophysiological Research, New Orleans, La.

Dement, W. C. (1960), The effect of dream deprivation. *Science,* 131:1705.

——— (1972), *Some Must Watch While Some Must Sleep*. Stanford: Stanford Alumni Association.

——— Fisher, C. (1960a), Studies in dream deprivation and satiation. *Psychoanal. Quart.*, 29:607–608 (Abstract).

——— (1960b), Studies in dream deprivation and satiation: an experimental demonstration of the necessity for dreaming. *Bull. Phila. Assn. Psychoanal.*, 10:30 (Abstract).

——— Henry, P., Cohen, H., & Ferguson, J. (1967), Studies on the effects of REM deprivation in humans and animals. In: *Sleep and Altered States of Consciousness*. eds. S. S. Kety, E. V. Evarts, and H. L. Williams. Baltimore: Williams and Wilkins, pp. 456–468.

Fisher, C. (1966), Dreaming and sexuality. In: *Psychoanalysis—A General Psychology. Essays in Honor of Heinz Hartmann*, eds. R. M. Loewenstein, L. M. Newman, M. Schur, and A. J. Solnit, New York: International Universities Press, pp. 537–569.

——— Byrne, J., Edwards, A., & Kahn, E. (1970), A psychophysiological study of nightmares. *J. Amer. Psychoanal. Assn.*, 18:747–782.

——— Gross, J., & Zuch, J. (1965), A cycle of penile erection synchronous with dreaming (REM) sleep. *Arch. Gen. Psychiat.*, 12:29–45.

——— Kahn, E., Edwards, A., & Davis, D. (1972), Suppression of REM sleep in a patient with intractable narcolepsy. In: *Sleep Research* Vol. I. eds. M. H. Chase, W. C. Stern, and P. L. Weaver. Los Angeles: Brain Information Service/Brain Research Institute, p. 159.

——— (1973), A psychophysiological study of nightmares and night terrors. II. The suppression of stage 4 night terrors with Diazepam. *Arch. Gen. Psychiat.*, 28:252–259.

Friedman, S. & Fisher, C. (1967), On the presence of a rhythmic, diurnal, oral instinctual drive cycle in man: A preliminary report. *J. Amer. Psychoanal. Assn.*, 15:317–343.

Karacan, I., Rosenbloom, A. L., & Williams, R. L. (1970), The clitoral erection cycle during sleep. Paper presented at 10th Meeting of Association for Psychophysiological Study of Sleep, Santa Fe, New Mexico.

Oswald, I. (1969), Human brain protein, drugs and dreams. *Nature, Lond.*, 223:893–897.

Passouant, P., Popoviciu, L., Velok, G., & Baldy-Moulinier, M. (1968), Étude polygraphique des narcolepsies au cours du nycthémère. *Rev. Neurol.* 118:431–441.

Rechtschaffen, A. (1973), The psychophysiology of mental activity during sleep. In: *The Psychophysiology of Thinking*. eds. F. J. McGuigan and R. A. Schoonover, New York: Academic Press, pp. 153–205.

Roffwarg, H. P., Dement, W. C., Muzio, J. N., & Fisher, C. (1962), Dream imagery: relationship to rapid eye movements of sleep. *Arch. Gen. Psychiat.*, 7:235.

Vogel, G. W., Thompson, F. C., Thurmond, A., & Rivers, B. (1973), The effect of REM deprivation on depression. *Psychosomatics*, 14:104–107.

——— Traub, A. C. (1968), REM deprivation: I. The effect on schizophrenic patients. *Arch. Gen. Psychiat.*, 18:287–300.

——— Ben-Horin, P., & Meyers, G. M. (1968), REM deprivation: II. The effects on depressed patients. *Arch. Gen. Psychiat.*, 18:301–311.

Wyatt, R. J., Fram, D. H., Buchbinder, R., & Snyder, F. (1971a), Treatment of intractable narcolepsy with a monoamine oxidase inhibitor. *New Eng. J. Med.*, 285:987–991.

——— Kupfer, D. J., & Snyder, F. (1971b), Total prolonged drug-induced REM sleep suppression in anxious-depressed patients. *Arch. Gen. Psychiat.*, 24:145–155.

20. The Brain as a Dream Machine: An Activation-Synthesis Hypothesis of Dreaming

J. Allan Hobson

The master of the school is gone and the boys are in an uproar.

          —THOMAS PAINE
          "An Essay on Dreams" (1795)

I can but give an instance or so of what part is done sleeping and what part awake . . . and to do this I will first take . . . Dr. Jekyll and Mr. Hyde. I had long been trying to write a story on this subject. . . . For two days I went about wracking my brains for a plot of any sort; and on the second night I dreamed the scene at the window, and a scene of turmoil split in two, in which Hyde, pursued for some crime, took the powder and underwent the change in the presence of his pursuers. All the rest was made awake, and consciously.

          —ROBERT LOUIS STEVENSON
          "A Chapter on Dreams" (1892)

All subjective experience, including dreaming, tends to be organized by the linguistic faculty of our brain-minds as a narrative-scenario. And we are so intensely involved—and in such peculiar ways—in these story-films that we tend to adopt an interpretive literary stance when reacting to our dreams. But just as literature and film—regardless of their content—may be profitably regarded as particular forms of expression, so may dreams also be profitably viewed as particular forms of mental experience. And it is this formal view of dreaming—as a particular kind of mental experience—that is enlightened by the reciprocal-interaction model of REM sleep physiology.

We begin by asking the most general and—we think—the most fundamental question about dreams: Where do they come from? Why are they so strange? Why are they so hard to remember? And what purpose do they serve? To answer these questions, we have developed the new dream theory called the *activation-synthesis hypothesis* (Hobson and McCarley 1977).

The recognition that the brain is switched on periodically during sleep answers the question of where dreaming comes from: it is simply the awareness that is normal to an auto-activated brain-mind. This causal inference is continued in the term *activation* in the new dream theory's title. The question of why dreams are paradoxically both coherent and strange is in turn suggested by the term *synthesis*, which denotes the best possible fit of intrinsically inchoate data produced by the auto-activated brain-mind.

The original dream theory thus had two parts: *activation*, provided by the brain stem; and *synthesis*, provided by the forebrain, especially the cortex and those subcortical regions concerned with memory. The physiology that is now in hand best supports the first part of the theory; much more work needs to be done on the synthetic aspects of the process. But I now add a third major component to the theory, the concept of *mode switching*, which accounts for the *differences* in the way the activated forebrain synthesizes information in dreaming (compared with waking): for the twin paradoxes of dream bizarreness and insight failure (where the system has lost self-reference as well as its orientation to the outside world) and for dreaming forgetting.

Brain-Mind Isomorphism

The simplest and most direct approach to the correlation of dream mentation with the physiological state of the brain is to assume a formal isomorphism between the subjective and the objective levels of investigation. By *formal isomorphism* I mean a similarity of form in the psychological and physiological domains. Such an approach begins with the general features (forms) of dreaming mentation and leaves until later consideration the narrative content of the individual dream.

As an example of the formal isomorphism approach, it may be reasonably assumed that subjective experience of visually formed imagery in dreams implicates activation of perceptual elements in the visual system during REM sleep. We may further assume that the visual-system activation of REM sleep must be formally similar to that of the waking state. We could not otherwise account for the clarity of our dream vision. Other details of psychophysiological correlation are assumed to obey the same general law; for example, the vivid hallucinated sensation of moving is assumed to be related to patterned activation of motor systems and of those central brain structures subserving one's perception of where one's body is in space. When we look at the physiological level, for patterned activation of the visual motor and vestibular systems, powerful, highly coordinated excitatory processes are found to be recordable in visual, sensory, and motor centers of the brain.

THE PSYCHOPHYSIOLOGY OF REM-SLEEP DREAMING

To conceptualize how the brain-mind is activated during sleep in such a way as to account for the distinctive cognitive features of dreaming, some of the physiological processes described by the reciprocal-interaction model have been converted into the intermediate language of systems theory. In using electrical-circuit and computer terminology in this section, I aim to facilitate understanding, not to reduce the brain-mind to an electrical circuit or a computer.

Brain-Mind Activation

The brain-mind has to be turned on and kept internally activated to support dream mentation throughout the REM sleep episode. A possible mechanism is the removal of inhibitory restraint upon many brain circuits consequent to sleep-related cessation of activity in a specific subset of neurons.

I propose that the *on-off switch* is the reciprocal-interacting neuronal populations comprising the aminergic neurons and the reticular neurons of the brain stem. While we do not yet know which of the two populations is the initiator, we have reason to favor the aminergic group for this role. Once the reticular system is disinhibited, its own energy will be capable of supplying the *power* to maintain neuronal activation throughout the brain.

The aminergic REM-off neurons are thought to exert a modulatory as well as an inhibitory influence upon the brain during waking. When this modulatory neuronal activity ceases in REM sleep, other brain ccells become spontaneously active. Not only are they more active, but the "mode" of their activity is changed: they run free of restraint from both external stimuli and internal inhibition. By such a mechanism, we may not only explain how the mind may be turned on during sleep but also account for its unusual operating properties during dreaming.

Sensory-Input Blockade

Access to the internally activated brain-mind by input from the outside world has to be excluded in order for sleep—and the illusions of dreaming—to be maintained. This appears to be accomplished in at least two ways. First, active inhibition of the nerves denies stimulus signals of peripheral origin access to the central nervous system; such *pre-synaptic* inhibition has been recorded at sensory-relay centers throughout the brain. The physiologist Ottavio Pompeiano, of Pisa, Italy, has shown that the nerve terminals from primary sensory neurons feeding information either into the spinal cord, or into certain brain stem and thalamic sensory-relay nuclei, are depolarized by signals coming from the brain stem (1978). The source of this depolarization is probably the same reticular neurons that constitute the on side of the power switch and include also the pre-motor neurons generating eye movements. Because of their depolarization by internal signals, the primary sensory neurons were rendered less efficacious in transmitting external information: there is simply less transmitter available for each of the externally excited volleys to release at the primary sensory endings.

The second mechanism for excluding external sensory signals is competition, or *occlusion,* by which the higher levels of sensory and associative circuits are kept so busy processing the internally generated messages that they ignore external signals. The net effect of occlusion is the outright neglect of external stimuli or the facile incorporation of them into the internally generated information stream of dreaming. In a REM-sleep dream, I once interpreted the buzzer (which timed our EEG records in the National Institutes of Health sleep lab) as a telephone ringing. Such stimulus incorporation into dreams not only helps preserve sleep, but also provides insight into the temporal aspects of brain-mind interaction in sleep.

Motor-Output Blockade

The internally activated but sensorially disconnected brain-mind must also quell motor output so as to prevent the enactment of dreamed motor commands—lest we all take off on dream walks, dream runs, or even dream flights four times a night! Motor acts appear to be canceled by inhibition of motor-command neurons in the spinal cord and brain stem. This output blockade also prevents the disruption of sleep by the sensory stimulation that such movement would necessarily feed back to the brain.

Here again it was Pompeiano who provided an explanation of this paradox (1978). In an elegant series of experiments, he convincingly demonstrated that the final common-path motor neurons of the spinal cord are actively inhibited via the physiological mechanism of postsynaptic inhibition. Pompeiano's evidence suggested that the origin of these postsynaptic inhibitory signals is, again, the brain stem. Some of the reticular neurons, activated via aminergic disinhibition, are sending "no go" commands down to the final common-path motor neurons in the spinal cord, while others are conducting "go" commands to upper levels of the motor system. This is a "zero-sum" game as far as motor output is concerned: internal motor commands are generated, but their external activation is effectively canceled by concomitant inhibitory signals.

By three processes, the brain-mind in REM-sleep dreaming is thus made ready: (1) to process information (activation); (2) to exclude sense data coming from without (input blockade); and (3) not to act upon the internally generated information (output blockade). (See figure 20.1). It remains to provide the activated but disconnected brain with internal signals and to make it process them as if they came from the outside world.

Internal Signal Generation

Dream stimuli appear to arise by the process intimately associated with the mechanism of brain activation. In most mammals, including humans, the so-called *PGO waves* (*P* for *pons, G* for [lateral] *geniculate,* and *O* for *occipital cortex*) present themselves as evidence for an automatic, internally generated information signal which originates in the brain stem. In precise association with the rapid eye movements, strong pulses of excitation are conducted from the brain stem to the thalamus. They are also sent via independent pathways to both the visual and the association cortex. It is now known that these PGO waves are generated by brain-stem cellular activity that faithfully replicates the direction of the rapid eye movements. Thus, not only is internal information generated in REM sleep but that information has a high degree of spatial specificity. According to the activation-synthesis hypothesis of dreaming, the now auto-activated, disconnected, and auto-stimulated brain-mind processes these signals and interprets them in terms of information stored in memory.

Synthesis: Switching the Mode of Information Processing

Although the precise cerebral basis of the distinctive cognitive disorders of dreaming is not yet fully understood, it is tempting to see these failures as perhaps related to the cessation of activity in the modulatory neurons. This arrest of modulatory neuronal activity would affect the entire brain including the cerebral cortex by depriving it of a tonic influence that may be essential to attentional processes, including the capacity to organize information in a logical and coherent manner and to achieve full self-awareness. This is what I mean by a change in mode of information processing: the brain-mind is active but, for some physiological reason, it lacks the capacity to test both external and internal realities.

During the waking state, the modulatory neurons are active; and the brain is thus set to perform its information-processing functions, including anaylzing incoming stimuli, integrating them with the priorities of the day, and producing the appropriate actions upon the environment. In the absence of both external information and the internal modulatory influence, the REM-sleep-activated brain interprets its internally generated signals as if they were of external origin. Both orientation-in-the-world and self-critical perspective are lost. By a similar mechanism, which we might call *demodulation,* it may be speculated that the synthesized dream product is unremembered. According to this view, the activated forebrain circuits that mediate the dream experience are simply not instructed to keep a record of the dream transactions, unless, of course, the dreamer is aroused and his or her modulatory neurons are turned back on. Thus the "remember" instruction (or mode) is also postulated as being carried out by signals from the modulatory interneurons in waking (when they are active) but not in dreaming (where they are inactive). All current models of learning and memory evoke the intervention of such modulatory interneurons, making the attribution of dream amnesia to the loss of aminergic modulation consistent with state-of-the-art hypotheses regarding learning and memory at the cellular level.

THE FORM OF DREAMS EXPLAINED

The activation-synthesis hypothesis can now account, in a preliminary but specific way, for all five of the formal aspects of dreaming as I have defined them: visual and motor hallucination; the delusional acceptance of such

Figure 20.1
REM Sleep and Dreaming

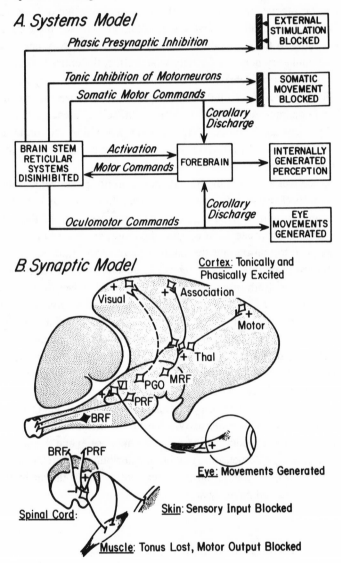

A. Systems Model

Phasic Presynaptic Inhibition → | EXTERNAL STIMULATION BLOCKED |

Tonic Inhibition of Motorneurons →
Somatic Motor Commands → | SOMATIC MOVEMENT BLOCKED |

Corollary Discharge

BRAIN STEM RETICULAR SYSTEMS DISINHIBITED — *Activation* / *Motor Commands* → FOREBRAIN → | INTERNALLY GENERATED PERCEPTION |

Corollary Discharge

Oculomotor Commands → | EYE MOVEMENTS GENERATED |

B. Synaptic Model

Cortex: Tonically and Phasically Excited

Visual
Association
Motor
Thal
MRF
PGO
PRF
BRF
BRF PRF

Eye: Movements Generated

Spinal Cord:

Skin: Sensory Input Blocked

Muscle: Tonus Lost, Motor Output Blocked

hallucinoid experience as real; extremely bizarre spatial and temporal distortion; strong emotion; and, finally, the failure to remember.

Hallucination

Mental activity in sleep is different from that in waking in that formed images arise in the absence of external sensory input and motor output: we see clearly, and motion is vividly hallucinated. In the waking state, we can fantasize scenarios; but even the fantasies of a Walter Mitty are not as intense as dream experience. According to the activation-synthesis hypothesis, the sensorimotor hallucinosis of the dream experience is the direct and necessary concomitant of the specific activation of sensorimotor brain circuits. These circuits link the brain stem to other subcortical centers and to the upper motor neurons and analytic sensory neurons of the cerebral cortex. If the higher-level neurons of the visual system are subjected to the same type of phasic excitatory signal that they "see" during the wake state, they will process that signal as if it came from the outside world. Our cortical neurons read the signals as visual sensory inputs. (See figure 20.2).

A. Systems model. A schematic representation of the brain processes underlying dreaming. Cessation of aminergic inhibition leads to activation of the reticular formation. The reticular formation turns on the cortex and sends it information about the rapid eye movements that it generates, resulting in visual perception. External stimuli and movement of it are both blocked by inhibition.

B. Synaptic model. Some directly and indirectly disinhibited neuronal systems, together with their supposed contributions to REM sleep phenomena. At level of brain stem, four neuronal types are illustrated.

MRF: midbrain reticular neurons projecting to thalamus that convey tonic and phasic electrical signals rostrally.

PGO: burst cells in peribrachial region that convey phase activation and specific eye movement information to geniculate body and cortex (dotted line indicates uncertainty of direct projection).

PRF: pontine reticular-formation neurons that transmit phasic activation signals to oculomotor neurons (VI) and spinal cord, which generate eye movements, twitches of extremities, and presynaptic inhibition.

BRF: bulbar reticular-formation neurons that send tonic hyperpolarizing signals to motoneurons in spinal cord. As a consequence of these descending influences, sensory input and motor output are blocked at level of spinal cord. At level of forebrain, visual association and motor cortex neurons all receive time and phasic activation signals for nonspecific and specific thalamic relays. *Source:* J. Allan Hobson and Mircea Steriade, "Neuronal Basis of Behavioral State Control," in *Handbook of Physiology—The Nervous System, IV,* ed. Vernon B. Mountcastle (Bethesda: American Physiological Society, 1986), fig. 44, p. 795.

Figure 20.2
Visual imagery and REMs

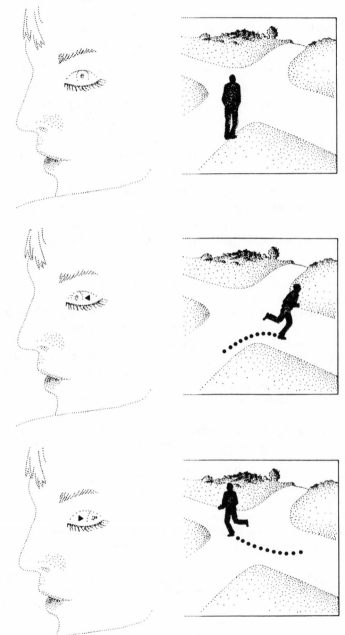

The brain-mind knows what state it is in only from its context. Since most organized percepts derive from the waking state, the REM-sleep-activated brain-mind assumes it is awake despite the distinctly different organization of experience. In REM sleep, the brain has no choice but to interpret its internally generated signals in terms of its previous experience with the outside world. According to activation synthesis, the change in mode of information processing caused by an arrest in aminergic neuronal firing contributes to this loss of self-reference.

Dreaming as Delusional

The internally generated signals are not only synthesized into extraordinary stories but are also accepted as experiential reality. The reason is that there is no external input to structure experience, and that only remote memory serves as a reference point. The past is thus interpreted as if it were the present. There are no external cues from which the brain-mind might construct a consistent orientational framework. And because the brain-mind has lost self-reference, it cannot provide internal stability, either.

In using the terms *hallucinoid* and *delusional* to describe dreams, I do not mean to imply that dreaming is psychopathological; it is a normal mental process. But that it is a valid model of psychosis, there can be no doubt. I think that understanding the dream process may better inform understanding of psychosis. Conversely, I believe that the ''psychopathology'' of these clinical states may probably best be explained by an extension of the kind of functional psychophysiological theory I am proposing here for dreams. While psychotic symptoms, like dreams, have individually specific meanings, it is not those meanings that generate the psychotic experience. Rather, the human brain-mind ascribes meaning to internally generated signals, whether it be normally deluded as in REM sleep, or abnormally deluded as in psychosis during the waking state.

How eye movement information may be related to visual scene construction in dreams is suggested by the change in position of a dream character with each change in eye position. While the data bearing on this specific question are still controversial, there is no doubt either of the strong correlation between eye movement and visual image intensity or that specific information about eye movement does reach the visual centers of the forebrain. Since the existence of an internal signal system has been known since the clinical observation of Helmholtz (1863), it seems likely that the visual brain uses its own eye movement data in dream scene elaboration. *Drawing by Barbara Haines.*

Disorientation: Distortions of Time, Place, and Person

The hallucinoid and delusional mental activity of REM sleep is the more extraordinary for its flagrant violations of natural law. There are discontinuities of all aspects of the orientational domain. Persons, places, and time change suddenly, without notice. There may be abrupt jumps, cuts, and interpolations. There may be fusions: impossible combinations of people, places, times, and activities abound. Other natural laws are disobeyed, and sometimes pleasantly so: gravity can be overcome in the sensational flying dream. We understand these remarkable dream features by adding to previous arguments the notion that the internally generated signals are qualitatively similar to, but quantitatively different from, those that arise from outside the brain. They are different in terms of intensity, of pattern, and of classes of sensory stimuli.

The eye movements of REM sleep in the cat have many oblique and rotational components, which may well generate an unusual sensory code for the forebrain to interpret. Thus, one aspect of spatiotemporal distortion, or dream bizarreness, may reside in the unusual nature of the stimulus source itself. Attentional processes also may be impaired (owing again to mode switching), making it more difficult for the brain to distinguish between different channels of information. In REM sleep, multiple sensory channels are simultaneously activated. Under such circumstances, the kaleidoscopic barrage of all internally generated information must be synthesized into a single plot. And despite the intense bizarreness of these hallucinoid experiences, we accept them as real. The changed mode of the synthetic analytic system may, I think, account for this marked loss of insight.

Intensification of Emotion

Activation synthesis ascribes the intense feelings (such as anxiety, surprise, fear, and elation) characteristic of some dreams to activation both of emotional centers, probably of the limbic brain, as well as of brain-stem "startle" networks. We also know that the autonomic motoneuronal system of the brain stem (which causes the heart to beat fast and the breathing to speed up) may be activated as an integral component of the brain-stem neuronal process responsible for REM. Hence there may be not only intensification of the central components of emotion via forebrain activation but also peripheral feedback from the autonomic mediators of emotional experience.

Amnesia

We can only speculate about one of the most striking cognitive aspects of dreams: that is, the failure to remember most of them. REM sleep is switched on, as I have said, when the firing of the brain stem's aminergic neurons is arrested. These *modulatory* neurons determine the metabolic mode of the brain. One aspect of this notion is that the mode selector (or controller) sends the instruction "Record this experience" (or, "Do not record this experience"). An analogy to a tape recorder is apt if overly concrete. In dreaming, the brain-mind follows the instructions: "Integrate all signals received into the most meaningful story possible; however farcical the result, believe it; and then forget it." The "forget" instruction is most simply explained as the absence of a "remember" instruction.

During REM sleep, the aminergic neurons do not send their "remember" instruction to the forebrain. If not told to remember, the forebrain will forget. I assume that the reason for such dream recall as we do have is that our dream experience is temporarily stored in a fragile short-term memory system, and that it can be more permanently stored only if an arousal occurs so that the aminergic neurons are reactivated. If, and only if, aminergic signals arrive at the many neurons storing that trace memory will the perceptual and cognitive experience of the dream be transferred into intermediate memory.

ACTIVATION SYNTHESIS AND PSYCHOANALYSIS

The activation-synthesis hypothesis assumes that dreams are as meaningful as they can be under the adverse working conditions of the brain in REM sleep. The activated brain-mind does its best to attribute meaning to the internally generated signals. It is this synthetic effort that gives our dreams their impressive thematic coherence: dream plots remain remarkably intact despite their orientational disorganization. And it may be that their symbolic, prophetic character arises from the integrative strain of this synthetic effort. The brain-mind may need to call upon its deepest myths to find a narrative frame that can contain the data. Hence, one can continue to interpret dreams metaphorically, and even in terms of the dynamically repressed unconscious, if one so chooses. But such a practice is no longer either necessary or sufficient as an explanation of either the origin or the nature of dreaming.

I differ from Freud in that I think that most dreams are neither obscure nor bowdlerized, but rather transparent and unedited. They contain clearly mean-

Figure 20.3
Activation Synthesis and Psychoanalysis

Psychoanalytical Dream Theory

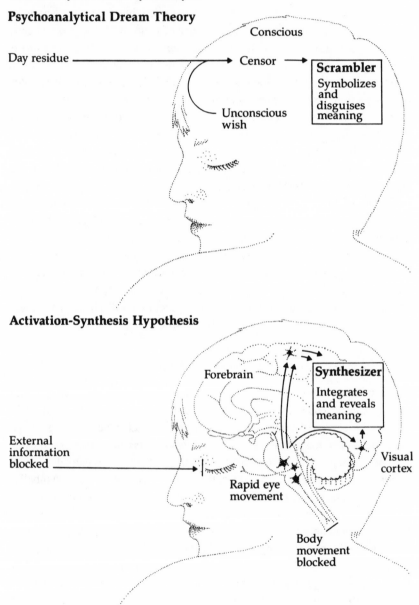

Conscious

Day residue ⟶ Censor ⟶ **Scrambler**
Symbolizes and disguises meaning

Unconscious wish

Activation-Synthesis Hypothesis

Forebrain **Synthesizer**
Integrates and reveals meaning

External information blocked

Visual cortex

Rapid eye movement

Body movement blocked

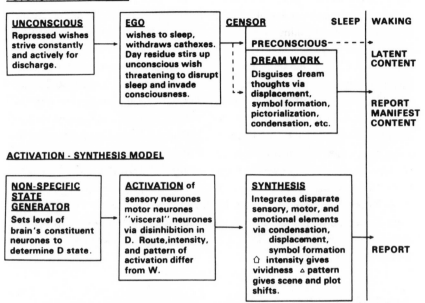

PSYCHOANALYTIC MODEL

UNCONSCIOUS	EGO	CENSOR	SLEEP	WAKING
Repressed wishes strive constantly and actively for discharge.	wishes to sleep, withdraws cathexes. Day residue stirs up unconscious wish threatening to disrupt sleep and invade consciousness.	PRECONSCIOUS - - - - - ● DREAM WORK Disguises dream thoughts via displacement, symbol formation, pictorialization, condensation, etc.		LATENT CONTENT REPORT MANIFEST CONTENT

ACTIVATION - SYNTHESIS MODEL

NON-SPECIFIC STATE GENERATOR	ACTIVATION of	SYNTHESIS	
Sets level of brain's constituent neurones to determine D state.	sensory neurones motor neurones "visceral" neurones via disinhibition in D. Route, intensity, and pattern of activation differ from W.	Integrates disparate sensory, motor, and emotional elements via condensation, displacement, symbol formation ⌂ intensity gives vividness △ pattern gives scene and plot shifts.	REPORT

The old psychoanalytic model and the new activation-synthesis model are sketched here to emphasize their differences. It is obvious that the old model has no brain basis: the strangeness of dreams is attributed to the active disguise by the censor of unacceptable unconscious wishes which, together with recent experience (''day residue''), constitute the instigators of dreaming.

The new model is brain-based: the strangeness of dreams is attributed to the distinctive physiological features of REM-sleep generation by which disparate and chaotic internal data must be integrated in the absence both of the structure of external space-time data and of the internal chemical controls necessary for logical thought, attention, and insight. *Drawing by Barbara Haines.*

The difference sketched above are emphasized here by showing, in parallel, the three critical steps in dream construction posited by each model. For psychoanalysis, the dream report is a symbolically encoded transformation of the true dream stimulus, needing interpretation to reveal the latent content. For activation synthesis, the dream as reported is the transparent and directly legible product of an unusual mode of information processing. The sense and the nonsense of dreams are both related to this change in brain-mind mode. *Source:* J. Allan Hobson and Robert W. McCarley, ''The Brain as a Dream State Generator: An Activation-Synthesis Hypothesis of the Dream Process,'' *American Journal of Psychiatry* 134, no. 12 (1977): 1346.

ingful, undisguised, highly conflictual impulses worthy of note by the dreamer (and any interpretive assistant). My position echoes Jung's notion of dreams as transparently meaningful and does away with any distinction between manifest and latent content. While contemporary conservative psychoanalysts continue to defend and apply Freud's dream theory without substantial modification, the more liberal (or hermeneutic) wing of psychoanalysis has explicitly divorced itself from neurology and the causal paradigm of physical science. Both groups may now wish to reconsider their positions in view of the new findings. To maintain their allegiance to Freud and his scientific style, the orthodoxy should welcome an updated dream theory that is compatible with an updated neurobiology (see figure 20.3). Because of its openness, the new theory gives the radicals the interpretive license they seek while offering a return to the safe harbor of classical science. To clarify the contrast, let me review the theory and examine the way in which its components are explained by orthodox psychoanalysis and the way in which we can now understand them.

Energy of the Dream Process

Freud's point of departure in the *Project for a Scientific Psychology* (1895) was rigorously scientific. He made it quite clear that his ambition was to establish a theory of the mind that was at one with his theory of the brain. The dream theory was a simple translation of those neurobiologically derived notions that he worked with in the *Project*.

Psychoanalytic dream theory is predicated on the erroneous idea that the nervous system, lacking its own energy, derives energy from two nonneural sources: the external world and somatic drives. We now know that the brain generates its own energy and, in so doing, is not dependent upon either the external world or somatic drives.

Nature of the Energetic Forces

The energy that activates the brain during REM sleep is neuronal, and the neuron is able to create its own information. The power demands of the energy system are relatively low; in Freud's view, they were high. Complementing this shift in emphasis, psychoanalysis sees the shaping of dream content as primarily ideational (the latent dream thoughts); activation synthesis sees it as strongly sensorimotor (there is no difference between latent and manifest content). Freud believed that unconscious wishes and day residues join forces to initiate dreaming. Activation synthesis sees wishes and day residues as two of many shaping forces in the synthetic process of dreaming but as having nothing whatsoever to do with generating the state in which such forces exert their influence.

Direction of Information Processing

Since the required energy (power) and the informational sources are of low level, activation synthesis sees dream construction as a *meaning-added process;* whereas for psychoanalysis, it is *meaning-substractive.* This is what I mean by contrasting synthesis with disguise-censorship of information. For psychoanalysis, the motive force of the dream is an idea whose meaning has to be concealed by a complex decoding process. While motivational forces and recent experience may enter into the synthetic construction of the dream, I hypothesize that dreaming builds up from signals of low informational order (the endogenous sensorimotor stimuli) to a higher-order final product (the dream as narrative).

The Sensory Aspects of a Dream

According to activation synthesis, the development of perceptions during dreaming is progressive, proceeding from primordial visual stimuli to perceptual imagery. By contrast, psychoanalysis sees the development of imagery as a regressive function from the ideational motive force of the dream to a perceptual experience: in dreaming, said Freud, we "regress" toward the sensory side. Activation synthesis has no need of a regression postulate: it is an intrinsic characteristic of the dream state to have a primordial sensory character, because the sensory systems of the brain are intrinsically and primarily activated. We view this sensorial aspect as progressive rather than regressive because the system is autoactive and autocreative.

Interpretation

Psychoanalysis sees dream bizarreness as a result of defensive encoding of unconscious wishes. By contrast, the activation-synthesis hypothesis sees the bizarreness of dreams as the unadulterted result of an imperfect integration of internally generated sensorimotor data which is processed under distinctive conditions: the space-time dimensions of the external world are absent; multiple sensory channels are activated in parallel; and attentional processes are impaired. Thus the disguise-censorship notion can be discarded as unnecessary and unwieldy. Discarded as unnecessary, because we have a more plausible alternative that fits with the neurophysiological facts. And discarded as unwieldy, because the new alternative theory achieves the same result by simpler means.

Meaning of Dreams

The brain in REM sleep, like the brain in waking, does its best to achieve a meaningful integration of data, even if it must resort to creative storytelling. The meaning of dreams for the activation-synthesis theorist is thus transparent rather than opaque. The content of most dreams can be read directly, without decoding. Since the dream state is open-ended, individual dreams are likely to reveal specific cognitive styles, specific aspects of an individual's projective view of the world, and specific historical experiences.

The notion that dream meaning is opaque is thus no longer either necessary or sufficient to account for the meaning of dreams; while apparent symbols in dreams may have multiplicity of "meanings," as opposed to many symbols being reduced to one or two instinctual drives or to sexual anatomy. Finally, in activation synthesis, it is not necessary to resort to interpretation via the technique of free association to find dream meanings.

Conflict in the Creation of Dream Plots

For the activation-synthesis theorist, conflict may enter into the plot construction of a dream. But conflict is only one of several factors used in constructing a dream plot and, as such, is neither necessary nor sufficient to account for the dream-fabrication process, as Freud assumed. Conflictual material occurs naturally in dreams, and may contribute especially to repetitive dreams since it may well have a relatively high priority in dream plot formation. Other factors include recency of input (the psychoanalysts' day residue) and what I would call *persistent concern* (the psychoanalysts' unresolved conflict).

When I was under consideration for the professorship I now hold, I had many vividly anxious and humorously absurd dreams of missing airplanes, boats, and trains. Should these dreams be regarded as symbolic translations of my professional self-doubt? Or do they more simply and directly reflect the fact that I was then traveling much more frequently than I had at any previous time in my life? And why should I need to disguise my concern about promotion? It was on my mind night and day, day and night, in undisguised form as evidenced by the many dreams of favorable—and unfavorable—votes on my candidacy that were mixed in, like double features, with the transportation comedies. And if the purpose of the disguise was to guard my sleep, I would be obliged to fire my censor, because having auto-suggested dream interruption in the interest of dream collection, I woke up with equal frequency from each scenario! I realize, of course, that the orthodox Freudian would seek an even deeper source of my travel and promotion dream anxiety. But I am inclined to see them both as realistic and undisguised variations on the theme of "incomplete arrangements."

To summarize, seven major points of difference with psychoanalytic theory characterize the new psychophysiologic model: the source of the energy for the process is seen as internal (not external); the nature of the energetic force, as neural (not ideational); the sensory aspects, as progressive (rather than regressive); the direction of the information processing, as elaborative (rather then degradative); bizarreness, as primary (rather than as the secondary outcome of defensive transformation); meaning, as transparent (rather than opaque); and conflict, as incidental (rather than fundamental to the process).

MOZART AT THE MUSEUM

The following is the transcript of a dream which I offer as a way of further clarifying the difference between the analytic position of the activation-synthesis hypothesis and Freudian orthodoxy.

My wife, Joan, and I are at the Museum of Fine Arts in Boston to attend a concert in the larger Remus auditorium. It is someone (perhaps John Gibbons) playing a Mozart piano (concerto?) on a large Steinway (no orchestra, but image vague anyway). [The piano is reminiscent of the large Steinway grand in the great hall of the Phillips Collection in Washington, which I visited the previous Saturday.] As is usual on such "museum" occasions, I am restive, feeling like the third wheel on Joan's business bicycle, and hence inattentive.

I decide to explore and go down to the smaller, older theater (near the

Question	Psychoanalysis	Activation Synthesis
Where does the energy for the dream process come from?	From an external stimulus that could not be discharged as a response because of conflict.	It is intrinsic to the brain.
What is the nature of the energy during this dream?	An unconscious idea: for example, a wish to kill my father so I can have my mother to myself.	From the neurons of the brain, each of which is an electrical generator and capacitator.
What is the cause of the sensory aspects of this dream?	Hearing music and seeing concert halls is a regression, to the sensory side, from the unacceptable ideational dream stimulus (such as a wish to kill my father).	The music I "heard" in the dream is quite familiar to me. I often listen to Mozart piano concertos while driving. The scenes (in the museum) are also familiar. I go there often with my wife, who is a program director. I have just been to the Phillips Gallery.
In what direction does information processing proceed?	The report is only the manifest content, which has been designed to conceal the dream's true meaning.	From low-level neural signals impinging on my mind and auditory cortex, I elaborate the sensations that cohere in a plot around the related themes: concern, Mozart, museum.
What accounts for the bizarreness of this dream; the corpulence of Mozart, for example?	Mozart is an obvious symbol of a powerful, venerated but unapproachable male—that is, my father. The fact that he is overweight clinches the argument (but my father is not overweight!)	Mozart is Mozart. I have seen the film *Amadeus* at a special museum showing, so he fits, although in the dream it was not a film. The body-type file has been opened and incongruous plot features are the result: *my* belly has begun to bulge!

Question	Psychoanalysis	Activation Synthesis
What is the role of conflict in this dream?	I want my mother, but my father is in the way. I have to knock him off, but that's not nice.	I am faintly distressed by the incongruities; no orchestra, wrong instrument; Mozart's corpulence (but my distress is not severe enough to make me doubt the dream's reality).
What does the Mozart dream mean?	Opaque: You hate your father and you want to kill him! But you can't face that base wish, so you turn him into a great man and laud him.	Transparent: I would love to see Mozart, to have my wife "score" by attracting him to the museum, and to discover him there so that I could report her coup to others.

Egyptian sarcophagi). This theater is now limited to small lectures but was, twenty years ago, the place where, as young members, Joan and I attended museum programs of the type that are now in Remus, and now under Joan's direction.

I hear music and the faint bustle of excitement. Opening the door a crack, I am amazed to realize that Mozart himself is on stage, playing the same concerto (again without orchestra) on an antique harpsichord from the museum collection (not the Mozart pianoforte). Although the door is open only for an instant, I notice Mozart's rich red brocaded frock coat (the curlicues are gold-embossed) and his white powdered wig. He has a beatific smile, and the arpeggios stream through the door into my ear. I also notice that Mozart has gotten a bit overweight, and wonder why.

I close the door with a shhh!, and try to figure out how to tell Joan of my discovery.

Then I wake up.

The preceding table may help to illustrate the practical differences between activation synthesis and psychoanalysis:

At a deeper level I am prepared to admit that this dream might have a psychoanalytic "meaning": I *am* ambitious. I *do* admire Mozart. I *would*, consciously, like to be as brilliant as Mozart. Some of my most devoted friends have even called me "Mozart." But to propose that Mozart is a stand-in for my father seems less plausible than to assume that, under the suspended cognitive rules of REM sleep, Mozart is Mozart. I saw him and heard him, discovered him even, in an obscure corner of the museum. I found the dream pleasant, surprising, and gratifying. I also enjoyed telling my wife this story. From a social point of view, my dream was a belated wedding present!

The examples just given serve as much to demonstrate the difficulty of deciding between alternative theories of dream interpretation as to convince us that one is better than the other. And in such a literary game, the eloquence and mystique of psychoanalysis are likely to win out over the plain talk and common sense of activation synthesis.

In order to transcend the anecdote and to elaborate an ample and detailed mental status inventory of the dream process, it was therefore necessary to develop a new, formal approach to dream content that would be isomorphic with physiology and share its systematic quantitative and experimental features.

In Part IV, I describe our strategy and preliminary results which support the activation-synthesis view of dreaming as organically driven and organically shaped so as to account for its distinctive cognitive features. Having defined, identified, and measured some of the items in reports that make them dreamlike, I then return to the narrative level and show that by regarding the dream story as transparent—and by looking deeply into it—one can discern significant personal meaning without either free association or the interpretation of putative symbols.

REFERENCES

Freud, Sigmund. 1895. "Project for a Scientific Psychology." In *The Origins of Psychoanalysis: Letters to Wilhelm Fliess, Drafts and Notes: 1887–1902.* Edited by Marie Bonaparte, Anna Freud, and Ernst Kris. Translated by Eric Mosbacher and James Strachey. New York: Basic Books (1954), pp. 347–445.

Helmholtz, Hermann von. 1863. "Sensations of Tone." In *Helmholtz on Perception: Its Physiology and Development.* Edited by R. M. Warren and R. P. Warren. New York: Wiley (1968).

Hobson, J. Allan, and McCarley, Robert W. 1977. "The Brain as a Dream-State Generator: An Activation Synthesis Hypothesis of the Dream Process." *American Journal of Psychiatry* 134:1335–68.

Hobson, J. Allan, and Steriade, Mircea. 1986. "Neuronal Basis of Behavioral State Control."

In *Handbook of Physiology,* vol. 4, *The Nervous System.* Edited by Vernon B. Mountcastle. Bethesda: American Physiological Society, pp. 701–823.

Pompeiano, Ottavio. 1978. "Cholinergic Activation of Reticular and Vestibular Mechanisms Controlling Posture and Eye Movements." In *The Reticular Formation Revisited.* Edited by J. A. Hobson and M. A. B. Brazier. New York: Raven, pp. 473–572.

PART IV

VISTAS

21. Emerging Perspectives on the Dream as an Investigative Tool

Melvin R. Lansky

I. THE PSYCHOANALYTIC STUDY OF THE DREAM

The psychoanalytic study of the dream involves both psychoanalytic investigation of the dream itself and psychoanalytically informed investigation that proceeds using the dream as an investigative tool. The dream, then, is both an object of study in itself and a tool for the study of the individual psyche, of the psychoanalytic process, of the overall clinical situation, or of the workings of the mind or even the brain generally. I will attempt a very selective overview that highlights both emerging trends and challenges for the psychoanalytic study of the dream as an investigative tool. I shall trace briefly the emergence and unfolding of three perspectives. The first concerns the psychoanalytic method and the study of the individual psyche. This was the investigative domain of *The Interpretation of Dreams*. I include in this section problems concerning the associative method and the rules of inference based on it. The second perspective concerns the psychoanalytic process. This includes the problem of interpretation as well as problems in conceptualizing both the nature of psychoanalytic process and the nuances of the transference relationship. The second point of view is that usuallly employed in psychoanaytic case reports. The third concerns the use of dreams in clinical and developmental contexts in which fruits of both psychoanalytic (i.e., associative) and naturalistic (i.e., developmental or general psychiatric) investigations are combined. The third point of view is closer to that employed in dynamically oriented general psychiatric reports.

I shall then touch very briefly on conceptual and methodological problems in the comparison of strictly psychoanalytic data about dreams with nonclinical data using nonpsychoanalytic methods, for example, electroencephalographic data from the sleep laboratory and anthropological data. I shall argue that the psychoanalytic study of the dream will increasingly need buttressing from a philosophical overview science or a metamethodology as strictly psychoanalytical (associative) data is used in contexts that combine more and more with other sources of data both to enhance our knowledge of dreams and to utilize dreams as investigative tools to enhance our knowledge of pathology, life predicaments, and the psychoanalytic process itself.

II. DREAMS AND THE PSYCHOANALYTIC STUDY OF THE IMAGINATION

In *The Interpretation of Dreams* (1900), the dream was hailed as the royal road to the unconscious, that is, the royal road to the investigation of the workings of the mind. The dream was a tool of investigation in the prepsychoanalytic activity of dream analysis that provided most of the data put forward in *The Interpretation of Dreams*. Dream analysis, as opposed to psychoanalysis proper, was a solitary endeavor in which the dreamer collected associations to elements of the manifest dream outside of a definable context for what was later to be recognized as the transference.

Not until the publication of the Dora case (Freud 1905) was the dream seen as the royal road to the investigation, not just of the mind looked at in relative isolation as it had been conceptualized using the results of dream analysis, but also of how the mind of the individual worked when that individual was considered as a self in relation to others, that is to say, in terms of the transference understood in the context of the psychoanalytic process.

The dream, then, when analyzed with the scrupulous use of the associative method has, since the inception of psychoanalysis, been a research tool that reveals the weavings of the imagination that both conceal and express repressed latent wishes. The dream, used psychoanalytically, illuminates the workings of repressed aspects of the mind. Historically considered, these workings were uncovered first in isolation and later in the context of the self in relation to the other.

Freud (1900) points out that it is a major psychological feature of dreams that the dreamer experiences them as discontinuous with the mainstream of that person's mental life: "the dream experience appears as something alien inserted between two sections of life which are perfectly continuous and consistent with each other" (10). And, again: "Our scientific consideration of dreams starts off from the assumption that they are products of our own mental activity. Nevertheless the finished dream strikes us as something alien

to us. We are so little obliged to acknowledge our responsibility for it that
. . . we are just as ready to say 'I had a dream' .   . 'a dream came to me' as
. . . 'I dreamt' '' (48). Clinically, we assume that such an experience of
discontinuity is the result of repression. Repression is the cornerstone of
psychoanalysis. That which is repressed is that which is discontinuous, that
is, dynamically walled off from the mainstream of conscious psychic continuity. Our awareness of the presence of repression results from our sensing
of discontinuity in the patient's narrative. In the analytic situation, the dream
is such a discontinuity. Indeed, the very presence of a dream recalled and
reported in the psychoanalytic situation is a signal that the stimulus for that
dream involves something about the process and about the nature of the
transference relationship that is disturbing and has been repressed. Working
with the dream reveals not only the *what* of such discontinuities—the repressed material—but also points toward the *how*—the nature of defense—
and the *why* of repression.

The Interpretation of Dreams, although it includes dream material from
therapeutic psychoanalysis, draws mostly from Freud's self-analysis, that is,
his attempts to analyze his own dreams. The fruitfulness of the prepsychoanalytic years from 1896 to 1899 is commonly underestimated. The fruits of
dream analysis—Freud's exhaustive investigations of his own dreams using
dream analysis—have illumined processes of dream formation and of the
workings of the imagination that simply could not be gleaned from a properly
conducted therapeutic psychoanalysis in which investigatory zeal would invariably be modulated by clinical conduct of the treatment.

Freud's answers to questions that he himself asks of the existing literature
in the monumental first chapter are answered largely with the results of dream
analysis, not psychoanalysis proper. These include investigations of material
and sources of dreams, memory and a moral sense in dreams, the relation of
dreams to waking life—topics pursued later, especially in chapter 5 ("Material and Sources") and chapter 6 ("The Dream Work").

Thorough investigation of the manifest dream for associative nodal points
indicative of condensation, for recent and indifferent impressions of the
dream day that find their way into the collage of the manifest content; detailed
explorations of calculations and speeches sufficient to demonstrate that synthetic activity is not formed by the dream work itself—all of these require
diversion into detail too painstaking and lengthy to be undertaken in therapeutic psychoanalysis proper.

The same is true of symbols. Symbols, it must be remembered, are not symbols in the everyday sense of the word nor even in the sense used by literary critics. Symbols in the context of *The Interpretation of Dreams* are dream elements that, after exhaustive associative anamnesis, are not derived from sensory experiences of the dream day. Only by such exhaustive use of the associative method—usage that would utterly preempt the flow of a therapeutic psychoanalysis—could the specific nature of symbols in dreams be investigated.

Freud made clear (chapter 7, section A) that his exhaustive work on dreams could often extend to several sittings and that he would often return to apparently unanalyzable dreams months or even years later.

With these considerations in mind, it should be clear that the investigations approached in chapter 1 and detailed in chapters 5 and 6 could not be done in the context of analytic work attuned, as all psychoanalysis is, to the nuanced vicissitudes of the transference. These prepsychoanalytic researches into the nature of the mind and of the imagination in particular can be verified by strictly psychoanalytic work, but they could never have been discovered in the context of therapeutic psychoanalysis.

It is also of note that, even at the very earliest stage of dream analysis, the psychoanalytic study of the dream overlapped with nautralistic and even statistical methods of data handling. One cannot know, for example, that a typical dream *is* a typical dream or a symbol a typical symbol unless the meaning of that manifest material has been demonstrated to be the same in a large enough number of cases to warrant adoption of an empirical generalization, namely, that this dream is an instance of a typical dream with a specific meaning or that the dream element is an instance of a typical symbol with a specific meaning. From the outset, psychoanalytic investigation blended use of the associative method with methods involving comparison and empirical generalization.

III. DREAMS AND THE PSYCHOANALYTIC PROCESS

The psychoanalytic study of the dream, historically, moved rapidly from a conceptualization of dream analysis both as a tool concerned with a one-party situation (since a good deal of Freud's transferences to Wilhelm Fliess were repressed), and, later, as a tool concerned with understanding the *self in relation to the others*, that is to say, apprehending the transference in the context of the psychoanalytic process. The shift was from an exclusive focus on how repression worked in *the individual* in (incorrectly presumed) isolation toward a focus illustrating the imminently object-related aspects of the psychoanalytic process, the transference conflictual enough to be repressed and represented in dreams. In every current school of psychoanalysis, it is now clear that the problem of *dream interpretation* must be understood in the context of the psychoanalytic process (Greenson 1970; Altman 1975; Meltzer 1984; Resnik 1987).

Since the Dora case, the dream has been a naturalistic research tool for the study of the analytic process. So it remains today, but the analysis of the dream as a tool for the understanding of the psychoanalytic process is often put forward without an adequate methodology for deriving inferences from such psychoanalytic investigations. We need a combination of associative and extra-associative methods—for instance, an overview of the progression of a case, including changes in states of mind and in external circumstances —to demonstrate convincingly the significance of a psychoanalytic process. The type of clinical contribution containing a few vignettes among many chosen by the author is methodologically inadequate. To be convincing, studies of dream interpretation within the psychoanalytic process would have to show, for example, that all or a preponderance of dreams changed in a specified way after a particular period of successful interpretive work.

The psychoanalytic study of the dream illuminates unconscious, that is to say, repressed or discontinuous, elements in the personality. By virtue of that illumination, the whole of the individual's psychic continuity and the signifi-cance of the psychoanalytic process becomes clearer and more continuous. Freud (1900), on the first page of *The Interpretation of Dreams,* asserts that "every dream reveals itself as a psychical structure which has a meaning and which can be inserted in an assignable point in the mental activities of waking life." In the context of the psychoanalytic situation, it may be said that the meaning of the dream cannot be considered apart from the meaning of the analytic session. What the session means is discovered by interpretive illu-mination of the conflict causing the repression, that is, the discontinuity in the patient's awareness of the state of the relationship at any one time. It is these conflictual or repressed aspects of the state of the transference or of the analytic process that, by their repression, render the transference or the analytic process indistinct, inexplicit, or obscure. It is a hallmark of psycho-analytic work with dreams that the dreamer does not simply see the "mean-ing" of the particular dream, but sees his or her entire mental life as more continuous after a dream has been successfully interpreted. The restoration of this continuity, of course, involves the acknowledgement of some aspect of the transference—that part currently in ascendancy in the analytic process —that had hitherto been repressed.

We cannot pursue psychoanalytic investigations that are truly systematic and generalizable without a more demonstrable grasp of what the psychoanalytic process is. Only then can we ask what are the essential features of change in the analytic process, where does dream interpretation fit in, and how do dreams serve to monitor both interpretation and the movement of the analytic process.

However, it is far from clear what a psychoanalytic process is. Although the dream in psychoanalysis ab initio has been a research tool, there are still formidable methodological problems to be faced concerning the use of that tool. That psychoanalysts have an intimate knowledge of the psychoanalytic process seems almost a truism. In fact, it is easy at first blush to overlook entirely the many difficulties in conceptualizing the psychoanalytic process (Compton 1990). To paraphrase St. Augustine, as analysts we know what a psychoanalytic process is as long as one does not ask us. But it is far from clear that one can describe the process so that (even psychoanalytically informed) observers can agree on essentials about either the nature of or significant changes in that process. Since *dream interpretation* depends upon the recognition of the nature of and changes in the process, the psychoanalytic use of dreams urgently needs a way of ascertaining and assessing the psychoanalytic process.

A host of questions arise in connection with difficulties in defining psychoanalytic process. For example, if we now understand that our knowledge of the meaning of a dream is contingent on our knowing the meaning of the analytic session as a whole, psychoanalytic understanding of a dream can only take place in the light of the entire session in which it is reported or perhaps an entire sequence of sessions that includes the session containing the dream. In this case, a usable methodology should contain some relatively unambiguous method of ascertaining the meaning of a session as a whole or the process as such. It might seem an obvious reply that it is precisely the associative method that provides such a procedure. However, the psychoanalytic literature contains little methodological discussion of the use of the associative method to reach decisions in cases in which presumably reasonable and competent analysts disagree. There have been scattered contributions on the use of the associative method (Freud 1900, chapter 2; Kris 1982) but surprisingly little detailing the way in which conclusions are drawn from that method. Despite the fact that decades of psychoanalytic practice attest to the practical usefulness of the associative method as we now use it, we are still far short of explicating a theory of evidence that transcends the personal style of the clinician using it. Thus, it is far from obvious, for example, how it is that an interpretation of a dream emerges from a sequence of associations, even from a presumably clear understanding of the psychoanalytic process. How, for example, do we know in any one dream which among many latent dream thoughts is the essential one or which conflict is the focal one (French and Fromm 1964) or which the clinically central wish. We need, therefore, a good deal of clarification of and rules of inference for the associative method before we are able to judge the presence of changes in psychoanalytic process.

Much of the clinical psychoanalytic literature on dreams reveals an amalgam of intuitive and associative methods. Anecdotal clinical material is frequently buttressed with vignettes, a surprising amount of which appear to be considered allegorically or on the basis of content that demonstrates the point the particular author is trying to make. Not uncommonly, conclusions from the analysis of one dream have been selected from among many dreams of the same patient to demonstrate the point at hand. While such anecdotal material may have clinical relevance and usefulness, vignettes from a single case have quite limited usefulness for the theory of dreams or the systematic study of the psychoanalytic process using the dream as an investigative tool.

Some of the same considerations apply to the problem of interpretation. We lack an agreed-upon notion of what interpretation is. In *The Interpretation of Dreams* (1900), ''interpretation'' has a simple and very concrete usage: interpretation is simply the reversal of the dream work, a going from manifest content to latent dream thoughts, just as the dream work fashions the manifest content out of latent dream thoughts. Certainly, in the context of the psychoanalytic process, interpretation is thought of as much more complex than it was in that original view. Explication of unconscious conflict, defenses against it, and perhaps a link to the individual's genetics is the very minimum requirement of psychoanalytic interpretation as such. But the ways in which interpretation actually serves to emancipate the patient from a process of which he or she is unaware needs a good deal more explication.

Essentially, psychoanalytic dream interpretation links the meaning of the dream and that aspect of the analytic process that is sufficiently anxiety producing to necessitate disguise and repression. Although most psychoanalysts would probably affirm such a view of dream interpretation, the methodological problem of studying different alternatives to the clinical approach to dreams is enormous. It cannot even be presumed that most analysts actually work in the way that they think they do. Since we lack operationalized empirical notions of how we *actually* work (as opposed to theoretical testaments to the way in which we think we work), we have very few studies of actual performative rules of dream interpretations—what recognized clinicians *actually do* when they interpret dreams as opposed to what they theorize that they are doing or what they think they are doing. There is also surprisingly little study of how it is that we acquire the conviction that we know the interpretation at hand, that is, the analyst's actual acquisition of conviction about the meaning of a dream. It is simply not clear exactly *how* the associative method gives rise to conclusions that clinicians put forward.

There have been noteworthy contributions to the study of the analytic process per se using dreams. Paul Bradlow (1987) studied manifest content of initial dreams in analysis. In a large psychoanalytic clinic sample, Bradlow found that initial dreams in which manifest murder content or explicit sexual activity with family members or very late occurrence of a first reported dream were meaningful prognostic indicators of unanalyzability. Using statistical methods, Milton Rosenbaum (1965) failed to verify the clinical precept that dreams in which the analyst appeared undisguised were indicative of an intensity of transference with uniformly poor prognosis for analyzability. Aspects of the process of termination in analysis were studied with the use of dreams by Oremland (1973) and by Cavenar and Nash (1976). French and Fromm (1964) have developed a method of studying integration and synthesis in terms of focal conflicts in dreams.

We know a good deal about the forces that promote and hinder awareness of the analytic process, but there still remains a good deal to be done on the nature of self-deception or repression, the essential aspect of which has tended to be obscured by the use of the term ''defense'' or ''defense mechanism.'' A well-analyzed dream in the context of the analytic sessions proximal to it gives us one of our best opportunities to study *what defense itself is* apart from what type of defense is typically used. Much has been written about defenses, but much less about the problem of defense per se, that is, self-deception in the service of lowering anxiety. Freud, in his earliest writings, emphasized that repression, the capacity to keep aspects of disturbing awareness out of consciousness, was the cornerstone of psychoanalysis.

The notion that primitive sorts of self-deception (e.g., those employing splitting) set apart a major type of disturbed personality organization (borderline or psychotic) from a less pathological form of self-deception (using defenses supporting repression[1]) (Klein 1946; Kernberg 1984) has been a major advance in psychoanalytic thinking. There is much in the philosophical (Fingarette 1969; Sartre 1943) literature, but rather little in the psychoanalytic literature on self-deception per se. "Defense" has become such a catch-all word in psychoanalysis that the essential philosophical nature of self-deception tends to be obscured. But the capacity to deceive oneself and the capacity to reverse such self-deception contain the key to both symptom formation and the process of cure. The lifting of repression in the analytic situation through psychoanalytic dream interpretation has provided a unique opportunity for the study of processes of self-deception.

IV. PROCESS AND PREDICAMENT

The dream, then, has been a major investigative tool in the study of how the mind works and what the psychoanalytic process is like. But neither the study of the mind nor the study of the process considered in isolation exhausts the investigative potential of the dream in psychoanalysis. Considering the dream as a research tool, it is clear that its use is limited neither to studies of the function and formations of dreams nor to the nature of the psychoanalytic process as such. The dream is a potential investigative tool for many syntheses of naturalistic observations and psychoanalytic data.

Psychoanalysts have usually been reluctant to see themselves as naturalists, and, with the exception of certain types of observations on child development, naturalistic observations have tended to be foreign to or even repugnant to the mainstream psychoanalytic thinking and writing. Psychoanalysis and clinical psychiatry have become increasingly polarized. I shall consider briefly the use of dreams in the investigation of development and the impact of significant life events, of psychopathology, and of trauma.

Developmental and Life Events

The study of *developmental* and of *significant life events* has been the one area in which psychoanalysts have integrated observational and associative methods of investigation. Mack (1965) has studied the development of night-

---

1. This sense of "repression" for one of many mechanisms of defense is in accord with current usage. It differs from that of repression used elsewhere in the text, which is the older, more general usage of "repression" and refers to the general capacity of the mind to deceive itself by removing painful awarenesses from consciousness.

mares or anxiety dreams in children at various ages and stages of development. The dream can be used to study separation and mourning, one's own impending death (Sharpe 1937) or the death of ones close to the dreamer, the birth of a child from the point of view of mother, father, siblings, or others; and these developmental and predicament considerations can also include biological processes, rhythms such as the menstrual cycle, organic disease, and the residues, for example, of deficit disorders and hyperactivity.

Psychopathology

Another major area, but, to date, a scantily developed one, in which the study of the dream may join with naturalistic observations is in the area of psychopathology. It still remains to be determined whether or not there are typical dreams or typical constellations of subject in relation to object that occur uniformly or even predominantly in different diagnostic categories.

Saul and his colleagues (Saul and Sheppard 1956) devised a method of quantifying cumulative hostility in manifest dream elements that meaningfully distinguished hypertensives from (poorly matched) normotensive controls. Langs (1966) found demonstrable differences in the manifest dreams of patients with paranoid schizophrenia, hysterical character disorders, and psychotic depression.

The question of the relation of dream to psychosis has a long history in the psychoanalytic literature. Frosch (1976), reviewing the topic of dreams and psychosis, concludes that the psychoanalytic literature does not support the notion that dreams have the same structure as psychosis. While some authors maintain that dreams may presage psychosis, data supporting this contention go beyond manifest content. Frosch also doubts that, using manifest content alone, schizophrenic dreams can be decisively distinguished from dreams of nonschizophrenics. Considering the manifest dream of the schizophrenic, Richardson and Moore (1963) found that judges could not accurately distinguish dreams of schizophrenics from those of nonschizophrenics. The authors conjecture that the failure of repression is not clearly revealed in the dreams of schizophrenics because defensive tones are relatively stronger during sleep than waking. They conjecture that bizarreness in these dreams may be due to a relative failure of secondary revision. In a nuanced clinical paper, Oremland (1987) has outlined constellations of self and object representations in the treatment of a schizophrenic patient. Summarizing a panel of the American Psychoanalytic Association, John Mack (Panel 1969) suggested that dreams of psychotic patients were characterized by heightened vividness, overwhelming anxiety, persistence of dream elements after awakening, loss of capacity to distinguish the dream from waking life, and the dreamer's sense of the prophetic nature of the manifest dream and its power to influence subsequent events. Robert Langs (1966) noted a proneness to conflict with others and a sense of the personal and impersonal environment as overwhelming and traumatizing.

Beck and his associates (Beck and Hurvich 1959; Beck and Ward 1961) conducted studies of depressive dreams and found a rather typical content among those dreams. The manifest dreams contained rejection, disappointment, humiliation, and similar unpleasant experiences in significantly higher numbers than dreams of nondepressed subjects (Beck and Hurvich 1959). Kramer and his colleagues (1965), in an inadequately designed study, noted a greater frequency of themes of escape and helplessness and hopelessness in dreams of depressed patients compared to nondepressed controls. Langs (1966) noted a defensive use of denial and decathexis of self and object representations in a group of psychotically depressed women and noted the usefulness of earliest memories as well as manifest content of dreams in groups of patients with psychotic depression, hysterical character disorders, and paranoid schizophrenia. These early efforts have still not been followed up with studies asking whether a change in the status of depression is revealed by a change in dreams (and, if so, what sort of change), or whether dreams as such could be used to monitor either course of illness, prodromal signs of illness, or the effects of treatment, psychological or pharmacological. There is no reason, in principle, why systematic studies of dreams cannot be used to study the nature and course of psychopathological entities.

Many of the major authors writing on character pathology tend to ignore dreams (e.g., Kernberg 1984). There is still an entirely unresolved question, for example, whether borderlines have "borderline" dreams. Oremland (1987) emphasizes the usefulness of typical self and object representations in selected dreams of psychotic and borderline patients in the context of the therapeutic process. Lansky and Bley (1990), studying nightmares, dispute the fact that "borderline" patients have typically borderline constellations of object relations in their dreams. Again, it is important to go beyond simple anecdotal material to develop a reliable methodology to evaluate systematically whether, for example, there is a consistent level of self and object differentiation in the dreams of borderline patients or whether typical pathological object relations appear under certain circumstances, what those circumstances are, and whether there is any change in response to treatment.

Kleinian authors (Bion 1977; Segal 1981) have pointed to evacuative and predictive dreams typical of persons in whom splitting is a major defensive operation. Segal (1981), following Bion (1977), emphasizes that primitive emotional tensions (beta elements) cannot be symbolized and transformed by primary and secondary processes until separation and the capacity for mourning are developed. Dreams of patients in primitive mental states serve to evacuate primitive tensions and to predict acting out, which discharges tensions that cannot be "metabolized" by the dream.

There still remains a good deal to be done on many aspects of character pathology that could be investigated by dreams. For example, Is there any significance or natural history to withdrawal dreams, that is, dreams occurring, for example, when drinking or compulsive gambling stops (Brown 1985), and does this tell us anything about the psychic processes or the course of illness or the response to treatment?[2] The relationship of dreams to medication is a complex area that tends to be poorly formulated, probably because people disciplined in the use of dreams tend not to have discipline in terms of research design and those capable of establishing medications protocols usually know very little about dreams. The whole problem of dissociation, incohesion, or fragmentation tends to be poorly studied in pharmacologic literature and perhaps might be better monitored by the sense of cohesion revealed in dreams or the presence of self-state dreams. The whole issue of dreams as monitors of medication effect or of prodromal symptoms of pathology that serve as indications for medication is a potentially important one, so that the dream can potentially touch on prodromal features, remission, change in illness, and effectiveness of treatment, no matter what kind.

Trauma

There is a paucity of literature on post-traumatic dreams as research tools. Weiss (1986), in discussing the function of dreams, has suggested that the dreams of prisoners of war differ depending on the predicament faced by the ego of the dreamer. The dreams of those in actual danger in the field differed markedly from those who were in prisoner of war camps, and those dreams

---

2. I am indebted to Dr. Richard J. Rosenthal for useful insights on the topic of withdrawal dreams.

in turn differed significantly from the dreams of those who had reached safety in the United States. Dreams could be used in studying anticipatory and reparative processes in different types of trauma without any presumptions that these traumata have the same effect on victims. These include physical and sexual abuse as children, rape, combat, internment in concentration camps during the Holocaust, and postaccident traumas.

The problem of the *reconstruction of trauma* belongs both to the study of the associative method (Dowling 1982) and of the psychoanalytic process *and* to the verification of the results of such studies (when possible) by use of extra-analytic data. Refined methodologies for such studies combining naturalistic and associative data can be expected to enhance our understanding both of dream formation and of the effects of trauma.

The topic of *predisposition to trauma* has been studied only very scantily in terms of its effect on dream formation (Lidz 1946; Lansky 1990; Lansky and Karger 1989; Lansky and Bley 1990).

Affects in traumatic dreams, of course, present major problems theoretically in the case of post-traumatic nightmares. On the surface these dreams would appear to be simple replays of the traumatic event, hence without latent content or dream work, and hence dreams that seem to generate rather than dampen affect. Close study of at least one type of these dreams (Lansky 1991) shows that the dream may indeed metapsychologically serve the function of wish fulfillment in that shame and the day residue are transformed into fear. As such, the post-traumatic nightmare would constitute a genuine psychoneurosis capable of analysis. In general, we need to know a good deal more about processes of a dissociation and of the nature of repetition (Levitan 1967; Stern 1988).

It is hardly questionable theoretically that extra-associative, that is to say, naturalistic data, are badly needed to complement purely psychoanalytic data in all these areas. The problem, of course, arises of how to integrate these data *with* strictly associative data concerning the course of the process, data from developmental observation and naturalistic observations of biology, pathology, and trauma. We need not only a method of integrating data, but a philosophy of science to integrate associative data with observational or naturalistic data so that we may reach decision procedures that are not simply arbitrary and derived from a fascination with the method at hand.

There is, then, a definite and expanding body of knowledge about the dream in developmental, pathological, and traumatic predicaments that amalgamates psychoanalytic methodologies with other methods of inference.

V. EXTRACLINICAL DATA AND PSYCHOANALYTIC DATA: THE NEED FOR A METAMETHODOLOGY

Data arising from sleep laboratories or using the electroencephalogram or neurophysiologic studies of sleep and dreaming are difficult to compare with data derived strictly from the psychoanalytic situation. A partisan of either of these methods risks becoming lost in or defensive of his or her own particular method. That risk, of course, includes losing sight of the all-important question, What in principle would answer the question at hand? Concerning the nature of dreams, for example, both sleep researchers and psychoanalysts risk ignoring questions that are out of the purview of their particular method. Accordingly, our need for a viewpoint transcending either specific methodology is intensified. Only with such a viewpoint will we be able to consider both frames of references and the nature of the data that emerge from them.

Take for example the quite basic question, What is a dream? There are different answers to this depending on what is the source of one's data. If one is a psychoanalyst or an introspective person interested in his or her own dreams, a dream is that—let us say small—percentage of the total dreams remembered and fixed in consciousness as material to be worked on in a process of self-inquiry, whether in analysis or self-analysis. If one is in a sleep laboratory, the context changes entirely. If, for example, when rapid eye movement is observed in an electroencephalographic recording of a sleeping person and that person is awakened, it is often the case that the sleeper will report that he or she was dreaming. Now, a dream in this sense is a vastly more extensive category of mental phenomenon than one observed in the psychoanalytic or self-analytic framework. It can usefully be asked, nonetheless, whether demonstrable psychoanalytic conclusions apply, in principle at least, only to dreams remembered for purposes of self-inquiry, or whether they apply beyond this small subset of dreams remembered and brought to analytic sessions. If psychoanalytic conclusions, that is to say, about overdetermination, wish fulfillment, and dream work do not apply to the entire domain of dreams, we are faced with the problem of deciding what falls within the psychoanalytic domain of dreams that have heretofore been limited to those seen in the clinical setting. Is this a disastrous problem for the theory of dreams or do we simply have to have a much more limited use of the word ''dream'' than does the sleep researcher?

Another question concerns the technology of the sleep laboratory. Is all dream activity in REM sleep? What about activity that is in non-REM sleep?

Are traumatic dreams, because they are not REM dreams, therefore not true dreams? Charles Fisher et al. (1970) assert this after laboratory investigation of these dreams. Detailed investigations of traumatic nightmares (Lansky 1990; Lansky and Karger 1989; Lansky and Bley 1990) have suggested otherwise. Where do self-state dreams and other post-traumatic nightmares fit into this schema? Does a distinction between REM and non-REM usefully distinguish between types of dreams? It is not clear at present that findings from the sleep laboratory are of sufficient pertinence to override careful clinical observations.

Regarding different frames of reference from which data are drawn, similar considerations apply to the problem of forgetting. Sleep laboratory studies convincingly show that considerably more dream activity takes place each night than is ever remembered. This observation would appear to decisively refute Freud's remarks about the role of repression in the forgetting of dreams (1900, 7A) unless it is realized that Freud is not discussing the topic of dream dreamed and never remembered at all. He addresses himself to (what we now appreciate to be) that small subset of dreams that one is sure that one has dreamed, but that one *doubts* that one can recall. Freud's essential point concerns *uncertainty and doubt*—in the service of resistance—functioning to deemphasize the partially recalled dream as a distinct mental activity. "Forgetting" for the psychoanalyst, then, has an entirely different context and frame of reference than it does for the sleep researcher describing dream amnesia.

I mention these points only briefly to stress the difference between the data themselves and a viewpoint towards all data that attempts to evaluate what kind of data they are as well as what can and what cannot, in principle, be inferred from them.

The need for a philosophy of integration of different types of data, a metamethodology as it might be called, becomes sharper, then, when psychoanalytic data is to be blended not simply with naturalistic observations or those from clinical psychiatry (for example, of observations of development, of naturalistic observations on pathology and trauma) but also with data arising from the use of completely different methodologies, for example, from a laboratory, and themselves in need of interpretation.

Our grasp of the nature of dreams or the use of dreams as tools can be rendered more effective only if we have a philosophy of science that addresses itself specifically to what different sources and types of data actually signify when they are integrated. Otherwise we are faced with the claims of competing technologies, each with its respective advocates overstating the importance of a particular method. These same considerations can be applied in principle when one applies the results of associative data to those not only of sleep laboratory data but also of development, of study of the process of the natural history of pathology or trauma, of neurophysiology, or of information processing. We need a methodology for the integration of different methodologies.

A more adequate dream theory needs to evolve with a philosophy of science integrating the types of data from different methodologies according to a metamethodology. Only if we can start with the premethodological question, What type of data, in principle, answers the major question at hand? can we avoid the inevitable temptation to adapt questions being asked so that they are framed totally in terms of one or another type of methodology. This is the major challenge of synthesizing data drawn both from the associative method and from other methods of investigation. We do not have much in the way of systematic inquiry about the significance of data gleaned from more than one method. As the dream emerges as a research tool that yields data that go beyond how one mind works or what the transference relationship is like at any one time, inferences will inevitably be made, whether those be comparisons of the analytic process currently with that in the past, of the patient's defensive organization with that of others, of the patient's level of development, or of data gleaned from completely different methods. The challenge of the future will be to evaluate the status of the fruits of dream analysis in wider contexts that include other types of data.

REFERENCES

Altman, L. (1975) *The Dream in Psychoanalysis*. New York, International Universities Press.
Beck, A., Hurvich, M. S. (1959) Psychological correlates of depression: I. Frequency of "masochistic" dream content in a private practice sample. *Psychosom. Med.* 21:50–55.
Beck, A., Ward, C. (1961) Dreams of depressed patients. *Arch. Gen. Psychiat* 5:66–71.
Bion, W. R. (1977) *Seven Servants*. New York, Aronson.
Bradlow, P. (1987) On production and the manifest content of the initial dream reported in psychoanalysis. In Rothstein, A. (Ed.), *The Interpretations of Dreams in Clinical Work*. Madison, CT, International Universities Press.
Brown, S. (1985) *Treating the Alcoholic: A Developmental Model of Recovery*. New York, Wiley.
Cavenar, J. O., Nash, J. L. (1976) The dream as a signal for termination. *J. Amer Psychoanalyt Assoc.* 24:425–36.
Compton, A. (1990) Psychoanalytic process. *Psychoanalytic Quarterly* LIX:585–598.

Dowling, S. (1982) Dreams and dreaming in relation to trauma in childhood. *Int. J. Psycho-Anal* **63:**157–66.

Fingarette, H. (1969) *Self Deception.* London, Routledge & Kegan Paul.

Fisher, C., Byrne, J., Edwards, A., Kahn, S. (1970) A psychophysiologial study of nightmares. *J. Amer. Psychoanal. Assoc.* **18:** 747–82.

French, T., Fromm, E. (1964) *Dream Interpretation: A New Approach.* Madison, CT, International Universities Press.

Freud, S. (1900) *The Interpretation of Dreams. Standard Edition, vols.* IV, V. London, Hogarth.

——— (1905) *Fragment of an Analysis of a Case of Hysteria. Standard Edition,* vol. VII:7–122. London, Hogarth, 1953.

Frosch, J. (1976) Psychoanalytic contributions to the relationship between dreams and psychosis: A critical survey. *Int. J. Psychoanalyt. Psychother.* **5:**39–63.

Greenson, R. (1970) The exceptional position of the dream in psychoanalytic practice. *Psychoanalyt. Quart.* **39:**519–49.

Kernberg, O. (1984) *Severe Personality Disorders.* New Haven, Yale University Press.

Klein, M. (1946) Notes on some schizoid mechanisms. *In V. J. Psychoanal* **27:**99–110.

Kramer, M., Whitman, R., Baldridge, B., Lansky, L. (1965) Depression: Dreams and defenses. *Am J. Psychiat* **122:**411–17.

Kris, A. (1982) *Free Associations.* New Haven, Yale University Press.

Langs, R. (1966) Manifest dreams from three clinical groups. *Arch Gen Psychiat* **14:**634–43.

Lansky, M. (1990) The screening function of post-traumatic nightmares. *Brit. J. Psychother* **6:**384–400.

——— (1991) The transformation of affects in post-traumatic nightmares. *Bull. Menninger Cl.* **55:**470–490.

Lansky, M., Bley, C. (1990) Exploration of nightmares in the treatment of hospitalized borderline patients. *Bull. Menninger Cl.* **54:**466–77.

Lansky, M., Karger, J. (1989) Post-traumatic nightmares and the family. *Hillside J. Clin. Psychiat* **11:**169–83.

Leveton, A. F. (1981) The night residue. *Int. J. Psychoanaly* **42:**506–16.

Levitan, H. (1967) Depersonalization and the dream. *Psychoanalyt. Quart* **36:**157–71.

Lidz, T. (1946) Nightmares and the combat neurosis. *Psychiatry* **9:**37–49.

Mack, J. (1965) Nightmares, conflict, and ego development in childhood. *Int. J. Psychoanal* **46:**403–28.

Meltzer, D. (1984) *Dream Life: A Reexamination of Psychoanalytical Theory and Technique.* London, Clunie.

Oremland, J. (1973) A specific dream during the termination phase of successful psychoanalysis. *J. Amer Psychoanal Assoc* **21:**285–302.

——— (1987) Dreams in the treatment of the borderline personality. In Grotstein, J., Solomon, M., Lang, M. J. (Eds.), *The Borderline Patient.* Vol. II. Hillsdale, NJ, Analytic Press. 81–102.

Panel (1969) Dreams and Psychosis. *J. Amer Psychoanalyt Assoc* **17:**206–21.

Reed, G. (1987) Rules of clinical understanding in classical psychoanalysis and in self psychology: A comparison. *J. Am Psychoanalyt Assoc* **35:**421–46.

Resnik, S. (1987) *The Theatre of the Dream.* London, Tavistock.

Richardson, G., Moore, R. (1963) On the manifest dream in schizophrenia. *J. Am Psychoanalyt Assoc* **7:**281–302.

Rosenbaum, M. (1965) Dreams in which the analyst appears undisguised: A clinical and statistical study. *Int. J. Psychoanal* **46:**429–37.

Sartre, J. P. (1943) *Being and Nothingness*. Hazel Barnes, tr. New York, Washington Square, 1956.

Saul, L., Sheppard, E. (1956) An attempt to quantify emotional forces using manifest dreams: A preliminary study. *J. Am. Psychoanalyt Assoc* **4:**486–502.

Segal, H. (1981) The function of dreams. In Grotstein, J. (Ed.), *Do I Dare Disturb the Universe: A Memorial to Wilfred Bion*. Beverly Hills, Caesura.

Sharpe, E. (1937) *Dream Analysis*. London, Hogarth.

Stern, M. (1988) *Repetition and Trauma: Toward a Telonomic Theory of Psychoanalysis*. Hillsdale, NJ, Analytic Press.

Weiss, J. (1986) Dreams and their various purposes. In Weiss, J., Sampson, H., *The Psychoanalytic Process*. New York, Guilford.

Appendix 1: List of Writings by Freud Dealing Predominantly or Largely with Dreams

[It would scarcely be an exaggeration to say that dreams are alluded to in the majority of Freud's writings. The following list of works (of greatly varying importance) may however be of some practical use. The date at the beginning of each entry is that of the year during which the work in question was written. The date at the end is that of publication. The items in square brackets were published posthumously.]

[1895   'Project for a Scientific Psychology' (Sections 19, 20 and 21 of Part I). (1950)]

1899   *The Interpretation of Dreams.* (1900)

[1899   'A Premonitory Dream Fulfilled.' (1941)]

1901   *On Dreams.* (1901)

1901   'Fragment of an Analysis of a Case of Hysteria.' [Original title: 'Dreams and Hysteria.'] (1905)

1905   *Jokes and Their Relation to the Unconscious* (Chapter VI). (1905)

1907   *Delusions and Dreams in Jensen's 'Gradiva.'* (1907)

1910   'A Typical Example of a Disguised Oedipus Dream.' (1910)

1911   'Additions to the Interpretation of Dreams.' (1911)

1911   'The Handling of Dream-Interpretation in Psycho-Analysis.' (1911)

1913   'An Evidential Dream.' (1913)

1913   'The Occurrence in Dreams of Material from Fairy Tales.' (1913)

1913   'Observations and Examples from Analytic Practice.' (1913)

1914   'The Representation in a Dream of a "Great Achievement." ' (1914)

1916   *Introductory Lectures on Psycho-Analysis* (Part II). (1916–1917.)

1917   'A Metapsychological Supplement to the Theory of Dreams.' (1917)

1918   'From the History of an Infantile Neurosis' (Section IV). (1918)

1920   'Supplements to the Theory of Dreams.' (1920)

1922   'Dreams and Telepathy.' (1922)

1923   'Remarks upon the Theory and Practice of Dream-Intepretation.' (1923)

1923   'Josef Popper-Lynkeus and the Theory of Dreams.' (1923)
1925   'Some Additional Notes on Dream-Interpretation as a Whole.' (1925)
1929   'A Letter to Maxime Leroy on a Dream of Descartes.' (1929)
1932   'My Contact with Josef Popper-Lynkeus.' (1932)
1932   *New Introductory Lectures on Psycho-Analysis* (Lectures XXIX and XXX). (1933)
[1938   *An Outline of Psycho-Analysis* (Chapter V). (1940)]

N.B—An unauthorized concoction of portions of *The Interpretation of Dreams* and *On Dreams* has appeared in two editions in America under the title of *Dream Psychology: Psychoanalysis for Beginners* (with an introduction by André Tridon). New York: McCann, 1920 and 1921. Pp. xi + 237.

Appendix 2: Psychoanalytic or Psychoanalytically Informed Books on Dreams

Altman, L. (1969) *The Dream in Psychoanalysis*. New York, International Universities Press.

Arlow, J. (Ed.) (1973) *Selected Writings of Bertram D. Lewin*. New York, Psychoanalytic Quarterly.

Breger, L., Hunter, I., Lane, R. (1971) *The Effect of Stress on Dreams. Psychological Issues* Monograph 27. New York, International Universities Press.

Fine, B., Joseph, E., Waldhorn, H. (1969) *The Manifest Content of the Dream*. Kris Study Group Monograph 3. New York, International Universities Press.

Fliess, R. (Ed.) (1953) *The Revival of Interest in the Dream*. New York, International Universities Press.

Fosshage, J. L., Loew, C. (Eds.) (1986) *Dream Interpretation: A Comparative Study*. New York, Spectrum.

French, T. (1953) *The Integration of Behavior*. Vol. 2, *The Integrative Process in Dreams*. Chicago, University of Chicago Press.

French, T., Fromm, E. (1964) *Dream Interpretation: A New Approach*. New York, Basic.

Freud, S. (1900) *The Interpretation of Dreams*. Standard Edition, vols. IV, V. London, Hogarth, 1953.

Garma, A. (1966) *The Psychoanalysis of Dreams*. Chicago, Quadrangle.

Grinstein, A. (1980) *Sigmund Freud's Dreams*. New York, International Universities Press.

——— (1983) *Freud's Rules of Dream Interpretation*. Madison CT, International Universities Press.

Hartmann, E. (1967) *The Biology of Dreaming*. Springfield IL, Charles C. Thomas.

——— (1984) *The Nightmare: The Psychology and Biology of Terrifying Dreams*. New York, Basic.

Hobson, J. A. (1988) *The Dreaming Brain*. New York, Basic.

Hunt, H. T. (1989) *The Multiplicity of Dreams: Memory, Imagination, and Consciousness*. New Haven, Yale University Press.

Jones, E. (1911) *On the Nightmare*. New York, Grove Press, 1959.

Kellerman, N. (Ed.) (1987) *The Nightmare: Psychological and Biological Foundations*. New York, Columbia University Press.

Kramer, M., Whitman, R. M., Ornstein, P. H., Baldridge, J. B. (Eds.) (1969) *Dream Psychology and the New Biology of Dreaming*. Springfield, IL, Charles C. Thomas.

Mack, J. (1970) *Nightmares and Human Conflict*. Boston, Little Brown.

Meltzer, D. (1984) *Dream Life: A Reexamination of Psychoanalytical Theory and Technique*. London, Clume.

Mendelson, R. (1990) *The Manifest Dream and Its Use in Therapy*. Northvale NJ, Jason Aronson.

Nagera, H., et al. (1969) *Basic Psychoanalytic Concepts on the Theory of Dreams*. London, George Allen and Unwin.

Natterson, J., Gordon, B. (1977) *The Sexual Dream*. New York, Crown.

Natterson, J. (Ed.) (1980) *The Dream in Clinical Practice*. New York, Aronson.

Palombo, S. (1978) *Dreaming and Memory: A New Information Processing Model*. New York, Basic.

Pontalis, J.-B. (1977) *Frontiers in Psychoanalysis: Between the Dream and Psychic Pain*. New York, International Universities Press.

Resnik, S. (1987) *The Theater of the Dream*. A. Sheridan, tr. London, Tavistock.

Roheim, G. (1952) *The Gates of the Dream*. New York, International Universities Press.

Rothstein, A. (Ed.) (1987) *The Interpretations of Dreams in Clinical Work*. Madison CT, International Universities Press.

Sharpe, E. (1949) *Dream Analysis*. London, Hogarth.

Waldhorn, H. (1967) *The Place of the Dream in Clinical Psycho-Analysis*. Kris Study Group Monograph 2. New York, International Universities Press.

Name Index

Subject Index

About the Editor

MELVIN R. LANSKY, M.D., is Adjunct Professor of Psychiatry at UCLA Medical School and founder/director of the Family Treatment Program at the Brentwood VA Medical Center. He is a teacher and practitioner of psychoanalysis, Training and Supervising Analyst at the Los Angeles Psychoanalytic Institute, editor of two books on psychopathology in the family setting, and author of award-winning articles on applied psychoanalysis.